Sal Maglie

Sal Maglie

Baseball's Demon Barber

Maglie

Judith Testa

NORTHERN

ILLINOIS

UNIVERSITY

PRESS

DeKalb

© 2007 by Northern Illinois University Press

Published by the Northern Illinois University Press, DeKalb, Illinois   60115

Manufactured in the United States using acid-free paper

All Rights Reserved

Design by Julia Fauci

Frontispiece: George Bruce

Library of Congress Cataloging-in-Publication Data

Testa, Judith Anne, 1943–

Sal Maglie: baseball's demon barber / Judith A. Testa.

      p.   cm.

Includes bibliographical references and index.

ISBN-13: 978-0-87580-367-8 (clothbound: alk. paper)

ISBN-10: 0-87580-367-9 (clothbound: alk. paper)

1. Maglie, Sal, 1917–92. 2. Baseball players—United States—Biography. I. Title.

GV865.M24T47 2006

796.357092—dc22

2006010844

To the memory of Joyce Dickey and Bill Brynteson,

dear friends and fellow baseball fanatics

CONTENTS

ILLUSTRATIONS

He looked like he came to kill you. Tall, gaunt, swarthy, and sinister, with a hawk-hook of a nose and hooded dark eyes, he had a tightly compressed mouth that now and then twisted into a sneer, or a fleeting smile about as friendly as the flash of an assassin's blade. His unshaven cheeks and jaw bristled with heavy black stubble, and his shadowy eyes beneath a frowning brow transfixed his victims with a baleful glower. Long arms, furred below the elbow with a thick growth of black hair, ended in hands whose fingers looked capable of snapping a man's neck. He radiated such murderous hostility as he stood on the mound that he might have been palming a dagger or a straight razor rather than a baseball. But in the right hand of Salvatore Anthony Maglie, known to fans in the 1950s as "Sal the Barber," a baseball often seemed like a deadly weapon, especially to batters whose chins endured a close shave from his terrifying high-inside fastball. As the sinewy arms rose, pumped above his head, and descended, as the right arm snapped back and then whipped forward, and the ball shot out toward the plate, the batter could only hope that The Barber had decided merely to shave his victim, not murder him. To the unnerved batsmen who faced him, there was something downright demonic about Sal Maglie's remorseless hatred of all hitters. But Maglie was not the devil in disguise, not a mass murderer who enjoyed slitting throats or splitting skulls. He just looked that way.

He was handsome as a movie idol. Tall and tanned, wide shouldered and narrow hipped, he exuded the sultry sex appeal of old-fashioned, smoldering stars like Rudolph Valentino and Robert Mitchum, or more recently, Sean Penn and the young Al Pacino. Black hair, glossy and abundant, cruised back from his forehead in deep waves. The term "bedroom eyes" might have been invented for him. Large, heavy-lidded, velvet-black, and framed with extravagantly long dark lashes, his eyes dominated even the generous nose that curved down from between his thick brows. That long nose with its beaked end gave his profile a keen, fierce quality, an eagle look at odds with those liquid eyes. Even freshly shaven, his face bore that basic badge of masculinity, the shadow of a dark beard. It might have been the face of a soldier of fortune or a Renaissance prince, and his slender, long-fingered hands could have belonged to a surgeon. But instead they, and all the rest, belonged to a baseball player, to that same, sinister Sal Maglie whose Medusa glare turned terrified batters to stone.

Even his name sounds tough. In the flat American pronunciation—"MAAG-lee" instead of the gentler Italian "MAHL-yeh"—the name brings to mind a man hard and craggy as a chunk of granite, and the bearer of the name was happy to perpetuate that image. But it was an image, not reality. Stone-cold ferocity and dark, demonic menace formed a mask that Maglie learned to wear when he pitched, a disguise that concealed, sometimes all too well, the man behind the mask.

Maglie was not, of course, the only ballplayer ever to project a tough and dangerous aura. The history of the game abounds in men who made instilling fear into opponents their stock-in-trade. The roll call of pitchers brings to mind hurlers whose mere presence on the mound brought out cold sweats in the batters they faced. They range from gentlemanly types like Walter Johnson, who greatly feared the consequences of hitting batters with his blazing fastball, but who clipped a record number anyway because they had no time to leap out of the line of fire, and Sandy Koufax, who hardly ever hit anyone; to the willowy, boy-faced fireballer Don Drysdale, who looked like an angel, pitched like the devil, and ran up a near-record number of hit batsmen; to the glowering Bob Gibson who seemed to hurl himself at hitters along with the ball, and blamed the batters if they failed to get out of the way.

With the exception of Gibson, whose black skin added to his aura as a pitching prince of darkness, no other pitcher who terrorized batters relied on his *appearance* to the extent that Maglie did. Unlike Johnson, Koufax, Drysdale, Gibson, and most other intimidating hurlers, Sal did not possess an outstanding fastball. What he had instead was superb control of a collection of curves, and a high hard one that topped out at around 85 miles per hour, combined with the kind of looks that convinced batters he was capable of using a baseball to smash their skulls. Eighty-five miles per hour is not so speedy by the standards of Johnson, Koufax, Drysdale, or Gibson, but plenty fast enough when the ball seems to be heading straight for the batter's ear. Where, when, how, and why Maglie developed these pitching skills, none of which came naturally to him, and the ways he put them to use in his career, form a part of the story recounted here, as does an analysis of the intimidating image that so dramatically increased the effectiveness of those skills.

But this is above all a book about a *man* who *played* baseball, rather than a baseball book. Red Smith observed that "sports is the real world. People we're writing about, they're suffering, living and dying, loving and trying to make their way in life, just as bricklayers and politicians are."

Because I believe that Maglie the man who played baseball—the man who lived, loved, suffered, tried to make his way in the world, and died—is as interesting as the game he played, statistics and material on the mechanics of pitching play a relatively minor role, and Maglie's life off the diamond receives attention along with his on-field exploits. In some ways Maglie's life forms a typical American story—if not precisely a rags-to-riches saga, nonetheless, the story of a man whose obscure beginnings, and years of mediocrity and failure, in no way prefigured his eventual success and fame. His is the story of a son of poor Italian immigrants who rose far beyond his own or his family's wildest dreams, who became wealthy and renowned, a star and a hero in the most quintessentially American of sports.

But as F. Scott Fitzgerald observed, "Show me a hero and I'll show you a tragedy." There is no Hollywood happy ending to Sal Maglie's story, and along with the highlights his life had its sad and even tragic side. Although Sal enjoyed some golden years when professional success and personal happiness coincided, there were also many years of frustration, disappointment, pain, and personal tragedy. During his time in the minors Sal struggled hard but rarely rose above mediocrity. His major league career, although successful, punctuated with memorable moments, and containing stretches of brilliance, was seriously shortened by his 1946 decision to leave the New York Giants in order to spend two years playing in the "outlaw" Mexican League. Banned from the majors along with the other players who had gone to Mexico, Sal lost another two years before the baseball commissioner lifted the ban and the Mexican League prodigals returned. Because he had taken so long to reach the Show, the further loss of four years from his major league career eliminated any possibility he might have had of qualifying for the Hall of Fame.

From 1950 through 1958 Sal played for five different teams, but he enjoyed his greatest success with the New York Giants. Maglie returned from Mexico transformed. He came back with baseball's most menacing demeanor and razor-sharp skills to match. He enjoyed three superb seasons with the Giants, from 1950 through 1952, but after that, hobbled by back problems, his effectiveness diminished, and he began to be passed around from team to team like a beat-up old used car. The Giants dumped him during the 1955 season, and he went to Cleveland, where the Indians, loaded with great pitching, had little use for him. Picked up on waivers during the 1956 season by the Brooklyn Dodgers, his archenemies when he was with the Giants, Sal experienced a last, unlikely comeback, pitching a no-hitter and leading the Dodgers to their final Brooklyn pennant. Late in the 1957 season, the Dodgers passed him on to the New York

Yankees, but he had little impact on the Lords of the Bronx. In 1958 the Yankees traded Maglie to the St. Louis Cardinals, where his career ended when he received his unconditional release after spring training of 1959. Sal then endured a checkered decade as a scout and minor league coach for the Cardinals, and an often-embattled pitching coach with the Boston Red Sox and the Seattle Pilots, before leaving major league baseball for good. He subsequently struggled to figure out what to do with the remainder of a life that had been devoted entirely to baseball.

On the personal level also Sal experienced both satisfactions and terrible reverses of fortune. His first wife, a lively and beautiful woman to whom he was deeply devoted, could not have children, and died when the couple was still in their forties. Sal recovered and remarried—another solid and satisfying union—but he later suffered the most devastating of all losses, the death of one of his children. That the son who died had been adopted made the loss no easier to bear. Sal's last years were a long nightmare of deteriorating physical and mental health, problems caused by brain damage that began with a cerebral aneurysm and ended by reducing the once powerful and active athlete to a near vegetative state.

Maglie's seasons in the sun shone with high baseball drama. He won brilliant clutch victories and suffered heartbreaking defeats. He pitched under all kinds of harrowing conditions, ranging from 110-degree heat in Mexico to snowfalls in Canada, often in the must-win pressure cooker of major league pennant races and sometimes despite the blinding pain of near-crippling injuries. His practice of throwing high-inside scared the living bejeezus out of hitters while it provoked brawls, collisions, and on-field exchanges of insults, obscenities, and vulgar gestures with opposing players. Other teams accused Maglie of throwing spitters and beanballs. Through it all he gained a formidable reputation as one of the all-time toughest customers ever to stalk out to a pitcher's mound. And yet, off the field he was a gentle, courteous, good-natured man whose voice one reporter described as "soft as a priest's in a confessional." The contrast between his ferocious on-field demeanor and behavior, and his gracious private persona, could not have been more dramatic.

Granted, Maglie is of interest because of his accomplishments as a major league pitcher. But he spent only a fraction of his life on the mound, and the roles he played in his life outside of baseball become interesting due to his achievements in the game. In addition to being a ballplayer, Sal was also a son and a son-in-law, a brother and a brother-in-law, an uncle and a great-uncle; a lover of who-knows-how-many women and the husband of two; an adoptive father and a stepfather; a teammate, a friend to a few, an acquaintance and bar-buddy to many, and a hero to untold numbers of fans who never met him; at different times a self-employed business owner and an employee of others; a church parishioner, a medical and dental patient, and for the last five years of his life a nursing home resident. All these aspects of Maglie's life receive attention here.

A classic piece of advice offered by traditional etiquette books is to avoid awkwardness and arguments in social situations by staying away from certain topics, chief among them politics, sex, and religion. To that list we could add race, money matters, and medical issues. But a biography is not a cautious conversation in which the author avoids controversial topics for fear of giving offense. Biography is neither an excuse for scandal-mongering and character assassination nor an exercise in reverence and hero-worship. Instead, it is an exploration of the subject's life, both public and personal, including areas the individual and his family might have wished to keep private. Politics proved an easy matter, since Sal was pretty much politically oblivious. He took no part in political campaigns and never even registered to vote. Sal did not brag, about sex or anything else, so information about that aspect of his life came to light indirectly, in hints and asides, and in greater detail from only one baseball source and one family member. In his religious life Sal was what might be called a reflexive Roman Catholic. He was baptized and married his first wife in a Catholic church, and was buried with Catholic ceremonies and in a Catholic cemetery, but he attended Mass only when someone else insisted. If asked, he would have identified himself as Catholic, but he was not pious, and he had no difficulty bending or ignoring Church rules when it suited him.

Sal's attitudes on racial matters can be garnered above all from his behavior. He avoided preaching and statements parading his tolerant attitudes; he simply lived a life on and off the diamond that remained free of even the smallest hint of racism. In the 1950s team officials rarely announced players' salaries the way they do today, but reporters of the time worked hard to learn how much the game's stars were receiving, and at least a good approximation of annual salaries often became public. Relative to today's baseball multimillionaires, Sal seems like a pauper, but his highest salary, the $37,500 he received in 1952, placed him in the top five percent of incomes in the United States for that year, and the salaries he earned throughout his major league career made him a wealthy man in comparison to his friends back home in Niagara Falls, many of them working in factories for hardly a dollar an hour. The most difficult matter to research is an individual's medical history, and recent privacy laws have made acquiring medical information even more difficult. Because the Maglie family declined to release Sal's medical records and death certificate, in discussing Sal's various health crises I have had to rely on newspaper reports, descriptions of those who saw Sal in old age and ill health, and whatever medical explanations I could find on my own or persuade medical experts of my acquaintance to provide.

Sal has already been the subject of two previous biographies, although neither does justice to the full extent of his life—a further reason for the present work. Today's libraries file *The Sal Maglie Story,* a slim 1957 volume by sportswriter Milton J. Shapiro, in their Juvenile departments, although Shapiro wrote the book for adult readers. Employing a semi-fictionalized approach, the author supplemented the facts of Maglie's baseball career with invented conversations in a style that resembles the stilted dialogue of 1950s television dramas. It is unclear how much input Maglie provided, although he must have given the author some information on his early life. In any case, the book has no bibliography and ends while Sal's career was still in progress, at the time of his comeback in 1956 with the Brooklyn Dodgers. A second biography, James Szalontai's *Close Shave: The Life and Times of Baseball's Sal Maglie,* appeared in 2002. This is a more ambitious work, but despite a length exceeding 400 pages, it covers only Maglie's playing career. The book displays an almost encyclopedic amount of research, bringing together material on just about every professional game in which Maglie participated. It is a valuable reference tool, and I have made use of it for that purpose. Many summary accounts of Maglie's games not covered in detail here come from Szalontai's book.

The present volume seeks to fill in the omissions, counteract the semifictions, and go beyond the time frame of previous biographies with an account of the realities of Sal Maglie's life, both on and off the diamond. Sal's family origins and background, as well as his childhood as a treasured only son, are treated in detail, because that aspect of his life has received no more than cursory attention in the past, even though his background helped shape so many of Maglie's later values and life decisions. Although Sal spent roughly twenty years playing minor and major league baseball, during the 1960s and through 1970 he also had a career as a scout and minor league coach for the St. Louis Cardinals, a coach for the Boston Red Sox and the Seattle Pilots, and, in a brief stint, the general manager of the minor league Niagara Falls Pirates. Sal's effectiveness, or ineffectiveness, in these positions has been little discussed. Outside of baseball he held a variety of jobs, few of which are noted in previous biographies.

Books and articles devoted to Maglie's baseball seasons furthermore make little room for material about Sal's life off the field during those years, and most mentions of his personal life are conventional comments on his attractive wife and happy marriage. Sal *was* happily married during those years, but it was a marriage shadowed and at times severely strained by the tensions arising from his wife's infertility and his own infidelities. These topics could not be acknowledged in publications of the 1950s. Shapiro's *Sal Maglie Story* described the Maglies, after ten years of childless marriage, as "not yet blessed with children." The lack of offspring drove Sal's wife to bizarre behavior and eventually led the couple to adopt two sons. The distinguished baseball writer Roger Kahn spoke for his generation of sportswriters when he declared that in the 1950s he would write about anything that occurred on the team he was covering—anything, that is, except "sex on the road."

Throughout this book I have supplemented written sources—books, magazine articles, and newspaper accounts—with personal interviews, on-site observations, recorded accounts of games, and film clips of Sal in action. Two extended visits to Sal's hometown of Niagara Falls, New York, permitted me to become familiar with the places where Maglie grew up and to meet some of those who grew up along with him. Conversations with Sal's old friends and nearly all of his surviving family members, including relatives by marriage, provided a perspective that supplements the picture offered by the news media. Interviews with some of Maglie's former teammates, as well as sportswriters and team officials from the 1950s and 1960s, further filled in the details of his professional life.

But such material has an intrinsic problem: people remember different things and remember things differently. As time passes "what really happened" becomes more and more a matter of what baseball historian Gabriel Schechter calls *hearsay history:* aging individuals' memories of the words and actions of others, now long dead. One rarely reads or hears the same story told the same way twice, even when the same person tells it. Most of the stories told about Sal Maglie by family, friends, journalists, and former teammates are probably true, although often difficult or impossible to verify. Other stories began as factual accounts, but have become exaggerated over repeated retellings, emerging as what I call "baseball fish stories." There are several of those about Sal Maglie. Sal himself was not given to a great deal of introspection, and interviews with him give few glimpses of his inner life. In some ways he became a prisoner of his own tough-guy image. In any case, we can never truly know what goes on in the minds of other people, and Maglie kept his thoughts to himself more than most. He rarely confided in anyone.

A word about quotations and notes: Excerpts quoted from taped or transcribed interviews remain as close as possible to the original, edited only for clarity and brevity. But in many of the instances when ballplayers of the 1950s were "quoted" by the news media, the reporters cleaned up the foul language to make their comments suitable for publication. In some of those cases—often in lines attributed to Leo Durocher, but sometimes in things said by Maglie and others—I have taken the liberty of restoring the quotations to something closer to their original form, which means a liberal dollop of profanity. In each case where I have changed a written quotation—by re-inserting the kinds of vulgarities those individuals typically employed—I have noted this, indicating that these are not direct quotations. Notes have been kept to a minimum, but all sources are listed in the bibliography, and on nearly every page I am indebted to the work of others.

Sal Maglie's lifetime spanned three-quarters of a century, and placing him within the context of his times means more than simply sketching in the baseball background. His life encompassed eras ranging from the outbreak of World War I, through the Great Depression, World War II and its aftermath, the apparently placid but often tension-ridden 1950s, the noisy and turbulent '60s and '70s, and on into the calmer waters of the 1980s and early 1990s. As the world changed during those decades, so did professional baseball. At the time of Sal's birth in 1917 major league baseball was a poorly paid sport played by white men of mostly southern rural backgrounds, who were entirely at the mercy of team owners and who performed in two eight-team leagues concentrated largely along the eastern seaboard. By the time Sal died in 1992 the national pastime had become a billion-dollar business that pays a diverse group of powerful and assertive black, white, Hispanic, and Asian athletes seven-figure salaries to play for almost twice as many teams, located in cities that span the continent. How events of the larger world in and out of baseball helped shape Maglie as both a ballplayer and a person is another concern of this book.

A biography should do more than merely recount the events in its subject's life; it should also illuminate his personality. Sal was a person, not a paragon, and he had his share of faults, failings, and foibles as well as numerous fine qualities of personality and character. Both Shapiro's and Szalontai's biographies of Maglie fall victim, in different ways, to the tendency to see Sal in terms of popular clichés. Shapiro frames Maglie's life within the traditional "comeback kid" genre. Szalontai offers a more complicated and contradictory picture. On one hand he claims that Maglie was a true American hero, a man who overcame early failures, blacklisting, injuries, and old age in order to forge a successful baseball career, and on the other he accepts the equally clichéd image of Maglie as one of baseball's most vicious headhunters. Sal shared many of the vices associated with baseball players of his own era and beyond: he smoked and drank heavily; wielded a colorful vocabulary of obscenities in two languages, with gestures to match; at one point gambled away a good portion of his earnings; and did his share of womanizing. But he never deteriorated into alcoholism; he confined his foul language to the company of men, mostly on the diamond; overcame his compulsion to gamble before it led him to economic ruin; and never flaunted his sexual conquests. Judging by two long marriages, each lasting roughly one-third of his life, and no divorces, Sal must have been a reasonably good husband. He displayed a typically Italian, absolute devotion to his family, not just his immediate family, but also his extended family of sisters, nieces, nephews, and relatives by marriage. His relatives recall his unstinting generosity to them during his major league playing career. Sal's relations also enjoyed his affection and personal attention, and his nieces and nephews remember the extraordinary warmth, gentleness, and generosity of their glamorous uncle. But Sal was less attentive to his own two adopted sons, and he spent so little time at home that his younger son claims to have no recollection of his father's presence during the first nine years of his life.

Sal's old friends, the men who had been the companions of his youth, remained his friends after he became wealthy and famous, and they adored the ground he walked on. Some considered Sal far too credulous and trusting in his business dealings, but for them he never ceased to be a hero. He made any number of unwise financial decisions, but no one ever accused him of dishonesty in monetary matters, and he never harbored hostility toward those whose poor advice he followed. Teammates and opponents, sportswriters and team officials remember him as a fierce competitor on the field, but relaxed and affable after hours, a man who did not nurse and rehearse the game's grudges over his evening cocktails. As noted, he was a man without prejudices, and although he absorbed his share of anti-Italian slurs, even in the heat of the most intense baseball combat no one ever heard him utter an ethnic or racial epithet. He did not have a Hall of Fame career, but it was a colorful and exciting career that spanned the 1950s, a decade many consider the best era in baseball history. Over the course of the intervening half century the image of baseball's demon barber has mellowed. Although he has been dead for more than a decade, friends and family in Niagara Falls, a generation of old ballplayers and baseball writers, and innumerable fans scattered all across America—myself among them—still remember "Sal the Barber" with admiration, affection, and love.

Sal Maglie

The Maglies of Italy and America

1

FAMILY ORIGINS

An exotic mix of blood flowed through Sal Maglie's veins. Although the press identified Sal as of Italian background, "Italian" in his case meant a stewpot of nationalities that included Greek, Roman, Slavic, French, Spanish, German, Albanian, Turkish, and North African Arab. He had the height and large-boned body associated with Albanians, Germans, and Slavs. The hawk-nosed profile, black curls, and dark eyes so often seen in Greeks, Spaniards, Turks, and Arabs contrasted with his fair skin, inherited from French and German ancestors, that nonetheless tanned to a deep brown.

In the early 1900s Sal's parents emigrated to America from Puglia, the southeasternmost province of Italy that forms the heel and several hundred miles along the back of the calf of the Italian boot. One of Italy's largest provinces and until recently one of its poorest, Puglia lacks natural defensive barriers, which accounts for the region's ethnic diversity. Its eastern coast lies about sixty miles from Greece and the former Yugoslavia, and its southern promontories are within sight of Albania. Visitors who venture much further south than the colorful old market town of Maglie, from which Sal's family takes its name, will find themselves in the Mediterranean Sea, only a few hundred miles north of Algeria and Libya.[1] A glance across Puglia's almost three thousand years of recorded history reveals colonizers, conquerors, invaders, and raiders, and all of them left their mark on the local population. The Greeks and Romans founded colonies, but the migrating tribes that disrupted and destroyed the Roman empire, the later Moslem raiders from North Africa, as well as marauding bands of Saracens and Slavs, and then German, Turkish, Spanish, Austrian, and French invaders, all devastated the impoverished land. Water grew so scarce that more peasants died of thirst than starvation.

The unification of Italy in 1860 ended the domination of Puglia by foreign powers, but officials of the new Italian republic were infuriated by the resistance of southerners to what they considered enlightened legislation. At the time of unification nearly 90 percent of Pugliesi were illiterate, and most agriculture so primitive that appalled agronomists from northern Italy compared the peasants' tools and methods to those of the Stone Age. Most boys left school and went to work around age eight, and conditions for peasant women were even worse. Few attended school, and many endured conditions little short of slavery. In the early twentieth century, Puglia had the highest death rate and the shortest life expectancy of any region in Italy. It contributed a smaller percentage of population to the great emigrant exodus of the nineteenth and early twentieth centuries than any other part of southern Italy, not because conditions were better in Puglia, but because they were worse. Most people who fled southern Italy were poor peasants, but they often owned a bit of land they could sell or put up as security for a loan, to raise the funds for steerage passage from Naples to New York. Few Pugliese peasants owned land—hence the relatively smaller number of emigrés.

Sal Maglie's parents, Giuseppe Luigi Maglie and Maria Immacolata Bleve Maglie, were among the more than 4.5 million Italians who entered the United States before 1930, but their reasons for emigrating were not the typical ones. Giuseppe's family was neither poor nor landless. They owned farmland outside Lecce, a sophisticated city in the extreme southeast of Puglia famous for its florid Baroque architecture, and there they grew olives and figs.[2] Giuseppe Maglie was born in 1883 in San Giorgio Jonico, a town on the opposite side of the peninsula from Lecce and about fifty miles distant. Decades later, Sal Maglie betrayed confusion regarding his father's birthplace. In 1951 he told an interviewer that his father had been born in "the Turin province, which is in the north of Italy, east of the Alps," about as far from San Giorgio Jonico as it is possible to go while still remaining on the Italian peninsula.[3] In 1968 he informed another writer that his father came from Foggia, a city in Puglia, but in the northern rather than the southern part.[4] Perhaps Sal confused it with the name of his mother's hometown: Faggiano.

According to a story preserved by Giuseppe's grandson Pascal (Pat) Grenga, Giuseppe graduated from the seminary in Lecce, the equivalent of a high school that also served as a boarding school for secular pupils.

Pat Grenga recalled that Giuseppe's brother Paolo received a university education, and became a professor and the dean of a private college, further evidence of the family's economic means and relatively high social standing. Since eldest sons in Italian families enjoyed inheritance rights that younger sons did not, it is likely that Giuseppe was a younger sibling. Many younger sons of Italian families chose emigration as a means of achieving the independence denied them in the rigid family structures of their homeland.

But Giuseppe had a more urgent and personal reason to emigrate. He had ignored a major social taboo by marrying one of his family's servants. This was his second marriage. His first wife, whom he married around 1905, had died in childbirth, leaving him with a son named Francesco. Giuseppe placed the boy in the custody of either his late wife's family or, in another version of the story, in the care of his married sister. While nobody would have condemned Giuseppe if he had engaged in casual affairs with servant girls while awaiting remarriage to a proper woman, it seems that there was something about Maria Immacolata Bleve that precluded such behavior, and it was not just that she was named after the Virgin Mary. Macolà, as she was known in the dialect version of her middle name, towered over Giuseppe by three or four inches. He was a compact, wiry man of average height for a southern Italian male of his era, about five-feet-four-inches tall. But in a time and place where peasant women rarely topped five feet, Macolà stood closer to five-eight, and in addition possessed a large frame and a strong will. She was also a striking beauty. With perfect skin, silky black hair, and enormous, piercing dark eyes under heavy brows, she looked less like a Pugliese peasant than an ancient goddess. Giuseppe followed her around as she performed her domestic duties, telling her, "I'm going to marry you someday." Macolà thought he was trying to seduce her with false promises. Outdoors, she responded to his advances by throwing stones at him.[5]

Born in 1890, Macolà was seven years younger than her suitor. She came from Faggiano, a town close to Giuseppe's birthplace, but even smaller and more remote. The town had an Albanian population, and Albanian blood may account for her unusual size. Her father, Salvatore Bleve, was a stonecutter. The entire family was illiterate, and Macolà never attended a day of school.[6] The best she might have hoped for was marriage to another peasant from her native village, but as events turned out, a very different fate awaited her. On July 9, 1909, Giuseppe Maglie married Maria Immacolata Bleve in Faggiano. The couple continued to live there, probably with Macolà's widowed mother, rather than at the Maglie family home across the peninsula, which suggests that the Maglies greeted Giuseppe's choice of a wife with something less than enthusiasm. On April 4, 1910, Macolà gave birth to the couple's first child, a daughter they named Santa Maria. Shortly after, leaving Macolà and their baby daughter behind in Faggiano, and his son, Francesco, in Lecce, Giuseppe departed for America.

"VIVA LA 'MERICA!"—IMMIGRATION AND RESETTLEMENT

Giuseppe's American descendants assume he emigrated in search of a better life, and in some senses he did. But his motivations were not the usual ones. Giuseppe came from a prosperous family and had no need to escape poverty. With his education, he could have found a profitable and secure position as a teacher or civil servant, but in America, his lack of knowledge of English would prevent him from finding comparable employment. Most emigrants left Italy convinced they would prosper more in the New World, but for Giuseppe, the opposite held true. Considering what he gave up by emigrating, he must have felt a strong need for a new beginning.

Aside from his education, Giuseppe was a typical Italian immigrant: strong, healthy, and young (27) when he arrived in America, and he left behind a wife and two children, with the intention of sending for them as soon as he earned enough money for their passage. Although he had no relatives in America, according to his grandson Pat Grenga, Giuseppe traveled with *paisani,* fellow townsmen who emigrated at the same time. As they watched the New York skyline appear and saw the Statue of Liberty, they no doubt added their own shouts of "Viva La 'Merica!" to the excited cries and cheers of other passengers. After disembarking in New York, they traveled to Pittsburgh, where they had heard there was work in the steel mills, but they learned there were greater opportunities in the flourishing industries of Niagara Falls, New York. Pat Grenga recalled Giuseppe saying that they worked their way to Niagara, hitchhiking from place to place. "He said they'd go a few miles, get a ride, stop at a place, and maybe there were Germans there. They'd have a beer, start singing German songs. Another place, a few miles away, the people might be Polish."[7] Giuseppe must have known hardships, but when he told the tale to his grandchildren, he made his first months in America sound like a grand adventure.

At some point in 1910 Giuseppe arrived in Niagara Falls, where he spent the rest of his life.[8] He could hardly have made a better choice. During the early years of the twentieth century Niagara Falls seemed like the center of the industrial universe. One-fifth of the fresh water on the planet lies within the four upper Great Lakes—Superior, Huron, Michigan, and Erie—and all of their outflow enters the Niagara River, more strait than actual river, and gathering speed as it drops sixty feet in half a mile of frothing rapids, plunges over the three spectacular drops known collectively as Niagara Falls. The shrewd eyes of industrialists soon assessed the potential of so much raw power. The original name they gave the town that later became Niagara Falls is revealing: they called it Manchester, after the English industrial city that inspired William Blake's poetic condemnation of its "dark, satanic mills."

Niagara Falls was a terrible-looking town. The same industries that brought prosperity, provided jobs for immigrants like Giuseppe Maglie, and made the region's engineer/entrepreneurs rich, also left a legacy of devastated landscapes and pervasive pollution. By the time Giuseppe Maglie arrived, much of the area on the American side of the Falls consisted of mills and factories, all running on the waterpower of the Falls, recently harnessed as electricity. That abundant, unending, inexpensive power source was a great incentive for chemical, paper, metallurgical, and even food industries to locate at Niagara Falls. The Pittsburgh Reduction Company (the aluminum-producing ancestor of ALCOA) moved to Niagara. Union Carbide, Carborundum, Olin, DuPont, International Paper, Norton Abrasives, Hooker Chemical, and Shredded Wheat also opened factories in Niagara Falls, and by the beginning of the twentieth century Niagara had become a leading production center. In 1910 it was a thriving city of 30,000, and by 1914 more than 11,000 workers held jobs created by hydroelectric power. In the 1880s the Niagara Preservation Movement, led by landscape architect Frederick Law Olmsted, secured strips of land adjacent to the Falls on both the American and Canadian sides, and persuaded the governments of the two countries to set the areas aside as parks. But beyond those few acres, the land around the Falls and the riverbanks exhibited a grim tangle of industrial buildings housing the companies that gave the world acetylene, alkali compounds, sodium, bleaches, caustic soda, and chlorine. All of them spewed a devil's brew of pollutants.

But hardheaded industrialists were not the only people interested in Niagara Falls. The place also attracted visionaries, crackpots, daredevils, and criminals. In the 1890s and early 1900s three men offered grandiose schemes to utilize Niagara's power. Leonard Henkle proposed the Dual Dynamic Palace and International Hotel, to be built at the crest of the cataract, where world leaders, pilgrims, and tourists would meet for spiritual resolution of the world's problems. King Camp Gilette, whose invention of the disposable razor had made him rich, envisioned the Falls as the center of a One World scheme, with the town of Niagara Falls expanding to become the only city in the world. William Love planned a canal that would utilize the drop of the upper and lower rapids of the Niagara River, as well as the Falls itself, to create an infinite power source, surrounded by an ideal town he named Model City. A mile of the canal was completed before Love's company went bankrupt. Decades later, Hooker Chemical used the canal bed as

a dumping ground for toxic wastes, and as a result the name Love Canal became synonymous with virulent industrial pollution.[9] The "mad water" of
the rapids of the Niagara River, as well as the heart-stopping drop of the
Falls itself, exerted a fascination for daredevil boaters, stuntmen, and persons in the throes of suicidal depression, as well as people wishing to rid
themselves of unwanted babies, and murderers disposing of the corpses of
their victims. People have thrown themselves (or others) over the Falls, gone
over in barrels, and tried to navigate the rapids in a variety of vessels, while
funambulists have spanned the gorge with tightropes and attempted, with
surprising success, to walk across. These activities contributed to a circus-like
atmosphere associated with the town of Niagara Falls, the alternate face of a
city otherwise known for its intensive industrial development.[10]

The more sinister side of Niagara, the thundering cataract's ability to de-
stroy just about anything cast into its waters, contributed to the area's attraction for criminals. Bootleggers did a brisk trade during Prohibition, ferrying
illegal alcoholic beverages across the Niagara River from Canada. Where
there are large amounts of money to be made in illegal enterprises, organized
crime is never far away, and the city of Niagara Falls has a long association
with that kind of criminal activity. Stories abound of gangsters tossing the
bodies of their victims into the obliterating waters below the Falls. Police reports from the early twentieth century note complaints from the town's Italians about threats from the "Black Hand," most of them attempts to extort
protection money from Italian families and businesses. As late as the 1990s
elderly residents of the Italian-dominated East Side could recall that the Black
Hand and other criminal gangs controlled illegal activities in Niagara Falls.[11]

Italians had begun emigrating to Niagara Falls in large numbers in the
late 1880s, drawn there by the promise of pick-and-shovel work and the expertise of some of them in bricklaying. Giuseppe Maglie first worked for
Union Carbide, shoveling iron ore. Since there was already an Italian community in Niagara Falls, Giuseppe found living quarters as a tenant of one
of those families. To earn extra money, many families rented out attics or
basements to immigrant men of their own nationalities. In return for a
small weekly payment, the men received meals and a narrow cot in an un-
heated room often shared with several others. There is no mention of
Giuseppe Maglie in the city directories of Niagara Falls during his early years
in the city, but he must have been one of the town's anonymous toilers, saving his meager pay, and looking forward to the time when his wife and
daughter, as well as his son from his first marriage, would join him.

By 1913 Giuseppe felt well enough established to send for his family, and
on September 16 they arrived in New York.[12] Overjoyed as he was to see his
wife and daughter, Giuseppe must have suffered a terrible shock when Ma-

colà emerged from the Ellis Island processing center with only one child clinging to her hand. Where was Francesco? Two family stories explain why he remained in Italy. According to one account, Giuseppe left the boy in the care of his sister, who became so attached to the child that she refused to relinquish him when Macolà announced she was taking her stepson with her to America. The more melodramatic version claims the boy had been in the custody of the family of Giuseppe's deceased first wife, but that Macolà had gotten hold of him and had the boy with her at the port of Naples as she prepared to embark on the ship that would take them to America. Then, a few minutes before they were to board, members of Francesco's mother's family rushed up and snatched the boy. Burdened with baggage, and the care of her three-year-old daughter, Macolà could do nothing to prevent Francesco from being taken away, and had no choice but to board the ship without him.[13]

Reunited with her husband, and settled in an apartment Giuseppe had rented in a house at 222 Fourteenth Street, Macolà gave birth to the couple's second child on August 15, 1914. By that time Giuseppe and his wife had become members of St. Joseph's Roman Catholic church, an Italian parish on the corner of Pine Avenue and Fourteenth Street, in the middle of a mostly Italian East Side neighborhood. The couple's first American-born baby, a daughter they named Carmen Josephine, was baptized there on September 6.[14] The first three months of 1917 culminated in American entry into World War I, and on April 6 the United States declared war on Germany. Giuseppe Maglie, who would have been drafted into the Italian army had he still been in Italy, was ineligible for the American draft.[15] He was 34, and had two young children, with another on the way. On April 26, 1917, Macolà gave birth to an eagerly awaited son. Since an Italian midwife delivered the baby at home—an apartment in a house at 366 Eleventh Street—no record exists of his size or birth weight, but he was probably frail. His parents must have feared for his life, because they summoned their priest from St. Joseph's church, Fr. Augustine Billerio, to the house the next day and had the boy baptized.[16] They named their son Salvatore, in honor of the Savior as well as Macolà's deceased father, and they gave him the middle name Anthony, after the saint who protects the sick. Maybe because the name Salvatore seemed a bit heavy for such a puny little mite, his parents called him "Sami" (pronounced *SAH*-mee), his initials with the softening Italian "i" at the end. They could only pray that their son would survive. Sal Maglie survived.

A CHILDHOOD IN THE FALLS

On June 1, 1915, a New York State census taker made his rounds in Niagara Falls, engaged in the trying task of extracting demographic information from the almost entirely foreign-born families in the town's East Side neighborhood. Italian names predominated, but there were also families from Syria, Russia, Poland, Ireland, Armenia, England, Canada, Scotland, Austria, Germany, and Bulgaria. Most of the men labored in the local industries. The Maglies made their first appearance as a family in the 1915 New York State census, and they were already beginning to Americanize. They lived at 366–R Eleventh Street, the "R" perhaps referring to a rear apartment in the multifamily house. Giuseppe was now known as Joseph Maglie, the English version of his Italian baptismal name. Macolà remained resistant to such changes. She must have struggled to pronounce "Immacolata" so that the census taker could spell it, but the best he could do was "Imiclator." He recorded Santa's name correctly, along with the little girl's age, five. The Maglies' second child, Carmen, was 10 months old. Joseph's occupation is given as "chemical worker," which suggests he was still employed at Union Carbide. The family also had four boarders, all Italian laborers.[17] Macolà supplemented the family income by taking in the same kind of lodgers that her own husband had been just a few years earlier.

The United States Federal Census of 1920 provides another snapshot of the Maglies, the first in which Sal appears. This time the census taker must have been inattentive, deaf, drunk, or entirely out of patience with Italians, because he transcribed every family member's name incorrectly, except for Joseph, who had already Anglicized his first name. Macolà became "Margaret"; Santa appears as "Sunday," Carmen as "Cosino," and the almost-three-year-old Salvatore as "Samuel," a common Americanization of a name with no English equivalent. By this time the Maglies had moved. They now lived at 225 Thirteenth Street, a house with a storefront that they shared with the Schiro family, who had six children, another family of three from Spain, and that family's three Spanish boarders. The Maglies also had two boarders, both Italian men listed as foundry workers. It is difficult to imagine 21 people, among them 10 children, stuffed into one small dwelling, but such close quarters were common among immigrant families. Others on the same block included people from Poland, Russia, Austria, Nova Scotia, and Canada.[18]

During the early 1920s Joseph Maglie left his job as a laborer at Union Carbide and opened a small grocery and meat market in the storefront at 225 Thirteenth Street. As a child, Sal sometimes delivered groceries by pedaling them to the purchasers on a three-wheeled cart. But the retail trade proved less profitable than the kind of work offered by the town's burgeoning industries. By 1928 Joseph had sold the grocery store and found employment with the city's aluminum-producing giant, ALCOA.[19]

By the time the 1930 United States Census took place, Joseph Maglie, again employed at Union Carbide, owned the two-family house at 222 Fourteenth Street, just east of Hymie Silbergeld's junkyard, which the Maglies earlier had occupied as tenants.[20] The house has since been torn down. On the part of Fourteenth Street where the Maglies lived, the section that extends from East Falls Street south to the New York Central railroad tracks, the homes were well kept two-family flats. But just one street away the residences were run-down and grimy with smoke from the railroad engines. That area was full of shady clubs, grubby restaurants, shabby stores, and—appropriately for the other side of the tracks—whorehouses. An old friend of Sal Maglie's, Jimmy Macri, owner of Macri's Palace restaurant in Niagara Falls, recalled with amusement that the houses of ill fame "looked just like any of the other houses—ya had to know which ones they were. Niagara Falls used to be *famous* for its whorehouses. When we were kids we'd go over there, and for a dime they'd let us watch. Then, when we got older, for a dollar we'd get laid."[21] Sal, too, no doubt received a youthful and rough introduction to sex in one of those same establishments.

In the upstairs apartment of the Maglies' property on Fourteenth Street lived a family of Serbians named Aiduk: two brothers and their wives, each with one child. The Maglies lived downstairs, and this time the census taker transcribed everyone's names correctly. By 1930 Sal's oldest sister Santa had married an Italian immigrant named Leone Grenga and had moved out of the family home. The census taker noted the value of the house at $8,000, that neither of the elder Maglies was an American citizen, that everyone in the household could speak at least some English, but that Italian was the language spoken in their home and that the family did not own a radio. The houses in the neighborhood had electricity, thanks to the cheap electric power generated from the Falls. They had running water and indoor plumbing as well, but no hot water, hence their designation as cold-water flats. The houses were heated by wood-burning stoves. Like the other addresses where the Maglies lived over the years, Fourteenth Street contained a broad ethnic mix. Benny Critelli, a childhood friend of Sal's, recalled the street: "There were all kinds of people. There was a black family named Grant. All kinds of people, but we had one thing in common—we were all poor. But we had respect for one another."[22] As a result of growing up in a peacefully mixed neighborhood, Sal Maglie developed into a man without prejudices, remarkable in an era when ethnic tensions in America ran high and racial and ethnic slurs were part of the common language. Although occasional flare-ups occurred, Niagara Falls had none of the tight ethnic enclaves and resulting hostilities that characterized life in larger American cities. Like his friend Benny Critelli, Sal remembered that "there were all sorts of people in the neighborhood—Italians, Poles, Jews. . . . The competition [among boys] was tough, but it wasn't between nationalities."[23]

By all accounts, Sal Maglie enjoyed a happy childhood, surrounded by love and affection, an upbringing reflected in a stable adult personality that was secure without smugness, confident without conceit, and unaffected by extraordinary personal success. His family may have been poor in contrast with the prosperity Sal later achieved, but "we always ate," as Sal put it in an interview many years later.[24] Although Sal's two older sisters both adored their doe-eyed baby brother, Carmen made him her special pet, and throughout her life felt she had a mission to take care of him. Macolà pampered him, too. As a child Sal harbored an extreme dislike for fish, and when his mother served it on Fridays he put up such a fuss, that rather than forcing him to clean his plate, his mother allowed him to fill up on vegetables, bread, and pasta, redistributing his portion of fish among the other family members. Sal's eldest nephew, Pat Grenga, who was only fifteen years younger, and regarded Sal more as an older brother, remembered being carried around on the shoulders of his teenage uncle. He also recalled everyone in the family catering to Sal. "Between my parents, my grandparents, and my aunt Carmen, they spoiled him. He was kind of a spoiled son, an only son."[25] But Macolà never allowed her boy to become a brat. She was not above giving Sami (as Sal was always called within his family) a couple of good smacks on the backside when she thought he deserved it. She once cautioned Pat Grenga's wife, Louise, never to hit her children with anything other than her hand. "She told me to use my hand, because that way you both share the hit," Louise mused. "That always stuck in my mind."[26]

One thing neither of the elder Maglies understood or approved of was their son's eagerness to play baseball. Sal did not have the kind of father that ballplayers like Bob Feller and Mickey Mantle had—men who groomed their sons almost from infancy for major league careers. Sal's background was more like Stan Musial's—mill town hardscrabble with immigrant parents suspicious of his passion for baseball. As far as Sal's parents were concerned, an occasional game of *bocce,* an Italian pastime similar to lawn-bowling, on a court the Maglies' son-in-law Leone Grenga had set up near their home, was all the athletics anyone needed.

Sal grew into a tall, skinny kid with coal-black curls and enormous eyes that gave him a gaunt, waif-like look, although he was healthy and loved sports. He soon learned to outrun his unwieldy mother, who had gained weight with each of her pregnancies. After a while she stopped chasing Sal as he ran off to sandlot baseball games. Sometimes, Macolà tried another way of keeping her son off the baseball diamond: she locked him in the basement. That worked only until he figured out how to pry open a cellar window, hoist himself up, and wriggle out. Another of Sal's escape techniques involved locking himself in the bathroom and opening the window.

Then he would unlock the door, scramble through the window, and dash away to join the neighborhood boys on the playing field. A less strenuous tactic was to excuse himself from the dinner table and sidle up to the front door, where he would stop and listen to see if he could hear his parents talking. If they were deep in conversation, he knew he could sneak out. He came home sooner or later to face a thrashing from his mother, which he accepted as the price for playing baseball.[27] Perhaps this was the beginning of Sal's remarkably high tolerance for pain. The sandlot games the boys played with such enthusiasm and dedication, despite their parents' opposition, also helped, as much as public schooling at the Thirteen Street School and South Junior High did, to turn Sal and the other children into Americans. Although they spoke their parents' native languages at home, neither Sal's nor his friends' English ever bore any trace of a foreign accent, and they grew up playing the quintessential American game of baseball.

Chet Grochala, another childhood friend of Sal's, recalled that in the summers he and Sal swam in the deceptively tranquil waters of the upper Niagara River, a pastime that must have left their mothers frantic with worry, since every year children drowned when they ventured too far downstream and were caught in the river's deadly rapids. Sal became a strong swimmer, and the exercise developed the muscles in his arms, chest, and shoulders. But baseball remained the boys' favorite sport. Chet remembered that he and Sal played on sandlot teams sponsored by local businesses. For a time Sal played on the Johnnie Ryans, a team that otherwise consisted entirely of Polish boys. Johnnie Ryan was a local soda drink company owned by a clever Polish American, Walter Janik, who had given his beverage an Irish name in order to market it more effectively to the local bars, most of which had Irish owners. What Chet remembered best about Sal was that "even when he was a kid, he pitched close to your nose. One time when we played against each other, I crowded the plate, and Sal threw the ball high, and I hit the only home run I ever hit. That night, Sal said to me, 'You little bastard! You ever crowd that plate again, I'll make you *eat* the ball!' The next time we played, I crowded the plate, and he had that ball whistling past my nose. I never crowded the plate on him again!"[28]

Perhaps Chet Grochala, who recollected the incident when he was 86 years old and in failing health, confused the mild-mannered Sal Maglie of his childhood with the ferocious major league nose-burner and chin-shaver Maglie later became, but this also could be an early instance of Sal's fierce competitive spirit. Nothing known about Sal's pitching skills as a schoolboy, however, suggests he was interested in or capable of pitching close to anyone's nose. Published mentions of Maglie's youthful experiences as a ballplayer agree that Sal was such a poor pitcher that even his sandlot teams rarely let him take the mound, relegating him instead to the outfield, first base, or the position nobody else wanted: catcher. One time while catching, Sal neglected to wear a mask, and a foul tip struck him in the mouth, leaving the lower part of his face a bloody mess and convincing him that he was, in his own words, "at the wrong end of this business."[29] Sal loved *throwing* a baseball. That interested him more than hitting, more than racing after fly balls, more than stretching his long legs to take throws to first, and much more than squatting behind the plate to catch other pitchers' tosses with his teeth. Sal played any position he was asked to fill, but when there was no one else around, he worked on his pitching, strengthening his arm and sharpening his aim by throwing rocks into the Niagara River. By the time he was in his late teens the men who ran the carnivals in Niagara Falls recognized him and refused to let him participate in games of skill that involved throwing balls, because he always walked off with the prizes. Another old neighbor and friend, Eddie Gadawski, recalled how "everybody used to watch him when he threw the ball, and knocked over all them little dolls."[30]

Niagara Falls High School did not have a baseball team. Boys could go out for wrestling, swimming, and basketball, but if they wanted to play baseball they had to turn to sandlot teams. During his high school years Sal played baseball with the Johnnie Ryans as well as with an American Legion team. Among the tallest boys in his class, Sal also went out for basketball. He excelled at that—and little else. A laudatory article in 1956 claimed he "did well in his studies, too, maintaining what approximated a 'B' average."[31] It is more likely that Sal managed a "C" average, and he must have failed several classes. His friend Benny Critelli recalled that he and Sal started kindergarten together at age five, and that they were still juniors in 1936, although they should have graduated in 1935. At that point Benny quit school and went to work. Chet Grochala, also born in 1917, recalled that Sal failed some courses and had to repeat at least one year of high school. Unless the Niagara Falls High School yearbook lies, Sal graduated in 1937, at the tender age of 20.

Sal appeared in his 1936 yearbook as a letterman in basketball for the 1935–1936 season. Next to his picture he signed Benny Critelli's copy of the yearbook with the name "Sam" Maglie. He was no longer the "Sami" of his childhood, but he had not yet assumed his adult nickname. The Niagara Falls schools encouraged children from foreign-born families to choose American equivalents or variants of their given names, which Sal did. At age 18, he was a work in progress. According to the yearbook, he stood six-feet-one and weighed 170 pounds, in contrast to his adult height of six-feet-two and a weight of around 185. Even his nose was still growing; it had not yet acquired the pronounced hook that characterized his adult profile.

1—Niagara Falls High School basketball team, 1936–1937. Sal Maglie, age 19, is second from left. Photo: collection of Daniel Bazzani.

In 1937 he was one of Niagara's basketball stars, along with Joe Morello and Dante Bazzani.[32] The team, called the Red and Gray, won their first five games, with Sal often listed among the outstanding players. In mid-January Sal received his first headline: "Maglie Stars As Mates Get Close Win Over Rivals." A few weeks later Sal grabbed another: "Maglie Tosses In 10 Points And Leads Falls Offense in Exciting Scholastic Game on Falls Court." On February 6, Niagara Falls dropped a game to Lackawanna High School, a contest in which Sal had three personal fouls called on him. The Red and Gray finished their season with 13 wins in 17 starts. Sal was the team's high scorer, with 137 points; Morello came in a distant second with 117, and Bazzani was third with 116. Sal also had the team's best foul-shooting record, scoring 27 out of 46 tries for a .587 percentage. Despite his outstanding play, the *Niagara Falls Gazette* did not choose Sal for its all-star squad. "But for the fact that overanxiousness caused Maglie to collect three personal fouls during the first part of several games, the Falls boy might have beaten Morello out for the other guard berth on the first team," the paper explained. Even at this early date, Sal had the aggressiveness that characterized him as a major league ballplayer. Maglie later looked back on his high school basketball career and observed, "I always played rough. . . . I scored because I used every inch of my body under the backboards. I pushed a little and elbowed a little and, finally, I scored. If the other team tried playing rough, I played rougher."[33]

After the basketball season ended, Sal, Joe Morello, and Dante Bazzani all received scholarship offers from Niagara University, a small Catholic institution in nearby Lewiston. Morello and Bazzani accepted the scholarships, graduated, and went on to successful careers as local businessmen. Sal turned down the scholarship, and he never regretted his decision. Although in Milton Shapiro's semi-fictionalized biography his parents urge him to attend college and display disappointment when he decides against it, in reality the elder Maglies, like many Italian immigrants of their generation, had little interest in higher education and considered Sal's high school diploma sufficient.[34] Furthermore, Sal knew he was no intellectual. He would have struggled in college and would have been there only because of an athletic scholarship. Beyond that awareness, there was also his stubborn allegiance to baseball. Although throughout high school he had played on baseball teams in and around Niagara Falls, Niagara University was interested in him only as a basketball player.

But the most pressing reason Sal turned down the chance to attend college was that his family needed his help. The 1930s was the Great Depression, and although Joseph Maglie had managed to hang on to his job, money was scarce. The Depression marked those who lived through it in different ways. Many emerged with habits of extreme frugality that stayed with them throughout their lives. Decades later, Maglie recalled that his friend and contemporary Phil Rizzuto, the New York Yankee shortstop, "was so cheap his pants had no pockets," Sal's humorous way of suggesting that the once poor but later prosperous Rizzuto never altered his early spending habits.[35] Sal, in contrast, reacted against his youthful poverty by becoming a big spender, taking pleasure in his ability to buy what he wanted, and to treat his family and friends to luxuries they could not have afforded on their own.

In addition to playing baseball and basketball, Sal worked for a short while at a local barbershop owned by Frank Dominic, because his father wanted him to learn the barber's trade. That line of work impressed the elder Maglie as secure and profitable, without the dangers involved in the heavy labor he himself performed. No matter what the economic times, he reasoned, people always needed haircuts. But Sal could barely be persuaded to show up at the shop. His tasks, which included polishing chrome, sweeping up hair, and emptying spittoons, disgusted and bored him. His tendency to slip out the back door and hurry off to play baseball ensured that his career as a barber's apprentice was brief.[36] Years later, the man who detested the idea of being an actual barber found himself the bearer of the nickname "Sal the Barber," a moniker that had nothing to do with his abortive barbering career.

After he graduated from high school Sal worked at Union Carbide; his father had moved on to a job at DuPont Chemical. But while the 54–year-old Joseph Maglie worked as a laborer, Sal received a cushy job as a clerk in the shipping department. Part of the reason was that he was a native speaker of English and had a high school education, but higher-ups at "The Carbide," as the workers called it, had another motive for hiring Sal: they wanted him on the plant's baseball team and for that reason did not want him injuring himself doing the strenuous manual labor most plant jobs required. Sal's friend Eddie Gadawski noted that "every plant in Niagara Falls at that time had a baseball team, a basketball team, a bowling team. All the guys that were good athletes—they're the ones that got the jobs. And the rest of the guys? Well, they just waited in line. Back then, if you were a good athlete, you got preference."[37] In the depths of the Depression Sal made $50 a week in a secure position at Union Carbide. By this time his pitching skills had improved enough that he made extra money playing local semi-pro ball. Pitching for teams such as the Simon Pures, sponsored by a Buffalo beer brewery, and another sponsored by Zito Realtors, as well as for the Union Carbide team, Sal picked up five or ten dollars an outing in addition to his salary, not an insignificant sum in the late 1930s. With his added income he could even take his girlfriend out on dates.

Back in 1934 when he was 16, and already a prominent student athlete, Sal had met the girl who later became his wife, his partner in a long and for the most part deeply satisfying marriage. Kathleen (Kay) Pileggi was a year younger than Sal, but due to whatever had held Sal back, they were in the same class at Niagara Falls High School. Sal was already a local celebrity, a young man with a "following," as his nephew Pat Grenga put it. The scrawny kid with the over-sized eyes had become a sturdy and strikingly handsome young man who did not lack for attention from the opposite sex. The only tactic Kay could think of for attracting his notice was to ask for his autograph. She had to wait her turn. "All the girls were crowding around to ask for his autograph, and I just followed suit," she told a reporter years later.[38]

She certainly caught his eye. Sal, who could have had his choice of just about any girl, lost no time in choosing Kay, whose good looks and Italian background matched his own. She was small, slender, and lively, with dark curls, large, wide-spaced brown eyes, and a big sunny smile. Kay was a generation more American than Sal. Her parents, Salvatore (Sam) and Philomena

(Mae) Pileggi, had been born in Canada, and emigrated to the United States in 1923. Sam Pileggi later returned to Canada, leaving his wife to support the couple's four children, which she did by working two and sometimes three jobs.[39] Not long after the autographing session, Sal began "courting" Kay in the quaint manner that now seems like something out of an old movie. He asked if he could walk her home from school, and offered to carry her books.[40] From then on they were inseparable.

Whatever Sal's earlier or later casual exploits, Kay was his first real girlfriend, his first love, and he never gave a thought to marrying anyone else. A contemporary of Sal's, American League catcher Birdie Tebbetts, confirmed the wisdom of that kind of choice: "The guy who marries his hometown sweetheart, that's the guy who is lucky. She's hometown, she's not Hollywood, she's not Broadway. But if you get a 'Baseball Annie,'—and everyone knows what they are, they are around every ballpark in the world—if you get tied up with one of those, it's not going to last too long and you are not going to have very much."[41] As for Kay, while the couple was still in high school, and long before marriage had crossed her boyfriend's mind, she announced to her family that she was in love with Sal and intended to marry him.[42] She did, but only after more than seven years. Sal was in no hurry to tie the knot. While his friends were marrying and starting families, Sal was trying to make it as a professional baseball player.

The Niagara Nugget Goes Nowhere

Sal's Career in the Minor Leagues

2

THE PERENNIAL PROSPECT

The Sal Maglie who picked up extra cash pitching for semi-pro teams in and around Niagara Falls in the late 1930s was a promising prospect, but the same cannot be said for Sal during his first, dismal years in the minors.[1] He had a good fastball and a natural curve tricky enough to fool a fair number of semi-pro batters, but there was nothing in his pitching arsenal to make a major league scout sit up and take notice. When he pitched at the minor league level he was at first so nervous his legs shook, and his control often collapsed in shambles. In addition, he was so emotionally invested in each game he pitched that he cried whenever he lost.

Sal once merited a quick look from a major league scout, but when the opposing team knocked out the jittery young pitcher in the first inning the scout turned thumbs down. Sal later filled out the story, with a touch of sardonic humor. "There was one time in Lockport, NY, when I was scouted in a semi-pro game by a very humorous guy, Darb Whalen, who, I think, was bird-dogging for the Dodgers. After the game he said to me, 'Kid, are you going to school?' I said, 'Yes.' He said, 'Keep going.'"[2] Jack Egan, a scout for the Boston Red Sox, also saw Maglie pitch during the same period, but thought Sal's jerky, snapping motion was a sure formula for future arm trouble and so passed on the chance to sign him. In 1937 Sal attended a tryout camp run by the Rochester Red Wings of the International League. At that time a struggling team hit hard by the Depression, the Red Wings could have used some decent pitching, but after Sal had thrown only three pitches, whoever was in charge had seen enough. "Next!" he yelled.[3]

A year later another opportunity arose when a group of local business-men developed a plan to bring high quality semi-pro baseball to Niagara Falls. The team was called the Cataracts, and organizers, hoping to lure lo-cal fans with local talent, offered Sal twenty-five dollars for each game he pitched and fifteen dollars for every game where he suited up, regardless of whether or not he pitched. That was big money—he would be paid as much for pitching one game as he received for half a week's work at Union Carbide, and the competition would offer more challenge than plant-sponsored baseball. Although Sal did quite well, the Cataracts failed to draw enough fans to cover the team's expenses, and before the first season ended the team disbanded.

But the venture was not a total loss for Sal, who acquired valuable play-ing experience. It may have been during his stint with the Cataracts that Sal pitched against one of the great Negro League teams, the Homestead Grays. Negro leaguers barnstormed all over the country in the 1930s and '40s, enduring taunts and discrimination as they took on local white teams. Sal remembered the Grays' catcher Josh Gibson, later voted into the Hall of Fame, predicting that he would hit a home run off Sal. He did, Maglie admitted, adding, "I guarantee that later on when I knew more about pitching he would have been in the dirt." Sal also recalled pitching against the Kansas City Monarchs, another topnotch Negro League squad, and claims he beat their legendary pitcher Satchel Paige, 1–0. According to Sal, Paige declared of him, "That guy should be in the majors," a day that was a long time coming.[4]

One further positive result came from Sal's partial season with the Cataracts: he caught the eye of Steve O'Neill, a former Cleveland Indians catcher then managing the Buffalo Bisons of the International League. O'Neill scouted some of the Cataracts games, hoping to spot promising tal-ent. Aware that the Cataracts were folding, O'Neill invited Maglie to work out at the Bisons' ball park, Offermann Stadium, and saw some promise in the high-strung youngster. To Sal's surprise, O'Neill offered him a contract for the remainder of the 1938 season. As he signed the contract for $275 a month—$75 more per month than his salary at The Carbide—Sal catapulted from a semi-pro team a few cuts above the sandlots to a Double-A minor league franchise just one step below the majors. He was, in every sense of the term, out of his league.

Baseball had been a colorful thread in Buffalo's historical fabric since 1877, when the Bisons began playing. Enthusiasm for baseball united the city's ethnically diverse population, which included a large Italian community. Among O'Neill's motives for hiring Sal was his hope that the young man with the Italian name and Latin good looks, who was already well-known for his high school basketball and semi-pro baseball exploits, would be a drawing card for the team. When Sal made his first trip to Offermann Stadium, he had never seen a professional ballpark. Not only had he never attended a major league game; he had never even watched a minor league contest. Now, he was about to participate in one.

Sal's debut was a disaster. Nervous to the verge of being sick, his knees knocking together, and without taking any warm-up tosses because he had no idea he was supposed to, the raw bush leaguer made his way to the mound on August 13, 1938, to face one of the best teams in minor league baseball, the first-place Newark Bears. Their lineup that day bristled with potential major leaguers, among them several future New York Yankees, including catcher Buddy Rosar and right fielder Charlie "King Kong" Keller. Even many of the lesser men in the lineup later enjoyed modest major league careers. O'Neill called Sal in as a reliever in the top of the third with nobody out and the bases loaded, a situation that called for a cool-headed competence Sal could not begin to provide. The trembling 21–year-old began his professional career with a wild pitch that scored the runner from third. He then walked the batter. Before O'Neill finally took him out, Sal issued two more walks, giving up a total of three runs. He failed to record a single out. Recalling the game thirty years later, Maglie deadpanned, "They didn't hit me. I walked them all, except for one I hit in the rear."[5] At another time he added, "I was so nervous that day I couldn't even see the catcher."[6] Sal remembered that inglorious inning as even worse than it actually was, claiming he walked four, and allowed four runs. According to the box score, he did not hit anyone—none of his pitches came close enough to the plate to do that particular kind of damage—and he walked three rather than four batters, allowing three rather than four runs to score. The Bisons, behind 5–0 when Sal came in, lost the game 10–2.

After such a dreadful outing it would have been no surprise if Sal had slunk off and disappeared. But Steve O'Neill, who had taken a fatherly liking to the quiet, intense Niagara Falls youth, was not ready to give up on him. He continued to use Sal in relief, and the pitcher showed marginal improvement. O'Neill kept him out of pressure situations. In his second outing, on August 20 against the Jersey City Giants, Sal came into a game where the Bisons were so far behind (12–2) that his performance would make no difference. In his mop-up role Sal pitched two scoreless innings. On September 2 the Bisons met the Brooklyn Dodgers at Offermann Stadium for an exhibition game. The fans had little interest in the meaningless contest. They were there to watch Babe Ruth, whose record of sixty home runs was under attack that season by the Detroit Tigers' Hank Greenberg. The Dodgers, then a mediocre team mired in seventh place, had brought in the decrepit old slugger as a coach, in the hopes that Ruth might boost their sagging attendance by putting on home run–hitting exhibitions. But he proved a pathetic shadow of his former self. He played in the exhibition game, which the Bisons *won,* defeating the big leaguers 7–5. Ruth committed an error, grounded out twice, and struck out. Maglie was the Bisons' third pitcher, entering the game in the ninth. He surrendered a home run to Goody Rosen but retired the side and wrapped up the win. During that outing he began what became a career-long habit of keeping mental notes on hitters. Aware that Rosen had homered on a low-inside fastball, he resolved that, should he face Rosen again, he would pitch him outside.

On September 4, Sal pitched the final three innings of the second game of a doubleheader against the Toronto Maple Leafs and allowed what had been a close game to turn into a rout. The Canadian team hammered him for eight runs, winning 12–3. With the season pretty much over, and the Bisons locked in fourth place, O'Neill figured he had nothing to lose by giving Sal a chance as a starter against the Montreal Royals on September 9. "After that first game," Sal recalled ruefully, "I don't see how anybody could ever have taken me seriously as a reliever."[7] Although he lost the Montreal game, 4–1, Sal turned in a passable performance. He worked the full nine innings, giving up six hits and three walks, and striking out two. In his first, partial season with the Bisons Sal had participated in five games and pitched a total of twelve innings, finishing with a 0–1 record and a respectable although not outstanding 3.75 ERA. It might seem that his ERA should have been higher, given the number of runs that scored when Sal was on the mound, but a significant number of those runs belonged to the pitchers he relieved. It had been his task to prevent those runs from scoring, and several times he failed to do that. In 12 innings pitched he had given up five earned runs and walked twice as many men as he struck out (eight walks, four strikeouts). He had also thrown a wild pitch and hit one batter. The best that could be said of Sal in 1938 is that he occasionally rose above incompetence and achieved mediocrity.

Since he had left Union Carbide with an agreement to continue to work for the company during the off-season, when his first term of professional ball ended Sal went back to his old job. At that point he had every reason to believe his brief career in professional baseball was over, and he held out little hope that the Buffalo club would want him back. But O'Neill surprised Sal by inviting him to return for a second season, a season that turned out worse than the previous one. Although Sal saw more action, his record did not improve, and he finished the 1939 season with three wins, seven losses, and a dismal 4.99 ERA.

In 1939 the Bisons enjoyed a slightly better season than they had in 1938, finishing third rather than fourth. Throughout the first half of the season Maglie slogged along, with no clear role on the pitching staff. Trying to find a comfortable berth for Sal, O'Neill sometimes used him as a starter, sometimes in a mop-up role, and at other times in middle relief. In all spots Sal remained inconsistent. Occasionally he turned in a good performance, as on May 21 when he started against Toronto, worked six innings, allowed three runs on seven hits, walked one and struck out four, gaining a 4–3 win. But in his previous start, on May 13, he had lost a 9–5 decision to Baltimore. He lasted eight innings, allowing only three hits and three walks (along with a hit batsman), but each of his seven runners scored as he gave up three base-clearing home runs. Later on Sal admitted that in his early years he lacked the finesse of a consistent winner. "I had a big curveball then, but after four or five innings they would get to me. It was inexperience."[8] He had the same problems as a reliever, sometimes stopping the opposition and other times blowing the game. On May 10 he pitched a perfect seventh inning against Syracuse and picked up the win, but near the end of June he was hit hard in two of his four relief appearances.

Around the middle of the season, after he had made about a dozen appearances, gained two wins, and suffered three defeats, Sal summoned the nerve to ask Steve O'Neill if he was ever going to see any regular work. He knew he would never improve by warming the bench. O'Neill's answer clarified why the manager was keeping him on the roster. He reminded the young pitcher that he was still very popular with his hometown fans. So *that* was the reason he was still with the Bisons—not because of his value as a pitcher, but because of his value as a drawing card. Sal must have known that to some extent—after all, Niagara Falls had already given their newly minted hometown hero a Sal Maglie Day, which was premature in view of his subsequent performances. Joe Calato, a friend of Sal's from Niagara Falls, remembered that the town held a parade for Sal when he was with the Bisons, with an open car in which Sal rode from The Falls to Buffalo, seated next to his proud mother. No one felt so proud later that day, when Sal was knocked out of the box early in the game. Learning the real reason for his presence on the club was a humiliation to Sal, but he swallowed it in the interests of remaining with the club. To have quit and returned home in the middle of the season would have been an even more humiliating and public admission of failure. He completed the season, picking up only one additional win and dropping four more contests.

Sal's roommate on Bisons road trips was another local boy, Dan

Carnevale, a Buffalo-born infielder who never reached the majors but who later managed the Bisons and also enjoyed a long career as a scout for the Cleveland Indians. The two young men, both from Italian families, had known each other since high school. Carnevale's most vivid recollection of Sal was of his friend's incessant smoking, an indication of the anxiety Sal was attempting to conceal. He recalled Sal as "a quiet guy, kind of distant, but very easy to get along with." Reminded of the adulation minor league ballplayers received on the road from local girls, the 86–year-old Carnevale growled, "I don't think he bothered with them much. Neither did I. We were all too busy playin' baseball! But I don't know what he did other times, when he wasn't with me."[9] Whether Sal was out sowing several acres of wild oats during road trips, or saving himself for the games and his girlfriend, is uncertain, but when the team was playing in Buffalo he lived at home. Someone from the team picked him up before each game and drove him to Offermann Stadium, then brought him back home after the game ended. At that time neither Sal nor anyone in his family owned a car.

Sal returned to the Bisons for the 1940 season, only to have his performance deteriorate still further. Steve O'Neill continued to profess his faith in his young prospect's eventual success. A 1940 program for the Buffalo Bisons contains a brief profile of Sal, and in it O'Neill insisted that "Maglie has as much 'stuff' as any pitcher on the Bison staff, but he still lacks the necessary experience to win regularly." He then went on to declare that "Sal has learned enough to be of great value to the team this season."[10] Perhaps the manager really believed what the program says, although it seems more likely he still hoped to use Sal as a drawing card for Niagara Falls fans. But the local hero was becoming a civic embarrassment. The setbacks he had suffered in the previous two years seemed mild in comparison to the disasters of his third year, when he lost seven games and failed to win even one. His number of innings pitched dropped from 101 in 1939 to 54 in 1940. Long stretches of inactivity separated his occasional and mostly unsuccessful trips to the mound, and his ERA soared to a grotesque 7.17. "As I lost the opportunity to pitch, my confidence went," Sal recalled.[11]

He was now 23, an age when most pitchers are either well on their way to a baseball career or headed for oblivion, and the latter seemed like it would be Sal's fate. Toward the end of the year Sal at last realized that the situation could not continue. Because he knew he was getting nowhere with the Bisons, he reached a painful but necessary decision: he told O'Neill he wanted to be sent down to a lower level of the minors. This was the humiliation he had been unable to make himself face in his previous two seasons, but now he understood that it was his only hope of continuing in professional baseball. If he could play at a level matching his skills, where he could pitch regularly and continue to develop rather than floundering around out of his depth, perhaps he might have a chance of working his way back up to Double-A and maybe even beyond—to the distant world of the major leagues, a realm he had visited only in his dreams. If three years of struggling in the International League had taught him anything, it was that he did not want to spend the rest of his life playing plant ball and pushing a pencil in the shipping office at Union Carbide. He had committed himself to professional baseball.

O'Neill agreed with Sal's self-assessment, and a few days later he sent Sal to the Jamestown (NY) Falcons in the Pony League. This was Class D baseball, as far down as the minors go. If Sal failed at this level, he was finished. He joined the Falcons' rotation but did not exactly burn up that lowly loop, either. In a game against the Batavia Clippers on August 22, 1940, he held the opposition scoreless for three perfect innings. Before the game the Batavia team had been a little in awe of Sal. They knew he had come from the Bisons, way up in Double-A, and they expected his offerings to give them trouble. But the second time through the order even the Class-D Batavians figured him out, scoring two runs in the fourth, two more in the fifth, and their final tally in the seventh, winning the game, 5–4. With the Jamestown team Sal managed to win three while losing four, but at least he brought his bloated ERA down to a more than respectable 2.73. He had seven starts and completed six of them, regaining both his confidence and his stamina.

Sal took his first step back up the baseball ladder the following year, when Jamestown sent him to the Elmira (NY) Pioneers, of the Class-A Eastern League (Figure 2). Elmira was another proud little baseball town, and its franchise had been in existence since 1923, the same year the Eastern League was founded. The teams played a 140–game season and there, in 1941, Sal finally hit his stride. He became the workhorse of the Pioneers' staff, hurling a league-high 270 innings, with 20 wins and 15 losses, and compiling an excellent 2.67 ERA. He appeared in 43 games, tops among pitchers in his league, and struck out 148 while giving up 107 walks. In one season he had gone from a sorry thrower to an accomplished hurler who grabbed his position's brass ring: a 20-game–winning season. Elmira enjoyed a strong season as well, finishing third and qualifying for the league playoffs. In the first round of playoff games Elmira defeated Wilkes-Barre three games to none, with one game ending in a tie. In the first game of that series Maglie came in to pitch to the final batter in the bottom of the tenth, preserving a 1–0 victory. This was precisely the kind of high pressure situation that had turned Sal to jelly a few years earlier. Now he handled it with aplomb. Elmira met Williamsport for the league championship, and won a closely contested

2—Sal as a member of the Elmira (NY) Pioneers. He joined the team early in the 1941 season, sent up from the Class D Jamestown Falcons. It is unclear why Sal, never much of a hitter, posed holding a bat. Photo: collection of John and Mary Pileggi.

seven-game series. Sal took a 2–1 decision in the second game and lost the sixth by the same score, but even the game he lost was not one that got away from him. He allowed a mere two runs on five hits in eight innings.

The successful 1941 season with Elmira came just in time. "I had just about reached the point of giving up baseball as a career," Sal recalled a decade later.[12] In the Eastern League he at last found the right level of competition: solid and challenging but not so overwhelming as to drive him from the field in disgrace. Sal never attributed his dramatic turnaround at Elmira to anything mystical—no strokes of luck or fate, no divine interventions or answered prayers. Nor did he ever describe his sudden success as a result of the game's clichéd answers: careful conditioning, clean living, courage, determination, and hard work. No doubt being freed from the strain of succeeding in front of his hometown fans played a part, but according to Sal, it was a simple matter of opportunity. "I got confidence from working. In professional ball you don't get anywhere unless you work. . . . I got to pitch. In Elmira they let me play. That was all."[13]

The spring of 1941 was also a busy time for Sal in his personal life. Even as he resolved that the upcoming season with Elmira would be do-or-die for his career in professional baseball, he and his longtime girlfriend Kay Pileggi eloped. On March 6 they were married by a justice of the peace in Lewiston, NY, a town about fifteen miles from Niagara Falls.[14] Since neither Sal nor Kay owned a car or even knew how to drive, the couple must have enlisted the help of one of Sal's friends in getting to Lewiston—one imagines an awkward threesome.

The first thought (or speculation) that comes to mind when we hear of an elopement back in the 1940s is that the girl must have been pregnant, or at least believed she was. Otherwise, why the rush? Such predicaments were not unheard-of, even in that sexually more conservative era. A year or so earlier, another aspiring young pitcher, also the son of devoutly Catholic European immigrants, had appeared at his minor league team's spring training camp in the company of his girlfriend, who was six months pregnant. Within a few weeks they married, and less than two months later the wife gave birth to a son. The ballplayer was Stan Musial.[15] If Sal and Kay had already become intimate, and given Kay's later, obsessive eagerness to bear children, it is possible she believed she was pregnant—the best of reasons for hurrying up their long-planned marriage. But more probable explanations also present themselves. Sal and Kay were both young, healthy, beautiful, and deeply in love. They had been a couple for seven years, and if they were not lovers, their physical attraction must have become an intolerable frustration. They were likely no strangers to each other's bodies by then, but still, in the 1930s "good" Italian Catholic girls did not go to bed with their boyfriends, and Sal could not support a wife on a minor league pitcher's pittance. So they married in secret, and Kay continued to live at home with her family while Sal, for the first time in his life, lived away from home, at a boarding house in Elmira (about 150 miles from Niagara Falls), during the baseball season. If Kay could sneak off to Elmira now and then, they could enjoy each other, secure in the knowledge that, legally at least, they were married.

But the charade ended one day not long afterward when Sal's mother discovered the couple's marriage certificate.[16] While Sal was away playing baseball, Macolà exercised the immemorial right of a mother to go through her son's possessions under the pretext of cleaning the young man's bedroom. Although illiterate, Macolà knew an official document when she saw one, and she brought the paper to her husband. When Joseph told his wife what it was she quickly concluded that such a *disgrazia* could not be allowed to continue. The couple must be properly married in a church and by a priest. But first, it remained to inform Kay's mother and to confront the guilty couple. The families had become acquainted during Sal and Kay's long courtship, and this prevented the situation from deteriorating into mutual recriminations. Instead, the two families agreed to do whatever was necessary to assure that the couple had a proper Catholic wedding. At the time Kay had a job at a local factory in order to supplement her family's income and earn money to pay for the lavish wedding she had been dreaming of for years. When she returned home from work that day, she found a committee of three elders awaiting her arrival. Shown the incriminating document, she offered a spirited defense. Both families knew Sal could not afford to support a wife. Would they prefer that the couple carry on an affair without benefit of *any* legal sanction? As far as the State of New York and the United States of America were concerned, she reminded them, she and Sal were man and wife.

But to people like the elder Maglies and Mae Pileggi, a secular marriage meant nothing. What counted was a church wedding, and they moved quickly to arrange that. The ceremony took place on May 31, 1941, at St. Joseph's church in Niagara Falls. In the parish register of marriages, the Maglie-Pileggi nuptials are squeezed onto the page in tiny, cramped script, among three other previously scheduled weddings on that day. Sal's nephew Pat Grenga, nine years old at the time, has pleasant memories of the luncheon reception—tables covered with a lavish spread of homemade Italian sandwiches and cookies and plenty of peanuts. The couple's formal wedding picture shows a radiant Kay in an elaborate white lace gown, with Sal wearing a rented tuxedo and a cat-that-swallowed-the-canary smile.

The newlyweds had neither the time nor the money for a honeymoon, and no inclination to spend their wedding night in a hotel in the "Honeymoon Capital of the United States," which happened to be their hometown. Someone in the wedding party, perhaps one of Sal's teammates, drove the couple to Elmira where, according to the recollections of Al Mallette, a retired sportswriter for the *Elmira Star-Gazette,* they had a second wedding ceremony in St. Patrick's church. This was a smaller and quieter function (probably a blessing of the couple by the parish priest rather than a second ceremony) for the benefit of teammates who could not attend the wedding in Niagara Falls. Then the couple changed into street clothes and hurried to the stadium, where, Mallette recalled, Sal pitched a game that night.[17]

3—Sal and Kay Maglie's wedding portrait, May 31, 1941. Sal's best man (left) is Kay's brother John Pileggi; Kay's maid of honor (second from left) is Sal's sister Carmen. Photo: collection of John and Mary Pileggi.

BASEBALL IN THE WAR YEARS

The year 1941 proved extraordinary in world events as well as in baseball, and it was significant for many more people than Sal Maglie. That was the year Lou Gehrig died—the "Iron Horse" who had played 2,130 consecutive games across 14 seasons succumbed to amyotrophic lateral sclerosis, the disease that now bears his name; the year Ted Williams batted .406, the last time any major league hitter achieved that plateau; and the year of Joe DiMaggio's unsurpassed 56-game hitting streak. It was the year when, for the first and only time, a major league game was halted so that an address by the President of the United States could be broadcast over the Polo Grounds PA system. Franklin Delano Roosevelt spoke of his determination to go to war against Germany, Italy, and Japan if he concluded that was necessary for the defense of America. That also was the year the Brooklyn Dodgers survived a tumultuous pennant race to win the National League flag for the first time in 21 years, only to lose their momentum in the World Series when what should have been a game-ending third strike slipped past catcher Mickey Owen, allowing the Yankees to rally and win the game. The next day the Yankees won the Series. Two months and one day after the end of the major league World Series and about three months after Maglie and the Elmira Pioneers had fought their way to the Class-A Eastern League title, the Japanese bombed Pearl Harbor. The conflict that followed permanently altered American society, and in the process it profoundly affected the game of baseball.

Born during the opening salvos of World War I, Sal Maglie began the final phase of his minor league career in the turbulent opening months of World War II. His performance with Elmira in 1941 had been just barely good enough to attract the attention of Eddie Ainsworth, a New York Giants scout, who gave the pitcher a lukewarm endorsement. "He hasn't much of a curve, but he could develop," Ainsworth wrote to the Giants front office.[18] With more and more ballplayers in both the major and minor leagues subject to military conscription, standards for the baseball draft were falling. On the strength of Ainsworth's so-so recommendation, the Giants drafted Maglie off the Elmira roster in 1942, assigning him to their Jersey City team. The Jersey Giants played in the Double-A International League. As the 1942 season began, Sal had made it back to the level where he had been when he asked Steve O'Neill to send him down to the lower minors. He had toiled for almost four years and was exactly where he had been when he started playing professional ball in 1938.

In the first months of the war there was some doubt as to whether baseball would (or should) continue. The commissioner of baseball, Judge Kennesaw Mountain Landis, a fierce conservative who despised Roosevelt, nonetheless swallowed his dislike and wrote to the President after the attack on Pearl Harbor, requesting guidance. After some personal persuasion from Clark Griffith, owner of the Washington Senators, Roosevelt responded on January 15, 1942, with his famous "green light" letter, in which he wrote that "I honestly feel it would be best for the country to keep baseball going."[19] The president was a baseball fan as well as a shrewd politician. He understood that baseball would provide a welcome distraction, giving everybody on the home front something to cheer about. It would take Americans' minds off the war, if only for a few hours a day, and confirm the belief that there were certain aspects of American life that could be counted on to continue, even in the darkest of times.

As the country geared up for war Sal Maglie behaved the way many ballplayers did: he tried to stay in baseball as long as he could. Although a few prominent stars, among them Detroit's Hank Greenberg and Cleveland pitcher Bob Feller, entered the armed services during the first few days of the war, most players waited, registered and ready to go when drafted, but in no hurry to speed up that moment. In spring training in Florida that year, as the Jersey Giants worked out with their parent team, Sal had his first taste of the majors, although mostly in the lowly capacity of batting practice pitcher for the New York Giants. When the season of exhibition games began he saw little action. The Giants' new manager, the team's popular outfielder and consummate hitter, Mel Ott (whose appointment as manager had been pushed off the front pages of New York newspapers by the attack on Pearl Harbor), paid little attention to Sal, and the quiet pitcher, never outgoing or self-assertive, was pretty much forgotten. He worked an intra-squad contest where he was knocked around and turned in a mediocre performance in relief in a game against an Air Force team at the Naval Air Station in Opa-Locka, Florida. He accompanied the Giants to Havana, Cuba, where he watched the Giants drop two exhibition games to the Brooklyn Dodgers. On April 13 Maglie received the news that he was being returned to Jersey City. But before he reported to Jersey City, he attended the opening game of the New York Giants' season at the Polo Grounds in New York City. As he sat in the storied stadium under the shadow of Coogan's Bluff, he had his first experience of a regular season game in a major league ballpark.

Sal absorbed the disappointment of being returned to Jersey City. He had not yet been called up by his draft board, and he enjoyed a solid season with the Jersey Giants, appearing in 50 regular season games, as well as in the league All-Star game, and becoming a dependable reliever. "I started a few games," Sal recalled later, "maybe three or four, but only when they were really stuck. I was strictly a relief pitcher."[20] He notched six straight victories in relief and ended with a respectable 9–6 record. The Jersey Giants finished in fourth place, good enough for a playoff spot, although they failed to win the Little World Series. In 165 innings Sal gave up 142 hits and struck out 92 batters while walking 74, and he compiled an excellent 2.78 ERA, a record that might have been good enough to recommend him to the New York Giants for their 1943 team under different circumstances.

But the circumstances at the end of the 1942 season were anything but normal. The call-ups to military service were increasing, shrinking the numbers of men available for major and minor league play. The manpower shortage became so serious that several minor leagues disbanded during the 1942 season. Sal received a summons to report for his pre-induction physical. Surprisingly, given his youth and apparent good health, he failed it due to a chronic sinus condition. Sinus problems, which can sometimes result in severe headaches, dizziness, and vision abnormalities, were one of the health factors the armed services deemed sufficient for deferment. Boston Braves slugger Tommy Holmes received a deferment for the same reason. But Sal's draft board informed him that it would not be appropriate for him to continue to play baseball while other young men from Niagara Falls were fighting and dying for their country and that he would lose his deferment unless he gave up baseball and went into defense work. His friends Chet Grochala, Eddie Gadawski, Benny Critelli, and others, were all serving in the military. As much out of embarrassment as patriotic fervor, Sal resigned from the Jersey City Giants and returned to Niagara Falls to take a defense-related job.

Beginning in 1942 industries in Niagara Falls had turned their production efforts to defense work, and Sal soon found a position. He worked for International Paper Company during 1943 and 1944 as a pipefitter—the industrial equivalent of a plumber—a trade he learned through on-the-job training. Although more hazardous than his old position as a shipping clerk at Union Carbide, the strenuous work enabled Sal to stay in excellent physical condition. "Most of my work was on construction jobs and I climbed girders and did heavy work every day," Sal recalled. "I had harder muscles and was in better condition than I was when I was in baseball."[21]

Although on the voluntarily retired list of professional baseball, Sal did not have to abandon the game during his years of wartime work. Instead, on weekends he played left field, pitched, and served as a pitching coach for the Welland Atlas Steels, a Canadian semi-pro team in Welland, Ontario, located just across the border from Niagara Falls and managed by future National League umpire Eddie Runge. Although the competition in the Niagara District League was hardly of professional caliber, participating enabled Sal to maintain his pitching skills. In 1943 the Welland team won the Niagara League title and went on to meet the Hamilton Co-ops in a best of three series for the Provincial championship. The Hamilton team took the championship, and Sal was the losing pitcher in both games. He blew the first game in relief in the ninth. In the second he pitched a complete game, but surrendered four runs in the bottom of the ninth to lose, 4–3. The following year, 1944, his team won the local league championship, and Sal compiled an 11–1 record. He was such a dominant figure that local newspapers dubbed the Atlas Steels the "Magliemen" or the "Maglie Maulers."[22] Years later a history written to celebrate the Welland centennial declared that "Maglie is the most prominent baseball luminary in the history of local sport. The Maglie era was without a doubt Welland's zenith in baseball."[23] Sal also made his mark in Canada as a basketball player. In the baseball off-season he was the captain of the Merriton Hayes senior team, sponsored by the Hayes Steel Company, and led the team to its first national title, the senior Dominion championship.

Meanwhile, major league baseball stumbled through the wartime years, making do with dubious talents and inferior equipment. There was a deepening concern that if the war continued for much longer, baseball would run out of men to play the game. Wartime players who otherwise would never have been in the majors included Pete Gray, a one-armed outfielder, and Bert Shepard, a pitcher with an artificial leg; a boy named Joe Nuxhall who had not yet turned 16 when he tossed two-thirds of an inning for the Cincinnati Reds, and grizzled oldster Hod Lisenbee, who made a comeback in 1944 at age 46; Chicago traffic cop Joe Miklos, who pitched two games for the Cubs before returning to his street corner; Eddie Boland, who played for the Washington Senators while on leave from the New York City Sanitation Department; Howie Schultz, a six-foot-six-inch first baseman for the Brooklyn Dodgers who was ineligible for the army because he was too tall; and a bespectacled violinist for the Buffalo Philharmonic named Eddie Basinski, who played shortstop for the Dodgers in place of Pee Wee Reese.

Commissioner Landis ordered teams to train near their home cities and to discontinue their trips to Florida and Arizona for spring training, because civilian train travel was being restricted due to the vast numbers of troops traveling by rail. Teams worked out as best they could in whatever facilities they could find, ranging from high school and college gymnasiums to the grounds of ramshackle estates, in chilly places like Bear Mountain, New York, and French Lick, Indiana. In addition to uncomfortable training quarters, the players had to endure baseballs made with a rubber substitute dubbed "balata," derived from the milk of a tropical tree, because the government had declared rubber a strategic material. Although Spalding, the maker of major league baseballs, claimed the substance would work as well as rubber, the artificial material around the ball's center hardened, leaving a dead-as-a-doornail baseball that one player compared to hitting a chunk of concrete. But with all its disadvantages, baseball continued. The New York Yankees defeated the St. Louis Cardinals to win the 1943 World Series, and in 1944 the St. Louis Browns, a perennial cellar-dwelling team, won the American League pennant for the first and only time in franchise history. In the World Series the Cardinals polished them off in six games.

War news eclipsed a major event in baseball history, the death on November 25, 1944, of the commissioner of baseball, Kenesaw Mountain Landis. The white-haired judge named after a Civil War battlefield had presided over the baseball world with imperial authority and a fierce rectitude equaled only by his rancid hypocrisy. Appointed baseball's first commissioner in the wake of the Black Sox scandal of 1919, Landis was a staunch public supporter of Prohibition who drank in private and an avid believer in racial segregation who managed to keep a straight face when insisting that no impediments existed to the participation of blacks in organized baseball. Major league club owners chose as the new commissioner Albert Benjamin "Happy" Chandler, a United States Senator from Kentucky and a strong supporter of wartime baseball, but a man with little knowledge of the game's inner workings.

Beyond the baseball world the tide of the war was turning in favor of the Allies, but there were more shocks to come. News of the D-Day landing on the beaches of Normandy on June 6, 1944, set off a national celebration, with the Statue of Liberty, kept dark since Pearl Harbor, illuminated again that night, although only for fifteen minutes. In January of 1945, while his long-suffering opponents writhed in helpless rage, Franklin Roosevelt was inaugurated for an unprecedented fourth term as President of the United States. He took the oath of office in a muted ceremony, with no formal attire, no parade down Pennsylvania Avenue, and no lengthy inaugural address. Less than three months later, on April 12, 1945, five days before the baseball season was to open, Roosevelt was posing for his portrait at his retreat in Warm Springs, Georgia, when he suddenly put his hand to his forehead, murmured "I have a terrific headache," and collapsed unconscious. He died a few hours later of a massive cerebral hemorrhage. But neither the death of the president, which plunged the country into a national state of mourning, nor a world war in its fourth year could prevent baseball from going about its business. Speaker of the House Sam Rayburn threw out the first ball at Griffith Stadium, since President Harry Truman was too busy with his new responsibilities to take on that ceremonial task. The subdued crowd observed a minute of eerie, absolute silence in FDR's memory; a bugler played taps, followed by the national anthem; and baseball once more began its annual cycle.[24]

A Taste of the Bigs

From the Jersey City Giants to the New York Giants

3

THE JERSEY CITY GIANTS

Shadowed by the country's grief at the death of Franklin Roosevelt, the 1945 baseball season began with neither players nor fans concentrating on the games. Both in Europe and the Far East the war was drawing to a close, and on May 8, President Truman announced the surrender of Germany. Amid jubilation over the victory in Europe and concern about the war against Japan, baseball began a slow journey back toward normalcy. The manpower shortage remained acute, and teams continued to make do with whatever players they could find, a state of affairs that worked to the advantage of Sal Maglie. Now 28 years old, with rusty skills and all the earmarks of a career minor leaguer, Sal registered yet another series of poor performances during a partial season at Jersey City, compiling a 3–7 record with an equally dismal 4.09 ERA. Incredible as it seems, in August of 1945 that was good enough to get him to the Show.

Sal could hardly wait to get back to baseball. On the assumption that the war was as good as over, he resigned his defense plant position in mid-June and returned to the Jersey Giants. He had missed spring training as well as several months of the season, and had been away from professional competition for more than two years. Although during his absence he had tried to maintain his form by playing semi-pro ball in Canada, he quickly learned that his skills had eroded. Although he won his first game, against the Buffalo Bisons, despite a mediocre performance in which he allowed three runs on 13 hits and issued four walks, the game was a disconcerting experience for Sal. "It was like starting all over again. I was rusty," he admitted later.[1] Maglie lost a game on June 24 when, after throwing four perfect innings, he broke down and gave up four runs in the fifth. He lost another game, this time to Montreal, on June 28. By the end of July he had lost six and won only three. He lost a game to Toronto on July 30, and on August 3 the Buffalo Bisons whacked Sal for nine runs in eight innings, collecting 14 hits and four home runs. Perhaps his disgusted manager left Sal in to take his lumps because he knew the same thing Sal knew, that the distracted pitcher had been called up to the "big" Giants. The New York club had a desperate need for pitching, and Sal, along with his Cuban teammate, lefthander Adrian Zabala, had received the answer to every bush leaguer's prayers: a summons to the Show. Sal Maglie had thrown his last minor league pitch.

THE 1945 NEW YORK GIANTS

In the final years of wartime baseball the Giants, like every other team, had struggled along with many players who had no business in the majors. Outfield aspirants in 1944 had included Bruce Sloan, an accountant with sketchy minor league experience; Steve Filipowicz, who had never played professional ball but had been a Fordham University star; and Danny Gardella, who had spent 1943 working in a shipyard and 1944 with the Jersey City Giants. "Dauntless Dan," as reporters dubbed Gardella, was a tough, colorful little New York native who hit the ball well, but whose fielding could charitably be described as uncertain. Pitching remained a problem. At the start of the 1944 season a gnarled 43-year-old named Lou Polli, who bore the cruel nickname "Crip," was a candidate for the bullpen, but he failed to last the season. His previous major league experience consisted of six innings of relief for the St. Louis Browns in 1932. Righthander Rube Fischer had shown promise, but a bizarre back surgery, in which doctors transplanted a part of his shin bone to his spine, ruined his effectiveness. As the 1945 season began only Bill Voiselle, whose severe deafness had kept him out of the service, was a reliable starter. Ace Adams had proven valuable in relief, leading the league in games pitched. Beyond those two, Giants pitching for 1945 remained in disarray. Righthander Van Lingle Mungo, a former Dodger more adept at bending an elbow on a bar stool than on the mound, had returned from the service, and the Giants hoped he might dry out and shape up. Harry Feldman, another wartime hurler, had compiled a mediocre 11–13 record in '44, and no one expected him to do much better in '45.

The Giants opened their last wartime season in strong style, winning eight of their first nine games, and by May 20 they were in first place. On May 30 the Giants' player-manager Mel Ott, who was leading the league in hitting, broke the National League record for total bases (4,888, established by Honus Wagner of the Pittsburgh Pirates), and on August 1 he belted his 500th home run, joining a select group that then included only Babe Ruth and Jimmie Foxx. On June 1 Ott made news for a different reason: the furious manager fined pitcher Bill Voiselle the astounding sum of $500 for ignoring one of Ott's orders. In a game against the Cardinals the manager had told Voiselle to waste an 0–2 pitch. Instead, Voiselle burned in a strike, the batter smacked it for a triple, and the Giants later lost the game. Normally, Ott fined his pitchers $100 for breaking that rule, and even though he later rescinded the fine, the punishment crushed the sensitive Voiselle. He had begun the season with eight straight victories, and his record had been 8–2 until that point, but he finished the year with a 14–14 record.

Voiselle's collapse proved symptomatic. Feldman and Mungo, after starting strong, were ineffective, and in June the New Yorkers lost almost twice as many games as they won. In July the team improved slightly, finishing the month with a 14–17 record. In early August, with his team mired in the middle of the league standings, Ott sent out another call to Jersey City. He had already brought up outfielder Whitey Lockman on July 1. Now Ott needed pitchers, and Maglie and Zabala looked like the best of a poor crop. Better yet, Sal was ineligible for the draft, since he had already flunked his physical due to sinus problems. Sal was so lacking in confidence that he thought Ott wanted the lefthander Zabala more than himself. Along with Maglie and Zabala, the Giants also acquired first baseman Roy Zimmermann from the Newark Bears.

Sal's career with the New York Giants began with no fanfare on a day and during a week notable for other reasons. On August 9 the Giants faced the Cardinals and their crafty southpaw Harry "The Cat" Brecheen before a modest crowd of 9,936. In the fourth inning the Cards knocked out Harry Feldman as they scored four runs, and with one down Ott called in Sal Maglie from the bullpen. Unlike his minor league debut, when the anxiety-ridden rookie fell to pieces, if Sal felt any nervousness this time, he knew how to conceal it. Although he walked a batter, he allowed no runs and recorded the final two outs of the inning. The Cardinals went on to win the game, 5–3. The public could be pardoned for failing to give much attention to Sal's major league debut. He was a nobody, another dreary journeyman pitcher coughed up by the minors in the final days of wartime baseball. But even had he been Christy Mathewson reborn, his debut would not have attracted much notice. Three days earlier, on August 6, president Truman had announced the dropping of an atomic bomb on Hiroshima, and when that cataclysm did not bring Japanese surrender, on that same August 9 when Maglie's major league career began, the president announced the detonation of a second nuclear bomb, this one on Nagasaki. During those tense days it is difficult to imagine many people making it to the sports section of their daily paper, tuning their radio dial from world news to ball games, or going out to the ballpark.

On August 14, after five harrowing days when the world held its collective breath, a dazed and devastated Japan at last surrendered, and the most terrible war in human history came to an end. And on that very day, as America and much of the world celebrated the Allied victory, as jubilant citizens poured into the streets, as church bells pealed and horns tooted, and the sidewalks of New York City disappeared under a blizzard of white ticker-tape, Sal Maglie continued to tag along with history, making his first major league start in a nearly empty stadium (3,038 attendees), and notching a victory of his own—his first major league win. Now, for the first time in a baseball career that had plodded on for almost eight years, Sal received attention not from the pipsqueak papers of little minor league towns, but from the New York dailies read by millions—the *Times, Daily Mirror, Daily News, Post,* and *Herald Tribune.* Those who made it past banner headlines trumpeting the war's end and reached the sports section found that writers had been impressed by this unknown hurler who emerged from the minors to whip the Cincinnati Reds, 5–2.

Reporters quickly applied ethnic stereotypes to Maglie. The *Daily Mirror's* Ken Smith introduced the new man as "Salvatore Maglie, a tall, 28-year-old Italian pitcher" and called the Giants' victory "a rousing day for the sons of Italy, as Danny Gardella, the little spaghetti eater from the Bronx, and fratello Ernie Lombardi" contributed hits to the Giants' victory. Dick Young, the popular and provocative sportswriter for the *Daily News,* called Maglie "the Giants' new spaghetti and curve ball bender." The *Herald Tribune's* Jesse Abramson dubbed the pitcher "swarthy Sal."[2] Although newspaper accounts agreed that Sal had triumphed over an easy adversary, a sorry Cincinnati team near the bottom of the league standings, reporters found Sal's performance impressive. He walked four, struck out four, and scattered eight hits as he pitched a complete game, giving up both runs in the fourth inning and otherwise holding the opposition to no more than one single in an inning. In the first three innings the Giants ganged up on Sal's mound opponent, Mike Modak, for five hits and five runs. Hod Lisenbee, born in 1898, and among the oldest men in the majors, relieved Modak in the fourth and shut out the Giants for the rest of the game, but five runs were enough to give Sal his first major league win.

Four days later, on August 18, he proved his first victory had been more than beginner's luck when he shut out the Pittsburgh Pirates, 6–0. Once again his teammates provided him with a comfortable cushion, pouncing on Pirates' starter Xavier Rescigno for six runs in the first inning, sending eleven men to the plate and the pitcher to the showers with only one out. Rescigno's reliever, Art "Cookie" Cuccurullo, then pitched eight and two-thirds innings of shutout ball in a losing cause, as his teammates failed to make a dent in Maglie. Sal struck out six, walked only one, and recorded one hit batsman, the first man to face him. He yielded three singles, one in the second and two when he wobbled briefly in the ninth. From the third inning on, Sal retired sixteen consecutive batters, until the first man up in the ninth, shortstop Vic Barnhart, hit a grounder that took a freak hop over second baseman George Hausmann's head and fell for a single. Sal retired the next two batters, but then right fielder Jack Barrett smacked a single, putting runners on first and third. Sal kept his cool and struck out third baseman Bob Elliott to end the game. Sal had a busy day at bat and as a fielder as well. He drove in a run with a sacrifice fly in the first, singled, covered first base for a putout, and had a hand in five of the Giants' 13 assists. On the basis of his recent performances the *Sporting News* in its August 23 issue named Sal their "Player of the Week," an unusual honor for a man in his first weeks in the majors, commenting, "He didn't make a spectacular entry with a ride in a barrel, or even float down the Hudson in a canoe, but he did come from Niagara Falls and now has the New York Giants sailing along on a second honeymoon. . . . [He] has been making the fans sit up and take notice in the Polo Grounds."[3]

In the last game of a successful home stand the Giants met the Brooklyn Dodgers on August 23, and Sal received his first exposure to one of baseball's legendary rivalries, a conflict so bitter that Dodger outfielder Andy Pafko declared it not rivalry, but civil war. In 1945 the man who later became the most successful Dodger-killer of them all had no idea of the two teams' long history of bitter conflict, an enmity that extended to the fans. Dodger rooters tended to stick together in the enemy territory of the Polo Grounds, congregating on the third base side of the center field bleachers, near the long set of steps that ran up from the field to the doors of the visiting team's clubhouse. (The home team's staircase was on the first base side.) From there they screamed abuse and rained curses on the Giants players. Bench jockeys were in full cry during the games, each side doing everything in its power to rattle the other with barrages of rude noises, insults, and obscenities. Beanball wars and spikes-up slides underlined the war of words, and had become a normal part of the teams' contests. Into the middle of this minefield walked an unsuspecting Sal Maglie, a rookie with no reputation for ferocity and no particular animosity toward Brooklyn. Manager Mel Ott took Sal aside soon after his arrival. "He had a talk with me," Sal recalled, "and told me . . . if you want to make money, you've got to beat the Dodgers.'"[4] He took the mound against the Dodgers on August 23, but lasted only three innings as Brooklyn roughed him up for three runs. Sal's opponent that day was a 19–year-old righthander who had once dreamed of being a Giant rather than a Dodger. Ralph Branca tossed a four-hitter, beating Maglie and the Giants, 4–1.

Sal won his third, 6–2, against the Phillies in the second game of a doubleheader on August 27. He hurled another complete game, had two hits and drove in a run. In each of his wins so far, Sal's opponents had been teams mired deep in the second division: Cincinnati, Pittsburgh, and Philadelphia. The 1945 Phillies were the bottom of the baseball barrel, on their way to finishing last for the seventh time in eight years. But the Brooklyn Dodgers were a different story. In his second outing against the third-place Dodgers, this time in relief, Sal again failed to still the Brooklyn bats. The game was the opener of a doubleheader played at the Polo Grounds on September 2, and it featured a near-brawl between the Giants' hot-tempered pitcher Van Lingle Mungo and Brooklyn's consummate bench jockey and all-around infuriator, their manager and third-base coach Leo Durocher. Only the determined efforts of two umpires, one restraining each of the potential combatants, prevented outright violence. Mungo had to leave the game in the eighth inning, with the score tied at 4–4, when he fell while fielding a ball and suffered a shoulder separation. After Ace Adams pitched the ninth Maglie followed with a perfect tenth, but he lost the game in the eleventh when the Dodgers scored three runs off him. Later on, Maglie traced his hatred of the Dodgers back to the humiliation of that particular defeat: "I walked [Eddie] Stanky and Augie Galan, and Dixie Walker got a hit that beat me. For some reason that made me resent the Dodgers. All the time I pitched for the Giants I hated the Dodgers."[5] Although he made no mention of it in regard to that game, one can imagine the jeers and howls from the Dodger bench that assaulted the rookie reliever as he handed the game to Brooklyn. The Dodgers had now defeated Sal twice, and in the process they made the mild-mannered pitcher angry. Sal, it turned out, had a long memory for insults and knew how to hold a grudge.

Once again facing the luckless Phillies in the second game of a doubleheader on September 3, Sal hurled another shutout as the Giants pounded their adversaries for nine runs. This time, the New York papers were not so generous toward Sal, as he notched an easy victory over the worst team in the league. Writing in the *Herald Tribune* on September 4, Harry Cross said of the Phillies, "It isn't difficult to beat them. The . . . games yesterday were just about as exciting as the Russian-American cable chess match." Hy Turkin, in the *Daily News* on the same date, merely noted that Maglie "held the visitors in tow all the way." Sal had more challenging opponents when the Giants traveled to Chicago to face the league-leading Cubs. The New Yorkers lost the first three games of the four-game series. On September 8 Sal saved the Giants from being swept when he pitched his third shutout, a 2–0 win in which he allowed six hits and one walk, and fanned eight batters. It was his second consecutive shutout, and this time the New York writers took notice. After seeing the Cubs savage the Giants three in a row, *Daily News* sportswriter Dick Young called Maglie the "magician responsible for the sudden and slightly miraculous transformation" of the Giants. Although he could not resist referring to Sal again as "the spaghetti and curveball bender," as he had in his report on Maglie's first game, Young expressed enthusiasm for Sal's pitching, wondering how it was possible that he had won only three games while with Jersey City. "His snapping hook lashed down seven [in fact, eight] Bruins on strikes," Young wrote in admiration. Sal retained his poise during an attempt at a rally by the Cubs in the bottom of the ninth. That inning opened with a single by Peanuts Lowery, but Sal struck out the next batter, pinch hitter Johnny Moore. Another pinch hitter, Frank Secory, batted for the catcher, Mickey Livingston, and forced Lowery at second. Cubs manager Charlie Grimm put in pinch runner Bill Schuster to run for Secory, and Schuster promptly stole second. With two outs and a runner in scoring position, a younger and less controlled Sal Maglie might have come apart. Instead, he fanned the final batter, pinch hitter Dewey Williams, to end the game.

Sal was not so successful in his next outings. Against the Cardinals on September 11 he left the game in the eighth inning, having allowed four runs and seven hits, but reliever Ace Adams took the loss. On September 16 Sal lost a close decision, 3–2, against the Pittsburgh Pirates, who had overtaken New York for possession of fourth place. With the Giants stumbling toward a fifth-place finish, Maglie lost his fourth game, 4–1, to the Boston Braves on September 23. In the Giants' final game of the year, also against the Braves, Sal pitched well, but the teams ended up knotted in a 2–2 tie when the game had to be called at sunset after seven innings of play.

Sal's first, partial season in the majors had concluded on a negative note, with two no-decisions and two successive losses. But despite his modest 5–4 record, three of his five wins had been shutouts, he had completed seven of his 10 starts, and his ERA was a superb 2.35, the best he ever attained. And, with help from Giants pitching coach Dolf Luque, he was beginning to learn about pitching high-inside. The Braves slugging outfielder Tommy Holmes was the first target of Maglie's knockdown pitches. In later years

Maglie claimed he prevented Holmes from winning the batting title in 1945 by knocking him down repeatedly that season, moving him off the plate, and breaking his concentration. Holmes lost the title by one point to the Cubs' Phil Cavarretta. Sal confessed that he had a particular reason for being so hard on Holmes: he wanted his fellow Italian Cavarretta to win the title. "If you were Italian," Maglie told Holmes many years later, "I wouldn't have decked you so many times."[6] One of the things Sal had to learn to deal with in the majors was the stream of ethnic slurs hurled from opposing teams' dugouts. Every ethnic group was fair game—Irish names brought forth shouts of "mick"; Germans heard themselves called "krauts"; Polish players were "dumb Polacks"; Italians had to listen to "wop" and "dago"; and the game's few Jewish players endured even more hostile snarls of "kike" and "sheeny." Evidently the ethnic abuse he had experienced during his first season in the majors had taught Sal solidarity with other players of Italian background.

Despite two fifth-place and two eighth-place finishes, at the end of the 1945 season the Giants rewarded the popular Mel Ott with a five-year contract and a substantial pay increase, which the team could afford, since their attendance had set a record, going over the million mark for the first time. The Giants finished the 1945 season in fifth place, behind the Pirates, Dodgers, Cardinals, and the pennant-winning Chicago Cubs. In the American League the Detroit Tigers came out on top. The World Series went to seven games, and Detroit won. Before the opening game, a colleague asked Chicago sportswriter Warren Brown which team he thought would take the Series. Brown summed up the quality of wartime baseball to perfection when he retorted, "I don't think either team can win."[7] But for most Americans the quality of play was less important than the simple, joyous fact that the Series was played in peace.

Almost obscured by the deluge of war news and the daily reports of games during the baseball season, several other events took place in baseball that had far-reaching repercussions. On August 14 the New York papers reported that a three-man syndicate consisting of Branch Rickey, John L. Smith, and Walter O'Malley had bought a controlling interest in the Brooklyn Dodgers, purchasing the stock from the heirs of Charles Ebbets, the team's founder. At that time Rickey was the club president, Smith the president of Pfizer, maker of penicillin, the wonder drug recently approved for general use, and O'Malley was an obscure Brooklyn lawyer who served as the club's secretary and attorney. With the purchase the group controlled 75 percent of Dodgers stock. The only other block stockholder was Mrs. James A. Mulvey, who held 25 percent. The *Herald Tribune* reported that Rickey, the only "baseball man" in the group, "now holds the reins [and] it seems unlikely that he will have any interference from his partners on any ideas concerning the ball club."[8] The reporter proved a poor prophet, as O'Malley later became one of the most powerful and prominent men in modern baseball. Branch Rickey, already known for his brilliant mind and innovative ideas, soon made a different kind of baseball history. He had found the man to break baseball's invisible but obdurate color line. On October 23, 1945, Rickey announced that the Dodgers had signed Jackie Robinson to play the next season for the Dodgers' Double-A affiliate, the Montreal Royals.

A third event bore a special significance for Sal Maglie. The December 27 issue of the *Sporting News* reported that Giants pitching coach Adolfo Luque would not return for the 1946 season. The Cuban-born Luque had accepted an offer to manage in Mexico in 1946, and he would spend the off-season managing a team in the Cuban Winter League. While he was still a coach with the Giants he had urged Maglie to keep his pitching skills sharp by playing winter ball in Cuba, an opportunity Sal was happy to accept. He liked Luque, despite the older man's gruff and sometimes forbidding manner, and Luque, who had worked with Maglie during the pitcher's two months with the Giants, liked the way Sal pitched. In Cuba, Luque was going to manage Cienfuegos, and he suggested that Sal play for his team. As a further inducement Luque reminded Maglie that the weather was beautiful in Cuba during the winter; Sal and his wife could enjoy a second honeymoon (or a first one, since they had never taken one at the time of their wedding); Cuban fans loved the game; and he would be paid the hefty sum of $400 a month for his services.

As America celebrated the end of the war and a long-awaited return to normal life, baseball had slogged through the 1945 season while anticipating the return of its familiar roster of stars and regulars and making plans to dispose of most of the assorted misfits who had populated the game for the past few years. "The boys" were coming back, and players such as Sal Maglie, despite credible performances, had reason to worry. Sal knew he was considered one of those disposable wartime players, and he hoped his season of winter ball in Cuba would keep him sharp and ready to compete successfully when the 1946 season began. But more important than the conditioning, the pleasures, or the pay, was the opportunity to work with Dolf Luque. In Cuba Maglie began a tough, demanding, and at times shock-inducing apprenticeship with Luque that transformed him from an ordinary pitcher into one of the most feared and fearless moundsmen of his generation.

The Cuban Winter League
and the Mexican Baseball War

4

LESSONS FROM DOLF LUQUE

When Sal and his wife departed Niagara Falls on their way to Cuba in October of 1945, the pitcher had no idea where his decision would lead him. He thought he was keeping himself in shape for the 1946 season with the New York Giants, giving his wife the gift of a vacation in a warm climate, and picking up extra money while learning more about pitching from Dolf Luque. Had he known he was setting himself up for a four-year exile from the same major league baseball he had struggled so hard to reach, he would never have set foot in Cuba. But had Maglie never gone to Cuba, he would never have played ball in Mexico, and if he had never gone to Mexico, he would not have developed into the superb pitcher he eventually became.

Cuban baseball boasted a long and proud history dating back to the 1860s, and Maglie was joining a class act. This was not the drab Cuba of the present Communist regime, but the glamorous, corrupt Cuba of dictator Fulgencio Batista—an island of luxury resort hotels, high-priced call girls, glittering gambling casinos under the control of mobsters, elegant restaurants, noisy nightclubs, and jam-packed baseball stadiums. During its heyday in the 1940s and '50s Cuba's capital city of Havana was not only a preferred winter haunt of the rich and famous but also the capital of Caribbean winter baseball. Four teams dominated—Havana's own Reds, the Almendares Blues, the Marianao Tigers, and the Cienfuegos Elephants. The intensity of fans' team loyalties equaled

4—Dolf Luque, Maglie's coach, mentor, and pitching instructor. The Cuban righthander passed on his expertise to Maglie during Sal's partial season with the New York Giants in 1945, in Cuban Winter League play, and during Sal's two seasons in Mexico. Photo: Transcendental Graphics.

the most fanatic loyalties of American baseball lovers, but one passion Cuban baseball never stirred up was racism. Cuban baseball teams were integrated, employing many Negro League stars from America during the winter season as well as Latinos of every skin color and a smattering of white players from the major leagues.

One of the most outstanding Cuban players, a man light-skinned enough to have been among the first accepted on the segregated big league diamonds of the United States, was right-handed pitcher Adolfo (Dolf) Luque (Figure 4). Born in Havana in 1890, Luque first broke in with the Boston Braves in 1914, then enjoyed a successful career with the Cincinnati Reds that extended from 1918 through 1929. He spent the closing years of his career, from 1932 through 1935, with the New York Giants, where he later served as a pitching coach. He won almost 200 games in his 18 years in the majors, and during that time he developed a formidable reputation for ferocity, both on and off the mound. Nicknamed "The Pride of Havana" by American fans, he preferred his Cuban nickname, "Papá Montero," after a mythic figure in Afro-Cuban folklore—a dancer, pimp, and all-around force of nature.

In 1923 Luque won 27 games for the Cincinnati Reds, and in 1933, while with the Giants, he notched a World Series victory, but he remains better known for his violent outbursts. Once, believing a teammate had made a derogatory comment about his Latin background, the enraged Luque hurled an ice pick at him. On another occasion, in 1922, hearing racial slurs coming from the New York Giants dugout, Luque stalked off the mound and into the dugout, where he punched surprised benchwarmer Casey Stengel, who had the bad luck to be sitting next to the man who had hurled the ethnic insults. Luque is also reported to have chased teammate Babe Pinelli (later a National League umpire) around the Cincinnati clubhouse, again wielding an ice pick, because he thought Pinelli had been lazy in fielding a ball hit down the third base line. Despite his reputation for violence, Luque was a skillful pitcher with a well-deserved reputation as a headhunter. A smallish man who stood only five-feet-seven and weighed about 160 pounds, he did not have an outstanding fastball. He relied instead on his sharp-breaking curve, pin-point control, and a reputation for pitching high-inside. His craggy, severe features, including narrow lips and penetrating eyes, enhanced the threatening image that underlined his aggressive pitching. This was the man who would mold Sal Maglie.

When Sal arrived in Cuba in the autumn of 1945 he was a big, good-natured bundle of pitching potential. At 28 he was a quiet, gentle, self-effacing man who adored his wife, remained unaware of his move-star good looks, and, after more than a decade of effort, had just begun learning how to pitch. Once Maglie joined the Cienfuegos team, Luque singled him out for special attention. Others had worked with Maglie in past years, but none before Luque had noticed Sal's possibilities as a mound menace. Luque took a good look at Sal—his unusual height, his black eyes, thick eyebrows, and heavy beard, his skin rapidly darkening in the Cuban sun—and saw a man who, with a little effort, could look thoroughly threatening. First, though, Sal needed to learn how to alter his appearance. This did not involve picking up a Carnival fright mask; instead, Luque showed him how to use his facial muscles to change his own features. He learned to press his lips together to form a thin, cruel, Luque-like line. His big, soft eyes, which could easily make him look dreamy and vulnerable, he narrowed to hostile slits, and he drew his brows into a deep scowl, except for moments when he stared down a batter—then he widened those eyes and froze the hitter with a poisonous glare.

But intimidating looks are of no use to a pitcher unless he develops an equally intimidating style of pitching, and here, too, Luque had a program. With Mel Ott's approval he had already begun working with Sal during the 1945 season, showing him how to brush back batters who took too firm a toehold at the plate. Sal's success with Tommy Holmes had proven the pitcher an apt and eager pupil. Now, as the season in Cienfuegos progressed,

Luque continued his lessons. The plate, the *whole* plate, he emphasized to Sal, belongs to the pitcher, and it is the pitcher's job to enforce his own possession of the strike zone. He must not grant the batter anything, not even those few inches on the outside part of the plate. Luque further insisted that for a pitcher to own the strike zone he absolutely *had* to learn to throw high-inside, not just a little bit high and inside, now and then, but often, and close enough to the batter's head that the man could feel the breeze from the ball, hear it hiss past his ears. The object was not to hit the batter and award the opposing team a base runner, and it was definitely not to "bean" the man and risk maiming or killing him. The motive was pure intimidation. The idea was to frighten the batter, shock him into moving back, and keep him from leaning in over the plate. Once moved back, the batter would no longer be in a position to hit pitches thrown over the outside corner of the plate. Hence the rhythm Luque inculcated: high-inside, low-outside, a sequence that became second nature to Sal. This kind of mound warfare did not require an overpowering fastball, but what it *did* require was extraordinary control.

Nowhere is baseball more a game of inches than when it involves pitching high-inside. The pitcher must be completely confident of his ability to put the ball exactly where he wants it. He cannot afford to be off by a couple of inches, because that is the difference between intimidation and serious or fatal injury. Although a pitcher may tell himself that if his pitch is too far inside he can rely on a batter's instinct to jerk his head back, there is always the possibility that the batter may "freeze" and fail to get out of the way. But there is more to it than that. Even a pitcher with pinpoint control may lack the temperament to pitch the way Luque taught. Just as many doctors never become surgeons because they cannot make themselves cut into living human flesh, so most pitchers never become headhunters because it requires a rare degree of nerve and cold-blooded calm to hurl a baseball again and again within inches of a man's unprotected skull. Batting helmets did not exist in the 1940s. Maglie the minor leaguer gave no indication that he possessed the temperament to become Luque's kind of pitcher, and might never have found out that he did, had he not encountered the flinty old Cuban in the latter's last season with the Giants and followed him to Cienfuegos and beyond.

Lessons in intimidation were only a part of what Luque offered. Sal already threw a good curve, but Luque saw a way to improve it. The Cuban took great pride in his own curveball and its remarkable provenance. Luque had been in his first year with the Cincinnati Reds in 1918, the last year of Christy Mathewson's futile fling at managing, and the legendary righthander took an interest in the young Cuban. During spring training Luque made a study of Mathewson's famous low curve and followed the older man's instructions until he mastered the pitch. Luque learned to throw a mean curve, and now, several generations later as generations are measured in baseball terms, and two decades after Mathewson's death, he handed it on to Sal Maglie.[1]

Along with teaching the secrets of successful intimidation and Christy Mathewson's curve, Luque also convinced Sal to throw from a variety of angles, ranging from strict overhand to full sidearm, to prevent the batter from concentrating on a single release point or predicting from what angle the ball would arrive at the plate. Luque further insisted that no pitch should ever be "wasted," a heretical view at odds with Mel Ott's order, enforced by stiff fines of Giants hurlers who ignored it, that a pitcher should always waste an 0–2 pitch—throw one far out of the strike zone to see if he could trick the batter into swinging at something unhittable. Luque believed that every pitch mattered. He of course did not insist that his pitchers try to throw only strikes, but when the pitcher was ahead in the count, and the batter expected him to "waste" a throw, that, according to Luque, was a good time to come inside with the high hard one, followed by a fastball away or a curve that caught the outside corner. In addition, Sal recalled, "Luque always insisted that pitchers must throw to exact spots, to batters' weaknesses, at all times."[2] Maglie absorbed each of Luque's lessons, and they stayed with him for the rest of his career. "I was just a thrower til I met Dolf," Sal confessed years later. "He made me a pitcher."[3]

Few details survive of Maglie's 1945 season with Cienfuegos.[4] Sal remembered winning nine games, and noted that Cienfuegos defeated Almendares for the championship. Maglie also beat the Havana Lions on several occasions. All his wins were complete games, and he lost six. Sal recalled Luque as "a tough, hard boss" who became furious at mistakes his pitchers made. When Maglie lost a 1–0 decision in the ninth because he gave up a single that rolled through an outfielder's legs, leading to the only run of the game, Luque stormed out to confront not the erring outfielder, but Maglie. "It was *your* fault," he shouted. "You *must* have done something wrong, or the batter would not hit you!"[5]

Sal's ability to beat the hated Havana team endeared him to the citizens of Cienfuegos, and once again he found himself celebrated as a local hero, the first time he had enjoyed that status since his short-lived celebrity with the Buffalo Bisons. But this time he earned his status through both his performance and his personal behavior. Since he already spoke Italian, Sal had little difficulty in picking up enough Spanish to make himself understood. His modest manner and ability to communicate made him even more popular with his Cuban fans. If not for his unusual height, the deeply tanned and darkly handsome *americano* could almost have passed for a Cuban.

Both of these factors—Sal's level of comfort in a Latino environment, and his success as a pitcher—recommended him to a pair of multimillionaire Mexican brothers who were about to give major league baseball its worst shock since the founding of the Federal League in 1914. Jorge and Bernardo Pasquel intended to use their family fortune to transform the insignificant Mexican League, which had existed since the early 1930s, into a rival of the American majors. Their plan of attack was simple: they would offer American ballplayers salaries, signing bonuses, and living accommodations beyond anything they could hope to receive in the States, thus luring them away from their American teams and into playing for teams in Mexico. They hoped to attract some of the game's leading stars, men like Ted Williams, Joe DiMaggio, Bob Feller, and Stan Musial, but they also were willing to settle for obscure players like Sal Maglie.

Bernardo Pasquel had come to Cuba to see what talent might be available in the Winter League, and Sal caught his eye. It was probably Luque who introduced his protégé to the Mexican baseball magnate. Since Luque had already agreed to manage in Mexico for the 1946 season, he would have been the logical intermediary between Maglie and Pasquel. "Bernardo offered me a contract for $7,500, plus a $3,500 bonus for signing," Sal related. "This was in February, 1946, but I wasn't interested because I had signed with the Giants for 1946 for $7,500. The only difference was the bonus and that wasn't large enough to make me throw over the big leagues and play ball under conditions which I knew nothing about. I asked him to double the offer and he said he couldn't, but he did give me his business card and asked me to get in touch with him if I changed my mind."[6] If these sums of money and offers made later by the Pasquels sound insignificant in comparison with the salaries of present-day ballplayers, it is important to keep in mind that $7,500 in 1946 had a purchasing-power equivalent to about $75,000 in today's currency, a solid middle class income, and vastly more than any of Sal's friends or relatives were making in Niagara Falls. Sal pocketed Bernardo Pasquel's card but forgot about it in the excitement of the season's end, the rush of packing to return to the States, and the opening of the New York Giants' spring training camp in Miami, where Maglie arrived a week late due to the length of the Cuban season. But the card from Pasquel soon came back to haunt Sal.

THE 1946 NEW YORK GIANTS

As the Giants prepared to open their training camp, baseball was not the only aspect of American life that was changing. Despite a fervent wish that everything would return to the way it was before the war had disrupted everyone's lives, nothing would ever be the same. Millions had died, and much of Europe, as well as parts of Japan, lay in ruins. During a speech in 1946 Winston Churchill summed up the grim new realities of relations between Russia and the West when he asserted that the Soviets had rung down an "iron curtain" that now separated eastern and western Europe. At home, the American government faced a rising crime rate, public transportation problems, and an acute shortage of housing as huge numbers of returning veterans sought to buy homes. The country also faced complex problems of wage and price adjustments. Prices, held in check by government controls during wartime, rose sharply in 1946, fueling an inflation rate of 18 percent. Labor unrest intensified as unions, freed from wartime restrictions, demanded long overdue improvements in wages and working conditions.

Among those workers who were beginning to think their employment issues should be addressed were major league baseball players. Team owners saw no reason to award raises to veteran players returning from wartime service, who had yet to prove that their skills had survived their long absences from professional playing fields. The idea had started to dawn on some ballplayers that they worked under conditions not far removed from slavery. A ballplayer was his team's property, what pitcher Mickey McDermott called "moveable meat," to be disposed of as that team saw fit. He could be sold to another major league team, sent to the minors, or released with no warning or discussion and without his consent. The standard player's contract used by every team did not permit players to change jobs and take advantage of higher salary offers or more attractive working conditions, as other Americans could. If a man did not wish to play for the same team the next year, the standard contract prohibited him from offering his services to any other team. If the player disliked that provision—known as the "reserve clause"—then he was welcome to take up some other line of work. Many players also wanted a pension plan, another benefit numerous other professions offered that baseball did not. Ballplayers had short working lives, and when their careers ended they would have nothing to fall back on except Social Security, then an untested program still in its infancy, and whatever they had saved.[7] Although there were a small number of highly paid players such as Babe Ruth and later Joe DiMaggio, Ted Williams, Bob Feller, and Hank Greenberg, most players received very modest salaries; some were paid as little as $2,500 per season, and others were rumored to make even less. The six-figure salaries now paid to bottom-level major league benchwarmers were still decades away.

Despite the turbulent times, the Giants were full of optimism as they opened their first postwar training camp under the sunny skies of Florida. This was no ordinary spring. Familiar figures had returned from military service, and a bumper crop of eager rookies added to the competitive atmosphere, crowding the camp with 60 potential players, a record number. Giants owner Horace Stoneham had acquired a massive six-foot-five-inch Texan named Clint Hartung, a *"phee*-nom," as the sportswriters called him, acclaimed as another Babe Ruth, who could both pitch and hit. In January Stoneham had paid $175,000 for Walker Cooper, considered one of baseball's best catchers. Other proven players were returning, among them sluggers Willard Marshall and Johnny Mize and outfielder Sid Gordon. Although infield prospects included the skinny, scrappy Bill Rigney—as well as a promising second baseman in Buddy Blattner—Roy Zimmermann and George Hausmann would not willingly step aside, and they were in no mood to let either rookies or returning veterans take over their positions. And the Giants' cup was running over with pitchers. There were 25 in camp, as many contestants for slots on the pitching staff as there are on a team's full roster of all positions for the season. Despite those numbers, the *Sporting News* singled out Sal Maglie, saying he "has been doing some brilliant pitching in Cuba this winter."[8]

Manager Mel Ott and his coaches had their hands full trying to evaluate so many players, pitchers in particular, and it was inevitable that some would be overlooked. Maglie, though, had good reasons to think he would make the team and enjoy a successful season. He had put in a solid partial season with the Giants in 1945, he was in excellent condition after his months of winter ball in Cuba, and he knew Luque's tutoring had improved his pitching. Sal signed his 1946 contract for an amount variously reported as $5,000, $6,000, $7,000, $7,500, or $8,000.[9] At that moment Sal was less concerned about how much money he was making than about how he could bring himself to Ott's attention. He was sure that all he needed was the chance to show his manager what he could do on the mound, and his place on the pitching staff would be assured.

Sal claimed that when he arrived in camp Ott greeted him with enthusiasm, exclaiming, "We're depending on you, boy!" and then forgot about him.[10] Maglie felt he had earned regular and frequent work, and he resented Ott for failing to give it to him. Sal did not appear in an exhibition game until March 14, almost a month after spring training began, and three weeks after his arrival in camp, and as a result he must have spent much of the time before that date stewing about Ott's lack of interest in him. But, just as he had remembered his first outing with the Buffalo Bisons as being worse than it actually was, Sal also recalled being treated worse during spring training of 1946 than the actual treatment he received. Thinking back to that spring several decades later he declared, "I pitched five innings in one game and struck out seven. And then I never got a chance to pitch again— not even batting practice. . . . Maybe [Ott] didn't like me. . . . I guess I was in his doghouse. Ott just ignored me."[11] In another interview, in the early 1980s, Sal complained again about being denied the opportunity to pitch batting practice: "Mel Ott set up a pitching rotation for batting practice for the purpose of getting a look at all the new pitchers, who were many. It was so bad that Ott would not even let me join the batting practice rotation."[12]

Without realizing it, Sal provided an explanation for why Ott had excluded him from the batting practice rotation; the manager was trying to get a look at the numerous *new* pitchers, and Maglie was a returnee. In fact, during March Sal saw action in some intra-squad contests as well as making three appearances in exhibition games. On March 7 the *Sporting News* noted him, along with several others, as having "pitched some fine ball in the intra-camp league games last week." Although not a large number of outings, the combined intra-squad and exhibition game appearances hardly constitute being ignored, especially considering that there were more than two dozen pitchers on the roster. In his first exhibition game, on March 14, Sal defeated the Boston Braves, 8–3, pitching five innings, yielding two runs on five hits, and issuing one walk. A week later the *Times* reported that Ott had pointed with pride to half a dozen pitchers on his staff whom he considered ready to begin the new season. One of those pitchers was Sal Maglie. On March 21 Sal lost a game in relief to the Philadelphia Athletics, 11–7, getting blasted for six runs in the eighth inning, giving up four walks, and committing a balk that brought in one of the runs. He pitched for the third time on March 30 against the Phillies, and won his second game of the training season with a deft performance in relief. Although he did not realize it, the next time he would pitch in a major league game would be almost four years later.

THE MEXICAN BASEBALL WAR

While Sal was struggling for attention from Mel Ott and nursing his resentments for what he considered the Giants' lack of appreciation of his efforts and abilities, major league baseball was under attack. The Pasquels were stepping up their campaign to lure American players to the Mexican League, making promises of extravagant monetary rewards for players willing to break their contracts and head south. Major league locker rooms, as well as the sports pages of major newspapers, buzzed with reports of the Pasquels' activities, along with rumors of their fabulous wealth and flamboyant lifestyle.

There were five Pasquel brothers—Bernardo, Jorge, Mario, and twins Alfonso and Gerardo—all born into substantial wealth in Veracruz, Mexico, in the early years of the twentieth century. Their father's cigar factory and customs brokerage firm had become the base for a business empire that included imports and exports, banks, cattle, publishing, movies, shipping, and automobile dealerships. Married to the daughter of a former president of Mexico, Jorge Pasquel also had business and personal ties with the man who became the next president of Mexico in 1946, Miguel Alemán. Jorge was a flashy dresser who considered a diamond stickpin, diamond cuff links, and a pearl-handled revolver essential parts of every sartorial ensemble. He was vain about his body, abstained from smoking, and maintained a regimen of exercise; he enjoyed fast women (especially Mexican movie actresses) and faster cars and was a big game hunter, an aviation enthusiast, and something of an expert on Napoleon. On the floor of his posh office in Mexico City lay the pelt of a gray mountain lion he had shot. He nicknamed it Ted Williams, in honor of his hopes of figuratively bringing down the great hitter and having him play in Mexico. He owned mansions all over the country.[13]

As a child Jorge Pasquel had developed a passion for baseball and had played on amateur teams, and as an adult he dreamed of making a name for himself in the baseball world. In the early 1940s he went on an eight-month tour of the United States to observe American major league baseball. He returned home with the idea of elevating the level of play in Mexico by bringing American players to the eight-team Mexican League, of which he was president. He also owned, or owned an interest in, several of the teams in the Mexican League, and he owned all the ballparks. Aware of the lower quality of the game in Mexico, Pasquel knew that the only way he could persuade American major leaguers to abandon their careers in the States would be to offer them enormous sums of money, and this he was prepared to do, with funds from his family coffers. In 1944 the Mexican League had convinced Rogers Hornsby to trade his American managerial career for one in Mexico, but the irascible Hall of Fame hitter, whose idea of constructive criticism of a losing pitcher was to follow the luckless fellow into the showers and urinate on his leg, got along no better with people in Mexico than he had at home, and he lasted only a year.[14] Pasquel began his own campaign quietly in 1945, luring several obscure Latino ballplayers to Mexico, defections that received little attention from the press. Jorge Pasquel's tactics changed radically in 1946. He realized that with baseball's veteran players returning from military service, there would be a surplus of talent, and he no longer had to settle for little-known players of Hispanic background. He launched an aggressive campaign that amounted to a declaration of war on American baseball. He was determined to stock his Mexican League teams with top American players, no matter what the cost.

Danny Gardella, the butter-fingered little New York Giants outfielder, was the unlikely gunner who fired the first shot in the Pasquels' baseball war. During the off-season Gardella worked as a trainer at Al Roon's Gym in New York City. There, during the winter of 1945–1946, he met fellow physical culture devotee Jorge Pasquel, who was in New York on business and needed a place to exercise. The Mexican millionaire grew incredulous when he learned that Gardella had to work at Roon's during the off-season because his salary from the Giants was not sufficient to last him through the year. Although Gardella turned down Pasquel's initial offer of employment in Mexican baseball because he was confident of his chances of making the Giants squad, he told Pasquel he would keep his offer in mind. Gardella then suffered a series of misunderstandings and conflicts with the Giants that left him so angry and frustrated that he decided to call his Mexican contact. A delighted Jorge Pasquel sent an agent to New York to escort Gardella—his first non-Latino recruit—to Mexico, where he signed a contract for $8,000 and was promised an additional $5,000 as a signing bonus. Because Gardella was a professional baseball player, he encountered a unique problem. Although he had not signed his New York Giants contract (for $5,000, he reported) at the time he departed for Mexico, the Giants considered Gardella tied to them by baseball's reserve clause. He had committed the cardinal sin of flouting that sacred text of major league baseball, and there were bound to be repercussions.

Before he left for Mexico on February 18 Gardella told reporters he had talked with other Giants players, and that two of them had also decided to sign contracts with the Pasquels: pitcher Adrian Zabala and Gardella's roommate, infielder Nap Reyes. Spring training had hardly begun, and the Giants had already lost three team members, but with their bloated postwar roster they were not concerned. Mel Ott scoffed that marginal players like Gardella were no longer important, now that the war was over. Ott did not realize that a new war had just begun.

By the time Maglie reached the Giants' training camp on February 22, Gardella was already gone, but he had left behind a camp abuzz with rumors of Mexican money. At first Sal ignored the stories, because he thought he had a good chance to make the team. He had already turned down the Pasquels once, and he felt he had worked too hard in hauling himself up to the majors to throw it all away. The story of what happened next remains complicated and full of contradictions, many of them created by Maglie himself as he told the story repeatedly over the years. In an early version, which he related in 1951, Sal cast himself in a passive role with regard to recruiting for the Mexican League. "I never gave a thought to Mexico until Hausmann and Zimmermann, who'd heard I'd had an offer, asked me how they could get in touch with the Pasquels," Sal recalled. "I remembered Bernardo's card, and I said I had his address and phone number in my hotel room."[15] It is worth wondering why Maglie so carefully held on to Bernardo Pasquel's card and brought it with him to Miami, if he had never given another thought to playing in Mexico. In an interview in 1952 Sal related a different story. He said that he had not been in Miami long when he received a call from Bernardo Pasquel. "He was looking for some ballplayers. I knew Roy Zimmermann and George Hausmann wanted to go, so I told them about Pasquel and they put through a call to him from my hotel room. After he got finished talking to them, Bernardo got on with me again and said, 'How about you?' I told him no, I wasn't interested at those prices, I'd be just as well off staying here. So he finally agreed to pay me what I'd asked [twice his Giants salary], and I said OK, he had a deal."[16]

Fifteen years later, Maglie told yet another story, in which he described himself as playing an active part, but with the call coming from Danny Gardella, not Bernardo Pasquel. In this version, one day when Sal was in his hotel room he received a phone call from Gardella in Mexico. "He said they needed players down there, and he wanted me to suggest some Giants who might be willing to go," Sal recalled in 1966.[17] Gardella told Sal the Mexican teams needed infielders but also wanted to know if Sal himself might be interested. Maglie said no, he was sticking with the Giants, but mentioned George Hausmann and Roy Zimmermann. Hausmann, the Giants regular second baseman in 1945, now being challenged for his position by Buddy Blattner and Mickey Witek, and Zimmermann, the marginal first baseman about to lose his job to returning star Johnny Mize, showed immediate interest. A few years before his death in 2004, the elderly George Hausmann related still another version of the Mexican recruitment story, in which he claimed that Maglie himself made two phone calls to Danny Gardella in Mexico and in the second of them also spoke with Bernardo Pasquel.[18]

Whether because Maglie had sought them out and personally urged them to contact the Pasquels, or whether they had heard through the team grapevine about Maglie's Mexican connections and gotten in touch with Sal on their own, can no longer be determined, but one thing is certain: the two infielders went up to Sal's hotel room and from there they, or Maglie, placed a collect call to Mexico City. They spoke to Bernardo Pasquel, who promptly offered the two men a $5,000 bonus each and salaries that were double the $7,000 they were making with the Giants, leaving them goggle-eyed at the amount of money suddenly at their fingertips. (Readers are reminded that such sums must be multiplied by 10 to reflect their current buying power, and should be considered without reference to the pay of present-day ballplayers.) Sal also spoke with Bernardo Pasquel during the same phone call. According to Sal's 1952 recollections, they came to an agreement that he would receive double his New York Giants salary, and Sal then accepted the offer. After his two teammates left Sal called Kay, and they talked the matter over at some length before deciding definitively—at least according to Sal's 1952 recollections—to take the Mexican offer. Sal later insisted, however, that they did not finalize anything, and he had not yet made up his mind concerning whether he would go to Mexico.

Meanwhile, even before Sal began weighing his options, and Hausmann and Zimmermann began crowing about their money, Mexican jumping beans had started sprouting all across the majors. More players, most of them marginal but a few of them quite prominent, announced they were leaving their American teams to play in Mexico for what sounded like astronomical salaries. Danny Gardella and his two Cuban teammates, Nap Reyes and Adrian Zabala, were already gone, followed shortly thereafter by Brooklyn Dodger Luis Olmo, a solid and versatile player who had led the league in triples in 1945. The Dodgers had offered Olmo $7,500; Pasquel signed the Puerto Rican native to a three-year contract at $15,000 a year. Dodgers president Branch Rickey protested the loss of Olmo, but there was nothing he could do beyond rumbling and grumbling. Rickey showed less concern about losing two French Canadian prospects from the Dodgers' Montreal farm club, outfielder Roland Gladu and pitcher Jean-Pierre Roy, but even the loss of the minor leaguers rankled. The Philadelphia Athletics lost Bobby Estalella, a Cuban utility player. A Mexican newspaper reported that Alex Carrasquel, recently waived by the Senators to the Chicago White Sox, had signed to pitch in the Mexican League. Two other obscure Latino players, infielder Chile Gomez of the Washington Senators, and catcher Chico Hernandez from the Chicago Cubs, also took off for Mexico.

At this point, the American majors could still afford to react with a collective shrug, as no teams had yet lost players of any real distinction. But that changed on March 30. On the same day Sal Maglie pitched his final game of the 1946 spring training season, the St. Louis Browns' 25-year-old shortstop Vern Stephens announced that he had signed to play in Mexico. He was a genuine, all-American star. In 1944 Stephens led the American League in runs batted in and narrowly missed being named the league's Most Valuable Player. In 1945 he led the American League in home runs. A handsome, incorrigible playboy who once defined infidelity as "getting laid in the same town where your wife is,"[19] Stephens had been chafing under both the pay cut and the strict supervision the Browns had imposed on him for the 1946 season, in the hope of curbing his wild night life. His contract contained a "good behavior" clause, and on road trips he was required to room with the manager.

Assured that $175,000, his salary for a five-year contract, had been deposited in an account in his name in a Mexican bank, and without informing his wife (yes, he had a wife), Stephens flew to Mexico City. He had hardly landed when Jorge Pasquel announced yet another surprise for American baseball: he had signed veteran Dodger catcher Mickey Owen. Newspapers reported that Owen received a bonus of $15,000 and was to earn $15,000 a year plus living expenses for himself and his wife, including a rent-free apartment. Rumors flew that the Pasquels were dangling offers huge enough to tempt even the game's superstars. They also made an offer to Jackie Robinson, whom Branch Rickey was protecting with the ferocity of a mother lion guarding a cub. When Rickey discovered a Mexican League agent attempting to sign Robinson, the burly former catcher ran the man out of the ball park. In any case the offer failed to tempt Robinson, who had his eyes fixed firmly on the prize of a future major league career. He said he would not accept even "if they gave me the $500,000 they [allegedly] offered Ted Williams."[20]

Although there was nothing illegal about Mexican baseball, now that the Mexicans had begun luring away important players, major league baseball labeled the Mexican League an "outlaw" and pilloried it at every opportunity. For a combination of hostility, sneering contempt, and sheer vindictiveness, it is hard to find the equal of major league baseball's response to the Mexican League jumpers. From the way the American baseball establishment reacted, it would seem that the men who went to Mexico to play baseball had deserted the American army and then used their American-made weapons to massacre American troops. The *Sporting News* published crude cartoons that made the Pasquels into caricatures of greasy, greedy Mexicans, out to fleece innocent Americans. One showed a stereotypical masked *bandido* brandishing a six-shooter and robbing an American businessman labeled "Organized Baseball." The articles, as well as those in American daily newspapers, brimmed with negative ethnic stereotyping of Mexicans. The Mexican papers fought back with cartoons and articles of their own. One cartoon showed Chandler and major league team owners turning players into human hamburger by feeding them into a meat grinder, and a newspaper accused American baseball of being "like a slave market."[21]

Team owners put pressure on commissioner Chandler to bar any players who jumped their contracts from returning to the majors. Chandler, still new to his job, had already stuck his neck out on the explosive issue of integration. A good-hearted man whose political stance could be described as moderate-populist, he had told members of the black press that as far as he was concerned, if black soldiers could fight in the war, then black athletes could participate in organized baseball, a statement that horrified the game's mostly ultraconservative and racist owners, who were already seething at Branch Rickey's signing of Jackie Robinson for his Montreal farm team. The Mexican crisis offered Chandler an opportunity to regain favor with baseball's most powerful men by taking a strong stand on the sanctity of contracts and the inviolability of the reserve clause, regarded by baseball magnates as the foundation of the game. Although reluctant to make any strong rulings, because he had not found anything in the rules that would justify extreme measures against the jumpers, Chandler nonetheless issued a statement on March 2, declaring that the jumpers had until Opening Day in the majors to return to their American teams or they would be barred from major league play for five years.[22] Given the brevity of the average major leaguer's career, a five-year ban was tantamount to a lifetime ban.

While Chandler and others in the baseball establishment were responding to the Mexican crisis, events continued to unfold at the New York Giants' Miami training camp.[23] Hausmann and Zimmermann, ecstatic over their good fortune, regaled teammates with the saga of their phone call to Mexico, and Pasquel's offers, no doubt including the detail that the call had been made from Sal Maglie's hotel room. The story reached Giants owner Horace Stoneham and also made its way to manager Mel Ott, who became furious at Hausmann and Zimmermann, but even more so at Maglie. He felt certain that Sal was serving as an agent for the Pasquels. The next day Sal entered a tense and silent clubhouse. Ott summoned Maglie to his office where, livid with rage, he shouted at Sal, accusing him of betraying his own team and stealing Ott's players. He used the phone call made from Maglie's room as incriminating evidence and assumed that Sal himself had placed the call. "That was what fucked me up with Stoneham and Ott," Sal recalled later. "I suppose the switchboard operator told somebody about the call, and since it came from my room the club figured it was me who made it. You know how word gets around a ball club."[24] Normally an amiable man, Ott was in no mood to listen to Maglie's claim that he had nothing to do with the call and that the men had used his phone to contact Pasquel merely because they happened to be in his room at the time.

Ott and Maglie had maintained cordial enough relations previous to this, but Sal had not enjoyed any special rapport with Ott, and he had been simmering with resentment toward his manager because of his treatment throughout spring training. Furthermore, Sal intensely disliked being bawled out as if he were a misbehaving child. Although slow to anger, he had a temper, and he hated being humiliated. Ott's accusations and his refusal to listen to any explanation made Sal as furious with his manager as his manager was with him. When Ott demanded to know the names of all the players Maglie had talked into jumping to Mexico, Sal snapped something to the effect that Ott could fucking goddamn well find that out for himself. Ott stormed out of his office, and sounding less like a manager than a drill sergeant, ordered his players to line up in front of their lockers.

Then he marched down the line, asking each man if he was staying or jumping to Mexico. Sal claimed in 1951 that it was only at that moment, after Ott had enraged and humiliated him, that he made his final decision. "I didn't know what I was going to say when he came to me. I was sore about the brush-off I'd been getting all spring, and I knew I was marked lousy for sure now. I could get almost twice as much money in Mexico as the Giants were paying me. I was twenty-nine, and I had only a few years left to build up a little nest egg for me and my wife. So when it came my turn, I told Ott I was going to Mexico."[25] Then, just as the tension seemed ready to explode, Bill Voiselle, the deaf pitcher who had not heard Ott's summons, and who was instead in the bathroom, obliviously shaving, began whistling a popular tune of the time, "South of the Border, Down Mexico Way." The meeting broke up amid roars of relieved laughter.

But nobody was laughing in the Giants front office. Team owner Horace Stoneham summoned the three players to Mel Ott's hotel room, there informing them that their careers with the New York Giants were over and they would not be welcomed back. Ott, still seething, ordered the locker room attendant to clear out the three players' lockers and throw their belongings in a heap outside the door of the clubhouse, a door they were all warned never to darken again. At Stoneham's orders the three men were told to vacate their hotel rooms. Sal made a quick call to Jorge Pasquel to let him know that he and his two teammates were on their way and to ask him to wire a cash advance to pay for the trio's transportation. None of the players had enough money to pay for the trip. Pasquel assured Sal that $1,000 would be waiting for them at the Western Union office that same day. Sal also called his wife to tell her to pack for a long stay in Mexico. When the three men arrived at the Western Union office they found the voucher from Pasquel waiting, but it was in Maglie's name, and the clerk wanted to see some identification before he turned over the money. According to George Hausmann's recollections, Sal said, "I don't have a driver's license—I don't drive."[26] He not only lacked a driver's license, he had no form of identification with him at all. A frantic scramble followed, as the men finally succeeded in finding someone who could vouch for their identities.

Unable to book a flight at such short notice the trio next tried to purchase train tickets, but they could not find seats on any train from Miami to Laredo, on the Mexican border, until George Hausmann remembered he knew an army officer in New York City who was in charge of military transports, who managed to procure the tickets for them. Before they left, Sal fired off a few more shots at the Giants, angrily asserting that his $5,000 Mexican bonus alone was more than his salary for 1946 and that every ballplayer should receive a minimum salary of $10,000.[27] By under-reporting how much the Giants were going to pay him, Sal left himself open for further furious retorts from his former boss. A few days later owner Horace Stoneham denied Sal's allegations and declared that if the jumpers returned to the Giants "I would sell the three of them to other clubs. I wouldn't want them with us." Then, sounding as if he looked forward to just the opposite, Stoneham sneered, "I hope the contracts signed by those players in Mexico are worth more than the paper they are written on."[28] What American news media called the Mexican Hayride had begun for three more obscure wartime players, and as the train pulled away Sal Maglie disappeared from major league baseball for four years. Hardly anybody noticed he was gone.

Down Mexico Way

Sal's Two Seasons
with the Puebla Parrots

5

THE 1946 SEASON

Sal and Kay arrived in Mexico City on April 1, 1946, he from Miami by way of Laredo, Texas, and she from Niagara Falls, both of them dazed by the sudden turn of events. Jorge Pasquel was there to meet them, and a limousine belonging to the Pasquels stood waiting to whisk Sal to another part of the Mexico City airport, where they picked up Kay. "I was sitting in the back seat where I must have been about two blocks away from [Pasquel]," Sal recalled, still awed by the memory more than 30 years later. The limo took the couple to a fashionable, fully furnished apartment, where they spent the next two weeks. One evening the dashing millionaire entertained the Maglies at his Mexico City mansion. Unused to luxuries, Sal was overwhelmed. "He had silverware—I swear it was piled up a foot high! We had a seven-course dinner, I'll never forget that. I didn't know what the heck kind of fork to use. They had four of everything. Really something!"[1]

Jorge Pasquel had his own reasons for keeping his American import in a golden cage: he had already lost his prize catch, Vern Stephens. After only a few days in Mexico the flashy shortstop had scrambled home, trailing horror stories of his brief stay south of the border, and had been welcomed back to the St. Louis Browns. Pasquel was therefore waiting for April 15, when the major league baseball season began in the United States, the deadline commissioner Chandler had set for players to repent of their Mexican sins and return to their American teams without incurring a five-year suspension. Once that date had passed, Pasquel distributed his collection of Americans among the eight Mexican League teams. Ignoring charges of favoritism, he assigned what he considered the best players to the Mexico City and Veracruz teams, which he owned, and others he thought were promising to the Torreón and San Luis Potosí teams, in which he held a financial interest. Other teams included Puebla, Monterrey, Nuevo Laredo, and Tampico.

Pasquel assigned Sal to Puebla, an indication of the pitcher's relatively low ranking. He was the only American-born player on the Puebla squad. The Mexican teams were all diverse in comparison to the segregated American major leagues. They included black and Hispanic players from Mexico, Cuba, Puerto Rico, and South America, a contingent of Negro leaguers from the United States delighted to be playing in a country free of racial discrimination, and a growing number of white players from the States. Monte Irvin, the Hall of Fame outfielder who played in Mexico in the early 1940s and was later Maglie's New York Giants teammate, recalled the relief he felt at the lack of racism in Mexico. "It was the first time in my life I felt really *free*," Irvin remembered, "because your skin color didn't make any difference. I could go anywhere and do anything." And then, as a sharp shard of bitterness pierced his gracious manner, he exclaimed, "I sometimes think I should have *stayed* down there!"[2]

Puebla, as Sal and Kay soon found out, was something less than a glittering metropolis, and Mexican baseball a far cry from its American relative. Although their pampered introduction to Mexican life did not prepare them for life outside the capital, especially the conditions on road trips, they both began their stay determined to make the best of whatever they encountered. The city of Puebla is in southern Mexico, about 60 miles southeast of Mexico City, and sits 7,000 feet above sea level in the Sierra Madre mountains. Jorge Pasquel provided the Maglies with a furnished apartment there, rent-free, and according to one account, even provided Sal with "a fat expense account." A newspaper story reported that Maglie quoted $13,000 per year as his Mexican salary, while another newspaper account a few days later gave the amount as $10,000, and a later American source claimed Maglie's salary was $15,000.[3] Whichever figure is correct, it was a lot more than he would have made with the Giants, and more than enough for the couple to live on while putting a substantial portion into savings. Pitcher Adrian Zabala, Maglie's former teammate from the Giants, also had been assigned to the Puebla squad. Since the Cuban-born Zabala was a native speaker of Spanish, and his wife Mary, who became Kay's friend, also had some knowledge of the language, their presence made life easier for the Maglies. Kay shopped for groceries and did the couple's cooking, as her husband was hardly capable of making himself a cup of coffee, and according to Sal's recollections, they ate and lived well. Once Sal became known as a winning pitcher, he was a local hero, congratulated on the streets and carried out of the ballpark on fans' shoulders after his victories.

Nonetheless, the culture shock was considerable, and Kay found the conditions much more difficult to adjust to than Sal did. The language barrier proved the least of their problems. Their furnished apartment lacked a refrigerator and was overrun with mice. Kay's younger brother Carl Pileggi visited during the 1946 season, and along with pleasant memories of fishing trips to nearby lakes and swimming with his sister in a pool in Puebla called Agua Azul (Blue Water), he also remembered "they had an apartment on the second floor and it had a little patio, but if you turned off the lights and then turned them on again, the patio floor was covered with mice—you couldn't get rid of them. My sister used to blow her top. She put up with quite a lot."[4] Bugs presented another problem. Players and their wives were driven to distraction by them, particularly at night, since the windows in their stifling living quarters had no screens.

An American newspaper article that appeared not long after the Maglies arrived in Mexico expanded gleefully on the difficulties the jumpers would face with regard to food. Vegetables, the paper advised, had to be soaked for three hours in chlorinated water before being cooked—provided chlorinated water could be found. Milk, the author warned, was not pasteurized, and the powdered variety was very expensive, as was butter. Sugar and bacon cost even more. Kay's other brother, John Pileggi, who also visited the couple, has vivid memories of accompanying his sister on shopping trips. "They used human, uh, manure as fertilizer. Kay used to buy fresh vegetables, but then she'd have to wash them and thoroughly boil them. If you wanted to buy a steak, they'd reach up on a rack and pull down a big chunk of beef all infested with flies and stuff. Kay couldn't take it."[5]

As long as the couple ate at home and drank bottled or boiled water they remained in good health, but when Sal began spending time at the Parrots' stadium and went on the team's road trips, the results were often disastrous. Without Kay to cook for him, unwise food choices in small-town restaurants and roadside *cantinas* or *taquerías* made him frequently and violently sick to his stomach. "The places where we'd stop," Sal recalled, "they never had ice. They didn't have any refrigeration or *nothing*."[6] Bad water, often the only kind available, brought on virulent attacks of diarrhea that left him feeling as if he had been reamed with a red-hot poker. Intestinal crises are a particular hazard for pitchers, obliged as they are to "bear down" each time they throw. "Y' cain't pitch with yer insides turned t' water," as later Mexican League jumper Max Lanier plaintively put it in his Carolina drawl.[7] According to novelist Mark Winegardner, Vern Stephens suffered the ultimate humiliation: "he crapped his drawers, right on the field."[8] If true, small wonder Stephens slunk home to the States after three days. In later years Sal always refused to admit how sick he became during his early days in Mexico, although he admitted to losing 15 pounds during his first season there, and pictures show him looking extremely thin and gaunt (Figure 5). It was Kay who spilled the beans, so to speak. In an otherwise perky first-person memoir that appeared in *Parade* magazine in 1956, Kay noted that she and Sal were both struck "deathly ill" repeatedly on road trips.[9] While he was visiting the Maglies, Carl Pileggi went to a restaurant with Sal during a road trip to Tampico and remembered being warned by his brother-in-law not to eat shrimp. "So Carl orders the shrimp. I was sick for two days, although I didn't wind up in the hospital," Carl recalled with a shudder.[10]

Queasy stomachs and wonky bowels were not the only problems American players faced in Mexico. Most of the ballparks were well below the standards of even the shabbiest minor league parks in the States. Delta Parque, in Mexico City, held 23,000 and was the best of the lot, the only one fitted with showers and locker rooms. Nonetheless, an American writer reported in 1946 that the Delta ballpark looked "like something discarded in Oskaloosa, Iowa, in 1915."[11] The Puebla park was much worse. Surrounded by a decaying fence, its rickety, unpainted stands held 8,000. The grandstand roof looked as if it had been built from lumber yard scraps and was covered patchily with sheets of rusted tin. The infield consisted of rock-hard bare dirt, and the outfield grass, pocked with gopher holes, was a sparse and dried-out layer over hard Mexican clay. No wonder the grass looked sparse—when the team was on the road the locals used it as a pasture for sheep and goats. The animals had to be shooed off the field before play could begin. The park provided neither locker rooms nor showers. Players had to change into their uniforms at home and return to their lodgings in the same reeking, sweat-soaked outfits, which they (or their wives) were responsible for washing. The rest of the ballparks in the league were little better and some even worse. The park in Tampico had railroad tracks running through the outfield, and games had to be stopped to let the trains pass. "And that wasn't the end of the field," Max Lanier recalled. "The outfielders had to run back over the tracks—it was terrible for them—they could trip and break a leg!"[12] Sal lost a game there when a line drive caromed off one of the rails and sailed over the outfielder's head. The ground grew so hot at San Luis Potosí that between innings players cooled their bare feet in buckets of water. In many parks the infield dirt was white, as well as extremely dusty, making it difficult for players to see the ball coming toward them. The many small stones scattered over the infields caused balls to take unexpected hops and bounces.

5—Sal pitching for the Puebla Parrots against Vera Cruz on May 23, 1946, at Mexico City's Delta Park. Notice the white dust covering his shoes and the extreme thinness of his arms. Photo: National Baseball Hall of Fame Library, Cooperstown.

Travel from one ballpark to another was even worse than the parks themselves. Teams took the longest trips by train, but more often they traveled by
bus. These were not private, air-conditioned coaches, but native rattletraps
where the players and their equipment competed for space in the stifling in-
teriors with rural travelers often accompanied by live poultry and other
small farm animals, the kind of buses where it seems that all along the way
more people get on, but nobody ever gets off. The heat, the changes in alti-
tude, and the constant rocking, jostling, and rump-rupturing bumps due to
the twisting, rudimentary roads and lack of springs in the seats, made some
American players dizzy and light-headed, and had others hanging out the
windows, convulsed with motion sickness. The buses caused back and but-
tocks miseries in other players, and scared the remainder half to death. Sal,
who insisted the bus trips never made him sick, admitted to being terrified.
"The buses were driven by madmen," Sal declared years later. "They used to
push those old wrecks as hard as they could on the narrow, winding roads
in the mountains."[13] Sal was afraid of heights, and repeated glimpses of the
sheer drops down hundreds of feet at the unprotected sides of those mountain roads were more than he could tolerate.

After a few hair-raising trips Sal concluded that if he had to be somewhere up high, and petrified every moment, it might as well be for a much
shorter time. So, swallowing his terror and the steep expense, he paired up
with Adrian Zabala, and the two of them chartered small planes to take
them from city to city on the team's road trips. Despite the cost, and alarming memories of big, black Mexican vultures waiting around as the planes
landed (as if they had calculated the crash odds), Sal considered the flights a
worthwhile investment. Without them, he might not have lasted two years
in Mexico. The hotels where the teams stayed during road trips were more
comfortable than the buses, but not by much. In some places the night life
beneath the hotel windows did not swing into high gear until around midnight and continued til dawn. The nights were hot in more literal ways as
well. Mary Zabala recalled their hotel room in Veracruz, which had no air-
conditioning: "At night you couldn't go to sleep, it was so hot. We'd have to
get up and take a shower, and then we would wet the towels and put them
around us to lay down to go to sleep."[14] No doubt Sal and Kay did the same.

And then there were the fans. Mexican baseball games in the 1940s were
less like sporting events than out-of-control carnivals. Food and drink ven-
dors swarmed the area outside the ballparks, cooking on portable stoves and
mixing the unidentifiable ingredients of their soft, and not so soft, drinks in
open vats. They hawked tamales, enchiladas, watermelon slices, chunks of
roasted pork and chicken, raw oysters in scorching hot sauce, roasted pep-
pers, corn on the cob, bananas, papayas, and cucumbers. The grandstands

had no aisles, and people had to crawl over or around one another to reach their seats on the rough bleacher boards. Sanitary facilities were almost non-existent, with predictably pungent results. Under a haze of heat thickened with cigarette and cigar smoke the nearly all-male crowds roared, howled, and produced ear-piercing whistles—the latter the Mexican equivalent of boos. Gambling was rampant, with fans betting not merely on which team would win, but on each pitch, on balls and strikes, on which player would get the game's first hit, what the final score would be, and just about any of the multitude of uncertainties the game produced. Because of the heavy betting, there were fans celebrating and grieving every pitch and every routine foul ball, as well as every play. An American reporter watched as gamblers shouted their odds on a pitch or an inning. Since they could not circulate through the crowded stands, they paid off the winners by tossing wads of pesos. "Some of the best catches aren't on the field," the reporter observed.[15]

Fans celebrated winning bets by hurling firecrackers onto the field. Max Lanier recalled that it was difficult to tell the difference between firecrackers and gunshots. "They liked to throw firecrackers out there, and you didn't know whether you was gettin' shot at or what. They'd scare you to death when they was throwin' some to the mound. . . . We'd pick them up before they went off and throw them back up in the crowd," he concluded.[16] Lanier was not displaying undue anxiety. Some fans came to the ballpark armed, and shooting pistols in the air was not unheard of, although there is no record of disgruntled fans plugging the players. Several American jumpers recalled that the Pasquels always carried revolvers, as did their bodyguards, often leaving them in plain sight during games. Pitcher Tom Gorman (later a National League umpire) saw Bernardo Pasquel shoot to death an unarmed intruder caught inside the grounds of one of the Pasquel mansions in Mexico City where Gorman was a guest, and another player reported that Mexicans in the stands "wore guns like we wear key chains or jewelry."[17]

THE DEVIL'S DISCIPLE—FURTHER LESSONS FROM DOLF LUQUE

These were the conditions that prevailed as Sal began his first season with the Puebla Parrots. To make sure he did not follow Vern Stephens and bolt for the border, Pasquel kept guards trailing Sal for the first 10 days of the season. He need not have worried. Although he did not realize it, Pasquel was doing the pitcher the greatest favor of his life by sending him to the team managed by Dolf Luque. The assignment may have been sheer chance, but it is more likely Luque requested that Pasquel send Maglie to Puebla, and that the baseball magnate agreed, since he did not care which team Maglie joined. With Sal in the Puebla fold, the lessons Luque had started drumming into him during Cuban Winter League play resumed and intensified.

Sal began his Mexican season in mid-April with a resounding 9–0 victory, then, according to his own recollections, "got my brains knocked out for a solid month."[18] In a game on April 28 the Puebla squad managed a 13–10 victory, but that was after Sal had been knocked out in the fourth inning. "It was the first time I'd ever known as many as six or seven batters in a row to hit line drives off me," he recalled. "Good, hard ones, too."[19] Sal had no idea what he was doing wrong. He was a curveball pitcher, and his best pitch refused to work. "My hook wasn't breaking at all," Maglie recalled. "It was just hanging, big and fat, over the plate," an invitation for hitters to tee off on him.[20] Dolf Luque stepped in with the answers. He pointed out to Sal that he was pitching under extremely different climatic conditions from game to game, and that those conditions had consequences for the way his pitches behaved. Puebla, Mexico City, Torreón, and San Luis Potosí, Luque reminded him, were high up in the mountains, but Veracruz and Tampico were low-lying cities. Sal had already noticed—how could he not?—that he gasped and struggled to fill his lungs with air in the high mountain ballparks and sweltered off 10 or more pounds per outing on the stifling coastal plains, where on-field temperatures sometimes reached 110 degrees. He was also well aware that in the highlands his curve hung on the thin air like a tactless remark, and in the lowlands his curve worked fine, but his fastball behaved as if he were throwing it under six feet of warm water. Pitching in both environments ruined his control, causing him to walk seven or eight batters in a game, and left him completely exhausted. Nothing in his minor league experience, his brief sojourn in the majors, or his Cuban season had prepared Sal for the variety and extremity of the climatic conditions he encountered in Mexico.

Luque lacked a degree in physics, but he understood from long experience the effects of the atmosphere on both pitched balls and batted balls in a way that Sal did not. He explained to the perplexed pitcher that the thinner air in the mountains kept his curve from breaking properly and also made it easier for batters to hit the ball harder—the thinner the air the less resistance the batted ball encounters. The advantage was that the thin air would also enhance the speed of his fastball. In the low-lying coastal regions the opposite held true. The heavier, moisture-laden air would help his curve, but slow his fastball, and batters would have a tougher time hitting the ball hard, since the humid air would slow it down. Luque's first advice to Sal was to stop seeing the thin or thick air as his enemy and start using the different atmospheric conditions to his own advantage by adjusting his pitches to the park where he was working. Luque instructed Sal to use his fastball more often when pitching at high altitudes, and to stop relying on his curve at those times—to just "show" the curveball to hitters now and then, when they were not expecting it, hooking it over the outside corner where it was most difficult to hit, and then coming in with the fastball. Although never a fireballer, Maglie had a good, live fastball that moved in and sank on right-handed hitters, and Luque began drilling him on improving his control of it.

A curveball specialist himself, Luque also went to work on Maglie's curve until Sal could bend it like a pretzel. Under Luque's tutelage Sal developed three different curves, one that broke across the plate, one that broke downward, and another that broke outside, depending on when he released the ball. "In Mexico I shortened up on my curveball so that it broke when it was almost on top of the plate," Sal explained.[21] He no longer threw a "roundhouse," a big, sweeping curve with a trajectory a batter could follow and hit, but one that came at the batter more or less straight, and then broke suddenly, at the very last moment, curving away and down from a right-handed hitter, making it difficult for the batter to react in time. Sal had been in the habit of releasing the ball high on the down-sweep of his arm, but Luque showed him how to release it slightly later, from in front of him, so that the ball seemed to come out from his white uniform, making it much more difficult for the batter to pick up. And he learned to throw his assortment of curves at different speeds and from different arm slots. "I saw that the Mexicans didn't like sidearm pitching, so I developed a cross-fire," Sal related.[22]

None of this came quickly or easily, and Luque worked Sal hard. He was not only teaching Sal how to pitch, he was also teaching him how to *think* when he pitched, the essential difference between a genuine pitcher and a man who merely throws the ball to the plate. Luque insisted that Sal remember the hitters from one at-bat to another, and from one game to another, keeping in mind what pitches he had thrown them, as well as where and how well they had hit those pitches. This would seem a prodigious feat of memory, but the keeping of mental "books" on hitters is an essential component of successful major league pitching. Sal had started collecting data when he was still with Buffalo, but Luque required that he master it in a more comprehensive way, and he grilled his charge constantly until Sal developed an encyclopedic memory. Years later he claimed that teammates could ask him about any game in which he had ever participated, and he could recount every pitch he had thrown that day.

Sal recalled Luque as a hard taskmaster. Maglie, an easygoing fellow at heart, lacked a natural tendency to bear down all the time when he pitched. "I was inclined to relax when I got ahead, especially against weak hitters," Sal confessed.[23] Not on Luque's watch, he soon learned. Just as the hardnosed Cuban had taught Sal never to grant a hitter the smallest fraction of the plate and never to waste a pitch, he also taught him never to let up, never to relax and coast along. No matter how far ahead he was, every pitch still counted, and if Luque caught Sal loafing on the mound, the pitcher heard about it, fast. Mickey Owen, who managed the Veracruz team for part of the 1946 season, observed Luque confronting Maglie and was amazed at how much Sal would take from his manager-teacher. "I think Luque was just like a dominant father with him when it come to pitching, and I think that Maglie respected his knowledge and his expertise and listened to him. . . . I've seen him get on Maglie—nobody would ever talk to Maglie like that except Luque, and I thought, boy, he's going to punch [Luque] any time now! Maglie wasn't afraid of nobody, but he'd just take it."[24]

From the tone of this recollection, offered more than 40 years after the event, it sounds as if Owen might have confused the tough, aggressive major league Sal Maglie of the 1950s with the much meeker student still learning from Dolf Luque in 1946, the way Maglie's childhood friend Chet Grochala recalled the teenage Sal already throwing high-inside fastballs. Nonetheless, Owen made a valid point with his identification of Luque as a parental authority figure to Maglie. Sal would never have dreamed of striking back at either of his parents when he was a boy, even when one or the other of them gave him a thrashing. Luque was 27 years older than Sal, old enough to be his father, but he was a much harsher disciplinarian than Sal's father. Luque was more like Sal's mother: a domineering individual with a set of scary eyes, a loud voice, and some very definite ideas. Sal understood what was at stake and accepted Luque's authority. His future as a pitcher was on the line, and to defy Luque verbally, not to mention slugging the smaller and older man, was out of the question. Sal "took it," as Owen observed, suppressing any anger or resentment he may have felt, in the interests of maintaining his working relationship with Luque. He knew he had found the teacher he had been looking for all his life.

There are several stories concerning how Luque enforced his lessons, stories that may well have some truth in them, although over the years perhaps they have been exaggerated in the telling. All of them involve guns. Luque was reputed to carry a pistol with him everywhere, including into the ballparks where his teams played. It is unlikely that Luque ever brandished a gun during his years in the majors—that would have made even bigger headlines than his exploits with ice picks—but he probably did pack a pistol in Mexico. Years later Maglie told a story about how Luque noticed a certain pitcher's attention wandering from the game while the pitcher was sitting in the dugout during his team's turn at bat, and he helped the fellow refocus by shooting a bullet into the floor right between the man's feet.[25] Sal did not identify that player as himself, but another and even more alarming variation of the tale has Sal as the object of Luque's sharpshooting. According to sportswriter David Falkner, when Luque grew impatient with Sal's faulty control during a bullpen warm-up session, he pulled out a pistol and shot at Maglie's feet every time one of his pitches missed its spot.[26] Maglie's New York Giants teammate Alvin Dark related another anecdote he heard from Sal himself, in which Luque ordered one of his pitchers (again unnamed) to throw knockdowns at the opposing team's pitcher. When his hurler refused, Dark continued, Luque "pulled out a pistol, shot at the mound, and *hit* the mound. The bullet ricocheted off and went *whizzzzzeeeeee*! And that was the last time he had any trouble getting his pitchers to knock down somebody. Pretty scary, huh?"[27] In his autobiography Monte Irvin recounted a story about a confrontation that took place between Luque and Negro League pitcher Terris McDuffie, in which Luque informed McDuffie that he had to pitch a particular game. When McDuffie refused, pleading a sore arm, Luque left the pitcher for a minute, then returned to McDuffie's locker. When McDuffie looked up, Luque was standing over him with a pistol. The petrified pitcher underwent an immediate change of heart. "McDuffie took one look at the pistol," Irvin related, "and said, 'All you gotta do is give me the ball.'"[28]

If Falkner's, Dark's, and Irvin's stories seem far-fetched, they are no more fantastic than an anecdote Mickey Owen related about the behavior of the manager of the Mexico City Reds toward a pitcher who failed to do his bidding. The Pasquels had invited Babe Ruth to put on a home run hitting exhibition in Mexico, and on May 16, 1946, Ruth appeared before a scheduled game. Owen, the Veracruz manager, had assigned pitcher Ramon Bragaña the task of serving up fat ones. But the once-great slugger could not get a good piece of the ball, although Bragaña was doing his best to provide something the Babe could blast over the roof. From the sidelines Mexico City manager Ernesto Carmona began heckling the sweating Bragaña, and finally stomped to the mound to tell Bragaña to leave; he was bringing in a pitcher from his own team who knew how to serve up a decent gopher ball. Bragaña responded by shoving Carmona, and the two men almost came to blows after the game. No sooner had Owen prevented the irate Mexico City manager from slugging his pitcher, when Carmona's brother burst in brandishing "an old-fashioned six-shooter." At gunpoint, he forced Bragaña to get down on his knees and apologize.[29]

Attempting to extract a modicum of both humor and wisdom from the story of Luque shooting at Maglie's feet, Falkner noted that the incident taught Sal an essential aspect of his later mastery over batters: "how to keep at bay guys with lethal weapons in their hands." Whatever the precise degree of truth in these anecdotes, they suggest the atmosphere of danger and the constant threat of violence that hung over Mexican League baseball. Sal had not led a sheltered life—the tough neighborhood of his childhood assured that he was no stranger to fistfights and rough competition—but he was a peaceable man who whenever possible avoided arguments, heated confrontations, and violence. Nonetheless, in order to survive and succeed with the Puebla team he had to adjust himself to the realities of Mexican baseball and not fall apart when faced with nerve-shattering experiences.

Unfortunately, Sal's wife Kay lacked her husband's resilience. Although she was a plucky and determined woman committed to sharing her husband's life, the cumulative experiences of their first few months in Mexico proved too much for her. She suffered a nervous collapse and had to return home. Kay made no mention of any collapse in her cheery published reminiscences of her months in Mexico, but Sal noted it in his 1981 interview with William Marshall, and her brother and sister-in-law, John and Mary Pileggi, remembered it vividly more than half a century later. Sal called what happened to his wife a "breakdown" and explained that Kay did not adapt well to anything in Mexico, despite her best efforts. The strange food and ensuing violent sickness, filthy conditions in the town markets, dangerous streets, mice in their apartment, suffocating heat, difficult travel, and dreadful hotel accommodations all took a toll on her. But one event pushed her over the edge. Mary Pileggi recalled, "When a man pulled a gun on Kay in Mexico, she practically had a nervous breakdown from fear and anxiety. She had to come home after that. She was so depressed and scared all the time, and it left her that way for months. Thank God she came home to us!" Kay's brother John added, "Can you picture her sitting a seat or two away, when somebody pulled out a big gun and started pointing it all around? She was terrified!"[30]

Although Sal related the story about Dolf Luque shooting at a player to get his attention, he never made any public references to someone threatening to shoot his wife. Perhaps it embarrassed him by making his own protestations of being well treated in Mexico ring hollow. Mickey Owen made an indirect reference to Kay's collapse, saying that life in Mexico was "too hard" for Sal's wife to tolerate and that Sal was "mad" at Kay, apparently for not holding up better under the rigors of Mexico.[31] Sal, who had never lived on his own, had become deeply dependent on Kay to keep his domestic life in order. But now Kay was leaving him stranded in a foreign country, at the mercy of Mexican restaurants, and vulnerable to the temptations of the numerous women attracted by his stylish wardrobe and sultry good looks (Figure 6). Art "Superman" Pennington, a big, handsome Negro League slugger who joined the Puebla team during the 1946 season and became friendly with Maglie, was an enthusiastic ladies' man. He recalled that Sal always seemed to be surrounded by beautiful women.[32] The last time young women had swarmed around Sal, they had been Niagara Falls high school girls asking for his autograph, but the women in Mexico were older and had other ideas. Although in his interview with William Marshall almost 35 years later Sal still stoutly defended Kay, calling her "a great person" who "understood" his situation in Mexico, he probably did resent her leaving him there to fend for himself. The teams played only four days a week, with the remainder of the time given over to travel or rest. Beyond playing baseball, there was little about Mexico that interested Sal. He did only a small amount of sightseeing, and he disliked the principal form of entertainment available—bullfights. He went once, and refused to return, although other players attended often. "Too *cruel!*" Sal exclaimed. Asked what he did to pass the time, he answered vaguely and perhaps a little evasively, "I don't know. Just go around, two or three fellows, that's all."[33] How Sal spent his long Mexican evenings after Kay's departure remains uncertain. When asked, Art Pennington merely raised a risqué eyebrow and smiled.

Adding further to the uncertainty surrounding the episode of Kay being shot at, in her 1956 article for *Parade* Kay claimed the traumatic incident took place not in Mexico but in Cuba and, perhaps at the magazine editor's advice, said nothing about it driving her back home. Given the nature of Cuban society in the mid-1940s, Cuba was an unlikely place for such an incident to happen. At that time it was a tightly run and repressive dictatorship where ordinary people did not dare to openly brandish weapons, particularly in the capital city, while Mexico in the same period was a disorderly democracy where anyone able to afford a weapon could carry one. Stories abound of the wild and even violent behavior of Mexican baseball fans, but there are no such tales about Cuban fans. Although it is risky to contradict an individual's first-hand account offered only ten years after the event, there is reason to believe the episode really did occur in Mexico, as Kay's brother and sister-in-law recalled, and that Kay, either unconsciously or for unknown reasons, moved it to Cuba.

Whatever Sal's feelings about his wife's return to the States, he put those emotions aside and concentrated on his work. His outstanding performance with Puebla in 1946 is the best indication of how well he succeeded. Playing a 90–game schedule (rather than the 154–game major league schedule) and having missed the first few weeks of the season, he still compiled a 20–12 record. Only one other Mexican League pitcher won 20 games that season. Between starts and relief appearances Sal appeared in 47 games and hurled a workhorse 285 1/3 innings for Puebla, topped only by Jorge Comellas of San Luis Potosí, who labored for 291 innings but compiled a poor 15–20 record. Sal's 3.19 ERA, although not brilliant, was respectable enough. He threw an impressive 21 complete games that included four shutouts, struck out 118 while walking 92, made no wild pitches, and did not hit a single batsman.[34]

6—Maglie in fashion-
plate movie star mode,
posing for a picture at
an unknown location
in Mexico, probably in
1946. Photo: collection
of John and Mary
Pileggi.

It is clear from his record that Sal had absorbed Luque's emphasis on control, and Sal's own recollections indicate that he had also learned the central tenet that underlay all of Luque's lessons: that the pitcher owns the plate, and batters who ignore that will receive a terrifying reminder in the form of a chin-grazing fastball. Sal recalled a game where Mexico City's Roberto Ortiz hit a home run off him, and then ran the bases roaring with laughter. Maglie, who rarely spoke to opposition players during games, shouted, "Ortiz, you'll never do that again. Whenever I see you, you're going down!" Sal kept his promise, flattening the bumptious outfielder at least once every time he pitched to him thereafter. "He didn't do any more laughing. He didn't hit another home run, either," Sal concluded with satisfaction.[35] Despite Maglie's efforts, Puebla finished in third place.

Sal enjoyed significantly greater success in 1946 than any of the other American pitchers who made the jump to the Mexican League later that season. Two of his Giants teammates, righthander Harry Feldman and reliever Ace Adams, unexpectedly left the Giants on April 26, and went to Mexico. The Giants had now lost eight players to Mexico: Gardella, Reyes, Zabala, Maglie, Hausmann, Zimmermann, Feldman, and Adams—four pitchers and four position players—almost one-third of a regular season roster. Assigned to the Veracruz club, Feldman compiled a dreadful 5–15 record, although his 3.79 ERA in 161 1/3 innings was not too bad. Adams, also pitching for Veracruz, had a sub-mediocre 5–7 record and a 4.09 ERA in 118 innings of work, during which he walked 77 batters while striking out only 48, hit four batsmen, and loosed five wild pitches, all particularly bad behavior in a reliever.

Pasquel's biggest coup among pitchers was his acquisition in late May of St. Louis Cardinals southpaw Max Lanier. Considered one of the National League's top hurlers, Lanier appeared to have a bright future in the majors. He sported a 6–0 record and a brilliant 1.93 ERA at the time he departed for Mexico in the company of teammates Lou Klein, an infielder who had lost his position at second base to Red Schoendienst, and rookie righthander Fred Martin. Despite a rural North Carolina background, Lanier was no innocent when it came to money. A tough-minded negotiator, he had been dissatisfied with his pay throughout his eight previous years with the notoriously stingy Cardinals and had clashed often with owner Sam Breadon over salaries. Newspapers reported that Lanier had agreed to a $150,000 contract for five years of play in Mexico, in addition to a $50,000 bonus, amounts that, if they were reported accurately, dwarf the sums paid to the less prominent and accomplished Sal Maglie.[36] Although Lanier maintained his low ERA in Mexico, he had his share of problems. "I sure did get sick a couple of times!" he admitted.[37] For a while he confined himself to eating out of cans—sardines and pork and beans—because he was afraid to try anything else, and later on he became an early model of the frequent flyer, going back to Texas to do his grocery shopping. Like Maglie, he found that his curve refused to break in the thin Mexican air, but he had no Dolf Luque around to offer any solutions. As a result, he injured his elbow, worsening an already sore arm in vain attempts to make his curve behave properly. He completed his 1946 season with the Veracruz Blues with an 8–3 record and pitched only 107 innings. Fred Martin also did quite well, winning 12 and losing 6 for the Mexico City team, with a fine 2.71 ERA over 169 1/3 innings. Neither Lanier nor Martin, however, came close to the number of innings Maglie put in, and both won far fewer games. In comparison to those who received much larger amounts of money, as well as the superstars who were offered enormous sums in unsuccessful attempts to lure them south of the border, Maglie had proven himself the Pasquels' best bargain.

ANOTHER WINTER IN CUBA

As winter approached, Maglie once again made plans to pitch in the Cuban Winter League, even though Cuba had become entangled in the political complications arising from the Mexican League fracas. American players were warned against playing on or against Cuban teams that contained any of the "outlaws" banned from organized baseball by commissioner Chandler—a measure that caused resentment among Cuban major leaguers, who could not return to play in their own homeland over the winter without risking suspension from their American teams. As part of its plan to exact revenge on the Mexican League, while attempting to keep the disgruntled Cuban players happy, organized baseball helped establish an alternative league in Cuba, called the National Federation, one in which eligible Cubans would have a chance to play. Cuban fans quickly voted with their feet. After two months of operation, National Federation games were attracting fewer than a thousand attendees per game, while the original Cuban Winter League, playing in the newly constructed Grand Stadium in Havana, attracted crowds averaging 20,000 for each game. The successful Winter League ignored the decree, which the Cubans felt smacked of American imperialism and which meant nothing to the Mexican League jumpers, since they were already banned from American baseball.

Sal returned to the Cienfuegos team in the Cuban Winter League, but Dolf Luque was no longer the manager. He had been transferred to the Almendares team. Sal was disappointed and tried to have himself reassigned to Luque's squad, but the transfer never took place. Sal's motivation was simple: he looked forward to continuing his work with Luque. But when the exchange failed to materialize he made no protest and spent the season pitching for

Cienfuegos and its new manager, Martin Dihigo. The brilliant Cuban, Mexican, and Negro League star, now nearing the end of his playing career, had taken over the team after Luque's departure. Decades before any American major league team had a black manager, Sal Maglie played on a team managed by a Negro League great, without any problems. Art Pennington recalled Maglie as the only completely unprejudiced white man he had ever met, so totally unaffected by racial considerations that for quite a while after meeting Maglie, Pennington thought the deeply tanned pitcher with the dark eyes and curly black hair was either Hispanic or a relatively light-skinned African American. He learned with surprise that Sal's background was Italian. Although not a deep thinker on the subject of racism and prejudice, Sal reacted to it with an instinctive revulsion. "He understood what was going on in the United States," Pennington declared. "He said it was *awful*! No way he was a racist, I can tell you that! He wasn't prejudiced *whatsoever*."[38]

No statistics are available on Sal's second season with Cienfuegos, but it seems to have been successful, even though Cienfuegos did not reach the league finals. The Almendares team, led by Max Lanier's brilliant pitching, won the league championship, and afterwards jubilant fans pummeled Lanier and almost tore off his uniform. He had pitched in tight pennant races and in World Series games, but he had never received such adulation. Like Maglie, he returned to Mexico for a second year.

THE 1947 SEASON

Much of the magic wore off during Sal's second season south of the border. Many of the American jumpers failed to return, leaving Sal even more isolated. Furthermore, although the Pasquels kept up a good front and continued to talk in grandiose terms about acquiring more high-priced American players, the Mexican League was in deep financial trouble. Players received less than their promised salaries, and expense accounts had to be cut. Although he admitted the Mexican League had lost $250,000 in 1946, Pasquel continued to advertise his ambition to sign big-name American players. Sal enjoyed another successful season, although he did not perform quite as well as he had in his first year.

In addition to financial problems, Pasquel had to contend with widespread unhappiness among his regulars—Negro Leaguers, Cubans, and native Mexicans who were angry that their salaries were so much lower than those of the American imports—as well as the loss of many of the American players recruited the previous year. Vern Stephens and Mickey Owen had already burned their Mexican bridges, while Max Lanier and Fred Martin were holding out for more money. On April 9 the *Sporting News* reported that only nine major leaguers were definitely in the Mexican fold for 1947. Oddly enough, the list did not include Maglie, although there is no indication that Sal was holding out for more money. He seems to have been forgotten. Jorge Pasquel called a meeting of his remaining American players just as the 1947 season began and explained that because of the losses he had sustained the previous year, salaries would be cut in half, and players would have to pay their own expenses. This made the players unhappy, but since they were all under Chandler's five-year ban, they were in a poor bargaining position. Even determined holdout Max Lanier capitulated in late May, when he realized there was no other way he could continue to play baseball, and signed for half his previous year's salary.

Sal started off the new season on the wrong foot, or perhaps on the wrong hand is more accurate. Despite an ongoing disagreement with his wife over his passion for playing basketball during the off-season, Sal insisted the activity kept him in shape. Kay saw it as just another distraction that kept her husband away from her and interfered with their social life. Sal recalled an instance when some basketball buddies interrupted the Maglie family's New Year's Day dinner and recruited him right from the table for a pick-up game. Kay was furious. After that, "my wife didn't talk to me for a few days," Sal admitted.[39] Only a week before his scheduled departure for Mexico, he fell on the basketball court and broke a bone in his right hand. The injury was serious enough that Sal was unable to drive, but because he wanted to have his own car with him in Mexico, he asked his friend Ernie Bevilaqua and his brother-in-law John Pileggi to drive him down to Puebla. After the war Sal had learned to drive, and he was the proud owner of a 1941 Cadillac, purchased second-hand from a friend in the Falls who had a used car lot. To men of Sal's generation a Cadillac was the ultimate status symbol, an indicator of the owner's financial success. Sal agreed to pay his two companions' air fare back to Niagara Falls, and Kay would follow him to Mexico later by plane.

At Sal's urging, Kay had decided to give Mexico another try. In 1947 the couple lived in an apartment in Mexico City rather than in Puebla, and Kay was delighted to find that it had a refrigerator and was free of mice. She often accompanied her husband on road trips (in the small planes Sal and Adrian Zabala rented, rather than by bus), but she reported that she and Sal still became sick on occasion and continued to be bothered by the extreme heat. "I'll never forget the games in Tampico and Veracruz," she recalled. "It was always above 100 degrees. Today, whenever I see a lobster boiling in a pot, I think of myself sweltering in the Tampico ball park."[40]

When Sal arrived in Puebla, manager Dolf Luque took one look at his bandaged hand and exploded. He informed Sal that he was useless to the team in his present condition and that the Pasquels were not going to pay him until he was able to pitch. At that point, at least according to Shapiro's account, Sal unwrapped his hand and heroically declared himself ready to pitch with three fingers.[41] Sal related a different version of the story, in which Pasquel made good on Luque's threat. "It cost me a month's pay from Pasquel. I couldn't throw a ball for the first month for the 1947 season down there, and they were determined not to start my pay until I began to pitch. I wanted that dough," Sal continued, "and I can still remember pitching when I could only get three fingers around the ball."[42] Since Mexican League records indicate that Sal pitched his first game in mid-April, perhaps the first month to which he referred was the training period. Evidently the fracture was not serious enough to require a cast. In contrast both to Shapiro's story and Sal's own account, a 1956 article in the *Niagara Falls Gazette* claimed that the injury was a wrist fracture that put Sal out of action for two months and that the wrist was set twice, first by a doctor in Niagara Falls and again by a doctor in Mexico. The author further asserts that the wrist fracture resulted in a change in Sal's delivery and an improvement in his control, with no credit given to Luque, a story that does not appear elsewhere. If it were true that Sal missed two months of the season, it would have been impossible for him to have compiled his 1947 record of 20 wins and 13 losses, especially given that the Mexican season was shorter than the American season: 120 games in 1947, in contrast to the major league schedule of 154 games. Even injuries, it seems, can be the origin of legends.

The 1947 Mexican League season finally opened in early April, and on April 17 Sal pitched a brilliant one-hitter for Puebla against the first-place Monterrey team, winning 3–0. On that same evening Mexican baseball ventured into night games, as Mexico City met San Luis Potosí at Delta Parque under what was supposed to be full illumination. Instead, the local electric grid could allow the park no more than 50 percent of the required power, with the result that the teams played in semi-darkness, a condition symptomatic of the overall state of affairs in the league. In early June the 57-year-old Dolf Luque enlivened the sports pages with news of his marriage to a glamorous young actress with the enigmatic name of Ivonne Recek Saade. His team celebrated by taking three out of four games from San Luis Potosí, with Maglie gaining one of the victories. But then Tampico defeated Puebla four straight, a circumstance that made Luque sick. Puebla's manager took to his bed with what was announced as "a bilious attack."[43]

On August 9 Maglie faced Mexico City's Fred Martin in a scoreless pitchers' duel that went on for 7 2/3 innings until the game was called on account of rain. Later in the month, in a four-game series against San Luis Potosí where two of the games were washed out by storms, Sal won his fourteenth game, an 18–1 romp that left Puebla in fourth place with a 41–40 record. On the last day of August Sal held Veracruz to four hits in a 7–2 win that put Puebla in third place. By the end of September Puebla surged into second place after taking four in a row from Tampico, as close as Puebla came to the pennant. In early October Monterrey swept four from Puebla, despite a valiant effort by Sal in one of those contests. He pitched a 14-inning game in which he also collected 2 hits and scored Puebla's only run, but he lost, 2–1. By the middle of October Puebla was out of contention for the championship, but Sal reached the 20–win mark. Puebla finished in third place.

Sal ended with a 20–13 record and a 3.91 ERA. Only one hurler exceeded his 20 wins: Mexico City's Negro League fireballer Theolic Smith, who won 22 despite an ERA of 4.09. Sal pitched the same high number of innings (285) his second year in Mexico as he had during his first year, but he walked more batters (108) and struck out fewer (105) than the previous year, when his ratio of walks to strikeouts was 92/118. In his second year he also hit three batters and tossed two wild pitches, in contrast to his immaculate record in those categories the year before. But these were minor lapses. Overall, Sal's record for his second year in Mexico was nearly as outstanding as his first. He had learned his lessons well.

During his two seasons in Mexico, as he absorbed more of Luque's methods and pitched under varied and often extreme conditions, an unrecognizably different Sal Maglie emerged—a grim, tough, ruthless competitor unfazed by weather, taunts, or pressure, a pitcher who could bend a curve three different ways at three different speeds from a variety of arm slots or send a batter sprawling with a fastball that grazed his chin. Of all the Americans who jumped to the Mexican League, only Maglie came back a better ballplayer. Long before anyone gave him the nickname "Sal the Barber," he was well on his way to becoming baseball's demon barber—a man different only in degree from Sweeney Todd, the "Demon Barber of Fleet Street," the legendary mass murderer who killed his victims while shaving them. Sal's close shaves never killed anyone, but he had gained a reputation as a headhunter and would use that perception as a tool of intimidation. His deadliest weapon lay not in his pitching arsenal but inside his opponents' heads. Maglie had learned Luque's ultimate lesson: he knew how to sow terror.

Knocking Around

The All-Stars, the Gas Pumps,
and the Drummondville Cubs

A FINAL SEASON IN CUBA

When Sal returned to Cuba in late 1947 for winter ball, he found Cuban baseball in conflict with the major leagues. American officials believed there was too intimate a connection between the Cuban Winter League and the Mexican League. The Cubans were aware that American baseball had been raiding Cuba and Mexico for years, signing players who looked white enough to "pass" in the segregated majors, so they were unconcerned about the Mexican League raids having turned the tables. Nonetheless, the Cuban Winter League caved in to pressure from American baseball and became part of the National Association of Professional Baseball Leagues, an American-controlled organization that regulated the activities of teams and players.[1]

The moment Cuba signed the pact with American baseball in June of 1947, the Mexican League jumpers who had played in the Cuban League the previous two seasons were out of a job in Cuba, since no organization that was part of the American baseball system would allow them to play. Because the ban also affected Cubans who had played in Mexico, it caused widespread bitterness and led to the formation of an alternative Cuban league called the Liga Nacional, which gave refuge to the outlaws from organized baseball. To counteract the new power of the Cuban League, which now had the might of American baseball behind it, the Liga Nacional relied on the prestige of its established Cuban players, the banned Americans Sal Maglie, Max

7—Maglie as a member of the Cuba team, Cuban Winter League, 1947–1948. Sal seems to be sitting on his glove, no doubt to protect his boney bottom from the hard cement of the dugout step. Photo: collection of Carlos Montfort.

Lanier, Fred Martin, Danny Gardella, and Lou Klein, as well as Negro League players who had gone to Mexico. The Liga Nacional fielded four teams, among them the shrewdly named Cuba, which could draw fans from the entire country. Sal played for Cuba, whose members included his old Giants teammates Danny Gardella and Nap Reyes, Canadians Roland Gladu and Stan Bréard, and Myron Hayworth, who had been a wartime catcher with the St. Louis Browns. Although the Cuba team came in second, Sal came out on top in two categories: he had the highest number of wins, 14, and the largest number of complete games, 20.

Before the Cuban season ended Sal knew he would not return to Mexico. Pasquel's dream of transforming the Mexican League into a rival of the American majors was crumbling. Maglie and Max Lanier voiced suspicions that the Mexican League venture had been a political scheme by Pasquel to drum up support for the political campaign of his childhood friend and business partner Miguel Alemán to become president of Mexico. According to that line of reasoning, once Alemán won the 1946 election, Pasquel had no further motive for his sham of running a baseball league. "The money the Pasquels were handing out that spring was all part of a big political coup to swing the presidential elections down there that were coming up the next year," Sal later asserted. "It was worked out so Alemán got the credit for us coming down there," declared Max Lanier. "And he did get elected. . . . After the election Pasquel started cutting everybody."[2]

But a simpler explanation is that Pasquel was running out of money to throw at baseball. Gate revenues did not offset the bloated payrolls caused by the salaries of his American recruits. When Sal and the few other Americans planning to return in 1948 learned they would have to endure still further cuts in their already reduced salaries, they called it quits. The Mexican League stumbled through a final season before collapsing in September of 1948. But by that time the Mexican Hayride was over for the Americans. The cart had overturned and left the jumpers scattered on the ground with no prospects of employment in baseball while Chandler's ban remained in effect.

MAX LANIER'S ALL-STARS

Before the Cuban winter season ended, Max Lanier hatched a plan to salvage his own and the other jumpers' careers. When it became clear that playing in Mexico was no longer an option, Lanier organized and outfitted a team he named Max Lanier's All-Stars, although in truth the only star was Lanier himself. With his Mexican League earnings he bought uniforms, equipment, and a used Trailways bus that he had painted in broad red, white, and blue stripes, with the team's name appearing in black block capitals. The big, comfortable conveyance bore no resemblance to the springless Mexican bottom-bruisers he and his American teammates had come to loathe.

The plan was to barnstorm—to tour small towns across the southern and midwestern United States, as far west as Iowa, Nebraska, and Michigan, as far north as Minnesota and Wisconsin, through Missouri and Arkansas, and as far south as Louisiana, playing against local competition. Barnstorming tours by major leaguers had been part of the game since the nineteenth century, and Lanier had every reason to assume that his team would enjoy success. He believed small towns would jump at the chance to see real major leaguers play and would be eager to challenge his team with their local squads. His team would finance itself by negotiating a guarantee and percentage of the gate for each game. They might even take on some of the top Negro League teams. Full of enthusiasm for his new project, Lanier enlisted 12 of the jumpers for his new team: pitchers Sal Maglie, Harry Feldman,

Fred Martin, and minor leaguer Homer Gibson; catchers Myron Hayworth and Jim Steiner; infielders Roy Zimmermann, George Hausmann, Lou Klein, and the Canadian Stan Bréard; and outfielders Danny Gardella and Murray Franklin. Both Maglie and Lanier agreed to do double duty, pitching one day and playing outfield the next. Sal also occasionally played first base. Maglie had last played the latter two positions in his sandlot days. Lanier planned an ambitious 100–game season and twice advertised his team on the pages of the *Sporting News*. The advertisement proclaimed, "Max Lanier's All-Stars—Greatest Attraction in Baseball History—Back From Cuban League—Entire Team Former Major League Stars—Why not promote this outstanding baseball event in your community?"[3]

At first the team planned—naively, in retrospect—to hold their spring training at Miller Huggins Field, the training site of the New York Yankees, since that team had vacated the field when the major league season began. But Chandler put a stop to the All-Stars' drills, citing the rule prohibiting the use of major league fields by ineligible players. Lanier had not anticipated the relentless hostility of major league baseball to any and all enterprises involving the Mexican League jumpers. Borrowing a term from contemporary politics, Tom Meany wrote that Chandler had "drawn an iron curtain around the suspended players."[4] Just as it had done in Cuba, organized baseball declared that any professional players or teams who competed against the banned players would themselves become subject to the ban. This stopped Negro League teams from competing against Lanier's squad. They could not risk their own livelihoods by making themselves ineligible to play against major league teams or to play in major league ballparks, where they drew their largest crowds. Lanier cut his team's schedule to 81 games, facing local semi-pro squads where the players did not have a prayer of reaching the majors or the minors, so they had no worries over the threat of banishment from organized baseball. Not surprisingly, considering the level of the competition, the All-Stars won all their games.

Again and again, as they traveled from town to town like a gypsy caravan, many players accompanied by their wives, and a few with children in tow, they encountered the long arm of the major leagues' ban. The best ballparks were unavailable, because town fathers or team owners were afraid of jeopardizing the chances of some local boy to make it in professional baseball if they allowed the All-Stars to use the only decent diamond in town. Places that had minor league teams could neither permit the All-Stars to play their teams nor allow them to rent their facilities. And so, men who had played in big league stadiums were reduced to playing on high school recreation fields or in municipal parks. As Sal recalled, "The places where we could have drawn the best gates were closed to us. We wound up losing money. At least, I know I did."[5]

The All-Stars' bus covered between 50 and 100 miles a day. The team members traveled in their uniforms, since there were rarely any locker-room facilities at the places where they played. They would arrive at the designated field around noon to play a team made up of local talent. The players' wives would station themselves outside the park and in the stands, where they sold souvenir programs. "Believe me, that money helped," Kay Maglie later recalled.[6] After the games the team members, still dressed in their sweaty uniforms, would collect their wives and children and climb back on the bus, riding another few hours until they came to a motel with enough rooms to accommodate them all. "Sometimes these places were nice," Kay remembered, "but mostly they were awful." She described a bleak motel in northern Wisconsin, where the roof was either being repaired or was not yet complete, so the ceiling had a big hole in it, and their room stood open to the night sky. "It was late August and cold, so cold that I went to bed wearing all the clothes I could find—including Sal's uniform," Kay recalled.[7]

Even with the discomforts, the All-Stars tour had its enjoyable moments. Kay retained affectionate memories of Sal singing Italian songs in his deep bass voice to his "girl," Danny Gardella, who would drape one of the wives' scarves around his head and convulse the whole bus with laughter as he rolled his eyeballs and batted his eyelashes at his "boyfriend" Sal. Gardella also sang, entertaining the group with renditions of popular songs and opera arias in his fine tenor voice. Sal recalled playing a lot of golf on the team's off-days. He added that playing three positions meant he was in every game and was "in better shape that year than I ever was in my life. All that base-running, . . . and pitching so often, I was really hard. I felt good."[8]

What none of the All-Stars realized was the full extent of the magical experiences their presence provided for people in the small towns where they played, towns most of them would never set foot in again but where memories of the big leaguers' appearance lingered for a lifetime. One such story concerns a game that pitted the All-Stars against the Fergus Falls (Minnesota) Red Sox. During the summer of '48 the semi-pro team included first baseman Richard Durrell, later the publisher of *People* magazine. In a 1988 article for *Sports Illustrated* Durrell recalled the game and the sense of danger involved in playing against Lanier's team of baseball outlaws. But the Sox faced a serious problem that day: they had no available pitcher. Their own mound staff was exhausted, or so the pitchers claimed, given the competition coming their way.

Just minutes before game time someone spotted one of the former Fergus Falls players in the stands, a local boy named Gordon Rothrock, who had played shortstop the year before and had thrown a little batting practice. The Fergus Falls manager promised Rothrock $50 and two cases of the local lager, known as Heine's Old Style, if he lasted three innings against the All-Stars. The young man, perhaps attracted as much by the beer as by the money and the challenge, climbed down out of the stands, donned a uniform and spikes, and tromped out to the mound to face a lineup of major leaguers. To everyone's amazement, no doubt including his own, Rothrock hung in there. He had a weird wind-up and put very little on the ball, so before long he had the big leaguers muttering over this strange-motion, nothing-ball pitcher. "I was fooling them with my assortment of noxious junk," Rothrock later proudly declared.[9] Although first one team and then the other grabbed the lead, the All-Stars pulled it out with two runs in the top of the ninth. Rothrock had never pitched a game before that memorable evening, and he never pitched again, except to demonstrate over subsequent decades his version of that unforgettable contest.

The All-Stars' season ended in late August in Madison, Wisconsin, when the team ran out of money and was forced to disband. Lanier had lost $8,000 on the venture, Sal about $2,000, and all the others were out various amounts as well. Nobody had made a cent. Recalling the ill-fated venture Sal reflected, "It really wasn't too bad. I look back on it as a sort of vacation. . . . We saw a lot of the country."[10] Sal made that statement in 1952, after his successful return to the majors, but in the autumn of 1948 his prospects had never looked worse. He had spent a decade in baseball and come tantalizingly close to a big league career, but now he was nowhere. He had taken the Mexican gamble and lost. Thirty-one years old, and facing another two years of suspension from major league baseball, he had no choice but to return home. Discouraged and depressed, he decided to give up his dream of playing baseball and find a real job.

THE GAS PUMPS AND A FAMILY CRISIS

Sal considered the months after his return from the failed Lanier All-Stars tour among the lowest points of his life. He lacked any non-baseball skills beyond those learned in wartime factory work, and he could not bear the thought of returning to that life. The one bright spot was the savings he had accumulated during his years in the Mexican League. According to his own accounts he used some of those funds to purchase a gas station on the corner of Pine Avenue and Fifty-sixth Street in Niagara Falls, although his childhood friend Benny Critelli claims that Sal did not own the place but only rented it, and another account states that Sal bought a half-share in the station.[11] Sal recalled that he "worked like a dog, from 12 to 14 hours a day, real grease-monkey stuff," adding that "working on the damp floors, under cars, brought on a case of rheumatism, and most of the pain centered in my right arm." Benny Critelli, however, recalled that "Sal just sold gasoline and oil—he didn't fix cars. He maybe changed the oil, but he was no mechanic."[12] Once again Sal recalled an episode from his past as worse than it was.

Whatever the exact nature of his work at the gas station, located in the bleak industrial landscape on the eastern outskirts of Niagara Falls, Sal hated every minute of it. To have gone from major leaguer to gas station attendant was a severe blow to his pride as well as his pocketbook. Every time he filled up a tank for friends like Benny or any of the Niagara baseball fans who recognized him, Sal received a reminder of how far he had fallen. Never an early riser if he could avoid it, Sal rose before dawn every day to open the station and returned home late in the evening, chilled and exhausted. He was short-tempered with his wife, who had never seen him like that, as well as restless and interested in nothing, pacing and wandering like a lost soul. At least now he had a place of his own to come home to. On April 28, 1948, he had used $10,000 of his Mexican League money to buy outright a house at 2727 Pierce Avenue in Niagara Falls. It was a very modest home: a small wood frame structure with five rooms on two floors, squeezed onto a narrow strip of land, similar to the places where he had lived as a child, although this house was not divided into apartments, and Sal and Kay occupied both floors.

But home ownership in his hometown brought Sal face to face with a problem he had avoided confronting during his years of traveling and striving to carve out a baseball career. From the first days of their marriage in 1941 Kay had been eager to have children. When Sal was barely making a living from baseball and the couple had no home of their own, it was understandable that Sal had been reluctant to start a family. But now the couple had settled into their own home and had substantial savings, and Sal had gone into a business that promised a steady income. They had been married almost eight years, and there was no reason to further postpone having children. The couple therefore could no longer avoid facing what they already knew: that Kay could not conceive.

The realization was shattering and heartbreaking for Kay. As for Sal, he wanted Kay to be happy, and if having children would make her happy, he would be delighted to do his part, but the issue did not obsess him. Nonetheless, by this point he must have heard about the subject from his imperious mother. One can imagine Macolà's perplexity, she who had become pregnant without the slightest difficulty, as she looked at her big handsome son and wondered what could be wrong with him or, more likely, with his wife. Kay's mother, who had borne four children, also fretted, concerned for her unhappy daughter whose lush body seemed to promise so much more than it delivered. Kay needed no prodding about pregnancy—the subject consumed her to the point where she lost all sense of appropriate behavior.

Kay's brother and sister-in-law, John and Mary Pileggi, offered powerful evidence of the extent of Kay's desperation when they revealed that Kay repeatedly begged them to *give her* one or more of their own children. According to Mary's recollections, Kay "couldn't get enough" of John and Mary's first child, their daughter Joanne, and she would say that they ought to consider giving her their next child. At first, the Pileggis did not believe Kay was serious. After John came home from military service in 1946, Mary became pregnant again, and Kay convinced herself that Mary would be willing to part with her second child. "While I was pregnant," Mary recalled, "Kay was rubbing my stomach and saying, 'Oh Mary, I've *got* to have this baby!' And I said, 'Kay, get it out of your mind.' And she says, 'But you can have children and I can't.'" When the couple's son John Jr. was born in 1947 Kay continued trying to convince Mary and John to give her their newborn son. Mary never for a moment considered such a transaction. "I said to her, 'No, *no,* Kay, you don't know what you're asking me. When they're your own, you just don't give them away!'" Despite repeatedly being refused by the Pileggis, Kay continued her efforts to persuade them to part with their children. When Mary became pregnant for the third time, in 1948, Kay was certain Mary would relent and give her the child. Mary experienced a difficult pregnancy and nearly died giving birth to the couple's second son. "Kay was so thrilled," Mary recalled. "She said that this time we couldn't refuse her." Sadly, the couple's infant son died several days later. John Pileggi emphasized, "We would never have given him up anyway! My poor sister—she was *desperate!*"[13]

Sal, too, envied the ability of his brother-in-law and sister-in-law to have children so easily. He once exclaimed to Mary Pileggi, "My God, Mary, it looks like you're a baby machine, because every time John makes a mistake, you're pregnant!"[14] In addition to John and Mary Pileggi, there was Sal's sister Santa Grenga, whose brood of five included four sons; Kay's other brother, Carl, who had a boy and a girl; and Kay's older sister Mary Villani, who had a son. As long as the couple remained in Niagara Falls they lived surrounded by relatives with children, a constant and painful reminder to Kay of her own childless state.

COMMITMENTS IN CANADA— SAL'S SEASON WITH THE DRUMMONDVILLE CUBS

The dreary winter of Sal's discontent and Kay's desperation ended at last, and in the early spring of 1949 Sal received an offer to pitch in the Provincial League, in Canada. He showed no hesitation in signing up. "Anything to get away from those pumps!" as he put it years later.[15] Although the Provincial

League was considered another outlaw league by major league baseball, Sal had nothing to lose by joining, since American baseball already considered him an outlaw. The offer came in a phone call from fellow Mexican League jumper Stan Bréard, then serving as player-manager of the Drummondville Cubs. The league operated in Quebec province, only a few hundred miles northeast of Niagara Falls, and was made up of teams from six neighboring towns—Drummondville, Sherbrooke, St. Hyacinthe, Granby, Farnham, and St. Jean. Sal sold the detested gas station and spent a couple of weeks whipping himself into shape, and then he and Kay headed north. Drummondville would pay him $600 a month—a comedown from his fat four-figure monthly income in Mexico, but at least he was back in baseball.

Canada's Provincial League had a history distinct from that of the Mexican loop Maglie had recently abandoned. Founded in 1934, it had been granted minor league Class-B status by American baseball in 1940 but retained that status for only a year, and during the period when Sal was involved it operated outside organized baseball. The Provincial League had officially disbanded for the duration of World War II. After the war, organized baseball refused to readmit the Provincial League for the now-familiar reason that the league permitted banned players to participate on its teams. Major league baseball defined as an "outlaw" any league that signed players banned for any reason from organized baseball. This rendered all the outlaw league's players, including those with no transgressions, ineligible to play for teams in organized baseball.[16]

The collapse of the Mexican League proved a windfall for the Provincial League. After the Mexican League demise, among those signed to play in Canada were Lanier, Zimmermann, Gardella, and Maglie. Drummondville was delighted by the team's acquisition of Maglie. On March 24 the French language newspaper *La Parole* reported, "The big news of the week for our baseball fans has to be the official signing of well-known pitcher Sal Maglie, formerly with the New York Giants of the National League. . . . Stan Bréard, who knows him well, is convinced that he will be a sensation in the Provincial League."[17]

Sal's 1949 season with the Drummondville Cubs *was* sensational, one of the best in his entire career, but unlike his victories in his top major league seasons, his Canadian triumphs have been for the most part forgotten, buried behind the bigger news during that summer of the jumpers' reinstatement by major league baseball. Many of the other refugees from the States returned home as soon as Chandler lifted the ban, deserting their Canadian teams, but Maglie honored his contract with the Cubs and stayed the full season, picking up 23 wins against 9 losses and proving himself essential to his team's championship. Perhaps because Sal's season in Canada has never been considered of much importance, records of it are often incomplete or inaccurate, and some statistics, such as his number of wild pitches, hit batsmen, and earned run average, are nonexistent. In his recent biography of Maglie, Szalontai reported that Sal "claimed to have won 23 games during the regular season, but records show only fifteen."[18] As the most recent research has shown, Sal's "claim" to have won 23 games was correct: he won 18 during the regular reason and a whopping five, with no defeats, in the playoffs. His 18–9 won-lost record for the regular season was the best in the Provincial League.

Sal began his Drummondville stint on Opening Day, May 8, picking up a win in relief. After a second relief appearance in which he was not involved in the decision, he began a five-game winning streak, and he did not lose a game until June 11. Although he was 3–4 for July, Sal had become the ace of the squad, with a record of 13–6. He notched another five-game streak between late July and early August, and in the last month won five while dropping three. He tossed two shutouts, as well as five other wins in which he allowed only one run, and led the Cubs to a first-place finish. In the Provincial League playoff system, which placed all six teams in postseason series, Sal distinguished himself further. In both of the two playoff series opponents took the Cubs to the full nine games. In the first series, against St. Hyacinthe, Sal won two games, and in the second, against Farnham, he won three. In each series Sal won the decisive final contest, and in the second playoff series two of his three wins were shutouts. Considering the hasty circumstances under which he began the season and all the outside excitement that enlivened the subsequent months, Sal could be forgiven if he had pitched poorly. He had not had much time to shake off the aches and pains and chilblains of his months in the gas station or to regain his stamina, and yet he became the staff workhorse, putting in a league-high 266 innings pitched and hurling an impressive total of 25 complete games. He struck out 205 batters, almost three times as many as the 69 he walked.

Sal dealt with plenty of distractions in those months. The entire season at Drummondville took place against a background of well-publicized legal actions in the United States, as several of the banned ballplayers attempted to sue organized baseball, actions which culminated in commissioner Chandler's lifting of the ban against the Mexican League jumpers. Danny Gardella had first instituted his $300,000 damage suit in 1947. His attorney, Frederick Johnson, a Harvard Law School graduate with a lifelong interest in baseball, recognized that Gardella had not broken his contract with the Giants when he went to Mexico, because he had never signed it, and his only violation had been of the reserve clause. Nonetheless, upon his return to the United States Gardella had found it impossible to make a living in baseball, and after Lanier's All-Stars disbanded he worked as a hospital orderly for $36 a week. Johnson believed Gardella's case offered an excellent chance to have the reserve clause overturned in court, a circumstance major league baseball until this point had avoided. The astute lawyer-fan realized that baseball had never claimed in a court of law that the reserve clause was binding on players; it stood as an honorary obligation or gentlemen's agreement. In the Gardella case Johnson argued that the reserve clause was a weapon used by organized baseball "contrary to settled principles of equity and to further a conspiracy in restraint of trade and commerce," and that it served to perpetuate an illegal monopoly the lawyer dramatically pictured as "stretching from Hudson's Bay to the Equator."[19]

In July of 1948 a judge dismissed the case. Undeterred, Johnson pressed on, and in November of 1948 he lodged an appeal before the Second Circuit Appellate Federal Court in New York's Southern District. On February 9, 1949, the three-judge panel announced it had voted 2–1 that Gardella's case was strong enough to warrant a trial. Major league baseball reacted with claims that the end of the game was at hand if Gardella won his case, but the most disheartening response, as far as Gardella himself was concerned, was the negative reaction of some of his fellow jumpers. Mickey Owen, Max Lanier, and Fred Martin visited Gardella at his home shortly after the Circuit Court's decision, urging him to drop his suit, because they believed that if he did, Chandler would reinstate all the jumpers.

Gardella refused to abandon his cause, but he must have impressed Lanier, because the ever-enterprising pitcher decided to try a lawsuit of his own and convinced Fred Martin to join him. They sued baseball for $2.5 million on the same grounds that Gardella had, charging that baseball was a monopoly in violation of antitrust laws and requesting reinstatement, even though both had broken signed contracts when they jumped to Mexico. In mid-March they went to court, but a New York judge denied their requests. Mickey Owen, with help from Fred Martin and Roy Zimmermann, drew up a petition for reinstatement that eleven players signed: Owen, Martin, Zimmermann, Max Lanier, Ace Adams, Harry Feldman, George Hausmann, Lou Klein, Murray Franklin, Luis Olmo, and Sal Maglie. On June 2, the United States Court of Appeals refused to order major league baseball to reinstate Gardella, Lanier, and Martin, upholding the decision that their cases should be settled by jury trial. Galvanized by the alarming thought that the reserve clause might be overturned if Gardella prevailed in court, on June 5, 1949, Chandler headed off that crucial legal test by announcing that the jumpers were free to return to organized baseball. He added that they were each entitled to a 30-day trial with their clubs, and that after that they could be retained, traded, or released. Although some hostile feelings lingered, the vendetta against the jumpers had ended.

Chandler's announcement was big news throughout the Provincial League, where 10 of the 18 former Mexican Leaguers were employed, four of them with Drummondville. Lanier and Maglie were delighted by the news, although Lanier was doing well in Drummondville, where the team provided him with a rent-free furnished house in addition to a $10,000 salary. In an interview after Chandler's announcement he said he had talked with the Cardinals about returning, but that they had not made him "a suitable offer." The *Sporting News,* never sympathetic to the jumpers, ran an article noting that history was against the jumpers' regaining their jobs—out of the 54 Federal League players suspended in 1915, only two enjoyed subsequent major league careers. The article listed Lanier, Olmo, Owen, and Martin as the best bets to resume successful major league careers, and suggested that Hausmann, Feldman, and Ortiz might possibly make it back. Sal Maglie's name was not even mentioned.[20]

Lou Klein was in such a hurry to return to the Cardinals that he bought back his contract from Sherbrooke. Zabala, Feldman, and Martin also left Sherbrooke. Lanier stayed in Drummondville initially, not out of loyalty but because he was still dickering with the Cardinals over his salary. Fred Saigh, the new Cardinals owner, reached an agreement with Lanier that would double Lanier's previous salary with the Cardinals, with a bonus if he reached St. Louis by the Fourth of July. The pitcher was gone from Drummondville by June 30. Zimmermann, Gardella, and Maglie remained to finish out the season amid rumors that they received fat bonuses, almost amounting to bribes, to persuade them to stay. Coco Tarte, a French Canadian player for the Farnham team, recalled hearing that Maglie received a $15,000 bonus (a fantastic sum amounting to five times his salary) as an incentive to finish the season with Drummondville, "and room and board for his wife and kids, too," the latter a detail that puts the accuracy of Tarte's claim further in doubt, since the Maglies had no children.[21] Years later Sal denied that he had received any bonus. "That kind of money simply didn't exist. We were lucky to be paid $250 per game," he snorted.[22] Sherbrooke's newspaper, *La Tribune,* reported that Sal had asked for a portion of Lanier's salary after Max had departed. This was a reasonable request, given how little Maglie had been paid—about $3,000 in contrast to Lanier's $10,000— and the fact that Lanier had reneged on his contract while Maglie had not. *La Tribune* reported that the extra funds from Lanier's account brought Maglie's salary to $8,000 for the season.

On August 23 Maglie made a trip to New York City, where he met with Fred Saigh, the owner of the Cardinals, and John L. Flynn, the attorney for Lanier and Martin in their lawsuit. Probably at the urging of Lanier, Sal had also met with Flynn at an earlier date, and he too may have been thinking about filing a lawsuit against organized baseball, although he later denied that, saying, "Since I left the Giants voluntarily while under contract to them, I would not have taken the team to court."[23] At another time Sal claimed that Mickey Owen, rather than Lanier, tried to enlist him in a lawsuit. "But I told him nothing doing," Sal said. "All I was interested in was in getting back. I'm no lawyer, I'm a ballplayer."[24] Saigh, after two months of secret negotiations, had finally convinced Lanier and Martin to withdraw their suits. Now he summoned Sal Maglie from Canada and told him that if he agreed not to go forward with his lawsuit, he could rejoin the New York Giants immediately for the remainder of the 1949 season. The offer came as Maglie was considering an opportunity to play in Venezuela when the Canadian season ended.

The temptation to shout *"Yes!"* and start packing his bags must have been powerful, but to his credit, Sal refused the offer. Although, according to Saigh, he agreed not to pursue the lawsuit, Sal told him he had "commitments in Canada that must be fulfilled" and that instead he would like to rejoin the Giants for their 1950 season.[25] In July he had given Provincial League president Albert Molini his word that he would not leave before the end of the season, and he did not go back on that promise. "I felt I should stay in Drummondville and help win the pennant for the only club that gave me a job when I needed one badly," Sal stated.[26] Although his decision to remain with Drummondville was an honorable one that reflects well on him, it was also a practical move. Ever the realist, Sal knew the competition in the Provincial League was not of major league caliber and that his skills were not sharp enough for him to be successful against big league hitters. If the Giants were going to give him one chance to succeed, he wanted to be at his best when he took advantage of that opportunity. Furthermore, the Giants had offered him only $5,000, and the cold weather in Canada had stiffened his arm. His wife recalled watching Sal pitch one of the last of the 1949 playoff games, against Farnham, on a day when the temperature was below freezing and snow fell throughout the game. According to Kay, Sal carried "a battery-powered hand warmer in his pocket" to keep his fingers from going numb.[27]

The two playoff series provided plenty of excitement. Drummondville's first playoff pitted the league's top-ranked team against the cellar-dwelling St. Hyacinthe Saints, with the first team to win five moving on to the finals. Although heavily favored Drummondville took an initial 4–1 lead in the series, the Saints roared back and evened the series at four games each. Fans of Drummondville were in a frenzy. Columnist Jean Barrette, reporting on the Cubs-Saints contests for the local newspaper, *La Patrie,* branded the series with a single, sinister word: *"Arrangé!"* (fixed). Although nothing was ever proved, rumors persisted that Albert Molini, the president of the league, hoped to recoup his losses by gambling heavily on the critical games. But in the final game Sal Maglie stopped the Saints, 7–1, to clinch the series for Drummondville. Fans celebrated, and admirers showered Sal with money and gifts, agreeing that he had saved the series.

The playoff finals for the league championship took place between Drummondville and Farnham. This time the Cubs faced a much tougher team than St. Hyacinche. The Farnham Black Sox were a solid squad that included many talented Negro League players. The Cubs took the first two games, with Maglie winning the opener, 7–0, but the Black Sox came back to take the next two contests. Sal returned on October 1 for the fifth game and spun another shutout, 2–0, giving up four hits and striking out 11—the game Kay Maglie remembered for its frigid weather and falling snow. The teams see-sawed for the next three games: Farnham took the sixth game, Drummondville the seventh, and Farnham won game eight. Once again the series came down to a ninth game, this one in Drummondville on the evening of October 4. More than 3,500 bundled-up spectators crowded into the stadium to cheer for their favorites, and once again Maglie took the mound, this time against Negro League veteran Willie Pope. Farnham scored once against Maglie and hung on to that lead, with Pope stifling the Drummondville batters until the bottom of the seventh, when the Cubs rallied and scored five. Sal did not allow another run and triumphed, 5–1, allowing four hits and striking out ten. The Cubs had needed ten wins to gain the Provincial League title, and Maglie had delivered five of them.

The next day the town of Drummondville held a reception for their team. Guests at the head table included Stan Bréard as well as Sal and Kay Maglie. Speeches lauded Bréard, and he was presented with the league trophy. Speakers also singled out Maglie for special praise, lauding him for his contributions to the team and the town of Drummondville. Sal had been instrumental in Drummondville's championship season, but Drummondville played an equally important part in Sal's career. If he had not received the invitation to play for the Canadian Cubs in 1949 and had instead spent that year pumping gas, changing oil, and moping, without an opportunity to keep in shape and maintain his baseball skills, it is unlikely he would have had much success when he returned to the Giants in 1950. Luque's lessons would have been lost along with all of Sal's own hopes and efforts, and that baseball legend, "Sal the Barber," would never have been born.

While You Were Gone...

Major League Baseball
from 1946 through 1949

During the four seasons Sal Maglie missed, several transforming events took place in baseball. Towering over everything, both in far-reaching significance and sheer human drama, was the integration of the majors by Jackie Robinson. Other events, less visible and dramatic, also began to change the national pastime. An attempt to form a players union failed, but players gained important rights. Although the game reached its peak of popularity in the second half of the 1940s, television began altering the economics of baseball and other facets of the game as well. The movement of millions from cities to suburbs, which began in the late 1940s and accelerated in the 1950s, affected attendance at games and later led to franchise shifts and league expansion. As America plunged into a postwar era of prosperity and world power, baseball continued to reflect the country's best—and worst—qualities.

THE 1946 SEASON—
RECOVERING FROM THE WAR

The best part of the 1946 season was the mere fact that it was normal, the first in five years that did not take place against a backdrop of war. Attendance soared, with nearly every team setting a new record. More than 90 percent of major leaguers had served in the military, and now droves of players rejoined their old teams but were angered to learn that owners had taken advantage of wartime wage controls to depress salaries. At a time when labor unions stood at their peak of strength, baseball had its own brush with unionization. Labor lawyer Robert Murphy founded the American Baseball Guild and tried to recruit major leaguers. The Pittsburgh Pirates came within a hair of a strike in June of 1946, but the effort fizzled. Not only did most Americans oppose the unionization of baseball[1]; there was also the game's own tradition of individualism. Those factors, coupled with players' suspicions that unions rewarded mediocrity and protected the unworthy, doomed Murphy's efforts. It would be another 30 years before baseball unionized. Nonetheless, owners met during the summer of 1946 and granted players new rights. They could choose representatives to meet with owners; they gained a minimum salary of $5,000 and a 25 percent maximum on cuts in salary from one year to the next; and most important, the owners agreed to establish a pension plan. Sal Maglie later claimed some credit for himself and his fellow Mexican League jumpers, declaring, "I was one of the instigators of having the pension."[2] Maglie was partially correct. Baseball owners had been prodded into action not only by Murphy's efforts, but also by the shock of the Mexican League raids.

When the minor league season began, the most closely watched game took place in Jersey City, where the Jersey City Giants faced the Montreal Royals. All eyes focused on the Royals' Jackie Robinson, the first black man to play professional baseball since the mid-1880s, when Cap Anson had shouted "Get that nigger off the field!" and baseball had cravenly complied.[3] Playing in an atmosphere of racial hostility whose intensity and viciousness is almost inconceivable today, but supported by enthusiastic black fans, loyal Canadians, and open-minded white Americans, he led his team to a pennant and a Junior World Series victory.

If Sal Maglie followed the fortunes of the New York Giants, he would have seen little to make him regret his decision to leave. By the time the season was a week old the Giants were in fifth place, and they never rose above that level, making a steady descent into the cellar. In the American League the Boston Red Sox walked away with the pennant, so the main excitement in baseball in 1946 came from a close National League race between the Brooklyn Dodgers and the St. Louis Cardinals. By the All-Star break the Dodgers held a seven-game lead over the Cards and Dodger manager Leo Durocher strutted around, full of confidence in his colorful crew. A source of delight to him was the success of righthander Kirby Higbe. Profane, a heavy drinker, and a womanizer of prodigious appetites, Higbe's nickname among his teammates was "Kirby Fucking Higbe" because of his persistent use of that expletive. Another Dodger character was Fred "Dixie" Walker. Brooklyn fans loved the Georgia native and nicknamed him in their local dialect "The People's Cherce." Dodger second baseman Eddie Stanky, an Alabaman who had started out as a wartime fill-in, was among the few wartime players with the talent to stick with the team after the veterans returned. Small, thin, and not particularly strong or fast, he always managed to make himself valuable. A pleasant man off the field, when he played, a personality emerged that seemed composed of equal parts of barbed wire, itching powder, and broken glass. Even some of his own teammates disliked him, but Durocher thought he was terrific. In contrast to these vivid personalities stood the steady Harold "Pee Wee" Reese. He had been the Dodgers shortstop since 1940 but had lost three years to military service, and 1946 was his first season back. An unassuming natural leader, the Kentucky-born Reese was considering how he would respond to the challenge Jackie Robinson might pose to his job when, inevitably, Robinson joined the Dodgers. Another quiet, determined fellow, right fielder Carl Furillo, who was a rookie in 1946, later became famous for the rifle-shot strength and accuracy of his right arm as well as his visceral hatred of two men: Leo Durocher and Sal Maglie.

The Dodgers and Cards ended the season in a tie, and for the first time, a major league championship was decided by a three-game playoff, as the winner of a coin toss decided where he wanted to play. The opening game could take place at home and the next two on the road, or the other way around. Durocher won the toss and decided on an opener in St. Louis, with the remaining games on his home turf of Ebbets Field. But the Dodgers dropped two in a row, and the Cardinals walked away as the National League champions. The 1946 World Series with the Red Sox went to seven games, and the underdog Cardinals won. During the pennant race, and throughout the Series, the last major story of the wartime era kept baseball grim company: the trial in Nuremberg, Germany, of 22 high-ranking Nazi officials for war crimes. The announcement that the Nazis had been hanged (except for Herman Goering, who committed suicide) shared the front page with the Cardinals' Series victory. The judgements at Nuremberg produced at least a symbolic sense of justice and closure to the war era.

THE 1947 SEASON—"WHEN ALL HELL BROKE LOOSE IN BASEBALL"

Never mind that the Dead Sea Scrolls were discovered in the Judaean desert in 1947, with profound implications for biblical scholarship; that India and Pakistan became separate, mutually hostile nations, with international repercussions; and that Thor Heyerdahl crossed the Pacific from Peru to Polynesia on a raft called *Kontiki*, revolutionizing archeologists' theories about prehistoric migrations.[4] In America the most significant event of 1947 took place on a baseball diamond. As Jackie Robinson, the first black man to play in the major leagues in the twentieth century, made history on April 15, 1947, by stepping onto the field in the uniform of the Brooklyn

Dodgers, America's ugliest side, its deeply ingrained racism, stepped out with him. Robinson's integration of the majors truly reshaped the game.

A forerunner of that reshaping was the appointment in 1945 of Happy Chandler as baseball commissioner, to replace the late Judge Landis, a rock-hard racist determined to preserve the game's segregated status. Robinson entered professional baseball literally over Landis' dead body. The real architect of baseball integration, however, was that remarkable character, Branch Rickey. The Dodgers' part-owner and president was baseball's resident intellectual, a brilliant, innovative, Ohio-born Methodist and tireless moralizer who was also a master of mesmerizing rhetoric, brilliant judge of baseball talent, shrewd businessman, and ruthless negotiator. No matter what his virtues, faults, and other achievements, it was his demolition of baseball's color bar that earned him distinguished baseball writer Donald Honig's highest accolade, "the Abraham Lincoln of baseball."[5] Historians still debate Rickey's motives for signing Robinson. Did he merely wish to exploit the untapped reservoir of baseball talent in the Negro Leagues? Did he view black players as just another weapon the Dodgers could use to defeat their rivals? Was he hoping to line his own pockets with money from the large audiences of black fans who would flock to watch Robinson (and later other black athletes) play? Or was he that rare phenomenon, a genuine idealist, a man whose actions were dictated not by expediency, advantage, or personal gain but by a higher vision of what is *right*? The most likely answer to all those questions is yes. Rickey was that singular American combination of piety and practicality, idealism and realism, a man whose passion for justice equaled his passion for profits.

Rickey had chosen Robinson with great care. If the man he had selected to integrate baseball could not play at the major league level while also bearing up under the torrents of racist filth, could not endure the spikes-up slides, the beanballs, and the death threats—if he lost his temper and fought back, or collapsed under the strain—then "baseball's great experiment" would go down with him, and there was no telling how long racists might maintain their grip on the game. He did not fail. In his year with Montreal in 1946, he displayed super-human restraint, ignoring the taunts and threats that rained down on him, and played brilliantly. As Scott Simon put it, Robinson was "first and last . . . a hard-nosed, hard-assed, brass-balled, fire-breathing *athlete*."[6] Robinson was ready for the Show.

But Rickey had badly underestimated the racial animosity of certain players. When Dodgers road secretary Harold Parrott learned from pitcher Kirby Higbe that a petition against Robinson was circulating among team members during an exhibition series in Havana, he contacted Rickey by phone in the States and alerted manager Durocher. Even though it was after midnight, Durocher hauled his players into the deserted hotel kitchen for a no-holds-barred harangue. Various versions of the tirade survive, and given that Leo possessed the foulest mouth in baseball, the more profane ones are no doubt the more accurate. He barked something along these lines: "Listen, you motherfuckers, I don't give a *shit* if this guy is black, yellow, green, or has stripes like a fucking *zebra*. I'm the manager of this fucking team and if I say he plays, he fucking *plays*. He can put an awful lot of fucking *money* in our pockets. He can make all of us fucking *rich*. And if any of you shitheads can't use the money, goddammit, I'll see that you're traded. And here's something else for you cocksuckers to think about. From everything I hear, he's only the first. Unless you fucking ass-holes wake up, they're going to run you right out of the ballpark! So you can take your fucking goddamn petition and *shove it up your ass!*"[7] End of meeting.

Details about the alleged petition remain uncertain, particularly in regard to the identities of its signers, since no copies have ever surfaced. Furthermore, trying to find old ballplayers who admit they opposed the integration of baseball is like trying to find old Frenchmen eager to admit they collaborated with the Nazis: "*Mais non, monsieur!* We were all members of the Resistance!" Many team members refused to have anything to do with the petition, and pitcher Ralph Branca, a New Yorker, does not even recall seeing it. "I guess they figured only the southern guys would sign it," he later speculated.[8] Rickey flew to Havana and acted quickly on Parrott's warning, dissuading several players from supporting the petition, but a few remained unswayed by Rickey's rhetoric and asked to be traded.

As if the potentially explosive situation with Robinson were not enough to keep the baseball pot boiling that spring, Durocher became entangled in difficulties that led to his suspension for the season, for "an accumulation of unpleasant incidents detrimental to baseball," conduct related to his alleged habit of consorting with gamblers.[9] On April 9, Chandler suspended Durocher for a year, leaving the Dodgers without a manager only days before the opening of the season in which Jackie Robinson was to make his major league debut. Undeterred, Rickey forged ahead. During an exhibition game the Dodgers were playing against Montreal at Ebbets Field, he had a team official tack an announcement on the press box bulletin board: "The Brooklyn Dodgers today purchased the contract of Jackie Roosevelt Robinson from the Montreal Royals. He will report immediately. [signed] Branch Rickey." The great experiment had begun. Rickey's friend Burt Shotton took over as manager of the Dodgers. An experienced baseball man, Shotton brought stability and calm to a tense Dodgers team. Jackie Robinson, after a slow start, and despite some of the most nauseating race-baiting ever to disgrace major league ballparks, began burning up the league. Along with the terrible indignities Robinson had to endure, he also experienced some gratifying support. Eddie Stanky defended Jackie, sometimes shouting back at those who taunted him when Robinson could not. Pee Wee Reese, another southerner, became Robinson's friend and one of his stoutest defenders, putting his arm around Jackie on the field in a public show of solidarity. Most heartening of all, in July Cleveland Indians president Bill Veeck broke the American League color line by bringing up Larry Doby.

As the train carrying the pennant-winning Dodgers pulled into Penn Station in New York City on the evening of September 20, thousands of fans crammed the station to welcome them back. They were the Jackie Robinson Dodgers—the team's single black player had come to personify them all. So many adoring fans mobbed Robinson that he needed a police escort out of the Station. How many people were "unwittingly snared into enlightenment," as Donald Honig put it, by Rickey's bold move of bringing Robinson to the majors, and by Robinson's own brilliant performances, cannot be measured. No one could claim that Robinson's success meant America had solved its racial problems. And yet, as the 1947 season went on, as white fans became accustomed to Robinson's fierce, electric presence, as they shared pride in his achievements with black fans sitting near them in the unsegregated Ebbets Field stands, some white fans came to conclusions that seem painfully obvious today, but that were new and astonishing insights in 1947: that black people were no different from themselves and that the treatment Robinson and others of his race endured from whites was unacceptable. Such changes may have been a mouse gnawing at the mountain of racism, but they were a start, and the start had been made in major league baseball.

With most of the dramas of 1947 in the Dodgers camp, Maglie's old teammates, the Giants, slugged and slogged their way though another mediocre season. Although they set a record for home runs, with 221, which led to their nickname, the "Windowbreakers," they were a slow-footed bunch who stole a total of 29 bases—the same number stolen by Jackie Robinson—and finished fourth. Their problem was still a lack of pitching. In September Mel Ott announced his retirement as a player after 22 years with the club. Despite another poor showing, the popular Ott was hired back as manager.

1948—THE SEASON OF THE BIG SWITCH

As spring training began the Giants were still desperate for decent pitching. They had a handful of pitchers—Dave Koslo, Monte Kennedy, Clint Hartung, and rookie Sheldon Jones—who had promise, but only one proven outstanding hurler, Larry Jansen. In their batting order the Giants still had Windowbreakers Willard Marshall, Sid Gordon, Walker Cooper, Bobby Thomson, and Johnny Mize, along with younger prospects Whitey Lockman and Don Mueller. The Giants started strong, but lackluster fielding and mediocre pitching took their toll, and by the All-Star break they were mired in fourth place. At this point owner Horace Stoneham began to think about the unthinkable, replacing Mel Ott with a manager capable of inspiring better play.

Meanwhile, in Brooklyn, the Dodgers were also sleepwalking. Integration proceeded at a slow pace as, in mid-season, the Dodgers brought up Roy Campanella, a cheerful, roly-poly catcher with a more relaxed personality than the tightly wound Jackie Robinson. The team was without Kirby Higbe, traded in 1947, and Rickey would also trade away Dixie Walker and pitcher Hugh Casey because of all three men's reluctance to play with Jackie Robinson. The Walker trade proved valuable, bringing the Dodgers two effective players: Preacher Roe, a scrawny southpaw from the Ozarks who concealed his college education and cultivated his hayseed image with the same good-natured guile he used to camouflage his spitball, and Billy Cox, a moody loner from Pennsylvania who became the National League's best third baseman. Eddie Stanky was gone as well, sent to the Boston Braves not because of his racial attitudes but because Rickey wanted Robinson at second base. Another change was to take place: Gil Hodges, a big, quiet Midwesterner of enormous physical strength, would be converted from a third-string catcher to a first baseman. A promising pitcher, Carl Erskine, also joined the Dodgers in 1948 and became a mainstay of the staff. A gentlemanly and deeply religious young man from Indiana with a fine overhand curve, Erskine formed a special bond with Jackie Robinson.

Durocher had returned from his suspension as abrasive and brassy as ever. To the dismay of Branch Rickey, for whom Durocher was a favorite reclamation project, the Dodger manager was soon up to his old tricks, consorting with gamblers and lowlifes. Durocher, for his part, was furious with Rickey for trading away Stanky. But in Rickey's eyes Durocher's worst sin was that he did not get along with Jackie Robinson. Durocher was many things and many of them bad, but he was not a racist. He and Robinson were intense men with highly competitive, bristling personalities that clashed rather than meshing for the common goal of winning games. Robinson was a grievance-storer who remembered every slight and insult, and Durocher was famous for his ability to get under anyone's skin. Robinson, accustomed to his team as a refuge from criticism and harassment, reacted with an aversion to the abrasive Durocher that hardened into hatred, and the resulting tensions affected the team's play. By the All-Star break the league champions were in sixth place, with a dismal 35–37 record.

At this point the inconceivable, the unbelievable, and the absolutely un-expected happened. Leo Durocher left the Brooklyn Dodgers and became the manager of the New York Giants. From the perspective of nearly sixty years later, with both teams long gone from New York, the switch no longer seems radical, but in 1948 it was mind-boggling. The animosity between the Dodgers and the Giants, and between the two teams' fans, was little short of war. In the 1930s a Dodgers fan drowning his sorrows in drink at a saloon shot and killed two Giants fans who had been tormenting him, and many others on both sides often had murder in their hearts. The two teams regu-larly engaged in beanball wars, and there was a vicious edge to all their com-petitions. Giants fans hated Durocher with a passion comparable to that di-rected at Hitler and Tojo. He was the *enemy*. His leaving the Dodgers for the Giants seemed unconscionable—as if in the midst of the war General MacArthur had defected to the Germans or the Japanese.

Part of the explanation for the Big Switch lies in the coincidence that the Dodgers and the Giants were both in the market for new managers at the same time. Each owner pondered the problem of finding an adequate re-placement. Ott apparently recommended Durocher to Stoneham as his re-placement.[10] Stoneham liked the idea but did not think the Dodgers would release Durocher to their bitterest rivals if he made a direct approach. Coincidence hastened events. On his way to the All-Star game, Stoneham encountered Frank Shaughnessy, president of the International League. Re-calling Shaughnessy as a friend of Rickey's, he asked Shaughnessy to sound out Rickey on whether Shotton might be available, but he said nothing about his interest in Durocher. Shaughnessy reported back that Shotton was unavailable, but would Stoneham be interested in Durocher? The delighted Giants owner declared that Durocher would do very well indeed. After all the fuss, neither the Dodgers nor the Giants underwent any immediate changes in the wake of Durocher's switch. Rickey hired back Shotton, and the Dodgers ended the season in third place. Briefly galvanized by Durocher's arrival, the somnolent Giants then slumped again and finished fifth, as the Boston Braves won the pennant.

THE 1949 SEASON—ENDINGS AND BEGINNINGS

The last baseball season of the 1940s featured tight pennant races in both leagues, and saw the problem of the Mexican League jumpers resolved, with the related issue that Danny Gardella's lawsuit was settled out of court, to the infinite relief of the baseball establishment. The 1949 season also began an eight-year period of domination of the game by all three New York teams, in particular the Yankees and the Dodgers. June started with Chandler's lifting of the ban on the jumpers, few of whom fans even remembered. Lost among the month's bigger stories was the New York Yankees' announcement that, for $1,000, they had signed a teenage boy from Oklahoma named Mickey Mantle.

Again answering Branch Rickey's call, Burt Shotton took over as Dodgers manager and led the team to the pennant. A great team was taking shape in Brooklyn, one that gripped fans' imaginations as no other ever has. Jackie Robinson, playing second base, was as responsible as anyone for providing the margin of victory in 1949, as he exploded into full stardom and full voice. Freed from the vow of silence Rickey had imposed on him, he ranted at umpires, wrangled with opposition players, and hurled obscenities back at those who taunted him with racial slurs. Fueled by his burning anger, Robinson led both leagues in hitting and was named the National League's Most Valuable Player. Campanella, the Dodgers' second black player, gained recognition as the National League's best catcher. Slugger Gil Hodges found his perfect niche at first base, Reese sparkled at shortstop, and Billy Cox proved a master of the hot corner at third. Edwin "Duke" Snider, a power-hitting young outfielder from California, took over in center field full-time, and Furillo established himself in right as a man with an uncanny knack for playing the balls that caromed off Ebbets Field's complicated right field wall and gunning them back to the infield with dazzling speed and accuracy. The Dodgers soon had their third black player, power pitcher Don Newcombe, who won 17 games in 1949, his first season in the majors.

Giants fans had problems adjusting to Leo Durocher. He was loudly booed the first few times he emerged from the dugout, although the team appreciated his baseball savvy and adjusted to his leadership style. When the Giants brought up their first two black players in July, Durocher welcomed Monte Irvin and Hank Thompson with a shorter and less vulgar version of the speech he had given to the Dodgers two years earlier: "I'm only going to say one thing about color: you can be green or be pink and be on this team. If you can play baseball and help this team you're welcome to play."[11] But Durocher was far from satisfied. He had told Stoneham that the Giants were not his kind of team. Lead-footed power hitters who were sluggish fielders did not meet Leo's standards, and he was eager to remake the team in his own image: scrappy, aggressive, and fast-moving. Stoneham finally asked him to write a report that included a list of who should stay and who should be traded. Durocher claims he turned in a four-word report: "Back up the truck."[12]

Stoneham liked his big, slow-moving sluggers Johnny Mize, Walker Cooper, Willard Marshall, and Sid Gordon, and Durocher had his way only gradually. First to go was Cooper, traded to Cincinnati, and toward the end of the season Mize was sold to the Yankees. Over the winter the Giants jettisoned two more sluggers, sending Marshall and Gordon to the Boston Braves, along with infielder Buddy Kerr. In exchange the Giants received the infield combination Leo wanted: shortstop Alvin Dark and Durocher's old favorite, second baseman Eddie Stanky. In an attempt to improve Giants pitching Durocher tried, but failed, to acquire Dodger righthander Ralph Branca.[13] It is interesting to contemplate how different the subsequent history of the Giants-Dodgers rivalry would have been, had that trade gone through. With his team under construction, the best Leo could do was a fifth-place finish. As the Giants entered the 1950s one of the most important factors in their rise to prominence would prove to be the return of a forgotten man who had not shown his face in New York in four years: Sal Maglie.

In a final coda to the Mexican League story, Danny Gardella settled his lawsuit out of court. Cardinals owner Fred Saigh, who had played an important part in negotiating the settlement, agreed to take Gardella, who had no desire to return to the Giants. Saigh's only regret was that he failed to pick up Sal Maglie, whom the Giants also wanted to unload. "That," Saigh declared in remorseful retrospect, "was one of the worst mistakes I made in baseball."[14]

The Birth of "The Barber"

Sal's 1950 Season
with the New York Giants

THE PRODIGAL SON RETURNS

The Sal Maglie who appeared in the Giants' training camp in the early spring of 1950 had pitched almost as many games outside the United States as he had in it. He had become a radically different and better pitcher than the one who left in 1946, but it remained for him to prove that to the dubious Giants. Sal knew the team had taken him back only because they had to under the terms of Chandler's amnesty for the jumpers, and they still saw him as the man responsible for persuading a large portion of the 1946 squad to defect to Mexico. Sal had a month to prove himself. After that the Giants could wash their hands of him, and his major league career would be over. He would turn 33 in April, and he was down to his last chance.

Sal's departure from the Giants had caused only a small stir, and his return caused even less. He had been so thoroughly forgotten that when he returned, a fair number of people thought he was a Cuban. Sal signed his 1950 contract, reported at $10,000, but did not see owner Horace Stoneham. Leo Durocher recalled that Stoneham had declared of Maglie shortly after the amnesty in 1949, "That dirty jumper's not going to be around here long. He isn't going to be getting *my* pay-checks."[1] But by the opening of the 1950 season the Giants owner had other things to think about. Not since John McGraw took over in 1902 had a manager made such sweeping changes in a New York Giants roster as Durocher was making. Aside from pitchers and catchers, only two players remained who had been regulars in 1949: outfielders Whitey Lockman and Bobby Thomson. Durocher had sacrificed power for speed and installed a completely new infield anchored by Eddie Stanky at second and Alvin Dark at short. Two young outfielders, Don Mueller and Monte Irvin, were primed to take over from the departed Willard Marshall and Sid Gordon. Wes Westrum was now the first-string catcher. Four proven pitchers were returning: Larry Jansen, Dave Koslo, Sheldon Jones, and Monte Kennedy, with more than half a dozen others, Maglie among them, hoping to remain in or enter the rotation.

At least Sal did not have to face Mel Ott again, since Durocher had taken over the helm of the Giants in 1948. Sal's decision to go to Mexico had not had any impact on him, so the manager harbored no animosity toward the returning pitcher. As the players were standing in the hotel lobby waiting for their room assignments, Durocher took note of Sal's excellent physical condition. "Leo walked up to me and shook hands and introduced himself. He banged me in the stomach. I was really hard. He looked surprised," Sal recalled. "'It won't take *you* long to get into shape,' he said."[2] The cordiality continued in the clubhouse, where Durocher made a brief speech welcoming back the returnees from Mexico (Maglie, Nap Reyes, and Roy Zimmermann), and Stoneham shook Maglie's hand in a let-bygones-be-bygones gesture. Most players who had been on the Giants' bloated roster in the spring of 1946 were long gone, and Sal encountered no hostility from his teammates, few of whom knew or cared about his Mexican adventures. And yet, he sensed that something was not quite right. "I had the feeling . . . they weren't counting on me," Sal recalled. "They were taking a look just because they owned me."[3]

Sal had never worked as hard as he did that spring. On the opening day of training, when Durocher called some pitchers to work off the mound, he did not include Maglie, but Sal volunteered anyway. Later that day the manager noted Sal's eagerness and commented, "I'm very happy to have you," adding, perhaps with a glint of amusement, "I see you like to pitch."[4] Sal confirmed that by offering to throw batting practice, a chore few pitchers seek out. Although lack of reliable pitching had been the Giants' chief weakness for years, Durocher had concentrated more on revamping other aspects of the team, and he seemed ready to continue relying on Jansen, Koslo, Kennedy, and Jones. Leo was merely looking for a fifth starter, rather than revamping his entire pitching staff. But as the training games began it became clear to Sal that Durocher had tagged him as a reliever, in that era not a respected specialty but a dumping ground for second-rate and over-the-hill hurlers. In the first game, an intra-squad exercise on March 5, Durocher divided the Giants into an A and a B team, and placed Sal on the B team, an indication that the manager did not consider Sal among his top pitchers.

In his first game of the exhibition season, on March 11 against the Cleveland Indians, Sal worked three scoreless innings, although he began his stint in a most unpromising way by committing three balks in the first inning. New balk rules had been instituted in 1950, the same that are still in force today: when pitching from the stretch pitchers have to pause momentarily before they continue their delivery. Umpires in Mexico had not enforced any such rule, and Sal had not developed the habit of pausing. Despite his having the balks called on him, hitting a batter, and issuing a walk, Sal did not allow a run to score. He overcame his initial difficulties and shakiness, a display of steel nerves that impressed Durocher. "Even after the third balk, he wasn't the slightest bit ruffled," the manager exclaimed. "I admired the way he controlled himself. You can imagine how some guys would blow their tops after being slapped for three balks."[5] Durocher continued to use Sal mostly as a reliever throughout March, and he was effective in all but one outing. The *Sporting News* greeted Sal's emergence as a reliever with enthusiasm, remarking that with his return the Giants had "plugged another old leak: the one in the bullpen." The writer also commented on the pitcher's exceptional poise under pressure: "Sal remained so cool while surrounded by base runners in his first two skirmishes . . . that he has typed himself as a fellow who can keep his head during an emergency."[6] As the Giants played their exhibition games, Sal earned his spot on the roster. He made more appearances and allowed fewer hits than any of the regular hurlers: in nine outings he pitched 32 innings, gave up 22 hits and 10 runs. Coach Freddie Fitzsimmons added his voice in praise of Sal. "He's a sound pitcher. He knows how to pitch and he is always around the plate. He has a good curve and he's sneaky-fast."[7] Although Maglie would have preferred not to be designated as a reliever, at least he was working and receiving positive attention.

In an interview with Arch Murray, Sal came as close as he ever came to apologizing for his decision to go to Mexico. Perhaps he realized that he needed to offer some sign of remorse in order to return to baseball's good graces, and Murray coaxed it out of him. "You never know what you are missing until you have been away," Maglie observed in Murray's formalized version of his speech. "I never knew how good I had it until I got to Mexico, and I'll pitch my arm off just to show the Giants how glad I am to be back. I knew I'd made a mistake a couple of weeks after I got down there. But there was only one thing to do and that was to make the best of it. There was no use grousing or moaning. The only thing to do was to try and learn all I could about pitching."[8] Whether Sal really concluded early on that he had made a mistake in going to Mexico is doubtful, especially since he returned for a second year, but the latter part of his statement is vintage Maglie: stoic acceptance, a resolve to make the best of the situation and learn whatever he could, and a refusal to whine or complain. Sal also told Murray, and through Murray, Leo Durocher, that he was happy to pitch out of the bullpen. "It makes no difference to me," Sal stated. "If Leo has four good starters and I can help him more in relief, that'll be fine."⁹ An amusing sidelight to Murray's article is the way Sal's recent successes repainted the pitcher's previous and for the most part undistinguished career in rosy colors. Murray confidently stated, "From the time in 1942 [sic] when he was signed to his first pro contract by Steve O'Neill, then manager of the Buffalo Bisons . . . Maglie has had all the earmarks of a pitcher with a future."¹⁰ A pitcher with a bleak future confined to the minors would have been more accurate, since little of Sal's minor league record pointed to his later success in the majors.

It would be nice to say that an impressively improved Sal Maglie marched right into the 1950 season and started mowing down the opposition, but for quite a while the opposite happened. The Giants began the season by falling flat on their faces, Sal along with them. The team lost four straight and finished April with a 1–6 record. On April 18, Opening Day at the Polo Grounds, the Giants absorbed an 11–4 shellacking from the Boston Braves. With Boston leading 7–2 Maglie made his return to the majors in relief of Larry Jansen, giving up three runs on three hits in his two-inning stint. Upon replacing Jansen, Sal promptly permitted a base on balls and two singles for the Braves' fifth run of the inning. In the sixth with one man on, Sal served up a fat pitch that Connie Ryan smacked into the left field stands. As sportswriter Jim McCulley noted with a trace of a sneer, "Maglie discovered quickly that he was not pitching in the Mexican League any more."¹¹ On April 21 the Giants came to Brooklyn, where the Dodgers mauled them, 8–1, and Sal made another unimpressive appearance in relief. In two innings he gave up two runs on three hits and walked two. The next day the Dodgers whacked the Giants again, handing them their fourth straight defeat, 7–6. In their first 36 innings of play, the Giants had given up 36 runs, a horrendous average of nine per game. And again, Sal Maglie had started off a new phase of his career by pitching poorly. He slouched in the bullpen, in daily dread of being told the Giants were sending him back to the minors, or even releasing him. He was so uncertain of his chances of remaining with the team that he and Kay were living in a hotel, afraid to tempt fate by leasing an apartment.

The Giants lost again on May 5, to the Pirates, but Sal put in two innings of scoreless relief, allowing no hits and striking out three, his first successful outing. The next day the Giants pulled out a 9–8 victory over Pittsburgh, thanks to a grand slam in the eighth by Bobby Thomson. Although Sal gained the win—his first—in relief, he needed relief help himself in the ninth. After completing a western road trip the Giants came back east to play the Phillies in Philadelphia. The National League's perennial cellar-dwellers had turned into pennant contenders. Maybe their snappy new uniforms gave them a brighter outlook, although the *Brooklyn Eagle*'s Harold Burr snickered that the off-white suits with red stockings, caps, and numerals made them look like "walking strawberry and vanilla ice cream cones."[12] But they were not melting like ice cream. They had won 14 of their first 22 games and were in first place, while the Giants were in seventh. Nicknamed the "Whiz Kids" by a Philadelphia sportswriter, the 1950 Phillies were a youthful, spirited, and determined team. The Giants dropped two of three to the Phils, with Sal putting in another mediocre relief stint in the first game, giving up two runs on two hits, including a home run, in two innings. With the season a month old Sal's performances had been mostly miserable, and the Giants were tied for last place.

In the second half of May the New Yorkers put together a modest four-game winning streak, their best effort of the season, but then went into a swoon and lost seven in a row. On May 21 the Giants dropped both ends of a doubleheader to the Pirates, the start of the losing streak. In the second game a desperate Durocher used seven pitchers in an 8–6 defeat, one short of a record for the National League. Sal was one of the seven and pitched an insignificant two-thirds of an inning. The Giants were doing everything badly. Their pitching was terrible, their hitting weak, and their defense full of holes. Dark and Stanky, Durocher's dream combo at short and second, were booting balls around the infield, and the team's fielding ranked sixth in the league. Durocher began throwing utility players and benchwarmers into games on the assumption that their play could not be any worse than what the regulars were doing. Monte Irvin, who had been sent down at the beginning of the season, was recalled from Jersey City in the hope that his bat might rouse the lineup into producing some runs. Sal perked up a little on May 27, working two scoreless innings in relief, but in a losing cause, as the Phillies whomped the Giants again, 8–5. He participated in another losing effort on May 30, when the Giants dropped the first game of a doubleheader to the Braves. Once more his performance was poor as he worked five and one-third innings in relief of Monte Kennedy and gave up three runs, six hits, and three walks, while striking out only two. Sal's discouragement deepened. Durocher was using him only sporadically. He had to pitch frequently in order to sharpen his skills, but because he was less than sharp Durocher did not use him often enough for him to improve. Leo did not see the undemonstrative Maglie as his kind of aggressive ballplayer. Sal began to wonder if his treatment was payback for his Mexican sojourn. Again, he asked to pitch batting practice, just to get in some pitching time. Burying his anxieties for the sake of Kay's comfort and peace of mind, Sal rented an apartment in late May, so the couple could stop living as if their stay in Manhattan might end at any moment.

In June the Giants improved. After splitting a doubleheader with Cincinnati on June 1 the New Yorkers reeled off seven straight victories. In the first game of the double bill with the Reds the Giants won, 8–7. Sal pitched to one batter in the top of the eighth, getting the out and receiving the victory, his second of the season. He also pitched a scoreless inning and a third in relief in the second game. The next day, still against the Reds, Sal tossed one and one-third scoreless innings in relief. On June 4, against the Pirates, Sal pitched only two-thirds of an inning, but notched his third victory in relief. Although each stint had been short, Sal had appeared in five of the Giants' last six games, and had been highly effective in all but one. He began to allow himself to think he might stick with the team.

Then, on June 4, the same day Sal gained his third victory, came the crushing news that the Giants had tried to unload him. While the team was in Pittsburgh Frank McKinney, president of the Pirates, contacted Horace Stoneham to discuss a trade. He had his eye on Alvin Dark, Whitey Lockman, and Bobby Thomson. Among pitchers McKinney suggested he might take Jansen, Jones, or Koslo. But Stoneham was not parting with any of his stars. "We might let him have the jumper," Stoneham responded. The deal fell through, with McKinney grumbling that "all [Stoneham] wanted to offer was second-rate players."[13] Sal had now seen that his boss considered him an inferior player, that Stoneham had neither forgotten nor forgiven his Mexican sins and was still trying to punish him by getting rid of him. That the Giants had not succeeded did not make Sal feel any more secure, although even success as a pitcher did not guarantee security. Earlier in the spring, with the Dodgers nosing around for a profitable trade, Stoneham reportedly had offered Larry Jansen to Branch Rickey in exchange for Ralph Branca and several other players, but the deal failed to go through. This was the second time the Giants had tried to acquire Branca. The Giants made another purchase during June, one that made no headlines because the player was an unknown outfielder with the Birmingham Black Barons who was destined for the Giants' Trenton farm team. The player was Willie Mays.

Almost a week passed before Sal appeared in another game, a 6–2 loss to the Cardinals on June 10 that broke the Giants' winning streak at seven. Sal relieved in the seventh and secured the final two outs in the inning. The Giants' record now stood at 20–23, and they had hauled themselves out of the cellar and into sixth place. On June 17 they lost to the Cubs, 9–7, but Maglie pitched six and one-third strong innings, allowing only one run on four hits and walking two. On June 19 New York played a single game against Brooklyn at Ebbets Field. Dodger righthander Ralph Branca took the victory, 8–5, notching 10 strikeouts. The victory was particularly satisfying for the Dodgers, not only because they defeated their hated rivals, but also because the win tied them with the Cardinals for first place. Sal entered the game in the third and worked through the fifth. He had endured two unsuccessful outings against the Dodgers back in 1945 and a third during the first week of the current season. There were a few Dodgers still around, among them Branca, who recalled the mild, ineffectual Maglie who had faced them five years earlier, but on this day they barely recognized the grim, glowering figure who stalked to the mound. Fighting for his very survival in the majors, Sal reached into the harshest of Luque's lessons. With an 0–2 count on Gil Hodges, Maglie had the hulking first baseman right where he wanted him. In the spot where Sal's former manager Mel Ott would have fined him $100 if he failed to waste a pitch, Sal did the opposite—he threw a "purpose" pitch. He knew from Luque's training that this was the perfect time for a fastball skimming the batter's chin and driving him back from the plate. But instead, Maglie's hummer sailed behind Hodges' head, the most dangerous place of all given the instinctive human tendency to pull back from an oncoming projectile.

Could Sal's control have faltered so badly at that moment that the ball came in almost a foot from where he had intended it to go? Or had desperation made him so reckless that he was willing, in the name of intimidation, to risk killing the first Dodger he faced? Neither batting helmets nor protective cap liners were in use at that time. In 1949 both leagues had issued a bulletin requiring the plate umpire to warn a pitcher after the kind of pitch that Sal had just thrown and to toss him out of the game and notify the league office if he repeated the offense. But a man's true intentions, like his good deeds, are often interred with his bones. It remains impossible to read Maglie's or any other pitcher's mind with regard to beanballs, and umpires are no better at it than anyone else. In this situation, with the Giants losing, and nothing much at stake in an early season game that had not featured any unusual displays of animosity on either side, to risk maiming an opposing batter by throwing behind his head would have been foolhardy, to say the least. But the pitch, whatever its intended location, had its desired effect. Although the plate umpire that day, Larry Goetz, treated it as an accident, he recalled that Hodges was visibly shaken, and Goetz himself acknowledged, "My heart was in my throat. I didn't think Hodges could get away from the pitch."[14] Hodges made an out.

Later in the same game one of Maglie's fastballs struck Carl Furillo between the shoulder blades. This may well have been deliberate, a payback for the homer Furillo had hit earlier in the game. The at bat was the beginning of a bitter animosity between Sal and the Dodgers' hot-tempered right fielder. Sal gave up three runs in his three innings against the Dodgers, and his outing could hardly be called successful. Harold Rosenthal, writing in the *Herald Tribune,* chuckled that Kirby Higbe, now a reformed drunk who had found Jesus at a Billy Graham rally, had pitched three scoreless innings after Sal's stint and was the only Giants hurler that day "who should not have been required to pay at least a junior admission to get into the park."[15] But Sal had put the Dodgers on notice of the rough treatment they could expect from him in the future—assuming he had a future.

Two days later, on June 21, Sal entered a rout that the Giants lost, 14–6, to St. Louis. He faced only one batter in a game where the fading Higbe was the starter. After the Giants had taken three of four from the Cardinals (Higbe's debacle was the only Giants loss), the New Yorkers split a four-game series with Cincinnati, winning the first two and then dropping both ends of a doubleheader on June 25. In the second game Durocher gave Maglie what he had been hoping for, his first start of the year. Pitching against the last-place team, Sal flubbed it. Ted Kluszewski, the Reds' first baseman whose physique was so massive that an awed opponent once described him as having muscles in his hair, tagged Sal for a homer, a huge blast over the right field roof, and two other Reds hit home runs off him as well. The final score, a 6–4 loss, was not terribly lopsided, but Sal was discouraged by his performance. "I was convinced I was on my way [back to the minors] after that game with the Reds," he recalled.[16]

But Durocher was too desperate for pitchers to consider demoting Maglie. He threw Sal into another losing game on June 30, against Boston. Monte Kennedy had been knocked out in the first inning, and Maglie followed him to the mound, keeping the Giants in the game for six and one-third innings in which he allowed only one run on four hits before being removed for a pinch hitter. The *Times* called his relief work "splendid." Sheldon Jones, relieving in the ninth, gave up a pinch-hit grand slam to Sibby Sisti that won the game for the Braves. Jones may still have been shaken by his beaning of Carl Furillo two nights before, a blow that sent the Dodger right fielder to the hospital and left Jones huddled in a corner of the Giants locker room trying to explain how the pitch got away from him. There, but for a few inches and Gil Hodges' excellent reflexes, might have sat Sal Maglie.

After his one unsuccessful start Durocher kept Maglie in the bullpen. Sal worked two innings in the first game of a doubleheader on July 2, giving up two runs on three hits and issuing one walk in a game the Giants lost. On

July 4 the Giants split a doubleheader with the Dodgers at the Polo Grounds, and Sal saw action in both contests. He tossed one scoreless inning in the first game and picked up the win, bringing his record to 4–1. In the second game, which Brooklyn won, 5–3, Sal pitched two and two-thirds innings and allowed one run. During the second game Dave Koslo hit Carl Furillo with a pitch. The battered outfielder, just back from his beaning by the Giants' Sheldon Jones, exchanged angry words with Leo Durocher and had to be prevented from attacking the Giants' manager. Furillo believed that pitchers were throwing at him on Durocher's orders. Leo's favorite expression was "Stick it in his ear!" Although Durocher himself always insisted this was nothing more than aggressive talk, and not to be taken literally as an order, Furillo was a literal-minded man who believed Giants pitchers really *were* trying to stick the ball in his ear. And he had a bruise behind his left ear to prove it.

The Giants continued to stumble in early July, losing six straight between July 4 and July 9. Sal plodded in to relieve Clint Hartung in the first inning of a game against the Phillies on July 5, working five and two-thirds innings. He did a credible job, allowing two runs on five hits. On July 8 Sal worked a scoreless inning in a game against Boston and then returned in relief the next day to pitch five and two-thirds innings, but he lost a heartbreaker, 3–2, in the thirteenth. At the All-Star break the Giants' record stood at a dismal 34–40, and Maglie's record at a modest 4–2. There seemed little reason to believe that either would improve in the next two and a half months.

In the week after the All-Star game the Giants resumed their losing ways, taking only three of their next nine and dropping both ends of two doubleheaders. One of the few bright spots was the game Sal pitched on July 14, a 7–5 win over the Pirates that was virtually a complete game, since he pitched eight and two-thirds innings in relief of an ineffective Sheldon Jones. But on July 16 Sal lost the second game of a doubleheader. He had worked five scoreless innings in relief, but gave up an unearned run in the twelfth due to an error by third baseman Hank Thompson. During the All-Star break the Giants had made an important addition to their beleaguered pitching staff by claiming burly righthander Jim Hearn from the Cardinals on waivers. An emotionally fragile man despite his imposing size (six-feet-four, 205 lbs.), Hearn had been ineffective with St. Louis, but he caught fire when he joined the Giants. With help from pitching coaches Freddie Fitzsimmons and Frank Shellenback, Hearn became one of the Giants' two most effective pitchers in the second half of the season. The other one was Sal Maglie.

The Giants split a pair of games with the Reds on July 17 and 18 and dropped a doubleheader to the Cardinals the following day, but then the Giants' fortunes underwent a dramatic change. After the doubleheader loss

Durocher held a clubhouse meeting with his dispirited players, telling them to forget about the day's disasters: to go out and have a good time—get loose, get drunk, get laid, do whatever they wanted, as long as they showed up for the next evening's game. The tactic must have worked, since the following night the Giants whacked the surprised Cards, 10–3. For the last game of the series with St. Louis, Durocher gave Maglie another chance as a starter, and Sal had every reason to believe it was his last. Although no longer so worried about being banished to the minors, Sal saw permanent residence in the bullpen as his fate if he failed in his second start. Durocher did not give Maglie the ball out of confidence that the pitcher would succeed. He thought he was scraping the bottom of the barrel. As the manager later put it, "This time I had no choice. . . . There we were in a terrible losing streak and I had to have a pitcher. I had no one else, so Maglie was it."[17]

In humid heat before a modest crowd in Sportsman's Park in St. Louis on July 21, Sal pitched the contest that turned his career around and sent him on his way to stardom. He threw a gritty, 11–inning complete game, defeating the Cardinals, 5–4, and toppling them into a tie with the Phillies for first place. It was the kind of game that became typical of Sal in his subsequent career. A little shaky at first, he recovered. He gave up a homer but remained unfazed. He administered at least one close shave. In the bottom of the last inning, with two outs and a runner on second, he fanned the final batter. The Cards quickly scored on Sal. He walked the leadoff man, Rocky Nelson, who stole second and raced to third when the Giants' first baseman fumbled a grounder by Red Schoendienst. Then Cardinals star Stan Musial brought Nelson home with a single. The Giants scored three runs in the third, but Sal failed to preserve the lead. With one out he walked Musial and Enos Slaughter before Tom Glaviano socked him for a long single that brought in two runs and tied the score. The Giants put up a run in the fourth to take the lead, and Maglie held it until the seventh, when Musial came to bat with two outs and crushed a hanging curveball onto the right field roof to retie the game.

The teams went into extra innings with the score tied, 4–4, and Sal beginning to tire. For a man who had not pitched a complete game all season, 11 innings was a marathon. In the top of the eleventh the Giants scratched out a run on a hit and a Cardinals error, and Sal came out to pitch the bottom of the inning. With one down on a fly to deep left, coach Freddie Fitzsimmons strolled to the mound to see if Sal felt he could finish and learned that nothing short of a gun in his ribs could persuade him to leave the game. After the coach's visit Maglie gave up a single to Eddie Miller, who took second on Del Rice's groundout to third. At Durocher's signal, bodies began to stir in the Giants bullpen. Stalling both to give Maglie a breather and to give the relievers more time to warm up, Fitzsimmons and Westrum lumbered out to the mound again to discuss strategy, but Sal already knew what he was going to do. As catcher and pitching coach debated the relative merits of Sal's fastball versus his curve, the exhausted pitcher cut in, "Shit, I don't care if this guy eats curves for breakfast. If he's gonna hit me, let it be my best pitch."[18] St. Louis manager Eddie Dyer sent up Eddie Kazak to pinch hit for pitcher Cloyd Boyer, and Sal ran the count on him to 0–2. Then, glaring down at Kazak, Sal sent him sprawling with a fastball at the chin. When the shaken hitter resumed his place Sal threw him a curve low and away. Kazak lunged at it and missed for the game's final out. Luque would have been proud of his star pupil.

Sal's performance won him admiring attention from a variety of quarters. The *Times* called Sal's effort "a magnificent exhibition of pitching guile and strength." "Where have you been keeping that guy?" Stan Musial asked Giants announcer Russ Hodges. "He's got the best curveball I've ever seen!"[19] The victory pepped up the entire club. As the happy crew traveled back east by train Sal received a reward from Eddie Brannick, the team's traveling secretary, who paid attention to newcomers only when they did something special to earn his notice. That night was Brannick's birthday, and as team members lined up for a slice of the cake, Brannick cut a big piece for Sal and personally brought it over to the pitcher who, with his customary reserve, had not joined the dessert line.

When a reporter asked Sal what accounted for his sudden effectiveness as a starter, the pitcher gave an honest answer, but it was one that angered Leo Durocher. Sal said he was pitching his own way, which Durocher interpreted as criticism of his managerial masterminding. "I wasn't popping off," Maglie insisted after he became aware of Durocher's displeasure. "I was just trying to say I was throwing my best pitch in the clutch. . . . You can give [the batter] a fastball or a curve. Well, I never had much of a fastball, even when I was a kid, and I didn't see any sense trying to fool anybody with it, but I threw it whenever it was called."[20] Although he did not say so, what Maglie was doing was following Luque's advice more closely than he was following Durocher's orders. Luque had taught Sal to rely on his curve, merely to "show" his fastball on occasion, and to develop his own mental book on hitters—independent habits of mind that could have put Maglie on a collision course with the imperious Durocher. Luckily, Maglie, Luque, and Durocher all agreed on the need to terrorize hitters with brushback pitches.

Seemingly inspired by Sal's performance, the New Yorkers steamed into Chicago and swept three from the Cubs. Back at the Polo Grounds the winning streak continued as the Giants took two from the Reds on July 25 and 26, and Maglie won his seventh, 3–2. By the time the Cardinals defeated them on July 30 the Giants had won nine straight. Sal made a brief, ineffective appearance in relief in that game, giving up three runs in just two-thirds of an inning and hitting two batters, his last stumble of the season. The month of August saw the Giants launch another impressive wining streak. Maglie picked up a complete game victory on August 2, defeating the Cubs, 8–6, for his eighth win as the Giants swept a doubleheader. They then topped that by steamrollering the Pirates four straight, with the last three games shutouts. Hearn won the second game, 5–0, and on August 6 Jansen won the opener of a doubleheader, also 5–0. Maglie took the second game, 3–0, for his ninth win. The Giants streak came to an end on August 9, when the Braves defeated them, 3–2. Despite the defeat, the occasion was less than a total loss for Eddie Stanky, since during that game the ever-annoying "Brat" discovered a new way to drive opposition hitters crazy. While Braves third baseman Bob Elliott was at bat, he asked second base umpire Al Barlick to move over, so he would not be in Elliott's line of vision as he batted. Stanky, noting the spot Barlick had vacated, promptly moved into it, distracting Elliott enough that he struck out. Stanky had just added a new weapon to his arsenal of annoyances.

As the New Yorkers moved on to Philadelphia to play the league-leading Phillies, the Giants juggernaut slowed down. The Phils took the first game of the series, but on August 11 Maglie won the second game, 3–1. Sal was not at his best—he gave up seven hits and issued seven walks—but he pitched his way out of one jam after another with what the *Times* called "a spine-tingling display of craft and courage." He made the Phillies waste their opportunities as they chopped his baffling assortment of curves into the ground and hit into three double plays.

Stanky had decided that his best bet for annoying the opposition was to stand at his second base position and do jumping jacks just as the pitcher delivered. His chosen victim that night was Braves catcher Andy Seminick. Bad choice. The tactic infuriated the tough Phillies catcher, a stoic former coal miner who once played for several weeks on a broken ankle. By his fourth at bat in the bottom of the eighth he was fed up. He turned to plate umpire Al Barlick and growled, "He can't do that!" Barlick responded that there was no rule forbidding such behavior. Stanky continued his waggling while Seminick steamed. Maglie, annoyed by the delay, made things worse by hitting Seminick on the elbow, a spot guaranteed to cause blinding pain. But the catcher refused to react. "You would have thought a fly landed on Andy's elbow when Maglie hit him," Phillies pitcher Bubba Church recalled in admiration. "He just ignored it and went down to first."[21] But Seminick was boiling mad. As he tossed and turned all night, unable to sleep because of the pain in his swollen elbow, he plotted his revenge.

Although Durocher had agreed to have Stanky stop his antics until a ruling could be obtained from league president Ford Frick, the next day Stanky continued waving his arms and, in the words of umpire Lon Warneke, "making a farce out of the game." The August 12 contest quickly deteriorated into violent confrontations capped by a near riot. In the second inning the revenge-bent Seminick thundered into third and slammed into third baseman Hank Thompson, scattering several of Thompson's teeth and knocking him unconscious. When Seminick came to bat in the fourth, Stanky, who really did not know when to leave well enough alone, began his wig-wag routine again, and this time umpire Warneke ejected him. Durocher replaced him with Bill Rigney. After Seminick reached base on an error, the next batter grounded to Dark, and the shortstop threw to Rigney for the force-out. Seminick barreled hard into the slender but feisty Rigney, who immediately tried to take on the Phils' burly catcher. Rigney was no match for Seminick, who began using him as a punching bag. Both dugouts emptied, fights broke out all over the field, and the umpires had to call in the police to break it up. Seminick and Rigney were both ejected. The Phils finally won in the eleventh, 5–4. Although it would be unfair to blame Maglie for a fracas clearly caused by Eddie Stanky, there is little doubt that Sal's hitting Seminick the day before was a significant part of what drove the Phillies catcher to such destructive fury. It would not be the last time Sal's pitching tactics had that effect.

The Giants split the next two games with the Phillies. Then they took on the Dodgers for a four-game series at the Polo Grounds. The Dodgers won three out of four, but the one Giants triumph was a 16–7 rout pitched by Sal Maglie. It was hardly the finest game Sal ever hurled, but it was his sixth straight win, and he went the distance, cushioned by the Giants' nine–run first inning. In the eighth, with the Giants enjoying a large lead, Gil Hodges had some payback for his near-beaning on June 19 by hitting his second home run of the game. Each of Hodges' homers came with two aboard, accounting for six of the Dodgers' seven runs. Those would be the last runs scored off Maglie for almost a month, through four subsequent starts and three appearances in relief. The righthander who had been just another name on the roster at the beginning of the season now rated as one of the team's top pitchers, and without any doubt its most intimidating.

On August 23 and 24 Sal made two brief appearances in relief. When he came into the game on the 23rd against the Cubs Sal had been idle for a week, and it showed. He took over for Sheldon Jones in the eighth with the Giants leading, 5–4, and allowed three hits while recording just one out. Monte Kennedy replaced Sal, and none of the runners scored. Kennedy's fine clutch pitching saved the game for the Giants. The next day, against the

Cardinals in St. Louis, Sal relieved in the bottom of the ninth with the winning runs on base and registered the final two outs. Two days later, on August 26, Sal shut out the Cards, 3–0, for another complete game and his twelfth win. The Giants collected only eight hits off the Cardinals' hurler, southpaw Harry Brecheen, but made them all count. Maglie needed only one run, and Alvin Dark provided that with a solo homer in the fourth. Sal struggled throughout the game, giving up 11 hits and two walks, but he stifled every attempt to score against him. The Cards had at least one hit in every inning, and although it seemed inevitable that they would be on the boards eventually, only one runner advanced as far as third. As baffled Cardinals sluggers chopped Sal's curves into mostly harmless grounders, the Giants turned three double plays. Even the *Brooklyn Eagle,* often a partisan of the hometown Dodgers, gave Sal credit, referring to his "air-tight clutch pitching" before an audience of "15,598 awed fans" in Sportsman's Park.

Sal hurled another shutout on August 30 against the Pirates, defeating the cellar dwellers, 4–0. This was his second consecutive shutout, and his streak of scoreless innings now extended to 20. He allowed Pittsburgh five hits and two walks and was never in serious trouble. He even helped himself by hitting a run-scoring double. But, for the first time in his career, Sal beaned a batter. The Pirates' rookie infielder Danny Murtaugh was no great threat at the plate, so one can only assume that in the fifth inning a fastball got away from Sal. The field was soggy due to a downpour earlier in the day, which may have contributed to the misplaced pitch. Murtaugh was carried from the field on a stretcher, but the team physician examined him in the clubhouse and pronounced him well enough to be taken home, rather than to a hospital. Although in later years Maglie admitted that hitting a batter in the head made him feel sick, Sal suppressed any upset the beaning might have caused him and continued his imperturbable pitching for the rest of the game.

The Giants returned to Philadelphia on September 4 to play a doubleheader, the first time they had faced the Phillies since the on-field warfare of August 12. There was no repeat of the violence as the Giants shut out the Phils twice. Someone sent a black cat scampering across the top of the Giants dugout, but it brought bad luck only to the Phillies. Jim Hearn stifled them, 2–0, in the first game, and Maglie needed a mere 98 pitches to dispose of them in the second, a 9–0 laugher. This was Sal's fourteenth win, his ninth in a row, and his third consecutive shutout. All nine wins had been complete games. Phillies pitcher Russ Meyer hit Maglie with a pitch in the fifth, bruising his right biceps, but Sal chose to ignore what may have been deliberate payback and did not retaliate, avoiding another outbreak of hostilities. Maglie had no interest in fistfights—he preferred to let his high-inside fastball do his fighting for him.

On September 8 Sal pitched a perfect ninth inning in relief of Jim Hearn, but the Boston Braves' masterful southpaw Warren Spahn defeated the Giants, 4–3. The next day Durocher chose Sal to face the Brooklyn Dodgers in a game at the Polo Grounds. Alvin Dark hit two home runs for the only scoring in the contest, as Maglie defeated Preacher Roe and spun another mesmerizing shutout, 2–0, allowing the Dodgers only four hits, all but one of them singles. Not a runner reached third base. The only time the Dodgers posed a threat was in the top of the ninth, when Gene Hermanski opened with a single and went to second on an infield hit by Duke Snider. Gil Hodges attempted a bunt, but Sal pounced on it and forced Hermanski at third, before persuading Furillo to fly out. Then Sal ended the game with pinch hitter Cal Abrams staring at a called third strike. Even many Dodger fans, not normally partisans of Maglie, cheered him as the game ended, and his scoreless streak continued. It was Sal's fifteenth win, and his tenth straight victory. He had now pitched four straight shutouts, and his streak of scoreless innings extended to 39. He had tied the National League record for most consecutive shutouts, joining Mordecai "Three-Finger" Brown and Ed Reulbach of the 1908 Cubs, Grover Cleveland Alexander of the 1911 Phillies, and Bill Lee of the 1938 Cubs in that exclusive pitchers' club. Doc White of the 1904 Chicago White Sox held the all-time major league mark of five consecutive shutouts. Sal also stood within reach of a National League record held by one of the most renowned Giants pitchers of the recent past, Carl Hubbell, owner of the National League record for most consecutive scoreless innings: 46 1/3. Walter Johnson, pitching for the Washington Senators in the American League, held the major league record of 56 consecutive scoreless frames, set in 1913.[22] Maglie was poised to make baseball history.

The Giants continued on a roll. From their former position in the league cellar they were now closing in on fourth place, which would put them in the first division for the first time all season. On a chilly, drizzly, windy September 13, in the second game of a four-game series with the Pirates at the Polo Grounds, Maglie took the mound again, hoping to break Hubbell's record. The great "Meal Ticket" himself, now the director of the Giants farm system, was on hand to watch Sal's performance. Despite the historic moment, the threatening weather, which had turned from drizzle to a steady downpour by game time, resulted in a small crowd of 11,684, leaving the Polo Grounds more than three-quarters empty.

In weather that would have resulted in most games' being called even before play began, Sal started on his quest to overtake Hubbell's record. Although he had no trouble retiring three Pirates in order in the top of the first, extending his skein of scoreless innings to 40, he had a close call in the second inning. He walked the Pirates' rookie right fielder Gus Bell, who went to second on a hard smash back to Maglie by shortstop Danny O'Connell, where Sal's only play was to first. The next batter, first baseman Eddie Stevens, beat out a grounder. With runners at first and third and one out, second baseman Johnny Berardino hit a fly to Whitey Lockman in left field. Bell tagged up and faked a dash for home. Lockman threw toward the plate to keep Bell in his place, but third baseman Hank Thompson tried to cut off the throw, and succeeded only in deflecting the ball away from catcher Wes Westrum, who was guarding the plate. Bell took off in an attempt to score. Maglie, who had alertly backed up his catcher on the play, pounced on the ball, and fired it to Westrum, who nabbed Bell at the plate to end the inning. From then on, as the rain grew heavier and the groundsmen packed the mound and the batter's box with sawdust in an attempt to provide some footing in the increasingly slippery muck, Sal kept the Pirates under his control. His teammates, meanwhile, put up three runs against Pirates pitcher Vernon Law. As the seventh inning began, Sal's streak stood at 45 consecutive scoreless innings. Four more outs and Maglie would equal Hubbell's record; five more and he would break it.

Gus Bell, who had nearly scored on Sal in the second, led off for the Pirates in the top of the seventh. The rookie outfielder, who had come up from Indianapolis to join the Pirates lineup in mid-season, had just returned from a five-day absence. He had taken the time off to have two wisdom teeth extracted, so perhaps Bell's dentist should be credited with an assist for what happened next. Sal, as he so often did, ran up an 0–2 count on the batter. This was his classic brush-back situation, but this time the strategy differed, and Sal broke one of Luque's central rules: *never waste a pitch.* Because he had been having good luck in getting the inexperienced Bell out with a low inside curve, Sal decided to see if the kid would bite again this time. The ball came in exactly where he wanted it. Bell, a left-handed hitter, seemed to fall away from the pitch, swinging awkwardly as he stepped back. He hit the ball on an arc toward the right field foul pole, a mere 257 feet away, where it landed just inches fair for a home run. It was the shortest possible homer, by 40 feet, in any National League park, and an out or a single in any other ballpark.

As Bell circled the bases to the sound of silence punctuated by occasional boos, Sal stared at his feet. The infielders trotted to the mound to offer their pats and efforts at comfort. Eddie Stanky rubbed up a new ball and snapped, "The pressure's off now. Bear down and get the side out, and let's win this fucking game!"[23] Only after Bell had crossed home plate and ducked into the Pirates dugout, did the Polo Grounds come to life, resounding with cheers and cries of sympathy for the new Giants hero, a drenched, dejected pitcher who had just lost both his chance to tie or break Hubbell's record and the possibility of a fifth consecutive shutout. Sal touched the brim of his cap and nodded acknowledgment of the crowd's applause, then went back to work, setting down the next three Pirates, at which point the umpires called the game. Afterward, senior umpire Babe Pinelli admitted that the game had been allowed to continue under almost unplayable conditions, explaining, "We felt the customers had come out to see Maglie set a record and they were entitled to a full break."[24] For his wet day's work Sal received credit for a complete game victory, his eleventh in a row and his fifteenth of the season.

Afterward came the inevitable interviews and photographs. Sal hurried himself into a pair of dry uniform trousers before posing, naked to the waist, shaking hands with a business-suited Carl Hubbell. Although commentators routinely referred to Sal as "swarthy," his torso proved to be surprisingly pale—the swarthiness of his face and forearms was all from the sun, and on his jaw was the smudge of his dark beard. Hubbell, the southpaw ace of bygone years, made the expected comments: "Records are made to be broken," and "I want a Giant to break the record and I sure thought Maglie would do it."[25] A little later, having added a dry uniform blouse, Sal posed playfully "strangling" Gus Bell, who had come to congratulate him. In the photograph the contrast between the peach fuzz–faced Bell, and Maglie with his heavy growth of dark beard, is dramatic and indicates Sal's practice of not shaving before games. In postgame interviews the pitcher was calm and gracious and sounded relieved. Now that the suspense was over he admitted to the tension he had felt. "It would have been nice to keep going a little longer, but I have to confess that the pressure was beginning to bother me a little," he said, adding with a smile, "Well, at least I can get a little sleep now."[26]

Most sportswriters sang Sal's praises. Ken Smith, in his column for the *Sporting News,* reviewed Maglie's achievements, and referred to the pitcher as "the stately Italian" and "this tall, slender, graceful curveball specialist," who had become "the champion pitcher of the majors." He ended by observing, "The magnificent Maglie has a grand curve and, Chum, he knows how to use it." Oddly, New York's greatest sports columnist, Red Smith, had trouble eking out praise for Maglie. He devoted a column to Sal's achievement but spent a good part of it noting how inferior Maglie was to Hubbell. Projecting his own sentiments onto an unidentified "incurable worshiper of Hubbell," he presented the idea of Maglie breaking Hubbell's record as "well, incongruous, not to say outrageous and downright obscene," which is strong language even if meant in a semi-joking way. After hastening to add that this was "no rap at Sal Maglie, a game and able guy," he went on to damn Sal with further faint praise, noting how meager Sal's natural gifts as a pitcher were in comparison with Hubbell's.[27] Years later Smith devoted another column to Maglie's shutout string and was no kinder. He described the mood at the Polo Grounds on the day Sal attempted to break Hubbell's record as one where "faint misgivings" existed among older fans who remembered Hubbell's years as a pitcher and were not eager to see his record overturned. Describing the challenger as "a darkly sinister stranger named Salvatore Anthony Maglie who had the audacity to challenge" Hubbell, Smith mused again about Sal's mediocre record and reminded his readers that Sal was "a renegade who had jumped to the outlaw Mexican League in 1946 and come skulking back" only after Chandler lifted the ban on "wetbacks like him." Smith ended his peculiar column with a description of Bell's home run: "Maglie threw, Bell swung, and there were lifelong Giant fans who actually smiled as the ball arched into the right-field seats."[28] Maybe Smith's words should not be taken seriously, although his veiled hostility is no less disquieting for being cloaked in humor. It suggests that he found something unworthy about a "darkly sinister stranger" challenging a record set by the impeccably American Hubbell. His words seem a throwback to the ambivalence toward Italian American ballplayers common in the sportswriting of the '30s and '40s.[29]

Although he won three more games before October, the rest of the 1950 season was an anticlimax for Maglie. He pitched again on September 17 as the Giants squeaked by with a 7–6 decision over the Cardinals, but Sal needed relief help from Monte Kennedy, who received credit for the win. Sal had been unsettled by the festivities held in his honor before the game. The last time anyone had organized a celebration for Sal had been 12 years ago, when a little parade wended its way from Niagara Falls to Buffalo, with the 21–year-old Sal, then a budding Buffalo Bison, riding in an open car with his mother. This time, more than 1,000 residents of Niagara Falls came to the Polo Grounds to celebrate Sal Maglie Day. As almost 22,000 fans looked on, the pitcher received a new car, a $2,500 war bond, and a variety of other gifts from his friends and neighbors, a radio from his teammates, and a wristwatch from fans in the Polo Grounds bleachers. (It was a tradition for fans to take up a collection to buy a watch for favorite players when they were being honored.) After the ceremony Sal offered a brief speech, and the Niagara Falls Boys Club drum, bugle, and glockenspiel corps serenaded their hero. No wonder Sal began the game so distracted that he gave up four runs in the first inning, although that was not entirely his own fault. He had loaded the bases after two were out, but three of the four runs scored on an error. "My friends made me feel as stage-struck as a high school kid in the senior show," Sal recalled. "I got out on the mound that first inning and couldn't find my feet."[30] Durocher almost took Sal out for a pinch hitter in the second when he was due to bat with two on and one out, but perhaps giving some thought to the occasion, Leo left Sal in, and he singled to score a run. Behind by two runs going into the bottom of the ninth, the Giants scored three to pull out the win.

Finally, on September 21, Sal suffered a defeat, as the Reds beat him, 8–5, and stopped his winning streak at 11. His record now stood at 16–4, and the Giants' late season surge had lifted them into fourth place, with a 77–66 record. On September 25 Durocher turned Sal loose against the Dodgers at Ebbets Field in the second game of a doubleheader. Brooklyn had taken the day game. In the nightcap Sal put on his grim game face and won his seventeenth, 4–3, in front of the kind of hostile, howling crowd that from then on formed the background to his outings against the Dodgers at Ebbets Field. Unlike the cavernous Polo Grounds, the Dodgers' intimate little stadium put the fans practically in the players' faces, with their individual shouts and carefully tailored insults fully audible to the opposition. Dodgers fans had reached a collective decision that the more abuse they heaped on Maglie, the poorer he would pitch. Instead, the opposite happened, and the abuse spurred Sal to greater excellence. "Of course I was hated in Brooklyn. At Ebbets Field they booed me, yelled at me, and I loved it. . . . The more they'd rip me, the more I just had that little bit extra," Sal recalled, still delighted by the memories almost two decades later.[31]

After dropping a game to the Dodgers on September 26, the Giants took on the Phillies for the two teams' last series of the season, two consecutive doubleheaders at the Polo Grounds. The Whiz Kids were faltering, and their once comfortable league lead had dwindled. The fourth-place Giants were hoping to play the role of spoiler in retaliation for the injuries Andy Seminick had inflicted. The Giants won the first game, 8–7, in ten innings. Sal came in to relieve Monte Kennedy in the eighth but poured gasoline on the fire by hitting Seminick in the ribs to load the bases. The aroused Phillies then smacked Sal for two hits before Koslo replaced him, and they closed the inning with the score tied at 7–7. In the tenth Alvin Dark drove Monte Irvin home with the winning run. But the game was not quite over. As Irvin tore around third and headed toward home, there was the brick wall of Andy Seminick, blocking the plate even though he did not yet have the ball. Just as it came in and Seminick reached out to catch it, the six-foot-one, 200–pound Irvin slammed into him, a high slide that sent the big catcher sprawling and left him with a broken ankle. But Irvin was safe, and the game was over.

In the second half of the doubleheader Jim Hearn blanked the Phillies, 5–0. The Giants also swept the second doubleheader, played on September 28, by identical 3–1 scores. Sal won his eighteenth game in the opener, his last appearance of the season. He threw another complete game and finished with a flourish, giving up just five hits and retiring the last 14 Phillies in order. The Giants also won their final two games from the Boston Braves, and completed the season on October 1 in third place. They had compiled a remarkable 22–11 record for September and nearly managed to deny the Phillies the pennant. The Phils held on, defeating the Dodgers on the last day of the season to sew up their first pennant since 1915. It was a valiant effort, but those habitual champions, the New York Yankees, won the World Series in a four-game sweep.

Sal Maglie had emerged from the obscurity of the bullpen, and from the doghouse where his Mexican League past had threatened to chain him up, to become one of the premier pitchers of the National League. Even though he had spent the first half of the season toiling in relief, he compiled an 18–4 record and led the league in winning percentage at .818. His ERA was a superb 2.71, second in the league only to teammate Jim Hearn's 2.49. Sal's five shutouts also led both leagues, as did his 11–game winning streak, and against the Brooklyn Dodgers he had been perfect, defeating them four times with no losses. He had thrown 12 complete games and won all of them. He pitched a total of 206 innings, allowing 86 walks and striking out 96.

Maglie had also established a reputation in another department: hit batsmen. Giants pitchers collectively (10 men) hit a total of 31 batters, with Sal accounting for 10, almost a third of the total, with one of them a true beaning, that is, hitting the batter in the "bean" or head with a pitch as opposed to bonking him somewhere else on his body. Only Cincinnati's Ewell "The Whip" Blackwell hit more batters, and he was notorious for his erratic control. Sal's 10 is a high number for any pitcher but is especially high for a curveball specialist known for his pinpoint control. It is difficult to avoid the conclusion that at least some of those hits were deliberate, although Sal remained reluctant to admit to that. "A ball will get away from you once in a while," he insisted. "No guy has perfect control. If you're pitching . . . high inside and it gets off a little, it's going to come pretty close to [the hitter] and cause him to hit the dirt. That's part of the game." Sal heatedly denied ever trying to hit a batter in the head: "I've been accused of throwing at guys' heads—which is almost like booking a fellow for attempted murder. This is my bread and butter. I'm not trying to kill anybody."[32]

According to the philosophy pounded into Sal by Dolf Luque, hitting a batter is less desirable than *almost* hitting a batter, since instilling fear, not causing physical injury or awarding the opposition a base runner, is the goal of high-inside pitches. Hit batsmen might be called collateral damage, a regrettable but inevitable side effect of Sal's pitching style. In an analysis of Maglie's pitching, Carl Prince claimed that intimidation was a less important motivating factor in the throwing of beanballs than the desire to arouse anger: "Anger, rabid, male anger, was Maglie's goal," according to Prince, who considered Maglie's pitching style mostly a lot of macho posturing.[33] Although ballplayers do on occasion try to anger their opponents, and some, like Eddie Stanky, make a specialty of it, most realize sooner or later that anger can be energizing, and making opponents angry often rouses them to better efforts rather than hindering their efforts. Fear, on the other hand, is paralyzing, as Sal Maglie knew very well and as the vast majority of the recipients of his high-inside fastball found out. Sal was less interested in angering his opponents than in scaring them out of their wits or at least out of their ability to hit his subsequent pitches. Sal the Barber did not waste time trying to make batters mad. He was too busy making them think he was going to kill them (Figure 8).

"THE BARBER" AND HIS BEARD

Sal Maglie owns one of baseball's best nicknames. In a sport that abounds in memorable monikers—from Buttercup Dickerson and Kewpie Barrett to Puddin' Head Jones and Wahoo Sam Crawford, among many others—Sal the Barber still stands out. The name has inspired a great deal of speculation and numerous attempts to track down its origin and significance. The questions of who first pinned the nickname on Maglie, and why, also remain uncertain, although there are more than enough stories to go around. The only aspect everyone agrees on is that the nickname originated after Sal's return to the Giants in 1950. In all his previous years of baseball nothing about the pitcher had been memorable enough to merit a nickname. Sal claimed he received his nickname from Jim McCulley, a writer for the *Daily News,* and that McCulley started calling him "The Barber" late in the 1950 season. According to Sal's account McCulley explained to the pitcher that he had given him the nickname because he "shaved the plate and came close to the hitters." Reminiscing about it in 1968, Sal added that he did not object and thought the nickname enhanced his reputation. "If hitters wanted to think I was going to shave them within an inch of the jugular vein, so much the better," he concluded.[34]

But Sal himself is not always the best source for that kind of information. The name seems to have had less flattering origins that Sal later may have preferred to forget. Giants broadcaster Russ Hodges thought Maglie received the nickname from Charles "Chub" Feeney, Horace Stoneham's nephew, who in 1950 was the Giants' vice-president. According to Hodges, during spring training Feeney remarked condescendingly about Maglie, whom he considered mediocre, "He may not be able to pitch, but I'll bet he could

8—"Expressionless as an executioner"—Red Smith's description of Maglie's menacing, stubble-shadowed game face. Photo: National Baseball Hall of Fame Library, Cooperstown.

always make a living. He looks like the barber who shaved me this morning."[35] Feeney, like his uncle Horace, was a wealthy man who could afford the luxury of having someone shave him every day, and the person who performed that menial task was most likely an Italian barber—a man of much lower social standing than Feeney himself. But Feeney was not prominent enough in 1950 for his comment to have become part of baseball lore. A more convincing source for a similar remark is Leo Durocher, who observed within hearing of Jim McCulley that Sal "looks like the guy at the third chair in the barber shop."[36] In this version, McCulley got the idea for the nickname from Durocher, rather than coming up with it himself, as Sal suggested, and then began using it in his writing.

Roger Kahn, always sensitive to the ethnic subtexts of seemingly bland remarks, noted Durocher's line as a disparaging "racial" comment, lumping Sal with the large number of Italian barbers in New York City, whom Durocher presumably saw as his social inferiors.[37] To Kahn's intuition could be added the existence of a hierarchy among barbers, with the "first-chair" man and his clients the most important, and the second and third-chair barbers less accomplished craftsmen whose clients were correspondingly less prominent. One of the participants in baseball's labor negotiations in 1989 noted, in relation to the importance of speaking directly to the commissioner, "Once you've been shaved by the head barber, you don't move down to the second chair."[38] Making Maglie a third-chair barber sounds like Durocher's dismissive way of suggesting Sal's lack of importance, as well as offering a casual ethnic put-down of Italians along the same lines as the remark attributed to Feeney. Often praised for his lack of prejudice against blacks, the famously foul-mouthed Durocher spouted just about every other kind of ethnic slur, although most of his comments came from that subcategory of careless prejudice born more from insensitivity than from any profound ethnic hostilities.

Late in his life Maglie offered a Canadian reporter still another version of the nickname's origin: "A New York *News* sportswriter looked at me sitting in the dugout and thought I looked like I was sitting in a barber's chair. And since I would shave the corners of the plate with my curve, he started calling me 'The Barber.'"[39] This seems to be a reference to Jim McCulley, who wrote for the *Daily News,* and who was the first to use the nickname in print. The nickname has even been credited to Giants pitching coach Frank Shellenback, a man not otherwise known for his wit. A more far-fetched version of the story claims that Maglie received the nickname because he was a real barber during the off-season. A pair of fans contacted Boston columnist Dan Parker, one of them insisting that he had actually had his hair cut and been shaved by Sal the Barber himself, a claim that shows how a legend can merge with a fantasy. "It is our understanding that Maglie is heartily ashamed that he is a barber, and refuses to answer any inquiries when the question arises," the fans wrote, and they asked that Parker settle the question of where Maglie's barber shop was located: Buffalo or Niagara Falls.[40] Parker checked with *Niagara Falls Gazette* sports editor Mike Quinlan, who quickly set the record straight. Sal was never a barber in either location, and the only chin-shaving he did was with his high-inside fastball.

When the nickname first reached Sal's ears he sensed it was not meant in a flattering way, and he reacted to being asked about it by answering that it was better "than somebody calling you a shoe-shine boy."[41] Since "shoe-shine boy" was one of the milder racial insults hurled at Jackie Robinson and other early black ballplayers, Sal must have known that his nickname, too, was not intended as a compliment and that it had a negative ethnic connotation—it implied that Italians, like blacks, were inferior people fit only for menial labor. But Sal soon became accustomed to the nickname, and even started to enjoy it. He realized it fit him for reasons that had nothing to do with ethnic stereotyping. Others began to associate the name with Sal's specialty of giving batters "close shaves" with his high-inside fastball, and also with his remarkable ability to shave the corners of the plate with his curve for called strikes.

Even his own decision not to shave before the games he pitched, and to allow his extremely heavy, dark beard to shadow his face, fit in with the nickname—when Sal pitched he looked like *he* needed the services of a barber. Although Maglie said he let his beard grow at first only because when he shaved before a game perspiration made his face sting and distracted him, he soon realized that his heavy, unshaven beard made him look a lot more threatening. Sal was neither the first nor the only player to appear on the field unshaven, although clean-shaven was the norm in the 1950s, and the vast majority of players of the modern era before the 1960s conformed to that standard. Since the 1960s, as every baseball fan knows, all kinds of bizarre hair sculptures have sprouted on players' faces. Burleigh Grimes, the bland-looking but belligerent spitballer who pitched between 1916 and 1934, was one of the few who let his beard grow on game days, a habit unusual enough to gain him the nickname "Ol' Stubblebeard." Finally, the association with razors lent Sal's nickname a sinister ring—something like Mack the Knife or the various violent nicknames of real-life gangsters—enough to make those who heard it think not so much of a man who shaved chins, as of a cold-blooded hired killer who made his living by slitting throats. Without realizing it Durocher (or someone) did Sal a tremendous favor by giving him an evocative nickname that enhanced his threatening image. One writer found something downright demonic in the sinister-looking pitcher's astonishing success after his return to the Giants, saying Sal "pitched like he had struck a deal with Old Scratch."[42] Once Maglie realized the nickname could help him, he was happy to be known as Sal the Barber, a name that would identify him instantly for the rest of his life.

At the Axis of Event, Part 1

Maglie and the 1951 Miracle Season

"To be a pitcher! . . . Standing at the axis of event."

Eric Rolfe Greenberg, *The Celebrant*

Nothing in the spring of 1951—certainly not Sal Maglie's performances—gave any clue that this would be Sal's greatest year and the New York Giants' season of miracles. But it was both. Time after time, Sal stood "at the axis of event," winning key games that enabled the Giants to overtake the Dodgers in baseball's most dramatic pennant race. The Giants' race for the pennant gains its drama from sheer improbability. The New Yorkers dropped 12 of their first 14 games, including 11 straight losses, sat in the cellar on May 15, were 13 1/2 games behind the Dodgers as late as August 11, came back to finish in a tie for first place with their crosstown rivals, and then won the pennant with a home run in the last inning of the last game of a three-game playoff.

Maglie asked for $20,000 but signed his 1951 contract for $15,000. Although his spectacular season in 1950 garnered him a substantial raise from the $10,000 he had made the year before, by comparison, Sal's teammate Larry Jansen received $30,000. When sportswriters asked if Sal was satisfied, he replied with sardonic humor, "I got no kicks. Of course, I'm getting from the Giants what I got in Cuba and Mexico five years ago, when nobody ever heard of me."[1] Sal had a poor training season and was hit hard in most games he pitched.

THE 1951 SEASON—THE RACE THAT BECAME A CHASE

Another event overshadowed April 17, Opening Day in professional baseball. Just a few days before, President Truman fired the grandiose but hugely popular military leader, General of the Army Douglas MacArthur, removing him from his Far East command despite howls of protest. The general soon came marching home again, where he gave a speech before a joint session of Congress to rapturous responses. "We heard the voice of God!" exclaimed an awe-struck representative from Missouri. Another gentleman from Missouri was less impressed. "It was nothing but a bunch of damn bullshit," snorted Harry Truman.[2] Undaunted by his firing, MacArthur participated in parades wherever he went, greeted cheering crowds that in New York City numbered in the millions, and, seated in private, flag-draped box seats, attended baseball games in all three New York parks.

In Boston Larry Jansen won the Opening Day game, spinning a five-hit shutout as the Giants beat the Braves, 4–0. Sal started in Boston the next day and pitched six mediocre innings, giving up four runs, although two were unearned. Removed in the sixth for a pinch hitter, he did not receive the loss as the Giants dropped the game, 8–5. The following day, April 19, the Giants split a doubleheader with the Braves, a pair of games that ended in a messy marathon. Jim Hearn defeated Warren Spahn in the afternoon game, 4–2, but in the evening the nightmare began, as the Giants lost by the grotesque score of 13–12. Although the New Yorkers did some great hitting, including a grand slam by Monte Irvin, their pitching gave it all away. The Dodgers meanwhile had gone to the very unusual length of canceling their game against the Phillies on April 19 on some slender pretext allegedly related to the weather, but really so the whole team could rest up for the coming contests with the Giants.

The Dodgers had experienced an eventful off-season. At the end of the 1950 season Branch Rickey departed to the Pittsburgh Pirates. After years of behind-the-scenes warfare with his co-owner and chief rival, the crafty Walter O'Malley had ousted Rickey. O'Malley fired Rickey's old friend Burt Shotton as manager, replacing him with Charlie Dressen, a peppery, egotistical little character who had been a Dodger coach during Durocher's tenure as Brooklyn manager. Dressen's great goal in life was to prove he was a better manager than his old boss. Frank Graham, Jr. provided a vivid thumbnail sketch of the new Dodger skipper: "Squat, sad-eyed, thin hair slicked back, Dressen seemed to cry out for sympathy. . . . A born loser who sometimes won."[3] He was also a man with some bizarre beliefs, among them a conviction that indulgence in oral sex weakens pitchers.[4] Whatever their sexual habits, Dressen's pitchers started strong, as the Dodgers took three from the Giants at the Polo Grounds in anger-fueled games that set the tone for the season.

The first of 22 episodes of the annual inter-borough warfare began on April 20, at the Polo Grounds, where the Dodgers put the Giants away easily, 7–3. The next day the Dodgers did it again, beating the Giants in a brawl of a contest by an identical score, this time with Gen. MacArthur in attendance. With Larry Jansen facing the Dodgers' Chris van Cuyk, the game contained enough combat to make the old soldier think he was back in Korea. Stanky slid into second on a steal and knocked the ball out of Pee Wee Reese's hand. Rocky Bridges bowled over Bobby Thomson at third on a pick-off attempt. Hank Thompson shouted obscenities at van Cuyk after the Dodger pitcher decked him with a fastball. Jansen, proud of his excellent control, had resisted Durocher's efforts to turn him into a brushback pitcher. But now, Durocher threatened to fine Jansen $100 each time he refused to throw a brushback. (Roughly equivalent to a $10,000–per-pitch fine at today's star pitchers' salaries.) With some reluctance the gentlemanly Giants hurler decked startled and angry Dodger catcher Roy Campanella. In a symmetrical payback, when Wes Westrum came to bat, van Cuyk sent the Giants' catcher sprawling. With the score tied at 3–3 entering the eighth, Campanella came to bat again, with Jansen still under orders to knock him down. When Campy had to hit the dust a second time he came up fighting, cursing at the closest Giant, catcher Westrum. Usually one of the best-natured men in baseball, the enraged Campanella shoved Westrum backward, right into umpire Augie Donatelli. Westrum bounced off Donatelli and shoved Campanella, propelling the rotund catcher toward the mound. Campy charged back at Westrum, who was already tearing off his equipment, preparing to trade punches with his Dodger counterpart. Donatelli, who had learned his trade in a German prisoner-of-war camp, separated the two men as players from both benches milled around. Campanella avenged his mistreatment by smacking a double into left field, and the Dodgers went on to score three runs, then added another in the ninth. Ralph Branca pitched no-hit ball in relief for the Dodgers in the last three innings and took the victory.

On April 22 it was Maglie's turn again, facing the Dodgers' Carl Erskine. After Maglie had set down the Dodgers in the top of the first, Dressen demanded to see the ball, accusing Sal of doctoring it and asking umpire Lee Ballanfant to inspect it. Durocher protested at great length, and Sal stood glowering as the umpire looked at the ball but found nothing wrong. Sal nursed a 3–1 lead going into the eighth inning, but then, after a heated argument between Maglie and Jackie Robinson over a fastball that hit Jackie in the back, the Dodgers scored two off Sal, one in the eighth and another in the ninth, to tie the score. The game continued into the tenth, when Sal lost it by giving up a home run to Carl Furillo. Maglie dropped his first decision of the season, the Dodgers swept the series, and the Giants had now lost four in a row. Maglie, who would turn 34 in a few days, was the second-oldest man on the squad—only Eddie Stanky was a few months older—and some speculated that age was beginning to affect his stamina. The carnage continued in Philadelphia, where the Phillies swept three from New York, bringing the Giants' losing streak to seven. The team returned to the Polo Grounds for a pair of games with the Braves, and dropped both of them. Maglie faced Boston's Johnny Sain on April 26 and suffered a 3–0 loss as Sain won his 100th major league game. Maglie's record stood at 0–2, and the Giants' losing streak had extended to eight. The next day the Braves walloped the Giants, 7–3, for New York's ninth straight loss.

As the disastrous month of April moved toward its close the Giants faced the Dodgers again, this time in enemy territory: the claustrophobic confines of Ebbets Field. The Giants dreaded playing on the Dodgers' home ground. Brooklyn fans were notorious for their raucous noise and nasty behavior toward all opposition players, but they saved their worst vitriol for the Giants. Durocher recalled how Dodgers fans spit at him, threw things at him, sprayed him with Coca-Cola, and called him "every filthy name they could think of." Monte Irvin declared that "it was an experience just going in and getting out alive."[5] Bobby Thomson remembered Durocher feeding his team a repetitive diet of hatred against the Dodgers, casting the Brooklynites not merely as rivals but as horrible human beings, creating an enmity that continued off the field. According to Thomson, Durocher claimed that the Dodgers were "the kind of guys who, if you take your eyes off them at a party, they start groping your wife's tits." Listening to such talk day after day, Giants players learned to despise the Dodgers. "We didn't even talk to those fellows," Thomson recalled, and he compared playing at Ebbets to "walking into a lion's den."[6]

This time, the lions ate the Giants two days in a row, devouring them by decisive scores of 8–4 on April 28 and 6–3 on April 29. The reeling New Yorkers' record was 2–12, and they had now suffered 11 straight defeats. They were in undisputed possession of last place, and the Dodgers rushed to rub their noses in the dirt of the cellar floor. Only a thin wall and a wooden door separated the home team and the visitors locker rooms at Ebbets Field, and after their victory on April 29 some of the Dodgers gathered in front of the door, taunting their vanquished opponents, hurling easily audible insults. Monte Irvin remembered hearing the voices of Carl Furillo and Jackie Robinson shouting "Eat your heart out, Leo, you sonofabitch. You'll never win it this year!" The addition of insults to the injury of defeat was too much for Durocher, who exploded at his team, using language that shocked even the toughest veterans of his tirades. According to Bill Rigney, Durocher "was so hot you could have fried eggs on the language coming out of his mouth . . . motherfucking this, cocksucking that." After ten minutes or so of Leo's scorching insults, an interruption by the bat boy with an innocent question caused Durocher to pick up one of the player's gloves and hurl it at the wall. But then a couple of well-timed comments by Dark and Stanky broke the tension, and suddenly everybody, including Durocher, was roaring with laughter. "[The Dodgers] must have been able to hear [Leo]," Rigney continued. "Now they hear this hysterical laughter. They must have thought we were all gone crazy, like maybe we murdered Leo and were all celebrating over his body."[7]

Durocher's tirade and its funny ending loosened the tension and broke the spell of defeatism. The next evening, April 30, they thrashed the Dodgers, 8–5, before an unhappy throng of 33,963 at Ebbets Field. Although he did not complete the game, the starter and winner of the contest that began the Giants' climb out of the cellar was Sal Maglie. The Giants gave Sal a comfortable cushion by pouncing on three Dodgers pitchers for six runs in the top of the first. The Dodgers counterattacked in their half of the inning as Gene Hermanski led off with a home run. Maglie's first pitch to the next batter, Carl Furillo, came closer to giving him a haircut than a shave and "almost turned Furillo's hat around," as the *Eagle*'s Tommy Holmes put it. The shaken Furillo flied out, but the Dodgers scored another run on a homer by Jackie Robinson. The Giants scored two more in the second, and the Dodgers chipped away at Sal for another run in their half of the inning. The pitcher's intimidation tactics failed to work on Pee Wee Reese. After Sal knocked him down Reese bounced to his feet, socked Sal for a double, and scored on a single by Rocky Bridges. In the top of the third, the fourth Dodger pitcher of the evening, Clem Labine, engaged in some payback by decking Bobby Thomson.

But the real nastiness began with Robinson's second at bat in the bottom of the third. Robinson had hit a home run his first time up, and this time on the first pitch Sal shaved Jackie's chin with a fastball. On Maglie's next pitch, a slow changeup, Robinson pulled a classic ploy: he dropped a bunt down the first base line, but then, instead of sprinting to first, he held back a little, gauging the distance and timing himself, watching Maglie as the pitcher charged off the mound to field the bunt. As Sal bent over near the foul line, his attention on the ball (which was rolling foul) rather than on Robinson, the 210–pound former football star gathered speed and barreled into Maglie. The force of the collision sent Sal sprawling in the dirt. Cursing a blue streak he scrambled to his feet and lunged at Robinson—the closest Sal ever came to an on-field fistfight. Members of both teams intervened to keep the two men apart, although the *Eagle*'s Tommy Holmes snidely implied that Maglie waited until his teammates had him well surrounded before making a show of trying to reach Robinson. Durocher hurried out to calm his furious pitcher, and plate umpire Babe Pinelli said a few words to the bristling Robinson. The game resumed, and Jackie tagged Sal for a single, but the pitcher struck out Hodges to end the inning.

The incident became one of baseball's fish stories, with the confrontation between Maglie and Robinson growing bigger in later retellings. Most newspaper accounts of the game, published the next day, took note of the clash, but none devoted much space to it, and the *Times* did not even mention it.[8] One later account contains numerous inaccuracies, including the claim that Robinson "made it to first," when in fact the ball rolled foul, and he returned to the plate. Another asserted that Jackie "barged into Maglie with crushing force" and that Maglie and Robinson "had to be pried apart by their teammates."[9] Historian Doris Kearns Goodwin, who claims eyewitness status, recalled that "Robinson's teammates had to pull him away from Maglie," although contemporary accounts indicate the two men never tangled. Joe Overfield claimed Robinson "body-blocked Maglie almost into right field," and Szalontai wrote that Robinson sent Maglie "flying into the air," both far-fetched images unsupported by newspaper descriptions. As a fish-story teller David Falkner topped them all by asserting that "Robinson left [Maglie] printed in the earth like a cartoon Road Runner."[10]

The flare-up had one immediate consequence: Ford Frick, president of the National League and soon to replace Happy Chandler as the new baseball commissioner, took Maglie's side against Robinson. Frick maintained that he had received no reports from umpires of pitchers "dusting off" batters and snapped, "I'm getting tired of Robinson's popping off. I have warned the Brooklyn club that if they won't control Robinson, I will."[11] Walter O'Malley, who disliked Robinson but disliked even more seeing one of his players singled out for criticism by the league's top official, insisted that Jackie had the full support of the Dodger organization. Robinson fired back, declaring, "Let Mr. Frick change the color of his skin . . . and go out and hit against Maglie."[12] Sal refused to be drawn into the war of words. He later noted that on the previous day, even though Jansen actually had hit Robinson, Jackie did not react. "But when I came close to him with an inside pitch." Sal continued, "he does everything but challenge me to a duel at 40 paces."[13] Although Robinson's implied charge of racism must have hurt Sal, who was the least prejudiced of men, he knew racism had nothing to do with his conduct toward Robinson. The only colors he paid attention to were the colors on a batter's uniform. Maglie was an equal opportunity intimidator.

In May the Giants posted a brilliant 18–9 record, with Sal accounting for a third of those wins as he notched six consecutive victories (seven, counting the game he won against the Dodgers on April 30). Sal faced Pittsburgh on May 4, and defeated them, 5–1, on a one-hitter. There was never any suspense about the game being a no-hitter or even a shutout, since the lead-off batter touched Sal for a triple and scored on an error by Irvin. Sal retired the last 18 Bucs in order. That same afternoon Cincinnati defeated the Dodgers in a game that featured a bitter disagreement between the Brooklynites and umpire Frank Dascoli. This would not be the last time the Dodgers clashed with that umpire, and before the season ended Dascoli would make a critical call at the plate that some claim cost the Dodgers the pennant. Against St. Louis on May 9, Sal sailed to his third straight victory by a score of 17–3. On May 13 the Giants swept a doubleheader from the Phils. Sal took the second game, 4–2. In Boston the Dodgers trounced the Braves to take over first place in a tight pennant race. In Cincinnati on May 18 Sal stopped the Reds, 4–3, for his fifth consecutive victory. On May 23 the Giants played a single game against the Cubs at Wrigley, and Maglie won it, 2–1. Sal took the win against the Phillies on May 27, a two-hitter, for his seventh straight win. For the first time the Giants' record rose above .500.

During the third week of May Durocher made a change that altered the fortunes of the Giants not only for the 1951 season, but for years to come. Leo convinced Horace Stoneham to bring up 20-year-old Willie Mays from the club's Minneapolis farm team to play center field. In the late 1940s Mays had played with the Birmingham Black Barons, and when the Dodgers passed on the promising outfielder because some half-wit of a scout reported the kid could not hit a curveball, the Giants snapped him up. He played for their Trenton team in 1950, and in 1951 he was hitting an astounding .477 with Minneapolis. Stoneham resisted Durocher's pleas at first. One excuse was that he did not want to damage the chances of his Minneapolis franchise by pulling their popular star player. Stoneham even placed an ad in a Minneapolis newspaper, apologizing for taking Mays away from his minor league team. But Stoneham's more pressing reason was racial. There were already four blacks on the New York roster—Monte Irvin, Hank Thompson, Rafael Noble, and Artie Wilson—and Stoneham did not wish to add a fifth, which meant the Giants might field a team with five of the nine positions filled by black players. Monte Irvin confirmed that this informal quota system existed in the 1950s.[14] Leo, on record as not caring if his team consisted of pink and green players with zebra stripes, had no sympathy with Stoneham's racial scruples. The two men at last agreed that the Giants would send one black player, Artie Wilson, to the minors when they brought up Mays.

Willie joined the Giants on May 25 in Philadelphia, playing center field, with Bobby Thomson shifted to left. In his first major league game Mays made an error and went 0 for 5 as the Giants lost to the Phillies, 8–5. On that day Brooklyn was in first place with St. Louis in second, two games out. The Cubs held third, half a game behind the Cards, and the Braves were in fourth, three games behind. The Giants were in fifth, but only 4 1/2 games separated them from the first-place Dodgers—the pennant race was that close. The Giants ended the month of May by losing two out of three to the Braves, leaving them still in fifth with a 21–21 record.

The Giants almost duplicated their sizzling May record during June, winning the same number of games, 18, while losing 11. Maglie began the month by beating the Pirates at the Polo Grounds, 8–2. The Giants hosted Cincinnati on June 5, and Sal extended his winning streak to nine as he defeated the Reds, 3–2. He allowed hits in seven of the nine innings, but always worked his way out of jams. On June 10 Sal faced the Cubs in the second game of a doubleheader, hoping to make it a three-game sweep, but lasted only until the fourth inning. The Cubs won, 7–3, handing Maglie his first defeat since April 26, and his third of the season. It was the first time the Cubs had beaten Maglie. On that same June 10 when Sal's winning streak ended, Brooklyn's Ralph Branca notched his fifth straight win and fourth consecutive complete game.

On June 13, in the second of three games in Cincinnati, Sal made his first relief appearance of the year, recording the final five outs in the Giants' 5–2 victory. On June 16 Sal became the first pitcher in the league to win 10 games, as he defeated the Pirates, 6–1. Willie Mays, who at last was starting to solve major league pitching, had two hits in the game and had hit safely in 11 of his last 12 games. Sal also had a good day at the plate, hitting his first major league home run. The Giants had climbed into second place, and trailed the Dodgers by five games. On June 18 the Giants pulled out a 5–4 win in 12 against St. Louis. Sal came into the game in the ninth in relief of Dave Koslo with the Giants leading, 4–2, and one man on base. After Sal induced the next batter to pop out, Stanky muffed a double-play grounder that would have ended the game. Before Sal could work his way out of the inning a single by Wally Westlake tied the score. New York scratched out a run in the twelfth, and Maglie held the Cards scoreless for the rest of the game for his eleventh win.

In the June 18 issue of *Newsweek* columnist John Lardner extolled Maglie's toughness in language that would have done Dolf Luque proud. Lardner placed the "grim-faced" Maglie in the John McGraw tradition of ballplayers "who believed in winning if you had to cut ears and gouge eyeballs to do it." Danny Litwhiler, a Cincinnati player, declared, "[Sal] scares you to death. He's scowling and gnashing his teeth, and if you try to dig in on him, there goes your Adam's apple. He's gonna win if it kills you and him both." The columnist then compared Durocher's long delay in 1950 before using Maglie as a starter to "benching a mongoose in a snake fight."[15] Luque's training had paid off for Sal: his intimidating appearance and even more terrifying delivery mutually reinforced one another.

On the trading deadline date of June 15, the Dodgers made a deal widely believed to have sewn up the pennant for them. The eight-player deal took place as the Dodgers were playing the Cubs at Wrigley Field, and it involved a straight four-for-four trade. Dressen called outfielder Gene Hermanski, pitcher Joe Hatten, infielder Eddie Miksis, and catcher Bruce Edwards into his office, telling them to clean out their lockers and move over to the Cubs locker room: they had just been traded. At the same time in the Cubs clubhouse four players—infielder Wayne Terwilliger, pitcher Johnny Schmitz, catcher Rube Walker, and outfielder Andy Pafko—were told they had been traded to the Dodgers. Players and sportswriters alike thought the Dodgers had gotten the best of the deal, particularly in acquiring Pafko, who was both a power hitter and an excellent fielder. Jim McCulley began his column in the *Daily News* by declaring that the acquisition of Pafko just about wrapped up the pennant for the Dodgers, and Pee Wee Reese recalled how players on other teams told him that with Pafko on their side the Dodgers would win the pennant by 30 games.

As the month of June wore on, the Giants could not gather any momentum. Sal started on June 22, against the Cubs in a game the Giants won, but he was taken out in the sixth and did not receive the decision. On June 26 the Giants were back at the Polo Grounds for a three-game series against the Dodgers for the first time since the tense, violence-spiked series in late April. Durocher chose Sal for the opener, and he did not disappoint Giants fans in the sellout crowd as he froze the Dodgers, 4–0. Both teams were playing under orders from league president Ford Frick to avoid the beanball wars that had characterized their previous meeting, but this did not prevent the usual Giants-Dodgers theatrics. There were at least half a dozen "discussions," as *Herald Tribune* writer Leonard Koppett delicately called them, concerning Maglie's close shaves and Preacher Roe's stealthy wet ones, but according to reporters present, neither pitcher threw any beanballs. Roy Campanella had a wonderful time chatting up Willie Mays each time the rookie came to the plate. Campy, an expert at the kind of carefully crafted chatter that distracted batters while seeming to offer them friendly pleasantries, asked Mays his opinion of Preacher Roe. When Mays admitted that Roe was a very good pitcher, Campy chortled, "Wait til you get Don Newcombe tomorrow. He *hates* colored rookies. He'll blow you down!" Possibly the raw Mays did not know that Newcombe was also a "colored" player. Another of Campanella's favorite subjects was sex. He enjoyed embarrassing Mays by ribbing him about his love life: "What d'you say, pup? When you going to get married?

You gettin' much?"[16] Campy's comic relief aside, Sal gave the Dodgers nothing to smile about. Not one of them reached third, and only one, Duke Snider, got as far as second, as Sal held Brooklyn's big bats to four hits, three of them singles. The game was Preacher's Roe's first defeat of the season after 10 victories but the third successive start he had failed to finish.

Small cracks such as Roe's failures were beginning to appear in the seemingly unbeatable Dodgers, but the Giants were unable to pry them open any wider. On the day following Maglie's victory the Dodgers bounced back to overwhelm the Giants, 10–4. The New Yorkers won the third game of the series, but then the Braves pounded them in Boston on June 30 by the embarrassing score of 19–7. The victim was Sal Maglie. The Braves jumped on Sal, scoring four in the first inning, but the Giants rallied to take a 7–4 lead. Maglie held Boston to just two hits over the next five innings, but collapsed in the seventh, giving up five runs and failing to get anybody out. Jones and Koslo tried to mop up, but the Braves pummeled them as well. It was Sal's fourth loss of the season, and he had yet to beat the Braves. The Dodgers were still in first.

In July the Giants posted a 17–11 record, but it was not good enough to gain ground on the Dodgers, whose pennant victory appeared certain. Against the Phillies on July 3 the Giants rallied in the thirteenth inning to win the game, 9–8. That same evening the Dodgers lost to Boston, 4–3. On the Fourth of July the Giants came to Brooklyn, and the Dodgers used them for firecrackers, taking both ends of a doubleheader, 6–5 and 4–2, and then burning up the Giants again the next day, 8–4, to sweep what many regarded as a crucial series. When it ended, a smug Charlie Dressen bragged, "We've knocked off the Giants. They won't bother us no more."[17] In the first game of the doubleheader Maglie had a four-hit shutout going until the eighth when he suddenly weakened and allowed a two-run homer by Campanella, who usually did not hit Sal well, and a solo shot by Pee Wee Reese. Taken out in the ninth with the game tied, Sal did not get the loss; Sheldon Jones was the loser in relief when the Dodgers squeezed home the winning run in the eleventh. Ralph Branca won the nightcap for the Dodgers in a game that featured the familiar arguments and mutual maneuvers by Durocher and Dressen in their efforts to outsmart one another. Amused by the spectacle, John Lardner devoted a column to the managers' machinations, observing that "the fun . . . lies in watching their brains collide in action, like a couple of runaway razor blades."[18] On July 8, in the last game before the All-Star break, the Braves defeated the Giants, 6–5, in 10 innings. Sal started, holding the Braves scoreless until the fourth, but was knocked out in the seventh. Former Giant Sid Gordon won the game for Boston with a homer in the tenth off Dave Koslo. Once again, Sal did not take the loss, and his record remained at 12–4. The second-place Giants' record at midseason was 43–36, but the Dodgers boasted a brilliant 50–26, and their lead was 8 1/2 games.

The National League All-Star squad, managed by Eddie Sawyer of the 1950 pennant-winning Phillies, reflected the quality of the Dodger lineup; the Phillies had deteriorated from the Whiz Kids into the Fizz Kids. There were seven Brooklyn players on the team: Roy Campanella, Gil Hodges, Jackie Robinson, Pee Wee Reese, Duke Snider, Don Newcombe, and Preacher Roe. Two Giants made the team: Alvin Dark and Sal Maglie. The Nationals won the game 8–3. Although his three-inning stint was not outstanding, Maglie was the winning pitcher, since it was during his innings (fourth through sixth) that the Nationals took the lead they never relinquished. Sal gave up two of the American League's three runs, both on homers, but he became the first New York Giants pitcher to win an All-Star game.

With the All-Star contest over, the Giants puttered along, winning and losing games in about equal measure. On July 15 the New Yorkers played a doubleheader against the Pirates at the Polo Grounds, with Maglie starting in the opener. The Pirates won, 7–6, in twelve innings. The Giants had given Sal a 6–2 lead, but he failed to hold on to it, and was taken out in the seventh after he had given up a homer, two walks, and a single. Pittsburgh tied the game in the ninth and won it in the twelfth, scoring the run off Dave Koslo, who took the loss.

Maglie started again on July 20 against Cincinnati, in a game where Durocher had made an important change in his infield. The manager had been frustrated by the uneven play of Hank Thompson in the hot corner. A troubled man with a history of violent behavior as well as a severe drinking problem, Thompson displayed moments of excellence but often seemed to be playing in an alcoholic haze. When he received a serious spike wound on July 18, Stoneham and Durocher used that as a reason to send Thompson down and to call up some pitching support: righthander Al Corwin. With third base open, Durocher assigned the spot to Bobby Thomson. This was the position Bobby had played at the start of his career, and he thanked Durocher for returning him there by banging out three hits and driving in two runs in the game on July 20 where the Giants piled up 11 runs. Sal won his thirteenth game, 11–5, his first victory since June 26. On July 24 the Giants split a pair with the Pirates. Sal won the first, 4–3, in 10 innings, as Willie Mays drove in the winning run with a single. Sal allowed four hits and two walks and struck out ten. In the third of a four-game series in Cincinnati, the opener of a doubleheader on July 29, Sal gained his fifteenth win, 3–1. On July 31, he secured the final four outs to preserve a 4–3 victory over the Cubs. Although the Giants played well during July, the Dodgers played better. Brooklyn stumbled briefly after the All-Star break, but won their last 10 games, finishing the month with a superb 21–7 record, and the pennant seemed even more firmly in their hands.

The Giants began August by losing seven of their first 10 games, digging themselves into a hole that looked like their own grave. They were 9 1/2 games behind the Dodgers at the start of the month, and their record for the next 10 days was almost as bad as it had been in the disastrous opening weeks of the season. Durocher sent Maglie to the mound against the Cardinals in St. Louis on August 3, and Sal pitched beautifully for four innings, nursing a 1–0 lead, but then collapsed in the fifth as the Cards scored five. The Cardinals won, 5–4, and Sal took his fifth loss. The Giants trounced the Cards in their next two games, and then returned to New York for another round of battle with the Dodgers: three games at Ebbets Field.

Because of a rainout on August 7, the teams played a doubleheader on August 8, and Brooklyn took both games. Feelings among the fans packed into the small park on the stifling August day ran so high that fights broke out in the stands as a counterpart to the battles on the diamond. Brooklyn took the first game, 7–2, with three Dodgers hitting home runs, and Carl Erskine pitching seven innings of superb relief for his twelfth win. Erskine was a principled man who refused to throw at anyone, but even he nailed a Giant, Monte Irvin, although it was certainly not intentional. Nonetheless, the Giants responded with tight pitches of their own, as Sheldon Jones knocked down Pee Wee Reese and Roy Campanella. The nightcap promised to be an even more bitter battle, with youth and power pitted against age and guile, as the Dodgers' Don Newcombe faced Sal Maglie.

Sal was not at his best that night, and he lasted only four innings, giving up five runs on seven hits. But while he was on the mound he and Jackie Robinson continued their warfare, and on this occasion Jackie came out on top. Newspaper accounts of the game are fragmentary, probably because it was a night game that lasted three hours, and reporters were in a rush to file their stories. Another reason they did not give much detail on this or other confrontations between Maglie and Robinson is that most of their exchanges were unprintable. Robinson was the one player who could "get to" Maglie, driving the pitcher to fuming, stomping, obscenity-spewing rage. Using his shrill, high-pitched voice to the best advantage, Robinson drilled Maglie's eardrums with a constant stream of abuse. "You fucking dago" was one of his milder epithets. Sal responded with gestures, snarls, and obscenities of his own, but he never returned ethnic slurs in kind.

Carl Furillo led off the first with a home run. With one out and a runner on second, Robinson came to the plate. Maglie decked him. Jackie regained his feet and took a step toward the mound where, according to Szalontai's account of the game, Sal greeted him by grabbing his crotch in what Leo Durocher labeled "the Italian salute."[19] In those testosterone-fueled tough-guy contests Maglie on occasion gave his groin a short, sharp shake, miming the derisive act of brandishing his genitals in the direction of whoever had angered him. Although four layers of material—jockstrap, protective cup, tight-fitting underwear, and baggy flannel trousers—combined to assure that the gesture never became more explicit, it was not the kind of act likely to be reported in 1950s newspapers. On Maglie's next pitch Robinson lined a run-scoring single to right, then stole second. By the time the inning was over the Dodgers had a two-run lead.

With two out in the third Snider walked, and Robinson came to bat again. This time he bunted down the first base line in an attempt to draw Maglie into fielding the ball, but Sal had learned his lesson in their April 30 collision and let Lockman handle the chance. By the time the first baseman came up with the ball Robinson was safe with an infield single. Snider and Robinson then both stole bases on the beleaguered Maglie and his battery-mate, utility catcher Sal Yvars. A single by Pafko followed, and the Dodgers had two more runs. As he reached the plate Robinson addressed a few more obscenities to Maglie before returning to the dugout, and Sal responded by pressing the fingers of his right hand into the crook of his left elbow and jerking his elbow at Robinson, a vulgar Italian gesture that means "up your ass!" Sal, still steaming, gave up another run in the bottom of the fourth. Maglie left the game after completing four frames, giving way to a pinch hitter in the fifth. As Sal marched to the dugout at the end of the inning, jeering Dodger fans pelted him with peanuts, mustard-smeared hot-dog rolls, beer cups, and any other handy missiles. After all the excitement Newcombe was within one out of a win when the Giants came back to tie the game in the top of the ninth. But with Dave Koslo on the mound in the bottom of the tenth the Dodgers loaded the bases, and Brooklyn third baseman Billy Cox knocked in a run to give the Dodgers a 7–6 victory. Roscoe McGowan began his account in the *Times* by suggesting, "Maybe the Dodgers wrapped up the pennant last night."

The Dodgers were still not finished humiliating the Giants. The following day, August 9, in a game widely regarded as the Giants' final chance to preserve any pennant hopes, the Dodgers beat them again, 6–5, to sweep the series and increase their lead to 12 1/2 games. The winning pitcher was Ralph Branca, who had not lost a game to the Giants at Ebbets Field since 1945. As the Giants returned to their locker room and began undressing in gloomy silence, they could hear the gleeful shouts from the Brooklyn side of the wall. They could not expect the Dodgers to be quiet out of respect for their feelings, but the way the Dodgers rubbed the Giants' noses in their defeat—and the evident death of their pennant chances—struck many of the Giants as excessive, unsportsmanlike, and unacceptable. In a louder and larger replay of the incident on April 29, a group of Dodger gathered in front of the door that separated the two clubhouses. They began shouting and banging on the door with their bats and then burst into a raucous and repetitious song: "Roll out the barrel, we got the Giants on the run!" Carl Erskine and Clem Labine, two Dodgers whose memories can be relied on, both recalled that Dressen egged his players on to taunt the Giants, rather than trying to prevent the incident. On the other side of the wall the taunts roused the beaten Giants to fury. Team captain Alvin Dark declared, "You can't treat human beings like they treated us and get away with it."[20] Durocher protested the incident to the league office, and shortly afterward the door and wooden partition were replaced by a brick wall. But the damage had been done—to the Dodgers, as it turned out.

The Giants also lost their next game, on August 11. When the Phillies' Robin Roberts shut them out, 4–0, and the Dodgers behind Branca won the first game of a doubleheader with the Braves, 8–1, the Dodgers held a 13 1/2–game lead over the second-place Giants. This was the largest lead they would have, and they held it for only a few hours, since the Braves beat the Dodgers in the nightcap and reduced the lead to 13 games. August 12 was Wes Westrum Day at the Polo Grounds, and the Giants made a special effort to win one for their popular catcher in front of his friends and family. Although Westrum went hitless in four at bats in the opener, Maglie made sure the Giants won the game against the Phillies, 3–2. He gave up the two runs early, but held the Phils scoreless in the last five frames. Rookie righthander Al Corwin turned in a fine performance in the second game, defeating the Phils, 2–1. The following day the Giants defeated Philadelphia again, 5–2, as Larry Jansen notched his fifteenth win, to sweep the series. Next came another series with the Dodgers, this one at the Polo Grounds. The games seemed of little significance in a pennant race considered already sewn up by the Dodgers, merely another opportunity for the bitter crosstown rivals to go after each other. Sportswriter Joe King sang the Dodgers' praises in several lyrical sentences that also contained an inadvertent prophecy: "It seems a cinch that nobody but the Dodgers can beat the Dodgers. Only through a cataclysmic blowup could they allow an inferior competitor to sneak in, and this Dodger team is so well-balanced, and so deep in great men, and so zestful in spirit that it hardly can collapse."[21]

The Giants won the first game of the series, 4–2, with a surprise starter, reliever George Spencer, who pitched a complete game. In the second game the Giants received a fine pitching performance from Jim Hearn. In the eighth Westrum touched Ralph Branca for a two-run homer, giving Hearn and the Giants a 3–1 victory. The third game, on August 16, matched New-combe and Maglie in a brilliant pitchers' duel between a pair of 16–game winners. Although lacking the on-field fireworks and beanball wars of previous games between the rivals, the game provided a dazzling display of pitching artistry as the Giants defeated the Dodgers, 2–1, to sweep the series. Sal allowed only four hits, two of them infield scratches, struck out three, and did not walk a batter. The Dodgers' only run came in the eighth on a bloop homer by the light-hitting Billy Cox that barely cleared the right field wall. Sal had the Brooklyn sluggers lunging for his snapping curves and turning most of them into harmless ground balls. "I felt better today than I have for the last two months," a pleased Maglie told reporters in the locker room.[22] Newspapers began to note that the Giants had cut the Dodgers' lead to 9 1/2 games, and that the Dodgers might not have the pennant sewn up after all.

In Philadelphia the Giants juggernaut rolled over the Phillies, sweeping another three-game series and extending their winning streak to nine. Back at the Polo Grounds on August 21 Sal faced Cincinnati but did not complete the game and was not involved in the decision. He gave up only three hits and four runs, but all the runs came on homers, and he left the game for a pinch hitter in the fifth. Trailing 4–1 in the eighth, the Giants came back to score six runs and win the game, 7–4. The next day they defeated the Reds again, 4–3, extending their winning streak to eleven games. On August 24 the Giants scored two runs in the bottom of the ninth to beat the Cardinals, 6–5, the fourth successive game in which they had come from behind in the late innings and won. On the following two days the New Yorkers played a pair of doubleheaders with the Cubs and won all four games, extending their winning streak to an astounding 16. Sal pitched an almost-complete game on August 26 (the first game of the first doubleheader) and was enjoying a three-run lead in the ninth when Chuck Connors tied the score with a three-run homer. The home run was his last major-league round-tripper; Connors soon left baseball, and later he gained fame as the star of the 1950s television western series *The Rifleman*. Westrum won the game with a two-out home run in the bottom of the ninth. Spencer, who recorded the final two outs in the top of the ninth, received credit for the win. In the *Times*, Louis Effrat wrote that "perhaps the Giants may yet make a close race of it." The winning streak finally ended on August 28 when the Pirates beat the Giants, 2–0, at the Polo Grounds. Afterward, Red Smith wrote that the Giants' pennant hopes were "only a dream. They can't really go far enough to crowd the Dodgers, not when they're chasing a team as strong as Brooklyn."[23] The Giants beat the Bucs the next day, and lost to them on August 30, completing a month of superb ballplaying that nonetheless left them still in second place, seven games behind the Dodgers.

The Giants began the last month of the season with a pair of Labor Day weekend games against the Dodgers at the Polo Grounds, and they buried the Bums in both. Maglie won his eighteenth in the first game, an 8–1 rout that saw Don Mueller blast three home runs in four trips to the plate and Alvin Dark and Eddie Stanky squelch a Dodger rally by turning a triple play. Sal issued no walks and silenced all of Brooklyn's sluggers, holding the Dodgers to seven singles, while his teammates pounded Ralph Branca for five runs in the first three innings, a drubbing that included a 400–foot, two-run homer by Bobby Thomson. Maglie's only shaky moment came in the third inning when, with two out and the bases loaded on three singles, Sal's first pitch to Jackie Robinson hit him, forcing in a run. The pitcher angrily argued, to no avail, that the ball had hit Robinson's bat rather than his hand. Warned by plate umpire Lee Ballanfant against throwing dusters, Sal stalked back to the mound and struck out Gil Hodges to end the inning. Given the circumstances, there is little likelihood that Maglie intended to hit Robinson and ruin his own shutout; it was another case of a high-inside pitch coming in a little too close to the batter. As the teams changed sides at the end of the third Robinson and Maglie exchanged angry words, but there was no repetition of their violent confrontation of April 30. In a postgame interview Robinson declared, "That pitch of Sal Maglie came right at me, but I'm sure he wasn't trying to hit me with the bases loaded. If I hadn't gotten my wrist up there, I'd have been hit right between the eyes."[24] Sal's reputation as a Dodger-killer was now firmly established. He had beaten the Dodgers in four of his five outings against them, the best record in the league, and his wins accounted for two-thirds of the Giants' victories over the league leaders.

The Giants won another the next day by the even more lopsided score of 11–2, a game that featured so many arguments and so much Dodger bench-jockeying that the exasperated umpires ejected not only Robinson and Dodger starting pitcher Don Newcombe, but also several men who were not even in the game, including Dick Williams, a future major league manager who referred to himself as "Dressen's DSA" (designated smart-ass). In response Dressen pulled another of his theatrical moves, ordering all remaining players not in the game to the clubhouse to prevent them from being kicked out. Since the clubhouse was some 500 feet from home plate, the migration took several minutes and disrupted the game as effectively as any argument. Such tactics did not win the Brooklyn manager many admirers. In his *Herald Tribune* column Red Smith wrote bluntly that Dressen "has been making a spectacular ass of himself." The Giants did some bench-jockeying of their own during the game. Maglie, usually among the quietest players, hit upon a way of unnerving Don Newcombe that was worthy of Eddie

Stanky. Instead of shouting obscenities at the thin-skinned hurler, Sal performed some effective pantomime—he put his hands around his neck in a throttling gesture that suggested to Newk that he was "choking," that he was going to fold under pressure. And fold he did on that occasion, as the Giants clobbered him for four runs. After stomping back to the dugout at the end of the sixth inning he was so angry he threw a catcher's mask onto the field, and umpire Al Barlick thumbed him to the showers. The Giants victory decreased the Dodgers' lead to five games.

The Giants took both ends of a doubleheader on September 5 against the Boston Braves. Sheldon Jones, inconsistent all season, and with a poor 5–9 record, pitched a complete game in the opener, winning it, 3–2. Maglie took the nightcap, 9–1, hurling another complete game for his nineteenth win. Sal overcame a career "hex" in this game, since he had never before beaten the Braves. The Giants defeated Boston again the next day to sweep the series. Durocher announced that for the remainder of the campaign he would use a three-man rotation: Maglie, Jansen, and Hearn. "I plan to go that way even if it means only two days rest between games for those fellows," Leo declared. "From now on it has to be all out if we want to . . . catch the Dodgers."[25] On September 5 Ralph Branca defeated the Phillies, 5–2, but it would be the Dodger righthander's last victory of the 1951 season.

On September 8 and 9 the Giants took on the Dodgers again at Ebbets Field, for the season's last two scheduled contests between the rivals. League president Ford Frick asked the players to refrain from making insulting remarks to each other during the course of the games. The biggest insult to the Giants was the trouncing they took in the first game at the hands of Don Newcombe and the Dodgers. The big righthander, showing no signs of choking, pitched a superb game, shutting out the New Yorkers, 9–0. He allowed only two hits, both singles in the second inning, as he chalked up his eighteenth victory. Once more, it looked like time to read the Giants out of the race. Ed Sinclair wrote, "Well, Sir, the Giants got caught up . . . just as many expected they would be and they now must wait till next year to bring their carefully nurtured pennant hopes out of their hope chest."[26] But once more Sal Maglie kept those hopes alive. Before almost 34,000 furious Dodger fans (few Giant rooters any longer wanted to brave the hostile territory of Ebbets Field) Sal mowed down the Dodgers, 2–1, becoming the National League's first 20–game winner of the season. His mound opponent was Ralph Branca, who pitched well enough to win in most situations, giving up only a two-run homer to Monte Irvin in the fourth. Bobby Thomson made a brilliant defensive play in the eighth that saved the game for Sal. After Duke Snider bounced a double off the scoreboard, Jackie Robinson smashed a triple that scored Snider and left Jackie dancing jubilantly on third base. With the count 1–1 on Andy Pafko, Durocher went to the mound for a visit with Maglie. The sight of the despised Giants manager in conference with the even more hated pitcher brought howls and jeers from the fans, accompanied by the waving of white handkerchiefs. A request over the public address system for the fans to refrain from their satiric salutes had the opposite effect, as even more white flags began waving. Pafko hit a hard grounder to Thomson at third. Bobby fielded the ball, and as Robinson flung himself back toward the base Thomson tagged him and staggered a few off-balance steps but threw accurately to Lockman, in time to get Pafko at first for the double play. Gil Hodges then fouled out to end the inning. Roscoe McGowan noted in the *Times* that the combination of Thomson, Irvin, and Maglie had "kept faint Giant pennant hopes alive."

At St. Louis Maglie lost the third game of a series on September 13. He was pitching on two days' rest, and the Cards knocked him out in the second inning, after he had given up five runs on two hits, issued two walks, and hit a batter. St. Louis went on to win, 6–4, and Sal's record dropped to 20–6. On September 16 the New Yorkers took a doubleheader from the Pirates. Jansen won the first game, 7–1, for his nineteenth victory, and a weary Maglie won the second, 6–4. Sal blew a 4–1 lead, but New York scored two in the top of the ninth to take the lead again. Sal yielded 12 hits in the game, and pitched out of trouble in the bottom of the ninth when the Bucs had the tying runs aboard. It was Sal's eleventh straight win over the Pirates and his twenty-first of the season. The day was cause for a modest celebration. The Giants had clinched second place, assuring them of their best finish since they won the pennant in 1937.

On September 17, when the Giants had an idle day, the Dodgers played the Cubs in Chicago, where they lost, 5–3. That day, the Dodgers lost more than a ball game when Turk Lown beaned Roy Campanella, a slip everyone agreed was accidental. Had his ear not cushioned the blow, there is a good chance the pitch would have permanently disabled or even killed the Dodger catcher. Instead, the seemingly indestructible Campy spent five days in the hospital and then returned to the lineup. The day after Campy's beaning the distressed Dodgers lost to the Cardinals, 7–1, as Ralph Branca dropped his fourth straight, and the Giants defeated the Reds, 6–5, to gain another game on the league leaders. The Giants had won five straight, and the Dodgers' lead now stood at three games. But then on September 20 the Giants lost to Cincinnati, and the Dodgers defeated the Cards. Once more the papers took up the cry that the Brooklyn bandwagon was rolling again, and the Brooklyn front office tempted fate by handing out applications for World Series tickets.

On September 21, with the Giants idle, the Dodgers took on the faded Phillies, expecting to make short work of the past year's champions. Instead,

Philadelphia shellacked the Dodgers, 9–6. The trouble began in the first inning when the Dodgers' rookie righthander Clem Labine found himself in a bases-loaded situation and gave up a grand slam to Puddin' Head Jones. What seemed to most observers nothing more than one bad pitch by a usually excellent young hurler turned out to have further ramifications. Labine had disobeyed an order from Dressen: the manager had told him to take a full windup when pitching to Jones, and Labine had refused, pitching from the stretch because he felt it improved his control. In the next inning the furious Dressen yanked Labine. It was time for him to come out, as he had just given up two more runs, but Dressen was not finished making an example of the cocky pitcher. For the rest of the season Labine might as well have not existed—no more starts, and just one relief appearance in the remaining games for a pitcher who had won four straight before his moment of defiance. "Charlie was a vindictive guy," Labine recalled. "He wanted to make sure I paid the penalty for not listening to what he said."[27] In the end it was the Dodgers who paid the penalty.

Starting on September 22 the Giants launched their final, amazing streak, taking every one of their last seven games. On the twenty-second Larry Jansen defeated the Braves for his twentieth win. The next day Maglie faced the Braves, who had often given him trouble, and beat them, 4–1. This was Sal's twenty-second win, the most victories for a Giant pitcher since Carl Hubbell had gained 22 in 1937. It was also Sal Maglie Day at the Polo Grounds (Figure 9). With his parents, his sister Carmen, his wife Kay, and a trainload of friends and fans from Niagara Falls proudly looking on, Sal received a Cadillac and numerous other gifts, while Kay received a watch and a diamond ring. In acknowledgment, Sal made a brief speech, thanking his friends and fans for their generosity, before taking the mound to stagger through to a victory.

On his first three pitches he gave up two singles, one of them to Sibbi Sisti, a good-natured utility player surprised to have gotten a hit off Sal so easily. From his perch on first base, Sisti called over to Maglie, "I suppose I'll never get a ride in that Cadillac now!" Sal was not amused. He whirled around, but instead of throwing the ball to first, he sent the base runner a filthy look. Sisti recalled, "I never got the ball out of the infield" for the rest of the game.[28] The Braves hit safely in seven of the nine innings, and in five frames they had two or more hits, for a total of 13. But Sal struck out seven and issued no walks. He managed to squirm out of each threatening situation, giving up only one run. The Giants gave Sal two insurance runs in the eighth, one of them on a triple by Bobby Thomson that scored Whitey Lockman. After the game Sal turned praise away from himself and onto Thomson: "Thomson is the big guy who's carried us on this surge," said Sal. "He's

9—Sal Maglie Day at the Polo Grounds, September 23, 1951. Sal receives a kiss from his wife Kay, while his proud mother and father and his sister Carmen look on. Photo: National Baseball Hall of Fame Library, Cooperstown/United Press/Corbis.

been a great third baseman and . . . his hitting has been wonderful."[29] Sal's struggles to win the game against the Braves led Barney Kremenko of the *Journal-American* to invent a new meaning for Sal's nickname. "Giving up that many hits and still sailing to victory is nothing new for the barber," observed Kremenko. "That's why they call him the barber, because he likes to shave his wins very close." The Giants won again the next day, to sweep the series. They were now 2 1/2 games behind the Dodgers, with four games left to play.

The next day, September 25, the Giants met the Phillies at Shibe Park, while the Dodgers played a doubleheader against the Braves in Boston. The Giants gave Jim Hearn a 3–0 lead, and he pitched shutout ball for his first six innings. When he weakened in the seventh Durocher called in Sal Maglie from the bullpen, even though The Barber had pitched a complete game just two days earlier. With two on and one out Sal persuaded Del Ennis to hit into a double play. He gave up only one hit in his two and two-thirds innings of relief and preserved the win for Hearn, who had left the mound in tears, thinking he had let his team down and deprived Maglie of a day of badly needed rest. As the Giants were winning their game against the Phillies, disasters befell the Dodgers in Boston. They lost the first game of their doubleheader to the Braves, 6–3, with a dog-tired Ralph Branca unable to make it out of the first inning. But even that defeat paled in comparison to the dreadful nightcap, a nocturnal Boston massacre where the Braves pounded Brooklyn to smithereens, and the Dodgers, playing like the nervous wrecks they had become, committed three errors, losing by the humiliating score of 14–2. The Dodgers' once invincible 13 1/2–game lead was down to one game.

On September 26 the Giants won again, pounding the Phillies, 10–1, and the Dodgers snapped out of their losing trance to trounce the Braves, 15–5. But in their eagerness to make up for their poor performance the previous day, the Dodgers made a mistake similar to the ones they had made by rubbing in the losses the Giants suffered at their hands earlier in the season. This time, the insult was on the field. With the Braves already badly beaten, Jackie Robinson stole home, just because he *could*. This infuriated Braves manager Tommy Holmes, who thought Robinson was "piling it on." "They may be sorry," Holmes growled after the game. "There was absolutely no need to put it on us that way. . . . They needed that run like a hole in the head. . . . It made my guys mad, and they're really gunning for them now."[30]

On September 27 the possibility of a tie between the Dodgers and the Giants, and the necessity of a league playoff, shifted from speculation to reality while the Dodgers were still in Boston. League president Ford Frick presided over a coin toss, to decide which team would have the home field advantage. Horace Stoneham represented his Giants, and Jack Collins, the Dodgers business manager, stood in for Walter O'Malley, who was out of town. Stoneham called the toss and when he lost, Collins chose Ebbets Field for the first playoff game; the Giants would host the second and the third, if the latter proved necessary. The Giants had two days off, September 27 and 28, before their final two games in Boston, while the Dodgers had games on both those days—and lost both of them. An angry Braves team was indeed gunning for the Dodgers. Although only 2,086 fans showed up on September 27, the Braves played as if before a packed house in the seventh game of the World Series, defeating the Dodgers, 4–3. With the game tied in the bottom of the eighth, Bob Addis led off against Preacher Roe with a single and raced to third on a single by Sam Jethroe. With Earl Torgesen at the plate Dressen pulled his infield in, wanting to keep Addis from scoring on a ground ball, and his decision seemed vindicated when Torgesen chopped an easy grounder to Robinson. Jackie threw to Campanella, who tagged Addis as he slid toward the plate. Although Campy believed he had Addis by a mile, the play was close, and plate umpire Frank Dascoli thought otherwise. He spread his arms in the "safe" sign. An incredulous Campanella blew sky-high, yelling "No! No! No!" and jumping up and down like a child having a tantrum. He slammed his glove to the ground, and Dascoli thumbed him out of the game, the first expulsion of his major league career. Furious Dodgers, cursing and shouting, poured out of their dugout, joined by angry infielders and a livid Preacher Roe. After order had been restored, and Rube Walker replaced Campanella, the inning ended without further scoring. When the Dodgers batted in the top of the ninth, Dressen sent up a pinch hitter for Walker, who would have batted in Campanella's spot. Reserve infielder Wayne Terwilliger grounded out. Then Pafko fanned for the final out, and the Dodgers had lost a vital game.

Did some chickens come home to roost here? The Dodgers had clashed repeatedly with Dascoli throughout the season. Whether the verbal abuse the umpire had taken from Brooklyn players had any impact on this particular decision can never be known, and naturally Dascoli never admitted to any bias. He described the play in detail to reporters after the game, insisting that Addis had avoided Campanella's tag. Writers and commentators discussed the play for days afterward, reaching the consensus that it was a judgement call and that Dascoli was an honest umpire. Photographs suggest that Dascoli's call was the correct one. Even worse than the call at the plate, as far as the Dodgers were concerned, was the expulsion of Campanella. Many writers, even some in Boston, agreed with the Dodgers that in such a close pennant race Dascoli should have been more tolerant. But Dascoli refused to give an inch. He reminded reporters that expulsion is automatic for glove-throwing, and added, "If you let them get away with that, the next thing they'd do is throw the center field bleachers at you."[31] The Dodgers compounded the problem after the game when a group of them pounded and kicked the door to the umpires' dressing room, splintering the wood and nearly breaking it down. The unsavory incident added anger, frustration, and sullen resentment to the burden of tension the Dodgers already carried. After all the hubbub they lost the next day's game to the Phillies by the same 4–3 score. If anyone was watching the American League race, they saw the Yankees clinch a tie for the pennant that same day, as Allie Reynolds pitched his second no-hitter of the season.

The Dodgers' once insurmountable lead over the Giants had dwindled to nothing. The rivals had identical 94–58 records, each with two games left to play. The Dodgers had two games against the Phillies at Shibe Park, and the Giants would play two against the Braves in Boston. To pitch the must-win game against the Braves on September 29 Durocher chose Sal Maglie. For the last time in regular season play Sal stood at the axis of event, facing the best the Braves could put up against him, their southpaw ace and future Hall of Famer Warren Spahn. Also in search of his twenty-third win, Spahn superstitiously wore teammate Johnny Logan's shirt that day, because it bore the number 23. In contrast, Sal harbored no superstitions. He wore no amulets and kissed no crosses. If he prayed, he kept his prayers to himself. Exhausted beyond anything a few days' rest could have cured (he had pitched a complete game on September 23 as well as two and two-thirds innings of relief on the 25th), and with his shoulder aching from an injury sustained during his relief stint in Philadelphia, Sal took the mound on a chilly, windy afternoon in Boston and accomplished what the *Herald Tribune* called "perhaps the finest pitching performance of his life." He shut out the Braves, 3–0, on five hits, all singles, and issued only one walk. Although the Giants scored three times, Willie Mays provided the only run Sal needed. In the second Willie walked and then stole second and third on Spahn, possessor of one of the best pick-off moves in the game. Mays scored on a single by Don Mueller. "How do I feel?" the usually taciturn Maglie responded to a reporter's question after the game. "How would you feel after the most important game you've ever won? Right now I'm the happiest guy in the world. . . . I've had better games, but this was the best clutch game. I had good control and felt strong all the way."[32]

For a few hours at least, the jubilant Giants were in first place, because the Dodgers' game in Philadelphia was an evening contest. Pitching on two days' rest in sudden-death pressure Don Newcombe came through again, hurling a brilliant five-hit shutout for his twentieth win as the Dodgers took the game, 5–0. The Dodgers and Giants remained in a tie for first place. On September 30, the final day of the season, the Giants' Larry Jansen defeated the Braves, 3–2, for his twenty-second win. When Jansen grew a little shaky in the sixth, Durocher sent Sal Maglie to the bullpen to warm up. Although Maglie had pitched a complete game the day before, Leo had more faith in him than in any of his relievers. Sal strode down to the bullpen in the dashing long black coat the Giants issued to each of their pitchers to keep them warm on chilly days. But the determined Jansen hung on to finish the game. Again the Giants had edged into first place, with their status dependent on how the Dodgers did in their final game with the Phillies. For a few heady hours it again looked like the Giants had the pennant, because in Philadelphia it was the seventh inning, and Brooklyn was down, 8–5. In a happy frame of mind, and with the champagne on ice if needed for a victory celebration, the Giants boarded the train for their return to New York. Giants broadcaster Russ Hodges listened to the Dodgers game via a telephone connection on the train (an unusual setup in that era) and related the play-by-play to Durocher and the coaches. While many players were enjoying dinner in the dining car, coach Herman Franks appeared with the astonishing news that the Dodgers had won their game with the Phillies, 9–8. Newcombe, relieving with *no* day's rest, had held off the Phils for five innings while the Dodgers clawed back into a game they won in the fourteenth inning on a home run by Jackie Robinson. The season was over, and the Dodgers and the Giants had finished in a dead heat. The pennant would be decided in a three-game playoff.

The Giants' "miracle" season was a combination of luck, skill, and determination, along with psychological and home field advantages (the latter discussed below). There was nothing supernatural about it, despite the dogged efforts of writer Thomas Kiernan to find some such component. In his book *The Miracle at Coogan's Bluff,* Kiernan attempted to find a magical or miraculous component, some quasi-religious dimension, to the Giants' pennant victory, even going so far as to track down the principal players more than 20 years later and hinting to them that perhaps God was a New York Giants fan. Sal Maglie refused to have anything to do with such an explanation—it would be fair to say that Sal did not have a mystical bone in his body. When pressed by Kiernan, he merely shrugged and stated, "It just happened."[33]

At the Axis of Event, Part 2

The Playoff, the Pennant, and the World Series

10

"Now the playoff comes. For the next few days . . . even the grimmest of worldwide news will have an overshadowing rival for attention in the whirl and clash of the great American game."

New York Times editorial, October 1, 1951

Of the two tired teams that finished the season tied for first place, the Dodgers were in worse shape than the Giants. They had watched the Giants gain on them, day by day, like the pursuing monster in a horror movie. During the 1951 season a film called "The Thing" was a hit in New York. "Astonishing! Fire can't burn it! Bullets can't kill it!" shouted an ad in the *Times*. For the Dodgers, the Giants were The Thing on spikes. While the Giants were winning their last seven games, Brooklyn lost four of their last seven and pulled out a tie only with superhuman efforts. Both teams reached the finish line physically exhausted, but the Dodgers were also emotionally drained in a way that the exhilarated Giants were not.

With almost biblical starkness the Dodgers' foolish pride had preceded their fall. Instances of arrogant behavior had antagonized other teams, motivating them to play even harder against Brooklyn, and it earned them the animosity of at least one umpire. They carried another burden as well. Although the presence of Jackie Robinson had gained the Dodgers black fans across the country, they were unpopular just about everywhere except in their home borough of Brooklyn. It often comes as a surprise to twenty-first-century fans to learn that the 1950s Dodgers were not as popular in their own time as they are today. In a testament to the power of words, the image of the Brooklyn Dodgers of the early 1950s was transformed by Roger Kahn, whose book *The Boys of Summer* enshrined the team in romantic legend. With the exception of Shakespeare, few poets have had lines of theirs become recognizable figures of speech, but thanks to Kahn, "the boys of summer," a phrase from a poem by Dylan Thomas, entered the lexicon of baseball as a synonym for the beloved and admired Brooklyn Dodgers of the early 1950s.[1]

The reality was both different and more complex. Many teams and their fans harbored a special dislike for the Dodgers that went well beyond loyalty to their own squads. The Dodgers were "the team everyone loved to hate," according to sportswriter Jack Lang, who covered the team as a young reporter in 1951.[2] In addition to their swagger and arrogance, there was another and even more important aspect of the Dodgers that drew hostility to them: Donald Honig called it "the Robinson factor." Although an eloquent advocate of Jackie Robinson, Honig acknowledged that Robinson's combative personality and aggressive play earned the Dodgers more than their share of enemies. Not even the vilest ethnic slurs directed at players of any other descent carried the historic freight of rage, fear, and hatred compacted into the insults hurled at Robinson during his first years in the majors, and he later took a fierce delight in returning those insults in kind, as well as through his breakneck style of play. Racial prejudices and animosities remained high among the reasons why many whites, both on the playing fields and in the stands, wanted to see the Dodgers defeated. Half a century later, former catcher Walker Cooper recalled the "racial feeling" the Dodgers inspired: "People today tend to forget that it was the Dodgers who had broken the so-called gentleman's agreement that was keeping blacks out of the majors. Rickey brought in Robinson and the rest of the league formed strong feelings about it. Those feelings—blaming the Dodgers for breaking the color line—were still lingering in 1951."[3] Many owners, managers, and players on other teams, as well as fans across a country where patterns of segregation remained largely intact, viewed the Dodgers with hostility and resentment rather than admiration for their role as pioneers of integration. In the south, announcer Nat Albright recalled, "You had whites praying for Big Newk and Jackie Robinson to lose."[4] All that, as well as a final month from hell, lay across the Dodgers' backs as the playoff began. The Giants were tired but happy, still riding the emotional high that their final, thrilling surge of victories had given them.

THE PLAYOFF—THE FIRST TWO GAMES

With the tie between the Giants and the Dodgers, all three New York teams finished in first place. This had never occurred before, and it would never happen again. In addition to the Dodgers and the Giants, who were about to extend their battle for the National League pennant into a playoff, the Yankees had clinched their third straight pennant in the American League a few days earlier. As if nothing of importance were going on anywhere else in the country or the world, New York threw itself into the final days of the baseball season. So many competing stations prepared to broadcast the playoff that listeners had a wide choice. Almost everybody in the metropolitan area owned at least one radio, and many also owned a television. American Telephone and Telegraph had completed a transcontinental cable a few months before the playoffs, allowing for nationwide broadcasts. In 1951 the Dodgers experimented with color television of sorts, sending out color wheels to 10,000 viewers so they could tint the images on their screens. Columnist Red Smith claimed to have found the color reproduction "only faintly phony." Dodger manager Dressen's white uniform, Smith insisted, looked "as immaculate as a prom queen's gown," until he stepped onto the grass, whereupon "he turned green, like cheap jewelry."[5]

Since the Dodgers had won the toss to decide where the opening game would be played and had chosen Ebbets Field, the playoff began on the Dodgers' home turf. Although writers debated why the Dodgers chose to open at home, nobody believed Brooklyn business manager Jack Collins had made the decision on his own. He must have consulted Dressen, who knew the Dodgers had beaten the Giants in nine of 11 contests held at Ebbets Field that season. Because the World Series was set to begin on October 4, there was no time to give the competing National League teams a day to rest. The regular season had ended on September 30, and the playoff began the next day, October 1.

New York City and Brooklyn came to a near halt. Newspapers filled their pages with playoff features. The *Times* ran an ad for televisions with a picture of Gil Hodges swinging a bat. The product was the (in retrospect) ominously named Black-Daylite Television. At the New York Stock Exchange the ticker-tape intermingled play-by-play with the Dow Jones averages. In the workplace, absenteeism soared and productivity plummeted. Despite the short notice, the first playoff game attracted a near-sellout crowd to Ebbets Field, with millions more glued to home radios or walking around with transistors pressed to their ears, parked in front of televisions at home or in neighborhood bars and barbershops, or standing in front of the windows of appliance stores where owners had placed televisions. Even inmates of the cities' prisons received permission to hover around their cell block radios. The weather was sunny and in the mid-70s, perfect for Dodgers devotees to visit their shrine, the site of the secular religion that united the diverse populations of Brooklyn in a single, fervent faith. As Alan Lelchuck recalled in his memoir *Brooklyn Boy*, "Ebbets Field demanded more devotion, afforded more pleasure, struck more pain, than any church or synagogue in the borough."[6]

In the ongoing battle of the managers between Durocher and Dressen, Leo had one apparent advantage. Thanks to the two days off that the Giants had enjoyed during the last week, he had a well-rested first-line pitcher, Jim Hearn, whose previous outing had been five days earlier. But Hearn was not as sound as he seemed. He had strained a ligament in his left side and had not told Durocher, although he confided in his catcher, Wes Westrum, and trainer Doc Bowman. At the park Bowman gave Hearn a broiling hot salve that hurt his skin so much it blotted out the pain of the injured ligament. The Dodgers' side of the pitching equation consisted mostly of a bleary collection of worn-out hurlers. Newcombe had pitched 14 2/3 innings in the previous two days. Overworked Carl Erskine and Preacher Roe had sore arms. An exhausted Ralph Branca had lost his previous five games. The Dodgers' one sound hurler, Clem Labine, was still in Dressen's doghouse. Having limited his options, Dressen named Branca, an odd choice, since Branca had also started the first 1946 playoff game and lost it.

Both Hearn and Branca pitched well in the opener, but the Giants' bats made the difference. Andy Pafko touched Hearn for a solo home run in the second inning, giving the Dodgers a narrow lead that lasted only until the top of the fourth when Branca nicked Irvin with a brushback and Bobby Thomson followed with a home run over the left field wall for two runs. It was Thomson's thirty-first of the season, a career best for him, and would stand for exactly two days as the most important hit of his career. Monte Irvin gave Hearn an insurance run with a solo homer in the eighth, making the score 3–1. The Dodgers' biggest deficit was the absence of a healthy Roy Campanella. The Dodger catcher had pulled a thigh muscle during a slide in the Dodgers' final game in Philadelphia, and he limped through the first playoff game half-crippled, with the injured area numbed by a shot of novocaine. He had no hits and grounded into one of the four double plays the Giants turned, snuffing each of the Dodgers' potential rallies. All the runs came on homers. Of the 18 gopher balls Branca gave up in 1951, 10 had been hit by New York Giants. After the game Branca remained stoical. "I pitched well," he stated. "We just didn't score enough runs."[7] Some Dodger fans took the loss with less grace than Branca displayed. While waiting at a Brooklyn Red Cross center to donate blood, a group of Dodger faithful watched the game on TV. In their midst sat a lone Giants rooter named Harry Friedman. When the Giants won, his taunts led the Dodger rooters to urge the nurse to drain all of Mr. Friedman's blood.[8] Hearn pitched the game of his life, overcoming nerves and ignoring his physical pain. Like Newcombe, he had sometimes been labeled as a pitcher incapable of "winning the big ones," but he had refuted that claim with a superb clutch performance. "He wore his guts on his sweaty right arm," wrote the *Mirror*'s Harold Weisman, employing an image a more alert editor would have killed.

Dressen and Durocher remained cagey about their pitching choices for the second game. Durocher would say only that he was still deciding between Sal Maglie and Sheldon Jones. That would seem an easy decision, given Maglie's 23–6 record in comparison with Jones' record of 6–10, but Leo now had a one-game cushion, so he could afford to give the bone-weary Maglie, who had pitched a complete game two days earlier, another day of rest, keeping him in reserve in case a third game was needed. If the Dodgers had won the first game, it would have been a different situation, and Maglie, no matter how tired, would certainly have gotten the call. Dressen indicated he would choose either his seasoned veteran Carl Erskine, or rookie Clem Labine. Unlike Durocher, he had little choice. Preacher Roe had pitched three days earlier and was complaining of arm pain. Newcombe was still recovering from his marathon 14 2/3 innings in two days. Branca had just pitched a complete game loss the previous day. Erskine had lost a game during the Philadelphia series and had pitched short relief two days before. Reliever Clyde King was sidelined with tendinitis. That left the most obvious choice, Clem Labine, but using Labine required that Dressen fetch the pitcher from his doghouse, where he had been sitting since the manager sent him there on September 21. Dressen at last recalled his exiled pitcher and handed him the ball for the second game. Durocher decided to go with Jones and save Sal Maglie. Just in case there should be a sudden-death, absolutely must-win third playoff game the next day, Durocher wanted his money pitcher ready.

Dressen's decision proved what a brilliant manager he was—in his own eyes. The healthy, well-rested Labine strolled to the mound and spun a six-hit shutout. How many games he might have won during the later part of the regular season, when Dressen was marching his weary quartet of Roe, Branca, Erskine, and Newcombe to the mound day after day, will never be known, but Labine's performance in the second playoff game suggests that the outcome of the pennant race would have been different had he pitched more often. Dodger hitters jumped on Jones and drove him out in the third. Spencer and Corwin followed, yielding eight more runs. Meanwhile, the Giants hit like they had holes in their bats and fielded like they had glue or grease in their gloves, committing a slovenly total of five errors. The Dodgers won, 10–0. Afterward Dressen offered reporters his usual "I-ful," taking credit for the win. Leo Durocher gave Labine credit. "The kid pitched a great game," The Lip rasped. But tomorrow, he warned the Dodgers, things would be different because "Sal the Barber will be shaving."[9]

THE "PLAYOFF-PAYOFF" AND THE PENNANT

October 3, 1951, was an eventful day. The United States government revealed that the Soviet Union had set off its second atomic bomb in two years, and America's monopoly in nuclear weaponry was gone for good. Fighting raged on in Korea, and the French reported a push by communist insurgents in Indochina, a region later to become better known as Vietnam. Readers of the *Daily News* could follow a scandal involving the murder of socialite Dorothea Hooker by her ex-bellhop boyfriend, and the tale of Texas oil heir Sheppard W. King, who declared himself more interested in marrying one of Egyptian king Farouk's former mistresses than in inheriting his mother's millions. But crowding other events in the headlines of papers not only in New York City but across the country the next day was the biggest baseball story ever: the New York Giants' come-from-behind victory on Bobby Thomson's home run in the bottom of the ninth in the final game of the National League playoff. Even the staid *Times* headlined the game on the front page in the same size type as that announcing the Russian nuclear blast. As far as baseball fans were concerned, Thomson's blast was the more memorable one.

Nobody wanted to admit to nervousness before the big game, least of all Sal Maglie. After the Giants' defeat by Clem Labine and Durocher's selection of him as the next day's do-or-die starter, Sal sat around nonchalantly in the clubhouse, sporting his favorite locker room attire and accessory—his bare skin and a big cigar. When a reporter asked him if he thought he would sleep well that night, Sal responded, "Why not? Who's worried?"[10] He had already beaten the Dodgers five times that season, so why not one more time? Years later he revealed that his pre-game words had been mostly bravura; in reality he was too tired to feel nervous. "I felt dead," he admitted, "and I didn't expect to last very long."[11] A picture of Maglie taken on September 29, minutes after he had completed his twenty-third and most important win of the 1951 season, revealed a man dazed with exhaustion (Figure 10). The photographer caught Sal in a candid moment, bare-headed and mopping his dripping brow in the crook of his right elbow. His eyes are wide and glassy, his jaw slack, his black curls glued to his head with sweat. He looks ready to drop. And yet, four days later, on October 3, Sal was back

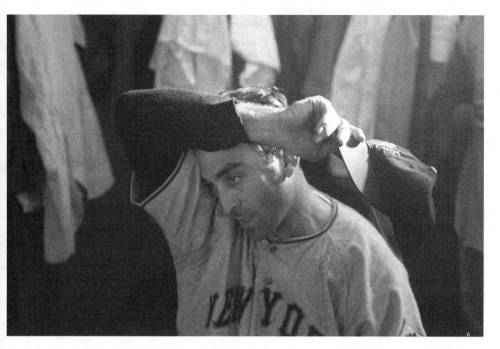

10—An exhausted Sal Maglie mops his brow after winning his 23rd game of the 1951 season, on September 29, against the Boston Braves. His 3–0 shutout assured the Giants of a tie for the pennant, and made the subsequent three-game playoff necessary. Photo: George Silk/Getty Images.

at the axis of event, on the mound in what many consider the single most dramatic game in baseball history: the third and final contest of the 1951 playoff between the Dodgers and the Giants.

None of the players stayed out late the night before the game. After a dinner in a Manhattan restaurant the Maglies retired to their apartment on West End Avenue in Manhattan, while players whose families lived out of town returned to their rooms at the Concourse Plaza Hotel. Sal had long ago learned to cope with the tensions of baseball. The tremulous, emotion-wracked boy of 15 years ago had given way to a man with iron nerves, who could coax his body into relaxation at night and whose game face gave nothing away. Two other men who would have key roles in the next day's game were both bachelors in their mid-20s who still lived with their parents, and neither were playboy night owls. Ralph Branca spent the night with his parents at their home in Mount Vernon, and Bobby Thomson turned in early at his parents' home on Staten Island. Thomson had no anxieties about the upcoming game, and Branca, who had pitched a complete game two days before, did not think Dressen would call on him if Newk ran into trouble. And so to bed.

October 3 in New York City was humid, in the 70s, and heavily overcast. Maybe the threat of rain kept attendance down, or maybe it was Giants fans giving up hope in droves after their team's 10–0 drubbing the day before, or many people feeling that so many other people would be trying to obtain tickets that the effort to get into the final game would be frustrating and futile. Whatever the reasons, there were only 34,320 paid admissions, which left the Polo Grounds about one-third empty. Although Russ Hodges' famous, thrice-repeated call, "The Giants win the pennant!" at the game's end was recorded by, of all people, a Dodger fan who taped the bottom of the ninth, hoping to preserve Hodges' anguish at the moment of a Brooklyn victory, no recording of the game by any of the local troubadours—Hodges and his partner Ernie Harwell, or Dodgers announcer Red Barber—exists. The only complete record of the third playoff game is that of Gordon McClendon, whose account the largest number of fans heard, since it was broadcast throughout the country on the 520 stations of the Liberty Broadcasting Network.[12] In the account that follows, excerpts from McClendon's call of the game appear in italics.

> *What happened before, even the Giants' closing rush from 13 1/2 out, will be forgotten when the final decision is rendered at the Polo Grounds this afternoon. Twenty years from now the fans will be talking about this afternoon's hero as yet unknown, but the man and the hour are about to meet. And if there's a goat, his name will echo down the corridors of time.*

On the mound in the top of the first, Sal wore his malevolent game-day scowl. He looked blue-bearded and sallow, with exhaustion adding to the sinister shadows around his eyes. He started by striking out the Dodgers' lead-off man, right fielder Carl Furillo. Although Maglie had never been able to intimidate the Dodgers' number two hitter, shortstop and field captain Pee Wee Reese, he gave it a try, throwing two brushback pitches, but Reese outwaited Sal, and the pitcher walked him. With Reese on, Sal walked Duke Snider. Even before Maglie's old adversary Jackie Robinson stepped to the plate, Larry Jansen began limbering up in the Giants bullpen. Jackie wasted no time—he smacked Sal's first pitch for a sharp single that brought Reese racing around to score and moved Snider to second. While the crowd roared in a frenzy of anguish and joy, Westrum and Durocher made their first visit to the mound, where Sal seemed to be faltering badly. But Durocher was not ready to give up on him, and he rewarded his manager's confidence by persuading the next batter, left fielder Andy Pafko, to hit a weak grounder to third. Thomson stepped on the bag to force Snider for the second out, but his throw to first was not in time to turn the double play. With Robinson twitching around on second, and Pafko on first, Sal faced another dangerous hitter, first baseman Gil Hodges, but he hit a weak pop-up along the third base line that Thomson gathered in for the third out. The damage could have been worse, but Sal had started poorly and left the mound with the Giants down 1–0. Don Newcombe, even less rested than Maglie, strode to the hill for the Dodgers. At six-feet-four and 225 pounds, the fireballing righthander towered over teammates and opponents alike. The Giants' lead-off hitter, second baseman Eddie Stanky, almost worked Newk for a walk, but instead hit a weak fly to left that Pafko caught. Alvin Dark turned Newcombe's first pitch into a sky-high pop that Billy Cox camped under and snagged near the mound. Then right fielder Don Mueller whacked a hard drive to left that Pafko nabbed, and the inning was over.

Sal opened the second inning in his time-honored way, with a high-inside fastball that backed Dodger third baseman Billy Cox away from the plate. Making good on his own claim that two successive brushbacks are better than one, because the second informs the batter that the first was no accident, Sal pushed Cox back again. On the third pitch Billy hit a soft one-hopper back to Maglie, who threw to first for the out. Rube Walker, replacing the injured Campanella as catcher, followed Cox, and Sal struck him out swinging. Newcombe, up next, lifted a high pop to Thomson that retired the side. In the bottom of the second left fielder Monte Irvin smacked the ball into the hole at short, where Reese scooped it up and fired to first for the out. The next batter, first baseman Whitey Lockman, lined a single into right field. Now Bobby Thomson came to the plate for his first at bat. He had failed to turn a double play in the top of the first and was eager to make up for his fielding lapse. He drilled a line drive down the left field line, good for a double, he was sure. Head down, arms pumping, he rounded first and headed for second. What he failed to notice in his eagerness for the extra base was that Lockman had seen the strong-armed Pafko field the ball and had decided not to try for third. The delighted Dodgers also saw what was happening. Reese took the throw from Pafko, and the grinning Brooklyn infielders caught the mortified Thomson in a run-down as he made a desperate effort to scramble back to first, where Hodges tagged him out. Thomson had committed the kind of bone-head blunder that would have embarrassed a Little Leaguer. After Thomson slunk back to the dugout, Willie Mays came to the plate and hit a long drive to left that took Andy Pafko back to the wall, where he hauled it in for the third out. After two innings the score remained Dodgers one, Giants nothing.

The day had grown so dark that at 2:04 p.m., just before the third inning began, the lights at the Polo Grounds were turned on. Sal wiped his brow as he faced Furillo again. The Brooklyn right fielder hit a weak bouncer back to the mound, and Maglie made a leisurely, contemptuous toss to Lockman for the out. Then Reese fouled out to Lockman, and Snider struck out to end the inning. After his shaky start Sal had retired eight in a row. Westrum opened the bottom of the third by drawing a walk, and Sal came to the plate with orders to lay down a sacrifice bunt. He laid one down, but directly in front of Newcombe, who pounced on it, whirled, and threw to second. Westrum barreled into Reese, who practically did a somersault, but held onto the ball for the force-out.

> *Newcombe made the ballplayer's play. If he had not made it good, if Westrum had been safe at second base, on what was a very close call down there, well, there might have been some more heads rolling as a result of this ball game. But Newcombe, taking the bit in his teeth, went for the ballplayer's play, the one with which you live or die, and got his man at second, 1 to 6.*

Stanky, up next, hit a sharp grounder to third that Billy Cox backhanded, then wheeled and whipped to Robinson at second. Jackie gunned the ball to first for an inning-ending double play. Three innings gone and the score remained Brooklyn one, New York nothing.

As Robinson stepped to the plate to open the top of the fourth, Sal greeted him with a strike, then brushed him back. He ran the count to 3–1 before Robinson hit a sharp liner that zipped over Sal's head. Stanky nearly lost it but recovered in time to throw Jackie out by a step. With one ball and one strike on Pafko the Dodger left fielder hit a rifle shot down the left field line that curved foul by no more than a few inches—a bullet that Sal dodged. He struck out Pafko and then disposed of Hodges on a weak bouncer to Thomson at third. Sal had retired 11 in a row since Robinson's one-run single in the first inning. The old Maglie magic had reasserted itself, and the Dodgers seemed unable to touch The Barber. In their half of the fourth the Giants failed to do Newcombe any damage, although they came close. After Dark hit a harmless pop fly that Robinson gathered in, Mueller smacked a sizzling line drive down the first base line that Hodges nabbed with a high-leaping catch. Irvin followed with a grounder to Cox, who threw him out easily. Still Dodgers 1, Giants 0.

> *These two teams struggling down through the years, playing shining, stumbling, faltering, blazing, shining again. Finally coming down here to the last day when only one game matters, when you can forget everything else, this is the only one.*

The fifth inning began with an oddity, when Billy Cox bunted Maglie's first pitch down the first base line, and Sal's throw to first hit Cox on the leg. The bunt counted as a single. Sal cut down the next batter, Rube Walker, with a strikeout. Newcombe then rapped the ball to the right, where Lockman backhanded it, and threw to Dark for the force-out at second. Next came Furillo. Sal had retired him easily in his previous two at bats, and this time the Dodgers right fielder was overeager. He swung hard on the first pitch, one of Sal's clever curves, nicking a weak, drooping liner that Irvin had to run hard for, but he made the catch to end the Dodgers' half of the inning. Lockman opened the bottom of the fifth by grounding out, Reese to Hodges, with Pee Wee fielding a grounder that took a wicked hop. Bobby Thomson stepped to the plate, already the goat of the game due to his base-running blunder in the second inning. He swung on Newcombe's first pitch, sending a whistling grounder past third base and into left field. With nobody on to impede his progress this time, he tore around first and dove into second with a headlong slide for a double. In the Dodger bullpen Erskine and Branca began warming up, but Newcombe overpowered rookie Willie Mays with fastballs and struck him out swinging. Dressen journeyed to the mound to consult with Newk, and they decided to walk the next batter, Wes Westrum, in order to get to Maglie. Dressen concluded that Durocher, no matter how badly he wanted a run, would not take his ace pitcher out for a pinch hitter. Dressen guessed right. Sal, hitting .155, came to the plate and chopped a dribbling grounder to Reese, who threw to Hodges for the third out. Still Dodgers one, Giants nothing.

If you could write the script for this one, how would you write it? If you were a Hollywood screenwriter . . . and Metro Goldwyn Mayer came to you and said, "Write me a script for a baseball picture; I want it to be the most thrilling baseball picture that you can imagine." What would you write? Why bother? Why not just copy the 1951 National League race? Wouldn't that be better than anything the most imaginative scenario writer could possibly drum up? This is the end of plots.

Sal began the top of the sixth working slowly, hoarding his strength, giving himself as much time between pitches as the umpires would allow him. He struck out Reese with a sharp curve over the outside corner, as the Dodger shortstop stood gaping in astonishment. Snider followed with a single, and that brought Jackie Robinson to the plate again as the stands resounded with the boos of Giants fans. With a 2–0 count on Jackie, a moment when the pitcher is almost obligated to come in with a strike, Maglie and Westrum instead went for a pitchout. They had scoped the Dodgers' strategy correctly—Snider was on his way to second in an attempted steal, and Westrum's peg from the plate caught him by 20 feet. But then Maglie lost Jackie, issuing him a walk, Sal's first base on balls since his wobbly first inning. Nothing unnerved Maglie more than Jackie Robinson dancing on first base, in constant motion, up and down, feinting toward second, scurrying back to the bag, never letting up for a moment. With Pafko at the plate, Sal scuffed around, glowering over his shoulder at the jiggling Robinson, before finally spinning and throwing to first. With two strikes on him Pafko ended the threat by hitting a high fly to Lockman. Sal had wormed his way out of another jam. Not appearing at all tired, Newcombe dispatched the Giants in the bottom of the sixth. Stanky hit a short blooper to left that Andy Pafko raced in and corralled. Following him, Dark hit a stinging drive toward third that looked like a sure hit, maybe a double, but Billy Cox speared it, and threw to first for the out, his second such save of the afternoon. Mueller then hit a pop fly to Hodges, and the inning was over, with Newcombe spending a mere five and a half minutes on the mound. The big righthander seemed to be growing stronger as the innings passed, keeping a tight hold on his one-run lead.

Sal had only a brief spot of trouble with the Dodgers in the top of the seventh. After Maglie retired Hodges on a pop-up behind the plate that Westrum nabbed, and Cox on a grounder to Dark, Rube Walker smacked a single to left. Just as Durocher had elected to send Maglie to the plate with a man on base, rather than going for the run via a pinch hitter, so Dressen did the same, sending Newcombe to bat with Walker on base. The Dodger pitcher hit a sharp ground ball to Stanky, who bobbled it briefly before throwing to first in time to get Newcombe, who gave up halfway down the line and headed for the mound, to a chorus of boos from fans who thought he should have run it out. But Newk knew he had no chance for a hit, and, like Maglie, was doing whatever he could to hoard his dwindling energies. Irvin opened the Giants' half of the seventh with a double. Pafko threw to second in an attempt to nail the fleet Irvin, but the throw was wild, and Jackie Robinson, ranging far over to the first base side of second, dove for the ball and came up with it, preventing Irvin from going to third. The next batter was Lockman, who bunted, a slow roller up the third base line. Newcombe dashed in for the ball and once again made the split-second choice to try and nip the lead runner, but this time he failed. Irvin had been off at the crack of the bat, and he beat Newcombe's throw to third. The next batter, Bobby Thomson, lifted a long fly to deep center. Snider caught it for the first out, but Irvin tagged up and came home as Giants fans roared in delight. The second inning's goat had just tied the game, 1–1. So great was the fans' joy, they hardly noticed that Willie Mays, up next, hit into an inning-ending double play.

Sal's eighth inning on the mound began with another triumph over Carl Furillo, but it was a costly one. The Dodger right fielder had done nothing with Maglie's deliveries all afternoon, and each easy out he made left him more determined to get a hit off his inscrutable adversary. He took a savage swing on Sal's first pitch, and sent a screaming, chest-high drive straight back at the pitcher. Pure instinct served Sal as he raised his glove to his chest in self-defense and snagged the ball. Had he not, it would have splintered his breastbone. One out, but Sal was shaken by the close call. Durocher, gauging the power of Furillo's drive and the sheer luck involved in stopping it, signaled for Jansen to begin warming up again. Reese, up next, smacked Sal's first pitch over Stanky's head and into right field for a single. With Snider coming to the plate, Thomson trotted over from third, and Westrum lumbered out to the mound, and then in came Dark, and finally Durocher joined the group. The real purpose of the meeting was less to discuss strategy than to allow the shaken pitcher time to pull himself together. Although Alvin Dark no longer recalls what they talked about, he remarked, "I can't imagine we were sayin' much, because with Durocher out there, *he* was doin' all the sayin'. The only thing I can think of is that we were tellin' Sal to slow down, take it easy, take a deep breath—things like that."[13] To give Sal even more time to recover, Westrum made a slow trip to the dugout and disappeared inside. Announcer Gordon McClendon speculated that the Giants were about to send in a new catcher, but apparently Westrum's excuse was that he needed to make some intimate adjustments of his catcher's paraphernalia, of the sort best not performed on national television. More time ticked past.

> *Throttling pressure. One of these two teams is at death's door in the National league in the eighth inning and we still don't know who it is. Still don't know. Would you care to hazard a guess? I wouldn't. I wouldn't have the vaguest idea. As far as I'm concerned, this one is completely in the laps of the gods.*

If all these time-consuming maneuvers had been made in order to give Sal an opportunity to calm down, they had little effect. Westrum had scarcely reassumed his crouch when Snider smacked Maglie's first offering into the hole, just beyond Stanky's reach, for a base hit. Reese tore into third, well ahead of the throw. With runners at first and third and one out, Jackie Robinson strode to the plate, his batting average at .337 and his first-inning single responsible for the only run Maglie had given up. Sal's first offering to Robbie was a ball, and then his second, incredibly, was a wild pitch, a low curve in the dirt. Of all the terrible times to uncork a wild pitch, this was it. Westrum tore after the ball, Reese raced in to score, and Snider, churning all the way from first, reached third ahead of Westrum's throw. The Barber had slashed himself with his own razor, and Dodger fans could smell his blood. Howling pandemonium engulfed the grandstands, and grew even louder as Sal, after another visit from Durocher, walked Robinson intentionally. Burning with disgust and rage at himself, Maglie slammed down the rosin bag in a rare display of temper. In the warm, humid air, evil-smelling dust rose from it to assail his nostrils, adding nausea to his misery. Sal claimed that the smell of rosin made him feel like gagging,[14] and that sometimes he had to struggle to keep from vomiting while standing in the most exposed place on the diamond. What happened next was enough to make any pitcher lose his lunch.

After Sal had gotten a called strike on Pafko, the Dodger left fielder beat a grounder down the third base line for what looked like an easy out, but Thomson failed to field the ball cleanly. It went for a scratch single that drove in Snider with the Dodgers' second run of the inning and sent Robinson to third. After Hodges popped to Thomson for the second out, Sal faced Billy Cox. The Dodger third baseman hit a bullet toward Thomson. Unable to get a glove on the ball the beleaguered third baseman tried to block it with his chest, but it shot past him into left field, and Robinson came home with the third run of the inning. The scorekeepers charged Thomson with an error. Sal disposed of Walker on a grounder to Stanky for the third out, but as he trudged off the mound the score stood at Dodgers 4, Giants 1, going into the bottom of the eighth.

With the Giants down to their last six outs, Durocher began sending up pinch hitters. He replaced Westrum with Bill Rigney, and Newcombe, still throwing smoke, struck him out on three pitches. Sal's bottom spot in the batting order came next, but there was no chance Leo would let Maglie take his turn this time. In his place he sent up Hank Thompson, who had been recalled late in the season. As Thompson walked to the plate Sal was officially out of the game. If the Giants pulled ahead in that inning, Sal could still be the winning pitcher, but if they did not, his last chance to emerge as the victor would disappear, although the game was still his to lose. Thompson hit a grounder to Hodges, who backhanded it and made a perfect throw to Newcombe, who covered first. Stanky, up next, sent off a futile little pop-up that Reese hauled in for out number three. Newcombe had never looked better, blowing away three Giants batters in under five minutes. Score still 4–1, Dodgers.

As the final act of the drama opened on the field, Maglie had already made his exit. After his disastrous top of the eighth and his removal in the bottom of the inning for a pinch hitter, Sal did not linger. He joined his teammates as they took the field for the top of the ninth, but instead of walking to the mound, he continued on across the outfield grass, traversing that endless swathe of turf on what Giants pitchers called the Death March. At first, while he was still on the field, the fans failed to notice him, but as he ascended the stairs to the clubhouse they spotted the disgraced pitcher. A few applauded, some in tribute to his strong but futile effort, others no doubt jubilant Dodger fans glad to see Sal gone. But nearly drowning out the scattered hand-claps came a chorus of boos from angry and disappointed Giants fans, so loud that radio announcer Gordon McClendon, at the opposite end of the cavernous Polo Grounds, heard and commented on it. Sal left the game having given up four runs on eight hits in eight innings of work; he had issued four walks, struck out six, and thrown a wild pitch—not a terrible job, but nowhere near good enough for the occasion. For once, Maglie had failed to come through when it counted.

Whether, late in the game, Newcombe believed he was reaching the end of his strength, and told his teammates so, remains one of those curiously uncertain stories. Some writers assert that Newk had begun complaining of fatigue as early as the seventh inning and that he repeatedly asked to be taken out of the game. According to these accounts, Robinson and Reese pleaded with him to stay in, with Robinson refusing to believe the pitcher's complaints, and screaming, "Don't give me that shit! Go out there and pitch til your fucking arm falls off!"[15] Other teammates, among them Snider, Pafko, and Dick Williams, have insisted that Newcombe never complained or asked to be replaced, and the pitcher himself denies all such stories.

For the top of the ninth the Giants inserted a new battery. Larry Jansen and Cuban-born catcher Ray Noble—pronounced NO-blay, as McClendon informed his radio audience—replaced Maglie and Westrum, who had left the game for pinch hitters. Dodger fans gave Newcombe a loud round of cheers as he came to the plate to lead off the inning, but he grounded out to Stanky on Jansen's second pitch. Furillo, impotent all day at the plate, hit Jansen's first pitch for a weak grounder that Dark fielded for the second out. Then Reese hit Jansen's first toss for a long drive to center that Mays gathered in, and the Dodgers were down on four pitches. The Brooklyn half of the ninth had lasted less than four minutes, the shortest half-inning so far, and the score remained 4–1 in the Dodgers' favor.

Whatever Newcombe himself or anyone else believed then or believes today about the big pitcher's condition when he took the mound in the bottom of the ninth, several facts remain beyond dispute: he had pitched a Herculean total of 22 2/3 innings in four days, every one of them under the most extreme pressure, and during that stretch he had given up exactly one run. He had hurled a complete game shutout on September 29, thrown 5 2/3 innings of scoreless relief the very next day, and now, three days later, had pitched eight innings and given up only a single run. If he was exhausted as he came out to pitch the ninth, he had every right to be.

Alvin Dark led off for the Giants in the bottom of the ninth, and Newcombe's first pitch to him caught the outside corner for strike one, another bullet, looking even faster in the murky late-afternoon light. But on the next pitch Dark reached out and hit the ball to the right side, a grounder that just made it past Hodges, squirting off his glove as he dove for it, and Dark was on with a single. Giants rooters, many of whom had begun leaving the stadium, paused to watch. Erskine and Branca started throwing again in the Dodgers bullpen. The next batter was Don Mueller, nicknamed "Mandrake the Magician" for his ability to follow Wee Willie Keeler's advice to "hit 'em where they ain't." As he approached the plate Mueller noticed something curious: Hodges was playing close to the bag, holding Dark on, although he was no threat to steal and represented an insignificant run. If Hodges had been playing further off the bag he would have been in a better position to field a ground ball, and perhaps start a double play. Instead, Mueller hit a seeing-eye single into right field, through the hole left by Hodges' attentiveness to Dark, who raced to third. After a short conference on the mound that included Dressen and the entire Dodgers infield, Newcombe reared back, and with one last spurt of energy he induced Monte Irvin to pop out to Hodges. Giants fans' cheering turned to groans, and Dodger fans sighed with relief, but not for long. Lockman stepped to the plate, and hit a double to left that had Mueller digging for third and scored Dark, bringing the tally to 4–2. Below the shrill cheers of Giants fans another sound could be heard—the low, communal moaning of Dodger rooters. At this exquisitely inopportune moment an announcement from the Dodgers office came over the loudspeaker in the press box: "Attention, press. World Series credentials for Ebbets Field can be picked up at six o'-clock at the Biltmore Hotel."[16]

Now came a strange interlude. Mueller had severely injured his ankle as he steamed into third and lay writhing on the ground, ignored for several moments in the prevailing frenzy of the Giants rally. When players and umpires realized Mueller had been hurt, time was called, and a hush came over the stadium. Mueller was loaded onto a stretcher and carried the long distance out to the clubhouse beyond center field. Durocher sent in a pinch runner for Mueller at third, Clint Hartung, the all-but-forgotten *"phee*-nom" of the wartime Giants, now reduced to an occasional role as a pinch hitter or pinch runner. Durocher had no immediate explanation for his choice of Hartung as a pinch runner. Years later, the Giants manager recalled he had assumed that Newcombe would remain in the game, and he also knew that, from his position in the third base coaching box, he had been taunting the Dodger hurler mercilessly throughout the contest. The diminutive Durocher was convinced the huge pitcher would attack him as soon as the game ended and chose Hartung because the six-foot-five-inch Texan was "the only man in the ballpark bigger than Don Newcombe."[17] Dressen had been busy as well. He concluded that Newcombe was finished. For several innings Dressen had been on the phone repeatedly with bullpen coach Clyde Sukeforth, asking in a frenzy of anxiety which pitcher the coach thought was throwing better. This time Sukeforth told Dressen that Erskine was bouncing his curve in the dirt, but that Branca looked good. "Gimme Branca," Dressen decided.

Wearing number 13 on his back, Branca began his walk from the bullpen to the mound as Newcombe started on his own long march to the clubhouse in center field. Like two big ships steaming in opposite directions, the two pitchers passed each other about midway in their respective journeys. Newk said a few words of encouragement to his replacement, and Branca offered reassurance to the man he was relieving. Normally, when a relief pitcher entered a game, Dressen issued detailed instructions to the new man, but this time, he merely flipped the ball to Branca from five feet away and muttered, "Here. *Get him out!*"—before hurrying back to the dugout. A ripple of alarm passed through the Brooklyn fielders, according to one of the two surviving members of that group. "I knew Charlie [Dressen] wasn't in full control at that point and I believe the rest of the team felt that way, too. It worried me," Duke Snider recalled.[18]

During the wait before play resumed, while Mueller was being carried off the field, Branca was taking his warm-up pitches, and in the on-deck circle Willie Mays was praying he would not have to come to bat, the next man up concentrated on the idea of getting a hit. Bobby Thomson knew that if the Giants lost he would be the goat, since he had made a stupid move as a base runner as well as an error and two questionable plays in the field. But he focused on the present, and tried not to be overanxious. "If you ever hit one, hit one now," Durocher muttered to him fervently. "Watch and wait for the ball. . . . Give yourself a chance to hit," Thomson told himself.[19] A few moments later Ralph Branca gave him that chance. After watching a big, fat fastball pump across the middle of the plate for strike one, Thomson stepped into Branca's next pitch, also a fastball, and hit it to Kingdom Come. Actually, he hit it on a rising trajectory toward the lower left field stands, where it disappeared, never to be recovered, soaring into the realm of myth.[20]

"Get down! Get down!" screamed Billy Cox as if addressing a badly behaved dog, but the ball winged over his head, and the roar of the crowd began to rise. "Sink! Sink!" Ralph Branca pleaded silently as he turned to watch the flight of the ball. "I can get this," thought Andy Pafko going back, and back, and then running out of space against the left field wall as he too raised his eyes and watched helplessly as the ball carried beyond his reach. "The Giants win the pennant!" New York Giants announcer Russ Hodges shrieked again and again. "Going, going, gone. The Giants win the pennant," declared Gordon McClendon to the nation. "It's in there for the pennant," said the Dodgers' Red Barber in a quiet voice, and then he fell silent, and let the hysteria of the crowd fill his microphone. In the Dodger bullpen, where all activity had ceased as the pitchers watched events unfold on the field, Carl Erskine turned to Clem Labine and commented wryly, "That's the first time in my life I've ever seen a wallet flying into the stands."[21] Labine was so mad he felt like taking a bite out of the bullpen bench. In center field Duke Snider ran toward left field, ready to play the ball off the wall if it caromed away from Pafko. As the ball disappeared into the stands, Snider made a sharp right turn and headed for the clubhouse. Branca picked up the rosin bag, flung it down, and began the longest walk of his life. As Thomson jogged, skipped, and in his own recollection floated around the bases on a cloud, only one Dodger, Jackie Robinson, remained in his place on the diamond. Shoulders straight, hands on hips, he watched to make damn sure Thomson touched every damn base. Then he joined his stunned teammates as they left the field of their broken dreams.

And what more can you say? That crowd down here has just seen the greatest baseball game I would daresay that's ever been played in our national pastime.

While the bottom of the ninth played out on the field, Sal Maglie mooched about aimlessly in the empty locker room, mad at the world. He was certain he would be the losing pitcher in the most important game he had ever pitched. He was not only distressed by his own failure at a most crucial moment but also disgusted with the sloppy fielding, bone-head base running, and lack of batting support the Giants had produced behind him. Now he slumped on a stool in front of his locker, stripped to a cigarette, a bottle of beer, and a layer of sweat, too exhausted and depressed to drag himself to the showers. At last, with his cigarette smoked, his beer bottle empty, and sweat drying to a chill on his back, Sal slid his feet into clogs and made his dejected way toward the shower room. He had almost reached his destination when he found himself face to face with the last person he wanted to see: New York Giants' owner Horace Stoneham. The naked, mortified pitcher had nowhere to turn. "H'lo Mr. Stoneham," he mumbled, glancing up, hoping the owner was headed somewhere else and would let him get on with his shower. Stoneham, however, had left his office and come to the clubhouse specifically to talk to Sal, not, as the pitcher no doubt feared, to berate him for his failure, but instead to praise him for his season-long efforts on behalf of the team and to console him for a tough final loss. Stoneham had prepared a little speech, and Sal listened to it patiently, because courtesy was part of his nature and his upbringing. Then, as Stoneham was talking, a sudden, sustained roar burst in from outside, so loud it captured both men's attention. They hurried to a clubhouse window, and from that vantage point watched the Giants win the game and the pennant.[22]

What happened next is not quite certain. Much later Maglie claimed he lifted the hefty Stoneham, who weighed well over 200 pounds, right off the ground in a jubilant victory bear hug, a detail Stoneham did not include in his own recollections of the moment.[23] If Maglie's story is true, it may explain some of the pitcher's subsequent back trouble. Nobody of Sal's slender build should have lifted the all too appropriately named Stoneham. The television and radio men were already trundling their equipment out of the Dodger clubhouse and over to the Giants' side as Sal raced back to his locker to pull on a clean undershirt and some uniform trousers so he would be decent for the cameras. A classic postgame photo (Figure 11) shows Sal in his clean, dry undershirt, with winning pitcher Larry Jansen and hero of the hour Bobby Thomson still in their full uniforms, all grinning and whooping it up. No other picture ever taken of Sal shows him with an expression of such radiant and unrestrained joy.

The hours after the Giants' playoff victory offer definitive proof that Tom Hanks's movie line, "There's no crying in baseball," is nonsense. Tears flowed everywhere, among players and fans on both sides. Some Giants supporters shed tears of joy. Many heartbroken Dodger fans, paralyzed with shock and grief, could not summon the energy to leave the Polo Grounds and sat weeping in their seats as ecstatic Giants rooters celebrated around them. Similar scenes played out all across New York and Brooklyn. Borough president John Cashmore considered flying the flags in Brooklyn at half mast. The celebration in New York City was the biggest since the end of World War II.

The clubhouses reflected the same contrast. In the funereal Dodgers locker room Dressen ripped off his shirt, buttons flying in all directions. Robinson slammed his glove into his locker. Many players removed their uniforms and showered hurriedly, any tears mingling with the streams of hot water, and left as soon as they had dressed. The inconsolable Ralph Branca was beyond concealing his devastated condition. He sank down on the steps leading up to the trainer's room, his head down almost between his knees. "Why me? Why me?" he sobbed. After a while Branca rolled over on his stomach, draping his long frame along six stairs, and buried his head in his arms, crying like a child. Next to him sat one of the Dodger coaches, kindly Cookie Lavagetto, sadly smoking a cigarette and keeping the

11—October 3, 1951—after "the home run heard 'round the world," and the New York Giants' pennant victory, Maglie jubilantly embraces his teammates: home run hero Bobby Thomson (left) and winning pitcher Larry Jansen (center). Photo: New York Daily News.

stricken pitcher company, but keeping his distance as well.[24] Lavagetto understood there was nothing he could say that would do any good but that it was important that Branca not be left alone with his grief.

After a while the pitcher composed himself, showered, dressed, and departed. His final words to reporters were those of a man about to be married: "I guess I'm just too lucky in love to be lucky at anything else."[25] Waiting for Branca in his car outside the park was his beautiful blonde fiancée Ann Mulvey, daughter of one of the part owners of the Dodgers, and her cousin, Jesuit priest Frank Rowley. Branca, a devout Catholic, asked Fr. Rowley the same question he had asked the empty air in the locker room: Why me? The priest suggested that "maybe God chose you because he knew your faith would be strong enough to bear this cross."[26] Evidently it was. A year later Branca looked back on the defeat, summoned whatever macho he could muster, and declared, "I felt bad for half an hour." Although Branca never escaped the notoriety that one pitch brought him, the pitch also brought him a paradoxical fame, and he has enjoyed the considerable compensation of living well. Still burly and handsome in his late 70s, he remains healthy, prosperous, and happily married.

(Years later, long after Branca and Maglie had retired, they ran into each other at a sports dinner where Branca was the featured speaker. Branca had answered a question about what kind of pitch he threw to Bobby Thomson on that never-to-be-forgotten day in 1951. "I decided to throw him a fastball up and in," the patient Branca once again explained, "so the fastball would move him away from the plate, and that would set up the next pitch, a curveball low and away, and I'd get him out." As he loaded up his plate at the buffet table after his talk, Branca felt a tap on his shoulder. It was Sal Maglie. As Branca turned to him Sal looked him in the eye. "If you're gonna get him with the fuckin' curve ball," Sal observed, "*throw* him the fuckin' curve ball.")[27]

In contrast to the silent Dodgers locker room, complete pandemonium reigned on the Giants' side, where it was less a clubhouse than a madhouse. Camera crews and reporters clutching notepads or microphones jostled one another and the celebrating players. Coach Herman Franks leaned against a wall and wept. Eddie Stanky cried, too, and said it was the first time he had ever cried over a baseball game. Even Durocher shed a few tears. Some of the Dodgers, including owner Walter O'Malley, manager Charlie Dressen, and Jackie Robinson, came over to offer the Giants their congratulations. Bobby Thomson, whose normal facial expression suggested wide-eyed surprise, was even wider-eyed, grinning and saying over and over again, "Gee whiz!" Outside the clubhouse an insistent crowd cheered and pleaded for the heroes to take a bow, and one by one they obliged. Someone had forgotten to put the champagne on ice, so after a few sips of the warm stuff the players turned to swigging cold beers. Hank Thompson persuaded Willie Mays to swallow some champagne, and Mays promptly threw up. When asked what was the first thing he did when he realized the Giants had won the pennant, Sal Maglie said he cracked open another beer. Sal also related a story for the occasion: "A way back in Philadelphia, Larry Jansen won a game. It was his fourth while I had nine. Larry said to me, 'I think I'll catch you before this is over.' I said to him, 'If you catch me, we'll win the pennant.'"[28] (Both Jansen and Maglie won 23 that season.) Nobody drank to excess, because the World Series began the next day.

Along with its heroics, joys, and sorrows, the third playoff game also generated some remarkable instances of nastiness and cruelty, indications of the ferocious intensity of feelings the Dodgers-Giants rivalry aroused. Not all

Brooklyn fans sank into passive despair. Some took out their frustrations by constructing stuffed effigies of the team members they considered responsible for the Dodgers' defeat and hanging them from neighborhood lampposts. A couple could be recognized as manager Charlie Dressen, but most, identifiable by the number 13 on their backs, were of Ralph Branca. A few fans went unconscionably far: they phoned the Branca family home, hissing and snarling at Ralph's mother (his *mother!*), asking her how she could have raised such a sorry excuse for a son or demanding to know why she had failed to teach her boy how to pitch. Even Sal Maglie, normally a kind man off the field, became caught up in the game's mean-spirited wake. He told a joke at Don Newcombe's expense, at once cruel, clever, and breathtakingly crude, that went like this: Question—what's Don Newcombe got in common with a queer? The answer: "Hah!" cried Maglie. "They both choke on the big ones!"[29] This does not sound like something Sal thought up. His preferred personal humor took the form of gentle, good-natured kidding, but reporters first heard the two-liner from him, and although for obvious reasons it never appeared in newspapers of the 1950s, it made the rounds and has remained associated with Maglie's name.

THE WORLD SERIES

After the drama of a playoff that brought the Giants their first pennant in 14 years, the World Series came as an anticlimax. Carried along on the adrenaline high of their playoff victory the day before, the Giants steamed into Yankee Stadium on October 4 and defeated the Bronx Bombers, 5–1. The new commissioner of baseball, Ford Frick, who had been chosen by the owners on September 20, threw out the first ball. The Giants' only rested pitcher, southpaw Dave Koslo, who had not participated in the playoffs, held the Yankees to seven hits as he defeated Allie Reynolds, whose previous outing had been his second no-hitter of the season. Larry Jansen pitched the second game and allowed only three runs on six hits, but Yankee junkman Eddie Lopat hypnotized the Giants with his slow stuff, and the Yanks squeezed out a 3–1 win. As the Series moved to the Polo Grounds for Game Three, the Giants came back and defeated the Yankees, 6–2, behind the pitching of Jim Hearn. The Giants enjoyed a five-run fifth, during which Stanky, apparently out in an attempt to steal second, kicked the ball out of shortstop Phil Rizzuto's glove with a hard slide. "It ain't a fuckin' tea party out there, not against my guys," Durocher growled when asked about the play after the game.[30] Mays had his first two World Series hits and batted in a run. Yankee legend Joe DiMaggio had gone hitless so far in the Series—he was 0 for 11. The Giants now led in the Series, two games to one.

Game Four was scheduled for October 7, but rain washed it out, giving both pitchers an extra day of rest. Allie Reynolds, who had lost the opening game, benefitted from the additional time off, but Sal Maglie, oddly enough, did not. In his first World Series outing, in a crucial game where a win would have given the Giants a commanding 3–1 lead in the Series, Sal turned in a poor performance. He lasted five innings (Durocher lifted him for a pinch hitter in the bottom of the fifth), giving up four runs on eight hits, walking two, and striking out three. As he had in the third playoff game, Sal struggled in the first inning. He walked leadoff man Hank Bauer, and although he did not allow any runs, the subsequent three batters fouled off several innings' worth of pitches. He needed ten tosses to strike out Joe DiMaggio for the third out. The Giants gained a run off Reynolds in the bottom of the first, but Sal gave it back in the top of the second. He allowed another run in the fourth, and in the top of the fifth, with catcher Yogi Berra on board with a single, Sal faced DiMaggio again. Sal kept working him low and away, but Joe refused to lunge. With the count at 3–1, Sal came in with a curve that failed to bend much. DiMaggio, who had broken out of his Series slump with a third-inning single, smashed the ball toward left. Monte Irvin turned and started back, but stopped after a couple of steps, and watched as the Yankee Clipper's last major league home run soared into the left field seats. Some say that was the Series, right there, the moment the Giants finally ran out of gas. The Yanks picked up two unearned runs in the seventh on a throwing error by Stanky, and the Giants scratched a second run off Reynolds in the bottom of the ninth, but they were out of miracles. They, and Maglie, lost the game, 6–2. Mays hit into three double plays, including the one that ended the contest.

Sal, miserable over his failure, declared it was one of his worst performances and that he had thrown only three good pitches in his entire five innings of work. Sal had gone through even worse outings, but never with so much at stake. Westrum, who once described Sal's control as so perfect that you could catch him while sitting in a rocking chair, agreed, saying "I never saw him with so little stuff."[31] The headline for Ed Sinclair's article in the *Herald Tribune* put it even more bluntly: "Maglie Had Nothing." Reporters speculated about why a pitcher who had won 23 games during the regular season would haven fallen apart. Jim McCulley thought the interruption in Sal's routine of pitching every fourth day threw him off stride, an explanation Sal himself offered years later. Sal also made a curious claim, saying he had overindulged in a big pasta dinner the night before at an Italian restaurant, and that the meal had left him "plain heavy."[32] Sal had been eating pasta all his life, so it is unclear why this particular meal would have stuck to his ribs in such unfortunate fashion. Roger Kahn, a cub reporter in the early

1950s and always an astute observer of Maglie, learned that on the day of Sal's World Series start the pitcher had been experiencing pain in the lower right portion of his back.[33] Whether it came from fatigue after his 298 innings pitched so far that year, or from his having hoisted Horace Stoneham four days earlier, is uncertain, but Sal was not the kind who complained about pain, and he would have gone to the mound crippled rather than admit to Durocher that he was unable to take his turn. This was the first known occurrence of the back problems that would plague Sal in future years, but at this point he dismissed it as nothing more than a passing twinge.

The loss of Game Four doomed the Giants, and they never recovered their momentum. In Game Five at the Polo Grounds the Yankees crushed them by the demoralizing score of 13–1, as Eddie Lopat again had Giants hitters swinging futilely at his tantalizing slow deliveries. The Yanks pounced on a weary Larry Jansen in the third for five runs and kept piling it on. The Giants' only run was unearned due to a first-inning error by Yankee left fielder Gene Woodling. But the Giants were not quite dead, and they made a close contest of Game Six. Behind 4–1 going into the top of the ninth, they loaded the bases with nobody out. Stengel replaced Johnny Sain with lefthander Bob Kusava, who persuaded Monte Irvin and Hank Thompson to fly out, with a run scoring on each sacrifice. With two out and the tying run on second, Durocher sent up utility catcher Sal Yvars as a pinch hitter. Involved in a long-running feud with his manager, Yvars had to borrow a bat, because he had broken all of his own in a fit of temper after a recent spat with Durocher. When Durocher called on Yvars to pinch hit, the catcher was in the bullpen, warming up none other than Sal Maglie, just in case The Barber might be needed should the game go into extra innings. None of the Yankees had ever played against Yvars, and so, to the utility catcher's delight, the lofty Yankees spent a long time discussing how to pitch to him. Yvars recalled, "I knew Kusava was going to throw me a fastball. . . . I guessed right and I hit a terrific line drive to right field. . . . [Bauer] makes this diving, shoestring catch. When he caught that ball I kicked first base so hard I could hardly walk for the next month."[34]

The World Series was over, and once again the Yankees had won the championship, but for the Giants their pennant victory had been so sweet that even the loss of the Series could not erase their joy. As Jimmy Cannon said in his *Post* column on October 11, the Giants "behaved like winners all the way from August to the last out in the sixth game." Worn down by a season in which he had pitched 290 innings, Sal Maglie was then unsuccessful in his playoff and Series games, but he had enjoyed the greatest season of his career, and his 23 wins played a crucial role in his team's pennant triumph. He went home happy.

THE SIGN-STEALING CONTROVERSY

No account of the 1951 National League pennant race can be complete without mention of a story that has been around for more than half a century: the claim that the New York Giants had a quasi-legal sign-stealing system that year, which enabled their hitters to know what pitches to expect. Rumors of the system had been circulating for years. Ralph Branca heard about it via the ballplayers' grapevine in 1954, but he kept quiet because he did not wish to sound as if he were making excuses for himself. In 1962 an Associated Press article reported that a spy in the clubhouse had helped the Giants win the 1951 pennant, but the vague account relied on an anonymous source and received little attention. In his book about the 1951 season, *The Home Run Heard 'Round the World,* published in 1991, Ray Robinson also devoted a couple of paragraphs to the story. But on January 31, 2001, just days before celebrations marking the fiftieth anniversary of the Giants miracle season were to begin, the *Wall Street Journal* published a detailed report on the scheme. It had involved a coach stationed in the Giants clubhouse in center field with a high-powered telescope trained on the opponents' catchers, picking up their signals and quickly relaying them to the Giants bullpen via a buzzer rigged up by an electrician. From there, utility catcher Sal Yvars passed them on to Giants batters. There is no longer any doubt that the system existed; since the publication of the 2001 article several members of the 1951 team have admitted both to knowing about it and to taking advantage of it, although Herman Franks, the coach behind the spyglass, went to his grave like a true undercover operative, refusing to admit his part in the clandestine operation.

Sign stealing has been around for as long as the game itself and has always been accepted as a legitimate tactic. Even stealing by various mechanical means has a long history and was not officially declared illegal until 1961. But legal and ethical are two different concepts, and no one claims any ethical high ground for the Giants. Although Bobby Thomson continues to hedge or outright deny that he knew the sign before he hit his game-winning home run off Ralph Branca, he admitted to taking the signs on other occasions, adding "I'm not particularly proud of that."[35] Sal Yvars, the man who provided the insider information used in the *Wall Street Journal* article, insists that Thomson *did* have the sign in the third playoff game. Yvars stated, "But if Bobby wants to say he didn't take the sign, let him say it. What else would he say in his position?"[36]

According to the *Wall Street Journal* account, the Giants first put their sign-stealing operation into effect on July 20, a home game where New York pasted Cincinnati, 11–5, and the winning pitcher was Sal Maglie. In later years no one thought to ask Sal about the sign-stealing scheme, probably be-cause it was an issue of greater relevance to hitters than to pitchers, al-though no pitcher is averse to his team's scoring extra runs for him. When the issue first surfaced in print in 1962 Sal was still in the majors, serving as a pitching coach for the Boston Red Sox, but by the time the more fully doc-umented article appeared in 2001, Sal had been dead for almost a decade. Even if he had been around to ask, the chances are he would have had little or nothing to say. Maglie knew how to keep his mouth shut.

The question of whether or not the sign stealing helped the Giants win the pennant is more difficult to answer than it might seem. Intuitively, one would think that for batters to know in advance what kind of pitches are coming would be a tremendous advantage, but that is not always the case. Some batters prefer not to know out of concern that the sign might be wrong or deliberately misleading, and the pitch different from what they were expecting, thus putting them at an even greater disadvantage than if they were unsure of what the pitch would be. Andrew Goldblatt published some calculations, reasoning that if the Giants gained an advantage from knowing pitches in advance, they would increase the number of runs they scored at home. Instead, he concluded, the opposite happened. Before the sign stealing went into effect the Giants scored an average of 5.46 runs per home game and afterward an average of 4.57. He also calculated batting av-erages, home runs, and RBIs for the Giants' batting order before and after the scheme began and found that most players did slightly *worse* after it started. Lockman improved slightly, as did Irvin (who said he did not care to know what was coming), but Bobby Thomson improved his average by a stunning 120 points, going from .237 before the signs became available to .357 afterward. Asked to explain his sudden improvement at the time of the first playoff game, Thomson attributed it to his move to third—he claimed he had to concentrate so hard on trying to keep from getting killed at third base that he had little time left to obsess on his hitting. He called it "a tri-umph of brawn over brain or muscle over mind," and perhaps it was.[37]

But what about that phenomenal 16–game winning streak the Giants put together between August 12 and August 28? All but three of those games took place at the Polo Grounds, which might suggest a whole new defini-tion for the term "home field advantage." But on the other hand, in the Gi-ants' final skein of wins from September 22 through the first playoff game against the Dodgers on October 1, five of the eight were played on the road. The Giants took 14 of their final 18 road games, obviously without the use of the telescope.

Still, the question remains and is likely to continue to remain: could the Giants have put up the record they did without their telescopic sign stealing? Ralph Branca, for one, would like to know. "It wasn't illegal, it was just immoral," he declared. "Without the sign stealing, could they have won?" Not according to baseball historian David Smith. "They only had to have one win that came from cheating in order to make the playoff happen," declared Smith.[38] And yet, because baseball is a game of infinite variables, any one of innumerable factors in any game could have tipped the balance, some of them having as much to do with how the Dodgers played as with whatever the Giants did or did not do. If the Dodgers had won just one more game, the playoffs would not have been necessary. Branca found plenty to criticize on both sides. "I blame the Giants management," he stated. "There was no law against it, because nobody thought anybody would be so despicable as to conceive of that system." But he was equally scathing in his criticism of Charlie Dressen's handling of Dodger pitchers during the 1951 season. "What he knew about pitching you could put on the head of a pin in the boldest print in the world and still have room for the Constitution," snapped Branca, who can still toss a sizzling phrase, if not a fastball.[39] Carl Erskine once said that *he* should be blamed for the Dodgers' losing the pennant. When asked why, he replied, "I lost on Opening Day." On another occasion Erskine suggested "The Cub Factor," a semi-serious theory offered by Chicago newspaper columnist Mike Royko, who claimed that any team having two or more players recently traded to them from the Chicago Cubs would find a way to lose the pennant.[40] The Dodgers had two former Cubs, Rube Walker and Andy Pafko, on the field in that fatal final game. Irving Rudd, publicist for the Dodgers in 1951, put the blame on General MacArthur. According to Rudd, the general was a jinx. He attended 13 games at Ebbets Field in 1951, and the Dodgers lost all of them. One could go on indefinitely, but in the end, as Branca admits, "It doesn't matter. Bobby still had to hit the ball."[41]

1952—A Season of Sun and Shadows

A HERO COMES HOME

After Sal's tremendous 1951 season with the pennant-winning New York Giants, the pitcher came home to a hero's welcome. On October 29, Sal rode in the place of honor in a parade to city hall, where the mayor offered him a warm welcome home on behalf of himself, the city council, and other civic officials. The mayor had proclaimed the date Sal Maglie Day, urging citizens to participate in the ceremonies and praising Sal for "his conduct on the baseball field and in the activities of everyday life [where he] has evidenced the highest qualities of sportsmanship and good character and has been a splendid example to the youth of the nation and an inspiration to the young people of Niagara Falls."[1] Throughout the day Sal was the guest of honor at civic and public functions, capped off with a testimonial dinner at the Century Club. An overflow crowd of more than 400 people—city officials, civic leaders, family, friends, and fans—filled the banquet hall and listened as a series of speakers lauded Sal for his achievements. Sal said a few words of thanks. A genuinely modest man, he was not much of a public speaker. When he had to give a talk longer than a few sentences, his wife wrote his speeches for him.[2] Sal was much happier surrounded by fans, especially kids, with whom he was always good-natured and patient.

In the autumn and winter months of 1951 and early 1952 Sal attended a round of testimonial dinners, award ceremonies, communion breakfasts, civic

association and Italian American organization meetings, and just about anything else to which he was invited, a practice he would continue throughout his career and beyond. Only on rare occasions did he ask to be paid, and
the only times he turned down requests for his appearance were when they
conflicted with something already scheduled. His courtesy and cooperative-
ness form a telling contrast to Joe DiMaggio's rudeness and hauteur. One
time at the height of Joe's career a member of the Yankee sales staff, who
was also a member of an organization called the Sons of Italy, approached
DiMaggio with the suggestion that the Sons of Italy would be honored to
hold a Joe DiMaggio Day at Yankee Stadium. DiMaggio brushed off the man
and his group with the crushing response, "They're not big enough."[3] No
group was ever "not big enough" to merit attention from Sal Maglie.

Sal remained a local hero because he always came home to Niagara Falls.
He and his wife continued to live in the modest home at 2727 Pierce Avenue that Sal had purchased with his Mexican League money. His parents,
sisters, nephews and nieces, and extended family of in-laws all resided in
the town as well, and some of Sal's star-dust rubbed off on his relatives, leaving them with fond memories of the '50s. Sal's niece Maria Grenga Rizzo,
daughter of Sal's sister Santa, adored her famous uncle. She considered Sal "a
true gentleman," kind and generous as well as glamorous, "handsome as a
movie star," and always beautifully dressed. "I don't think he even *owned*
a pair of jeans!" she exclaimed.[4] He always wore suits, or dress slacks and a
sweater, and dress shoes to family gatherings. On visits to the Grenga home
during the winters Sal never put his overcoat in the closet. Instead, he hung
it on the post at the bottom of the stairwell bannister. He purposely left
small change in the pockets, and the Grenga children would then "raid"
their uncle's coat pockets. They did not learn until years later that he had
intended them to find and keep the money—his way of giving them a little
gift each time he came to their house. Another niece, Kathy Pileggi Peller,
daughter of Kay Maglie's brother Carl, remembered herself as a shy little girl
awed by her famous uncle but enthralled by her beautiful aunt Kay, for
whom she was named. "She was like an angel," Kathy Peller recalled. "She
was wonderful. I remember her baking—that was her big thing. Also, she
used to take me to downtown Buffalo, me and my cousin, uncle John's
daughter Joanne, and she would buy us dresses, beautiful dresses." She
added that "Sal and Kay were always very generous. At Christmas there'd be
presents all over, from them. It was sort of like a fairy tale, really."[5]

The early 1950s were golden years for Sal and Kay Maglie, a "fairy tale"
existence of success, fame, and financial prosperity shadowed only by their
lack of children. Maria Grenga Rizzo recalled the deep mutual affection and
attraction between her aunt and uncle. She had never seen a couple so

much in love. Although Sal was hardly the wealthiest man in Niagara Falls, his income put him in a class with the town's physicians, lawyers, and small-business owners, a long way up the social and economic ladder from where he had begun in his days as a shipping clerk, pipefitter, and gas jockey. Unlike many men made arrogant and snobbish by sudden wealth and fame, Sal did not change. "Fame never went to his head," recalled nephew Dennis Villani, son of Kay's older sister. "If you talked to him, you'd think maybe he worked in one of the factories around here. He was the most gentle man you could ever want to meet. *Gentle.*" Dennis, who was on tense terms with his parents after they divorced, spent several years of his childhood in the early 1950s living with Sal and Kay and stayed with them on and off through the mid-60s. "They treated me like I was their son," Dennis declared, adding that "Kay was more of a mother to me than my own mother was."[6] Dennis clearly served as a surrogate son, particularly for Kay, still desperate for children.

As the wife of a famous baseball player, she not only had her own and Sal's family members and their children around her, but also the families of Sal's teammates. Many of the team social events that the Maglies attended included the players' families, and baseball players tend to be, in Jim Brosnan's phrase, "famously procreative." The early 1950s was, moreover, the height of the postwar baby boom, the era novelist John Updike evocatively recalled as "when everyone was pregnant." Everyone, that is, except Kay Maglie. Almost all the married Giants players had at least one child, some had three or four, and one, Sal's roommate Larry Jansen, had seven. (He eventually became the father of 10.) In the 1950s Jansen liked to joke at picnics that he would be happy to allow other Giants families to take home some of his children. He had no idea that Kay Maglie would have been overjoyed to find he was serious.[7] Larraine Day, the film star wife of Leo Durocher, also noticed the baseball baby boom. "It seems to me," Day wrote in her memoir, "that hardly a day passed without glad tidings from the delivery room for some hard-hitting, fleet-footed fly catcher."[8] Sal's teammates Don Mueller and Whitey Lockman both became fathers during the 1951 season and marked the occasion with celebrations in the clubhouse. One of the reasons given for Philadelphia's failure to win another pennant in 1951 is that the team was distracted because 11 Phillies families had newborns or were expecting babies during that season. Although ballplayers of the 1950s like to claim they talked about nothing but baseball in the locker rooms, on train trips, and in their hotel rooms, they also talked about their growing families. Sal, quiet to begin with, could contribute nothing to those conversations. In baseball he was surrounded by men who had no trouble procreating, even when they did not plan on it. Yankee pitcher Mickey McDermott once overheard a phone conversation between his roommate, catcher Yogi Berra, and Berra's wife in which, when Carmen Berra finally came to the point of the call, Yogi bellowed, "Whaddya mean you're pregnant again? You *can't* be! I *bought* you a *diagram*!"[9]

Although it is unlikely that anyone made direct remarks or addressed prying questions to Sal about his childless marriage, ballplayers noticed such things and came to their own conclusions about the causes. Pitcher Jim Brosnan, writing in the late 1950s, took note of the Cincinnati Reds' trade of infielder Alex Grammas and wondered if it had anything to do with Grammas' 10–year childless marriage. Brosnan remarked, "On the Cincinnati club if you don't have at least three children you're not even average. Some people doubt your virility then, and it's only one step further to doubting your own ability. My conclusion is fairly obvious, isn't it?"[10] By 1952 the Maglies had been married and childless for 11 years, and hints of their distress come through. Roger Kahn, calling to mind the Sal Maglie of 50 years ago, remembered the pitcher as bothered by his childlessness, although "not inordinately."[11] But the mere fact that Kahn, then an obscure young reporter, was aware of the issue at all is an index of how much it bothered Sal, who was not prone to confide such matters to the press. Clearly, the word had gotten around. An article from 1952 noted Sal's sister Santa's brood of five. "Sal envies her," author Ed Fitzgerald wrote with surprising candor. "He and Kay are still hoping they will have kids of their own."[12] By this late date, both Sal and Kay knew that was not going to happen.

THE 1952 SEASON

At the start of the 1950 season Sal had been in no position to make salary demands, but before the beginning of the 1952 season his situation was a lot more favorable. In the spring of 1950 he knew he was lucky to be back in the big leagues, so he swallowed his disappointment and accepted the $10,000 the Giants offered him. As a result of his successful return to the majors in 1950, the Giants gave him a substantial raise, bringing his salary in 1951 to around $15,000. He then enjoyed a star-quality season in 1951, when he and teammate Larry Jansen led the majors in wins. Now, for the first time, Sal found himself in a strong bargaining position and made the most of it. In January, as contract negotiation time came around, Maglie told the Giants he wanted them to more than triple his salary, and pay him $50,000 for the 1952 season. The Giants front office professed itself shocked at Maglie's demands, and in response offered him $35,000 or $27,000, according to a different report. Another news story gave Maglie's initial demand as $40,000 and the club's offer as $33,000.[13]

This time Sal was prepared to dig in and test Horace Stoneham's resolve. Maglie believed the Giants were failing to keep their promises to him. Given his outstanding record, he felt he had been grossly underpaid in the previous two years, and he was eager to make up for that. "When I was reinstated in 1950, they told me if I did okay they would take care of me," Sal told the *Herald Tribune*'s Ed Sinclair. "Well, they're taking care of me to a certain extent, but it doesn't seem quite enough." Sal reminded everyone of his cooperation in past years, saying he was one of the first Giants to sign his contract in 1950. Furthermore, Sal continued, gathering steam, "I kept my word with them. I never refused a manager anything in my life because I always was and always will be a team man. I pitched out of turn, I worked in the bullpen with a sore arm. Anything they wanted of me I did and we made out pretty good, didn't we?" On a more conciliatory note Sal added, "If they meet me half way, I'll be satisfied."[14] Aware of his advancing age (he would be 35 early in the 1952 season), Sal realized that this might be his last chance to give his salary a significant boost, while he was still a top performer. He believed he was as valuable to the Giants as Larry Jansen, who had made $30,000 the previous year and was reported to have signed for $35,000 in 1952.

The Giants retaliated for Sal's holdout by informing him that he would not be allowed to report to the team's training camp until he had signed his contract. "It doesn't take me long to get in shape," he assured everyone, adding that he had remained close to his playing weight, his arm felt fine, and he was working out regularly at his hometown YMCA.[15] The Giants opened their training camp on February 14 without Maglie. By this time the Giants' offer stood at $35,000, with Maglie holding out for $40,000. Within a week they reached a compromise, and Sal signed, reportedly for $37,500. The salary—the most Sal would ever receive—made him the highest-paid Giants pitcher in 1952 and one of the highest-paid pitchers in the history of the ball club. As a comparison, in 1951 the average public school teacher's salary was $3,000.

Maglie also received extra income from product endorsements. The year 1952 was a good one for Giants players in that regard, as they had made national headlines in October of 1951 with their sensational playoff victory over the Dodgers. During 1952 Sal appeared in an advertisement that many players would have avoided: he posed in an ad for Mennen spray deodorant for men (Figure 12). Although less embarrassing than—for example—Rafael Palmeiro's endorsement of Viagra, an advertisement that featured Sal in his New York Giants uniform, with his right armpit coming toward the viewer, hardly qualifies as glamorous. The ad copy had Sal repeating one of the company's slogans: "Are you **sure** you don't need **a man's deodorant**?" The

12—Despite his successful 1951 season, Maglie received few contracts for endorsements. Here, he appears in an advertisement for Mennen Deodorant for Men, a product that could have capitalized on Sal's ultramasculine appearance. Instead, designers softened Sal's image by lightening his dark beard.

advertising artist who created the image "touched up" Maglie's face, removing the scar on his right eyebrow, smoothing out the lines around his mouth and eyes, and eliminating his black beard. With his cap pushed up far enough that the bill does not shadow his face, Sal looks surprisingly benign and almost bland.

Given his fame, we might expect that Maglie would have been more sought after by advertisers. But Sal's reputation for ferocity on the field caused advertisers to shy away from him. The gentleness of personality so often noted by his friends was not evident in Sal's appearance. The famous beard was an asset on the field, adding to his forbidding image, but off the field it was a liability. Sal had the kind of ultra-heavy, dark beard that made him look as if he always needed a shave. In the 1950s that was not a desirable look for a ballplayer. Maglie may have been a model American citizen, but those who wrote about him often found it easy to describe him as looking like an Italian gangster. Although no sportswriter is more sensitive to ethnic insults than Roger Kahn, even he once described Sal (who at the time was losing money in a low-stakes blackjack game) as glowering "like Il Patrone of Cosa Nostra."[16] In an era long before *The Sopranos* made gangsters glamorous, companies did not want their products promoted by people whom the media had described as looking like criminals.

With his contract signed, Sal reported to the Giants training camp a week late and found that management had made some significant changes. Eddie Stanky, the sparkplug at second base, had gone to St. Louis, where he would be the Cardinals' player-manager. In exchange the Giants acquired outfielder Chuck Diering as well as Sal's old buddy from the Mexican League, lefty Max Lanier. To replace Stanky at second the Giants called up Davey Williams. With Willie Mays scheduled to enter the army in May, the Giants also planned to bring up Dusty Rhodes, an excellent left-handed pull hitter but a man with the fielding skills of a grizzly bear who was another of baseball's epic elbow-benders. Except for the addition of Lanier, the core of the pitching staff remained the same: Jansen, Maglie, Hearn, Koslo, and Kennedy. The Giants also added a haughty, elegant-looking knuckleballer named Hoyt Wilhelm, a reliever beginning his major league career at age 29. With Lanier's arrival, Sal remained the Giants' second-oldest player; in 1952 Lanier, like the departed Eddie Stanky, was 36.

True to his word that he had kept himself in shape during the off-season, Sal pitched brilliantly in most of his spring training games. At one point he had a scoreless streak of 19 innings and did not walk anyone for a month. Durocher was delighted. "If I had to pick one guy in the league to win 20 games, it would have to be Maglie," he exulted.[17] But as the Giants wound up their training season with a trip north in the company of the Cleveland

Indians, disaster struck in an unexpected place. Monte Irvin caught his spikes on third base while trying to take the extra base on a single by Willie Mays. He sustained an ankle fracture and dislocation so severe that a shard of bone protruded through his skin. "They're carrying our pennant chances off the field," was the unspoken thought that beat writer Arch Murray attributed to the Giants team. The injury occurred on April 2, and although Irvin returned toward the end of the season, the Giants would miss his batting skills. To fill the gap in the outfield the Giants obtained Bob Elliott from the Boston Braves in exchange for pitcher Sheldon Jones.

Durocher chose Maglie as the Opening Day starter against the Phillies on April 16, and he did not disappoint, beating Philadelphia ace Robin Roberts, 5–3. Sal came through again on April 20, invincible as ever against the Dodgers on their home ground. Before the game he told the *Times'* John Drebinger, "I guess it's about time that somebody gave these fellows a shave and cut them down to size."[18] By this time Sal himself was routinely using his reputation as "The Barber" to enhance his menacing image. Then he went out and did what he promised, spinning a dazzling two-hit shutout and defeating Brooklyn, 6–0, the first time anyone had shut out the Dodgers at home since August of 1949. If there was a flaw in his performance, it was his wavering control: he walked an unusually high number of batters, six, and threw a wild pitch. He also hit one batter, perhaps deliberately, as a gesture of contempt and a sharp reminder that he could inflict that punishment at will. With two out in the bottom of the ninth and a count of 0–2 on Gil Hodges, Maglie treated himself to what the *Eagle's* Tommy Holmes believed was a deliberate knockdown, not a mere brushback. According to Holmes, Maglie's pitch "turned Hodges upside down, catching him on the left hand as Gil brought it up hurriedly to protect his face."[19] Sal fanned eight and, just to put his seal on his mastery of the Giants' traditional rivals, struck out a frustrated Carl Furillo four times. Maglie had yet to lose a game at Ebbets Field.

Sal picked up his third win against no losses on April 29 against Cincinnati by a 2–1 score. With the game tied 1–1 in the top of the ninth, Sal singled with Dark on second, driving in what proved to be the winning run. Throughout the game Cincinnati manager Luke Sewell complained that Maglie was throwing a spitter, but the umpires sided with the pitcher, insisting he was merely blowing on his hand, not spitting on it. After the game umpire Lee Ballanfant declared that Sal is "just a great pitcher. . . . Every time Sewell complained tonight, Maglie's curve got a little sharper." Sewell backed off, grumbling that one way or another Sal "gets just enough moisture on [the ball] so that he can grip the seams a little tighter."[20] When a manager is reduced to claiming that the opposing team's pitcher is *breathing* on the ball, one can sense a certain desperation. Thanks in part to Sal's excellent pitching, the Giants finished April with a fine 7–4 record.

Beginning with Sal's victory over Cincinnati on April 29, the Giants went on a seven-game winning streak. Maglie won again on May 3, defeating the Pirates, 3–2, for his fourth straight win and his twelfth consecutive victory over Pittsburgh. Once again Sal singled, and he scored what proved to be the winning run. In the fourth inning Sal beaned weak-hitting Pirate in-fielder George Strickland. This was the second—and last—time Sal struck a batter in the head. Unlike his beaning of Danny Murtaugh, this time the skulling was more serious. Sal hit Strickland in the back of the head, knock-ing him unconscious. He had to be removed from the field on a stretcher and taken to a hospital. Although X-rays revealed no skull fracture, Strick-land suffered a concussion and remained hospitalized for two days for ob-servation. He said he never saw the pitch coming. "It was just a fuzzy blur," he related.[21] Strickland's injuries occurred despite Branch Rickey's order, first issued in 1952, that all Pirates players wear protective batting helmets. Such helmets were in the early stages of development, unwieldy, and not very ef-fective. Furthermore, many players thought it was "sissy" to wear one, and it is unknown whether Strickland was wearing the protective gear when he was beaned. Imperturbable as ever, Sal suppressed the sick feeling he experi-enced when he struck a batter in the head and continued to pitch. His iron nerves served him well, and he completed the game without further diffi-culty. Sal won his fifth straight on May 7 against St. Louis, although he did not complete the game. With the Cards threatening in the ninth, Durocher called in Larry Jansen to finish, and Maglie recorded another win, 3–1. His record stood at 5–0 and his ERA at a spectacular 1.02.

As his string of consecutive wins grew longer, baseball writers began pay-ing closer attention to Sal, marveling at his control, his variety of curves, and his sense of pace. They also noted his cumulative won-lost record, pointing out that, as of early May, Sal owned the best lifetime percentage of all active major league pitchers. He had a four-year record of 64–22 for a .744 mark. He had a better than .500 record against all rival clubs except one; Sal had lost to the Boston Braves four times and won only three games against them. The Phillies had never defeated Sal; he was 9–0 against them. His record stood at 13–1 over Pittsburgh, 10–3 over Brooklyn, 8–3 against Cincinnati, 5–2 over St. Louis, and 3–1 over Chicago. If Sal were to lose fewer than five games during the 1952 season, he would set an all-time record for fewest losses over a three-year period among pitchers who had pitched at least 154 innings per season. Two pitchers, Ed Reulbach of the early Chicago Nationals in 1906–1908 and Lefty Grove of the Philadelphia Athletics in 1929–1931, had both lost only 15 times over three years. Since

Sal had lost only four games in 1950, and six in 1951, and had yet to drop a decision in 1952, he seemed like a good bet to break the record. Sal's "stuff" did not seem formidable, and yet he could use it with such artistry that he left opposing players grinding their teeth in frustration. Sportswriter Joe King thought Maglie's secret lay in his "exquisite sense of pace." He always seemed to have something left, no matter how tough or long the game. Sal explained it with a guy-from-the-garage image: "It's like driving a car. If I'm going along at 50–60 miles an hour in a car which can do 80, I have the situation under control. I can drop back to 30–40 miles if that's wise, and I have plenty in reserve to go up to 80 in an emergency. But if I go 80 all the time I have nothing in reserve and I'm going to find it hard to get down to 30–40 in a hurry if I should want to. Many of the young pitchers try to go 80 all the time, and as a result they either run out of gas, or have no change-of-speed or reserve power to get through nine innings."[22]

On May 14 Sal defeated Cincinnati, 8–3, for his sixth straight victory, with the Giants' barrage of hits behind him giving him a comfortable cushion. Just as in Sal's game against the same team on April 29, the Reds repeatedly asked the umpire to examine the ball, with the same negative results—the arbiter found nothing wrong. But the constant delays interrupted Sal's rhythm and annoyed him so much that after Cincinnati pitcher Frank Hiller, batting in the fifth, told umpire Augie Donatelli that he wanted to inspect the ball personally, Sal registered his disgust by firing the ball over his catcher's head. In the next inning Durocher tried the same tactic against the Reds, asking the umpire to inspect the ball after every pitch, slowing the game to a crawl. When Sewell began his routine again in the seventh, Donatelli had taken enough nonsense. He ordered Sewell back into the dugout and informed him that Maglie was striking out the Reds on curveballs, not spitballs. Sportswriter Jim McCulley noted that Sal had not recorded any strikeouts and that the pitcher "didn't seem to have an awful lot . . . yet he won with ease." With the season almost a month old, the Giants were in first place, leading the Dodgers by two, and had won 12 of their last 13. Maglie, McCulley concluded, "gets more amazing every day."[23]

On May 19 Sal continued his skein of victories, shutting out the Pirates on seven hits, 4–0, with only one batter getting past first base, for his second shutout of the season. Maglie won his eighth in a row on May 23, defeating the Boston Braves, 5–3. Four days later, on May 27, Sal faced the Dodgers and shut them out again, 3–0. His record was now 9–0; he had 12 straight wins dating back to the previous season, seven straight victories over the Dodgers, and a string of 18 scoreless innings pitched against the Bums. This time, the Dodgers managed four hits, twice as many as in Sal's previous game against them, but Maglie allowed only one Dodger base runner to advance as far as third. He issued four walks and struck out six.

The Dodgers, no doubt aware of the Reds' lack of success in pinning the spitball label on Sal, tried another tack: they insinuated that he cut the baseballs. Several Dodgers rummaged through a bag of balls used in the game and discovered that five had conspicuous cuts on them. "I've never seen such cuts on a ball before,"one anonymous Dodger declared ominously. "I'm not saying Maglie made those cuts, but he certainly took advantage of them."[24] Dodgers manager Charlie Dressen, who realized that anyone on either team could have made the cuts, or that they may have happened by accident in the course of play, minimized the importance of his players' discovery. Some newspapers also reported that Jackie Robinson had again raised the spitball accusation against Sal, but Robinson denied it, saying he suspected Sal of using cut balls but that any pitcher could benefit from nicks in the horsehide. Larry Jansen added his own sardonic comment on the spitball controversy by asking what the Dodgers thought Preacher Roe was throwing. Sal, half annoyed and half amused by the flap, insisted he did not even know how to throw a spitball. As for the cut ball business, "I didn't see any cut-up baseballs," he stated. "But if I had, I certainly would have taken advantage of it."[25]

Led by Maglie's brilliant pitching, the Giants achieved a 20–6 record for May and were in a close race with the Dodgers. Although no one suspected it while Sal was rolling up one victory after another, he was beginning to experience discomfort in his back. Major league pitching is rarely a pain-free occupation, and it can sometimes seem less like a sports activity than a process by which a small number of adult males gradually tear their arms out of their sockets while also often ruining their backs, shoulders, necks, elbows, knees, and ankles. Sal first had begun to notice an unusual stiffness in his back during the early part of May, but because he was loathe to complain or admit to any ailments, he had ignored it. Rather than mentioning the problem to Durocher, he told pitching coach Frank Shellenback, but the coach did not take him seriously—after all, Sal was winning game after game.[26] How could he do that if there were anything seriously wrong with his back? So Sal went on pitching and ignored his body's warning signals.

His first loss of the year could be blamed less on his own problems than on sloppy fielding by his teammates. Facing the Cardinals in St. Louis on June 2, the Giants committed two errors and handed the Cards a 5–4 win. The victory over Maglie completed the Cardinals' sweep of a three-game series. The game began well for Sal, as the Giants picked up three runs off Cards southpaw Harry Brecheen in the first three innings. But in the bottom of the third Dark made a wild throw on what should have been an inning-ending double play, and St. Louis scored two runs, one of them unearned.

With two out in the sixth, right fielder Don Mueller hesitated on a high pop fly by Peanuts Lowery, and the ball bounced off his glove. The scorekeeper called it a double rather than an error, and it led to a three-run sixth for the Cards. Sal rarely showed any emotion on the mound, no matter what kind of fumbling took place among the fielders, but this time he was visibly upset. Clearly, he needed all the fielding support he could get, and the Giants were failing to provide it. In the seventh, with two on and none out, Durocher removed Sal for pinch hitter Bill Rigney, who grounded into a double play. Max Lanier completed the game.

The defeat was a particularly galling one for the Giants. They had failed to support their ace pitcher and could not take advantage of a Dodger defeat the same afternoon. Willie Mays was gone to his army service; they had lost five of their last six games, and the whole team appeared to be in a slump. After the game Sal was disconsolate. He tried to be philosophical, saying the usual "You've got to lose one sooner or later," but he slouched in front of his locker looking as if he had lost the deciding game of the World Series rather than an early season contest. "My control was off a little," he admitted, trying to explain what had happened to him. "If I'd had my control, I'd have been all right, but I was in trouble in every inning." Sal's control was not too bad; he walked only four, one of them intentionally, but registered no strikeouts. "I've always missed the breaks with this club," Sal grumbled, in a rare moment of self-pity.[27] Even if the results were less than disastrous, Maglie sensed that something was wrong with him.

On June 6 the Pirates, the team that had beaten Sal only once in 14 tries across three seasons, pounced on The Barber and knocked him out in the fourth inning. Sal gave up five runs, two of them unearned, on six hits, walked three and struck out three. The Giants defense continued to be poor; this time they committed three errors, and Pittsburgh waltzed away with an 8–1 victory. On June 10 the Giants lost a 14–inning game against Cincinnati, 6–5, a game that took four and one-third hours to complete. Sal lasted seven mediocre innings in the marathon contest, giving up four runs on eight hits, walking four, and striking out five. Shapiro, in his 1957 biography of Maglie, gave a detailed, behind-the-scenes account of Sal's back problems before and during the series with Cincinnati, including extensive dialogue between Maglie and coach Frank Shellenback, and harrowing descriptions of Sal's back pain during that time, but it is unclear how much of the material is based on fact, and how much is imaginative semi-fiction. Sal was not revealing any such agonies to reporters.

A real blowout of a game took place on June 15 at the Polo Grounds. A large crowd turned out to watch the Giants play, and after three innings it looked like the fans would go home happy, since the New Yorkers had blasted their way to an 11–0 lead over St. Louis. With Maglie on the mound, a rally by the Cards seemed unlikely, but rally they did, knocking Sal out with a seven-run fifth inning. The Cards scored three more in the seventh, then Solly Hemus tied the game with a lead-off homer in the eighth. He hit another round tripper in the ninth to increase the Cardinals' lead to 14–11. Although the dazed Giants started a modest rally in the bottom of the ninth, scoring one run, the Cardinals took the game, 14–12. Durocher's pennant winners had blown an 11–run lead; the team's best pitcher had gotten his ears pinned back, and once again the Giants had played sloppily, committing three errors, including one by Maglie.

Some of the reporters covering the game thought that Durocher should have taken Sal out earlier than he did, before the Cards pounded him for seven runs. In the *Times*, John Drebinger observed that "the skipper had only himself to blame for allowing Maglie to stagger through that nightmarish fifth inning." After the game Sal told the assembled sportswriters, "With that big lead, I was sure we had this one stowed away, so I just let up. Then I couldn't get going again."[28] Maglie faced the Cards in a brief appearance in relief the next day and hit Tommy Glaviano, who had homered against him the day before. Sal took on the Cubs on June 20, and although New York won the game, 4–3, in ten innings, Sal lasted only two innings. He allowed three runs on four hits and issued one walk. Max Lanier followed him to the mound and turned in eight innings of shutout pitching to gain the win.

Sal had not completed a game or won a game since his shutout of the Dodgers on May 27. In five starts and one relief appearance the once-invincible pitcher had been hit hard even by ordinary batters. He could no longer be relied on to come through in clutch situations, and the Giants had fallen into second place. Although he was not talking about it in public, his back was still bothering him, and once again he took his troubles to Frank Shellenback, asking the pitching coach to watch him warm up, to see if he could spot any problems in his delivery. Shellenback watched Sal throw for ten minutes, then offered a diagnosis. "You're cramping your follow-through. Until the last couple of weeks, you had a nice, loose, easy move following through. Now you've been putting a hitch in it."[29] Apparently Sal had been favoring his aching back, and now he worked hard at following Shellenback's instructions on how to iron out the kink in his delivery. He hoped he had found the solution to his problem.

On June 26 against Brooklyn at the Polo Grounds, The Barber emerged with his razor freshly sharpened. Despite speculation before the game that the 35–year-old pitcher had reached the end of the line, Sal proved he still held the Dodgers in the palm of his pitching hand. Since his victory over Brooklyn on May 27 Maglie had failed to win a game and had been knocked out in five straight starts, but this time, sweating copiously in the 100–degree heat, he hurled a three-hit shutout that was a no-hitter until Jackie Robinson broke it up with a single in the seventh inning. Sal's mastery over the Dodgers was beginning to seem supernatural—he had become the Demon Barber of Brooklyn. The win was Sal's seventh in a row over the Dodgers and his third of the current season, added to four in the latter part of 1951. In addition, he had now hurled three consecutive shutouts against the Dodgers. Sal did not attribute either his ability to defeat the Dodgers or his sudden return to form to anything supernatural. With sweat still streaming down his face he answered reporters' questions in his usual matter-of-fact way, saying, "I made up my mind to just throw that ball with a good follow-through. I just decided to throw hard as long as I could and let them hit it. Then we'd see what happened." What happened was mostly nothing, as far as the Dodgers were concerned. Sal needed only 85 pitches to dispose of the Bums, who flailed harmlessly at Sal's offerings. "The fewer pitches, the better off you are on a hot night like this," Sal declared, still wiping away sweat. "Now I'm out of the slump. Everything is going to be all right."[30]

But everything was not all right, either with Sal or with the Giants. Maglie took the mound on June 30 in the first game of a doubleheader against the Boston Braves and eked out his eleventh win, 8–7. Sal had a shaky time, lasting seven innings and giving up six runs on eleven hits, while walking three and recording five strikeouts. Durocher removed him in the eighth after he walked Eddie Mathews and Jack Daniels touched him for a double. The Giants finished June in second place with a 17–12 record, to which Sal had contributed only two wins in seven outings.

On the Fourth of July there was cause for great rejoicing in Brooklyn. Before a crowd of nearly 50,000 at the Polo Grounds, where by 1952 only the appearance of the Giants' crosstown rivals brought out fans in large numbers, the Dodgers finally defeated Sal Maglie. It was the first time they had bested The Barber since April 22, 1951. Sal began with his control in tatters, as he walked the first four batters, forcing in a run. In the second, with Billy Cox on with a single, Reese poled a homer into the left field stands. Sal managed to complete the inning, but Durocher removed him for a pinch hitter in the third. By the time the umpires called the game after eight innings due to rain, the Dodgers led, 5–1, and Sal received his third loss. Since he had pitched only two innings on July 4, Durocher started Sal again on the sixth against the Phillies, in the last game before the All-Star break. Sal had a perfect lifetime record against Philadelphia, 9–0, but this time they beat him, 4–1. He lasted seven and one-third innings, giving up three runs on five hits.

Sal was one of five New York Giants chosen for the 1952 All-Star game. Along with seven Brooklyn Dodgers, the two New York teams contributed almost half the members of the National League squad, an indication of their continuing dominance in their league. Leo Durocher, helmsman of the 1951 pennant-winning Giants, was the manager. For this one day, seven All-Star Dodgers would be under his control, five of them chosen by Leo—Gil Hodges, Pee Wee Reese, Duke Snider, Carl Furillo, and Preacher Roe—while two more, Roy Campanella and Jackie Robinson, were chosen by the fans. From his own team Durocher picked only Sal Maglie for his first-string team. It is possible that Leo was resting his own players over the All-Star break while making the Dodgers work. The fans chose Whitey Lockman and Bobby Thomson, and Durocher added Wes Westrum and Alvin Dark to his reserve squad. Although newspapers reported that Maglie would probably be the National League's starting pitcher, Sal did not appear in the contest, a rain-shortened five-inning game that the National League won, 3–2.

After the All-Star break the Giants dropped three of their next four games. On July 11 Sal lost to last-place Pittsburgh, 6–2, a particularly disheartening defeat. He lasted seven innings, allowing all six of the Pirates' runs and giving up ten hits. Durocher, frustrated with his club's performance, called up Dusty Rhodes from Nashville, commenting that he could lose just as well with new men as with the ones he had been playing. As far as anyone knows, Sal had not yet discussed his back problems with Durocher directly, but he seems to have confided them to pitching coach Shellenback. In the newspapers, writers could only speculate. Some made excuses for Maglie, claiming that his setbacks could be attributed to the Giants' sloppy fielding and poor hitting, or the loss to the team of Mays and Irvin. Others implied that Sal's decline began when accusations by the Reds and the Dodgers focused close attention on Maglie's quasi-legal pitching methods, obliging him to clean up his mound routines and thereby lessening his effectiveness. Leo Durocher was a smart, experienced, and highly observant baseball man who must have been aware that there was something wrong with Sal. A pitcher does not go from winning nine straight, and being virtually unhittable, to five straight losses, failing to complete all but one game, and being smacked around even by mediocre hitters, just because his teammates make a few errors behind him or fail to pile up a lot of runs. Perhaps Durocher, like Sal himself, was in a state of denial: ignore the problem and maybe it will go away.

Durocher gave Sal an extra day of rest before sending him to the mound again on July 16 to face the Cardinals at Sportsman's Park. The Giants pulled out an 8–7 win in ten innings of a nasty contest that took almost four hours to complete. Maglie faced Wilmer "Vinegar Bend" Mizell, a rookie southpaw with an unraveling pretzel windup and a sizzling fastball. Like Maglie, Mizell had no inhibitions about brushing back batters, and he welcomed Dusty Rhodes to the majors by decking him in the second inning. Maglie tried to retaliate, but instead nicked Cardinal third baseman Billy Johnson with a pitch. In the top of the third Mizell nailed Sal hard on his left arm. Maglie tried to remain in the game, but the combination of back pain and the added injury to his arm proved too much for him. He retired the first two batters in the top of the fourth, but then Mizell, who was batting .044—an awful average even for a pitcher—touched Sal for a triple. Although Sal had not given up any runs, he was in serious distress, sweating profusely as well as moving stiffly and with great difficulty. Durocher knew it was time for Maglie to come out and went to the mound personally to remove Sal from the game, a task he usually left to his coaches. Sal's condition was hardly a secret, and the masquerade had gone on long enough. The next day's *Times* reported this was the fifth straight start Maglie had failed to finish "because of a crippling pain in the lumbar region that will keep him idle until the Giants return home."[31] The searing pain in his back would keep him idle for longer than that. Within days, Sal was in the hospital, and he did not return to the mound for a month.

How—and why—had Durocher avoided dealing with his star pitcher's problems for so long? The most likely answer is that Sal concealed them so successfully. A quiet, determined man of stoic disposition who detested acknowledging any ailment or weakness, Maglie had plodded to the mound again and again, his back ablaze with pain, insisting he felt fine. Sportswriters were baffled. Phil Allen interviewed Durocher after Sal's "strange slump" had begun, but before the pitcher broke down completely, and received some revealing answers. "When Maglie suddenly lost his touch," Durocher related, "I asked the trainer whether anything was wrong with his arm, whether he complained of any illness, whether he was worried over anything, and the trainer told me there was nothing wrong." Asked if he had spoken to Maglie about possible problems, Leo had a ready response. "I never said a word to Maglie. I never ask a pitcher. They won't tell you anything. . . . If anything is wrong they'll generally tell the trainer where they won't tell me, but Maglie never told the trainer anything." Durocher concluded by shrugging off Sal's difficulties. "I've seen Maglie in slumps like this before and he always comes out of them sooner or later. I'll just have to be patient." Allen ended his article by suggesting that Maglie's real problem was old age. "Maybe a 35–year-old arm gets tired after nine straight wins."[32]

At the time Durocher was answering Phil Allen's questions, neither man knew how serious Sal's problems really were. Shortly after his abbreviated outing on July 16 the Giants realized that Sal's back was not going to improve if they continued to ignore the problem. From St. Louis, the team sent the pitcher to the Chicago Medical Center, where doctors found a lump the size of a lemon near the base of his spine. It was not a tumor, they assured him, but they diagnosed his problem as a badly strained ligament. Sal had suffered a serious joint and muscle strain in his lower back, which he had ignored, and the lump was due to a severe reflexive spasm of the lower back muscles as they attempted to "guard" the injured ligaments and joints that Sal continued to stress when he insisted on pitching through his pain. The recommended therapy was known as diathermy, an electricity-based treatment commonly employed by physical therapists and sports trainers in the 1950s. A large and awkward machine was used to create heat in the affected body tissues in order to stimulate blood flow to the injured area and promote muscle relaxation and healing. Sal spent two restless and unhappy weeks undergoing diathermy treatments in Chicago, all the while fretting over his inability to help the Giants when they needed him most. As July crawled to its end, the Giants played .500 ball, and the Dodgers tightened their hold on first place.

At last, the doctors in Chicago allowed Sal to return to New York, but he was not yet ready to go home, much less back to the mound. He was sent to Harkness Pavilion, part of New York's Columbia Presbyterian Medical Center. There, the medical staff continued the diathermy treatments and also put Sal's back in traction. As used in the 1950s, this was a procedure where the patient lay on his back in a bed with a harness around his waist. Two ropes were attached to the harness, running along the side of the patient's legs and over a pulley at the end of the bed, with weights attached to the end of the ropes to create a long axis of pull, or traction force, on the spine. The effect was to provide a gradual, sustained pull on the spine to relax the muscles, take the weight off the vertebrae, and stretch the joints of the spine. During the course of treatment, which could go on for several days or weeks, the patient remained in bed.[33] Fortunately for Sal's strength and stamina, the traction therapy lasted only three days, and when it was over he returned home to his apartment in Manhattan, with strict orders not to exert himself too much or too quickly. The doctors told him it would take at least two weeks of gradually increasing exercise for his back to be able to endure the strain of pitching, and longer than that before he could participate in an actual game. Frantic to return to baseball, Sal was in uniform and back at the Polo Grounds the next day.

As the Giants stumbled through the first two weeks of August, winning five and losing eight, Sal tried to regain his form. He wanted to pitch during the three-game series against the Dodgers in the first week of August, but his back was too stiff. He tried warm-up pitches from the mound, but as a result he could hardly move the next day. Even without Sal, the Giants took two of the three games against the Dodgers. The New Yorkers were not so lucky in Boston on August 8, 9, and 11, as the Braves swept four straight. On August 13 the Giants returned to Brooklyn and split a doubleheader with the Dodgers. The next day, almost a month after he had last pitched a game and less than two weeks after he had left the hospital, Maglie took the hill to face the Dodgers. Although his back was too stiff for him to bend down to field bunts, and he had to squat to reach the rosin bag, his razor remained sharp. He lasted six innings and held Brooklyn scoreless for the first four, securing his twelfth victory, 4–3, with help from Al Corwin. Dressen, aware of Sal's back problems, had his hitters bunting, but Giants infielders covered for the hobbled pitcher, and Sal tossed enough brushbacks to keep his opponents on notice against crowding the plate. The *Eagle*'s Tommy Holmes noted that Sal threw stiffly and unnaturally during the game but accused the notorious Dodger-downer of hurling "unmistakable beanballs" at Reese and Robinson in the first inning. Half-crippled though he was, Maglie's mere presence on the mound paralyzed the Dodgers. They had yet to defeat him in their own backyard.

The Giants swept a doubleheader from the Cubs on August 19. In the opener Sal looked like his old self, tossing an eight-hit shutout, 5–0, for his thirteenth win, his first complete game since June 26. His teammates made his life easier by scoring four runs for him in the first inning. Sal claimed he felt fine and strong after the game, and if he had experienced any back pain it did not show up in his performance. Maglie started another game on August 24, against the Reds in Cincinnati, but did not figure in the decision. He worked five and one-third innings, giving up three runs (one unearned), as the Giants lost, 5–4. The Giants defeated the Dodgers, 4–3, on August 30 at Ebbets Field. Once again, the winning pitcher was Sal Maglie, whose record improved to 14–5. In late August the Dodgers led the league by eight games over the second-place Giants, but with their 1951 collapse still fresh in their minds, the Dodgers were nervous. Lacking Maglie's services from mid-July to mid-August had cost the Giants several games—they were 11–14 during that period—and they had been unable to put together a winning streak long enough to enable them to gain ground on Brooklyn.

In September Maglie returned to his familiar role of workhorse. Of the last 29 games the Giants played, Sal participated in nine, making six starts as well as three appearances in relief. Sal started the first game of a doubleheader on September 3 and shut out the Phils in the first four innings. In the fifth, however, Philadelphia scored three runs, only one of them earned, as Sal and third baseman Bob Elliott both committed errors. Sal left for a pinch hitter in the bottom of the fifth and did not figure in the decision as the Giants went on to win, 4–3, in 10 innings. Two days later, with the Giants leading 5–4 in the ninth, Sal came in to relieve Al Corwin with one out and runners on first and third. He struck out both batters he faced to end the game. With The Barber back, Durocher refused to concede the pennant. "I'll give up when I read in the papers that Brooklyn clinched the flag. . . . If we ever take those Dodgers again, there'll be 100,000 suicides in Brooklyn!"[34]

Beginning on September 6 the Giants played an unusually long five-game series against the Dodgers at the Polo Grounds that included a single game sandwiched in between two doubleheaders. Dodgers owner Walter O'Malley tried to galvanize his slumping squad by sending a sharply worded telegram addressed to manager Dressen that was intended for the entire team. In it he declared, "We have to beat the Giants. If we don't—then we don't deserve to win. . . . We need courageous pitching and free and vicious hitting. . . . We have enough guys who want to win to do the job."[35] Despite O'Malley's efforts, the Giants swept the first twin bill on September 6, reducing the Dodgers' lead to four games. On that same date, the citizens of Niagara Falls gave Sal another "day," honoring him for the third time in three years (Figure 13). Almost 500 showed up for the celebration, led by the city's police chief, two city councilmen, and Sal's old friends Carmen Caggiano and Dominic Iannuzzi. Gifts included a heavy gold ring and a check for $700. Sal announced that he was donating the check to the Boys Clubs of Niagara Falls, an organization in which he had been active for several years.

It is fortunate that the Niagara boosters chose September 6 for their celebration, since the Giants won two games that day and Sal could relax—he was not pitching. On the following day, when Maglie faced the Dodgers' Preacher Roe, he was not so lucky. Sal gave up solo homers to four different Dodgers, while Roe limited the Giants to a single run, handing Sal his sixth loss. On September 8 the two teams played another doubleheader. The rivals split the twin bill, and seemed intent on splitting each other's skulls and skins as well. The day game was an ugly business that featured hit batsmen, beanballs, a spiking, and the ejection of a pitcher. The Dodgers ran roughshod over the Giants, winning 10–2, and clobbering five Giants hurlers, beginning with Max Lanier. In the course of the afternoon Bill Rigney had to leave the game after he received a spike wound from Gil Hodges as Hodges slid into second; Hoyt Wilhelm hit Hodges with a pitch; Dodger pitcher Joe Black decked Giant right fielder George Wilson, and Monte Kennedy did the same to Hodges and Black; and finally, with two out in the top of the ninth, umpire Lee Ballanfant ejected an astonished Larry Jansen for hitting Billy Cox with the first, and what turned out to be the only, pitch Jansen threw.

13—Boy meets hero. Shy, seven-year-old Vince D'Anna, son of Russ D'Anna, one of Maglie's Niagara Falls friends, is introduced to Sal during the Sal Maglie Day celebration at the Polo Grounds on September 6, 1952. Photo: collection of Vince D'Anna.

The nightcap, in contrast, was a tense contest the Giants won, 3–2, in the bottom of the ninth on a double by Don Mueller. Almost as dramatic as Mueller's clutch hit was the courageous relief pitching of Sal Maglie, who entered the game in the seventh with the score tied, 2–2, nobody out, and Brooklyn's lead run on third. Because Sal had pitched the previous day, he was not even in the bullpen. He had to hurry down there to warm up as the inning started badly for Al Corwin, who first gave up a single to Hodges. When a triple by Pafko tied the score, Maglie was brought to the mound. Although Sal's back problems were still obvious enough that reporters watching the game noticed his altered motion and reduced power, the crafty pitcher put out the fire. In his three innings of relief he gave up two hits and two walks but no runs. In the bottom of the ninth Hank Thompson singled and scored the winning run on Mueller's double, giving Sal the satisfaction of notching his fifteenth victory and once again defeating the Dodgers.

Despite the close pennant race, only 3,094 fans showed up at the Polo Grounds on September 11 to watch Sal face Pittsburgh and struggle through five innings to notch his sixteenth victory. The Dodgers lost that day, and Sal's win cut Brooklyn's lead to 3 1/2 games. On September 12 the Giants played a doubleheader against Cincinnati, and took the first game, 4–2, extending their winning streak to five. In the second game Sal appeared in relief, although he had pitched five difficult innings the day before. He came on in the eighth and managed to retire the Reds, but in the ninth he allowed two successive doubles, and the Reds went on to win, 8–7, handing Sal his seventh loss on a day when the Dodgers won. In the clubhouse Maglie spoke to reporters. "I'm dead tired," he admitted. "My arm feels heavy. I didn't have much."[36] Not a word about his back problems. Then, as if to disprove any notion that his back was still troubling him, on September 15 Sal pitched a complete game against the Cards that was as solid as any he had hurled since being sidelined in mid-season. He gave up one run on six hits while his teammates blasted five St. Louis pitchers for 12 runs. The win brought Sal's record to 17–7.

After the New Yorkers split a pair with the Cubs at home, they traveled to Philadelphia, where the Phillies swept three games and buried the Giants' pennant hopes. Sal lost a heartbreaker on September 19, a classic pitchers' duel between Maglie and Curt Simmons. The one run the Phillies scored came in the first inning on a disgraceful error by Clint Hartung in right field. After Sal had given up a walk to Richie Ashburn, Mel Clark lifted a routine fly to right that any competent fielder should have caught. Instead, the ball bounced off Hartung's knees, and Clark was safe. On the mound, Sal cursed in disgust. When Ashburn scored on a single by Del Ennis, that was the ball game. Although he had pitched seven fine innings before being removed for a pinch hitter and had given up only that single unearned run, Sal took his eighth loss, bringing his record to 17–8. As the season drew to a close there was no longer any hope of overtaking the Dodgers, who clinched the pennant on September 23. On September 24 the Giants hammered Boston, 11–8, but Sal was knocked out in the first inning after retiring only one batter, as the Braves scored three runs. This was the shortest outing so far in Sal's major league career. Despite all his problems, Sal closed out his 1952 season in strong fashion, with an 8–0 shutout of the Phillies. He lasted almost seven innings and perhaps could have finished the game, but he left in the seventh so Hoyt Wilhelm could come in and break Ace Adams' record, set in 1943, of 70 relief appearances. Sal pitched before an almost-empty stadium: attendance for the meaningless game was 1,684. His win was the last Giants victory of the season as they dropped their final two games to the Phillies and finished the season in second place, 4 1/2 games behind the pennant-winning Dodgers. The 1952 Dodgers, the legendary "Boys of Summer" in their full flower, took the Lords of the Bronx to seven games in the World Series but lost again as the Yankees won their fourth consecutive championship.

Sal Maglie had now completed three full seasons in the majors, the minimum sportswriters required to take a player seriously as an established star and not just a bottle-rocket who flares briefly before disappearing. In each of those years Sal had posted an outstanding record, and his winning percentage remained among the highest for active pitchers. Although back problems hampered him severely for most of the season and he failed to break the mark for fewest losses over a three-year period, he still posted a superb 18–8 record. Only Philadelphia's Robin Roberts, who led both leagues with 28 victories, won more games. Sal posted an excellent 2.92 ERA, among the ten best in the league. Had Sal enjoyed a healthier 1952, the Giants might well have overtaken the Dodgers and repeated their 1951 miracle, but that possibility was now no more than fuel for the Hot Stove league.

MOTIVATING MAGLIE—SAL'S RELATIONSHIP WITH LEO DUROCHER

On the August day Sal came home from the hospital he gave a long interview at his apartment to the perceptive columnist Milton Gross, a man with the unusual ability to persuade Maglie to speak frankly about the problems he was experiencing.[37] Gross described Sal lying on the couch in his living room, with his feet elevated and pillows under his back. He did not, Gross observed, look like a man who would be back on the mound any time soon. "It's more serious than I thought, I guess," Sal admitted reluctantly. He then related the history of his back problems, acknowledging that he had been experiencing stiffness in his back even before it became obvious in his pitching performances. He recalled running in the outfield in Cincinnati during a workout in the second week of July and feeling discomfort in his back. The problem worsened that night, he said, due to the chill from the air-conditioning in his hotel room, and when he tried to pitch on July 16, the pain finally became unbearable. That was when Durocher took him out of the game, even though he had not yet given up a run. Asked when he thought he might be ready to pitch, Sal answered, "I can't even say when I'll pitch to the hitters, because now I don't even know if I can stretch my legs. [Last week] I couldn't bend over to touch my knees. I'd go into the bathroom to wash and my back'd stiffen and I'd just stand there splashing water on my face, unable to straighten up. Maybe tomorrow," Sal sighed, "Maybe tomorrow after I exercise I'll be able to tell you." The final question Gross asked was whether Maglie had ever told Durocher what was happening to him. "No," Sal replied. "I was worried, but I didn't complain. Everybody takes their turn. I'm no different. I didn't want them to think I was alibiing."

Other reporters had been unable to find out much about Sal's condition, beyond the fact that he had been experiencing back pain, but Gross not only presented the specifics of Sal's physical condition, he also offered pertinent insights into the relationship between Maglie and his manager. Sal's description of his refusal to say anything to Durocher about his condition, for fear he might be accused of making excuses for his poor performances, mirrors Durocher's own earlier comments to interviewer Phil Allen that pitchers "won't tell you anything."

Sal, in particular, must have been reluctant to tell his manager anything that might imply he was less than willing to take his turn, because he knew that Durocher had already decided he was a slacker, a pitcher who had to be urged to "bend his back." There are two curious references to Maglie in articles about the use of hypnosis in sports, where the authors claim that in 1952 Durocher thought Sal's problems were more mental than physical and sent the pitcher to a hypnotist named Arthur Ellen, whom Leo had encountered doing a stage show at the Chase Hotel in St. Louis. According to these accounts, Ellen hypnotized Sal, and then showed him he was being overprotective and that there was nothing physically wrong with him.[38] There *was*, of course, something wrong with Sal physically, and the problems were not going to disappear, no matter what Sal may have claimed while under hypnosis.

The relationship between Durocher and Maglie, alluded to in Milton Gross' column, was complicated, and it resists easy generalizations. Different observers who knew both Durocher and Maglie, and watched the two men interact, came to different, even opposite, conclusions. The common thread that connects the disparate observations and opinions is an awareness that both men were ferocious competitors whose desire to win trumped any other consideration. Durocher was willing to go to unethical if not illegal lengths to win ball games by any means, including the use of his spyglass and buzzer system. Maglie was willing to risk destroying his own body in that same pursuit and took the risk of maiming or killing his opponents with knockdown pitches for the same reason. And yet, despite Maglie's menacing reputation on the mound, Durocher felt the pitcher lacked sufficient competitiveness.

Durocher, although he would not have put it in these terms, considered himself a motivational psychologist. He believed that different players required different approaches by the manager in order to perform at their best. Some needed to be coddled; others, Leo was convinced, needed a swift kick in the behind, and Durocher fancied he could distinguish who needed which kind of treatment. He was brilliant in his handling of rookie Willie Mays, understanding that the naive young man with prodigious natural gifts needed constant praise, reassurance, and fatherly support. He also correctly assumed that the older and more emotionally mature Monte Irvin did not need any hand-holding and only wished to be treated with respect. When Durocher sized up Sal Maglie he saw a tough, seasoned veteran, a mature man who was already an experienced pitcher when he rejoined the Giants in 1950. But perhaps because he knew Maglie had played for two years in Mexico, a country renowned in American ethnic stereotyping for laziness and torpor, Durocher became convinced that Sal needed a fire built under him in order to perform to the utmost. Maglie's personal reserve, his reluctance to be a "holler guy," may also have led Durocher to suspect that Sal lacked sufficient enthusiasm and desire to win. Finally, as Sal himself admitted, he had a tendency to ease up when he was far ahead in a game. Durocher must have noticed that as well.

Whatever his reasons, Durocher concluded that Maglie required rough treatment. "Sal Maglie you had to stay after," Leo declared in his autobiography. "You had to needle him, you had to make him mad."[39] Durocher claimed, with evident pride, that he sometimes infuriated Maglie so much that the pitcher retaliated by giving his manager the "Italian salute"—Leo's name for Sal's gesture of grabbing his crotch. Some of Sal's teammates on the Giants confirmed Durocher's habit of "riding" certain players. "I have a very clear recollection of Durocher's *modus operandi*," recalled Whitey Lockman. "Don Mueller, Wes Westrum, and Sal Maglie were three guys where he used the reverse psychology routine to try to motivate them. He would ride them, and try to get them mad at him. He thought it would inspire them, or motivate them to perform better. Maybe it worked with Maglie—he certainly pitched well for Leo!"[40] Monte Irvin agreed with Lockman, saying "that's the way Leo *was*. Sometimes Leo would get on you just to make you mad, and make you try harder."[41] Larry Jansen, who recalled getting along well with Durocher, described him as a manager who would "chew your butt real good if you screwed up, but the next day he'd forget about it."[42] Even catcher Sal Yvars, who called Durocher "a vulgar, filthy guy who treated me and Maglie like dirt,"[43] acknowledged that Leo tried "to win any way he possibly could." Yvars also confirmed Durocher's (and Maglie's own) perception that Sal would let up when he was four or five runs ahead, "so we'd get on him a little bit—throw the ball back to him real hard—wake him up."[44] Alvin Dark did not recall Durocher singling out Maglie for any special abuse and believes the two men had a good relationship. Durocher, according to Dark, "knew which ones he could get on and he knew which ones he should not get on, and he was just one of those managers who would do anything that would help win a ball game."[45]

Roger Kahn declared that Durocher believed in motivating Maglie with the verbal equivalent of a lash—a lash embedded with barbed ethnic insults. A manager today who abused a player with a hail of ethnic slurs would have a lawsuit on his hands, face discipline from the commissioner's office, or be out of a job, but not in the 1950s. Without a trace of embarrassment Durocher confided to Kahn in the early '50s his method for bringing out the best in Sal Maglie: "Now the dago pitcher," Durocher began, "is a different kettle of fish [from Willie Mays.] If I let him get happy, he don't pitch good. So I get him mad. I say, 'Watsa matter, you stupid wop, you choking?' He gets so mad he wants to kill me, but he don't. He takes his dago temper out on the fucking hitters."[46]

As Kahn records it, Durocher was not describing an isolated incident, but the typical way he treated his ace righthander. How Maglie felt about being obliged to listen to those kinds of insults for years is unknown, because Sal remained silent on the subject. Although he may have growled some responses to Durocher's goading, he never retaliated or complained about his manager's treatment of him. Throughout his life he rarely criticized Durocher, insisting that Leo had given him his chance as a pitcher. Durocher, not surprisingly, tried to exonerate himself in his autobiography, claiming that Sal understood perfectly well what his manager was doing, and why.[47] The treatment enraged Sal, but in Durocher's version of events, Maglie admitted its effectiveness. What toll it may have taken on the pitcher to keep that rage bottled up inside him remains a question for psychologists to answer.

1953—Sal's Season in Hell

12

The biggest baseball news of 1953 seemed to have nothing to do with the New York teams. For the first time since 1902—when the Baltimore Orioles moved to New York City and later reemerged as the Yankees—a major league franchise changed cities. The Boston Braves, who had long performed in the shadow of the more popular Red Sox, moved to Milwaukee, a transfer closely watched by other restless owners. This marked the beginning of a series of moves that would see big league teams migrating around—and across—the country. In 1952 the Red Sox had drawn more than a million fans and the Braves a paltry 281,000. But in the beer capital of America the Braves enjoyed a season attendance record of 1,826,397, almost a quarter of a million more than the world champion Yankees drew in 1953 in a park twice the size of Milwaukee's. Urged on by wildly enthusiastic fans, the Braves surged from seventh place in 1952 to a second-place finish in 1953. The Dodgers took over first place in late June and won the pennant on September 12. The Giants, still without Willie Mays, and plagued by pitching problems that included the collapse of Sal Maglie, finished fifth.

After his disappointing but far from disastrous 1952 season, Maglie considered himself cured and pushed aside suspicions that he might be near the end of his career. "I don't think so," he told the *Niagara Falls Gazette* in October after his return home. "I feel swell and my back ailment is just about over. I don't think it will be chronic. The way I feel, I don't see why I shouldn't have a lot of good years ahead. . . .

A player doesn't just fade out of the picture overnight." Sal was right about one thing: he did not fade out of the picture. Throughout his hellish 1953 season, as his back ailment and other miseries beset him and his effectiveness plummeted, the publicity never lessened. Sal experienced the other side of fame. When he was the triumphant pitcher spinning shutouts and strikeouts and streaks of scoreless innings, the fans, photographers, and sportswriters pursued him with praise and celebrated his accomplishments. But when he collapsed, when his control crumbled and his curve failed to break, when he was shelled off the mound again and again, barely able to retire a single batter, it all happened under the same pitiless glare. Now, though, writers hovered like vultures, each wanting to be the first to break the story of The Barber's retirement. Although the 1953 season was the worst Sal had experienced up to this point, he had fought too hard for his major league career to give it all up.

As the 1952 season ended, sportswriters' speculation centered on the New York Giants. Some stories concerned possible trades the Giants might make to shore up their tattered pitching staff, which had been a big disappointment in 1952. Jansen as well as Maglie had suffered a back injury, with Jansen's effectiveness limited even more sharply than Maglie's. Jim Hearn had fallen apart in August, other starters had been erratic, and only reliever Hoyt Wilhelm had been outstanding. In an article for the *Sporting News* Arch Murray listed five Giants as "untouchable," that is, not to be traded: Irvin, Thomson, Lockman, Dark, and Maglie, implying that any other player might be traded in the search for better pitching. A few months later Murray reported that doctors declared "there is nothing organically wrong with Sal Maglie. His arm is still strong and the back . . . is sound again."[1]

There was also speculation about whether Maglie's salary would be slashed in 1953 as a response to his less than brilliant 1952 season. During the second week of January, Maglie attended the New York Press Photographers Association dinner, and while in New York he also planned to confer with Horace Stoneham about his 1953 contract. He told reporters he had been spending a quiet off-season, avoiding his usual round of public appearances in the interest of giving his body a thorough rest. But he had stayed in shape. "Have I been keeping in trim?" Sal answered the question by patting his flat stomach. "Even over Christmas and New Year's," he assured his listeners, no small feat given the multicourse feasts Italian families consume on those holidays. Asked if he expected to take a cut in salary, Sal answered that he did not think he would be asked to accept a pay cut, and he was right. To everyone's surprise, he signed his contract that same evening at the Photographers Association dinner. Stoneham had brought the paperwork with him to the banquet and signed Sal when the pitcher came over to his table to exchange greetings. The announcement, made during the dinner, left reporters scrambling to the telephones to pass in the news to their editors and distracted everyone from the purpose of the dinner, which was to present Maglie, Dodger shortstop Pee Wee Reese, and Yankee shortstop Phil Rizzuto with plaques as the athletes most cooperative with photographers.[2]

As usual, no one would reveal the exact amount of the contract, but it was announced that Sal had received the same terms as the previous year, estimated at between $35,000 and $37,500. Maglie exclaimed afterward, "I'm as happy as I am surprised," which suggests that, contrary to his earlier statement, he expected a salary cut. His swift signing contrasted with his tense contract negotiations the previous year. Sal also revealed that, as a result of having three teeth extracted, "my back feels better than ever."[3] What causal connection Sal thought existed between his troublesome teeth and his aching back is anybody's guess, but pitchers are willing to submit to just about anything short of castration if they think it will improve their mound performance. Perhaps Sal had suffered toothaches that compounded the discomfort caused by his back problems. And if he *believed* that having the teeth removed made him feel better, that was almost as good as a sound medical connection between his back and his jaw.

As the Giants' spring training season began Sal's performances were erratic. He started off strong, pitching three scoreless innings against the Cubs on March 9. Interviewed afterward, Sal was elated. "I would say it was an entirely satisfactory workout," he declared with a smile. "I wasn't at all tired and could have gone on for another three innings." Then, however, Sal admitted to a problem: "I still can feel a hitch just above my right hipbone when I stride on that leg. . . . I'm not worried about it at all, but I'll let the doc work on it a little."[4] As the training season went on Sal would win a game and then lose one, be entirely in control or find himself being hammered. During several appearances his back stiffened and he departed early. He finished spring training with a 4–2 record, and although he talked an optimistic line, his back was still bothering him.

On Opening Day, April 14, Durocher gave the ball to Larry Jansen, because he wanted to save Sal for the Giants' home opener against the Dodgers. The Giants began their home schedule on April 17 with what had always been a guarantee of a big turnout—a doubleheader against the Dodgers with Sal the Barber set to shave Dem Bums in the opener. But a crowd of only 18,307—less than half the Polo Grounds' capacity—showed up for the games. The opener had been billed as a duel between aces, with Maglie facing Preacher Roe, but the Dodger southpaw called in sick with an upset stomach, so Dressen replaced him with a rookie making his major league debut: a pallid, blond, 20–year-old lefthander named Johnny Podres, who looked like he needed to shave maybe once a week. Sal, black-bearded and sinister as ever, began the game in brilliant fashion and seemed on his way to inflicting the ultimate humiliation on the Dodgers: for six and two-thirds innings he had a no-hitter going. But then, with two out in the sixth, Jackie Robinson hit a little wind-blown fly into left field that eluded Monte Irvin. Robinson, always a brilliant base runner, took a wide turn at first, drawing a wild throw from Irvin that allowed Robinson to race all the way to third. Campanella followed with a triple for the first Dodger run. But the Giants had already scored three times by that point, and they picked up three more in the eighth. Although Sal began the top of the ninth with a five-run lead, by that time his back had stiffened. He retired the first batter to face him, but then gave up four successive singles and two runs before Durocher summoned Wilhelm from the bullpen to shut the door. The Giants won, 6–3, and Maglie had beaten Brooklyn yet again. Although he wavered in the ninth, he had pitched eight superb innings and shown excellent control: he struck out only three but did not issue any walks. Maglie's magic spell over the Dodgers remained intact. As Red Smith put it, "Maglie opened the Manhattan baseball season as skillfully as a barber opens a jugular."[5] Smith's chilling, demon-barber analogy could only add to the Maglie myth. Sal pitched again on April 21, against the Pirates, who had always been among his easiest victims. But this time Pittsburgh pulled out a 5–4 win. Sal lasted only four and one-third innings, giving up five runs on nine hits.

The annual Dodgers-Giants war heated up during a three-game series at Ebbets Field. On April 24 the Dodgers pounded the Giants, 12–4. The game on April 25 turned into one of the nastiest contests ever played between the two clubs. Maglie took the mound against newly acquired Dodger hurler Russ Meyer, nicknamed "Mad Monk" because of his hot temper, but it was not Meyer's temper that flared during the contest. The score seesawed in the early innings. The Dodgers scored once on Maglie in the bottom of the second, but the Giants promptly took the lead back with two runs off Meyer in the top of the third. So far, the game seemed tranquil enough, but trouble began brewing in the bottom of the third. With two out Snider smashed a triple off the right center field wall. Sal walked Jackie Robinson, then decked the next batter, Roy Campanella, with his classic high-inside fastball. But Campy, often unnerved by Sal's tactics, bounced back with a sharp single to left that scored Snider and tied the game. Shuba then plunked a double just inside the left field foul line, scoring two more runs. Irvin tried to catch Campanella with a throw to the plate, but the ball skipped past catcher Sal Yvars, and Shuba raced around to score as well as the ball rolled into the Brooklyn dugout for an error. The Dodgers now led, 5–2, a development that left Sal in a rage, stomping around and kicking at the dirt on the mound. He was not accustomed to losing control of a game against the Dodgers, especially not at Ebbets Field, where they had never beaten him.

The next batter was Carl Furillo, and Maglie loosed a fastball that buzzed just over the Dodger right fielder's head. It is difficult to believe that Maglie intended to bean Furillo with a pitch that—had it been a few inches lower—could have killed him, but there is no doubt he intended to frighten Furillo, who had already been beaned five times in his career. The two men glared at each other for a moment before Furillo loosed a string of loud profanities at the pitcher. Sal said nothing, but his next pitch was his contemptuous answer, the classic Maglie follow-up to a brushback, a curve low and outside. Furillo took a vicious cut and missed by two feet. As he swung, the bat either slipped out of his grasp—his hands may have been sweaty after his close brush with a beaning—or the infuriated Furillo purposely let go of it, hoping it would smack Sal in the shins. The bat sailed toward the mound like a whirring helicopter blade at the level of Maglie's knees. He avoided it successfully, but a dramatic photograph in the *Herald Tribune* suggests a near miss. It shows the bat still in the air, just behind Maglie's left knee, and Sal looking as if he had barely avoided the oncoming missile by jumping over it.

While the fans howled and members of both teams came pouring out of their dugouts, Furillo advanced slowly toward the mound, where Maglie stood his ground, glowering. Catcher Sal Yvars hurried to Furillo's side, trying to assure him that Maglie had not meant to bean him. Furillo ignored the distraction and kept advancing on Maglie, but before he could reach the mound, umpire Larry Goetz and players from both teams blocked his path. The umpire managed to restrain Furillo, but he nearly broke away when he spotted Durocher, whom Furillo considered the real force behind Maglie's beanballs. It took an armlock applied by the powerful Gil Hodges to keep Furillo from charging the Giants' manager. Furillo was persuaded back to the plate, and Maglie struck him out to end the inning. Sal was removed for a pinch hitter in the sixth, when the Giants scratched out a run, and the New Yorkers garnered two runs to tie the game in the seventh on a two-run homer by Monte Irvin. In the eighth Joe Black relieved Meyer and gave up two more runs, the Giants' winning margin. Wilhelm, who had replaced Maglie, shut out the Dodgers for the remaining frames and gained the win. Even though Sal had failed to defeat the Dodgers this time, his perfect record at Ebbets Field remained intact.

After the game, all the reporters wanted to talk about was the near-beaning and the bat incident. Dick Young, under the mistaken impression that he knew a few words of Italian, framed the Maglie-Furillo confrontation as a blood feud between a pair of hot-tempered Italian primitives: "Carlos" Furillo and Salvatore Maglie. When the game ended, Young was one of the sportswriters who listened with a certain degree of skepticism to the two men's stories and the side remarks of other participants. Once the heat of the moment had passed, neither Maglie nor Furillo would admit to any evil intentions. Maglie denied he had thrown at Furillo's head, and Furillo denied slinging his bat at Sal. "Perish the thought," wrote Young, dripping sarcasm. "They're paisons [sic]. They say so."[6] When asked by Roger Kahn if he had thrown at Furillo, Maglie retorted, "That's ridiculous. If I was going to throw at him, I would have come a lot closer." He said something similar to Dave Anderson. "It was way over his head," sniffed Sal. "If I was throwing at him, he'd have known it." Asked the same question by Dick Young, Sal elaborated, "I never threw at Carl in my life. I don't think I've ever hit him. Look it up—I bet I never did." But then he added in a harder tone, "I'll tell you one thing, though, if that bat had ever hit me, it would have been a different story." Sal Yvars offered another distinction: "Carl didn't even go down. Campanella, he went down."[7] In baseball parlance, in order for a batter to claim he has been thrown at, he must "go down," or hit the dirt, in order to escape the pitch. If he can avoid it merely by ducking or jerking his head back, then, by definition, the pitch is not a knockdown.

Furillo had even less to say about the incident than Maglie. "The bat slipped out of my hands, that's all," he muttered. When Kahn asked Carl if he had also slipped out to the mound, Furillo offered the bland reply, "I was just going out to get my bat." Plate umpire Larry Goetz, who had not ejected either Furillo or Maglie, dismissed the whole incident. "That's all there was to it. The ball slipped and the bat slipped," he insisted. Although no one had accused him of anything, Durocher felt compelled to proclaim, "I had nothing to do with it." Walter O'Malley put a fitting capstone on the incident right after the game by sending Furillo an envelope containing $50. "It's for catching the largest bass in Vero Beach this spring," the Dodger owner announced with an innocence matching Durocher's.[8] Almost lost in the hubbub of the on-field brawl was a statement by Horace Stoneham denying that he was considering shifting his club's home to Yankee Stadium. "Such a story is purely speculation, and is utterly without foundation," Stoneham stated.[9]

Sal ended April with a superb six-hit shutout of the Milwaukee Braves, the seventeenth of his career. Bobby Thomson hit a solo homer in the ninth for the game's only tally, and Sal walked away with a 1–0 victory in his first complete game of the season. So far he had won two and lost one, but the Giants finished April in sixth place with a 5–9 record. On May 6 Sal started a game against the Cubs at the Polo Grounds but lasted only four innings, giving up four runs on six hits. The Giants eventually won, 8–5, but the win went to Al Corwin. Sal threw another brilliant shutout on May 10 in the first game of a doubleheader against the Pirates at the Polo Grounds. He gave up only three hits, walked six, and struck out nine. His ERA of 1.18 was the second-best in the league on that date. Despite a couple of stumbles, Sal seemed on his way to regaining the championship form of his 1951 season.

Sal pitched a complete game on May 16 but lost to St. Louis, 5–2, at the Cardinals' recently renamed stadium. Formerly known as Sportsman's Park, the site had been renamed Busch Stadium in honor of the team's new owner, August "Gussie" Busch, who owned the Anheuser-Busch beer company. On May 21 Durocher sent Sal to face the Dodgers at the Polo Grounds, but this time the fabled Maglie mojo was nowhere in sight. While warming up for the game Sal strained a muscle on the left side of his back. He recorded only one out before giving up a single to Pee Wee Reese, a home run to Duke Snider, and a double to Jackie Robinson. Al Corwin hurried in to replace Maglie and recorded his fourth win as the Giants notched a 7–2 victory. Sal described his back problem as "twitches and kinks," whatever that might mean. Even Sal's loyal hometown booster, *Niagara Falls Gazette* sportswriter Mike Quinlan, noted that "the idea persists that the 'miseries' in his back are giving him more trouble than he bargained for."[10] Sal missed two subsequent turns as a result of re-injuring his back. The Giants lost their last three games in May. They had a 14–10 record for the month, finishing it in fifth place. For the season so far, the team's performance was mediocre, hovering around .500.

Sal did not take the mound again until June 4, and when he did, he was not impressive. His control was poor and he gave up three runs, all on solo homers, on six hits before giving way after five innings to Hoyt Wilhelm, who picked up the win in an 11–3 blowout against Cincinnati. The following day the Giants beat the Cubs, 11–1, behind the pitching of righthander Ruben Gomez, a rookie from Puerto Rico who won his first major league game. Gomez was a pitcher on the Maglie model, unafraid of brushing back hitters. On June 8, in the opening game of a three-game series, the rejuvenated Milwaukee Braves trounced Maglie and the Giants, 12–8, for Sal's third straight loss, dropping his record to 3–3. Sal lasted seven innings, allowed eight runs, although only four of them were earned, and gave up six hits. The team failed to support Maglie in the field, as they committed three errors in the sixth inning. After the game Sal insisted he had felt fine and that his back had not given him any trouble. The Braves swept the series.

On June 14 the Giants dropped both ends of a doubleheader to St. Louis, and Sal lost a 1–0 heartbreaker in the first game. The defeat dropped his record to 3–4, the first time he had fallen below .500 since rejoining the Giants in 1950. In his first appearance at Milwaukee's County Stadium, on June 19, Sal turned in another fine performance as the Giants crushed the

Braves, 15–1. Maglie allowed four hits and contributed three singles of his own to the Giants' onslaught. Sal tossed another beauty of a game on June 24, shutting out the Cardinals, 3–0, on eight hits, to bring his record up to 5–4. In his last three starts Sal had given up only two runs and had gone 19 innings without walking a batter. Durocher decided that Sal was his old self at last and announced that he was returning to a four-man rotation: Maglie, Jansen, Hearn, and Gomez. With lefty Dave Koslo's record at 1–8, Leo dropped him from the rotation. "I can't afford to give Maglie and Jansen any additional rest," Durocher stated. "They'll have to work every four days because I simply haven't any more starters."[11]

Despite Durocher's declared intention of moving to a four-man rotation, Sal did not appear in another game until July 5, an 11–day break during which the Giants won four and lost five. Their record for June was 15–14, and the team's overall record continued to hover just above .500. Perhaps Leo was hoarding Sal's energies for another round against the Dodgers, and if so, his hunch proved correct. Sal took on Brooklyn at the Polo Grounds on July 5, and the Giants made the Dodgers look even worse than bums, steamrollering them, 20–6. Considering that the 1953 squad was among the finest the Dodgers ever fielded, on this particular day it was amazing that the Giants reduced them to bush leaguers. Sal did not pitch an outstanding game—he allowed six runs on nine hits—but with the kind of batting support his teammates gave him, Sal did not need to be too sharp. His record against the Dodgers in 1953 was now 2–0. Durocher, for once, found nothing to argue about. As one Giant runner after another pounded across the plate, he stood in the third base coaching box roaring with laughter.

Sal's victory over the Dodgers marked the beginning of an eight-game winning streak for the Giants, the longest they put together all season and one that stirred talk of another 1951–style miracle comeback. Once again Durocher held Sal out of the rotation until it was time for the Giants to take on the Dodgers on July 10 at Ebbets Field. The largest crowd in two years, 32,889, came out to cheer the Dodgers and jeer at Maglie, and once more their efforts were in vain. Sal foiled the Dodgers again, allowing them just one run, a homer by Roy Campanella in the second inning, while the Giants piled up six tallies. Dodgers rooters took out their frustrations by throwing beer cans at umpire Artie Gore after he called Robinson out on a close play at third in the seventh inning. After the game Durocher gloated that "Sal pitches against [the Dodgers] like it means life or death."[12] Over the course of five seasons, dating back to 1945, Maglie had been involved in eight decisions at Ebbets Field and had won all of them. The few times he was knocked out on the Dodgers' home ground he had managed to dodge the losses. His record against Brooklyn now stood at 18–3.

Sal won his fifth straight on July 16, an easy 10–3 victory over the Cubs at the Polo Grounds, bringing his record to 8–4. Although Hank Sauer touched him for a three-run homer in the first inning, Sal settled down and pitched shutout ball for the rest of the game. He did not allow a hit for the last five innings. It seemed there could no longer be any doubt that Sal had fully recovered from his back problems and might even go on to win 20 games. No one, least of all Sal himself, could have predicted that his July 16 win over the Cubs would be his last victory of the 1953 season and that the subsequent two and a half months would be a long nightmare of pain, humiliation, and failure. Although Sal put on his customary, fear-inducing mask along with his uniform each time he took the field, now the man behind that mask was becoming frightened, depressed, and outraged that his body was betraying him.

The bell began to toll for Sal Maglie on July 21 as he faced the Cardinals at the Polo Grounds. Fresh from his fifth consecutive win in his previous game against the Cubs, Sal was hoping to pick up win number nine. Instead, he retired only one batter as St. Louis pounced on him for four runs on five hits. The Cards won, 10–6. On July 26 Sal tried again, this time against the Reds, but he left after four and two-thirds innings and was not involved in the decision. He allowed five runs, only one of them earned, on seven hits, and was also charged with an error. On July 30 Sal faced Milwaukee and again lasted only a third of an inning, allowing three runs on three hits and issuing two walks, for his sixth loss of the season. This time, Sal complained of soreness in his shoulder rather than his back. "My arm hurt me every time I tried to throw too hard," Sal reported after the Milwaukee disaster. He said he had first noticed the pain in his shoulder on July 10 during his win over Brooklyn and said it had been bothering him ever since, making it impossible for him to throw his curveball. "The sore shoulder," he explained, "has affected my curve because I can't snap. I more or less have to push the ball because I've been favoring my back," he admitted, making reference to his ongoing problem, which had never disappeared, although Sal had been trying hard to pretend that it had.[13]

Despite Sal's stumbles, the Giants played well during July, compiling an 18–10 record and managing to stay in the pennant race. But August proved disastrous for the New Yorkers, as they finished the month with a terrible 10–25 record. Hitting was not the problem—the Giants' team batting average of .285 was the highest in the league. The problem was a pitching staff that fell apart. As Durocher realized that any chance for the pennant was gone, he lost interest in managing. As if to prove his indifference, he sometimes turned over his managerial duties to one or another of his players, including Alvin Dark, Whitey Lockman, Bill Rigney, and Wes Westrum, all of whom later became major league managers. Although rumors flew that Durocher would be fired, Stoneham offered him a two-year extension of his contract through the 1955 season.

Sal made his first August start on the fourth, against the Cubs in Chicago, and once again he was hit hard. The Cubs knocked him out in the fourth inning after he had given up two runs on four hits. The Giants lost, 5–3, and Sal's record fell to 8–7. Even his hometown newspaper began to wonder if his days as a mound star were over. Noting that the current summer had been a rough one for Sal, *Niagara Falls Gazette* sportswriter Mike Quinlan suggested "maybe it's time that Sal was given a chance to be a relief pitcher." Quinlan also pointed out that Sal's excellent control and wide knowledge of National League hitters would be an advantage to him in the bullpen, where he could "be a big help to Hoyt Wilhelm." And of course, Quinlan concluded, "Durocher could always save Sal for the Brooklyn games."[14] If Sal had happened to see Quinlan's well-intentioned article (which he probably did not, since he rarely came home during the season), he would have cringed. To have been demoted in the eyes of a once-worshipful local writer from the ace of the Giants staff to a second-string reliever who might possibly give Wilhelm some help was a long fall.

As if he were taking Quinlan's advice, Durocher saved Sal for the Giants' next game against the Dodgers, which took place a week later on August 11 at the Polo Grounds in front of 45,604 fans. This time, the Dodgers turned the tables. Not only did Brooklyn win, but Carl Erskine shut out the Giants, 4–0, as the Dodgers finally defeated Sal Maglie. Erskine pitched the kind of game against New York that Maglie used to pitch against Brooklyn: the slender righthander with the classic curveball threw a complete game shutout in which only seven Giants reached base and only one advanced as far as second. Sal did not pitch badly. When he left the game he had given up only two runs, although the Dodgers had smacked him for nine hits. He was warming up before the fifth inning when he began experiencing pains in his shoulder, so Durocher replaced him with Wilhelm. The Giants' team physician described Sal's ailment as a tightened muscle over the right shoulder blade, adding that it was nothing serious. The Dodgers went on to sweep the series. Brooklyn now led the league by 7 1/2 games over the Braves, and the Giants were mired in fifth, an insurmountable 17 1/2 games out.

Rumors continued to fly that Sal's pitching career was over. The day after his defeat by the Dodgers, Maglie gave an interview to sportswriter Joe Reichler. Referring to Maglie as "the one-time pitching ace of the New York Giants," Reichler said Sal still believed he could return to his winning ways, despite his advancing years (he was 36) and the physical ailments that had so radically reduced his effectiveness. Maglie blamed his sub-par 1953 season on his failure to get himself into proper shape during spring training, adding that this had been a costly mistake he would not repeat in the following year. "You remember I hurt my back last summer," Sal explained. "Well, I worried about it all winter, and when I reported to camp last February naturally I favored it. I was reluctant to bear down in exhibition games. As a result, when the season started, I was not in shape to go nine innings. I felt weak and tired." Then, just as the pain in his back began to disappear, his arm became sore. "That's because I wasn't pitching properly," he continued. "I had been pitching too much with my arm only. I was using very little body motion. . . . As a result I strained a muscle in back of my right shoulder just above the shoulder blade." But the proud pitcher declared that he would retire if he could not regain his prior form. "I will never take money under false pretenses, " Sal promised. "If my back hurts so I can't follow through, or my arm does not act right in training camp next spring, I will turn in my uniform. I'm not going to go through such a year as this again, no matter how much they pay me." Asked about the rumors of his retirement, Maglie responded, "I know what they're saying about me. They think I'm through. They may be right, but I don't think so. If I did, I'd quit right now. And I'd admit it because I never have tried to fool myself."[15]

This was the most extensive interview Sal had granted in a long time, and clearly he wanted to dispel the rumors that his career was over. For the most part Sal was honest and forthright with Reichler on what is always a difficult subject for a ballplayer, but there was one moment when he fell prey to an almost universal illusion among aging athletes: the belief that they will know when the time has come for them to quit. Sal declared that he had never tried to fool himself, but on the contrary, he had become a specialist in fooling himself, minimizing his ailments, insisting he felt fine, and pitching through periods of intense pain, until agony overwhelmed him, and his body would no longer obey him. "I know I've been going bad," he told Reichler, the urgency and sincerity in his voice jumping off the printed page, "but deep down in my heart I also know I can still pitch well enough to win."[16] Somehow, Sal had managed to disconnect his mind and emotions from his failing body.

According to Reichler, doctors had advised Maglie that the only cure for his ailments was steady work rather than extended rest. Despite this, Durocher held Sal out of the pitching rotation for 11 days before giving him a start against the Phillies in the first game of a doubleheader on August 22. The game did not provide an entirely fair test of Sal's recovery, since the Giants' poor fielding and weak hitting compounded the pitcher's problems. Maglie gave up two runs in the first inning. After a leadoff double by Ted Kazanski, Ashburn dragged a bunt to the right, forcing Sal to make an unsuccessful attempt to field it. With runners on first and third, Earl Torgeson lifted a blooper to left, where Don Mueller was unable to catch up with the ball, which bounced past him for a two-run double. In the second inning, a single and an error by Lockman again put runners on first and third. A single that bounced off the tip of Hank Thompson's glove at third drove in a run, and the next batter squeezed another bunt past the stiff-backed Maglie, giving the Phillies a four-run lead. At this point Maglie departed, as Durocher replaced him with Ruben Gomez. The Giants lost, 7–1, and Sal's record dropped to 8–9. Before the game Maglie insisted his arm felt good. Asked if another failure would prompt him to call it a season and return home, he replied, "That would be up to Durocher." When reporters put the question to the manager, he replied curtly, "No, I do not plan to send Sal home."[17] Nevertheless, the game had made clear that Maglie could not field his position adequately. Although he had not been charged with errors, he had been unable to handle either of the bunts the Phils had laid down. Durocher had little choice but to drop any pretense that Maglie was part of the regular rotation, and he relegated him to the bullpen. On August 30 Sal threw one and one-third innings of scoreless relief in a game against the Cubs where the Giants had a huge lead.

Perhaps Durocher saw Sal's brief performance as a positive enough indication that he was willing to give him another chance as a starter. On September 1 Sal made his last start of the season, against Chicago at the Polo Grounds, and the Cubs mauled him. He lasted two and one-third innings, giving up six runs on eight hits, three of them homers, including a round-tripper by the opposing pitcher. Although the Giants came back to win the game, 10–9, taking Sal off the hook, he had been totally ineffective. His dismal performance was mirrored in the day's attendance figures: a mere 1,406 fans bothered to show up, meaning that roughly one seat in 40 was occupied.

The only occasion that could still bring fans to the ballpark, even with the pennant race all but over, was a series between the Giants and the Dodgers. In their last meetings of the season the old rivalry flared again, fierce as ever, although this time the warfare did not involve Maglie—at least not directly. On September 4 the Dodgers defeated the Giants, 8–6, in a game full of umpire-baiting, beanballs, and bunts motivated less by strategy than malicious intent. After Larry Jansen decked Duke Snider in the eighth, both Snider and Robinson bunted down the first base line hoping to run down the pitcher, but Jansen, having observed the tactic employed against Maglie, eluded both runners. The next day Brooklyn crushed New York by an embarrassing 16–7 margin.

That left one last game between the inter-borough enemies, a contest on September 6, with Ruben Gomez on the mound for the Giants. In that game animosities boiled over into one of the worst on-field brawls in baseball history. In the second inning Carl Furillo came to bat against Gomez, to the familiar background noise of Durocher shouting "Stick it in his ear!" Whether or not Gomez was following Leo's instructions, his first pitch struck Furillo on the wrist. At first Furillo seemed set to charge out to the mound, but he contented himself with shouting at Gomez before proceeding to first base. Unfortunately, first base was adjacent to the Giants' dugout, and now Furillo turned his attention to Durocher. The two men exchanged insults along these lines:[18] "I know fucking goddamn well that was you, Leo, you cocksucker. You fucking *told* him to do that," accused Furillo. "That's right, you fucking dago prick," replied Durocher, "and the next time you come up I'm going to have him do the same goddamn thing!"

As this exchange of pleasantries went on, Gomez was pitching to Billy Cox. With the count 2–2, Furillo called time and pointed toward the Giants' dugout. At that moment Durocher crooked his forefinger in a "come here" motion, daring Furillo to come after him. With no one to restrain him this time, Furillo bolted toward Durocher, who rose to meet his adversary. "Knowing Furillo," Pee Wee Reese recalled, "I would not want to get him too upset, because Furillo would fight a buzz-saw, and of course Leo never backed down from anyone."[19] Despite a phalanx of Giants players around their manager, the maddened Furillo charged into them, pushing Durocher's defenders aside and flinging himself on the Giants' manager. Before anyone could stop him, he clamped a choke hold on Durocher, whose bald pate went from pink to red to purple. According to Duke Snider's account, umpire Babe Pinelli abandoned his responsibility for stopping the melee. Instead, he rushed over and yelled, "Kill him, Carl, *kill* him!"[20] As players struggled to pull Furillo off Durocher, someone stepped on Carl's left hand, breaking a bone in his little finger and putting him out of action for the rest of the season. When the melee ended, both Furillo and Durocher were ejected from the game, which the Dodgers won, 6–3, for their ninth straight victory over the Giants. Although Maglie played no part in the brawl, he bears some responsibility. As the Giants' leading brushback pitcher since 1950, the cumulative effect of his high-inside fastballs was to pile up the fuel that Gomez ignited.

But for the moment, Sal was finished throwing brushbacks. Durocher parked him in the bullpen and called on him only twice for the remainder of the season, both times in meaningless games. As far as Durocher was concerned, all the remaining games in the 1953 season were without significance, and he turned most of them over to his various player-managers. Sal pitched four innings of scoreless relief against Chicago on September 11 in a losing cause as the Giants dropped the game, 5–2. On September 22 he gave up three runs in three innings against Philadelphia in his last outing of the season. The Giants finished fifth with a 70–84 record. Sal posted his worst major league numbers, a dismal 8–9 record and a 4.15 ERA. Although it was no consolation to the Giants, in 1953 the superb Dodgers team once again went down to defeat in the World Series, beaten by the baseball equivalent of General Motors. Stengel's unstoppable Yankees machine won a record-breaking fifth straight championship.

When the season ended the Giants embarked on a barnstorming tour to Japan, Korea, Hawaii, and the Philippines, where they played exhibition games against local and military teams and entertained American armed services personnel. Japan was returning to its prewar enthusiasm for baseball, and in July the Japanese government had extended the invitation. Sal initially signed up for the journey, but as it turned out, he was so exhausted, emotionally distraught, and pain-wracked by the time the season ended that he was in no condition to go anywhere. Kay was disappointed, but she had always put her husband's needs before her own. If she could not nurse a baby, she could at least nurse her weary, worried husband back to health, and Sal sank gratefully into her care.

Once home, Sal realized that most people in Niagara Falls thought he had gone on the trip to the Far East, and he took advantage of the downtime to collect himself mentally and rest his aching body. He welcomed the silence, the lack of the usual flood of phone calls and invitations. In a rare burst of domesticity, he even did some house painting, and to his relief the exercise did not do any harm. "I could hardly lift my right arm when I got home," he admitted to Mike Quinlan. "My back ached, and I felt all washed up. But the quiet helped, . . . and right now the future looks a lot brighter for me than it did a couple of months ago."[21]

1954—The Giants Take It All

13

BASEBALL IN THE MID-1950s

The national pastime had not participated fully in the prosperity that characterized the 1950s. Attendance at major league games was decreasing, and many minor league franchises were disbanding, unable to compete with the lure of major league games—and everything else—on television. But the success of the Braves' move to Milwaukee seemed to have reversed that trend, and in 1954 another team changed cities. The St. Louis Browns, one of baseball's worst teams, and no match for the Cardinals in popularity, moved to Baltimore, where the team exchanged its bland name for the cheerier moniker Orioles. The transfer was a huge initial success. The Orioles drew almost 1.1 million fans their first year, a fourfold increase over the Browns' gate in 1953. A similar process took place in the American league in 1955, as the Athletics abandoned Philadelphia to the Phillies and moved to Kansas City. In New York, the only city with two major league teams in the same league (Brooklyn is technically a part of New York), the Dodgers still played to nearly full houses at little Ebbets Field, but the Giants had seen their attendance drop so much that on game days the Polo Grounds sometimes stood 80 percent empty.

The year 1954 saw significant developments for the future welfare of ballplayers. Player representatives drew up the constitution and bylaws of the Major League Baseball Players' Association, avoiding the use of the word "union" in their name. Although the group's demands were modest—improvements in pensions and an increase in the minimum major league salary—team owners rejected them all. Eventually, however, owners agreed to improvements in the pension plan, using some of the money from television revenues. The reserve clause remained untouched.

BEFORE THE BIG SEASON

Horace Stoneham's decision in 1953 to grant Leo Durocher a two-year contract had repercussions in a predictable place: Brooklyn. Charlie Dressen, always in competition with Durocher, decided he also deserved a multiyear contract, and tried one-upping Leo by demanding a three-year pact from O'Malley. Never fond of Dressen, and angered that the manager had twice failed to bring a world championship to Brooklyn, O'Malley saw a chance to rid himself of a tiresome fellow. When Dressen insisted on a three-year contract or nothing, O'Malley gave him nothing. In his place the Dodgers hired Walter Alston, a veteran of the Dodgers organization with many years of experience managing in the minors, but a man whose major league career had consisted of one inning with the Cardinals in 1936, where he had two fielding chances and flubbed one of them, and a single at bat, in which he struck out. He was totally unknown to fans and sportswriters. Despite his thinning gray hair and Midwestern schoolmaster's face, Alston was a massive bull of a man built on nearly the same scale as Don Newcombe. But Newk had the face to go with his physique and Alston did not, hence the assumption that Alston was a milquetoast who could not control a big league ball club. Over the course of 23 one-year contracts, he proved he could do that and more, piloting the Dodgers to four world championships.

The Giants organization kept busy in the off-season as well. They made an unsuccessful effort to obtain Milwaukee Braves ace Warren Spahn. On February 1, anticipating the return of Willie Mays from army service, Horace Stoneham made the difficult decision to send the team's 1951 hero, Bobby Thomson, to the Milwaukee Braves in exchange for a pair of desperately needed southpaws, Johnny Antonelli and Don Liddle. There was a whiff of the west in the air as the Giants moved their 1954 spring training site from humid Florida to the warm, dry climate of Phoenix, Arizona.

Returning for the start of his fifth full year with the Giants, Sal Maglie had to fight for his place on the pitching staff. Although no stranger to such struggles earlier in his career, he had enjoyed several years of security in New York, hailed as the ace of the Giants' staff, listed as untouchable in terms of trades, and assured of a place on the roster. But his collapse in 1953 had reacquainted him with the prime reality of the professional athlete's life: he is only as good as his most recent performances. Giants vice-president Chub Feeney stated, "We aren't counting on Maglie. . . . Even though his back seems to be better, we just can't count on him."[1] After his dismal 1953 season, the Giants slashed Maglie's salary to $28,000 from its high of somewhere between $35,000 and $37,500. He would turn 37 in April of 1954, an age when most men are entering their prime earning years but that in baseball often signifies old age and impending retirement.

In an attempt to come to terms with the approaching end of his career, Sal invested in a liquor store in Niagara Falls that would bear his name, the first of many businesses in which he invested over the years. Unlike Stan Musial, who bought into a St. Louis restaurant that cashed in on his name and provided him with substantial earnings in addition to his baseball salary, Maglie achieved no financial success through his business ventures. Due to the red tape involved in obtaining a liquor license and the necessity of his being present for his store's grand opening, Sal reported to spring training a week late. He had explained the situation to Stoneham and had received the owner's permission for his late arrival. But no one had told Durocher, and the manager was furious, blasting Sal in his customary caustic manner. "Maglie should have been the first man to get here," Leo fumed. "How do I know he can pitch at all? Maybe he thinks he's got a job won and he can do what he wants. . . . What's Maglie more interested in? The liquor business or baseball? Maybe he doesn't know it, but he hasn't won any job. . . . Maglie's fighting for his job. Right now he isn't doing very well," he concluded with a sneer.[2]

Rather than a real fit of temper, this may have been another of Leo's efforts to anger Maglie, to push the pitcher into exerting himself even more when he finally did appear, but Sal took it seriously. He arrived in Phoenix by train on February 27, the day after Durocher had sounded off to reporters. Informed of Durocher's tirade, Sal stopped at his hotel only long enough to drop off his luggage. He was in uniform, on the field, and participating in his first workout within an hour of his arrival. Angrily, Sal assured reporters that he had received permission from Stoneham to report late, explained the difficulties of obtaining a liquor license, and added that the store "represents a $20,000 investment, and I'm in no position to kick that kind of money around carelessly."[3]

Sal also noted quietly that another event had delayed his departure: his father had suffered a heart attack. Joseph Maglie was 71 years old and had been retired since 1950. He and Sal's mother (no longer known as Immacolata, but as Mary, the English translation of her first name) had moved into a home on Linwood Avenue in Niagara Falls, a nicer neighborhood than Fourteenth Street, the location of their previous house. Sal and his sister

Carmen, who worked throughout her adult life, had purchased the home for their parents, and she had continued to live with them until her marriage in 1953. Although they had Americanized their first names, Joseph and Mary Maglie never became American citizens, and neither received Social Security benefits.[4] Joseph may have had a small pension from his years of work at Union Carbide and DuPont Chemical, but without help from their children, the amount would not have been sufficient to support the couple in their old age.

Sal did not tell reporters about the overwhelming emotional experience that may have triggered Joseph Maglie's heart attack: Francesco, Joseph's son from his first marriage, had come from Italy to Niagara Falls to meet his father for the first time since Joseph had emigrated to America in 1910, when Francesco was a small child. As recounted in Chapter One, this was the man who, as a boy, had either been left behind with Joseph's sister, or had been torn from his stepmother's grasp just as she was about to take him aboard the ship that would bring them to America. Joseph's heart attack and hospitalization occurred shortly before Francesco arrived, but father and son later enjoyed a deeply emotional reunion.[5]

Family matters aside, Sal offered some big news to the sportswriters buzzing around him. He had found out the source of the back miseries that had been hobbling him: a displaced pelvic bone. Since doctors had been unable to find anything wrong with him, during the winter Sal had turned in desperation to a Buffalo osteopath (sometimes identified as a chiropractor) named Vincent Konschaft, who X-rayed Sal's body and discovered what all the doctors had missed—Sal's right leg was three-eighths of an inch shorter than his left. This inequality put undue strain on the left side of Sal's back and had resulted in what threatened to become scoliosis, a permanent side-curvature of his spine. Dr Konschaft manipulated Sal's spine in order to realign his pelvis and then gave Sal a three-eighths inch leather lift to wear in his right shoe, to reduce the stress on his spine. Although it might seem incredible that such a simple and noninvasive treatment could have such dramatic results, the effect of wearing the shoe-lift was "really remarkable," according to Sal. "I felt like I was a new guy almost overnight. I'm putting the same lift in my baseball shoes, and I'm sure it's going to make a big difference."[6] On March 1 Durocher watched Sal throw, and forgot all about his pique at his pitcher's late arrival. "He was throwing almost as hard as he did at any time last year," declared the happy manager. "He had his good curve going, and he had the hitters fishing for it like he used to do."[7] Pitching coach Freddie Fitzsimmons summed it up: "Boys, he was *firing*."[8]

If any news made Durocher even happier than seeing Sal Maglie regain his old form, it was the return of Willie Mays. After his discharge from the army, Mays arrived in the Giants training camp on the morning of March 2. His delight at being back in baseball was equaled only by Durocher's delight in seeing him again. Onlookers recall Leo swooping down on Mays and embracing him like a long-lost son. Accounts of Willie's first appearance in Phoenix have taken on the quality of legend—the story of the hero's return. Roger Kahn recalled being in the clubhouse when Mays walked in and seeing Sal Maglie come bursting out of the showers "buck naked" to shake Willie's hand. Arch Murray offered a version of the encounter in which Willie greeted his naked, dripping teammate by shouting, "Say, hey, where've you been?" When Sal answered, "In the showers," Murray's version of Willie had a witty reply ready: "That's just what I thought. Knocked out again!"[9] Still another story has the whole Giants team pretending not to remember Mays. In that account, Sal Maglie came clomping into the room wearing a rubber weight-loss shirt and dripping sweat, threw Mays a brief look and then turned to the clubhouse attendant and asked, "Who's this? Some new busher?" When Willie yelled, "Maglie! It's me!" Sal shrugged and turned away. The charade continued until Mays had taken a couple of swings in batting practice, and hit each ball out of the park. Then his teammates crowded around him to welcome him back.[10] No matter which version of the story is true, the Giants were glad to have Willie again, and pitchers were especially grateful. "It's different pitching with the kid in center field," Maglie remarked. "All I gotta do with Willie there is keep the baseball in the park."[11]

Sal began the new year with a resolution not to worry. He was feeling better than he had in a long time, strong, confident, and pain-free. He told the *Sporting News,* "Last summer I was troubled with my sore back and that trouble, together with my constant worrying, combined to give me a bad time on the mound."[12] In retrospect, then, Sal admitted that chronic anxiety had compounded his physical problems. He had walked to the mound for much of the 1953 season not only in physical pain but riddled with anxiety and fear that he could no longer perform adequately, and, like a man who fears impotence in his sexual performances, those emotions helped create a self-fulfilling prophecy. Roger Kahn, always aware of the undercurrents, asked Giants vice-president Chub Feeney why Maglie had won only eight games in 1953—was it a sore back or "emotional problems"? Ignoring the issue of emotional problems, Feeney assured Kahn that Maglie's back would improve as soon as Willie Mays started playing behind him again.[13] Feeney's attitude was typical; Kahn's interest in a player's psychological health remained rare among sportswriters of the 1950s. Sal's problems in 1953 had been a complicated combination of physical and emotional elements, and both needed tending before he could return to his old form.

With his leather shoe-lift in place, and his back giving him no trouble, Sal took the mound for spring training stints in a positive frame of mind. He felt relaxed and confident enough of his abilities that he did not brood over a bad outing, as he had done the previous year. Although the Baltimore Orioles smacked him for four runs on seven hits in three innings in his first appearance, on March 9, Sal shrugged it off, declaring there was nothing serious wrong with him. As if to prove his point, he threw four scoreless innings a few days later. Win or lose, Maglie remained optimistic. Even being struck on the forearm by a sharp comebacker off the bat of Willie Mays during a batting practice session failed to slow Sal down. The X-rays were negative, and he did not miss a turn in the exhibition rotation, pitching five scoreless innings against the Indians three days later. By the end of spring training he had worked 33 innings and had an ERA of 3.00. In comparison, the previous year he had worked one-third of an inning more but had had a poor ERA of 5.79. Sal felt ready for another star season.

THE 1954 SEASON

Leo Durocher was convinced that this was going to be the Giants' big year. Monte Irvin had recovered from his ankle fracture. Willie Mays was back, breaking the fences with his bat and running down everything in center field. Leo finally had a pitching staff he could count on, one that included two reliable lefties as well as a rejuvenated Sal Maglie. Opening Day at the Polo Grounds on April 13 featured the classic cast of characters: the Giants against the Dodgers, with Maglie on the mound for New York and Carl Erskine on the hill for Brooklyn. Although "Oisk," as Dodger fans called their beloved righthander, held the Giants to only four hits, and Sal allowed Brooklyn eight safeties, the Giants won, 4–3, by making every hit count. Three of the Giants' four hits were home runs, a two-run shot by Alvin Dark with Maglie on base with a single, a solo round-tripper by Hank Thompson, and a monster 440–foot blast by Willie Mays into the left field upper deck. Maglie was not especially sharp—he gave up two home runs to Roy Campanella—but as usual he was good enough to beat the Dodgers. He was hanging on to a 4–3 lead when he weakened in the seventh and needed Marv Grissom to bail him out of a bases-loaded jam. Grissom held the Dodgers scoreless, and Maglie rose from the grave (or so it must have seemed to the Dodgers) and beat Brooklyn once again. What did they have to do to defeat Sal? Drive a stake through his heart? After the game, most of the Dodgers gave Sal credit for good stuff, but his old adversary Jackie Robinson refused to concede anything. "He's not going to get out of those jams all the time," Jackie sniffed. "Not with the junk he was throwing me."[14]

Just as he had in previous years, Durocher made sure Maglie was ready for the Brooklyn home opener against the Giants at Ebbets Field on April 18. Again Sal faced Carl Erskine, and once again, not brilliant but more than adequate, Maglie bested the Bums, 6–3. Roger Kahn's account of the game highlighted Maglie's menacing appearance. "Sal Maglie, a name used by mothers in Brooklyn to frighten disobedient small boys," Kahn's report began, "was in the Giant lineup at Ebbets Field yesterday." He described Sal as "the same old Maglie," glowering and peering darkly at Dodger batters, and "throwing just enough high, tight pitches to keep them thinking." Brooklyn had not seen a villain to match Maglie since Frankenstein's monster, Kahn observed, concluding that the Dodgers' only effective weapon against Sal was rain.[15] In the third inning, with the bases loaded and nobody out, Sal walked in a run, but then forced Campanella to pop up, persuaded Hodges to foul out, and struck out Furillo on three pitches, while the Dodgers fans packing Ebbets Field groaned in despair. Sal also hit Campanella with a pitch, possibly as a payback for the two home runs the Dodger catcher had hit in the Polo Grounds opener. Sal enjoyed toying with Campy, upsetting the usually composed catcher with high-inside pitches, "setting him up to hit the breaking ball, which he couldn't hit," Sal explained years later.[16] Often during Campanella's first at bat, Sal would send a screamer several feet over his head. Although in no danger of being hit by such a pitch, the Dodger catcher was so nervous facing Maglie that he would hit the dirt anyway, much to Sal's amusement and the Dodgers' dismay. "All the Dodgers would start screaming," Sal recalled. "They'd get so damned angry that they'd try to kill me with home runs—be the big heroes—and they'd break their backs swinging at bad balls. They didn't get anything. I had their number."[17] Sal certainly had their number in early April of 1954. The Dodgers had lost only two games during the first week of play, both of them to Sal Maglie.

As the season entered its second week, the Giants, with a 3–5 record, appeared to be floundering. But then the Phillies came to the Polo Grounds, and the Giants starved them to death in a three-game series in which Philadelphia failed to score a single run. On April 24 Marv Grissom hurled a 1–0 shutout, and the next day the Giants took a doubleheader, with Johnny Antonelli and Sal Maglie pitching shutouts. Maglie and Antonelli limited the feeble Phils to a total of eight hits—five off Maglie and three off Antonelli. Maglie, who had his 37th birthday on April 26, celebrated a day early by outpitching Curt Simmons for his third straight victory and his first shutout of the season. Maglie's win over the Phillies made him the second-highest-ranking active pitcher in the majors in terms of won-lost percentage. His record of 75–31 produced a .7075 average. Only former New York Yankee ace Vic Raschi, with the Cardinals in 1954, and holder of a 121–50 won-lost record, had a fractionally better percentage of .7076. Sal would need only one more victory to top Raschi, and he gained it on April 30 when he defeated the Cubs, 4–2, in a 14–inning complete game, the longest of his career. The only walk he gave up was intentional. He had already chalked up half the number of victories he had won in all of the previous season, with five months still to go. He had resumed his workhorse status, having pitched more innings than any other pitcher in either league. Sal was starting the season in spectacular fashion. His record stood at 4–0, three of his four starts had been complete games, and his ERA was a fabulous 1.87. But despite all his gleaming numbers, Maglie was the oldest man on the Giants squad.

No pitcher could sustain such a record indefinitely, certainly not one who had just turned 37 and whose body had seen the wear and tear that Sal's had. On May 5 Cincinnati smacked Sal for seven runs on 13 hits in seven innings, and the Giants lost, 7–1. Maglie defeated the Pirates, 5–1, on May 9, another complete game. On May 14 the Giants defeated the Cubs, 9–6, for their sixth straight win, and climbed into second place. Sal started the game, but left for a pinch hitter in the fifth. Although the Giants were ahead when Sal departed, Grissom could not hold on to the lead. After the Giants took the lead again by scoring three runs in the seventh, Hoyt Wilhelm closed the door on the Cubs to earn the win. Sal faced the Cardinals' Vic Raschi on May 19 and allowed the Cards only three runs, but Raschi pitched a five-hit shutout, defeating the Giants, 3–0. Sal started again on May 24 in a 5–4 win over the Phillies, but he did not figure in the decision. On May 29 the Dodgers beat the Giants, 4–2, an especially sweet victory for Brooklyn, since they defeated Sal Maglie. Even with that loss, Sal still held a 20–7 edge over the Dodgers.

Sal suffered a terrible outing on June 3, when he lasted only one and two-thirds innings and gave up six runs. But the Giants pounded back to defeat the Cardinals, 13–8, with Grissom earning the win in relief. On June 7 Sal redeemed himself with a strong showing against Milwaukee, taking the game, 4–2. Five days later Sal pitched the Giants into a tie with the Dodgers for first place as he tossed seven scoreless innings in 90-degree heat against the Cubs at Wrigley Field. Wilhelm finished the last two innings, and the two men combined to complete a 5–0 shutout. On June 15 Ruben Gomez defeated Cincinnati, 5–3, to give the Giants undisputed possession of first place, a spot they had not occupied since 1951. Sal faced off against the Cardinals' Harvey Haddix on June 18. Performing with the kind of brilliance that had characterized Sal during his scoreless streak in 1950, Haddix hurled his third consecutive shutout and ran his string of scoreless innings to 32, defeating the Giants, 5–0. The Giants lost the game in the first few minutes of play, when Sal gave up a homer to lead-off man Rip Repulski. Hurrying to cover first on a ball hit to Lockman by Musial, Maglie tripped, pulled a muscle in his left thigh, and had to leave the game. The loss dropped Sal's record to 7–4, and the injury caused him to miss a turn. The Giants' lead over the Dodgers decreased to one game.

Maglie recovered just in time to face the Dodgers on June 29 in a nail-biter that went 13 innings before a near-capacity crowd at the Polo Grounds. Jim Hearn had been scheduled to pitch, but had injured his back, so Sal stepped in. When Snider hit a 440–foot triple in the first inning—a smash that would have been an inside-the-park home run if not for a sensational throw by Mays that held the Duke at third—it looked like the Dodgers had solved Sal. But Snider failed to score, and the Giants held a 2–0 lead as the game entered the top of the ninth. Tired, but determined to conserve his energy, at the end of each inning Sal made his way to the dugout at such a slow pace that one time Willie Mays, running in from center field, passed him before the pitcher reached the bench. With two outs and Robinson on first with a single, Sal had two strikes on Campanella, and was one strike away from a shutout victory when Campy got hold of a hanging curve and sent it over the roof in left to tie the score. The Giants put a man on with one out in the bottom of the ninth, but Irvin grounded into a double play. In the tenth, with Grissom replacing Maglie, the Dodgers loaded the bases with two out, but Robinson flied out. In the Brooklyn half of the eleventh, with one out and Campanella on second, Grissom struck out the next two batters. In the bottom of the eleventh the Giants loaded the bases with two out; then substitute catcher Ray Katt grounded out to end the inning. With the winning run on third in the Dodger twelfth, Robinson hit into a double play. With two outs in the top of the thirteenth, Don Hoak, among the weaker Dodger hitters, lucked into one of those miniature home runs possible only down the right field line at the Polo Grounds, putting Brooklyn ahead 3–2. Then, in the bottom of the thirteenth, with the Giants down to their last out, they loaded the bases against Billy Loes, and Durocher sent up Dusty Rhodes as a pinch hitter for Ray Katt, leaving the Giants without a catcher if the game continued another inning. Rhodes took two called strikes, and with the Dodgers needing one more strike to win, Rhodes singled to center, driving in two runs and winning the game for the Giants, 4–3. Grissom gained the victory, but once more Maglie had cast a spell over the Dodgers. The Giants also took the next two games to sweep the series.

The Giants and the Dodgers squared off again a week later, this time for a three-game series at Ebbets Field. In the opener on July 6 Maglie faced the Dodgers' Preacher Roe. Just as in the previous week's game, Brooklyn threatened to knock Sal out in the first inning, scoring two runs before Sal retired a batter, but Durocher left him in, and he wormed out of the jam. Unable to knock Sal out in the first, despite having him on the ropes, the Dodgers could do no further damage to The Barber until the ninth, when three singles loaded the bases with none out. With the partisan crowd howling, Durocher replaced Maglie with Grissom, who retired the final three Dodger batters and preserved a 5–2 win for Maglie, improving Sal's record to 8–4. Against the Dodgers at Ebbets Field Sal was still perfect: 10 wins, no defeats. After the game a reporter asked Maglie how many games he thought he might win before the end of the season. The normally serious Sal grinned and declared, "If Grissom holds out, there's no limit."[18] Inspired by Maglie's victory, the Giants again swept a series from the Dodgers. They had now beaten the Bums six straight and increased their league lead to 6 1/2 games. Alston was so furious with his team after the last loss that he closed the clubhouse and gave the Dodgers a taste of his temper. He then chased his abashed crew out onto the field for a session of postgame batting practice.

Sal won the opening game of a doubleheader against the Pirates on July 11 by a sloppy 13–7 score. He lasted eight and one-third innings, and the Pirates scored all their runs off him, six of them earned, on 11 hits. In St. Louis on July 16 Sal started but lasted only three and one-half innings and did not figure in the decision, as the Giants dropped a game to the Cardinals, 5–4. On the eighteenth he tossed two innings of scoreless relief against Cincinnati to preserve a win for Jim Hearn. Sal defeated the Cubs on July 21 at Wrigley Field, 2–1, for his tenth win, throwing a complete game and allowing only four hits.

After Sal's win over the Cubs, the Giants slumped in late July, losing six in a row. The fifth of those losses, on July 26, was something of a historic landmark: the first time the Dodgers had ever defeated Sal Maglie at Ebbets Field. A jubilant crowd of 33,251 witnessed the event. Rain delayed the game for an hour and perhaps took the edge off The Barber's razor; or maybe the law of averages caught up with him. Sal lasted five innings and allowed four runs before he was removed in the top of the sixth without recording an out and with the Dodgers leading, 4–1. The racket that accompanied Sal's departure was extraordinary, even by the raucous standards of Ebbets Field. Fans hooted and jeered, horns tooted, cowbells jangled, members of the Dodger Sym-phony created happy disharmony, and so many handkerchiefs waved Sal good-bye as he walked to the dugout that *Post* columnist Jimmy Cannon said "it looked as though a great flock of one-winged gulls were flying through the stands." Although the Dodgers trounced the Giants, 9–1, on Carl Erskine's five-hitter, nobody left early. It was as if the fans would not believe Sal was really the loser until the announcement came over the public address system at the end of the game and made it official: "Losing pitcher, Maglie."

Sal's finally losing to the Dodgers at Ebbets Field did not prove any jinx to the Giants. Although they lost their sixth straight the next day to the Cardinals, on July 28 they defeated St. Louis, 10–0. Dusty Rhodes hit three consecutive home runs, and Johnny Antonelli—the new ace of the Giants staff—gained his tenth straight victory, bringing his record to 15–2. On the final day of July, pitching in 100–degree heat, Sal picked up his tenth win, beating Cincinnati, 7–0. He pitched seven and one-third innings, scattering three hits, before giving way to Grissom. As the month ended, Larry Jansen, who was three years younger than Maglie but was rendered ineffective by persistent back, shoulder, and arm problems, announced his retirement, remaining on the staff as a pitching coach. The Giants brought up Al Corwin from their Minneapolis team to replace him.

Sal began August badly, as the Cubs knocked him out after one and one-third innings in a game on August 4 at the Polo Grounds. The Giants came back to win, 4–3, in 11 innings, so Sal did not figure in the decision. After that win the Braves swept a three-game series at the Polo Grounds on August 6–8. In the last of the three games Maglie faced Warren Spahn, and the Braves' ace southpaw bested him, 5–2. Sal allowed three of the Braves' five runs before being taken out in the seventh. At the same time, Brooklyn pounded Cincinnati, 20–7, reducing the Giants' lead to three games. Like the league-leading Dodgers of 1951, the Giants were beginning to hear footsteps behind them.

On Friday, August 13, the Giants and the Dodgers opened a three-game set at Ebbets Field, and once again Durocher sent his Dodger-killer to face Carl Erskine. Both Erskine and Maglie put up goose eggs until the bottom of the sixth, when the Dodgers scored a run. The Giants then scored two off Erskine in the seventh, to pull ahead. But in the bottom of the seventh, after Grissom had replaced Maglie, Carl Furillo smacked a two-run homer to give the Dodgers a 3–2 win. Grissom took the loss, and Sal again managed to wriggle off the hook at Ebbets Field. The next day the Dodgers won, 6–5. When they swept the series by pounding the New Yorkers, 9–4, the next day, the Giants' lead dropped to a mere half-game. All the Dodgers needed was some momentum, and they could overtake the Giants, but instead they went flat. It seemed as if they expended all their energy in defeating the Giants and had nothing left for other teams.

The Giants, in contrast, bounced back from their thrashing by the Dodgers and won their next seven games. On August 18 Maglie defeated the Phillies, 6–2. The game featured one of the rare humorous intervals in Maglie's pitching career, a carnival of foul-offs by Phillies leadoff man Richie Ashburn. "One afternoon I fouled off 18 or 19 pitches off of him on a 3–2 count," Ashburn recalled. "He had excellent control and so did I. After a while he just started laughing. Then he would throw me another pitch and

I would foul it off. That was the only time I ever saw Maglie laugh on a baseball field."[19] Maglie finally lobbed one to the plate, and the surprised Ashburn hit a two-hopper back to the mound, by which time both men were laughing. On August 22, while the Dodgers were dropping a doubleheader, the New Yorkers took both ends of a twin bill from Pittsburgh, but Sal was knocked out in the fifth inning of the second game. The Giants came from behind to win it, 5–3, with Wilhelm posting his ninth victory. On August 27 Sal won his thirteenth as he bested the Braves, 3–1. He was injured twice during the game: Braves righthander Gene Conley struck Sal on the left shoulder with a pitch in the sixth inning, and in the eighth he was hit on the right thigh by a line drive he failed to field. Despite the bruises, he held on to pitch a complete game. As had become his habit, Durocher rested Maglie for the upcoming Labor Day weekend series with the Dodgers, sending him back to New York to recover from his bruises while the team was still in St. Louis (Figure 14). The Giants took two out of three from the Cards.

14—The softer side of Sal Maglie. Sal's wife Kay hands her husband a cup of coffee in their Manhattan apartment on September 3, 1954, before a game against the Dodgers. Photo: National Baseball Hall of Fame Library, Cooperstown.

The Giants-Dodgers series began at the Polo Grounds on September 3, with Sinister Sal facing Brooklyn righthander Billy Loes. Sal had problems in the first inning, when the Dodgers scored twice against him. He lasted six innings, allowing Brooklyn four runs on six hits, before Wilhelm took over and held the Dodgers scoreless. The Giants tied the game in the sixth. In the seventh, with two on and two out, Durocher allowed Wilhelm to come to the plate, and the pitcher, whose batting average lurked somewhere around .088, connected for a single to drive in the lead run. The Giants won the game, 6–4, with Wilhelm picking up the win. Unhappy about being kept out of the rotation in order to be ready for his start against the Dodgers, Maglie said his problem had been too much rest. "I hadn't thrown a ball in a week, and I couldn't get loose at first," he grumbled after the game.[20] The next day the Giants exploded for seven runs in the seventh inning and trounced the Dodgers, 13–4. Although the Dodgers pulled out a win in the third game, with Podres beating Antonelli, 7–4, the Dodgers left the Polo Grounds further behind than when they arrived. The Bums were four games out with 19 left to play. In his next start Sal was not involved in the decision. He worked seven innings against the Braves on September 14 but left with the score tied, 1–1. Wilhelm won the game in relief. Afterwards someone in the locker room called out to him, "You were great! [The win] should have been yours!" Sal responded with typical modesty and generosity, "That would have been nice, but the main thing is we won. All I care about is this," and he pointed to the name "Giants" on his shirtfront.[21]

Starting on September 20, the Dodgers hosted the Giants for the two teams' last series of the season. It was sudden-death time for the Dodgers—if they did not win the game on September 20, they would be eliminated from the pennant race. For that crucial game Durocher once again gave the ball to Sal Maglie. An extremely superstitious man and a devout believer in the old Maglie magic, Durocher was horrified to find that his black-stubbled demon barber had *shaved* before this most important game. Sal realized he was going to be photographed after the game, win or lose, and had decided that, for once, "I wanted to look nice."[22] If Durocher could have figured out a way to do it, he would have hammered the hairs back into Maglie's face. "What the fuck did you do *that* for?" Leo screamed, furious at Sal for eliminating the central aspect of his supernaturally sinister image.[23] As if in fulfillment of Durocher's fears, Sal began by walking the first two Brooklyn batters. But then Duke Snider grounded into a double play, and Maglie struck out Gil Hodges. The only run the Dodgers could scratch off of Sal was in the third. After the sixth, Maglie gave up no more hits or runs. Starting in the second, the Giants smacked three Dodger pitchers for seven runs, and Sal won his fourteenth game, pitching the Giants to a 7–1 victory that clinched the pennant.

Durocher attached a curious story to the pennant-winning game, involving his conviction that Maglie was a sluggard who had to be prodded into giving his full measure of effort, an assessment no one else agreed with, but one to which Durocher clung tenaciously. In his autobiography, composed 20 years later, he recalled going to the mound in the first inning after Sal had walked the first two batters. Leo decided that Sal was "pitching easy, not bending his back," and needed to be shocked. "Get a pitcher ready!" Leo shouted (in his version of events). "Let's go! You're through, Maglie! *Out!*" Sal, according to Leo, responded that there was no way he was leaving after facing only two batters. "I don't *need* you," Durocher sneered back. "I got eight other guys out here who want to *win* this game. Out!" At this point Maglie supposedly shouted at his manager, "Get back in that dugout, Durocher! You manage! I'll pitch!" And Durocher allegedly answered, "You will, huh? I'll tell you what you'll do. You'll bear down on this next one. You'll bend your back and shake your ass, or you're *through!*"[24] Newspaper accounts confirm that Durocher made a quick trip to the mound in the first inning and that there was activity in the Giants bullpen, but they make no mention of any shouting match between manager and pitcher, an unusual enough occurrence that reporters would have noted it. Even Dick Young, owner of New York's sharpest eyes and keenest ears for baseball scandal or dissension, saw and heard nothing unusual. Durocher made several even more extraordinary claims. First, he insisted Sal was so angry that when the manager returned to the dugout, Sal gave him his "Italian salute," the vulgar gesture of grabbing his crotch. Durocher claimed that a photographer caught Sal in the act but that such a crude picture could not be published. When the inning was over, Leo recalled, Maglie stormed back to the dugout and stalked to the water cooler, where he filled his mouth with water which he spat all over Durocher's pants and shoes.

The story of the photographer catching Maglie in the act of grabbing his crotch—not the photo Sal had in mind when he shaved before the game—probably has its origins in a marvelous but ambiguous picture, proof that the supposedly objective camera can create a thoroughly confusing impression. Photographer Yale Joel snapped a picture of Maglie on the mound on September 20, wearing a ferocious scowl, with his lower lip thrust out in an expression of extreme displeasure (Figure 15). His glove dangles from his left wrist, and his left hand clutches the ball as if he is about to rub it up, as was his habit. By a strange trick of shadow, light, and arrested motion, it appears that Maglie's right hand is indeed grabbing his crotch, but a closer look at the photo also discloses a ghostly image of Sal's right hand, chastely located at the level of his belt.[25] Possibly the crotch-grabbing motion was so quick that the camera captured both images. The

15—The side of Sal the Dodgers saw on September 20, 1954, as he defeated Brooklyn, 7–1, to clinch the pennant for the Giants. This photograph seems to show Sal giving his "Italian salute." Photo: Yale Joel/Getty Images.

photograph appeared in *Life Magazine,* illustrating an article about Maglie with the punning title, quite daring for 1954, "Mean Man in a Clutch."

The story of Maglie spitting water on Durocher was met with incredulity, but also with a possible explanation, by Giants players with clear memories of being in the dugout that day. Alvin Dark exclaimed, "Oh my goodness! I never heard of anything like that! I never heard of *anybody* spittin' water on Durocher. I don't think a player would do that to Durocher—'less he was ready to fight," Dark added with a chuckle. "I don't think a ballplayer would want to take a chance on breaking his fingers. I think if it had happened, everybody in the organization would have heard about it."[26] Whitey Lockman agreed. "I wouldn't think a player could get away with that with Leo, for sure!" Lockman then speculated, "But it could be that Sal did it in such a way that it looked accidental, or wasn't a direct hit, or something like that. But I don't recall that incident happening."[27] Furthermore, the incident as Durocher described it is completely out of character for Maglie. Sal had a temper, but he also had a sullen respect for authority. Managers in Sal's era were, moreover, much more powerful than they are today and were usually the highest-paid member of the team, in contrast to the present, when star players often make as much as ten times more than their managers. No matter how angry Leo's taunting made him, the chances are slim that Sal would have risked his hard-won career by doing something as potentially dangerous as spitting on his temperamental manager. But Durocher was not averse to stretching the truth, especially in the interest of telling a good story.

The Giants celebrated their pennant with the usual champagne in the clubhouse—on ice this time, and not warm as it had been in 1951—but first they had to get to the clubhouse. As the game ended, the players piled on top of one another in their efforts to congratulate Maglie. His teammates pummeled, pounded, patted, backslapped, hugged, and practically smothered Sal. A quick-handed Giants fan snaked into the melee and stole the pitcher's cap. When the team finally reached the clubhouse, Sal answered a reporter's inane question, "Did you feel tired out there?" by sighing and murmuring "I guess so." "They were great! They were all great!" burbled Durocher. "Sal Maglie," said coach Frank Shellenback, "he's the one who did it. He did a helluva job for us when it meant the most. He pitched the big games, the ones we had to win, like this one tonight. . . . He's still the best."[28]

The remainder of the season was a matter of playing out the string of six games. Sal put in one more appearance, on September 25, in a game the Giants lost, 2–1, to the Phillies in 11 innings. Sal worked only two innings, giving up one run on two hits before being removed. Durocher wanted to give Maglie some exercise but saw no reason to tire him in a meaningless contest. Sal's final record for the season stood at 14–6 with an ERA of 3.26, neither as brilliant as his 1951 season nor anywhere near as bad as his 1953 performance. Although at the same time the previous year, it was doubtful if Sal could continue to pitch, in 1954 he was Durocher's most likely choice to open the World Series.

This time, New York City rolled out a royally red carpet for the new National League champions. There had been no time for ceremonies in 1951, with the World Series starting the day after the playoff. On Monday, September 27, one day after the regular season ended, more than a million New Yorkers watched a tickertape-festooned parade of 12 open cars make its way up Broadway. Each car contained several Giants players, all in full uniform, except for their spikes. At City Hall Park, the team members were introduced one by one and then received greetings and congratulations from New York Mayor Robert Wagner and other civic dignitaries. With a surer sense of protocol than that of the parade organizers, Durocher refused to ride in the lead car. "No," the manager insisted, "that first car is reserved for Willie Mays and Al Dark."[29]

THE WORLD SERIES

In 1954 a humorous fantasy novel appeared, called *The Year the Yankees Lost the Pennant.* Under the snappier title *Damn Yankees,* Douglas Wallop's novel about a baseball bargain with the devil became a popular musical comedy and later a movie. Much of the success of all three stemmed from the coincidence that in 1954 the Yankees really *did* lose the pennant. The Cleveland Indians won a record-breaking 111 games and left the stunned Yankees, with a mere 103 wins, in second place. Cleveland's crown jewels were its pitchers: Early Wynn and Bob Lemon, who each won 23 games; Mike Garcia, who won 19 and had the lowest ERA (2.64) in the American League; and Art Houtteman as well as the aging but still able Bob Feller. Relievers Don Mossi, Ray Narleski, and Hal Newhouser backed up the starters. Collectively, the Cleveland pitching staff led the league in complete games, least runs allowed, and least bases on balls. The Indians' batting order included American League batting champion Bobby Avila; Larry Doby, who led the league in home runs and RBIs; and Al Rosen, who batted .300. Odds ran heavily in favor of the winningest team in American League history making short work of the Giants.

To pitch Game One, Cleveland manager Al Lopez could choose from his embarrassment of pitching riches. Both his ace righthanders, Lemon and Wynn, were rested and ready. Garcia was set to go as well. Bob Feller, a year younger than Sal Maglie but in the twilight of a Hall of Fame career that had begun in the mid-1930s when he was in his teens, was eager to pitch in a

World Series. Lopez eventually settled on Bob Lemon. Durocher, too, had his choice of several pitchers but decided to go with his money pitcher, his sinister, black-bearded Barber.

The Fall Classic began on September 29 before a crowd of 52,751 at the Polo Grounds.[30] The only dark clouds were the ones that seemed to hover around Sal Maglie. Although he said little about it, he had pulled a muscle in his back while at bat during the pennant-clinching game against the Dodgers and was concerned that it might interfere with his effectiveness during the upcoming game. But as always, Sal would have dragged himself to the mound half-dead rather than ask out of a game. Sportswriter Arnold Hano watched Maglie warm up for his Series start and began worrying. Hano thought Sal looked "as if each pitch hurts someplace," and the pitcher seemed to be having trouble with his control.[31]

Sal confirmed Hano's worries as the game began. He threw three consecutive balls to the Indians' leadoff hitter, left fielder Al Smith, then struck Smith in the ribs. Roger Kahn speculated that Sal, frustrated and angered by his lack of control, may have hit Smith on purpose, perhaps thinking something like, "If I'm going to walk you, I might as well hurt you."[32] Although usually an insightful student of Maglie's psychology, Kahn's guess at Sal's motivation in this case seems inaccurate. Sal saved his *very* occasional, deliberate plunking of batters for instances of payback—punishment exacted for previous home runs or the opposing pitcher's throwing at Giants batters. To open a World Series game by awarding the opposition's leadoff man a base seems more the product of shaky control than malevolence. The next batter, second baseman Bobby Avila, socked a line drive into right field for a single, and when Don Mueller fumbled the ball for an error, Smith raced to third. Giants fans groaned in dismay, Sal slammed down the rosin bag in disgust, and in the Giants bullpen lefthander Don Liddle began warming up. After that, Sal snuffed center fielder Larry Doby on a pop foul that Hank Thompson grabbed behind third, and he took out third baseman Al Rosen on an infield pop to Whitey Lockman. But Maglie's troubles were not over. The next batsman, large, left-handed–hitting first baseman Vic Wertz, smashed a triple to deep right center, scoring Smith and Avila. The top of the first ended when right fielder Dave Philley hit a long drive that Don Mueller hauled in for the third out. Sal stalked back to the dugout disgusted, with the score Cleveland two, New York nothing.

The Giants failed to make more than minor dents in Bob Lemon in the bottom of the first, and neither Cleveland nor New York scored in the second. Sal set down the Indians in order in the top of the third, and in the bottom of the inning the Giants scored two off Lemon, tying the game. Wertz made his second hit off Maglie, a single in the top of the fourth, but could advance no farther than second. The Giants threatened in the bottom of the fourth but failed to score, and Cleveland did the same in the top of the fifth, when a pair of bloop hits put two men on base, but Sal wriggled out with no score. Lemon continued to frustrate the Giants in the bottom of the fifth.

The sixth inning began with the unwelcome sight of Vic Wertz, the one Cleveland hitter who had no trouble solving Sal Maglie. This time up Wertz hit a single to right that landed in front of Mueller. As Wertz lumbered into first and made a wide turn, Mueller threw to Lockman, hoping to catch Wertz off the bag, but the throw sailed over Lockman's head and rolled toward the plate. There, Westrum, in the process of picking up his mask rather than backing up the play, spotted the ball, lunged for it, and missed. The ball continued on its merry way toward the Cleveland dugout, where Westrum finally caught up with it, preventing the slow-footed Wertz from going to third. The next batter, Dave Philley, drove a hard smash back to Maglie that Sal pounced on and fired to first to retire Philley, with Wertz moving to third. Following Philley to the plate was George Strickland, whom Maglie had beaned in 1952 when the Cleveland shortstop was with the Pirates. He hit a weak pop to Dark for the second out, and then Hank Thompson made a fine play on a sharp bounder to third by catcher Jim Hegan for the third out. At bat in the bottom of the sixth with two out, Sal tapped a weak little dribbler that rolled between the mound and first base. Wertz and Lemon handled the play with ease, and Sal stopped his slow jog halfway to first base. The game had been underway for almost two hours, and Maglie was growing weary. He had retired the Indians in order in only one inning, the third. Arnold Hano, watching Sal closely, noted how exhausted he looked. Despite his ferocious scowl and black stubble, Maglie was sweating profusely, and his pitching motion was growing labored, "the throwing of a man who is made up of two parts, his arm and his heart, and one of them is going fast," Hano observed.[33]

After Maglie retired the Indians in the top of the seventh, and the Giants again failed to score in the bottom of the inning, Sal took the mound to begin the top of the eighth. The first batter he faced was American League home run king Larry Doby. After Doby fouled off Sal's first delivery and failed to be tempted by an outside pitch, Sal unleashed one of his classic high hard ones, putting Doby in the dust as the crowd gasped. But the pitch failed to accomplish its purpose, and Maglie, his control faltering, walked Doby. Grissom and Liddle began throwing in the Giants bullpen. Al Rosen came to the plate and smashed a drive into the hole between short and third that Dark stopped with his bare right hand. He managed to hold Rosen to a single, and kept Doby from advancing to third, but the batter due up next was Vic Wertz, who had owned Maglie all day. That, and the plain fact that Sal was worn out, brought pitching coach Freddie Fitzsimmons to the mound. As Westrum joined the conference, the three men fiddled around for a while, buying time for the bullpen, before Fitzsimmons carried out Durocher's order and called for the lefthander, Don Liddle, to face the left-handed–hitting Wertz.

Sal slumped on the side of the mound, waiting for Liddle to arrive before setting out on that long walk toward the clubhouse in center field. The sympathetic crowd began to applaud him as he plodded across the grass. As he approached the bleachers the applause grew louder, and fans rose to their feet to cheer him. The sad, exhausted pitcher walked slowly, limping a little, shoulders hunched, head bowed, his dark-bearded face glazed with sweat. He did not raise his head to acknowledge the fans' tribute. Possibly he was too moved by it to trust himself to look into that sea of sympathetic faces, or maybe he was just too tired and disheartened. But because courtesy was an integral part of Sal's makeup, he could not ignore the cheers and managed a little wave of his right hand before climbing the stairs to the locker room and disappearing inside. The base runners were his responsibility, and the game was his to lose.

The single pitch Don Liddle delivered to Vic Wertz was sufficient to engrave Liddle's name in baseball history. It was not a good pitch. From the Giants' point of view, it was the worst possible pitch, something like the fat one that brought Ralph Branca an unfortunate form of baseball immortality in 1951. But the consequences of Liddle's pitch were different. Wertz took a mighty swing and hit the ball squarely on a high line toward the deepest part of center field for what looked like a sure triple, if not an inside-the-park homer, and at least two guaranteed runs for Cleveland. Most center fielders would not have been able to get anywhere near the ball, but most center fielders are not Willie Mays. Running with his back to the plate, as if he had eyes in the back of his head to track the ball and tell him where it would come down, Mays lifted his hands to the level of his left shoulder and made one of baseball's most sensational catches, well over 400 feet from the plate. He then whirled around and followed that feat with an equally sensational throw, dead accurate, all the way to second baseman Davey Williams. Doby tagged up and moved to third, but Rosen retreated to first. All Wertz had accomplished was a long, loud out, moving to third a runner who would soon prove meaningless. His mission accomplished, Liddle left the game and was replaced by Marv Grissom.

Another of baseball's persistent legends clings to Liddle and that single pitch. Supposedly, when Grissom reached the mound, Liddle handed the ball to coach Freddie Fitzsimmons, and as he turned to leave, remarked, "Well, I got my man."[34] Years later, Liddle clarified that he would never have made such a light-hearted crack in a Series game when the situation was tense, with two men on and only one out. Instead, Liddle recalled, he made the comment to Durocher in the clubhouse after the game. "It was a joke, of course, because it was only because of Willie's great catch. . . . Leo's the one spread that around."[35] As the game continued, and Grissom took over as the Giants' pitcher, Lopez sent up a pinch hitter for Dave Philley, left-handed–hitting Dale Mitchell, who drew a walk. Cleveland still threatened, but Grissom slipped a third strike past Dave Pope, another pinch hitter, batting for Strickland. Then catcher Jim Hegan flied out to Irvin in deep left field. The inning was over, and the Indians had blown what seemed like a sure opportunity to crack the game wide open.

The Giants failed to score in the bottom of the eighth, and neither team scored in the ninth. In the top of the tenth, leadoff batter Vic Wertz made his fourth hit of the day, a double that fell between Irvin and Mays. Willie uncorked another perfect throw to third that deprived Wertz of a triple, and again the Indians failed to score. In the bottom of the tenth, with Lemon still on the mound, Don Mueller struck out. Willie Mays, up next, walked and stole second. Hank Thompson received an intentional walk, which would have brought Monte Irvin to the plate. Instead, Durocher sent up his only pinch hitter of the game, the best pinch hitter in baseball that year, happy-go-lucky Dusty Rhodes, on intimate terms with bars and broads but a stranger to jitters and big-game tensions. He had pinch-hit 45 times that season and delivered in 15 of those at bats. He knew what he had to do, and he did it, lofting Lemon's first pitch down the short right field line, where it traveled less than 260 feet and landed just over the wall, barely fair. It was a home run, and before most fans realized what had happened, the Giants had won the game, 5–2. An outraged Bob Lemon tossed his glove high in the air—grounds for expulsion were the game still in progress—but it was over.

Although he had not gained the win, which went to Grissom, Maglie was in a much better mood in the jubilant Giants clubhouse after the game than when he had left the mound. Sal grinned ruefully when asked about Wertz's hits against him and managed a little joke: "In spite of it all, Wertz showed bad judgment, don't you think? He hit a 470–foot out, and a 420–foot double. He should have done it the way Dusty did." Turning to 24–year-old Johnny Antonelli, Maglie said with a laugh, "Well, John, us old gaffers won the first one. So now it's up to you to get us another win tomorrow."[36]

Antonelli did just that, beating the Indians and their co-ace, Early Wynn, 3–1, the next day. Although Al Smith smacked Antonelli's first pitch for a home run, that was the last scoring the Indians managed. Dusty Rhodes came through again, this time with a pinch-hit single in the fifth to tie the game. The Giants put across a second run for Antonelli, and Rhodes, who remained in the game, added icing to the cake with a solo homer in the seventh. The Series then moved to Cleveland for the third game, on October 1, and this time the Giants pasted Mike Garcia, coming away with a decisive 6–2 victory. Al Lopez, who had toyed with the idea of starting the once-great Bob Feller in the third game, but had gone with Garcia instead, turned again to Bob Lemon for the must-win fourth game. The Giants clobbered the weary righthander, who had pitched 10 futile innings only three days earlier. Durocher gambled on Don Liddle, who had been something less than untouchable in his brief appearance in Game One, and the lefthander came through, giving up only one earned run, along with three unearned ones, in six and two-thirds innings. Wilhelm and Antonelli combined for scoreless relief, and the Giants took it all, winning the game, 7–4, and the World Series in a four-game sweep.

Hardly a week after the parade in honor of their pennant victory, New York City again welcomed the Giants with another huge tickertape parade. The Giants organization held a victory party for the team, with Horace Stoneham cutting an enormous cake with a Giants cap made of sugar icing perched on top. Durocher kept bursting into tears and hugging Willie Mays. It was Durocher's first—and only—world championship, and the first the Giants had won in 21 years. Rumors flew that the team was thinking of leaving New York for California. "There is nothing, absolutely nothing, to it," declared Horace Stoneham.[37]

1955—Troubles, Travels, and a Transformed Family

14

Sal's fine 1954 record, combined with the Giants' world championship, assured that Niagara Falls would honor Maglie again. The celebration was even bigger than the event after the 1951 season. The mayor proclaimed December 1, 1954, Sal Maglie Day, with a schedule of festivities that culminated in a testimonial dinner at the Century Club, just as in 1951, but this time the events included both a luncheon and a dinner, as well as Sal's participation in an assembly for the awarding of athletic letters at Niagara Falls High School. The day's activities began with the assembly at the high school. Along with the presentation of letters to student athletes, the school honored Maglie as a former pupil and member of the Red and Gray basketball team. Knowing better than to bore the students with a long speech, Sal said a few words, drawing a parallel between the high school's winning football team and the New York Giants.

Sal's next stop was City Hall, where another ceremony took place, and Sal was presented with a certificate of merit. Then came a luncheon where he and Niagara University basketball coach John J. "Taps" Gallagher were co-guests of honor. Gallagher had scouted Maglie for the Niagara University basketball team, although he had not convinced Sal to attend the college. After a break of a few hours, the evening's festivities began with a cocktail party at the Century Club, followed by a dinner for more than 400. Present were Sal's old Buffalo Bisons teammate Dan Carnevale, who had just been named manager of the Bisons, as well as another Italian American ballplayer and friend of Sal's, Sibby Sisti, recently named manager of the Quebec team of the Provincial League. Sal's mother and father, his wife, and the rest of his extended family also attended, listening proudly as a series of speakers lauded Sal. "The youth of the Falls look up to you and follow you and your exploits in baseball. You are a fine example to the youth of the city and the youth of the entire country," declared Harold Herkimer, the director of health and physical education when Sal was at the high school. Msgr. Pascal Tronolone reminded the audience that Sal "owes everything to his mother and father from whom he inherited the spirit of Christian humility." Sal, as usual, kept his remarks brief, thanking everyone who had helped to make the occasion "one of the best days of my career."[1]

A few weeks later Sal received a tribute which must have amused as well as gratified him. The Niagara Falls Barbers Union, local 780, awarded him a full membership. When the union held a meeting to install its new officers, it bestowed their "order of the scissors and shears" on Sal, along with a certificate of full membership. The virtually all-Italian union was delighted to welcome the city's most famous barber to its ranks, and, provided he did not have to wield any actual scissors and razors, Sal was happy to accept the honor.

As the round of laudatory events ended and spring training loomed, Sal once again had to face his advancing age and declining skills. Although the Giants still claimed to consider him one of their "Big Four" pitchers for 1955, there were whispers of changes. Sal signed for a salary higher than the one he had received in 1954, but lower than his top salary. He had insisted on a raise, and the Giants gave it to him, bringing his 1955 pay up to around $32,000. Joe King assured his readers that, judging from Sal's performance in 1954, there was "no reason to fear The Barber is wearing out." But a week later the same writer sounded a note of doubt, reporting that the Giants organization would be on a hunt for "a potential new Maglie. They realize Sal the Barber, 38, cannot go on forever."[2] The Dodgers were less concerned about facing him. Gil Hodges scoffed, "As for the Giants, I don't think some of those fellows can repeat what they did last year . . . and maybe Sal Maglie won't be as tough for us as he has been in the past."[3]

SAL'S 1955 SEASON—THE NEW YORK GIANTS

As spring training opened, Willie Mays appeared in camp after a season of winter ball in Puerto Rico and announced he was "bored with baseball." Mays lacked Maglie's solidly grounded personality, which enabled Sal to accept the publicity, personal attention, adoration, awards, and flattery that stardom brought without becoming a different and less approachable person. The priest who praised Sal's "Christian humility" during Sal Maglie Day ceremonies had been correct. Sal's humility was genuine. No matter the honors heaped on him, Sal remained the same person, disarmingly unaffected by it all. Mays, on the other hand, responded to the overwhelming publicity and adulation he had received since his return from military service by becoming petulant, suspicious, and cynical. Although he continued to play brilliantly despite his comment about boredom, the innocent, laughing boy was gone forever, and with him went the spirit that had inspired the 1954 world champions.

New York put up a successful spring training record of 17–13, but Sal experienced unspecified arm problems. Although he pitched some strong innings, he was hit hard on several occasions and on another was the cause of a flare-up, despite having left the game several innings earlier. On March 13, after Sal had pitched four scoreless innings against Cleveland in an exhibition game, Giants pitcher Al Worthington beaned Wally Westlake, which led to a heated argument between Durocher and Cleveland third baseman Al Rosen. Fortunately, a new rule had just gone into effect in the National League, requiring batters to wear protective helmets, and Westlake was not hurt. The argument was less about what Worthington had done in actually hitting a batter in the head, than about what had happened several innings before, when the Indians protested that Maglie was throwing at Larry Doby, although Maglie had not hit Doby. Sal's reputation as a thrower of beanballs superceded the reality that he rarely hit anyone, in the head or anywhere else.

The Giants opened the 1955 season on the road on April 13 against Philadelphia and lost to the Phillies, 4–2, with Robin Roberts carrying a no-hitter into the ninth before Alvin Dark ended it with a single. Johnny Antonelli took the loss. The next day the Giants opened at home against the Dodgers. The weather was chilly and drizzly for the ceremonial raising of the pennant and world championship flags, and a disappointing crowd of only 29,124 enjoyed the historic moment, made all the sweeter because it took place in the presence of the Dodgers. As expected, Durocher started Sal Maglie against the Giants' chief rivals, with Don Newcombe on the mound for Brooklyn. The flag-raising was the end of the Giants' good times that day, as the team played poorly, and Sal was ineffective, although he would have done better if the Giants had refrained from costly errors. Maglie allowed four runs, none of them earned, on four hits, gave up two walks, and struck out three in four innings of work. The final score was a messy 10–8 victory for the Dodgers. The next day columnist Jimmy Cannon, as if sensing that Maglie's defeat by the Dodgers meant his days as a Giant were numbered, wrote a nostalgic piece evoking the qualities that made Maglie so memorable. He noted, as others had done before, the dramatic contrast between the man Sal was off the field and his evil reputation on the mound.

"There is a haunting quality about him," Cannon wrote. "There, standing on the little knoll the pitchers use, Maglie turns into an image of menacing solitude. He creates a climate of wickedness for himself although I know him to be a man of courteous impulses."[4] Brooklyn beat the world champions the next day as well, as Billy Loes pitched a 3–0 shutout and defeated Ruben Gomez. The Giants had started the season with three straight losses.

The Dodgers, in contrast, began by breaking a National League record, winning their first ten games. Never relinquishing their hold on first place, they ran away with the pennant. The team was much the same one the Giants had beaten the previous year, but there were also some differences. It had taken him a while, but the quietly forceful Walter Alston had won the respect of the team's veterans. Don Newcombe, who had failed to win even 10 games in 1954, roared back in 1955 and won 20, with only five defeats. Although Carl Erskine, Johnny Podres, and Billy Loes all suffered arm problems, the Dodgers turned to their minor league system and brought up two strong young arms, Don Bessent and Roger Craig. In December of 1954 they had signed an 18-year-old lefty named Sandy Koufax, a Brooklyn native with a dazzling fastball and a hair-raising lack of control. Across the board, the Dodgers were the best team in the league: they led in team batting average, homers, doubles, runs, slugging percentage, and stolen bases. Their pitchers had the lowest collective ERA, struck out the most batters, and gave up the fewest runs.

The Giants lost five of their first six games, and at the end of the first week of play the champs found themselves tied for sixth place. On April 17 they dropped a doubleheader to the Phillies, with Antonelli losing the first game to Robin Roberts and Maglie losing the second to Murry Dickson, a durable veteran a year older than Sal who had been in the majors since 1939. The score in both games was 4–2. Maglie's record stood at 0–2. If it was any comfort to Sal, a newspaper article that day noted that Vern Stephens had been released by the Baltimore Orioles and that Maglie was now the only former Mexican leaguer left in the majors. Beginning on April 22 New York played a three-game series against the Dodgers at Ebbets Field and took two out of three. Jim Hearn won the first game, beating Johnny Podres and breaking the Dodgers' ten-game winning streak. New York defeated Brooklyn again on April 24, but in between, the Dodgers handed Sal Maglie his third defeat. During the game on April 23 the ugliest of the many incidents between the two teams took place, and Sal was right in the middle of it.

At first, the game promised to be merely another in the long line of Maglie victories over the Dodgers. The Barber's razor was sharp, and he began shaving Brooklyn chins in the first inning, drawing flinches, stares, and growls. Maglie responded with gestures meant to indicate that the ball was slipping and the close shaves were accidental (no doubt to keep the umpires off his back), but both he and the Dodgers hitters knew that was not true. Sal was doing what he always did—frightening and humiliating the Brooklyn batters. Sal threw brushbacks "whenever they didn't expect it. That way I had them looking to duck all the time."[5] Although Sal's fastballs, coming in at the chin or the temple, *looked* frightening to the batter as they whizzed toward the plate, as long as the batter could see the ball, he could move his head out of the way. But when Jackie Robinson came to bat in the second, Sal unloosed a fastball that came in behind Robinson, just at the level of his shoulders. That, as Roger Kahn observed, "*is* truly dangerous, a killer pitch. As a batter strides . . . he loses height. A normal reflex is to fall backward. When a pitch is shoulder-high behind a man, he ducks directly into the baseball."[6] Robinson started to duck, but thanks to his extraordinary reflexes, he did not flinch backward. Instead, he hunched his shoulders and froze as the ball sailed behind him, so close he must have heard the hiss and felt the wind. He held that pose and glared at Maglie, who went through his usual fidgets, refusing to acknowledge that anything out of the ordinary had happened. *Had* anything out of the ordinary taken place, beyond an accidentally misplaced pitch? It is worth pausing to consider the issue in greater detail.

Sal's pitches so rarely sailed behind batters' heads that when they did, they could almost be explained as slips of the hand. Almost, that is, because— although it is extremely unlikely that Maglie was a homicidal maniac intent on murder—ultimately no one can read a pitcher's mind.[7] Judging by his numbers of hit batsmen in general (there is no separate statistic for beaning), Sal's reputation for hitting batters was far worse than his numbers indicate. He never led the league in hit batsmen, and even in 1950, his peak year for hitting batters, he struck 10, while Ewell Blackwell topped the National League with 13, and in the American League Tommy Byrne also hit 13. It should be kept in mind, however, that both Blackwell and Byrne were notoriously wild, while Sal was a control pitcher. This leads to the suspicion that Sal hit some batters intentionally, marking his territory, so to speak. From then on Sal lived off the reputation he established in 1950. He understood the art of intimidation: no batter hits as well if he is afraid the pitcher is going to throw at him. If the pitcher can make the batter dread being thrown at, that is as effective as actually throwing at him. Once Sal had established his fearsome reputation in 1950, it was no longer necessary, except on rare occasions, for him to reinforce it by deliberately hitting a batter. He later admitted to hitting Stan Musial intentionally on one occasion in the second game of a doubleheader in 1954, during which Stan the Man had hit a record-breaking five home runs.[8] The plunk was pure payback.

In 1953, when Sal's control presumably was at its worst due to his back injury, he hit only one batter (league leader Gerry Staley smacked 17), creating the suspicion that many of Sal's hit batsmen could not be blamed on the pitcher's lack of control. Sal's 1954 total of hit batsmen was three, well behind National League leader Brooks Lawrence, who struck eight, and the American League's Steve Gromek, who bonked 13. Furthermore, in his entire career Sal beaned only two batters. Despite this, Maglie maintained his reputation as a headhunter. The menacing image he had so carefully cultivated over the years went a long way toward perpetuating his reputation. As Roger Kahn observed, "Let a lean young pitcher with a crew cut [that is, a typical, clean-cut "American" type] knock down a hitter, and someone may suggest the ball slipped." But "whenever Maglie throws within three feet of a batter's chin," Kahn continued, everyone is certain he is a cold-blooded killer trying to murder the batter.[9] Szalontai, who in his biography of Maglie made a special effort to keep track of Sal's alleged beanballs, which he invariably characterized as "vicious," mentioned only a few instances of the ball sailing behind a batter's head. One of them was the pitch to Jackie Robinson on April 23, 1955.

Robinson took no immediate action against Maglie after his near-beaning in the second inning of that game, and Sal struck him out. But, according to Robinson's recollections, when Jackie returned to the dugout, Pee Wee Reese declared that the Dodgers had to do something to retaliate against Maglie and instructed Jackie, "When you come up [again], drop one down the first base line and dump him on his butt."[10] Robinson agreed, although the action was not, in his version of events, his own idea. The next time he came to bat, in the fourth inning, even before Sal had thrown a pitch, Robinson began screaming at him: "You dago bastard! You couldn't hurt me if you hit me! I'm gonna bunt down the first base line and knock the shit out of you!"[11] As good as his word, Robinson bunted along the first base line. He had tried this tactic on Maglie twice before—the first time he had collided with Sal and sent the pitcher sprawling; the second time, Sal had avoided fielding the bunt.

Baseball games are like snowflakes—no two are alike, and this time Robinson's bunt traveled not toward the mound but toward Whitey Lockman. As Jackie saw the first baseman rush forward to field the ball, he was certain that this time, although Maglie would not be in his way on the base path, Sal would have to leave the mound to cover first. There, he would be directly in front of Robinson, now running full tilt toward first base, where he intended to crash into Maglie. But once again Maglie refused to move. He knew exactly what Robinson planned to do. Noticing that Maglie was not moving, second baseman Davey Williams tore over to cover first, and just as he was reaching for Lockman's throw, Robinson barreled into him, head down, using his shoulder to smash into the smallish Williams with the full force of his 210 pounds in rapid motion, all of it intended to maim Sal Maglie. Instead, the impact spun the unsuspecting Williams around, and he landed in an awkward heap. Both dugouts emptied, and it looked as if an all-out brawl would ensue. But after writhing on the ground for a few moments, Williams staggered to his feet and grimly insisted on continuing to play, although he was out for two weeks after the game. He was not, as one later account claimed, carried off the field on a stretcher.[12] Already suffering from back problems before the collision, he never fully recovered and retired that same year, at age 28. Robinson was sufficiently bruised by the collision that he did not play the next day. Physically at least, Sal Maglie was unscathed.

Here was a play where, technically, Maglie was not involved at all, beyond having thrown the pitch that Robinson bunted. But it is the pitcher's job to cover first when the first baseman is drawn far enough off the bag when he fields the ball that he has no chance of making the putout unassisted. It is not up to the second baseman to race all the way over from his position to make the play. Literally, the innocent Williams took the fall for Maglie. In Roger Kahn's judgment, "at a critical moment, The Barber lost his nerve."[13] The best that can be said in Sal's defense is that he showed a reasonable interest in self-preservation. He knew from past experience that Robinson's intention in bunting was to lure him into fielding the ball and then to collide with him, injuring him if possible or at least shaking him up and giving him a lesson in Dodger vengeance. Instead, by declining to put himself in Robinson's way, Sal was the indirect cause of a career-ending injury to a player with no involvement in the bitter Giants-Dodgers feud. He had saved his own delicate back but at the expense of someone else's. Decades later, the incident still rankled, and Maglie remained on the defensive about it. In a rare display of ill humor, during a 1974 interview he refused to discuss it.[14]

Robinson bears a much greater responsibility than Maglie for the injury to Davey Williams. He was the one who inflicted it, and he expressed regret. A few days afterward he apologized to Williams, saying he was sorry that Davey had been hurt, "but when Maglie threw behind me, he was starting a really dangerous business, and I was going to put a stop to it before he hit Gil or Campy or Pee Wee in the head." And then, puffing air through his cheeks, he added as if speaking directly to Maglie, "Don't ever throw that fucking baseball behind me."[15] To sportswriter Joe Reichler Robinson explained, "When I dropped that bunt I had no intention whatsoever of knocking down anybody but Maglie. I was charging with my head down and didn't even know it was Williams I bowled into until he was sprawling on the ground."[16] In retrospect, Robinson came to believe that mistakenly running down Davey Williams was his worst moment in baseball, worse than all the racism he had endured in his early years in the game, because it put him, not his adversaries, in the moral wrong. He wondered aloud, "What the hell am I doing this for? I don't need it. I don't need the money. What for?"[17] The man who for years had inhabited the heart of the hatred between the Dodgers and the Giants had begun to question why such over-the-top hostility should continue.

Those sobering thoughts came to Robinson later. As the game on April 23 went on, the vicious cycle of payback continued. Monte Irvin recalled the aftermath of the incident. As soon as the inning ended Durocher motioned his team off the bench and into the tunnel that led from the dugout toward the clubhouse. He snarled at his players, "Are you going to let this son of a bitch run us out of the ball park? The first man up that gets on, I want you to just keep running and I want you to give [Robinson] what he gave to Davey." Aware of the racial issue in anything involving Robinson, Durocher turned to Irvin and asked, "How do you and Hank [Thompson] feel about it?" Irvin answered for both of them: "Leo, we've got *Giants* written on our shirts."[18]

The first man up in the next inning was Alvin Dark, who hit a double to left field. Following the plan put into effect by Durocher, Dark sped around second and tried to reach third, guarded by Jackie Robinson. The relay reached Robinson in plenty of time, and he stationed himself as if to take the full impact of Dark's spikes-up slide. That would have been the collision of two former college football stars, each prepared to encounter the other, but as Dark began his slide, Robinson stepped out of the way and jammed the ball against Dark's nose. To Jackie's dismay, the ball slipped out of his hand, and Dark was safe. The umpires intervened to prevent a fistfight between the two men. The Dodgers won the game, 3–1. Afterward, Alvin Dark made an excessive comment, comparing Robinson to Hitler, although Robinson asked sportswriter Joe Reichler to tell Dark he had no interest in fighting. The rest of the Dodgers were jubilant, both at their victory and at Robinson's rough play. They stood in line to shake Jackie's hand, slapping him on the back and shouting, "That's the way to play if they want to get nasty about it!" and laughing about Jackie having "put the fear of God into Maglie."[19] Asked about the incident, Leo Durocher's comment was a curt "No comment," and Sal Maglie confined himself to a single, dismissive syllable: "Eh."[20]

Sal did not pitch again until May 5, when he won his first game of the season, 6–3, over the Chicago Cubs. In a game delayed several times by rain, and despite a stiff neck, Sal pitched six innings, allowing two runs on five hits. His victory brought the Giants over .500 for the first time. Without saying much about it, Durocher dropped Maglie from his regular rotation, which now consisted of Antonelli, Gomez, Hearn, and Liddle, and used Sal as a spot starter and in relief, a demotion from his starring role. With a 1–3 record, Sal was in no position to complain. During a doubleheader with the Pirates on May 8 at the Polo Grounds, Maglie wasted a scoreless ninth inning's worth of work in the opener, which the Giants and Ruben Gomez lost, 7–5. In the nightcap he relieved Don Liddle in the fifth with two out and the bases loaded and persuaded Pittsburgh third baseman George Freese to fly out to Mays. Sal completed the game, picking up his second win.

For the rest of May Durocher used Maglie more regularly, and he responded to more frequent work by earning four straight victories, bringing his winning streak to six games. He tossed his first complete game of the year against the Cubs in the second game of a doubleheader at Wrigley Field on May 15, defeating Chicago, 9–4. He won his fourth on May 22, beating Pittsburgh, 3–2. On May 27 Sal regained his old mastery over the Dodgers, defeating Carl Erskine, 3–1, and confining Brooklyn to seven hits. After the injury to Davey Williams and the near fistfight between Alvin Dark and Jackie Robinson during Sal's previous start against the Dodgers a month earlier, the game was peaceful. Sal curved the Dodgers to death with an assortment of slow stuff and threw only one pitch high and tight, which bounced off the handle of Roy Campanella's bat for an easy out. Although the first three Dodger batters in the first inning combined a walk, a base hit, and a fly ball to produce a quick run, after that Sal did not permit a runner to advance past second. Sportswriter Robert Creamer noticed that Sal was still laughing at the Dodgers. "When things work right . . . the Maglie mouth splits into the Maglie grin, which to Dodger eyes looks like an open sneer."[21] On May 31 Sal gained his sixth win, a neatly pitched 2–1 effort against the Phillies in which he allowed Philadelphia five hits and gave up his only run in the first. The win brought his record to 6–3.

Sal attributed his turnaround after three straight losses at the beginning of the season to his study of films made of his deliveries by Frank Bergonzi, a jack of all trades employed by the Giants front office. Beginning in 1950, Bergonzi shot film footage of all the Giants pitchers. In the company of pitching coach Frank Shellenback, Sal watched Bergonzi's film of him, and the two men spotted the problem: Sal's follow-through had changed since 1951. "I had a very long stride then," Sal explained, "and a full follow-through. Another later movie showed me with a curtailed stride and a sort of timid follow-through. . . . With a longer stride my body comes down lower to the ground on delivery, enabling me to get the maximum action on the ball. . . . Since I saw the pictures and got back to the old way of throwing the ball, I feel stronger and more confident."[22]

The Giants had played fairly well in May, compiling an 18–13 record and maintaining their position in third place, but in June they fell out of contention, putting together a miserable 10–17 record. By June 19 they were in fourth place, and by the end of the month they had slumped to fifth. Maglie began the month strongly with a 3–2 victory over the Cubs in the opening game of a doubleheader, another complete game, and his seventh consecutive win. The Cardinals came to the Polo Grounds for a doubleheader on June 12. Maglie started the second game and lost it, 6–5, in 13 innings. Sal gave up a run in the top of the first, but the Giants scored four runs in the bottom of the first and another in the second, giving Maglie a 5–1 cushion, usually sufficient for him. This time, though, he failed to hold the lead. The Cards scored two in the third, and in the sixth rain delayed the game for half an hour. When Sal resumed pitching, there was a freak play in the seventh inning that confused the pitcher. With New York leading 5–3 and two out, Solly Hemus stroked a low line drive down the first base line for what appeared to be a double. Sal started toward the area between second and third, to back up a possible overthrow to second base from right field. But the ball never reached right field. It struck the foot of first base umpire Lee Ballanfant and rebounded into the hands of first baseman Gail Harris, who was too far from first to make an unassisted play, and who could not throw immediately to Maglie because Sal was on the far side of second. Sal raced over to cover first, but Hemus easily beat him to the bag. Instead of being out of the inning, the rattled Maglie had to pitch to Stan Musial, who homered to tie the score. The Cards won it in the thirteenth, and Grissom, who had relieved Maglie in the seventh, took the loss.

Durocher singled out Maglie and that particular play for special, public scorn. For years Leo had lashed Sal behind the scenes, calling him a "stupid wop" and a "dumb dago," justifying his abusive language by claiming it was a tactic and that Sal pitched better when he was angry. But this time Durocher really believed Sal had been worse than stupid; he thought he had been lazy, and if there was one thing Durocher could not endure it was a player's failure to give his full effort. After the game Leo blamed Sal for the Giants' loss, fuming to reporters that "Maglie was too lazy to cover first base." He added, "I'm real sore at Maglie, because he blew an easy play."²³ The unfairness of Durocher's singling out Maglie's performance on a freak play, and labeling it lazy, is obvious. The Giants manager seemed to be looking for reasons to tear Sal down. Perhaps his real beef was that Sal was no longer invincible where it counted most: against the Dodgers.

On June 18 Sal faced the Braves and fared poorly. Although he was not involved in the decision, in five innings he gave up four runs on ten hits, walked three, and made a fielding error. Milwaukee won, 7–4. Maglie's next outing was more successful, as he snapped the Giants' six-game losing streak by beating Cincinnati, 4–3. He pitched a complete game, bringing his record to 8–3. No pitcher on the struggling club had a better record. But then the Dodgers defeated Sal again on June 28, 6–5. Sal lasted six innings, giving up five runs, four of them earned, on six hits. To the surging Brooklyn team, Sal was no longer a figure of menace but had become just another aging hurler. The Barber had lost four games so far, three of them to the Dodgers.

Maglie had a busy month of July. With the Giants in fifth place, and the pennant as good as lost, Durocher seemed determined to squeeze every last bit of use out of the oldest man on the team. In scorching heat on July 2, Sal pitched the Giants to a 6–1 victory over the Phillies, improving his record to 9–4. Although he gave up nine hits in eight and one-third innings, the one run the Phils scored was unearned. The Giants had put together a modest four-game winning steak when Sal took the mound against the Dodgers on July 8 at the Polo Grounds. The game turned into a more than three-hour debacle where the two teams used a combined total of 37 players, including 11 pitchers. The Giants chased Don Newcombe with four runs in the second and two more in the third, a surprising feat, considering that the big righthander's record was 14–1. Sal did not do much better, giving up five runs in the fourth, then leaving for a pinch hitter. As he made the walk to the clubhouse in center field, Dodger fans gave him their favorite good-bye, waving white handkerchiefs and jeering at the battered Barber The Dodgers finally won, 12–8, with Gomez taking the loss. Just two days later Durocher sent Sal out to face Brooklyn again, and he made a gallant effort in the last game he ever pitched against the Dodgers while wearing the black and orange–trimmed white uniform of the New York Giants. He left in the fifth with the Giants behind, 2–1, but New York scored two in the bottom of the ninth on a lucky play to pull out a 3–2 win. A fragment of the Maglie magic remained to the end.

Sal had another outing against the Braves on July 16, facing Warren Spahn. The Giants won, 8–7, but Sal was not involved in the decision. His performance was mediocre, as he allowed four runs in seven innings, three of them coming on homers. The Giants defeated the Cardinals, 6–5, at the Polo Grounds on July 21. Sal started but lasted less than two innings, allowing four runs, only one of them earned, on four hits. Despite the suffocating heat, Durocher threw Sal into another game the next day, against Cincinnati. If he was trying to wear out the exhausted veteran, he was succeeding. Sal lasted three innings and was taken out after he gave up three runs: a two-run homer by Wally Post, followed by a solo round tripper from Reds slugger Ted Kluszewski. The Giants pulled out the win, 6–3. Sal next faced the Cubs at Wrigley Field on July 26, where he lasted two and two-thirds innings, allowing three runs on five hits, including two homers. Once again the Giants came from behind and won, 6–5. Although Sal was not losing games, he was not winning them, either. His last victory had been on July 2. The Giants climbed into third place in July, but several victories had come in spite of Sal's poor pitching. Maglie hit bottom on July 30. In a game against the Braves at County Stadium he failed to record a single out. After walking the leadoff man, he gave up three successive hits, and Durocher took him out. All the runners scored, and the Giants lost, 5–3. Sal's record fell to 9–5, the best on the team, but for a variety of reasons Sal had pitched his final game as a member of the New York Giants.

SAL'S 1955 SEASON—THE CLEVELAND INDIANS

On July 31, shortly after New York had defeated Milwaukee, 7–3, the Giants front office announced that Sal Maglie had been sold to the Cleveland Indians on waivers in a straight cash deal with no other players involved. The price the Giants received for Sal was first reported as $25,000, a figure later revised downward to $10,000 cash, plus about $11,000 remaining on Sal's 1955 contract, which then became the responsibility of the Indians. The deal was not quite as simple as it seemed, either in the actual transaction or the motives of the parties involved.

Along with the reserve clause, the waiver system in place at that time points up the chattel status of major leaguers in the 1950s. One of baseball's more complicated set of rules, waivers is a system by which all the teams in a league have a chance to bid on a player about to be released or included in a trade. When a club fails to act on its right to purchase a player's contract, that club is said to "waive" the right. Before a player can be released, all teams in the league must grant waivers, in reverse order of their league standing. In the 1950s a team could ask waivers on a player they considered superfluous without the player's consent and without even informing him. The player himself might only find out he had been placed on waivers when another club claimed him, or when no club wanted him, and he was released. Sal was sitting in the dugout in Milwaukee on July 31, the day after his miserable showing against the Braves, when Durocher informed him that he had been sold to the Indians. He also told the pitcher that he had been on the waiver list for six weeks.

Cleveland's shrewd general manager Hank Greenberg, the Hall of Fame hitter who had made a successful second career for himself in upper level management, was less interested in what Maglie could do to improve Cleveland's already outstanding pitching staff than he was in denying the Yankees a chance to get hold of Sal. Although in the 1950s there was no George

Steinbrenner spending millions to acquire the best players for the Yankees, the team was so dominant that others were eager to deny the Bronx Bombers the chance to further strengthen their team by picking up players on waivers from National League teams late in the season. Greenberg campaigned successfully for a change in the waiver rules. Under earlier rules, if the Giants had found that no National League club wanted to claim Maglie, they could have sold him to any American League team, regardless of that club's standing. Under the new rules, the dominant clubs in both leagues could no longer snap up the other's league's players offered on waivers. Under the new rules, the teams lowest in the league standings had first choice of whether to take players offered on waivers. Since Cleveland was in third place when Maglie became available, and no team below Cleveland in the standings wanted Sal, the Indians could claim him. The Yankees, because they were in first place, could not muscle in and purchase Maglie.

The Giants had a number of reasons for wanting to get rid of Sal. There was the persistent rumor that Durocher had turned against Maglie after that game on June 12 when Sal failed to cover first and Leo blasted him for being lazy. But there were reasons that went well beyond managerial spite. With no chance to win the 1955 pennant, the Giants were cleaning house, preparing for a future where they saw no place for the 38–year-old Maglie. Attendance at the Polo Grounds had continued to decline, and Stoneham, whose only income came from the profits his team made, was looking for ways to cut costs. Maglie's salary was among the higher ones on the club and seemed like too much for the team to be paying a creaky old pitcher. Better to let Sal go, the front office concluded, and make room for younger pitchers who needed the experience and could be paid much less. The sale came as a surprise to Sal, but he concealed whatever emotions the news aroused in him and expressed no displeasure. He was, after all, being sent from a team with no chance at the National League pennant to a team in contention for the American League flag. "It was a shock to learn I was sold, but I'm really glad to come to the Indians," Sal said, expressing confidence that he could help Cleveland win a second straight pennant. "They talk about my age, but I've got plenty of good pitching left in me," he declared.[24]

On August 2 Maglie joined the Indians, who were playing the Yankees at Yankee Stadium. Although Sal said he hated to leave the Giants, claiming "it was like saying good-bye to your family," he later recalled his departure quite differently, claiming that only Durocher, who had alternately befriended and bedeviled him, bothered to say good-bye. "Before I left, Leo thanked me for all the help I'd given to the Giants over the years, but no one else from the ball club ever said a word to me."[25] This is another instance of Maglie's remembering an event in his past as worse than it was.

According to a report at the time, many of Maglie's Giants teammates said good-bye and wished him well. Alvin Dark shook Sal's hand and told him he would assure the Dodgers "they can relax until October when they'll be seeing you again [in the World Series]." Others echoed Dark's sentiments and noted how much Maglie would be missed. Whitey Lockman said sadly, "It's going to be awfully funny going into a Brooklyn series without Sal out there starting it," and Don Mueller declared, "He was the one who won the big ones for us."[26]

Sal was polite during his sudden transfer to an American League team, but not long after joining the Indians he unloaded to a New York reporter: "I'll never forgive Leo for the incident when he called me lazy. . . . He saw an opportunity there to embarrass me. The only way I can figure it is that the Giants already had waivers on me, and Leo was building it up so that I could be let go."[27] Maglie felt his manager had deliberately and publicly humiliated him, and that made him angrier than any private rebuke. Although the incident increased his dislike for Durocher, Sal's 1955 blast was one of the few times he made any public criticism of the Giants manager.

Sportswriter Joe King offered an eloquent and prophetic epitaph on Sal's years with the Giants: "The close of Sal Maglie's career as a Giant very likely was also the end of the one brief glorious spell the club enjoyed since the faraway days of John McGraw. . . . Sal was the most valuable Giant . . . because he alone could control the team to beat, the Dodgers. He held the key to the pennant, and when he lost it this year he was expendable."[28] King was very nearly right. More than fifty years have passed since the Giants sold Sal Maglie, and during those decades they have won only two pennants and never another World Series.

In the two months remaining in the 1955 season, Sal saw light action in 10 games with the Indians. Although he was not in completely foreign territory—he knew the Cleveland players from the years of spring training exhibition games the Giants and the Indians had played—he did not know the American League hitters, and he found the junior circuit umpires less inclined to give him the corners on their calls. Sal made an effort to bring his ferocious reputation with him. He noticed that Ted Williams always tried to get as close to the plate as he could while an opposing pitcher was warming up. He would sidle up alongside the batter's box and time the pitcher's speed by swinging as the ball reached the plate. Maglie issued a public warning that the first time Ted tried that with him he was going to throw the ball at his head. Sal was not about to have his territory invaded by the twentieth century's last .400 hitter.

Maglie's first outing with the Indians came on August 5, and he made a mess of it. He started but lasted only two innings, allowing four runs (two earned) in the first inning and another in the second before being taken out. Sal lost, 7–5, to the worst team in the league, the Washington Senators. On August 7 Sal threw one inning of scoreless relief in another game the Indians dropped to Washington, 9–3. During the second week in August the Indians went on a six-game winning streak and fought their way into first place in the tight American League race. Cleveland led the second-place Chicago White Sox by one game, and the Yankees were in third, only a game and a half out. The Indians swept a doubleheader from the Kansas City Athletics on August 12. The first game was a 17–1 laugher, and with the victory safely in the bag, Lopez gave Bob Lemon the rest of the afternoon off. Sal pitched the final three innings, giving up the A's only run, which was unearned, and allowing three hits. Maglie made another relief appearance on August 16 as the Detroit Tigers' Billy Hoeft defeated Early Wynn, 7–0. Sal tossed three and two-thirds innings of scoreless relief in a lost cause, as the Indians tumbled back to third place and the Yankees took possession of first.

In Cleveland on August 21 the Indians defeated the A's again, 9–4, and Maglie pitched two scoreless innings in relief. The Indians took on the Yankees in Cleveland on August 25. Stengel's league leaders knocked out Early Wynn, taking the game, 5–2, as Sal wasted three and one-third innings of scoreless relief, handling the league leaders "with the same insolent ease with which he used to make life miserable for the Dodgers."[29] Cleveland regained first place by defeating the Yankees on August 22 as their rookie fireballer Herb Score beat the Yankees' erratic righthander Don Larsen. But on August 28 Cleveland dropped both ends of a doubleheader to the pesky last-place Senators and tumbled back into third again. In the second game, in which the Senators pasted the Indians, 13–4, Sal pitched two and two-thirds ineffective innings, allowing four runs.

With the Yankees and Indians tied for second place, just half a game behind the White Sox, Lopez decided to take a chance and gave Sal a start against Chicago. He suffered another poor outing. He lasted only three and one-third innings, giving up three runs as the White Sox defeated Cleveland, 8–1, dropping the Indians back into third place. Sal's record with the Indians was now 0–2. He made two more brief appearances. On September 5 the Indians split a doubleheader with Kansas City. In the opener, which Cleveland lost, 5–4, Sal came in to face one batter and recorded the out. Against the Orioles in Baltimore on September 8 Sal threw four and one-third innings in relief, allowing one run. The Indians won the game, but Sal was not involved in the decision. In the final weeks of the season he warmed the bench as the Indians slugged it out with the White Sox and the Yankees. The Tribe took over first place for a few days in mid-September but could not hold on to it and finished second, three games behind the Yankees.

Over in the National League, with the Curse of the Demon Barber lifted off their backs, the Dodgers' hour came round at last. They not only won the pennant, they finally beat the Yankees in the World Series. Johnny Podres pitched a 2–0 shutout in Game Seven that brought Brooklyn its first and only World Series title. Amid hysteria and drunken craziness, observant and sensitive teetotaler Carl Erskine uncovered something like a religious experience: "It was such an emotional finish. . . . There was a lot of celebration, naturally, but . . . the key guys on that ball club were very quiet because this was like a spiritual experience more than a celebration."[30]

As for everyone else, unrestrained jubilation was the rule. Next year had arrived. Firecrackers exploded, horns honked, spontaneous motorcades formed and went blaring through the streets. Total strangers hugged and kissed one another. Brooklynites rushed out onto their doorsteps screaming and banging flatware against pots and pans. Blizzards of tickertape and every kind of torn paper from toilet tissue to telephone books rained from the windows of downtown office buildings. Schools had ceased any pretense of teaching, and their public address systems carried the seventh game to students. When the school day ended, kids raced home to catch the final innings with their families. Restaurants and diners gave away free food. Jubilant drunks, crazed with joy, staggered from bar to bar.

Police tried to barricade the Bossert Hotel in Brooklyn, where the Dodgers' victory party was going on, but ecstatic fans swamped them, surrounding the players as they stepped from their cars. A representative of the *Tonight* show tried to carry off Series hero Johnny Podres to New York for a television appearance, but Dodgers general manager Buzzie Bavasi stepped in, explaining with admirable understatement that Johnny had "had a few drinks, and I don't know what he's liable to say." The show's producers were hoping to entice the girl-crazy pitcher with a pretty blonde who was to escort Podres to Manhattan, riding with him in the back seat of the limo. "That would make it worse!" Bavasi exclaimed, having an excellent idea of what would transpire en route.[31] As the party rolled on toward dawn, Johnny Podres, exhausted, exuberant, and falling-down drunk, his suit soaked with champagne, remained happily unaware of the old adage that alcohol adds to the inclination while taking away from the performance. He tried to give his hotel room key to the daughter of one of the Dodgers' vice-presidents.[32]

THE NEW MAGLIE FAMILY—"EVERYONE ELSE JUST HAS BABIES"

Sal Maglie could be forgiven if his mind was not entirely on baseball during the latter part of the 1955 season and if he ignored the World Series. After almost 15 years of childless marriage, he and Kay were at last in the process of adopting. They seem to have come to the decision reluctantly. After Kay had tried to convince John and Mary Pileggi to give her their second son (who died a few days after his birth), Sal declared to Mary, "we've made up our minds. We're going to Buffalo, to Catholic Charities," the local religiously affiliated agency that handles adoptions.[33] Despite what seemed like a firm decision, Sal and Kay did not begin adoption proceedings until several years later and did not complete the process until late in 1955.

Sal had always been reluctant to discuss personal problems with anyone outside his immediate family. Larry Jansen, Sal's roommate on the Giants for several years, could not recall Sal ever bringing up the subject of his own lack of children, although at that time the Jansens were adding a new baby to their large family almost every year, and the subject of children must have come up on occasion. "No, uh-uh, no. We didn't talk about that." Jansen insisted. "Pretty much just all baseball."[34] Sal and Kay had made efforts to determine the cause of their infertility. John Pileggi recalled hearing an explanation of his sister Kay's childlessness resulting from an "infantile womb," a medical condition in which the woman's uterus fails to develop properly, and pregnancy is impossible. With little reliable information available, Sal and Kay groped their way among the myths and prejudices that clouded the subject of infertility but were unable to accept the medical verdict. Instead, they kept hoping they would conceive a child and therefore continued to put off beginning the adoption process.

In the 1950s adoption did not have the positive connotation it does today. Many saw it as decidedly second-best, an admission of failure by couples who could not produce children of their "own." As it became obvious to the Maglies that their union was not going to produce children, they encountered the powerful issue of blood kinship, strong in American society and even stronger in Italian peasant culture, where it carries an almost mystical weight. The news that his son was going to adopt a child pleased Sal's father but was less welcome news to Sal's mother. Mary Maglie, from a peasant family, could not fathom why Sal and Kay would want to raise a child physically unrelated to them. "It's not your *blood*," she would remind them whenever the subject of adoption came up.[35]

Adoption is a long, arduous, and emotionally trying process for the couple seeking a child. Not only did Sal and Kay have to choose a child; they also had to be "chosen." As one weary adoptive mother expressed it, "everyone else just has babies."[36] In the 1950s, adoption agencies had rigid criteria that prospective adoptive parents had to meet. The couple had to have been married long enough to give evidence that the marriage was both durable and had proven childless. The husband had to produce evidence of sufficient income to assure long-term financial security for the child. Both husband

and wife had to undergo physical examinations to show they were in good health. The wife was required to be at home and able to give full-time care and attention to the child. Adoption agencies also expended great efforts to "match" adoptive parents and children. Many states had laws requiring children be placed in a home of the same religion as that of the birth mother, but even more important, in the eyes of the social workers who controlled the adoption process, was that the child and the parents resemble one another physically.[37] The purpose of this was to inject naturalness into a family form which at that time was still stigmatized as artificial, not quite as good as a "real" family.

On the face of it, Sal and Kay Maglie would seem to be just the kind of devoted, stable, prosperous couple that adoption agencies hoped to have as clients. And yet there were other issues that may have concerned the social workers who conducted the Maglies' "home study," as the process of evaluating potential adoptive parents is called, and delayed their approval as adoptive parents. Although Sal was prosperous in the 1950s—his salaries in the $30,000 range made him wealthy by the standards of the time—the agency understood that a baseball player's earning years are brief. It is unlikely that Sal could have provided any guarantee that he would continue to enjoy his current standard of living after his career ended. Further, in their pursuit of assuring a narrowly defined normalcy in the home life of the adopted child, the agency workers would have noted that Sal was away almost eight months of every year. The other issue that may have played a part is ethnicity, part of the agencies' obsession with "matching." Both Sal and Kay were distinctly Italian-looking, and there were hardly any babies of Italian origin available for adoption. Few girls of Italian background became pregnant out of wedlock, and either those who did were rushed into marriage, or someone in the girl's family assumed responsibility for the child. Putting a baby up for adoption was not acceptable.[38] Blood kinship, as Mary Maglie understood, took precedence over the moral issue of illegitimacy, so finding a baby who "matched" the Maglies was not easy.

Mary Pileggi remembered the efforts of Catholic Charities of Buffalo to find a child for Sal and Kay. "They called and said they had a little girl who matched Sal perfectly. Not just dark curls, but black hair on her arms and face," Mary recalled. No doubt the couple had already seen pictures of the child, since the next step after the home study is the agency's selection of a child for potential placement in that home. Next, a meeting was arranged to bring prospective parents and child together, always an emotionally fraught moment for the adopting couple. When Kay Maglie saw the little girl in the flesh, she realized the social workers had done their job too well—this was more matching than she could handle. A hairy husband was one thing, but a hairy little girl quite another. Kay took one look at the child, cried "Oh my God!" and burst into tears. The offended social worker informed Kay and Sal that there were many other couples who would be eager to have the child they had rejected.[39]

According to Mary Pileggi's recollections, that same day the Maglies had a chance encounter with the infant they eventually adopted. As they were walking down the hall after their traumatic meeting with the child Kay could not bring herself to accept, they spotted another baby. "Sal says to the social worker carrying the baby, 'I'll take this little one here,' and he pinches the baby's cheek," Mary related. The social worker explained that the baby had just been placed with Catholic Charities and they had no details on him yet. "Well, when you find out the details, we'll be back," Sal said. Current staff at Catholic Charities of Buffalo doubted that the event could have occurred in the way Mary Pileggi remembered hearing it recounted to her, since the "intake" of babies being relinquished for adoption does not occur in the same location where prospective parents go to meet the children ready to be placed for adoption.[40]

Nonetheless, whatever way the Maglies first saw that particular child, he was the one they adopted, although he did not "match" them physically. Possibly the couple's prominence in the region played some part in the agency's decision to bend the rules on their behalf, or perhaps their enthusiasm, eagerness, and immediate bonding with the baby convinced the social workers to overlook the lack of physical resemblances; it is impossible to know. What is certain is that on November 17, 1955, Sal and Kay brought home a chubby, cheerful six-month-old boy with fair skin, blue eyes, and a fuzz of reddish-blond hair. They named their adopted son Salvatore Anthony Maglie, Jr. In the family he quickly became known as "Little Sal." Maglie wanted a son to carry on his name, a boy to share his passion for baseball, and now he had one. As soon as the child could toddle around, Kay dressed him in a miniature baseball uniform, and Sal was out in their backyard teaching the little fellow the game that filled his own life.

If Sal was delighted to become a father, Kay was ecstatic to be a mother. It was far more important to her than all the wealth and fame Sal's baseball stardom had brought her. At age 37 she threw herself into motherhood with the passion of one whose heart's desire had been too long denied. Members of the Maglie and Pileggi families all praised Kay's abilities as a mother, and although the elder Mrs. Maglie was dubious at first, even she responded to the adorable child. Sal was moved by the baby in ways he had never experienced. He had always enjoyed children and loved his nieces and nephews, but this was different, a child who was his own in every way but blood, and blood meant nothing to him. "The little guy makes a difference right in there," he told reporters, pointing to his heart in a rare public display of private emotions.[41]

But as every new father finds out, the arrival of a baby alters the relationship between the husband and wife. Kay's universe had a new center. Although she remained a loving and devoted wife, Sal was no longer the exclusive object of his wife's attention. She now had less interest in going with her husband on his baseball travels. When Sal rejoined the Indians in 1956, Kay and Little Sal were going to remain in the couple's home in Niagara Falls. But then Sal realized he could not bear to be away from his son for all those months, and he persuaded Kay to pack her bags and the baby and come with him to Cleveland. His feelings had caught up with hers—Sal too had fallen head over heels in love with his little boy.

1956—The Artful Dodger

Sal Comes "Home" to Brooklyn

15

"There is absolutely nothing to the report that the Dodgers got Sal Maglie to have him stuffed and mounted in the plastic dome atop O'Malley Gardens."

Red Smith, *Herald Tribune*, May 16, 1956

THE HUNDRED-DOLLAR HONEY

Few expected Maglie to last long with the 1956 Indians, but nobody could have predicted where he would be within a month of the season's start. Cleveland's pitching remained solid, with Wynn, Lemon, Garcia, and Score all going strong, and Narleski, Mossi, and Cal McLish backing them up in the bullpen. The Tribe was hoping Bob Feller would retire, since they were loathe to trade away the Cleveland idol. That left Maglie as the most vulnerable member of the Indians pitching corps. During the winter Sal received a letter from Hank Greenberg, informing him that his salary would be cut for the coming year, down to around $24,000 from his previous year's $32,000. "From the tone of the letter," Sal recalled, "it didn't look as if I'd even make it to their training camp."[1] When his contract arrived, Maglie signed it without protest, knowing he was lucky to have been offered a contract. Unknown to Sal, the Indians were trying hard to unload him, even before spring training began, but they had no takers.

Still, Maglie remained determined to prove he could pitch. He reported to the Indians' training camp several days early, and he even gave up smoking, a habit to which he had been addicted since his teens, in the hope that it might increase his stamina. His spring training performance was good enough to win him a place on the Cleveland roster, but that place was in the back of the bullpen. Sal made two brief appearances as a reliever. On April 21 he was ineffective in a game where the Tigers defeated the Indians, 7–6. He pitched three innings, allowing two runs on six hits, and throwing a wild pitch. Against the Orioles on May 4 he tossed two innings of scoreless relief in another losing cause, as the Orioles won the game, 4–3. Maglie was not involved in either decision. The only event that broke the boredom of those early weeks was when teammates Mike Garcia and Herb Score presented Sal with a cake on his thirty-ninth birthday. They put the number 29 on it, figuring the pitcher would appreciate losing 10 years.

Just when it seemed Sal was headed for baseball's scrap heap, the Indians unintentionally did him one of the biggest favors of his life. Not wanting to waste the team's first-line starters in an exhibition game on April 30 against the Dodgers, Lopez used three pitchers he could afford to throw into a meaningless contest: the fading Bob Feller, rookie hopeful Bud Daley, and Maglie. The game took place on a chilly night, before a sparse and bad-tempered crowd, in an unlikely location: Jersey City. The previous August, Dodgers president Walter O'Malley had rattled his Brooklyn cage by announcing that in 1956 the Dodgers would play seven games in Roosevelt Stadium in Jersey City, as a way of showing his discontent with his situation in Brooklyn.

Jersey City was an old-time baseball town that had been the home of the Giants' top farm club, the Jersey City Giants, where Maglie spent his last months as a minor leaguer. Roosevelt Stadium was also where Jackie Robinson made baseball history in 1946, when he became the first black man in modern times to play in a minor league game. Now both men were returning to the old ball park in the twilight of their careers, and the Dodgers would be facing the one pitcher they hoped they were rid of forever. As Yogi Berra would say, it was déjà vu all over again. Sal entered the game in the seventh, after Feller had hurled three perfect innings to start the game and Bud Daley had allowed the Dodgers no runs on two hits in his three-inning stint. Sal pitched through the seventh, eighth, and ninth in the biting cold without allowing a run. With one out in the eighth, he gave up a single to Randy Jackson, who stole second and went to third on an overthrow, but he fanned Gino Cimoli and retired Charley Neal to get out of the jam. The Indians scratched out a run in the tenth that proved sufficient, as Maglie set the Dodgers down in order in the bottom of the tenth to win the game, 1–0.

The Dodgers were amazed. They thought Sal was dead, but evidently someone had forgotten to drive that stake through his heart. After the game Campanella wondered why anyone would think The Barber was finished—

his curve was just as sharp and baffling as ever. "I'm glad he's in the other league now," declared Pee Wee Reese.[2] Maglie's performance was not lost on Dodger management. They knew Cleveland was eager to unload the veteran and that they might be able to pick him up at a bargain price. With last year's mound hero Johnny Podres in the Navy, only Don Newcombe was a reliable starter. All the other Dodger pitchers seemed to have one arm ailment or another. Brooklyn had sold Billy Loes to the Orioles, so they were one man short on their pitching staff.

As the May 15 deadline for trimming rosters approached, Hank Greenberg called Dodgers general manager Buzzie Bavasi, asking if Brooklyn might be interested in Maglie. Knowing he was in an excellent bargaining position, Bavasi did not jump at the suggestion. He told Greenberg he needed to check with others. First he asked manager Walter Alston's opinion, and Alston said, "Grab him. I think he can help us."[3] Bavasi then took the team's temperature on the purchase. Would the Dodgers throw a collective fit at the thought of Maglie on their squad? He asked Reese, the level-headed team captain. "He looked like the same guy to me," Reese replied. "I'd like to see him on our side."[4] Bavasi also received approval from the one man whose consent was essential. Walter O'Malley thought the sight of the erstwhile Dodger-killer in a Brooklyn uniform would sell extra tickets, especially in games against the Giants, and O'Malley was never averse to raking in more money.

Bavasi called Greenberg back, and the Cleveland general manager, no amateur bargainer himself, informed Bavasi that he wanted $100,000 for Maglie. "Get lost! You've gotta be out of your friggin' mind!" Bavasi shot back. Greenberg promptly reduced Sal's selling price to $10,000. Bavasi, realizing he was now in the driver's seat, said no deal. "How much *will* you give us for him? Please, give us *something* for him," Greenberg pleaded. Barely able to contain his glee, Bavasi said he would give Greenberg $100 for the man who once had been the most feared hurler in baseball.[5] To save the dignity of everyone involved, including Maglie, Bavasi agreed to say that the Dodgers had paid $10,000 for Sal. Cleveland, however, let it be known that Maglie had been sold to the Dodgers for $100,000, and a white-as-a-sheet Walter O'Malley stormed into Bavasi's office, wanting to know how in hell he was going to come up with such an exorbitant sum. When Bavasi confided the pitcher's actual purchase price, O'Malley's color improved immediately. That same day Bavasi received a phone call from Maglie, who was in Cleveland, already packing up his apartment. He was happy to accept the position with the Dodgers but asked to postpone his arrival in Brooklyn for a day, because his father was ill, and he wanted to go home to Niagara Falls to see him.

Now it was the turn of the New York columnists to write their riffs on the astounding development. Red Smith's one-liner appears at the head of this chapter. Sid Friedlander devoted his *Post* column on May 18 to a comically stilted fantasy dialogue between the newly arrived Maglie and various Dodgers. In it, Campanella recalls Maglie's beanballs, saying "It was just deuced awkward of me to have my ears sticking out so often right where the ball was being pitched." "I am glad you are with us, Mr. Maglie. You have always been my ideal," murmurs a demure Carl Furillo. "I am glad to hear you say that," Sal replies. "It has always been my desire in life to be loved by everybody." The column ends with the team linking arms and waltzing onto the field singing "Your Side Is My Side, My Side Is Your Side." Jimmy Cannon devoted one of his classic columns to the event, claiming he was now prepared to believe absolutely anything. "I'm a changed guy," he wrote. "I intend to call every telephone number I see on the television commercials. . . . Tell me the Daughters of the Confederacy are building a monument to General Grant in Richmond and I'll bite. . . . *Maglie now coming in to pitch for Brooklyn.* . . . I'd keep my mouth shut if a movie company planned to revive King Kong with Liberace in the title role. . . . Perhaps the English are celebrating the Fourth of July this year. . . . I'll take your word that the Queen of England is in a Charleston contest at Roseland. . . . *Maglie now coming in to pitch for Brooklyn.* . . . Louis Armstrong is a tenor. . . . Harry Truman is a Republican. . . . All horse players die rich. . . . I look like Gregory Peck. . . . New York's a city in California. . . . Casey Stengel may quit the Yankees to teach English at Yale. . . . *Maglie now coming in to pitch for Brooklyn.*"[6]

Fan reaction was equally colorful and varied. Nothing in baseball, not even the Dodgers' later and long-rumored move to Los Angeles, created quite the same shock as the news that Sal the Barber would now be trimming beards for the Brooklyn Dodgers. Anthony Puccio, a long-time Dodger fan, asked in disbelief, "Is Maglie really one of us? Has The Barber become a Bum? I've booed him for so long, how can I bring myself to cheer him? How can you love a guy you hate?" From the other side, Giants fan Louis Keppel moaned, "How could they do this to me? What do those Bums want from us—blood? . . . All that's left now is for The Barber to pitch against us and beat us. If that should happen I'll borrow his razor and cut my throat."[7] A Jewish Dodger fan observed that hearing the news of Maglie joining the Dodgers was like hearing that Hitler had converted to Judaism. The analogy is extreme, but the event seemed every bit that incredible.

The Dodger team members, who had advance notice from Reese and Alston, were reserved in their comments to the press, although all agreed that Maglie could help the club. "Based on what he showed me in Jersey City a couple of weeks ago," said Reese, "he's got to help us." Campanella agreed. "He showed me he still knows how to pitch. I've said all along I couldn't understand why the Giants let him go last year." Jackie Robinson added,

"I'm glad he's with us. He's still a good pitcher, and you know what a great competitor he is."[8] Among the Brooklyn regulars, only Carl Furillo expressed displeasure. When he heard about the deal he phoned Bavasi and shouted, "Buzzie, you have to be the dumbest dago around. The guy can't pitch anymore and furthermore, I hate his guts!"[9] Although Furillo had calmed down by the time he spoke to reporters, he remained unenthusiastic about the prospect of Sal as his teammate.

On May 18 the Dodgers held a news conference in Brooklyn to introduce Sal. For several hours the pitcher patiently answered reporters' questions and posed for photographers in his Dodgers uniform. He responded to questions in his deep, surprisingly soft voice. Although reporters had been interviewing Sal for years, they remained amazed by the contrast between the fierce man on the mound and the gentle soul they encountered in the clubhouse. When asked why he had "hated" the Dodgers so much, Sal smiled and said thoughtfully, "Hate is just a word, I guess. I don't hate anybody. But I've always borne down harder against the top teams—and Brooklyn is a top team."Asked about his feud with Carl Furillo, Sal raised his eyebrows and responded, "Furillo? To tell you the truth, I've never spoken to the fellow. I don't know him. I didn't throw at him." The latter comment must have raised a few eyebrows among reporters, because Sal offered a revealing amendment. "At least I haven't [thrown at him] in the last four years," he clarified, a tacit admission that he *had* thrown at Furillo during his own first few seasons with the Giants.

Although reporters were aware of it, Sal made no mention of his recent bereavement. His 72–year-old father, whom he had hurried home to visit several days before, had died of a heart attack earlier that same day. But Sal did not cancel out on the press conference. He absorbed the hammer blow of shock and grief and went through with his commitment, flying in from Niagara Falls in the morning, then flying back again that same evening. Sal had remained close to his parents, despite his absences from home. During the winter months, even with his busy schedule of appearances, he came by their house every day for a chat and a cup of strong Italian coffee. He helped them with odd jobs or drafted one of his nephews to assist them. The nephews, Joseph's grandsons, called their grandfather "Papanone," the Italian equivalent of "Big Daddy."[10] Despite his short stature, he had loomed large in their lives.

Over his decades in America Joseph Maglie had learned to understand and enjoy baseball, and he had been immensely proud of his son. Sal's friend Eddie Gadawski, whose in-laws owned a bar-restaurant in Niagara Falls about a block from where the elder Maglies lived, remembered Joseph Maglie as a regular customer. "Very nice man. Spoke broken English. He'd come in to see the guys. The old-timers would get together, the old Italian guys, the old Polish guys. They'd have a good time, have a few drinks, sit around and talk, play cards. Sal's father used to come in and listen to baseball games on the radio, at the bar. He was a big fan—he followed Sal's career. 'Dat's-a my boy!' he'd say, 'Dat's-a my Salvatore!'"[11] After a funeral mass, Sal's father was buried in St. Joseph's Cemetery in Niagara Falls. Familial duties accomplished, Sal tucked away his grief and returned to New York. Rather than rent in unfamiliar Brooklyn, the Maglies again took an apartment in Manhattan. But Sal had already given his heart to Brooklyn. As he told *Niagara Falls Gazette* reporter Bob Lowe, "It will be just like going home."

WITH THE 1956 DODGERS—SAL'S SEASON OF HAVING EVERYTHING

Personal satisfaction and professional success coincided for Sal in 1956. He and Kay had the child of their dreams, and because Kay's happiness was complete, so was Sal's (Figure 16). Although he did not win 20 games during his abbreviated season with the Dodgers (he had already done that in 1951), Sal achieved several other milestones every pitcher hopes to reach: he won his 100th game, threw a no-hitter, and won a World Series game, the latter after a loss in 1951 and a no-decision in 1954. And most important of all, Maglie, the indomitable old veteran and former enemy, inspired an aging and faltering Dodgers team to its final Brooklyn pennant.

The question that intrigued everyone as Sal joined the Dodgers was: How would Maglie and Furillo get along? The Dodger right fielder had expressed hostility at the prospect of having his old enemy as a teammate, and team members felt uncertainty and anxiety about how Furillo would react to the sight of Sal. There are several versions of the moment when Maglie and Furillo first met, although it appears that only one is based on actually witnessing the event. The others are examples of "hearsay history." The earliest account of the meeting to appear in print is Frank Graham Jr.'s column in the September 1956 issue of *Sport* magazine. In that version, there is no tension at all: When Furillo saw Maglie enter the clubhouse he walked over grinning and said, "Hey, you're supposed to be my enemy. Hello, Sal. Welcome aboard." Other Dodger players then entered the locker room like actors receiving their cue to come onstage, and they welcomed their new teammate with equally jovial remarks. More recently, however, Graham acknowledged that the article was based on the report of another sportswriter, who was not present when Furillo and Maglie met, but who had heard the story from someone else.[12]

In 1989 Jack Lang, a retired sportswriter who covered the Brooklyn Dodgers in the 1950s for the *Long Island Daily Press,* wrote an obituary for Carl Furillo. In it he related a less positive version of the meeting between

16—Three generations of the Maglie-Pileggi family pose for a picture in 1956. Left to right: Kay Maglie's mother, Mae Pileggi; Sal; the couple's adopted son, Sal Jr.; Kay Maglie; and Sal's mother, Mary Maglie. Photo: collection of John and Mary Pileggi.

Furillo and Maglie. According to Lang, Furillo was sitting at his locker lacing up his spikes when Maglie walked in. When he looked up and saw Sal he "snarled in disgust and went back to tying his shoes." In a recent interview, Lang insisted he was in the clubhouse when Maglie entered.[13] Roger Kahn, writing in the early 1990s, did not claim he was present. Describing the atmosphere as "electric," he noted Furillo's hostility. In Kahn's account, as Maglie came into the room, and other Dodgers looked on anxiously, Furillo greeted Sal, not warmly, but civilly, one Italian to another. "'Hello, Dago,' Furillo said. ''Lo, Skoonj,' said Maglie."[14] Skoonj was one of Furillo's nicknames, a reference to scungilli, an Italian seafood dish whose main ingredient is snails, and was a comment on Furillo's slowness as a base runner. His other nickname, "The Reading Rifle," referred to his Pennsylvania origin and the legendary strength and accuracy of his throwing arm.

The most detailed and likely the most accurate account comes from Tom Villante, the executive producer of the Dodgers' television and radio broadcasts in the 1950s, who happened to be in the clubhouse by chance at the moment Maglie arrived. He was not a newshound sniffing out a story but had merely gone down there to pick up a sandwich and a soft drink. The only other person present was Charlie "The Brow" DiGiovanna, who had graduated from being the world's oldest bat boy to second in command in the clubhouse. Furillo, Villante recalled, was the first player to return from practice. He sat down at his locker with his back to the entrance and lit a cigarette. Just at that moment, the door opened, and in walked Sal Maglie. "The Brow and I looked at one another and wondered, Oh my God! What's gonna happen when Furillo turns around?" Maglie realized that the one player in the locker room was Furillo, because he saw the number 6 on his back, and he stopped at the doorway, venturing no further. Maybe Furillo heard the door open, or perhaps he sensed something. He turned around, and the two men glared silently at one another for what seemed to Tom Villante like eternity. Then Charlie DiGiovanna yelled, "Don't do it! We're all dagos in here!"[15]

Whatever Furillo intended to do—grab Maglie by the throat, curse at him, or who knows what—when The Brow said "Don't do it," he was warning The Rifle not to mess with The Barber. They were teammates now, as well as fellow Italians, whatever their personal feelings about one another. After a few more endless seconds had ticked by, Furillo rose to his feet, went over to Maglie, and shook his hand. The two men laughed, a little uneasily, and that was that. "What was interesting," Villante recalled, "is that The Brow broke the tension of the moment with that funny little line. It was funny because the four of us were all Italians. Then the other guys started to come in and got introduced to Sal, and the next thing you know, Furillo and Maglie are friends." Villante then observed, "I don't know what The Brow and I would have done if Furillo had grabbed Maglie around the throat. There's no way we could have stopped him. That added to the drama—the ferociousness of Furillo."[16]

Buzzie Bavasi came up with his own scheme for promoting harmony between the two men. He handed Furillo $200, a considerable sum in 1956, and told the tight-fisted right fielder to take Maglie out for dinner at Toots Shor's, the fabled Manhattan watering hole, more men's club than restaurant, where sports stars always received a warm welcome. Despite the fortune in his hand, Furillo's initial reaction to Bavasi's suggestion was, "You've gotta be fucking *nuts!*"[17] But after Furillo concluded that dinner for two would cost only about $20, and he could pocket the remainder, he agreed to Bavasi's request. Meanwhile, Bavasi called Shor and told the owner to put the two men's meals on his own tab but to let the players think that Shor himself was paying for their dinners. Neither man ever learned about Bavasi's tactic, and Furillo spent the rest of his life thinking he had taken the Dodgers' general manager for an impressive sum of money. Reflecting on the episode almost half a century later, the 90–year-old Buzzie Bavasi concluded, "Maglie cost me $300. One for his contract and two to Carl. I would have to say it was the best $300 I ever spent in baseball."[18]

The dinner had its intended effect, cementing what became an enduring friendship. Jack Lang recalled spending an evening in Furillo's hotel room in June of 1956, sharing ribs and beer with the two players, listening to them talking baseball and exchanging stories like a couple of life-long buddies. Donald Honig reflected on the unlikely friendship: "The fact that they became friends tells you a lot about Maglie. It tells you that Maglie had to have some depth of character. He was more mature than Furillo. Maglie could just have avoided Furillo, not had anything to do with him. Of course, I give Furillo some credit, too, for recognizing that Maglie was a good man—one who didn't carry a grudge. Sal was the ultimate professional and a gentleman."[19]

Had Maglie and Furillo ever really hated each other? It is unlikely that Maglie hated Furillo. Sal always insisted there was nothing personal in his treatment of the Dodger right fielder. He did not brush him back—or throw at him, depending on one's point of view—any more often than any of his other favorite Dodger targets, such as Reese, Hodges, and Campanella, and he liked to remind reporters that he had never hit Furillo with a pitch (although he had, once, in 1950). Moreover, Maglie was a man who did not bring his on-field animosities with him into his off-field life. But Furillo's dislike of Maglie extended beyond the playing field, as witnessed by his angry phone call to Bavasi, protesting the Dodgers' purchase of Maglie.

Although sportswriter George Vecsey suggested that Maglie and Furillo were both unforgiving types, that was much more true of Furillo than Maglie. Tom Villante recalled Furillo's personality: "He was like a bulldog—he'd get a hold and he would *not* let loose. There was real bad blood [between Furillo and Maglie] that went way back. You were dealing with a guy who was like a pit bull. He wasn't a guy who'd easily forgive and forget." Sal was a different type. "With Maglie," Villante continued, "you were expecting somebody *satanic*. He was one mean guy on the mound, and yet off the field he was a sweetheart. I think that's why people who got to know him loved him so much, because he was so completely different from what they were expecting."[20] George Vecsey wondered if the two men understood that they were "merely disposable warriors, used by club owners to sell tickets to a spectacle."[21] Although this poignant image brings to mind a pair of battered gladiators in an ancient Roman arena, fighting each other to the death for the amusement of the audience, and then being forgotten as soon as their mangled bodies are hauled out across the blood-soaked sand, it seems doubtful that Maglie and Furillo possessed sufficient detachment to see themselves in that light.

Columnist Dick Young speculated that Maglie and Furillo might become roommates, but that did not happen. With a 25–man roster, somebody always had a room of his own, and in 1956 that player was Carl Furillo. In an era when double rooms were the rule, Furillo was a loner, as well as a man known for his violent temper, so he was the obvious choice for a single. Maglie was paired with 25–year-old Roger Craig. The lanky, good-natured righthander from North Carolina found Maglie a congenial roommate. He also found Sal a wonderful source of pitching lore. Although Craig was not a rookie—1955 had been his first year with the Dodgers—he believes he was assigned to be Maglie's roommate so that Sal could "help me along and teach me the ropes, and help me with my pitching, which he did." Craig described Maglie as "a very quiet guy. He wouldn't talk much unless I asked him questions. But when Sal talked, you listened. I was asking him all kinds of questions, because I wanted to be as good a pitcher as I possibly could. He took me under his wing. I guess that with me he found someone who admired him and liked him. He and I hit it off and we hung out together. We'd go out after a road game once in a while and have a beer, by ourselves, and we'd sit and talk."[22] Craig had joined the Dodgers too late to have seen the full force of the animosity between the Dodgers and Maglie when Sal was with the Giants, but he was aware of its existence. "I think he was trying to feel the situation out," Craig reflected, "not trying to start anything. He waited and let people come to him. He never tried to push himself on anybody—that's the way he was. I think he must have said to himself, 'I'm just going to do my job, keep my mouth shut, and help them win.'"[23]

During his first two months with the Dodgers Sal was not much help. Following his well-established pattern of a slow start, his performances were something short of spectacular. He began his tenure with the Dodgers by pitching batting practice, and with his first pitch he knocked down Pee Wee Reese—perhaps from force of habit. Reese regained his feet and drew his hands across his chest, underlining the lettering on his uniform blouse. "Hey," he exclaimed, laughing but startled, "we're on the same team, Dodgers!"[24] Sal apologized. Alston remained cautious about putting Maglie into his starting rotation. The new Dodger pitcher made his first appearance as a reliever on May 24 in Philadelphia in a game where rookie fireballer Don Drysdale was the starter and loser, as the Phillies defeated the Dodgers, 6–4. Sal pitched two innings in his Dodger debut, giving up two runs on four hits—hardly a brilliant beginning. The next day an annoyed New York columnist wrote, "Using Maglie in a game in Philadelphia means that he can't be used in the impending series with the Giants. And if Sal wasn't bought to be used as a publicity gimmick when the Dodgers play his old teammates, what on earth was he brought to Brooklyn for?"[25] To his credit,

Alston ignored those urging him to treat Maglie as a circus sideshow attraction. He had a more vital role in mind for the veteran hurler.

With the Dodgers floundering in the lower middle of the league standings in a close race—although only three games out of first, they were in fifth place during the last week of May—Alston tried Maglie as a starter on May 30 in Philadelphia in the first game of a doubleheader. Sal lasted four innings, allowing three runs on four hits and striking out five. He began by striking out the side, but he gave up a homer to the leadoff hitter in the second and another with a man on in the fourth. Don Bessent took over for Maglie in the fifth, with the Dodgers behind, 3–0. In the sixth the Dodgers jumped on Robin Roberts for six runs and won the game, 6–5, but Sal did not receive the win. The Phillies pounded Don Drysdale in the second game, winning it 12–3.

The two pitchers' problems may have had something to do with how they had spent the previous evening. Despite the 20–year difference in their ages, Maglie and Drysdale became friendly soon after Sal joined the team. The rookie Drysdale, only 19 years old, saw in the veteran Maglie a role model who confirmed his own ideas about on-field ferocity, and Sal recognized in Drysdale a kindred mound temperament as well as a dazzling but still undisciplined talent. Both men arrived in Philadelphia by train ahead of the rest of the team, as Alston wanted them to have a good night's sleep before the Memorial Day doubleheader. After dinner, they were at loose ends for something to do, so Sal suggested they walk off their heavy meal. They made stops at numerous bars along their meandering route, with Sal having his favorite drink, a dry martini (or two) at each watering hole, and Don downing a couple of beers. After a while they were both feeling tired, not to mention looped, and decided to return to their hotel. "How do we get back there, kid?" asked Maglie, who had been coming to Philadelphia for years. "You're asking *me*?" replied Drysdale, who had no idea where they were.[26] They took a cab to the hotel, and for understandable reasons, neither man was at his best the next day. In his autobiography Drysdale recalled that he and Maglie pitched complete games on May 30, but the record shows that both men were taken out well before the ends of the games they started.

Drysdale considered Maglie an important and positive influence on him. "I learned more from Sal than any other single individual," he told Roger Kahn. "The greatest thing Sal taught me was this: The hell with all hitters. The hell with *all* of them. Except the hitters on your own club. They're the ones who put up the runs that you need."[27] In his autobiography Drysdale elaborated on what he had learned from Maglie: "One of the best early lessons I got about pitching was from Maglie, on how to move a batter off the plate. There were many times when I'd be out on the mound . . . and I'd peer into the dugout, looking for The Barber. And there he was, giving me a little nod, or whistling. That meant it was time to send a 'message' to the batter. . . . I was developing the same ideas as Sal."[28] Those ideas were not as simple as merely throwing high-inside. Drysdale talked endlessly with Maglie about how to "work" batters, how to move the ball around, how to keep a batter from digging in. When Drysdale made a mistake on the mound, after the inning ended Maglie would take the younger man aside and analyze what he had done wrong.

Once, when a batter had gotten a solid hit off Don, Sal asked him if he recalled what pitch he had thrown. Drysdale said the pitch had been a curve. "Right, and you had him leaning over like he had lumbago," Sal pressed. "So why did you throw him another curve? Once you got a batter leaning in, jam him with your fastball. If he hits your fastball, he'll have to do it with his knuckles." After games, they went through the same drill, going over pitch selections. Sal still had his knack of remembering pitches, even when they were not his own. "'You remember when it was 2–2 on so-and-so?' he'd say. 'Why did you throw what you did there? What were you thinking about?'" Drysdale's locker was next to Maglie's, another advantage to the rookie pitcher. "He knew I was eager to learn and listen," Drysdale recalled, "and whenever we had some free time, I'd pull up a stool and go to school with Sal the Professor."[29] Drysdale, who delighted in his later reputation as one of baseball's most notorious headhunters, was the first *Maglie cum laude* graduate of The Barber's Shaving Academy. In honor of his mentor, Drysdale asked for the number 53 on his uniform—Sal's 35 reversed—and kept it throughout his career.

As Drysdale's education in big league pitching continued, so did Maglie's comeback. On June 1 Sal pitched two scoreless innings in relief against the Cubs in a fifteen-inning heartbreaker that the Dodgers lost, 4–2. Brooklyn lost two more to the Cubs before finally pulling out the last game of the series on June 3 behind Sandy Koufax, as the fast but wild southpaw won in his first start of the year. Koufax, like Drysdale, was one of the youthful Dodger pitchers who learned from the veteran Maglie. Although Sal did not become as close with the reserved Koufax as he did with the outgoing and hard-drinking Drysdale, the two men liked and respected one another. Maglie recalled with pleasure the hours he spent "talking pitching" with Koufax.[30] As would become clear in later years, one area where the two men disagreed concerned their willingness to risk hitting a batter. Koufax, possessor of one of the greatest fastballs in the history of the game, hardly ever hit anyone, although he agreed with Sal on the importance of intimidation as a tactic. He once described pitching as "the art of sowing fear,"[31] a concept Maglie would have agreed with completely. What aspects of pitching the two men talked about are unknown, but Maglie probably emphasized the importance of control, something Koufax at that time had yet to master.[32] Koufax likely heard about Maglie's back trouble, if not from Sal himself, then from others, and about how the older man had pitched despite severe pain. Although he did not realize it at the time, that was a lesson Koufax would learn by living through it. When asked in later years who had taught him the most about pitching, Koufax mentioned Carl Erskine, Don Newcombe, and Sal Maglie.

From Chicago the stumbling Dodgers, still in fifth place, moved on to Milwaukee to take on the league-leading Braves in a four-game series. If they failed, they would fall out of contention for the pennant. Although he had pitched only three days earlier, Maglie came to Alston and asked for a start in the first game against the Braves on June 4. County Stadium was the site of a major humiliation, the last game Sal had pitched for the Giants, when he had been knocked out in the first inning without retiring a batter and had been sold to Cleveland that same evening. Since the Giants had unloaded him, Sal had not had an outing that lasted more than four innings, but he told Alston he felt ready to go nine, and he did. Before a noisy sellout crowd of Braves fans, he spun a three-hit shutout. The only hits he gave up were singles, and only one runner made it as far as second. Sal struck out five and issued one walk. He had last pitched a complete game on June 22, 1955, had last won a game on July 2, 1955, and had not thrown a shutout since April 25, 1954. He was happy with his performance, telling reporters afterward, "My arm feels great. They've been patient with me. Alston let me come along gradually, two or three innings here and there. That's what I needed."[33] Maglie also expressed confidence that he could take a regular turn in the pitching rotation, pitching every four or five days. Pee Wee Reese paid Sal a succinct tribute: "*This* is a pitcher."[34] Revved up by Maglie's victory, the Dodgers took three out of four from the Braves.

For the rest of June and on to the end of July Maglie pitched regularly and well, but the Dodgers did not give him much run support. He started nine games, won two and lost three, and brought his record to a mediocre 3-3, but that record was stronger than it appeared. In the three games Sal lost, the Dodgers scored a total of only four runs. In those games Maglie was removed for a pinch hitter, not because the opposition blasted him off the mound. Alston showed his confidence by saving Sal to face the toughest teams; eight of his first fifteen starts were against the Dodgers' two closest contenders, the Braves and the Reds. Sal's next start after his shutout of the Braves came on June 9 against the Reds in Cincinnati. He pitched seven strong innings, shutting down the Reds' power hitters as the Dodgers built up a 5-0 lead. But in the eighth Sal faced muscleman Ted Kluszewski with the bases loaded. Big Klu, who was the same height as Sal but outweighed him by 40 pounds, powered a pitch into the right field bleachers for a grand slam. Clem Labine then replaced Maglie and gave up another run to tie the score, but the Dodgers came back with three runs in the tenth for an 8–5 win. Labine rather than Maglie notched the victory. The game was the beginning of a six-game winning streak for the Dodgers that propelled them from fifth to second in the tightly packed pennant race.

When the Dodgers returned from their road trip they had won four in a row, and Alston handed Maglie the ball in an effort to extend that number to five. This was Sal's first appearance at Ebbets Field in a Dodgers uniform, and the biggest crowd of the year, 26,784, came out in the steaming heat on June 15 to give their former nemesis a hero's welcome. As Sal strode to the mound the old ballpark erupted in a resounding ovation. Whatever their initial dismay, Dodgers fans had taken Sal to their hearts. As with the blossoming relationship between Maglie and Furillo, there is no friend like a former enemy. After he donned a Dodger uniform Maglie was at first bemused but finally touched and enthralled by the intensity of the Brooklyn fans' affection for him. Most Giants fans had admired Sal, while remaining just a bit in awe of him, but Dodger fans adored him. "All of a sudden I was a hero with the fans, who used to boo me mercilessly," said Sal, recalling his Dodger days. "Giants fans were marvelous, but Dodger fans were better, possibly because I had come over from the other side." He was one of them, or *shudda* been, all along, as Maglie later admitted. "Those were great days with the Dodgers," Sal recalled. "In fact, I got more of a kick out of them than I ever did in all my years with the Giants."[35]

Sal gave the fans their money's worth through seven innings, although he was not at his best. He gave up three runs in the third and allowed another in the seventh, when the Braves loaded the bases and scored on a sacrifice fly. Maglie showed he had kept his razor sharp, as he decked Braves pitcher Lew Burdette twice in the third inning, to cheers rather than jeers from the Brooklyn faithful. But then he walked Burdette, as well as the next batter, setting the scene for Bill Bruton's three-run homer. Sal departed after the seventh, replaced by Labine with the Dodgers losing, 4–3. In the ninth, Brooklyn pulled out a dramatic finish, as substitute catcher Rube Walker hit a bases-loaded single to win the game, 5–4. This time the winning pitcher was reliever Ed Roebuck, who pitched the top of the ninth.

Sal did not start again until June 22, when he had the hard luck to face Cincinnati's Brooks Lawrence, who had an 8–0 record coming into the game and a 9–0 record when it was over. The Reds righthander retired the first 11 batters and tossed a two-hitter, tumbling the Dodgers back into third place. Sal lasted four and one-third innings, giving up five hits and five of the Reds' six runs. The Dodgers lost, 6–0, as Sal's record fell to 1–1. Four days later Sal returned to the mound to face the Cubs, and this time the Dodgers pounded the cellar dwellers, 10–5. Although less than brilliant, Sal's performance was good enough. His record improved to 2–1. On July 1 he nursed a 4–2 lead into the ninth inning, but then his control slipped, and Alston replaced him with Clem Labine, who gave up four runs as the Phillies won the game, 7–4. Labine took the loss. In early July the Dodgers won two out of three from the Giants, losing a single game on July 2 at Ebbets Field to their old rivals, and then sweeping a July 4 doubleheader at the Polo Grounds. So far, Alston had not sent Maglie out against his old teammates.

On July 8 Maglie lost to the Phillies, 3–2, in the second game of a doubleheader. Sal pitched well early on but gave up all the Phillies' runs in the sixth and left the game in that inning. His record fell to 2–2. After the All-Star break, the Braves swept a four-game series from the Dodgers, who remained in third as Milwaukee took over first. Sal suffered another tough outing on July 14 in the last game of the series. He pitched a shutout for six innings but then allowed a two-run homer by Joe Adcock in the seventh. He left in that inning with the score tied, and Don Bessent lost the game in the tenth, 3–2. The Dodgers defeated the Cubs in their next two games, but then they dropped two out of three to the Reds. On July 19 the Dodgers lost the final game of the series, 7–2. Sal lasted six innings, giving up three runs on five hits, and his record fell to 2–3.

This was not what the Dodgers had in mind when they purchased Maglie. He was beginning to look like a waste of 100 dollars. In addition, Cincinnati general manager Gabe Paul accused Sal of firing fastballs at the scoreboard clock in Crosley Field, causing the clock to stop. "Officials of the Brooklyn club are being advised of this act of 'senior delinquency,'" huffed Paul. Maglie and Ken Lehman, another Dodger pitcher under suspicion in the clock-breaking incident, treated the matter as a joke, claiming they both had been a wee bit wild recently.[36] Although uncharacteristic of Maglie, the incident suggests that the usually reserved and serious veteran had loosened up enough as a Dodger to take part in the kind of hijinks more typical of rookies. He was having fun.

Or maybe it was something in the air. Late July of 1956 may have set a record for bad behavior by baseball players. In addition to Maglie's alleged clock destruction, Duke Snider scuffled with a fan who called him gutless and dropped the man with a left to the jaw. Ted Williams celebrated his 400th home run by spitting at the writers in the Fenway press box. Worst of all, on July 24 Giant pitcher Ruben Gomez became involved in a violent brawl with Joe Adcock of the Braves. After Gomez hit Adcock in the ribs, the enraged slugger charged the mound. Gomez threw the ball at Adcock again, this time hitting him in the hip. The terrified pitcher then fled toward the Giants clubhouse in center field, with Adcock in pursuit. Players from both teams milled about as the Polo Grounds organist tried to bring order by means of an emergency rendition of "The Star-Spangled Banner." A few minutes later Gomez emerged, this time brandishing an ice pick. Shades of old Dolf Luque. Saner members of both teams intervened to restrain the two players. On the same day Gomez was disgracing himself at the Polo Grounds, his old teammate Sal Maglie defeated the Reds at Ebbets Field, 10–5. Sal allowed 13 hits, but he did not walk a batter, and he struck out six as he went the distance for his third win, the sixth straight for the Dodgers.

Carl Erskine defeated the Cubs on July 27, and Sal turned the same trick the next day, pitching his second complete game victory in less than a week and bringing the Brooklyn winning streak to seven. The Cubs had not beaten Sal since 1953. Brooklyn scored two in the bottom of the first, two more in the fourth, and another pair in the seventh. Sal confined the Cubs to three runs and took the win, 6–3, improving his record to 4–3.

Now, when the Dodgers needed him most, Sal hit his stride, putting together a comeback that must have left New York Giants management banging its collective head against a wall for having tossed away such a treasure. Counting his victory on July 28, and through August and September, Maglie compiled a superb 10–2 record with a brilliant 1.88 ERA for that period. The two games he lost were by scores of 2–1 and 3–2. On 12 occasions during the final two months he pitched on only three days' rest, winning the big must-win games as well as the less crucial ones in between. On August 1 the Dodgers defeated the league-leading Braves, 2–1. The game was a tension-filled duel between Maglie and Lew Burdette. Sal allowed only one (unearned) run in the six and one-third innings he pitched. Dale Mitchell, recently purchased from the Indians, won the game with a pinch-hit single in the eighth, and Labine, who relieved Sal, was the winner.

Maglie took the mound again on August 5 in the first game of a doubleheader against the Cardinals. Facing Murry Dickson, the oldest starting pitcher in the majors (and Sal's senior by only 10 months), the artful Dodger tossed a four-hit shutout for the twenty-second shutout of his career and his 100th win. Sandy Amoros and Roy Campanella hit two-run blasts, and Duke Snider contributed two solo home runs to Sal's 7–0 victory. Stan Musial, who usually murdered Dodgers pitching, went 0 for 8 in the doubleheader. Sal reacted to his 100th victory with his customary calm. "When the Giants traded me away in 1955, I never expected to win 100," he said. "But I knew I'd do it with the Dodgers, particularly when they started letting me pitch in turn."[37] Sal had always done best with regular work, and now he had the chance to pitch in the regular rotation. On August 10 Maglie lost a game to Philadelphia, 3–2. Although he lasted only one and two-thirds innings and gave up all three Phillies runs, he was unfazed by the defeat.

Four days later, on August 14 at Ebbets Field, Sal finally faced his old teammates. Although the Giants were in last place, they still took pleasure in playing hard against their perennial rivals. For six innings Maglie and Jim Hearn kept a tight pitchers' duel going, with each man giving up four hits, and neither allowing a run. In the bottom of the seventh, with a runner on second, Alston sent up Dale Mitchell to pinch-hit for Maglie. The crowd roared and booed its disapproval—they wanted to see Sal, their new favorite, continue his shutout. Mitchell fouled out, but the Dodgers scored a run. Labine came in to pitch the top of the eighth and promptly blew the lead, along with Sal's chances for a victory. With a man on, Gino Cimoli, filling in for a flu-struck Carl Furillo, misjudged a fly to deep right, and the Giants tied the score. Then, with two out and one man on, Willie Mays hit a two-run homer. New York won the game, 3–1, with Labine taking the loss. Maglie had pitched seven scoreless innings in a losing cause, but once again he had avoided defeat at Ebbets Field.

Sal made his next start on August 18, against the Phillies, and came through with a 9–2 victory for his sixth win. In his hometown paper, sports columnist Mike Quinlan proudly noted that the Dodgers might well have purchased the pennant when they bought Maglie. When Don Newcombe defeated the Phillies the next day, the Dodgers climbed into second place. On August 24 Sal extended the Dodgers' winning streak to six and notched his seventh victory, 6–4, in a game against Cincinnati. Duke Snider, who was batting .500 against the Reds, belted a run-scoring double in the first, and in the third he smacked a three-run homer. Sal lasted six and one-third innings, long enough to gain the win, as Don Bessent held the Reds scoreless the rest of the way.

On August 28 the Dodgers split a doubleheader with the Cubs at Wrigley Field. In the first game Maglie faced rookie righthander Moe Drabowsky, who held the Dodgers to one run on six hits in seven innings, and Brooklyn trailed, 2–1, when Sal left the game for a pinch hitter in the seventh. Alston threw Ed Roebuck and Ken Lehman into the game in an effort to keep the Cubs in check, but finally had to call on Don Newcombe, who had pitched five innings as a starter the previous day, to stem the tide. The Dodgers rallied to win the game, 6–4. Instead of Maglie, Newcombe picked up the win, his twenty-first. Although the Dodgers dropped the second game, Milwaukee lost to the Pirates, and the Dodgers gained a half-game, creeping up to 1 1/2 games behind the league leaders.

Maglie started against the Giants at the Polo Grounds on September 1 in the second game of a doubleheader. After the Dodgers had taken the first game, Sal faced Max Surkont in the nightcap. The game began as a pitchers' duel, with Surkont holding the Dodgers hitless for five innings and Maglie allowing only one scratch single. But in the top of the sixth the Dodgers clipped Surkont for three runs. Despite his three-run lead, Sal still must have felt tremendous pressure as he faced his old teammates, since he blew a gasket in the bottom of the sixth. With one out, he ran up a 3–1 count on Foster Castleman. With each pitch that plate umpire Artie Gore judged a ball, Sal became more agitated.[38] Hands on hips, he glared at Gore or turned his back on the plate and stared at the scoreboard, as if he could not believe the count Gore was ringing up against him. When Gore called Maglie's fifth pitch a ball and waved Castleman to first, Sal exploded. He fumed, stomped, cursed, shouted, and finally slammed his glove to the ground. Gore thumbed Maglie to the showers, the first and only time Sal was ever thrown out of a game. Although the Dodgers protested loudly and at length, Gore's decision stood, and Bessent finished, combining with Maglie for a two-hit shutout. The win brought Sal's record to 8–4 and kept Brooklyn close behind the Braves. The Dodgers were not so fortunate the next day, when they played another doubleheader with the Giants and New York took both games. Following that setback, the Dodgers won two out of three from the Pirates, with Sal winning the third game on September 5. The Dodgers held a 4–2 lead going into the ninth, when Maglie faltered a little, allowing two hits and a run. Again Alston brought in Bessent, and the rail-thin righthander struck out the final Pittsburgh batter to preserve Maglie's victory, 4–3. The game brought Sal's record to 9–4, and it was his fourth straight win.

Robert Creamer contributed a small gem to *Sports Illustrated,* in which he described what each Dodger did on September 4, the team's day off between games two and three with the Pirates. Nearly all were snapshots of family activities—Reese took one of his daughters for a medical checkup; Robinson and his wife went with their children to the theater; Erskine and his family went shopping; Campanella took his brood for a trip on his boat; and "sinister, blue-jawed Sal Maglie . . . took his 15–month-old son to the park and pushed him gently on the swings."[39] Happy at home and comfortable with his niche on the Dodgers, Sal was growing stronger as the season went on. In his last ten games he had complied a brilliant 1.96 ERA.

After Sal's victory over the Pirates the Dodgers hosted the Giants in a four-game series at Ebbets Field, where Brooklyn took three out of four. Sal did not appear in any of the games. Although local reporters still longed to see Maglie in contests against the Giants, Alston refused to waste him. The New Yorkers were near the bottom of the standings, and Alston wanted Sal ready for tougher teams. On September 11 Sal tossed one of his most crucial games of the season, against the Braves at Ebbets Field. It was the first of a two-game series, the last contests of the year between the first and second-place teams. The Braves' lead over the Dodgers had shrunk to one game, and a Dodger win in the opener would put the teams in a tie for first. The Braves, who evidently had not learned from the experience of the 1951 Dodgers, announced they would begin selling World Series tickets the following week. If Sal Maglie had anything to say about it, those tickets would be worthless. As they say in Brooklyn, Braves fans could use them for "terlet paper."

In his Manhattan apartment, Sal had unusual difficulty in falling asleep the night before the game, tossing and turning for hours until finally dropping off around 6 a.m. He slept until noon, and around 3 p.m. he ate his usual pregame meal: a large steak. September 11, 1956, was a Tuesday, but even if it had been a Friday, Sal would not have deviated from his pregame diet. Larry Jansen told an amusing tale of Sal's dedication to his game day beefsteak, despite the prohibition then in effect in the Catholic Church against eating meat on Fridays. When the two men were with the Giants they were having dinner at a restaurant on a Friday. Jansen, a devout Catholic, ordered salmon. Sal ordered filet mignon. Jansen chided Maglie about disobeying the Church rule, but Sal persisted. When the waitress brought their dinners, Sal stood up, made the sign of the Cross over his steak, and intoned, "Swim, you son of a bitch, *swim!*"[40] The jovial Jansen has told this story at numerous baseball events, sometimes presenting it as true, other times as a joke. It sounds like the kind of thing Sal Maglie might do. He did not take religion too seriously, especially when it got in the way of baseball. If Maglie were Jewish, he most likely would not have done as Sandy Koufax later did, and taken himself out of the rotation on Yom Kippur. For Sal, "the great god Baseball" reigned supreme over every other deity.

Sal came to the clubhouse in a relaxed mood that day, chuckling over how his son had chewed a cake of soap. Baby behavior that was routine to others was still new and enchanting to him, and the little boy's antics helped keep the pitcher's life in perspective. He was no longer pitching just to win. Now he had his son's future to consider. A crowd of 33,384, the largest of the season, jammed into Ebbets Field on September 11 to cheer the team and its newest hero, and Sal did not disappoint. Facing the Braves' Bob Buhl, who had beaten the Dodgers seven times that season, he pitched a magnificent game.

Although he gave up a solo home run to Eddie Mathews in the second, Sal held the Braves scoreless for the next six innings with his baffling assortment of curves. The Dodgers, meanwhile, were not doing much with Buhl despite the Milwaukee pitcher's poor control, so Sal took matters into his own hands in the fourth, driving in his first two runs of the year with a bases-loaded single, giving the Dodgers a 2–1 lead. Dodger fans roared with joy, hailing Sal as their savior as they hugged one another and danced in the aisles. Maglie wormed out of minor jams in the fifth and sixth, but the Braves gave him a close call in the eighth. After a single and a sacrifice, Henry Aaron stepped to the plate, but Sal persuaded the Braves future Hall of Fame hitter to ground to Gilliam for the second out. With the tying run now at third, next up was Eddie Mathews, who had already hit a home run and singled. His fights and feuds with Maglie forgotten, Jackie Robinson strolled to the mound from third to give Sal a breather. Reese joined them at the same leisurely pace, and tucked a little white feather he had found into Sal's back pocket. "That's for good luck," he told the pitcher.[41] The men continued to chat until Alston emerged from the dugout and made it a foursome. The manager asked Sal what he wanted to do. "I got to pitch to this guy," Sal told him.[42] Alston returned to the dugout, Reese and Robinson resumed their positions, and Mathews grounded to Gilliam to end the Braves' half of the inning.

In the bottom of the eighth, Robinson led off with a single and then gave the Braves a lesson in aggressive base running. After Amoros had sacrificed him to second, Jackie taunted Braves reliever Ernie Johnson into trying to pick him off, then raced home on Johnson's wild throw to second. Hodges followed with a solo homer off the rattled Johnson, and the Dodgers led, 4–1. With a three-run cushion, Sal took the mound in the top of the ninth to a standing ovation from ecstatic Dodger fans. He then gave up a home run to leadoff hitter Joe Adcock. Unruffled, Maglie dispatched the next three Braves, among them one-time Giants hero Bobby Thomson, to wrap up his tenth victory and put the Dodgers in a tie for first place. After the game, Sal was in a terrific mood. The usually reserved pitcher joked with reporters, calling out to the writers gathered around him, "How about that hitting? Somebody say something nice about my hitting!"[43] He admitted that his back still hurt sometimes, but he swore his arm had never felt better. His teammates heaped praise on Sal for his clutch performance. "What curves that man throws," exclaimed Roy Campanella. "They take off like they have wings!" "Lordy, Lordy," sighed Pee Wee Reese. "What a job that man can do." Jackie Robinson added, "We wouldn't be anywhere near where we are if it weren't for Sal. He's a great guy to have on your side."[44] In the *Daily Mirror* columnist Sidney Fields observed, "When Maglie was a big, bad Giant, Dodger fans crossed themselves whenever they heard his name, as if exorcising the devil and all his plagues. But today even the most rabid Dodger rooter is willing to forget and forgive the deadly razor Sal the Barber used on their team. The seventh-place Giants are gnashing their teeth because they sold Sal to Cleveland last year; and Cleveland is trying to figure out the lapse of sanity that let them surrender Sal to the Dodgers."

The Dodgers' tie with the Braves was short-lived. The next day Milwaukee's Lew Burdette defeated Don Newcombe, and the Braves regained first place, although not for long. The Dodgers took two from the Cubs on September 14 and 15, edging the Braves back into second. On September 16 Maglie faced off against the Reds and defeated them, 3–2, before another adoring crowd at Ebbets Field. Sal nearly blew the game in the ninth—he had a shutout going and had two outs and two strikes on Wally Post when the Reds' right fielder scratched out an infield single, followed by a Smoky Burgess home run. Again Don Bessent put out the fire, and Sal had his eleventh win. After the game a reporter asked Cincinnati manager Birdie Tebbetts if his players had made any comments on Maglie's pitching. "No," Tebbetts sighed wearily. "Swearing is all."[45] Where, Dodger fans wondered, had their pal Sal *been* all their lives? The love affair between Brooklyn and The Barber was growing stronger. "Coming to the Dodgers was the luckiest break I ever had," Sal told *Sports Illustrated*. "This gave me a chance to prove to myself that I could still pitch and win."[46] Years later Maglie exclaimed, "I don't care how cheaply they got me. That was the biggest and nicest break of my big-league career. I wouldn't have believed it—me, the old Dodger hater—but I was made for Brooklyn and Brooklyn was made for me."[47]

The Dodgers held on to first place as September counted down toward October, but it was not a firm hold. On September 21 Sal faced the Pirates in Pittsburgh and lost a close, fiercely fought game, 2–1. Maglie brought a sharp razor with him. In the first inning he decked Pittsburgh's right fielder Roberto Clemente, and he offered further close shaves to others throughout the contest, but this time his strategy backfired. The Dodgers could cadge only one run off the Pirates' Ron Kline, and in the seventh Frank Thomas clipped Sal for a two-run homer that won the game for Pittsburgh, ending Sal's winning streak at six. Afterward, Pirates' coach Clyde Sukeforth, fired by the Dodgers in the wake of their 1951 playoff loss, commented angrily on Sal's brushbacks. "The whole ball club got sore. I haven't seen the team so riled up all season. You don't throw at a second-division club. It's not good policy."[48] The loss shook the Dodgers, and they dropped two of their next three games to the Pirates, who relished their role as spoilers. Their manager, former Dodger Bobby Bragan, treated the team to beer after every late-season win, and after their third victory over the Dodgers one Pittsburgh player chortled, "My God, they're out there playing for $10,000 [a World Series share] and we're out there playing for a bottle of beer."[49] After their loss to the Pirates on September 24, Brooklyn fell to second, half a game behind the Braves. With five games left and the pennant race in a dead heat, every contest became a must-win situation. Now, more than ever, the Dodgers needed a "money pitcher," a man who could win the big games, and that man was Sal Maglie.

1956—Money Pitcher

Maglie's No-Hitter, the Pennant, and the World Series

16

As little as three months earlier, no one could have imagined the Dodgers would be counting on Sal Maglie to carry them into another World Series. But when the Brooklyn club was on the verge of collapse, Maglie the 39-year-old money pitcher won the games that had to be won. As the 1956 season wound down to its final five contests, the Dodgers took four of them to win the pennant, with Maglie accounting for two of the four victories. One of those victories was a no-hitter, and the other clinched a tie for the pennant. But that was in the future. When the dazed Dodgers returned home from their thrashing at the hands of the sixth-place Pirates, they were in second place, half a game behind the Braves, and if they failed to win their upcoming game against Philadelphia, they could kiss their pennant hopes good-bye.

THE NO-HITTER

The contest with the Phillies on September 25 was a night game, and the Braves had already won their game that same afternoon, increasing their lead over the Dodgers to one full game and increasing the pressure on the Dodgers to defeat the Phillies. On three days' rest, Sal Maglie took on the task of winning. The weather was awful—a cold, damp, late-September night—and Ebbets Field was not even half full. There were 15,204 bundled-up fans on hand, with the Dodgers Sym-phony and the Seventy-Seventh Division Army Reserve band providing music to keep chilly toes tapping. Sal added a second undershirt beneath his uniform, and the Dodgers provided him with an electric blanket to huddle under while Brooklyn was at bat. Enthusiastic Dodger rooters warmed their hands applauding him as he walked to the mound, while Robinson, Reese, Gilliam, and Hodges warmed the ball. As they snapped it around the diamond, each man rubbed it up briskly before it finally made its way to the pitcher's hand. The intensity of the moment, the urgency of winning, gave Maglie's long, dark-bearded face "the look of a Sicilian bandit chief," according to a writer for *Newsweek,* who perhaps was thinking of another Salvatore—Salvatore Giuliano, the real-life Sicilian bandit chief whose death in a hail of police bullets had made international headlines in July of 1950. Because of Sal's baleful game face, some journalists still compared Maglie's appearance to that of an Italian criminal.

Sal retired leadoff hitter Richie Ashburn on a pop-up to second. The next batter, the Phillies' first baseman Marv Blaylock, connected solidly, lining what looked like an extra-base hit into the left field corner, but fleet little Sandy Amoros raced over to make a diving catch. In the top of the second Puddin' Head Jones poked a sharp one-hopper between Gilliam and the second base bag, but Reese—playing his 2,000th game for the Dodgers—raced in back of second, scooped up the ball, and flipped to Hodges at first in time to nip Jones. The Dodgers reached rookie righthander Jack Meyer for three runs in the bottom of the second, as Jackie Robinson started things off with a double. With one out, Hodges walked, and Robinson began his pitcher-rattling routine at second. Both runners advanced when Meyer threw the ball into center field in an attempt to pick off Robinson. Furillo then drove in the first run with a grounder to short, where Smalley had no play except to first, and Robinson scored on a fielder's choice. Then, with Hodges on, Campanella blasted a home run into the upper left field stands, and the Dodgers led, 3–0. Brooklyn picked up two more in the third, but Sal already had more runs than he needed.

Maglie walked the third man to face him in the third inning, pitcher Jack Meyer, but stranded him when Ashburn grounded out. In the fourth Sal induced three easy ground-outs, and he set the Phillies down in order in the fifth and sixth, picking up two strikeouts along the way. By the time he walked Puddin' Head Jones to lead off the eighth, Sal had retired 13 batters in a row. After Jones walked, Elmer Valo popped out to Reese. The next batter, second baseman Solly Hemus, hit a hard grounder down the first base line, but Hodges nabbed it and fired to second to begin a 3–6–3 double play. Hemus screamed at umpire Augie Donatelli that the ball had been foul and underlined his claim by giving the umpire a hard shove. Donatelli thumbed him from the game, and Hemus concluded his evening on the field by throwing his batting helmet at the umpire. Even before the scene ended, Sal was in the dugout, watching Hemus' hysterics in amusement from under his electric blanket.

Ever since the sixth inning the fans had been cheering Sal wildly each time he retired a batter, and as the top of the ninth opened, everyone in the park, Maglie included, knew he was three outs away from a no-hitter. But Phillies manager Mayo Smith refused to fall in with that plan. As the first batter he sent up Frankie Baumholtz, a veteran left-handed hitter, in place of shortstop Roy Smalley. Baumholtz lifted a high foul back toward the Brooklyn dugout. Campanella raced toward the dugout as his teammates rose from the bench and put out their hands to keep him from falling into their midst as he made the catch. Next, Smith used pitcher Harvey Haddix, another lefty, as a pinch hitter for reliever Jack Sanford. Sal struck him out. The third batter was another left-hander and the Phils' top hitter, the pesky Richie Ashburn, who was batting .308. Jackie Robinson came out to the mound, rubbing up a new ball for Sal. The pitcher glanced at him with a small smile. "This is the guy I got to get," Sal said.[1] Ashburn fouled off four of Sal's pitches, then Maglie put his fifth one low and too far inside, clipping Ashburn on the foot. The fans groaned, but not in sympathy, as Ashburn hobbled to first. That brought up Blaylock, who hit a grounder to Gilliam. The second baseman fielded it cleanly and fired to Hodges for the final out. "I watched that ball bounce all the way," Sal said after the game. "I watched every damn hop until Gilliam got it and Hodges grabbed it and the ump's arm went up for the last out."[2] When he saw that signal, Sal let out his breath, chopped at the air with his right fist, and shouted, "I got it. My God, I got it!"[3] Then, oblivious to the roaring crowd and his teammates converging on him, he blew a kiss through the TV cameras to his wife, who was home with a bad cold, watching the game on television. Sal's teammates, along with as many fans as could elude the lax police cordon, rushed to overwhelm the pitcher with hugs, back-pounding and kisses. The *Daily News* on September 26 carried a banner headline "SAL'S OUR PAL!" and below it a photograph of a surprised-looking Maglie being smooched on the cheek by Campanella. The caption said "Campy Pitching—Maglie Catching. It's a kiss, not a beanball" (Figure 17).

Inside the locker room, "Senator" John Griffin, the portly clubhouse manager who suffered from a heart condition, fainted from all the excitement and had to be taken to the hospital, which delayed and subdued the celebration of Sal's feat. Team president Walter O'Malley peeled off five 100–dollar bills from his wad of walking-around money and handed them to Sal. Reporters surrounded the pitcher, peppering him with questions. He calmly answered queries about what pitches he had thrown to which batter, and when he had started to think about the possibility of a no-hitter, and so

17—Maglie gets a kiss on the cheek from Brooklyn catcher Roy Campanella after pitching a no-hitter for the Dodgers against Philadelphia on September 25, 1956. Photo: Frank Mastro/ International News/Corbis.

on and on. "The main thing is that we won the ball game," Maglie asserted. "I knew I had a no-hitter going all the way. No one had to tell me. I've been around baseball too long not to be aware of something like that."⁴ He also posed for photographs. When Carl Erskine, who had pitched his second no-hitter earlier in the same season, hugged and kissed Sal, it was not one of the usual posed shots, but an expression of unfeigned joy and real affection. All the Dodgers affirmed that, without Maglie's efforts, Brooklyn would be in the second division instead of inches away from the pennant. Furillo, who had become Maglie's closest friend on the Dodgers, declared, "I been in six no-hitters, but this is the easiest I seen. I never saw one before where you didn't have to go back to pull a few down." He added that Sal "deserves the most valuable player award on this club."⁵

A no-hitter represents a pinnacle of achievement for the pitcher who accomplishes it, always giving him a special place in the record books. At the time Sal tossed his gem, only one man had thrown a no-hitter at an older age than 39. Cy Young, back in 1908, had accomplished the feat at age 41. Since 1956, three other pitchers over 39 years old have turned the trick: Warren Spahn in 1961, when he was 40, Nolan Ryan in 1990, at age 43, and Randy Johnson in 2004, at age 40. No-hitters also have elements of luck as well as superb defensive play, and Sal's was no different. Maglie was fortunate that Baumholtz's pop foul in the eighth drifted toward the Dodgers dugout, and not to the opposite side, where the Phillies would have watched Campanella take a header and lose the ball rather than holding him up as he secured an out. A fine catch by Amoros prevented a hit in the first inning; a sparkling bit of fielding by Reese choked off another in the second; and Hodges' handling of the hard grounder by Hemus in the eighth turned what would have been a run-scoring double into a double play.

By the time the clubhouse festivities ended, it was close to midnight. Sal then showered, shaved, dressed, and returned to the apartment in Manhattan that he shared with Kay and their son. Also staying with the Maglies were Sal's mother, Mary Maglie, and Kay's mother, Mae Pileggi. Sal did not like to leave his recently widowed mother alone in her house in Niagara Falls, so he had invited her to stay with him in New York that summer, and Kay's mother had begun living with the couple shortly after they adopted their son. One newspaper thought the story of Sal's no-hitter might continue, even after the clubhouse closed. The *Post* sent a woman reporter to the Maglies' apartment—unusual in the 1950s, particularly in reference to a sports-related story—to record Sal's homecoming after his memorable achievement. The reporter, Nancy Seely, gave readers a glimpse into Sal's private life and a vivid, if typically 1950s-style, portrait of the woman who shared that life.⁶ Seely noted Kay's beauty and charm, her ladylike poise, and her pride in her husband's achievements. She noticed how Kay greeted Sal when he finally arrived, without squeals or screams or even congratulations—just a kiss, a warm, private smile, and a quiet "Hi, darling." When asked by Seely what the secret of her happiness was, Kay offered the classic wifely response of that era: "I want what he wants."

The reporter then turned her attention to the other members of Sal's family, admiring the couple's adopted son, now 16 months old and the picture of health and contentment. Dressed in yellow leggings and a yellow sweater that Kay had knitted for him, the little boy happily went along with being tossed in the air by Sal and obligingly planted a kiss on his father's freshly shaved cheek. When not the center of attention the baby occupied himself with rolling a baseball around on the floor or cuddled in the lap of one or the other of his grandmothers. The multi-generational family that Nancy Seely revealed to her readers was not unusual among Italian Americans of that era. Grandparents living under the same roof as their adult children and grandchildren was the rule rather than the exception.

Seely ended her article with a summary of the Maglies' interests, noting that they "like to play bridge, to dance, read, and swim. They go to the movies, and when they're in New York they try to get to the theater frequently. But their favorite pastime is visiting their many friends, and entertaining them [at their home.]" Kay added that since they had adopted their son, they "spend an awful lot of time just enjoying Sal Jr." The pastimes listed are all conventional, attractive ones, and probably do represent a selection of things the couple enjoyed, but in reality some of Sal's other interests were less clean-cut. Bridge was not Sal's card game—he liked to gamble and preferred blackjack or poker.[7] Throughout his marriage a source of conflict with Kay when they were home in Niagara Falls was Sal's practice of staying out late in the evenings with his male friends, drinking and playing cards. Often he did not return until well after midnight, and he usually came home more than a little drunk. Sal's nephew Pat Grenga recalled that the only harsh words he ever overheard Kay and Sal exchange were on the subject of Sal's night-owl habits.[8]

THE PENNANT

For all the celebration that attended it, Sal's no-hitter was only one win, and the season was not yet over. As a special reward for his achievement, and in acknowledgment of the early morning hour when the elated pitcher's day finally ended, the next day Sal was allowed to arrive at the clubhouse late. *Times* columnist Arthur Daley reported the banter over Maglie's absence. Reese had given Sal a private nickname, an indication of the affectionate regard Maglie's teammates had for him. "Where's the great MaGoo?" Pee Wee asked, noting Maglie's vacant locker. "Time off for good behavior, I guess," chuckled Jackie Robinson. Before the game began Sal appeared, and the season went on. That same day, September 26, the Phillies battered the Dodgers and Don Newcombe, 7–3, and Brooklyn fell another half-game behind the Braves. Because reporters knew there was no talking to Newcombe after the loss of such a crucial game, Jimmy Cannon approached Jackie Robinson for insights into Newk's state of mind. Robinson replied that he thought Newcombe resented all the attention and credit Maglie had been getting. "Look, I know that without Sal we wouldn't be where we are. . . . But along the way, they should have given some credit to Newk. . . . If I was in his spot, doing what he's been doing for the ball club and I wasn't given the credit, I'd be burned up, too."[9] Although Robinson did not mention it, Newcombe was by far the most successful black pitcher of his time, and perhaps he suspected a racial motive in the failure of the press to give him sufficient credit for his achievements. But there was a nonracial reason for the different ways the press treated Newcombe and Maglie. Newk, who had been with the Dodgers since 1949, had already won an astounding 26 games that season, but he was a young, huge, formidably strong flamethrower, so he was expected to win with ease. Sal the Barber was old, was not spectacular in his physique, threw a fastball that had seen better days, and was both a new member of the team and a former enemy, so his skein of victories for the Dodgers came as a gratifying and newsworthy surprise.

After their split with the Phillies, the Dodgers had two days off, one scheduled and one due to a rainout—a two-day respite where they could gather their energies for the last, vital games. Milwaukee, in contrast, had to play the Cardinals in St. Louis. The youthful Braves team could not keep from chattering about a pennant and a World Series win, while the Dodgers had long ago learned not to tempt fate that way. "Just think of all that money," babbled outfielder Chuck Tanner. "We're just a couple of days away from it. I never saw that kind of money in my life."[10] The winner's shares in the 1956 World Series would be around $10,000, which was something like three years' wages for Sal Maglie's factory worker friends in Niagara Falls.

The only way the Dodgers could win the pennant was if they took all three of their games with Pittsburgh and the Braves dropped two out of three to St. Louis. Recalling what Pittsburgh had done to the Dodgers the last time the two teams met, it seemed unlikely that the Dodgers could accomplish a sweep, and even less likely that the Braves would fail to take two out of three from the Cards. But on September 28, while rain washed out the Dodgers-Pirates game, the Cardinals defeated the Braves, 5–4. The Cards took little pleasure in their victory, because they wanted to see the Braves win the pennant. The unpopularity of the Dodgers in places other than Brooklyn continued, especially in cities with a southern orientation such as St. Louis. The Dodgers had not only brought integration to baseball; those integrated squads had also won too many pennants. Some St. Louis newspapers even published anti-Dodgers editorials. "Most people believe the Bums have won enough for the time being, at least," harrumphed one daily.[11]

On September 29 the Dodgers and the Pirates played a doubleheader in order to make up the game lost to rain the day before. The date was a Saturday, the weather cool and sunny, and 26,340 enthusiastic paying fans packed Ebbets Field, eager to watch The Barber wield his razor. Ladies' Day attendees and Knothole Gang youngsters brought the attendance to an over-capacity 34,022. With three days' rest and fresh from his no-hitter, Sal started the first game and gave up a two-run homer to Frank Thomas in the top of the first. Brooklyn scored three in the bottom of the first, two of them on a homer by Amoros, and before the game was over had added three more. After the first, Maglie gave the Pirates next to nothing. They scratched out four hits but no further runs. As Sal registered Pittsburgh's final out and walked off the mound, fans at Ebbets Field rose to give him a roaring, standing ovation. He had pitched the Dodgers into a current tie for the pennant, ending the season with a 13–5 record and an ERA of 2.87. The Braves looked on in dismay. Their only game, against St. Louis, was scheduled for the same evening.

In the second game of the doubleheader Pirates manager Bobby Bragan chose Ron Kline, who had baffled the Dodgers in his previous outing against them, while Alston counted on Clem Labine, a reliever who had made only a few starts. Like Maglie, Labine came through when it counted, in a game enlivened by several altercations. Campanella homered in the third to give the Dodgers a 1–0 lead. In the fifth, Campy managed an infield single, and Labine then attempted a sacrifice bunt, but Pirates catcher Hank Foiles threw to second, hoping to catch the lead runner. The throw was high, pulling shortstop Dick Groat off the bag. As far as anyone other than the umpire could see, Campy was safe, but umpire Vic Delmore called him out. Alston and Campanella protested, but the loudest objections came from the solidly partisan crowd, which refused to accept the verdict. The chorus of boos grew deafening, and the white handkerchiefs that used to wave in derision at the hated Sal Maglie now came out against the umpire. Usually such protests fade away between innings, but Dodgers fans carried this one into the top of the sixth, when they began hurling wadded paper, garbage, and beer bottles onto the field. The situation became so bad that umpire crew chief Jocko Conlon had announcer Tex Rickart tell the crowd over the public address system that the umpires would forfeit the game to the Pirates if fans failed to quiet down. The threat of such a disaster restored order. In the bottom of the sixth it was the Pirates' turn to howl. With Robinson on first and Amoros at bat, plate umpire Stan Landes ruled that catcher Hank Foiles had interfered with Amoros' swing and awarded Sandy first base. Pittsburgh manager Bobby Bragan and Foiles argued so vehemently that both were ejected. Gil Hodges, up next, smashed a triple that scored his two teammates and gave Labine a 3–0 lead. The Pirates scored once in the ninth but could not get a rally going, and Labine completed the game, a 3–1 victory.

That night in St. Louis, the Braves blew a game they absolutely, positively should have won. The Cardinals were not going to hand their opponents the win, but in this particular game they would not have minded being beaten. Instead, the Braves beat themselves. The game went 12 innings, with the Braves' great lefthander Warren Spahn, who had won his 200th game late in that same season, facing the Cards' Herm Wehmeier. On an ordinary day Wehmeier was hardly Spahn's equal, but on this occasion both men were brilliant and carried a 1–1 tie into the twelfth inning. In the bottom of the twelfth, Stan Musial doubled, and Spahn walked Ken Boyer to set up a potential double play. The next batter was Rip Repulski, and the center fielder did just what Spahn wanted him to do: he chopped a little bouncer to Eddie Mathews at third that was tailor made for a double play. But the ball took a bizarre carom off Mathews' glove, hit his leg, and rolled into left field. Musial scored, and the Cardinals won, 2–1. Warren Spahn sat in front of his locker and cried. "The whole country is going to be sore at us for spoiling it for the Braves," gloomed Cardinals slugger Hank Sauer. "Everybody wanted them to win."[12]

Not quite everybody. The Dodgers now led by one game, and nobody in Brooklyn was complaining. The "woist" that could happen to the Dodgers now was that if they lost their final game and if Milwaukee won theirs, the two teams would finish in a tie. If both teams won, Milwaukee's victory would be meaningless. In that last game of the season, on September 30, Alston sent Don Newcombe to face the Pirates' Vernon Law. Suffering from a severe cold and pumped full of penicillin, Newcombe was not at his best. Although the Dodgers had compiled a 7–2 lead by the sixth inning, Newk let much of it slip away. A spectacular leaping catch by Duke Snider in the seventh prevented more damage, but by then Pittsburgh had narrowed the gap to 7–5. In the top of the eighth Newcombe gave up a solo home run to Lee Walls, bringing the score to 7–6, and Alston went to his bullpen, calling on Don Bessent. The reliever came in with one out and immediately surrendered a single. Then Robinson bobbled a sure double play ball at third. Bessent had two base runners, but he persuaded Jack Shepard to fly out and struck out Dale Long to end the inning. Amoros added a Dodger insurance run in the bottom of the eighth with a solo homer. As the ninth inning opened, the score stood at 8–6, Dodgers, and the scoreboard showed Milwaukee leading the Cardinals. The Pirates did not go down easily. Roberto Clemente led off the ninth with a single. Bill Virdon hit a smash that would have been a sure hit, except that it went directly at Gilliam, who turned it into a double play. Then Bessent struck out Hank Foiles, and it no longer mattered what happened with Milwaukee in St. Louis. The Braves were welcome to their empty victory. The season was over and the Dodgers had won the pennant.

Campanella lumbered out to the mound, engulfed the scrawny Bessent, and lifted him off his feet. As players and fans surged onto the field, Sal Maglie pushed through the throng, and wrapped his arms protectively around Bessent, who was in danger of being crushed. In the clubhouse, happy chaos reigned. The Dodger Sym-phony rushed inside and began blaring away. Walter Alston hurried around the room, shaking each player's hand. Duke Snider doused Don Newcombe's head with champagne, and the big pitcher paraded around in a pair of pink shorts, with a silly hat pushed down over his face. Sandy Amoros, who spoke hardly any English, sat in his usual silence, but with a big grin on his face and an equally big unlit cigar in his mouth. Fans continued the celebration across Brooklyn, unless they had already joined the long line for World Series tickets, which did not go on sale until the next day (Figure 18). Horns honked, bars offered free drinks, and in downtown Brooklyn a big bonfire burned far into the night. Mayor Robert Wagner of New York sent a telegram of congratulations. Walter O'Malley also offered a few words. He praised Alston and added that "real progress" was being made on his proposal for a new Dodger stadium in downtown Brooklyn. Amid all the jubilation, no one had any spare grains of salt with which to season his statement. He knew, as the celebrating Brooklynites did not, that this would be the last pennant celebration for Brooklyn's Dodgers.

The Dodgers held their pennant victory party at the Lexington Hotel in New York City rather than at a site in Brooklyn. As each player and his wife entered the room, the band played an appropriate song. For Carl and Betty Erskine it was "Back Home in Indiana"; for Duke and Bev Snider, "California, Here I Come"; for Pee Wee and Dottie Reese, "My Old Kentucky Home"; and for Carl and Fern Furillo, "The Pennsylvania Polka." The band was stumped for a state song when it was Sal and Kay Maglie's turn—somehow "New York, New York" would not have been quite right for a Brooklyn event, so they struck up an Italian melody. Duke Snider thought it might have been "Arrivederci Roma." To the other Dodgers' surprise, Sal swept his smiling wife straight out onto the dance floor. Who knew The Barber could also cut the rug?

18—Although tickets did not go on sale until the next day, avid Dodgers fans wait in line on September 30, 1956, to purchase World Series tickets after the Dodgers won the pennant that day, in the last game of the season. The sign proclaiming Maglie for the "Rookie of 1956" award suggests the affection of Dodger fans for their former enemy. Photo: National Baseball Hall of Fame Library, Cooperstown.

THE 1956 WORLD SERIES

A two-page-wide illustration accompanies an article in the October 1,1956, issue of *Sports Illustrated,* about the disorderly National League pennant race in comparison to the Yankee walk-away in the American League. On the right-hand page it shows the Yankees dressed as ancient Roman legionnaires, lined up in orderly ranks, their identical shields emblazoned with NY, their centurions planting the 1956 pennant firmly in the ground, and standing at the front, Casey Stengel dressed like Julius Caesar. On the left-hand page, a disorderly mob fights it out for a distant flag labeled "1956 Championship." Braves in feather headdresses brandish tomahawks, axes, and spiked war clubs against paunchy, determined fellows wearing Brooklyn tee-shirts and other scruffy characters carrying Cincinnati banners. The men attack the Braves and each other, with weapons ranging from monkey wrenches and hubcaps to broken bottles and toilet plungers, while the Yankees wait impassively for a winner to emerge from the chaos. The Dodgers eliminated their rivals and won the pennant in an exhausting final week, but then they had to face the well-rested Yankees, who had clinched the pennant on September 18. This would be the seventh and last time the Brooklyn Dodgers faced the New York Yankees in a World Series.

The Series opened at Ebbets Field on October 3 before a packed house. From his flag-draped box seat President Eisenhower threw out the first ball. Campy caught the toss. The ball snapped around the diamond and then into the hands of the Dodger pitcher for Game One: Sal Maglie. Alston could have started Newcombe, whose record was a brilliant 27–7, but instead of the temperamental Newk, he elected to go with his money pitcher. Opposing Maglie was young Yankee southpaw Edward "Whitey" Ford, a future Hall of Famer whose record was 19–6.

Sal began badly, and he kept the faithful on edge all afternoon. Dodger fans groaned in anguish as Mickey Mantle, a Triple Crown winner that year with a .353 average, 52 home runs, and 130 RBIs, came to bat in the top of the first with Enos Slaughter on with a single. Mickey promptly hit one out of the park, with the ball bouncing across the tops of vehicles in a used car lot on Bedford Avenue. But the Dodgers lost little time in racking Whitey Ford. Nicknamed "Slick" by his teammates, Ford did not succeed in slipping much of anything past the Brooklyn hitters. Robinson led off the second with a home run, Hodges singled, and Furillo brought him home with a double to tie the score. In the third the Dodgers continued to pound Ford. After Reese and Snider singled, Hodges homered to give the Dodgers a 5–2 lead, and Maglie had all the runs he needed. Ford was done for the day.

The Yankees kept threatening to blow Maglie off the mound—in Red Smith's words, Sal spent the afternoon "pinching out burning fuses"—but New York managed only one more run, a solo homer in the fourth by Billy Martin. It was also Martin who suspected Maglie of doctoring the ball, either with spit or pine tar, and twice called on the plate umpire to inspect it, with the usual negative results. In the fifth Sal flirted with disaster. Hank Bauer opened with a single to left, and Slaughter cracked another single. But Sal tantalized and hypnotized Mickey Mantle with curves, then slipped an unexpected fastball past the youthful slugger for a third strike. Next up was the always-dangerous Yogi Berra, who came to the plate with two on and one out. Alston made a trip to the mound to see how Sal was feeling. The pitcher admitted his arm felt "a little stiff" but insisted he could take care of Berra. Alston left Maglie in, and Berra went to a full count before flying out to left. So did the next hitter, Bill Skowron, to end the inning. While the Dodgers batted in the bottom of the fifth, Brooklyn trainer Harold "Doc" Wendler gave Sal's aching arm a quick rubdown, then applied some of the blister-inducing mystery salve that produced enough pain to distract a pitcher from whatever was ailing his arm. After the game a reporter asked Sal if his arm had felt especially stiff. "It's always stiff, mister," Maglie replied. "At my age it just don't get loose."[13] Brooklyn scored one more run, but Sal kept the Yankees guessing and pitched a complete game that ended when Mickey Mantle hit into a double play. The final score was 6–3. Sal gave up nine hits, walked four, and fanned 10, his highest number of strike-outs for the season. He also threw 148 pitches, an unusually high number for his own time and an almost unheard-of total for a present-day hurler.

Enos Slaughter, a tough old former Redbird recently dealt to the Yankees, said of Sal after the game: "He's a smart one. His fastball is gone but he runs you crazy with those sliders and sinkers. And he's always feeding you a bad ball, hoping you'll bite on it." Although he had three singles off Sal that day, Slaughter added, with the admiration of one veteran warrior of the game for another, "He'll murder you—take everything away from him and he'll claw you with his bare hands."[14] Hank Bauer, another seasoned Yankee veteran, said of Maglie, "He fights you on every pitch."[15] The usually re-served Walter Alston waxed effusive in his praise of Maglie: "I just can't say enough for him. I just don't know what to say. . . . He gives you all he's got and he's wonderful. He gets in trouble and then he strikes someone out."[16] The win was Sal's first World Series victory. "I don't have a complaint in the world," Sal told a United Press reporter. "I got what I always wanted and I know a lot of guys who go all their lives and never will be as contented as I am now." The weary but delighted pitcher added, "This was my greatest thrill. Yes, even more of a thrill than my no-hitter. They claim you can't have everything you want in life, but believe me, with this World Series vic-tory, I have close to all I ever wished for."[17]

Jimmy Cannon, who possessed a rare and happy talent for writing about sports heroes with an unabashed sentimentality that never slipped into mawk-ishness, meditated on the autumnal quality of Maglie's triumph. He noted Sal's aging and weakening arm and the stiffness of his muscles and move-ments, but he described him as "a man made spectacular by desire." He lifted Sal's achievements out of the comparatively trivial realm of sports and into the greater context of all human striving against mortality, the drive to achieve one's goals before old age put them forever beyond reach. "No man is small," Cannon wrote, "who does what he is paid for with an artist's pu-rity. We should all be joyous because one of our species has dignity and fights off the years which are mankind's most ferocious enemies. . . . We are all improved by the likes of Sal Maglie, . . . because this is a rare man who knows the foe is time but works at his job with a manual laborer's splendor. . . . I consider him a glorious man."[18]

19—Jackie Robinson and Gil Hodges congratulate Sal Maglie after his 6–3 victory in Game One of the 1956 World Series. Happy camaraderie has replaced the bitter antagonism that once existed between Robinson and Maglie. Photo: National Baseball Hall of Fame Library, Cooperstown/Associated Press/Corbis.

Casey Stengel took the Yankee defeat in stride. He wasted no time analyzing Whitey Ford's failure but instead announced that his pitcher for Game Two would be "that feller which pitched three four-hitters and I don't want to hide him."[19] That feller was six feet four inches tall, weighed 225 pounds, and lived a headline-prone life that made him difficult to hide. That feller was Don Larsen. A career underachiever notorious for heavy drinking, womanizing, and total indifference to curfews, a man whose preferred reading matter was comic books, the 27-year-old Larsen was best known in 1956 for a spring training exploit in which he ran his car off the road in St. Petersburg at 5:30 a.m., hitting a telephone pole and destroying a mailbox. In 1954, while with the Baltimore Orioles, Larsen had compiled an unenviable 3–21 record to lead the American League in losses. He came to the Yankees in late 1954, and although his record improved with New York, particularly after he adopted his no-windup delivery (he was 11–5 in 1956), Larsen was considered mediocre, a playboy pitcher who had never lived up to his potential.

He certainly failed to live up to it on October 5 in Game Two of the World Series, a contest delayed a day due to rain. With an over-capacity crowd of 36,217 in attendance at Ebbets Field, the Dodgers blasted the Yankees, 13–8. The wild game lasted 3 hours and 26 minutes, a record for a nine-inning World Series contest. The Yankees set another record by using seven pitchers, and those hurlers set still another by giving up 11 walks. Larsen did not make it past the fourth inning. In a bad portent for the Dodgers, Don Newcombe failed to get past the second. Newk gave up a run in the first and five in the second, four of them on a grand slam by Yogi Berra. Removed from the game with the Dodgers behind 6–0, the distressed pitcher broke protocol and left the clubhouse, refusing to wait for the end of the game. When the attendant at the parking lot where he had left his car taunted him, Newcombe punched the man in the stomach. He should have stayed around, as his teammates made a thundering comeback from their 6–0 deficit, shelling Larsen and de-vouring half a dozen more Yankee pitchers on their way to their 13–8 victory. The Dodgers now enjoyed a 2–0 lead in the Series.

The Yanks evened things up when the Series moved to their home ground. Yankee Stadium had more than twice the capacity of Ebbets Field and none of its intimacy. Freed from the telephone booth confines of the Dodgers' playing field, Whitey Ford was slicker than a snake in silk pajamas, going the distance for a 5–3 Yankee victory in Game Three and defeating Brooklyn's Roger Craig. The 40-year-old Enos Slaughter, the only man on either team older than Sal Maglie, sparked the New York offense with a three-run homer. The Yankees also won Game Four, 6–2, with Tom Sturdivant, supported by home runs from Mickey Mantle and Hank Bauer, besting Carl Erskine.

With the Series tied at two games each, Game Five began in Yankee Sta-dium on October 8, a sunny Monday afternoon. This was a crucial game—the team that took it would be favored to win the Series. To everyone's sur-prise Stengel took a risky gamble. After keeping his pitching choice a secret from everyone, including the pitcher himself, he gave the ball to the man the Dodgers had blasted off the mound in Game Two: Don Larsen. Or, more precisely, Stengel had pitching coach Jim Turner place the ball in Larsen's shoe, the manager's quaint way of informing a hurler he was pitching that day. Larsen's teammates Hank Bauer and Bill Skowron were standing near the pitcher's locker when he saw the ball in his shoe, and they recalled the look of shock and disbelief on Don's face when he made the discovery.

The question of what Larsen, whose nickname for himself was "The Night Rider," was doing the evening before the game, and how late he stayed out in pursuit of whatever it was he was doing, is among the most contradictory of baseball myths, a muddle of hearsay history and revisionist autobiography unlikely ever to be sorted out. One story, told by Toots Shor to New York columnist Bob Considine, placed the pitcher at Shor's restaurant, downing drinks with Shor and hobnobbing with Earl Warren, baseball fan and Chief Justice of the Supreme Court. In this version of Larsen's evening, Warren told Shor that he would not attend the next day's game, because Larsen was obviously going to be out all night drinking and would be incapable of decent pitching. Mickey Mantle claimed that Larsen had dinner with friends, then sat around with his friends and Mantle at a local saloon, drinking *ginger ale.* A third version comes from columnist Arthur Richman, who wrote that he shared a cab back to the Bronx with Larsen after sharing a dinner and a couple of beers with him earlier in the evening. Richman claimed that, during the cab ride, Larsen said he might pitch a no-hitter the following day. Still another story comes from Yankee outfielder Bob Cerv, who claimed he went out for drinks that night with Larsen and several other Yankees and gave the following terse account of the evening: "I left him at 4 a.m."[20] Another Yankee, pitcher Bob Turley, also claimed Larsen was out drinking and that he slept only about half an hour the night before the game. Larsen insists all these stories are inaccurate, and that he returned to the Yankees' hotel before midnight. As for drinking himself into a stupor, he commented in righteous retrospect, "I would never have gotten myself out of top physical or mental condition on the eve of such an important game."[21]

Other weird tales accompany Larsen into Game Five of the 1956 World Series. Teammate Andy Carey told of how his father, in town for the Series, had a fake newspaper front page printed at a novelty shop in Times Square the evening before the game. It read, "Larsen Pitches No-Hitter Against Dodgers." The elder Carey tucked the page under Larsen's hotel room door, but then he had second thoughts, afraid the headline might jinx the pitcher. Still in the grip of superstition, he retrieved and destroyed it, flushing the page down the toilet. In another part of New York City, Bob Wolff, announcer for the Washington Senators, was preparing to call the fifth game for the Mutual Broadcasting System. Huddled with the Senators' publicity director Herb Heft to go over his notes for the game, Wolff commented, "Wouldn't it be something if Sal Maglie pitched a no-hitter against the Yankees?" Heft laughed and replied, "Nobody pitches no-hitters in the World Series!"[22]

Larsen was sharp in his first inning of work, but his pitching did not suggest a masterpiece in the making. He struck out leadoff man Junior Gilliam but went to a full count on Pee Wee Reese before striking him out as well. Duke Snider hit a hard line drive to right that Hank Bauer corralled with a knee-high catch. In the bottom half of the first, Sal Maglie made his first appearance on the mound at Yankee Stadium. Thanks to a rain day before Game Three, he had enjoyed a five-day rest, and as usual, he was relying on his assortment of baffling curves, with the occasional fastball at the chin.

Hank Bauer, leading off for the Yankees, tried to bunt Sal's first offering but fouled it off for strike one. Sal's second pitch to Bauer was a fastball that brought a loud gasp of horror from the stands, full of Yankee rooters unused to Sal's pitching tactics. In the words of broadcaster Bob Neal, it sailed "*way* inside and behind him, and Bauer ducks out of the way."[23] The announcer then described Maglie looking at his hands to indicate that the ball had slipped. Had it? Or was Sal taking another terrible, calculated risk in order to announce to the Yankees that his razor was as sharp and potentially deadly as ever? In the high tension situation of a crucial World Series game, and keeping in mind Maglie's frequent shakiness at the start of many of his games, it is unlikely that he intended the ball to go behind Bauer's head, although it is safe to say he certainly did intend it as a high-inside warning to the hitter. After the game Maglie explained, "The call was for an inside pitch. I threw it too high and it got away."[24] Bauer, whose face someone described as looking like a clenched fist, clenched his face even further and glared out at Maglie. The Barber glowered back, and on his next pitch Bauer popped out to Reese. The next batter, first baseman Joe Collins, also tried to bunt his way on, but Robinson threw him out at first. Mickey Mantle lofted a fly to Sandy Amoros in left to end the inning.

First up in the top of the second was Jackie Robinson, batting cleanup, and he came close to changing the course of the game. The Dodger immortal, older and slower, his hair graying and his middle thickening, now in the final days of his Hall of Fame career, smashed a smoking drive at third baseman Andy Carey. The ball was hit so hard that it ricocheted off Carey's glove. But instead of bounding out into left field for a single, it bounced to shortstop Gil McDougald, who scooped it up and fired to Skowron at first. Robinson was out, but barely—a few years earlier he would have beaten the throw. "Jackie Robinson hit the shit out of the ball," Andy Carey later remembered.[25] It was the first of several crucial plays. After that moment of excitement, Hodges struck out, and Amoros sent a little pop fly toward the area just beyond second base, but well away from where right fielder Hank Bauer was playing. It might have fallen for a bloop single, but second baseman Billy Martin backpedaled and snagged it at the last moment. Sal made equally short work of the Yankees in the bottom of the second. Yogi Berra popped out to Reese, Enos Slaughter flied out to Amoros, and Sal struck out Billy Martin. Furillo opened the top of the third by flying out to Bauer in right. Campanella was called out on strikes. Maglie sent a harmless fly to Mantle, who was playing shallow in center, for the third out. The bottom of the third was similarly uneventful. After McDougald grounded out to Robinson, Carey and Larsen both fouled out to Campanella, and the game was one-third over, with neither pitcher having allowed a base runner.

Top of the fourth, top of the order again for the Dodgers. Larsen needed only two pitches to dispose of the first two batters, as Gilliam and Reese both grounded to Martin for easy outs. Then came Snider, and Larsen fell behind on him, 2–0. Knowing that Larsen had to come in with a good pitch, Snider readied himself and smashed the next offering toward the right field stands. Everybody, including Larsen, thought it was a sure four-bagger. The Duke was already into his home run trot when the ball hooked slightly before landing in the stands. Umpire Ed Runge declared it foul. As Dodger fans groaned and Yankee rooters sighed in relief, Snider returned reluctantly to the plate. Two more pitches, a called strike and a foul-off, then Larsen caught Snider with a called third strike to end the inning.

The bottom of the fourth began well for Maglie, as Bauer grounded out to Robinson and Joe Collins was called out on strikes. Sal had retired 11 consecutive batters when Mickey Mantle stepped to the plate for the second time. Sal worked him carefully, mixing curves and fastballs. Then, with the count at 2–2, Sal hung a curve, and Mantle smacked a home run into the lower right field seats. It was not one of Mickey's out of the park blasts. It carried only a little beyond the foul pole at the 296–foot mark, but as Hamlet said of his unspectacular yet fatal wound, "T'will serve." Sal had thrown only one bad pitch so far, and it had cost him, although there is no way he could have known it had cost him the ball game. He gave the rubber a kick and went back to work. Yogi Berra, up next, hit a drive to center that looked like it might fall for extra bases, but a racing Duke Snider made a sensational catch to end the inning. The Yankees led, 1–0, but the lead did not seem insurmountable.

The Dodgers did not go quietly in the top of the fifth. If they ever had a chance to get to Larsen, that was the time. Robinson fouled off several pitches before hitting a fly to deep right field for an out. Then Hodges, on a 2–2 count, drove the ball into the far reaches of left center field, the vast expanse of turf that visiting outfielders called "Death Valley." It looked like a sure extra-base hit, but Mantle came tearing across the field and at the last second made a backhand catch some 400 feet from home plate. The ball would have been a home run in almost any other park. Mantle recalled later, "If I'd started a split second later, or been a step slower, of if I hadn't shaded over on Hodges, the ball would have dropped for at least a double. It was the best catch I ever made."[26] Amoros followed Hodges to the plate, and he too nearly broke the spell. With the count 1–1, he clobbered a Larsen fastball toward the right field stands, another shot that had home run written all over it. But at the last moment it hooked foul. Extra World Series umpire Ed Runge—who had been Maglie's manager when Sal was doing defense work and playing ball in Canada during the war—made the call from his position on the right field line. He later told plate umpire Babe Pinelli the ball had been foul by no more than four inches. Pinelli responded that if he had called that one from the plate, he would have awarded Amoros a homer. Like Snider's blast in the fourth, it was nothing but a long, loud strike, and Amoros had to return to the plate. Two pitches later, he grounded out to Billy Martin to end the Dodgers' half of the inning. To open the bottom of the fifth, Maglie walked Slaughter, the first pass given up by either pitcher. Martin then laid down a sacrifice bunt, but Maglie scuttled off the mound, snatched the ball, and fired it to second to force Slaughter. With Martin on first, Gil McDougald stroked a wicked line drive that seemed headed for left field, but Reese leaped into the air, deflected the ball, and caught it. The shortstop then threw to first to double up Martin for the third out.

The bottom of the Dodger batting order gave Larsen no trouble in the top of the sixth. Furillo and Campanella both hit pop-ups to Billy Martin for two quick outs. As he came to the plate, Maglie was in no mood to stand there passively and let Larsen strike him out. Sal swung hard at Larsen's first two offerings but missed. He laid off the next pitch, and fouled off two more before letting ball two go by. Then he made another vain swing at a Larsen fastball for strike three. Larsen had retired 18 in a row, and he left the mound to a huge ovation. Sal took the mound for the bottom of the sixth, and had a tough time of it. On his first pitch he gave up a single to third baseman Andy Carey. Larsen came to the plate next, to the sound of another roaring ovation, and with orders to bunt. After he missed twice and Maglie had an 0–2 count on him, the Dodgers decided Larsen would no longer attempt a bunt, and Jackie Robinson moved back to his normal fielding position. But Stengel kept the bunt sign on, and Larsen succeeded in his third try, laying down a perfect sacrifice bunt in front of the plate. Maglie and Campanella both scrambled for it, but Campy's throw was too late to get the runner at second. Hank Bauer, up next, slapped a single to left. Maglie hurried over to cover third, but Carey scored easily. Sal gave up another single, this time to Joe Collins, moving Bauer to third. Alston came to the mound to talk with Maglie and give the sweating pitcher a few moments of rest, while the relievers had a chance to warm up. But the manager did not take Maglie out. "Take Sal out?" Roy Campanella exclaimed after the game, "the way he was pitching?"[27] Alston returned to the dugout. Now Mickey Mantle was up with two on and one down, and the Yankees' opportunity to blast Sal out of the game was at hand. His first pitch to Mantle was a ball; then he threw a pair of strikes, one called and one swinging. Mantle hit Maglie's next pitch sharply to Hodges at first. He stepped on the bag for an easy out before throwing to Campanella. Now the Dodgers had Bauer hung up between third and home.

Campanella and Robinson played a clumsy game of catch, with one of Campy's throws sending Jackie sprawling in the dirt to retrieve it, before Robinson finally tagged Bauer for the third out. The game was two-thirds over, and the Dodgers had yet to have a man reach base.

Larsen continued to baffle Brooklyn in the top of the seventh. Gilliam grounded out, Reese flied out to Mantle in center, and Snider lifted a tame fly to Slaughter in left. The radio and television announcers, loathe to break the taboo about mentioning a no-hitter in progress, merely noted that Larsen had now retired 21 men in a row. Larsen's teammates refused to say a word to him, and the usual dugout banter turned to dead silence. Everyone on the team made sure they took exactly the same seat in the dugout in each inning. Anxiety spread to the usually relaxed and nerveless Larsen, who ducked into the dugout tunnel between innings to suck on a cigarette. On the Brooklyn side, Sal Maglie refused to concede anything. In the bottom of the seventh he retired the dangerous Berra and Slaughter on routine fly balls. He gave up a single to Billy Martin, the fifth and last hit the Yankees would get, and then walked Gil McDougald, but Andy Carey hit a grounder to Reese, who threw to Gilliam to force Martin, and the inning was over.

As the top of the eighth opened, a continuous roar shook Yankee Stadium, like a huge, noisy engine running. Jackie Robinson stepped to the plate, determined to do something to break Larsen's hypnotizing rhythm. After taking a called strike, he called time, stepped out of the batter's box, walked back to the on-deck circle, and said something to Gil Hodges. The fans booed him for his delaying tactics. After fouling off the next pitch, Robinson rolled a weak grounder back to Larsen, who lobbed the ball to first for the out. Gil Hodges strode to the plate, muttering to no one in particular, "I'll get this guy!"[28] He almost did. Hodges smashed a low liner toward third base, where Andy Carey lunged for it and speared the ball at his shoe tops. Unsure of whether the umpire would claim he had trapped the ball, he threw to first to make sure of the out. Later Carey kicked himself for throwing to first: "Oh, you son of a bitch, what if you had thrown the ball away!"[29] Hodges stopped halfway down the line, gave Larsen a queer look, and headed back to the Dodger dugout. Sandy Amoros ended the top of the eighth with a fly to Mantle, and Larsen had retired 24 consecutive batters. When he retired Hodges, Larsen set a new World Series record for consecutive outs.

Sal Maglie was the last man to emerge from the Dodger dugout in the bottom of the eighth, and the first batter to face him was Don Larsen. The roar of the crowd reached a deafening pitch, but none of the applause was for the forgotten Dodger pitcher. Sal had a five-hitter going and had given up only two runs—a performance good enough to win most games, but not this one. At bat, Larsen was too nervous to concentrate. This might have been an excellent moment for Maglie to throw a brushback, but Sal refrained, perhaps out of respect for a fellow pitcher's achievement. Instead, he struck Larsen out on four pitches. Hank Bauer and Joe Collins followed Larsen to the plate, and Maglie struck them out, too. "I figured," he said later, "that for me, either way, it was the last inning, and I didn't have to save anything."[30] As he returned to the dugout after striking out the side, the crowd suddenly noticed the heroic old hurler and accorded him a portion of their cheers.

Maybe it was the belated cheers that did it, or perhaps the realization of the historic moment of which he was a part, even as he was losing a vital game, but Maglie was overwhelmed. As he left the field he went down the steps and through the dugout without pausing, continuing into the runway that led back to the clubhouse. According to Roscoe McGowan, who had no business being where he could see what he saw and later reported in his *Times* account, Sal walked to a point well out of sight of his teammates and sat down on the low wall bordering the runway. He stayed there for about half a minute, with his head bowed and his hands clasped in front of him, before returning to the dugout to watch the top of the ninth. McGowan thought Sal might have been praying, though he knew better than to ask. But prayer, especially the silent kind, does not require the solitude Sal sought.

It is not unheard-of for pitchers to cry after a particularly rough loss. Ralph Branca's emotional meltdown in 1951 is the classic instance; Roger Kahn once caught tough, cocky Clem Labine in tears after a World Series defeat; and even the stoical Warren Spahn gave way to weeping after his heartbreaking loss to the Cardinals near the end of the recent pennant race. But nobody had ever seen Sal Maglie's eyes so much as mist over, even after the most wrenching losses. But now, as he sat alone in the dim hallway, head bowed, hands clasped at his knees, if a couple of tears trickled into the sweat-glazed stubble on his cheeks, no one will ever know. One thing is certain: Sal needed those moments alone to regain his composure. His was more than the ordinary exhaustion of a 39-year-old man who had just pitched eight intense innings. He had been hurling the ball, and his heart, for all those futile innings against the blank, unyielding wall of Larsen's perfection. Did Sal realize on some level that his career was effectively over? That there were no more miracles in store for him? That he had stood for the last time at baseball's ultimate axis of event and thrown his last pitch in a World Series game?[31] If he did, he quickly buried those thoughts. He knew he would need all his poise, all his courtesy and generosity of spirit, to get through the next few hours.

At three minutes before 3 p.m. Don Larsen walked to the mound on rubbery legs to face the last three Brooklyn batters. Billy Martin gathered the Yankee infielders and gave them an ultimatum: "*Nothing gets through.*" On the Dodger side, the team's irrepressible publicist Irving Rudd shouted: "To hell with history! Let's get a hit. Get a fucking hit!"[32] The crowd was no longer roaring. Instead, a breathless hush engulfed the huge stadium. "Tension kept mounting until it was as brittle as an electric light bulb," *Times* columnist Arthur Daley wrote. "The slightest jounce and the dang thing might explode. Or perhaps it was more like a guy blowing air into a toy balloon. He keeps blowing and blowing . . . but every puff might be the last. Larger and larger grew Larsen's balloon. It was of giant size at the start of the ninth." Larsen, a Lutheran choirboy in his youth but no choirboy as an adult, mumbled a prayer: "Help me out, somebody, please help me out. Get me through this!"[33] The first man up, Carl Furillo, displayed his bulldog qualities, refusing to let go of his last chance to bat. "The guy's got good stuff, huh?" Berra grunted from his crouch. "Yeah, not bad," Furillo growled, refusing to be distracted.[34] He took one pitch for a ball and fouled off four more before meekly flying out to Bauer in right. The crowd, quiet as the inning opened, began to roar again. Larsen then disposed of Campanella. After lining a hard foul to deep left, Roy sent a tame grounder to second base that Billy Martin fielded and threw to Collins for the second out.

There was no chance that Maglie would come to bat. Sal watched from the dugout as pinch hitter Dale Mitchell stepped to the plate in his place, the twenty-seventh batter to stand in against Don Larsen. A veteran left-handed hitter, Mitchell had been in the majors since 1946 and had joined the Dodgers in July. He held a lifetime batting average of .312, and although he hit few home runs, he rarely struck out—only 119 times in more than 3,000 at-bats, which is fewer than some sluggers ring up in a single season of swinging for the fences. Larsen went to a 1–2 count on him. The batter fouled off the next pitch. Something close to total silence prevailed at Yankee Stadium. Larsen paused to remove his cap, and wipe the sweat from his forehead, stooped to pick up the rosin bag, then tossed it down. Yankee fielders fidgeted. Berra signaled for a fastball, and Larsen delivered. Mitchell hesitated, then committed himself to a futile half-swing. Larsen's ninety-seventh pitch thudded into Berra's glove at the same moment Babe Pinelli's arm went up to signal "Strike three." The stunned Mitchell turned to argue the call. To the end of his life he would insist it was an outside pitch, but he was protesting to the empty air. Pinelli was walking away, and Berra was trundling out toward Larsen, leaping into the dazed pitcher's arms. It was Mitchell's last at bat in the majors, and for Pinelli, who was set to retire, his last game behind the plate. In the broadcast booth Vin Scully captured the moment, saying, "Ladies and gentlemen, it's the greatest game ever pitched in baseball history."[35]

The game had repercussions in unexpected places and in unexpected ways. A boy named Steve Siegel was sitting in the stands that day, allowed the rare privilege of missing school so the whole family could attend the game. The elder Mr. Siegel saw the opportunity to teach a lesson. "In the eighth, my father started pounding me in the shoulder, yelling 'History in the making, history in the making! Stevie boy, . . . you're seeing history in the making.'" His father's words made an impression. "I must have listened," recalled Steve Siegel, "because I became a history teacher."[36] At Columbia Presbyterian Hospital in Manhattan, another boy lay in a coma after being hit by a truck while riding his bicycle. Doctors had given up hope for his recovery, advising the boy's parents to place him in a long-term care facility. On the day the boy was scheduled to be transferred out of the hospital, Game Five of the World Series was on the radio at the nursing station, just outside the boy's door. Although no one at the hospital knew it, the kid was an ardent Yankee fan. As the game ended, he sat bolt upright, opened his eyes, and cried out: "He did it! He pitched a perfect game!" The whole floor went wild, and the boy eventually went home.[37]

Nobody could argue with Vin Scully's assessment of the importance of Larsen's achievement. It was the first, and still the only, perfect game ever pitched in World Series competition, the first perfect game in the majors in 34 years, and at the time only the sixth perfect game in modern baseball history. As Joe Trimble observed in the *Daily News,* "The unperfect man pitched a perfect game." And unperfect Larsen remained, never again approaching the pinnacle he reached on October 8, 1956. The "perfect Yankee" was well below perfect in his personal life as well. The footloose bon vivant of 1956, who liked to present himself as single, had an estranged wife and a child. On the same day Larsen pitched his perfect game, Vivian Larsen obtained a court order to have his World Series share withheld on the grounds that he was in arrears in his support for her and their 11–month-old daughter. She also charged that, three months after their marriage on April 26, 1955, Larsen left her, and that he "brazenly suggested that when the child was born it be given out for adoption." It is easy to imagine how eagerly Kay Maglie would have snapped up Don Larsen's unwanted daughter. Several hours after his big game, Larsen wrote a check for the money he owed his wife and sent it to her through her attorney.

While Larsen was accepting congratulations, answering reporters' questions, posing for pictures, picking up endorsements, and paying his debts, Sal Maglie was dealing with his role as the pitcher who lost to perfection. Not quite two weeks ago, Sal had been the center of attention as the "Cinderella pitcher," the man plucked out of the ash heap by the Dodgers, who had hurled a no-hitter at age 39. It was a mere five days since he had beaten the Yankees in Game One. Now, shaved and showered, Sal sat at his locker naked, in no hurry to dress and make the obligatory visit to the Yankee side to congratulate Larsen. Evidently he was hungry after his exertions. Writer Murray Kempton recalled him "tearing his lunch off a long Italian sausage," an uncouth image that makes one wonder if Kempton, a noted egalitarian, might have fallen victim to a tendency to see the well-mannered Maglie as an Italian roughneck.[38] It is impossible to *tear* an Italian sausage; the casing is too strong, and furthermore, where would Sal have acquired that delicacy? In the days before specialized diets and players with personal nutritionists, players did not bring their own food into the locker room. Either of the Dodgers' two solicitous clubhouse men, "Senator" John Griffin or Charlie "The Brow" DiGiovanna, may have made Sal a favorite sandwich, and if Kay Maglie had decided Sal needed a personal postgame snack, she would have sliced it neatly and not simply handed her husband a length of sausage to gnaw on. Neither general manager Buzzie Bavasi nor Tom Villante, producer of the Dodgers' radio and TV broadcasts, put any credence in Kempton's story of Sal and the sausage.[39] A small detail, perhaps, but one that reveals how even a liberal writer could fall victim to ethnic stereotyping, inventing a "colorful" detail out of his own preconceptions.

Polite and patient as always, despite his exhaustion and disappointment, Sal answered reporters' questions. Someone asked if he was "satisfied" with the game he had just pitched, a query that must have struck him as silly. Maglie was the money pitcher, the man who wins the big games, and he had lost this one. How was he supposed to feel satisfied with a defeat? "But you got to adjust yourself," he stated, and in his voice one can hear the shrug of his tired shoulders.[40] Asked if he had thought about his own no-hitter as the tension mounted in Larsen's game, he answered, "I know just how he felt in the ninth inning and, in a vague way, I didn't want to see his no-hitter ruined. It would have been impossible, of course, but I wanted to see us win it without spoiling his performance." Almost inaudibly, Maglie mused, "That's the way it goes. What can you do against a once in a lifetime performance? I gave it my best shot."[41]

After answering reporters' questions, Sal dressed and made his way from the subdued Dodgers dressing room into the uproar of the Yankees' quarters. Sal shook Larsen's hand, posed for more pictures, managed that sad-eyed smile that identified him like a number, and said the right things. "I felt sorry for you in the ninth, Don," he commiserated, "because I knew what was going through your mind." Then he added, gracious in defeat, "You were the best and there was nothing we could do about it."[42] A few days before the World Series began, Maglie had offered an assessment of himself that proved prophetic. "I've learned and I'm still learning, and I've been getting to be a better pitcher all the time. But I think now I'm as good as I'm gonna get."[43]

After all the hoopla surrounding Larsen's perfect game, the concluding games of the 1956 Series were an anticlimax. "As for the rest of the World Series, well, who cares?" asked an editorial in the October 9 edition of the *Herald Tribune*. For the record, the Dodgers broke the spell Larsen had cast and won Game Six at Ebbets Field in 10 innings, 1–0, behind the superb pitching of Clem Labine. But the next day Game Seven was a Yankee rout, as the Bronx Bombers again pounded Don Newcombe, who lasted only four innings, giving up a pair of two-run homers to Yogi Berra and a solo shot to Elston Howard. Again Newk left the stadium early. In the company of his father and sympathetic but observant reporter Milton Gross, he cried all the way home. In the seventh Bill Skowron hit a grand slam off Roger Craig to make the final score 9–0. In the last at-bat of his career, Jackie Robinson struck out to end the game. Johnny Kucks pitched a three-hitter, and Stengel had another world championship. As the disappointed Dodgers fans filed out of Ebbets Field after what would prove to be the last World Series game ever held there, Walter O'Malley was already negotiating with Los Angeles to build the team a big, modern stadium 3,000 miles away. On October 31, 1956, just three weeks after the Dodgers' defeat, O'Malley sold Ebbets Field to a real estate developer.

The day after the Series ended the Dodgers left for a series of exhibition games to be played in Hawaii and Japan. Each player received an extra $3,000, plus expenses, for making the trip. Carl Furillo, who had fought in the Pacific in World War II, refused to go. So did Sal Maglie, who had a pressing reason for staying home: he and Kay were beginning the process of adopting a second child. Delighted with their adopted son, they were eager to expand their family before they became too old to be considered for another child. In the 1950s adoption agencies were reluctant to permit couples over 40 to adopt, and Sal would reach that milestone on his next birthday. But, just as had occurred with their first adoption, the Maglies encountered obstacles and delays. Although the *Niagara Falls Gazette* reported that the second adoption was underway in late 1956, less than a year after they had adopted their first child, the couple did not bring home another child until the summer of 1963. By that time, both their lives had changed dramatically.

1957—"The Calendar Never Killed Anybody"

Sal at 40 as a Dodger and a Yankee

17

ON THE BANQUET CIRCUIT

With the completion of his 1956 "Cinderella" season, Sal Maglie picked up still another round of honors, more than he had received in all his previous years. In a late October Associated Press poll of members of the Baseball Writers Association of America to select a major league All-Star team, Sal was the runner-up to Don Newcombe as the team's right-handed pitcher. The dream team included future Hall of Famers Mickey Mantle, Ted Williams, Henry Aaron, Stan Musial, Willie Mays, Duke Snider, Yogi Berra, and Whitey Ford. On November 1, the Baseball Writers Association gave 159 out of a possible 199 votes to Maglie for the group's Comeback of the Year Award. Sal also received an avalanche of awards and recognitions from other local and national sports organizations.

In July of 1956 baseball commissioner Ford Frick had announced that the Baseball Writers Association would reward the best pitcher in the major leagues with the newly founded Cy Young Award. (Until 1967 only one Cy Young Award per year was presented; since then one is given in each league.) The awarding of the first Cy Young trophy caused some confusion, because it included both a popular vote from fans, conducted by the *Sporting News,* and a separate vote by the Baseball Writers Association. The fans, whose votes came from their hearts rather than from attention to performance statistics, overwhelmingly chose Sal Maglie. The Brooklyn pitcher received 12,839 votes, while runner-up Warren Spahn received

6,742. Don Newcombe, never a fan favorite due to his harsh temper, was fourth, with only 2,937 votes. The letters fans sent with their selection contained eloquent tributes to Maglie. James Moss of St. Cloud, Minnesota, wrote: "His undaunted spirit moved from season to Series. A losing cause there? Think! He was splendid in victory—magnificent in defeat."[1] Even Ty Cobb, not known for his admiring attitude toward players of the 1950s, whom he considered softies and sissies in comparison to the cutthroat types of his own era (like himself), had high praise for Maglie. When he learned Sal was the popular choice for the Cy Young Award, Cobb compared Sal favorably to the greatest pitchers of the past: Cy Young, Grover Cleveland Alexander, Walter Johnson,* and Christy Mathewson. "Maglie," the Georgia Peach declared, "has the stamp of the old-time greats." Commenting on Maglie's performance against Don Larsen, Cobb observed, "Real champions are not easily discouraged. Maglie is of that stripe—a craftsman and a competitor."[2] It is easy to believe that Sal found compliments from Cobb more gratifying than anything writers, fans, or banquet speakers might say about him.

But in the official Baseball Writers Association balloting, conducted before the World Series, Don Newcombe was the clear winner of the Cy Young Award. Despite Newcombe's late-season failures, the Dodger righthander's 27–7 record was the best in either league and assured him the prize. Running a close second to Newcombe in the balloting was Sal Maglie. Although Maglie's record did not approach Newcombe's, the writers were aware of how many big games Sal had won for Brooklyn during the regular season. Newcombe also received the 1956 Most Valuable Player Award, and again Maglie was the closest runner-up.

Starting as early as October, when the World Series ended, Sal's round of award ceremonies began. The town of Niagara Falls held another Sal Maglie Day on October 27, with a motorcade around the city. In the evening there was a dinner in the pitcher's honor at one of his favorite haunts, the Como Restaurant. After a multicourse Italian dinner came the award ceremony, where Msgr. Pascal Tronolone presented Maglie with his gift, the keys to an Oldsmobile station wagon, a typical suburban family car chosen in recognition of Sal's new role as a father. In his speech of thanks, Sal spoke more about being a new father than about baseball. "I still can't believe it," he told the audience of family and friends. "Ever since the adoption of Sal Jr., I've had new determination. The coming of this boy into our home has changed our lives. Now I'm aiming for three more years in the majors, and then I'll have enough to give him the best start in life, and take care of Kathleen [Kay] and myself." He also told why he had not gone to Japan with the Dodgers after the Series: he needed to be present to sign the papers finalizing the adoption of Sal Jr. as well as to continue with the process of adopting a second child. "His name will be Joseph Maglie," Sal announced, "in honor of my father, who died suddenly this summer."[3]

More awards followed. On December 11 Sal was honored as western New York's athlete of the year at the Buffalo Athletic Club's annual Sports Night. Presented with a plaque, Sal noted, "I'd rather pitch against the Yankees than come up here and speak . . . but this honor makes me very proud."[4] The Touchdown Club of Washington, D.C. honored Maglie at a banquet in Washington on January 12. Sal was chosen for the Clark Griffith Memorial Award for his "sensational string of victories" in the last month of the National League pennant race. On January 20 Sal traveled to Chicago to share honors with Casey Stengel, as both men were honored by the Chicago chapter of the Baseball Writers Association at their annual Diamond Dinner. The group presented Maglie with the William Wrigley Jr. award for making "the comeback of the year." On January 31 Sal was in New York City for the annual dinner of the New York Sports Broadcasters Association, where he and Mickey Mantle received awards for outstanding achievement during 1956.

At home, the Niagara Rapids Athletic Club honored Sal as their "Athlete of the Year" in a dinner and ceremony at the Century Club on February 6. Among those attending were Dodgers scout Al Campanis and Cleveland Indian outfielder Gene Woodling. Fr. Thomas Kelley of Bishop Duffy High School presented the award to Sal. Maglie's talk, as usual, was brief. As he related how he had been waived by the Indians to the Dodgers, he interrupted his prepared talk to exclaim with heartfelt intensity, "God Bless Brooklyn!" Woodling's talk was less inspirational and more realistic. The outfielder, who had been in the majors since 1943 and had bounced around among several teams, had been Maglie's roommate when Sal was with Cleveland. He warned his audience, and indirectly the evening's honoree, "Don't expect security or sympathy in professional baseball. Neither of them exist. You can be fired from your job tomorrow, and you'll never get any sympathy when you're at the end of the trail."[5] One wonders if Sal was paying attention.

During the off-season, Sal the Barber had been cultivating a beard—not the sinister, unshaven look familiar to fans from his mound appearances, but a neat, pitch-black, and formidably thick Vandyke. Anything relating to Sal's beard always aroused interest, and when asked about it by sportswriters, Maglie explained that he was growing the beard in order to shave it off during a television commercial for Remington Rollectric razors. When National League president Warren Giles spotted the beard during Sal's appearance at the Chicago sportswriters dinner, he told the pitcher, "That looks very nice, but you'll have to shave that thing off before you start pitching."[6] (Imagine any league official today presuming to tell a player what kind of facial hair is or is not appropriate on the field.) Maglie assured Giles that the beard would be gone before spring training ended. A special advantage of the product Maglie was endorsing was that it could be run off the current provided by an automobile cigarette lighter. Sal's nephew Dennis Villani recalled accompanying Sal to the set where the commercial was being shot. "He was sitting in the car on the sound stage," Dennis remembered with amusement, "and they're making like they're driving the car. But there are two guys in the back, rocking the car, to make it look like the car was moving."[7]

In addition to the pitcher's brief career as a pitchman, Sal received a more enduring tribute: he appeared, only thinly disguised, as a major character in the novel *Schoolboy Johnson*, by John R. Tunis. The author, among the most successful writers of sports fiction for young people in the 1940s and 1950s, produced a series of novels about a semi-fictional Brooklyn Dodgers team of that same era. The title character is based on the young Don Drysdale, and the character of Speedy Mason is a version of Sal Maglie—they even share the same initials. Schoolboy, whose nickname suggests his immaturity, is a tall, handsome, blond young man from California, with an eye for the ladies and a quick temper, while Tunis describes Speedy as "the big fellow with the dark unshaven cheeks," a veteran of the Mexican League who glared at batters, all details borrowed from Sal Maglie.[8]

As the plot unfolds, the hotheaded Schoolboy learns from his veteran teacher and friend how to control both his temper and his pitches, and as a result he wins the pennant-clinching game. Although the year is not specified, the story amounts to a novelistic retelling of the Dodgers' 1956 season, with a few fictional twists, such as Drysdale/Schoolboy's winning the pennant-clincher. The story is gritty and more than a little melancholy in its contrast of youth and age, of a brilliant career just beginning, and another, fine but not quite brilliant, coming to a close. The Schoolboy learns his lessons, and Speedy Mason also learns some hard lessons about the abrupt end of playing careers. "This apparent cruelty, this impersonal method of tossing you out, is a part of baseball. Don't ever forget: baseball is a business. You don't like it? Go run a filling station." The old veteran muses about his own release: "I knew it was coming, of course I knew, how could I help knowing? I thought I was ready for the bad news any time, yet when it came I wasn't ready for it at all."[9] The novel, written in 1957 and published in 1958, is eerily prophetic in its description of Mason/Maglie's inability to accept the end, even when he knew it was approaching.

The biggest story in major league baseball during the winter of 1956–1957 had nothing to do with Sal Maglie, although Maglie had a definite reaction to it. On December 13, 1956, the Brooklyn Dodgers announced the trade of Jackie Robinson to the New York Giants. Like Durocher's switch of managerial allegiance in 1948 and Maglie's appearance in a Dodger uniform in

1956, the story created a sensation in New York. As one Dodger fan proclaimed, "I'm shocked to the core. . . . Jackie Robinson is a synonym for the Dodgers. They can't do this to us!"[10] Of course "they" could, and did. The trade was not such a complete surprise to Robinson as it was to his fans. He had never gotten along too well with Walter Alston, and the more important Walter—O'Malley—intensely disliked him. Robinson, for his part, thought O'Malley was a racist. At the time he learned of the trade, Robbie had already decided to retire, and he had made two business deals to assure his future financial security: he had agreed to take a job with Chock Full O'Nuts, the restaurant and coffee chain, and he had sold the exclusive rights to his retirement story to *Look* magazine. Just hours after he had signed his contract with Chock Full O'Nuts, Robinson learned he had been traded to the Giants. He had not told the Dodgers of his intention to retire because the contract he had signed with *Look* stipulated that his retirement must first be announced in the pages of that magazine. When the magazine article came out in January of 1957, the situation made Robinson appear to be in the wrong and obliterated the blatant cynicism of the Dodgers in setting up the trade.

After his retirement, Robinson made several comments about former Dodger teammates, including one suggesting that Roy Campanella's career was pretty much over. Campy, not an easy man to upset, was hurt and angry. Robinson also mentioned that he would like to return to baseball as a major league manager. When told about Jackie's ambitions to manage, Maglie had some uncharacteristically sharp comments, asserting that he did not think any team would hire Robinson. "I believe Jackie ruined his chances of becoming a manager because of all that popping off he's done lately. . . . You couldn't get anybody to play for him after the way he's been rapping on other players." He added that Robinson never was very popular, even among his own Dodger teammates, but made it plain he had nothing against Robinson personally. "I always sincerely admired him as a player because of his fierce determination to win. I like to play that way myself," Sal declared.[11] There was no hint of racial animosity in Sal's observations about Robinson. He merely noted what even those who were closest to Robinson, such as Pee Wee Reese, had said in the past: that Jackie was a difficult man to get along with. But without Robinson, the Dodgers were a team without its flaming heart.

Maglie did not press too hard in his 1957 contract negotiations with the Dodgers. Considering how valuable he had been to the team in 1956, he might have held out for a lot more money, but instead he merely asked that the Dodgers restore the cut Cleveland had made in his income. The Dodgers did not quite come up with an increase that would have negated the amount Hank Greenberg had slashed from Maglie's pay, but they did sign Sal for an estimated $30,000. Although not too imposing in comparison with the salaries of the game's superstars—Ted Williams' 1957 contract was believed to call for the eye-popping sum of $100,000, and Mickey Mantle was making $60,000—Maglie's salary was not bad for a pitcher with chronic back trouble who would be 40 on his next birthday. Sal said he was satisfied and ready to report for spring training.

SAL'S 1957 SEASON—THE BROOKLYN DODGERS

As the Dodgers' training camp opened in mid-February, reporters asked Walter Alston what he thought about his pitching staff. He professed himself optimistic, listing Newcombe, Podres, Erskine, Maglie, Craig, and Labine as starters, although he suggested Labine might be more valuable in relief and that Erskine and Maglie might need more rest between starts. Dodger photographer Barney Stein was busy during spring training in Vero Beach, Florida, producing images for a "Family Album" to be included in the 1957 Dodger Yearbook. Pee Wee and Dottie Reese introduced their nearly newborn son; Clem Labine posed between his two daughters; and Sal Maglie, a father at last, grinning and glowing with pride, showed off Sal Jr. while holding the little boy in the middle of a huge sombrero.

Eager to begin, Sal asked to pitch batting practice on February 24, the same day he arrived in camp. The next day, Maglie put in some throwing time despite a steady rain. He threw batting practice on March 2, and after inquiring of Sandy Amoros, no doubt in some combination of sign language and Spanish, if the Cuban outfielder was wearing his batting helmet, proceeded to plunk Sandy in the rump with the slowest of his slow curves. Amoros, realizing that this was a joke—Sal's way of welcoming him back—took it with good humor. When Sal spoke with reporters he sounded upbeat, telling them he saw no reason why he could not pitch for three more years. "I have no more back trouble," he assured them. "I feel fine and my arm feels good."[12]

The National League champion Dodgers did not play like champions during their spring exhibition season, ending with a 16–17 record. Sal's performances were spotty. His first outing, on March 8, was a disaster, as the Braves clobbered him for seven runs when he gave up three homers in the fourth and failed to retire a batter. This seemed like cause for alarm, but Sal said he just needed more outings to sharpen his control. On April 6 he went six innings against the Braves, giving up only one run on six hits, but in his last exhibition outing, against the Yankees on April 13, he was smacked around again, giving up four runs on five hits in five innings.

The 1957 season was a sad and listless one for the Brooklyn Dodgers. The aging squad had become one of baseball's "twilight teams," caught in a kind of suspended animation, waiting to learn what the Dodgers' fate would be. Would they remain in Brooklyn, in a new stadium at some as yet unagreed-on location? Or would the once inconceivable happen—would the Dodgers abandon the borough where they remained baseball's most beloved team? As the weeks and months went on, it slowly became clear that the *Brooklyn* Dodgers were doomed. No amount of protests from fans, no piles of petitions, no eloquent appeals to tradition and loyalty would keep the team in Brooklyn, especially not with Los Angeles beckoning. But regardless of what was going on behind the scenes—and a recent study suggests that New York State parks commissioner and power broker Robert Moses was at least as much to blame as Walter O'Malley for the death of the Brooklyn Dodgers[13] —the team had a season to play, and they played it as best they could. The Dodgers were in first place for all of four days during the first week of the season; after that they sank to second and then third, and for a few dismal days in June even hit fifth place before creaking their way back up to third, where they finished, eleven games behind the pennant-winning Milwaukee Braves.

The Dodgers opened the season in Philadelphia on April 16, where they took 12 innings to defeat the Phillies, 7–6. On April 18 they came home to Brooklyn for Opening Day ceremonies. The weather was chilly and wet, and Ebbets Field was barely one-third full—only 11,202 fans came to watch the pageantry. Assisted by a Marine Color Guard, Walter Alston raised the sixth National League pennant to fly over Brooklyn in the last ten years. Emmett Kelly, the mournful clown who for a brief time found a second career as the "Brooklyn Bum," meandered sadly around the field. He appeared to plant seeds behind home plate, but whatever the intended symbolism, it was lost on the audience.

There was never any doubt who the starter would be in the Dodgers' home opener. Sal Maglie toed the slab for Brooklyn and pitched a superb game, beating the Pirates, 6–1, for his 109th major league win. Pittsburgh scored its only run in the eighth, thanks to two consecutive errors by Don Zimmer, filling in at short for Pee Wee Reese, who had injured his back. Sal threw a complete game, allowing only four hits. A writer for *Sports Illustrated* noted that Maglie had been born 20 days after the United States entered World War I, and that he pitched against a team where many of the players barely remembered World War II. When asked if Zimmer's errors had bothered him, Sal was gentle with the eager little benchwarmer who had tried too hard to fill Reese's shoes. "Hell no," Sal said. "I'm sorry for Zimmer. I know how hard he tries. He's a good ballplayer."[14] (That good ballplayer and self-described baseball "humpty" would still be in the game, serving as a bench coach, into the twenty-first century.) After his initial win, Maglie began to be bothered by a stiff neck. He missed his turn in the rotation and pitched his next game on April 30 against the Cubs at Ebbets Field, as Brooklyn defeated Chicago, 10–9. Sal lasted five and two-thirds innings, giving up five runs on six hits. He issued two walks, struck out one, and hit a batter. He was not involved in the decision.

Between his first two starts Sal turned 40. On his birthday, April 26, his oldest nephew Pat Grenga and his wife Louise welcomed their first child, making Sal a great-uncle. The coincidence delighted Maglie, and years later, when his memory had grown dim, he still remembered Cecilia Grenga, born on his fortieth birthday. A few days before his birthday Sal gave an interview to Murray Robinson of the *Journal-American*.[15] When asked how he felt about turning 40, Maglie answered, "I'm not so sure life begins at 40, but there's no reason why it can't go on at 40. The calendar never killed anybody, even in baseball." He then related to his interviewer how a whole new life had opened up to him when he and his wife adopted their son. In the months before they brought the boy home late in 1955, Sal had been riding the bench in Cleveland, discouraged and disgusted, almost ready to quit baseball. "But then we adopted the baby, and life really began for me. My whole outlook changed. I felt strong, my arm as good as ever. I made up my mind I'd stay in the game no matter what [Indians manager Al] Lopez thought of me—for the baby's sake. I wanted to secure his future." Sal told Robinson he planned on staying in baseball through the 1959 season, as either a pitcher or a coach. "I've got to go through 1959," he explained, "to qualify as a 10–year man for my pension. I have to think of these things because of my family." At that time, a player who had put in 10 years in the majors received a pension of $175 a month. Sal also offered a glimpse of his fierce concentration on baseball: "I don't read anything but the sports page, and I don't have any hobbies outside my profession. Music? I can take it or leave it." The author's report on Maglie's private life offered the usual sanitized details: that Maglie "takes an occasional drink before dinner" (Sal did his heavy drinking after dinner), that he smoked "sparingly" (the first indication that he had not totally given up smoking, as he claimed to have done in 1956), and that he refrained from eating spaghetti during the baseball season, as if the consumption of the one dish Americans considered typically Italian would be the culprit that caused his weight to balloon. Robinson reported that Sal's sole extravagance was his collection of 34 suits. Sal's reputation as an elegant dresser remained intact.

Brooklyn had opened the season strongly, with an 8–3 record for April, but they were in second place. They continued to play well in May, compiling a 15–12 record, but failed to gain any ground on Milwaukee. Sal took the mound again on May 5 at Ebbets Field but lasted just three innings in a game against the Braves. He allowed three runs, only one of them earned, and six hits, before giving way to Bessent, the first of four unsuccessful Dodgers relievers. The Braves won, 10–7, but Sal did not figure in the decision. On May 10 he lost a tough game to the Giants at the Polo Grounds, 2–1. Sal departed after four innings, after giving up six hits and both of the Giants runs, for his first loss. The Giants took two out of three in the series. Still bothered by stiffness in his neck, Sal dropped out of the Dodgers rotation and did not appear in another game until May 25, when he pitched two scoreless innings in relief as the Dodgers defeated the Giants, 8–7. Sal had a good outing on May 30, when he went seven and two-thirds innings against the Pirates, allowing three runs on seven hits and only one walk. The Dodgers won, 4–3, and Sal's record improved to 2–1. The pitcher seemed to be achieving his desired form. But then a series of ailments, none of them major, but in combination enough to disable him, began to plague Sal. The soreness in his neck persisted; his right shoulder hurt; and while shagging fly balls in the outfield in Philadelphia he jammed his right thumb. As a result, he did not pitch in June. The Dodgers did poorly without him, compiling a 14–17 record and ending the month in fourth place.

In early June the National League owners met in Chicago and made a historic decision: they gave both the Dodgers and the Giants league approval to move their franchises—the Dodgers to Los Angeles and the Giants to San Francisco. Previous franchise transfers—the Braves' move from Boston to Milwaukee, the Philadelphia Athletics' to Kansas City, and the St. Louis Browns' to Baltimore where they became the Orioles—did not have such a profound effect. Boston, Philadelphia, and St. Louis could support only one team, and the teams that moved had been in perilous financial shape. Moreover, none moved such a vast distance as the Dodgers and Giants did. Those two teams had played in a huge metropolitan area; the Dodgers were among the most financially successful teams in National League history. They were still prospering when they decided to move, and they moved some 3,000 miles to the opposite side of the country. Although the Dodgers' profit over the years 1952–1956 had been $1.7 million *more* than the Yankees', who played in a stadium better than twice the size of Ebbets Field, the management of both the prosperous Dodgers and the less successful Giants had become convinced that they could profit more if they moved from the congestion, racial tensions, and political squabbles of New York to the burgeoning, beckoning west. With their fate as good as sealed, the Dodgers played out their final season in Brooklyn.

During July, when Sal rejoined the regular rotation, the Dodgers finally caught fire and compiled their best month of the season, wining 20 games while losing only 10. After defeating the Cubs on June 30 and the Giants on July 1, with Don Drysdale hurling a 3–0 shutout in the latter game, Sal Maglie returned to the mound on July 2 to face the Giants. He pitched a superb four-hit shutout, defeating the New Yorkers, 6–0. He issued no walks, hit one batter, and struck out three. No Giants reached third. Despite the month he had lost, Sal's 1957 record of 3–1 put him ahead of where he was in 1956, when he did not post his third victory until July 24.

Sal lost a close game to the Phillies on July 7 due to an embarrassing lapse of concentration of the kind that would never have happened a year or so earlier. Duke Snider hit a line drive to the shortstop in the first inning with a man on first and, thinking the ball had been caught, turned and walked toward the dugout. The astonished but delighted Phils completed a quick double play. Sal lost the game, 2–1, with his record falling to 3–2. The Barber pitched again a week later, on July 14 against the Braves at Ebbets Field, when Gil Hodges hit a two-run blast in the ninth to give Brooklyn a 3–2 win. Sal had left the game in the seventh inning with the score tied, and Johnny Podres picked up the win. On July 19 the Dodgers took a doubleheader from the Cubs. Maglie won the second game, 5–3, although he gave up home runs to Ernie Banks and Bob Speake during his six-inning stint. Maglie lost his third game on July 24, when he went up against the Cardinals' Larry Jackson, who hurled a three-hit shutout. On July 30 Sal enjoyed another excellent outing. Although Labine finished the game for him, Sal allowed no runs on six hits in seven innings, and struck out seven, for a 1–0 victory over the Cubs at Wrigley Field. His record now stood at 5–3.

Even as he was pitching well, Sal began turning his mind to the future. "I Can't Pitch Forever" was the title of an article that appeared under Maglie's byline in the *World Telegram and Sun* in July of 1957. In it, the pitcher explained that, although he hoped to help the Dodgers win another pennant, he was also thinking about his future beyond baseball. Sal was aware of the increasing role television was playing in the lives of Americans. He pointed out that it is easy to tell when a player has had a good season—his image (and sometimes his wife's) will appear in a television commercial. "There I am in one," he reported, "shaving my van Dyck for Remington Rollectric, and there are Kay and other baseball wives endorsing beer. Ball players and other athletes are cheering for cigarettes all over the place."[16] Sal revealed his own recent move to help assure future financial security for his family. He had invested in a soft drink company, inking a business contract with the Johnny Ryan beverage firm in Niagara Falls. As a boy, Sal had been a member of the Johnnie Ryans baseball team, sponsored by the same company. Although the drink was something of a specialized taste in the Niagara Falls area, the company had plans to broaden its base, with an endorsement from Sal Maglie as part of its sales pitch. Sal also noted that he was part owner of a liquor store in Niagara Falls, as well as having an association with Spalding, the sporting goods manufacturer. He appeared to be taking care that, as his career wound down, his financial status would remain secure. Because he and Kay were adopting another child, Sal had further reason to make sure he had sources of income when his baseball career ended. He even had a go at acting, appearing as himself in a television drama called "The Littlest Little Leaguer" about a studious Jewish boy whose family takes him to a game at Ebbets Field in an effort to interest him in a less intellectual pursuit, and as a result the boy becomes a Dodger fanatic.

As the month of August began, the Dodgers were still in third place, but only two games separated them from first. Their excellent play in July had lifted them into pennant contention. After they split the games on August 2 and 3 with the Braves, Maglie faced Milwaukee's Bob Buhl on August 4, with the hope of making it two out of three for Brooklyn and putting the Dodgers within striking distance of first place. But Sal had nothing that day. He lasted only an inning and two-thirds, giving up four runs on five hits, including two home runs, as the Braves won the game, 9–7, and Sal's record dropped to 5–4. The Dodgers slumped badly, losing three of their next four games to the Giants. Drysdale won the first game of the series, but Podres and Newcombe failed to stop New York in the next two. On August 8 it was Sal's turn to try to defeat his old teammates, but they battered him even worse than the Braves had. He failed to survive the first inning, allowing four runs on three hits and giving up two walks in a game where the Giants gave the Dodgers a 12–3 thrashing. The loss dropped Sal's record to 5–5. On August 13 Alston gave Maglie another chance against the Giants, this time at the Polo Grounds. He did a little better, allowing two runs in two and two-thirds innings in a game the Giants won, 4–2. Sal did not receive a decision in the game, but the loss dropped the Dodgers to five games off the pace. The fading veteran redeemed himself in the first game of a double-header with the Pirates on August 18, throwing a six-hitter and winning 2–1. His mound opponent, Bob Friend, threw a two-hitter, but one of those hits was a two-run homer by Duke Snider. Sal pitched a complete game, walked two, and struck out six, to improve his record to 6–5.

The next day, August 19, the New York Giants' board of directors met, and announced that they had voted to move the club to San Francisco for the 1958 season. Horace Stoneham told reporters that the city had agreed to construct a new $5 million stadium and lease it to the team for 35 years at the modest rent of $125,000 per year. The deal was a fine bargain for

Stoneham, who was guaranteed a profit of somewhere between $200,000 and $250,000 per year, in contrast to the $81,000 in profits the Giants took in during 1956. "We're sorry to disappoint the kids," declared Stoneham in answer to a pointed question from a reporter, "but we didn't see many of their parents out there at the Polo Grounds in recent years."[17]

Meanwhile, the Dodgers' season slogged on. They struggled to stay in the race, but this time they did not have a nearly unbeatable Sal Maglie to carry them along. He could no longer be counted on to win the big, late-season games, and he could barely dream of working complete games on three days' rest. Sal started against Milwaukee on August 22. He lasted five innings, giving up four runs on five hits and two walks. Henry Aaron hit a home run in the first, as the Braves defeated the Dodgers, 6–1. Sal's record fell to 6–6, and the Dodgers dropped to 7 1/2 games out of first. Still, The Barber had a few tricks left in his shaving kit. On August 25, just three days after his unsuccessful start, Sal came in from the bullpen in the bottom of the ninth with two out and the bases loaded. He struck out Ken Boyer on three pitches to preserve a 6–5 Dodger win over the Cardinals in the last game the two teams played at Ebbets Field (Figure 20).

20—"Top of the Ninth." In the Dodger bullpen, the future and the past work side by side as Sandy Koufax (left) and Sal Maglie (right) warm up on August 25, 1957, during the last Dodgers-Cardinals game played at Ebbets Field. Photo: Vince Walsh, copyright Ebbets Field Color Photos Inc.

In the Dodgers' front office, team officials concluded that Sal had outlived his usefulness and put him on waivers. The 40-year-old Maglie went to the mound one last time as a Brooklyn Dodger on August 31, appropriately enough against the Giants, in the next-to-last game the Dodgers and Giants played at Ebbets Field. A crowd of more than 23,000 was on hand, but the number was deceiving, since it included Ladies' Day customers and a large contingent of Knothole Gang youngsters. The paid admissions numbered only 14,222. Sal lasted five and two-thirds innings and might have endured longer, but the Giants scored three unearned runs when the Dodgers' normally solid defense crumbled behind the tiring pitcher. In the sixth, with Whitey Lockman on with a single, Reese, who was playing third, muffed a sure double play ball from Valmy Thomas. The ball bounced off his shin for one error, and he then compounded his bobble with a wild throw to second. After Lockman at third scored on a sacrifice fly by Gail Harris, and Maglie walked the next man, Danny O'Connell, Sandy Koufax came in to relieve Sal. At this point the Dodgers went into another defensive doze. When Don Mueller hit a fly to left center, Duke Snider and left fielder Gino Cimoli let it drop between them, scoring Thomas from second. Then, to top off the mess, Gilliam missed Snider's throw to the infield, allowing O'Connell to score all the way from first. Despite ineptness, the Dodgers hung in and won the game, 7–5, as Ed Roebuck held the Giants scoreless in three and one-third innings of relief to take the win. Sal had given up five runs (only two of them earned) on seven hits. Perhaps some small, final shred of the Maglie magic remained—Sal's mysterious ability to so often avoid defeat at Ebbets Field.

In the *Herald Tribune,* Tommy Holmes speculated on whether the fiasco while Sal was on the mound might have affected Maglie's market value, in case the Yankees decided to buy him. He noted that the time limit on a deal that would have left Sal eligible to pitch in the World Series (assuming the Yankees won another pennant) had expired at midnight the previous day. In his partial season with the Dodgers, Sal had pitched only four complete games in 17 starts, for a total of 103 1/3 innings. His ERA was an excellent 2.93 but his record a mediocre 6–6. Buzzie Bavasi knew this was the ideal time to sell Sal, when several teams desperately needed pitching for their pennant drives. The Dodgers' asking price for Maglie was said to be $40,000.

SAL'S 1957 SEASON—THE NEW YORK YANKEES

On September 1, 1957, the New York Yankees bought Sal Maglie from the Dodgers for a reported $25,000 ($37,500 in another report) and two minor league players to be named at a future date. Either price would have brought the Dodgers a sizable return on Bavasi's $100 investment. There were whispers that the Dodgers had deliberately held on to Sal until after the deadline for World Series eligibility had passed, because they were afraid the pitcher might come back to haunt them if, by some remote chance, they won the pennant and had to face the Yankees in the Series. Red Smith, who at times had been less than enthusiastic about Maglie, called his sale to the Yankees an "unconditional surrender" by the Dodgers, saying Brooklyn had conceded the pennant to the Braves when they sold Sal and that the White Sox had surrendered the pennant to the Yankees when they let the sale go through. Brooklyn players complained as well, less from any sentimental attachments than because many still believed Sal could help them win the pennant or at least climb into second place.

In joining the Yankees Sal became the fifteenth and last player to wear the uniform of all three New York teams (Figure 21). The group includes some forgotten figures, but also some of the game's most colorful characters, among them Wee Willie Keeler and spitballer Burleigh Grimes. Three prominent modern managers had also been associated with all three teams: Charlie Dressen had played for the Giants, coached for the Yankees and the Dodgers, and managed the Dodgers; Leo Durocher had played as both a Yankee and a Dodger and had managed the Dodgers and the Giants; and Casey Stengel, manager of the Yankees, had also managed the Dodgers and played for both the Dodgers and the Giants.

Sal took the trade in stride. He had loved playing for the Dodgers, but he understood the realities of baseball life. The Dodgers were rebuilding, and the Yankees were hoping to pick up some pennant insurance in the form of an aging but knowledgeable and skillful hurler who welcomed the opportunity to pitch in the pressure of a pennant race. Few and far between are the ballplayers who object to donning Yankee pinstripes. The Yankees had enjoyed fairly strong pitching in 1957 from Whitey Ford, Tom Sturdivant, Bob Turley, Bobby Shantz, Bob Grim, and Don Larsen, but Shantz was having arm trouble, and Ford had developed shoulder problems, so the Yankees needed another hurler for the last month of the season. As soon as he was informed of the trade, Sal packed up his belongings from his locker at Ebbets Field and drove to Yankee Stadium. He reported to Casey Stengel 10 minutes before game time with a big grin on his face, and asked, "Skipper, when do I work?"[18] He donned the uniform the Yankee clubhouse attendant gave him, with the number 21 on it, and went to the bench. Shortly after the start of the game on September 1 with the Washington Senators, an announcement came over the public address system that Maglie had joined the Yankees. Cheers for the pitcher rang out all over the vast stadium. Yankees fans, who had not watched Sal torment their team year after year as Dodgers fans had when Maglie was with the Giants, accepted Sal immediately. As the cheers

21—Sal manages a smile as he displays his Yankees uniform after the Dodgers sold him to their perennial American League rivals in August of 1957, a day too late for Maglie to be eligible for participation in the World Series. Photo: George Brace.

and applause continued, the modest pitcher needed some urging from his new teammates before he agreed to step out in front of the dugout and tip his cap. He hastily withdrew but later admitted that the reception had moved him deeply. His popularity now transcended his team identification. Over the years Sal the Barber had become a New York legend.

Once again, reporters swarmed around Maglie, wanting his reaction to the trade. Asked how long he expected to last with the Yankees, he replied, "I think that I can pitch for another two years. . . . I was hurt a couple of times [this year], but they weren't the kind of injuries that will hurt me next year." Informed that the White Sox had tried to snatch him away from the Yankees, Sal declared that he would have retired rather than go to Chicago. From his bitter experience in Cleveland, Sal had learned that teams sometimes grab a player not because they want or need him, but merely to prevent another team from having him, and he hoped that was not true of the Yankees. "I didn't pitch for [Cleveland,]" Sal related. "A few relief jobs, yes, but I'm a starter. I have to work regularly." The pitcher was convinced he could continue in the starter role despite his age. "When you're young," he told reporters, "you depend mainly on your arm. . . . As you get older, you depend more on your head—what to throw and where to throw it. That's why I feel that I can still take a turn as a starter every fourth day." Along with the chance to be a starting pitcher on a pennant-contending team, Sal had a further reason to be happy about rejoining the American league. With the Giants moving to San Francisco, every National League team now would have to fly to the West Coast. With no American League teams yet located in the West, flying was an option but was not obligatory. "There wouldn't have been any way out," admitted the flying-phobic pitcher. "I'd have flown, all right, but I wouldn't have liked it!"[19]

Although Stengel did not place Sal in his starting rotation, he put him to work. Between August 30 and September 2 the first-place Yankees had lost four out of five games to second division clubs, but they reversed that downward spiral on September 3, when Tom Sturdivant and Sal Maglie combined to pitch a seven-hit shutout of the Baltimore Orioles. With the Yankees leading 2–0, Sturdivant began the bottom of the ninth by giving up a single, and Stengel replaced him with Maglie. Sal made another of his inauspicious debuts by giving up a second single. But with two on and none out, Maglie then retired the side. It was the tenth shutout of the season by Yankee pitchers but the first that had employed the services of more than one hurler.

Sal's first start as a Yankee came on September 6 against the cellar-dwelling Senators at Griffith Stadium in Washington. About the only team the Senators seemed able to beat regularly was New York. They had taken five of their last six games with the league leaders, and they took this game as well, 4–3, thanks to a costly error by Yankee second baseman Jerry Coleman. Maglie did a fine job for six innings, allowing only one run on four hits, while the Yankees collected three runs. The one run Maglie allowed came in the fifth inning, as the result of a balk. With Bob Usher on base with an infield single, Sal was pitching to Rocky Bridges. He stopped in the middle of his windup, and whirled to throw to first. Usher went to second on the balk, and Bridges then singled him home. When Washington opened fire in the bottom of the seventh with successive doubles that brought in another run, Stengel replaced Maglie with Art Ditmar, who allowed the tying run to score. With the bases loaded and two out in the bottom of the ninth, Milt Bolling hit a routine grounder to third baseman Jerry Lumpe, but second baseman Jerry Coleman dropped Lumpe's throw, allowing the winning run to score. Bob Grim, rather than Maglie, was the losing pitcher.

After the game, Sal admitted to a sense of awe at finding himself in pinstripes. "This time is kind of different from the others," Sal mused about his most recent change of teams. "I mean, it's different being a Yankee."[20]

Stengel gave Maglie another chance as a starter on September 11 at Yankee Stadium against his former teammates, the Cleveland Indians, now languishing in fifth place. It was Sal's first Stadium appearance since October 8, 1956, when he had been the victim of Larsen's perfect game. Facing Early Wynn, Sal responded with a superb three-hit shutout, defeating the Tribe, 5–0, despite suffering from a severe cold. He gave up two hits in the second and did not allow another until the ninth. It was Sal's first American League shutout and the twenty-fifth of his career. Although he fanned only one batter, he tied the Indians in knots with his still potent collection of crackling curves, and he kept them off balance throughout the game with his changeup. On September 14 Sal made another relief appearance, tossing two scoreless innings to preserve a 5–3 victory for Bob Turley over the Kansas City Athletics. Maglie gained his second win as a Yankee on September 18 as the Yankees defeated Detroit, 4–3, at Yankee Stadium. Sal pitched seven and one-third innings, giving up three runs (two earned) on ten hits, and issuing two walks. On September 22 Sal made a successful appearance in relief, retiring two batters as New York beat the Red Sox, 5–1.

As the season drew to a close, Maglie received an invitation to attend a game at the Polo Grounds, not as a player but as a spectator to the last game the New York Giants played at their old ball park. A paltry crowd of 11,606 (above average for the Giants that year) showed up on September 29 to watch the Giants take on the Pirates. Greats and fan favorites from every era of Giants history were in attendance, and announcer Russ Hodges introduced each one at home plate to cheers from the fans. Sal received one of the biggest ovations. He sat with 88–year-old Jack Doyle, the oldest surviving Giant, born just a few years after the end of the Civil War; pitching immortals Carl Hubbell and Rube Marquard; Monte Irvin, the team's first black ballplayer; and "Windowbreakers" Willard Marshall and Sid Gordon. Heading the assemblage was Blanche McGraw, widow of the greatest Giants manager, John McGraw, and a faithful attender of Giants games in the decades since her husband's death. Manager Bill Rigney put as many oldtimers in the lineup as he could. Bobby Thomson and Whitey Lockman, who had recently returned to the team, were on the field, as were Willie Mays, Dusty Rhodes, Don Mueller, and Wes Westrum, with Johnny Antonelli pitching. The Giants were in sixth place that day, and the last-place Pirates defeated them, 9–1. When the game ended the players made a dash for the clubhouse as fans poured onto the field, tearing up and taking away anything they could carry. They made off with telephones and signs; they tore up and carried off home plate, the pitcher's rubber, and the bases, and even gouged out sections of the outfield grass. A few angry types gathered in front of the clubhouse in center field, shouting "Hang Horace!" but their protest did not amount to much. Blanche McGraw was the last person to leave. In tears, she lamented, "I still can't believe it. This would have broken John's heart. New York will never be the same."[21]

A few days before the funeral game at the Polo Grounds, the Dodgers played their final game at Ebbets Field. On September 24 they defeated the Pirates, 2–0, before a pathetic handful of 6,702 Flatbush faithful. The Dodgers staged no special ceremonies, as the Giants had done, because—although the deal with Los Angeles was as good as final—management had made no official announcement that the Dodgers were leaving Brooklyn. Most fans left the park quietly, while a few stood by the gate leading to the Dodger clubhouse with tears streaming down their faces. Others ran onto the field and, like certain Giants fans, tore up whatever they could to keep as souvenirs. In the quiet clubhouse a determinedly cheerful Roy Campanella held a little party for players and sportswriters. And so a unique era in Brooklyn history ended without fanfare, overshadowed by brutal news earlier that same day from Little Rock, Arkansas, where President Eisenhower had ordered out 1,000 federal troops to protect nine black students at Central High School from violent mobs of enraged whites determined to prevent the integration of their school. Major league baseball was integrated, but the racial harmony and equality briefly embodied by the Jackie Robinson Dodgers seemed further away than ever. On October 8, while the World Series was going on, the news everyone in Brooklyn had been dreading came in a statement from the absent Walter O'Malley, handed out to reporters by Dodger publicist Red Patterson. In dry legal language the statement made it official: the Dodgers were moving to Los Angeles. A fan summed up the impact of that move better than any historian: "It wasn't just a franchise shift. It was the total destruction of a culture."[22]

Milwaukee, meanwhile, had captured the National League pennant. The Braves took Stengel's Yankees to seven games, and on October 10 they won the World Series, bringing home a championship for the first time since 1914, when the team was still in Boston. For the first time since 1948, a world championship flag flew west of the Hudson River. All in one season New York had lost the World Series and two of its three baseball teams. The period Roger Kahn later dubbed "The Era—When the Yankees, the Giants, and the Dodgers Ruled the World"—was over. Safely ensconced (for the moment) with the Yankees, the only major league team left in New York, Sal Maglie was a relic of that era. Baseball is sometimes called America's secular religion, but religions revere and preserve their relics. Baseball merely considers them old.

1958–1959—Sunset at the Show

Maglie's Last Year as a Player

18

FINAL WEEKS WITH THE YANKEES

How does a ballplayer know when the end of his career is at hand? There are as many answers as there are ballplayers and body parts that break down, but the short answer is that most players do *not* know, and the end comes as a rude and often devastating shock. Catchers and outfielders claim their legs will tell them when to quit; infielders say their slower reflexes will send the message; sluggers say they will know when they can no longer connect on the fat ones; and pitchers offer a variety of end of the road signs, ranging from sore arms and aching legs to negative reinforcement in the form of hitters belting their best pitches. Detroit Tigers trainer Jack Homel knew Hal Newhouser's days as a pitcher were over when the southpaw started talking about donating his left arm to science.

Many players *say* they will know when to quit, but when the moment comes, few recognize it, and those who do often try their best to ignore it. Some hang on for financial reasons, but many others stay because they cannot imagine any life but baseball. Sal Maglie was one of those players who claimed he would know when to quit, but he did not act on that awareness. Asked by sportswriter Milton Richman, Maglie responded: "I think my arm will outlast my legs. My legs will tell me."[1] That is an odd response from a pitcher who had suffered serious back problems, as well as neck and shoulder trouble, but who had never voiced any complaints about his legs.

Furthermore, Sal was accustomed to ignoring pain until the agony became so acute that it practically paralyzed him. As he moved toward his forty-first birthday, he remained convinced that he could look forward to a few more good years in the Show.

Sal had spent only one month with the Yankees in 1957 and was ineligible to participate in the World Series, but his new teammates voted him a half-share of their World Series money, a generous decision, considering the short time he had spent with the club. After the Series, Casey Stengel claimed he had tried to obtain Sal before the August 31 deadline, but that the National League had blocked the sale. Sal's reputation for ferocity, the threat of his still sharp razor, evidently were enough to make National League officials afraid of the damage he could do in the World Series when pitching for the other side. If true, that is quite a compliment to the 41–year-old hurler. Whitey Ford offered Sal another kind of compliment, disclosing after the Series that Sal's savvy had contributed to his own success. "He helped me more than anybody. He went over the Braves hitters with me and when I got through I felt as if I'd been pitching against them for years," Ford declared.[2]

The Yankees' spring training camp for pitchers began on February 22, but Maglie arrived a couple of days late. Although he had already signed his contract, he had been delayed by obligations concerning his liquor business in Niagara Falls, which was not doing well, as a price war among competing liquor stores had cut into his profits. "How can they do it?" he asked in a worried aside to a reporter. "They're selling the stuff cheaper than I can buy it."[3] Neither Sal nor the Yankees put up impressive numbers during the training season. The team ended with a 14–16 record, and Sal was hit hard, both as a starter and in relief.

As the 1958 season began, the lack of competition from the Dodgers and Giants should have given Yankees attendance a dramatic boost, but it did not. Fans of the two vanished New York teams were no friends of the Yankees and refused to come out and root for the only team in town. Nonetheless, Stengel's ball club tore out of the gate at full speed. The Yankees were in first place by the fourth day of the season and never gave up that spot. Once again, the Yanks were running away with the American League pennant, to such a degree that one disgruntled sportswriter called the rest of the league a seven-club second division. The Yankees had the advantage of strong pitching from all their regulars: Whitey Ford posted the league's top ERA, 2.01, and Bob Turley (21–7) was the league's only 20–game winner. Bobby Shantz, Johnny Kucks, and Don Larsen were also doing well, and the Yankees had additional help from rookie Ryne Duren, a fireballing reliever who terrorized hitters with his wildness. With so much pitching excellence available, the Yankees had little use for Maglie's services, and Sal spent April and early May as a benchwarmer.

On May 12 the Yankees played an exhibition game against the Braves in Yankee Stadium, with the proceeds donated to charity. Unwilling to waste regular starters, Stengel put Maglie into the game. Sal had not pitched in over a month—his last trip to the mound had been on April 9, when he had been knocked around in a spring training game. Aware of the deadline when teams had to cut their rosters down to 25 players—and that he was a leading candidate to be cut—Maglie pitched as if he were in the World Series. In seven innings he allowed only two runs on four hits, walked three, and struck out three. The Barber shaved enough chins to convince the Braves his razor was still sharp. After keeping the world champions guessing for seven innings, he turned the game over to Johnny Kucks, who gave up two runs, as the Braves pulled out a 4–3 win.

Sal finally received an opportunity to start on May 18, in a game against the Senators in Washington. Sal had turned 41 on April 26, making him one of the oldest men in the majors. Maglie pitched another strong game, lasting eight innings in a 5–2 Yankee win in the opening game of a double-header. As he often did, Sal faltered at the start, giving up a run in the first. He gave up another in the bottom of the fifth, but that was after he had helped his own cause in dramatic fashion by smacking a three-run homer in the top of that same inning, the second and last round-tripper of his career. With two runs in, one out, and runners on second and third, Senators pitcher Pedro Ramos felt safe in pitching to Maglie. But he made the mistake of grooving one, and Sal parked it in the bleachers, providing his own margin of victory.

Maglie's next start came on May 24, in a game in Detroit against the last-place Tigers. Sal pitched a good game but lost, 3–2. The defeat ended the Yankees' 10–game winning streak, as well as the Tigers' nine-game losing streak. A one and one-half inning fragment of that game is the oldest regular season play-by-play baseball action that exists on film.[4] It is also the only extended visual record of Maglie's pitching. All other films of him on the mound provide only glimpses, but this sequence shows him throwing almost two full innings, unfortunately at the end of his career rather than at the height of his powers. The film fragment begins with one out in the bottom of the second, New York leading 1–0, and Detroit's Reno Bertoia at bat, with Charlie Maxwell on second and Al Kaline on third. Kaline had beaten out a bunt, Maxwell had walked, and Ray Boone had sacrificed the runners to second and third. Announcer Mel Allen commented that Sal's control was off that day, but that crafty and experienced hurlers like Maglie "can often get by on pitching savvy on days they don't have their stuff." With the count at 2–2, Bertoia beat a little worm-killer into the grass between the mound and first base. Both Maglie and first baseman Bill Skowron charged after the ball, but Maglie scooped it up, then found nobody covering first, so he raced over to make the putout himself, tagging Bertoia on the face as he tried to avoid the tag by sliding. Kaline scored on the fielder's choice. Mission accomplished, Sal turned and walked nonchalantly back to the mound.

The account of the game by *Times* sportswriter John Drebinger, who presumably was present, overdramatized the play and makes one wonder how many other plays in other games were jazzed up by writers as a way of holding their readers' interest. In the *Times,* usually a source of sober sports reporting, Drebinger described Maglie as making the putout on Bertoia "with a headlong dive," although no such dive appears in the film. The writer then stated that Maglie "picked himself up [and] appeared badly shaken." Since Sal did not fall, he did not have to pick himself up (Bertoia was the one on the ground), and although his heart was no doubt pounding from his sudden burst of exertion, the pitcher gave no evidence of being badly shaken up. Sal walked the next batter but then Detroit pitcher Frank Lary grounded out to end the inning.

Nonetheless, plays like the one involving Bertoia can be rough on a 41-year-old. Sal was the first man up in the top of the third. He schlepped to the plate and slumped there like an advertisement for the designated hitter, shoulders sagging, abdomen protruding, the bat lolling on his shoulder, as if his arms were too weary to hold it upright. But he was not indifferent to his turn at bat. He took a called strike, then checked his swing on the next pitch, correctly judging it to be a ball. He swung and missed on the third, for strike two, let ball two go by, and then took a solid swing and fouled one off before ending his at bat with a clumsy lunge, for strike three.

The film also records Sal's repertory of mound fidgets. Sportswriters often commented on how long Sal took between pitches, and the film shows why. On each pitch he went through an elaborate routine of touching his fingers to his mouth, picking up and dropping the rosin bag, wiping his fingers on his shirt front, touching the bill of his cap, slipping his glove down onto his wrist, and rubbing up each new ball. Sal's delivery had never featured a high leg kick—he was no Warren Spahn or Juan Marichal—but by May of 1958, suffice it to say that if he were a dog he would not have been able to lift his leg high enough to water a fire hydrant. He seemed slow and stiff, barely able to get through his wind-up, appearing to push the ball toward the plate rather than hurling it, and in the bottom of the third several Tigers hit him hard.

The first man up, Detroit's slick-fielding second baseman Frank Bolling, took a sidearm fastball for strike one, fouled off the second pitch, and then smashed a drive down the left field line that went foul by inches. Sal decided it was time to send the cocky youngster a message. Only once in the filmed sequence of innings did the old Barber flash his razor, and that was on his next pitch to Bolling, who jumped back, jackknifing away from the fastball that buzzed his chin and falling to the ground. When he stood in again, he hit a harmless pop to Mantle in shallow center for the first out. After former Yankee Billy Martin grounded out, Detroit slugger Harvey Kuenn smacked a home run into the upper left deck to give Detroit a 2–1 lead. Al Kaline followed with a sharp single to left, and Charlie Maxwell cracked Maglie's first pitch for a double, putting runners on second and third. Al Ditmar began warming up in the Yankee bullpen, and Yogi Berra trotted out to the mound to talk with Sal. They issued the next batter, Ray Boone, an intentional pass, bringing up Reno Bertoia, who hit a sharp drive to Jerry Lumpe at third for the third out. As Sal walked slowly back to the dugout, Phil Rizzuto, who had become a Yankees announcer, commented: "You never see Sal get excited. He takes things in stride, which is the mark of a true champion." Detroit picked up another run off Sal in the seventh. He left the game for a pinch hitter in the eighth, and Ditmar finished, pitching two scoreless innings. But Frank Lary made the Tigers' margin hold up and pitched a complete game for the victory. Sal's record was now 1–1.

On May 27 the Yankees lost to the Kansas City Athletics, another of the league's weaker teams, and on the following night the A's won again, defeating the Yankees, 4–3. Sal pitched two scoreless innings of relief. The Yankees dropped a doubleheader to another inferior team, the Washington Senators, on May 30, for their fourth straight defeat. The Yankees lost the opener, 13–8. Maglie was the fifth Yankee pitcher in that game, and he failed to stop the bleeding, as he allowed two runs on three hits in an inning and one-third. On June 5 the Yankees split a doubleheader with the White Sox, taking the opener, 12–5. Sal pitched one inning of scoreless relief in the second game, but the White Sox rallied to win it, 3–2. The Yankees dropped both ends of a doubleheader with the Indians on June 8, the first by the embarrassing score of 14–1. The second game was closer, 5–4, but Maglie proved ineffective as a starter, allowing four runs on five hits and two walks in three innings of work. Johnny Kucks took the loss. In another doubleheader on June 12, against the Kansas City A's, the Yankees lost the first game, 4–1, with Maglie contributing an inning of scoreless relief, and notched a 3–2 win in the second contest.

On June 14, after the resurgent Detroit Tigers had beaten the Yankees, 5–4, Casey Stengel called Maglie into his office to tell him that he had been sold to the St. Louis Cardinals. The Yankees announced the sale to the press the same day, stating that the Cards had paid slightly more than the waiver price of $20,000. Sal had made only three starts and pitched only 23 1/3 innings for

22—Passed on to the St. Louis Cardinals by the Yankees in 1958, Maglie assumes a pitching pose. Photo: George Brace.

the Yankees. His record was an undistinguished 1–1, and his ERA a poor 4.70. According to news reports, Sal took the news calmly, although when he learned that the Yankees had shunted him aside to make room for 39–year-old pitcher Virgil Trucks, he displayed some anger. "I knew all along the Yankees were going to let me go at cut-down time," Sal admitted. "But I was astonished to learn they had acquired [Trucks] to replace me. I can do a better job than he can. . . . And just wait til I start pitching for St. Louis. I'll prove to the Yankees they made a big mistake," he exclaimed to reporters.[5] Before joining his new team Sal took a couple of days off to move his family back to Niagara Falls, where he also needed to tend to some dental work, and an unspecified income tax problem. When he reported to the Cardinals on June 19, Sal had reached his last stop as a major league ballplayer (Figure 22).

BEHIND THE SCENES

The most difficult time in a baseball star's life is not at the beginning, the years of obscurity and hardship and striving as he struggles to reach the top, but near the end, when he is struggling to keep from hitting bottom. His goal is merely to survive another season in the game that has dominated his life. The stresses associated with the end of a player's career can be overwhelming, and they rarely bring out the best in the men experiencing them. Jovial and talkative players turn surly and uncommunicative, while silent types retreat into even deeper silences. Others take out their fears on rookies, becoming resentful and critical of younger players they know are intent on taking their places. Some begin drinking heavily, or if already barroom regulars, slide into alcoholism. Gamblers spend more time at the card tables or playing the ponies. Men who were reasonably faithful husbands turn into compulsive womanizers, seeking in bedroom athletics the affirmations they no longer find on the field. At a time of life when most men are reaching their prime, major league baseball players face professional oblivion. Age is writ large and with pitiless clarity on ballplayers; the decline of their skills happens in public, and no place in baseball is more public than the pitcher's mound.

Although Maglie had already stated in a 1957 article that he knew he could not pitch forever, he convinced himself that his time in the Show was not over yet and that he could squeeze a few more years out of his worn-out right arm. Why would he want to? Financial worries may have played a part, since none of Sal's investments had paid off, and some had resulted in the loss of considerable sums. His liquor store, as noted above, was losing money. Sal's old friends are unanimous in remembering him as a hopelessly poor businessman. Joe Calato, owner of a prosperous manufacturing company, recalled that certain friends of Sal's "got him into this and that; he was losing money all over the place." Another of Sal's friends, Jimmy Briganti, noted how some of Sal's friends and business acquaintances took advantage of Maglie's trusting nature in order to involve him in dubious schemes. "He never held that against his friends, though. He was a warm, generous person—maybe too generous," Briganti concluded. Benny Critelli, a friend of Sal's since childhood, recalled a notorious financial fiasco known among the old gang as "the onion deal." Some friends, again unnamed, convinced Sal to invest in an onion farm. "Somebody came through selling futures on onions," Benny recalled. "They said if you invest $5,000—well anyway, they pulled the rug out from under them— the ones who sold them the futures. Sal was in a lot of businesses. People took advantage of him. They used his name. He was always more of an athlete than a businessman." Jimmy Macri, another old friend and owner of a successful restaurant, was even blunter: "Sal was always too trusting. It wasn't just that some of his friends involved him in unsuccessful businesses. They robbed him. *They robbed him blind!*"[6]

But money alone was not enough to keep Sal in baseball beyond the point where he should have seen that he was at the end of the road. Although a modest man, Maglie nonetheless had an ego, and for much of his life he had been a star. As far back as high school he had been an athletic hero, with girls crowding around asking for his autograph and glowing reports of his basketball prowess in the local press. For most of the past 15 years he had been a baseball star, acclaimed in Cuba, Mexico, and Canada, as well as in the major leagues. Unlike many stars, who become bored and impatient with signing autographs and the myriad other forms of attention and invasions of privacy that fame brings, Sal never minded any of that. He was not like Ted Williams, who craved fame but resented and rejected its consequences. Sal enjoyed being famous and was not eager to exchange fame for has-been status.

It is not unusual for a ballplayer to turn to alcohol as a means of drowning anxieties about the approaching end of his career. Like all but a very few ballplayers, Maglie enjoyed drinking. He had grown up in an Italian household, so he was used to consuming wine, and he knew how to hold his liquor. There are no anecdotes that report or even hint at Sal getting out of hand or abusive as a result of drinking. Nonetheless, there is evidence that Sal's drinking increased during his last seasons in the majors. The Yankee teams of the late 1950s harbored some legendary boozers, so on road trips Sal found himself in the company of men for whom heavy drinking was routine. He went out with Mickey Mantle, Whitey Ford, Eddie Lopat, and others known to down a few, and introduced them to the pleasures of his own favorite drink, an extra-dry martini, which—the way Maglie liked it made—is a glass of straight gin over vermouth-bathed ice cubes.[7] Clearly, Sal had no trouble keeping up with his drinking companions.

One area where a once-celebrated ballplayer nearing the end of his career is particularly vulnerable is in his marriage. For as long as there has been baseball there have been women who make themselves available to ballplayers, but the insecurities that surface at the end of a player's career make him more vulnerable to the siren songs. The 1950s was a more sexually conservative era than subsequent decades, and players' dalliances more discreet, but baseballing was no less common. Carol Decker, who in the 1950s worked as a waitress in one of the bars in Vero Beach, near the Dodgers' training camp, recalled that most of the players were married but that their married status failed to slow them down. Local girls swarmed around the players, vying for their attentions. "My God," she exclaimed, "it was a feather in your cap if you had a Dodger!"[8] One could extend that observation to every major league team.[9]

Despite obvious and copious evidence to the contrary, in the 1950s sportswriters presented ballplayers to the public as clean-cut paragons of virtue and marital fidelity and made it a rule not to write about players' sexual adventures.[10] Some even denied that such activity existed. The problem, according to one indignant male author of the era, lay not with the ballplayers, but with women: the aggressive temptresses who threw themselves at these poor, innocent fellows at every turn. The writer warned that ballplayers had to be protected from scheming, dangerous females. "They can't afford to have their futures ruined by silly, sex-crazed girls parading around making idols of men who happen to be in the public eye," the reporter huffed.[11] Nonetheless, the players were hardly innocent, put-upon paragons of virtue, trying to maintain their vows of on-the-road celibacy and marital fidelity. Many players, then as now, were more than happy to sample the sexual smorgasbord offered them wherever they went.

Players nearing the end of their careers often find that women offer a badly needed reassurance no longer available to them on the field. Roger Kahn, who in the 1950s had refused to write about players' sexual activities, later published a story about pitcher Early Wynn near the end of his career, terrified of facing the rest of his life and desperate to escape his fears through sex and alcohol. Kahn recalled that after losing to the Yankees, Wynn "wanted a woman." The helpful sportswriter arranged a date, but it fizzled when Wynn behaved crudely. Hours later, in a Greenwich Village nightclub, he collapsed in tears, admitting his career was over. Kahn gently reminded Wynn that he was 40 years old and that he must have known this was going to happen. In naked despair the pitcher sobbed, "But now it's *happening!*"[12]

Although Sal Maglie held no tearful sessions of soul-baring with reporters, it was *"happening"* to him as well, and his private behavior seems to have changed during his time with the Yankees. Before then, Sal had no reputation as a woman-chaser. Although he was not a puritanical blue nose—he once informed the young Roger Kahn that "English girls are all frigid," leading one to wonder what experiences led him to that conclusion—he was not a playboy pitcher of the Don Larsen and Johnny Podres stripe.[13] Still, Sal was tall, dark, and dangerous-looking and had always exerted a powerful attraction for women. "Gorgeous Gussie" Moran, a tennis player of the 1950s as famous for her beauty and daring court outfits as her playing prowess, listed Maglie among her "Ten Most Exciting Men in Baseball," a ranking based purely on the players' sex appeal.[14] If from time to time in his earlier years Sal took advantage of what women offered him, he did not brag about it. One should keep in mind, however, that most players from the

'50s still observe a strict code of silence on that subject, whatever their own private behavior may have been. Faithful husbands do not tell tales about unfaithful ones. And even long after their careers have ended, the womanizers keep quiet about their postgame games and would rather die than rat out a fellow philanderer. Information often appears indirectly, in some other context, such as when Don Newcombe, still bristling decades later at the racial prejudice and insults he endured in the 1950s, took defiant note of the number of women back then, both black and white, who eagerly shared his bed.[15] There are also players who blurt simple amazement at a teammate's sexual shenanigans. A broad hint about Maglie's sexual behavior during his time with the Yankees comes from his roommate Bill Skowron. During an informal conversation, Skowron is reported to have recalled Sal in a way that brings to mind Babe Ruth, saying that on road trips Maglie was so often out all night with women that he felt like he was rooming with Sal's suitcase.[16] Although it is unlikely that Maglie engaged in the perpetual round-robin of bedroom adventures attributed to Babe Ruth, his promiscuity was noteworthy enough for Skowron to remember it decades later.

An incident previously tucked away under Family Secrets also sheds light into this dark corner of Maglie's life. Although the specifics remain uncertain, there is no reason to believe the story is fabricated, since its source is Sal's wife Kay.[17] At some point in the late 1950s, Sal had a brief affair that resulted in the woman claiming Sal had made her pregnant. The most likely time and place for this to have occurred would be during Sal's stint with the Yankees. He realized his position there was tenuous, which would have added an edge of desperation to his life that was less overt but no less intense than the one Roger Kahn witnessed during his evening with Early Wynn. Furthermore, Sal was spending time with a group of teammates notorious for their heavy drinking and flagrant womanizing.

For any ballplayer of Sal's era, but for a married one in particular, a pregnant woman accusing him of fathering her child was a nightmare on a par with a crippling injury. Both could be career-enders. Such disputes generally dissolved into heated and sordid she-says-he-did, he-says-he-didn't debates. Between the late 1940s and the early 1950s three members of the Brooklyn Dodgers, all of them pitchers—Hank Behrman, Hugh Casey, and Billy Loes—became entangled in paternity suits, and Dodgers management lost no time in trading them away.[18] None of their careers ever recovered. In Sal's case, the issue never reached the ears of management or anyone else connected with the team, but it was resolved in a brutal way that left nobody involved looking good, except for Sal's extraordinarily loyal and loving wife.

Sal responded to the woman's accusation with disbelief and outrage. Evidently the affair had been a fleeting one, probably a couple of nights with a

Baseball Annie—and Sal had no reason to believe he was any more likely to be the father than any other ballplayer. He was furious that the woman had singled *him* out. Fuming over what he regarded as the unfairness of the situation, Sal confided his problem to some Niagara Falls buddies. Happy to help their famous friend, they offered to "take care of it" by making sure the woman had an abortion, although at the time abortion was illegal and took place under furtive and often appalling conditions. Sal agreed to turn the matter over to his eager friends. Their idea of solving Sal's problem was to get hold of a couple of local thugs, then send them off to confront the woman and "escort" her to the nearest abortionist. In that era, it was often the sleaziest characters who knew where to find the abortion providers.

Somehow, Kay Maglie found out about the situation. No one, least of all Sal, was prepared for her response. Unhappy, hurt, and angry as she was when faced with irrefutable evidence of her husband's infidelity, she nonetheless grasped at the chance to acquire a second baby, this one actually fathered by Sal. The adoption application the couple had filed might take years to provide them with another child, but now they could add to their family in just a few months' time. Instead of confronting her husband with threats of divorce, she begged him to tell the woman to have the baby and to assure her that he and Kay would then adopt the child. A much more devout Catholic than her husband, Kay was horrified that Sal would even consider pushing the woman to have an abortion, especially when the situation presented them with such a perfect chance for a private adoption. But Sal refused his wife's pleas. Although he admitted to the affair, he insisted the child was not his or that there was no guarantee that it was, and he wanted no reminder of the humiliating experience of having been caught in such sordid circumstances.

If the woman were to have the child and hand it over to the Maglies, the risks of such an arrangement are obvious. Along with the uncertainties involved in private adoptions, there is the issue of inherited resemblances. Suppose the child really was Sal's and turned out to be what the Irish call the "dead spit" of its father? People both in and outside the Maglie and Pileggi families would notice and whisper their speculations about the child's paternity. But as it turned out, the woman was not pregnant. Confronted by the threatening characters Sal's friends had sicced on her, the frightened woman admitted to fabricating the pregnancy story in the hope of extorting money from Sal, a cynical ploy that has been used on more than one straying baseball husband.

And so the unhappy situation dissolved and disappeared, and the episode remains the closest Sal ever came to biological fatherhood. His marriage withstood the impact, largely due to Kay's determination. Like most baseball wives, she had long ago learned that putting up with on-the-road philander-ing was part of the unwritten contract that came with being married to a baseball star.[19] She may have been further helped in coping by the sensible distinction Italians often make between fidelity and loyalty, where a man is not necessarily expected to be faithful to his wife as long as he remains loyal to her and does not break up his family by desertion or divorce. If there was one thing Kay could be sure of, it was that Sal would never abandon her and their son. The couple buried the painful episode and went on with their lives.

LAST STOP—THE ST. LOUIS CARDINALS

When he came to the Cardinals from the Yankees, Sal went from a fabled champion team firmly in first place to a second-division club stumbling along in fifth place. The team's single superstar was Stan Musial, who achieved his 3,000th hit during the 1958 season and who received the Na-tional League's only $100,000 salary. The relatively weak St. Louis pitching staff included Sam "Toothpick" Jones (14–13), Larry Jackson (13–13), Wilmer "Vinegar Bend" Mizell (10–14), Lindy McDaniel (5–7), and reliever Jim Brosnan (8–4). Sal might prove an asset in such a group. He felt a rap-port with Cardinals manager Fred Hutchinson, a former pitcher who imme-diately placed Sal in his starting rotation. On June 22, within three days of his joining the team, Sal was on the mound against Milwaukee. He pitched seven strong innings, gaining a 2–1 victory. Along with the single run, he gave up five hits and a worrisome five walks, while striking out one. His was the second victory in what became a six-game Cardinal winning streak that lifted the team from fifth to second place. Sal pitched again on June 28 against the Phillies and tossed a complete game five-hitter, defeating the Phils, 8–1. Now only 1 1/2 games behind the Braves, the Cards looked like strong pennant contenders, and Maglie appeared to be an important part of the St. Louis surge. But that game was Sal's last major league victory.

In early July the Cardinals flew to the West Coast to play the transplanted Dodgers and Giants. On July 3 the Cards and Dodgers split a doubleheader. St. Louis took the first game, 4–2, with Sam Jones picking up the win, but Sal Maglie lost the night game, 3–2, although he did not pitch badly. He lasted eight innings, gave up three runs (two earned) on seven hits, walked three, and struck out four. Sal's defeat was the beginning of a four-game los-ing streak for the Cardinals that included two successive defeats by the Gi-ants. Home in St. Louis on July 10, Sal faced the Phillies. They bombarded him and a succession of other Cardinals pitchers for a 13–3 win that pushed the Cards down into third place. Sal took the loss, allowing five runs on four hits and a disturbing total of six walks in three and two-thirds innings.

Throughout his career, Sal could always baffle hitters with his assortment of slow stuff and "junk," but without his pinpoint control, he was ineffective. Manager Fred Hutchinson understood Maglie's eagerness to continue pitching, and for lack of anyone better, he kept Sal in the starting rotation, even as his effectiveness diminished. Milwaukee defeated Sal, 4–1, on July 15. He lasted five innings and gave up all four of the Braves' runs, on five hits. His record fell to 2–3.

Shortly after his defeat on July 15, a family crisis occurred that caused Sal to hurry home. Kay had not accompanied her husband to St. Louis—the first time she had not followed him to wherever his career took him—but after Sal's sale to the Cardinals, she had returned with their son to Niagara Falls. Kay had been diagnosed with breast cancer, and had to undergo immediate surgery. In the 1950s cancer was literally unspeakable, so neither the local newspaper accounts of Kay's surgery nor Sal's later memoir specify the nature of her illness. The surgery was supposed to be a simple one to remove the tumor, but instead a mastectomy was necessary. "They took her breast," said Kay's brother John Pileggi, as if describing robbery rather than surgery.[20] Although Sal implied in his memoir that he rushed to his wife's bedside, according to Kay's family, he did not arrive until a day or so after the operation was over. Kay's sister-in-law Mary Pileggi was at Kay's bedside when she came out of the anesthesia. Mary described Kay as "devastated, *devastated*" by the unexpected outcome of the surgery.[21] The few family members who knew the nature and extent of Kay's surgery kept it concealed, both from public knowledge and even from other family members. Sal, according to his sister-in-law, was reassuring and compassionate toward his wife's distress. He stayed with Kay for two weeks, then on July 29 he rejoined the Cardinals, who were playing in Philadelphia.

Sal had been completely inactive for two weeks, and he found it impossible to whip his body back into condition. The Cardinals were faltering as well. When Sal had last pitched, in mid-July, St. Louis was only 3 1/2 games out of first place, but when he rejoined the team, the Cards were 7 games out and in the middle of an eight-game losing streak that would plunge them into last place. The Pirates strangled the Cards four times in a series that opened the month of August and included three consecutive shutouts. Maglie was the victim of the third of them, in the opening game of a doubleheader on August 3. He gave up only two runs on four hits and issued no walks in six innings, before being removed for a pinch hitter. The loss dropped his record to 2–4. Sal pitched another hard luck game on August 9 against the Cubs at Wrigley Field. Again he gave up only two runs on four hits, this time in seven innings, but a ninth inning home run by Curt Flood won the game for Chicago, 3–2. Sal was not involved in the decision.

The Cardinals managed to haul themselves out of the cellar, and for a few days in mid-August they held on to fourth place. But then they lost to the Giants on August 14 and fell into fifth, where they pretty much remained for the rest of the season. On August 15 the Cards dropped both ends of a doubleheader to the Dodgers in Los Angeles. Larry Jackson lost the first game, 4–3, and Maglie dropped the second, 5–3, bringing his record to 2–5. He lasted only four innings, allowing five runs on five hits, along with one walk and a hit batsman, Charlie Neal. The Dodger second baseman was the forty-fourth and final batter Maglie hit in his major league career. It is difficult to believe that those last few plunks were deliberate, since Sal's control had been slipping throughout the 1958 season, but on the other hand, he had a reputation to maintain. He was pitching meaningless games for a fifth-place team, so perhaps he thought it was worthwhile to put a man on base, to inform batters that they still had to pay for crowding the plate on The Barber.

After more than a week of idleness, Maglie took the mound again on August 23 against the Phillies in St. Louis. This time he was whacked, giving up three runs on three hits, and recording only one out in the first inning before being removed. The Cards lost, 4–2, and Sal's record dropped to 2–6. Still, Fred Hutchinson was not ready to give up on the stubborn old veteran. He gave Sal one last start on August 31, against the Cubs, a team Sal used to have eating out of his hand. Not any longer. Cubs hitters teed off on him for three homers in the three innings he pitched and went on to win the game, 8–5. Although Sal did not receive the loss, he gave up five runs (two earned) on four hits, walked two, struck out one, and committed an error. When he left the mound that day, he had thrown his final pitch in a regular season major league game. He warmed the bench for the rest of the season, watching the Cardinals plod to a fifth-place finish, 20 games behind the Braves, who won their second straight pennant. This time, after being down 3 games to 1, the Yanks came back and won the World Series. Although the Yankees had released Sal in mid-June, his old teammates generously granted him a half-share of their Series-winning money, the last such winner's windfall of his life.

A SHORT SEASON—SPRING TRAINING 1959

When Sal reported to the Cardinals' spring training camp in St. Petersburg, Florida, in February of 1959, he reported to a new manager. Fred Hutchinson had been replaced by Solly Hemus, a former utility infielder of mediocre ability six years Sal's junior, known for his loud mouth and racist attitudes. Hemus' repeated use of racial slurs soon alienated a proud and prodigiously talented black rookie righthander named Bob Gibson. Not surprisingly, Maglie noticed Gibson's blazing fastball and took an interest in the young man.[22] Like Don Drysdale, Gibson would carry Maglie's intimidating pitching philosophy into the next decade. Still determined that his career would continue for another year so he would become eligible for a pension, Sal reported to spring training vowing a comeback. He had absorbed another substantial pay cut, although not the maximum 25 percent. His salary was estimated at about $28,000. St. Louis general manager Bing Devine told the press he had sent Maglie a letter explaining the pay cut but assuring the veteran hurler that he still had confidence in his ability to return to form. "I deserved it," Sal admitted, referring to the trimming of his salary, "but I'm looking forward to next season. . . . My arm and my back feel fine."[23]

Regardless of how he felt, or said he felt, Sal was among the oldest players in the majors, one of only eight active players over 40. Red Smith, watching Maglie work out under the hot Florida sun in the company of youngsters not even born when he first became a professional pitcher, wrote a column that reads like an elegy. In one of the odder comparisons concerning Sal's appearance, the noted columnist who had never quite warmed up to Sal remarked that Maglie "looks like a Roman friar in one of those orders that specializes in jumping on grapes or maybe illuminating the parchment pages of sacred writings. There is an old testament cast to the elongated visage with the deep and mournful eyes. The hair, thinning a trifle more noticeably with each passing year, makes way now for a monk's gleaming tonsure behind two dark tufts which top the lofty brow." Smith went on to note that the gentle, monk-like appearance vanished the moment Maglie stepped onto the pitcher's rubber. "What the batter sees is a tall figure of menace, expressionless as an executioner, who throws too close."[24] He might have been describing Maglie almost a decade earlier. In appearance at least, The Barber's menace remained intact, but it was an illusion that would soon be shattered.

A remarkable record of Maglie's last days, and even his last minutes, in the majors appears in the journal kept by pitcher Jim Brosnan during his 1959 season. Published as *The Long Season,* this literate and insightful work contains two sections devoted to Maglie: one describes Sal's arrival at the Cardinals' spring training camp, and the other details the disastrous exhibition game that ended Sal's career. With bemused humor, warmth, and compassion, and without a trace of condescension or cruelty, Brosnan catches the poignancy of Maglie's final, futile struggle to hang on just a little longer.

Brosnan recalled Maglie's arrival in the Cardinals' clubhouse in St. Petersburg on February 24, the beginning of spring training for pitchers. It seemed to Brosnan that the veteran pitcher knew everybody. Sal walked down the aisle between the lockers, shaking hands right and left, and Brosnan was thrilled when Maglie greeted him. For him, Sal was still a celebrity,

a baseball legend. He noted, as so many had before him, the contrast between Maglie's appearance and his personality. "Sal is not a pleasant-look-
ing man—he looks like an ad for the Mafia," Brosnan observed, employing
the familiar Italian gangster image, "but he has a nature that transforms his
face in the light of any friendship."[25] When the admiring Brosnan asked Sal
how he was feeling, the veteran confided a complaint that he did not offer
to sportswriters: "Well, I tell you, driving down here . . . I felt my back going stiff on me. Feels like pleurisy, or something." Later, as they ambled
across the outfield, Maglie groaned to Brosnan, "This gets harder all the
time. . . . If I didn't have to work to eat, I don't think I could take it."[26]

A month later, Brosnan returned to Maglie in his journal, recording in
vivid detail the veteran pitcher's last appearance on a major league mound.
The game took place on Sunday, March 29, with the Cards facing the
Phillies. After rookie righthander Ernie Broglio had taken his turn, and with
the Cardinals holding a 3–2 lead, Sal came in to pitch the seventh. Brosnan
noted the big ovation Sal received when his name was announced but also
soon noticed that Maglie was hanging his curve. Although he gave up a
walk and a single, Sal wormed out of the inning without allowing any runs.
"Can't get my rhythm," he gasped to Brosnan on the bench. "I'm wild high
and can't get my breaking stuff where I want."[27] The younger man observed
that Sal was already sweating heavily and looked as if he had pitched seven
innings, instead of only one. Nobody, rookie or veteran, wanted to witness
the spectacle of a disintegrating Sal Maglie, for none wanted to acknowledge
that they would someday be where he was, sitting alone on a dugout bench,
soaked in flop-sweat, and staring at the end of their dreams. But Brosnan
watched. Sensing the desperation, the tension of Sal's tightly strung nerves,
he noted, "When a pitcher starts doubting his own stuff, he prays for an
easy inning. He needs one."[28]

But there were no easy innings left for Sal Maglie. In the eighth, he gave
up one run, and then Philadelphia loaded the bases. Sal was no longer the
smooth, imperturbable craftsman Brosnan had once loved to watch. He was
still trying though, determined to the end, shuffling through his repertory
of pitches, mixing his stuff—a curve, then a fastball, a slider on the hands,
or a slow curve change-up, a final flash of his rusty razor for a brushback.
But the Phillies were hitting him no matter what he threw. With the bases
loaded, pinch-hitter Dave Philley smashed a high fastball over the right field
fence for a grand slam. Before Sal finally ended the agonizing inning, he
gave up another home run with a man on, for a total of seven runs. With
those runs went the ball game (the Phillies won it, 9–5), and any hope Sal
had of remaining with the team. After the game, Brosnan walked to the
parking lot with Sal and watched the weary pitcher getting into "his big

spotless Cadillac," that gleaming symbol of his years of major league stardom. Sal was still not ready to give up. "I need more work," he told Brosnan. "I have to be sharper than that. Think I'll ask Solly if I can pitch some batting practice."[29]

But St. Louis did not consider Sal worth retaining. After his disastrous outing, manager Solly Hemus washed his hands of the veteran pitcher. "I'm afraid The Barber has had it," Hemus told reporters, "and it's a shame for two reasons. He has been a great competitor, a great pitcher, and we could use the protection of a skilled veteran." Having paid Sal the conventional compliments, Hemus reached his real reason for getting rid of Maglie: "Where possible, though, I'd like to go with the younger fellows who have a future."[30] Hemus' last remark summed it up: Sal no longer had any future—only a past. A few days later the Cardinals handed Maglie his unconditional release. There were rumors that he might catch on with some other team as a spot starter, but this time, when Sal was put on waivers, no club in either league wanted him. Cardinals general manager Bing Devine offered Maglie a position with the St. Louis farm system, a vaguely defined combination of coaching and scouting designed to provide the veteran with a tenth year of employment in the majors, and to make him eligible for his pension. Sal initially showed little interest, because he thought the job entailed too much traveling, but even more importantly, because he thought he could still pitch. "I don't think I'm all through. I'm ready to give it one more whirl," the stubborn veteran insisted.[31]

Sal delayed responding to the offer from the Cardinals. He hung around for a while, staying in a motel in St. Petersburg. "I don't know what I'm going to do," Sal admitted to a reporter. "They tell me I can coach minor leaguers, but I'm used to doing things myself, not showing other guys." Sal pleaded with whoever in baseball management might be reading his words, "I'll relieve, I'll start, I'll play it any way they want." He turned to point at his motel room telephone. "But right now there's nothing I can do except wait for that phone to ring, and hope."[32] And so he settled into a hopeful holding pattern, waiting for the phone calls that never came. At last, Sal more or less accepted that his pitching career was over. On April 13 he came to terms with the Cardinals, who had left their offer open, and accepted a position as traveling pitching coach and scout for their minor league farm system. "It's a new job for the Cardinals and they haven't ironed out all the details as yet," Sal said. The job was indeed new—the St. Louis organization had invented it just for him. "My job will be to work with all the pitchers in their farm system. I'll drop off at a club, check with the manager on how his pitchers are going, and work with the younger hurlers."[33] But Sal still harbored hopes that he might continue to pitch. After telling another reporter,

"I like to work with the kids, and I think I can teach them a lot," with his next breath he uttered a wistful comment that revealed his continuing emotional connection to the Show: "I'm going to stay in shape and maybe I can help some club in July or August."[34]

Sal disliked his jerry-built coaching and scouting position, and he quit at the end of one season. Among his objections to the job was the incessant traveling—not weeks, but months away from his wife and son, this time without the companionship of teammates. Despite his reputation as a loner—more a product of his forbidding appearance than his actual behavior—Sal was a gregarious man who had spent his entire life in close quarters with other people. He did not relish being alone. He put 24,000 miles on his own car, driving around from one St. Louis farm club to another, ranging as far north as Rochester, NY, as well as across the entire south. Roger Kahn summed up the scouting life as "sitting on creaky wooden benches in a hundred bush-league fields. Driving the two-lane blacktops through the night. Tank-town meat loaf. Dingy bars, where your drink came with a wooden swizzle stick and the blondes had crackly hair and sandpaper skin. You saw that when you got them in the light."[35] It was a rude comedown from the life of a major league star to a life like that of a traveling salesman, selling baseball dreams instead of dry goods.

Sal found the coaching component of his position equally unsatisfactory. Most of the minor leaguers considered Sal's advice irrelevant. He was a faded figure whose starring seasons they barely remembered. "It was not too rewarding a job," Sal later admitted. "The minor league pitchers would do what you taught them just as long as you were with them, but they lapsed back into their own habits once I left. Seldom would they show any improvement from one visit to the next."[36] How different that situation was from his own younger years, when he had worked month after month under the close tutelage of Dolf Luque. The harsh old Cuban had cuffed and cursed him, shouted and maybe even shot at him, and made him into an iron-tough major league star, but he had not accomplished the feat with fleeting four-day visits every few weeks. When Sal's contract with the Cards was up, he did not renew it. If he was going to remain in baseball, it would have to be in the bigs.

1960–1962, 1966—Coaching the Kids

Four Seasons with the Boston Red Sox

19

During 1959 Maglie collaborated with sportswriter Dick Schaap on an article that summed up his pitching credo. Bluntly titled "I Always Threw Beanballs," it dealt with the cut-throat, high-risk game of physical intimidation and psychological terrorism that Sal had played so successfully. He recalled how Dodger fans believed that when he pitched against Brooklyn, he threw at the heads of Dodger batters. "This was their belief," Sal stated, "and I can't really blame them. *They were 100 per cent correct.*" From that chilling statement, he went on to defend the knockdown as the best pitch in baseball because of its efficiency in backing batters off the plate. Despite the provocative title, Sal insisted he never threw at opponents' heads with the intention of *hitting* them in the head. He noted that a pitch thrown toward a batter's head is easy to get away from because the hitter can see it coming. He also offered insight into his motivation. "I couldn't stop throwing the knockdown," he confessed. "That would be the same as if Marilyn Monroe stopped wearing sweaters."[1] Without realizing it, Sal revealed that he had become a prisoner of his tough-guy image as surely as Monroe became locked into her buxom sex-kitten role. Maglie without his knockdown would be like Marilyn in a burlap sack—why pay attention to either without the feature that made them famous? Sal concluded with a pledge that as a coach he would teach young pitchers to hang tough, move the ball around, and master the fierce art of the knockdown.

THE 1960 SEASON

The article may have helped launch the former pitcher on the next phase of his career. On October 20, 1959, less than two months after the article appeared, the Boston Red Sox hired Maglie as their pitching coach (Figure 23). A few days later Jerry Nason wrote in the *Boston Globe:* "Will some of Sal Maglie's desire rub off on the Red Sox pitching staff he will now coach? . . . Notorious for his knockdown pitch, this was merely an example of The Barber's cup of desire running over. He hates to lose."[2] Nason filled out his article with quotations from the Maglie-Schaap piece. Maglie was the choice of Billy Jurges, who had replaced Mike "Pinky" Higgins as the Rex Sox manager in early July of 1959. Jurges, who had enjoyed a successful career as an infielder, had been Sal's teammate on the 1945 New York Giants. The new manager declared: "I expect a lot more from the whole staff now that I've hired Sal Maglie as my pitching coach."[3] Despite his age (he would be 43 in April), Sal clung to his dream of continuing to pitch. In a November speech at a sports dinner, Sal declared that he intended to "get in shape with the idea of being ready for relief work in mid-season," adding, "I believe I can still help . . . I think I could pitch for another five years." "Just coach," Billy Jurges told him.[4]

Maglie was glad to have a position with a major league team again, since he had taken on the financial obligation of a new home. After more than a decade in the modest little house on Pierce Avenue, in 1958–1959 Sal and Kay had a luxurious and much larger home built at 2413 Park View Drive, an attractive street on the outskirts of Niagara Falls, backing up to a park and a golf course. In a continuing effort to build a financial base for his postbaseball years, in May of 1960 Sal opened a tire business in Niagara Falls, in partnership with a friend, building contractor Sam Infantino. Sal was the figurehead, the famous name that others hoped would sell the product.

Sal also engaged in another activity during the 1960s, one that adversely affected his financial situation: he developed a gambling habit. He had always preferred card games that involved money, but for many years he confined himself to low-stakes games played for amusement. His friend Mickey Rizzo remembered Sal as "a lousy card player. He was too easy—he just played for the sake of playing—he didn't care if he won."[5] As the 1960s began, however, Maglie became involved during the off-season in serious gambling in Niagara Falls. During the mid-sixties as well, when he lived at home year-round, he took part in high-stakes card games with men whose financial resources were much greater than his own. According to an individual familiar with the gambling scene in Niagara Falls during the 1960s, "there was a group of guys in a private club, that cleaned Sal out a couple of times a week."[6] At some point Maglie must have realized that gambling was leading him to financial ruin, and he broke himself of the habit.

23—Relaxed and ready to start a new phase in his major league career as pitching coach for the Boston Red Sox in 1960, Maglie no longer felt obliged to glower at the camera. Photo: George Brace.

The Red Sox team that Maglie joined in 1960 had not done too badly in the late '50s, finishing third in 1957 and 1958 and fifth in 1959. Maglie remained upbeat about the Boston pitching staff, although he admitted that it consisted mostly of inexperienced young hurlers. "I just try to put across the technique of pitching," he said. "They all have arms but need to work to develop their rhythm and correct minor mistakes in their delivery, stride, or release of the ball." He concluded by saying, "I definitely want to stay in baseball. It's my life."[7]

As the Bosox manager, Billy Jurges found himself in trouble from the start. His players complained that he was incapable of controlling a major league team and also accused him of making downright dumb managerial decisions. Jurges lasted less than two months, leaving the team on June 8. His departure was explained as due to illness. With the Red Sox in last place, owner Tom Yawkey rehired his old pal Pinky Higgins, under whose leadership the team climbed all the way up to seventh, where they finished. The most significant event of the Boston season took place on September 25, when the Sox announced that Ted Williams, the mercurial star who had been the one steady, shining light on a team riddled with disappointments, would retire at the end of the season. Sal did what he could for his young pitching staff, but with few tangible results. As usual, the Yankees won the American League pennant, but in the 1960 World Series the Pittsburgh Pirates defeated New York, and the loss cost the old master Casey Stengel his job. After 12 years, 10 pennants, and seven world championships, the 70–year-old Stengel departed, although baseball had not seen the last of him.

INTO A NEW ERA—THE 1961 AND 1962 SEASONS

The year 1960, often remarked upon as the beginning of a new era in American political and social history, also marked a distinct dividing line in baseball history. On the national level political power passed from the old, conservative order represented by 70-year-old Dwight Eisenhower to the youthful and vigorous liberal vision personified by the 43-year-old John F. Kennedy. The much-discussed sexual revolution was just beginning to be noted. In baseball, league expansion began in 1961. The neat pattern of two eight-team leagues playing a 154–game season disappeared. In July of 1960 the two leagues met separately and authorized expansion to 10 teams beginning in 1962, but the American League moved up its schedule, adding two teams in 1961. The Senators abandoned the nation's capital for Minneapolis, where they emerged as the Minnesota Twins, with an expansion team replacing them in Washington. The other new team appeared in the lucrative West as the Dodgers shared territory with the Los Angeles Angels. The following year the National League added a team in Houston, initially called the Colt 45s, but later renamed the Astros, and New York rejoined the National League with the Mets, managed by the resilient Casey Stengel.

Ever-hopeful Red Sox fans looked forward to a 1961 season where young players, particularly pitchers, would lift the team higher in the standings, but again they were disappointed. The Bosox had several pitching prospects. In addition to Bill Monbouquette, who had been the team's leading winner in 1960 with a 14–11 record, the Sox pitching staff boasted Tracy Stallard, a 23–year-old righthander who had impressed Sal Maglie during spring training the previous year. Maglie told a reporter he was positive that Stallard had "a big league arm."[8] Manager Pinky Higgins declared himself satisfied with his coaching staff of Rudy York, Billy Herman, and Sal Maglie, and happy with the addition of former back-up catcher Len Okrie as his bullpen coach. There had been rumors that Higgins would dismiss Herman and Maglie, but in reality Higgins did not much care who his coaches were, and in any case, the coaches' competency had little impact on the fortunes of the Red Sox in 1961. It was a season dominated by frenzy over whether Mickey Mantle or Roger Maris, or both, would break Babe Ruth's record of 60 home runs. In the season finale, Red Sox pitcher Tracy Stallard, touted by Maglie as a rising star, assured himself of a different kind of baseball immortality when Maris thumped one of his pitches into the right field stands of Yankee Stadium for his sixty-first home run to set a new record.

Although the Red Sox finished sixth, and the Yankees won another pennant, Maglie reaped some satisfying rewards. The outstanding member of the Boston pitching staff, 24–year-old Bill Monbouquette, responded to Sal's mound tutoring by setting a new team record for most strikeouts in a game. "Monbo," a homegrown product from nearby Medford, MA, made history on May 12 in a game against the Senators as he whiffed 17 batters on his way to a 2–1 victory. Not even such Sox greats as Cy Young, Smokey Joe Wood, or Lefty Grove had accomplished the feat, and Monbo just missed tying the modern major league strikeout record of 18, then held jointly by Bob Feller and Sandy Koufax. The pitcher gave Maglie credit for helping him gain both the skills and the confidence he displayed on that remarkable night. "Sal told me I hadn't been warming up enough," Monbo explained after the game. "He told me to warm up for 17 or 18 minutes and to take my time doing it, rather than rush through 13 or 14 minutes . . . before the game. It sure worked. . . . Sal also told me to end my pre-game workout by throwing a lot of breaking stuff. . . . I've worked very hard on my curve ball. They've been hanging a lot, but Sal got me to bring my arm way down on the curve, and it sure had my curve rolling and cracking."[9]

But those were not the only lessons the Boston pitcher learned from Maglie. Sal had been working with Monbouquette since the previous spring, passing on his accumulated wisdom to his most promising protégé. Monbo had a reputation as a hothead who would charge off the mound and engage in nose-to-nose confrontations with umpires. Sal taught him to channel his aggressiveness and to see the batter, not the umpire, as the enemy. "If he saw me getting mad, he'd come out to the mound and tell me, 'Frenchy, it's not gonna help. It's only gonna make it worse,'" Monbouquette recalled. "Sal was very influential in my career as far as settling me down. Sometimes he'd come out and just say some silly thing like 'This is a lovely night,' and then walk away. He'd break the tension, and I'd relax."[10]

Maglie also sensed Monbo's toughness and came down hard on the younger man. Sal told him that whenever he lost a game, it was his own fault, the same point Luque had never tired of making to Maglie. "What he meant," Monbouquette clarified, "was that, as a pitcher, you're not entitled to make a mistake. If you make a good pitch and you make an error—well, make *another* good pitch. You don't give in to the hitter. Sal used to say to me all the time: 'Remember—you're not entitled to a mistake. You make a bad pitch and you get away with it, you better be smart enough to know that.'"[11] Sal also realized that Monbo was the combative type who could profit from reverse psychology. "He knew I was a mentally tough kid," the former pitcher recalled. "If a certain guy came up, he'd taunt me. He'd say, 'Aah, you can't get this guy out!' And Sal always had this little smirk on his face, because he knew I liked the challenge. What he tried to do was make you take it up another level. He wanted you to recognize how good your stuff was. If I proved him wrong, he had this big smile on his face, and a little chuckle—'all right, so you proved me wrong, but let's try something else.' There was always something else, there was always a challenge with him. That's what I really liked about him."[12]

And of course Sal passed on Luque's harsh lessons about pitching inside, *far* inside, and often. Sal convinced the hurler that he had a terrific fastball, and even more important, to throw it high and tight. Monbo began emulating Maglie. "I wasn't afraid to throw the ball inside and back you off the plate. If you didn't like it, it might be worse than backing you off," he added, sounding The Barber's familiar, intimidating note.[13] "Sal talked about a lot of stuff, like 'move this guy off the plate, move his feet, move his legs,' and oh, he *did* preach: '*throw that ball inside!*' And he didn't mean pitch to get a strike on the inside corner of the plate. He meant you've got to set that hitter up with a pitch *way* inside!"[14] Luque would have loved every minute of it.

Bill Monbouquette's generous praise of Maglie's role in his success had positive postseason results for Sal. After the Series ended, the Minnesota

Twins tried to obtain Maglie's services as their pitching coach for 1962, but Sal had no interest in changing teams, particularly if it involved moving to the Midwest. Maglie rented an apartment in Boston, a city within driving distance of Niagara Falls, where Sal's wife, son, and mother-in-law now lived year-round, in the Maglies' handsome new home on Park View Drive. Sal Jr. was six years old, a sturdy, handsome, happy boy with straight, strawberry blond hair and so many freckles that his uncle Carl Pileggi nicknamed him "Frek." The Maglies, now in their mid-40s, were still waiting on their application to adopt a second child.

The Red Sox' 1962 season was much like their previous one, except they ended even lower in the standings, finishing eighth in the expanded 10-team league. Although Bill Monbouquette won 15 games, he lost nearly that many as well. The Sox staff included two other impressive pitchers, righthanders Earl Wilson and Dick Radatz, and Maglie went on with his efforts to mold an effective pitching staff. Monbouquette continued to benefit from Sal's attention, as did Wilson and rookie Radatz. Despite the team's poor record in 1962, Red Sox pitchers enjoyed several stellar moments. Dick Radatz emerged as Boston's ace reliever, and in a rare achievement for members of a second division club, two Red Sox pitchers, Wilson and Monbouquette, threw no-hitters.

Earl Wilson had been, technically, the first black player signed by the Red Sox—a team with a long and disgraceful history of racism—but military service delayed his appearance with the team, so Pumpsie Green beat him to Boston in 1959. A six-foot-three-inch flamethrower, Wilson had a temper similar to Monbouquette's. Sal worked with him as he had with Monbo, calming him down in tense situations, and teaching him to put his intensity to use against hitters. Sal's lack of racial biases meant he could deal with a sensitive and short-tempered black man without the situation deteriorating into racial animosity. Other men, liberal on the surface, might betray their real attitudes when confronted with a difficult personality in a minority player, but Sal never had those problems, because he had no hidden prejudices. Maglie further served as a buffer between the pitcher and manager Pinky Higgins, who was notorious for his bigoted racial attitudes. Sal also helped Wilson make a change in his pitching motion. Maglie observed that Wilson had been pitching directly overhand but thought Wilson might be more effective if he lowered the position of his pitching arm. Pitching with his altered delivery, Wilson enjoyed his most successful season with the Red Sox, compiling a 12–8 record. Now that Boston had a dependable reliever in Radatz, Maglie urged Wilson to forget about pacing himself but instead to throw as hard as he could for as long as he could. Wilson did not complete his first nine starts in 1962, and his no-hitter on June 26, against the Los

Angeles Angels at Fenway Park, was his first major league complete game. Wilson walked four, but no batter advanced beyond second. After the game Wilson called the no-hitter "the greatest thing that ever happened to me."[15] With his usual reserve, Maglie stayed in the background, claiming no credit for his pupil's success.

Less than five weeks after Wilson's no-hitter, Monbouquette did the same, defeating the Chicago White Sox, 1–0, on their home turf. Monbo fell short of a perfect game by issuing one walk. The achievement was especially sweet for the pitcher, because he had been stumbling through the season. His pitching had been so poor he had been dropped from the American League All-Star squad. He had not pitched a complete game since June 29, and had not won since July 8. His record stood at 8–10, and he had been knocked out of four straight games. Perplexed by his failures, Monbo again turned to Sal for advice and credited the old master with putting him back in form. "Maglie helped me a lot," Monbouquette declared after his triumph, "especially with coordination. I was throwing with my arm coming around way ahead of my body. But Maglie helped me so that I had my body out front and then the arm whipped around like it should."[16]

Now that two of his pitchers had reached one of baseball's rarest achievements, Sal felt more comfortable in fielding reporters' questions about his own role in their success. "I can't take much credit for their no-hitters," Sal said. "I've never taught anyone to pitch a no-hitter. All I try to teach 'em is to pitch to win. . . . The basic thing to me is to win. That's all I ever tried to do when I was pitching." Sal added that he had passed on another bit of wisdom to the elated young hurlers, reminding them to keep their achievement in perspective, that even a no-hitter is only a single win and is never a completely individual achievement. "Baseball is a team game," Sal stated. "Sure, every player likes to accomplish something in the way of individual honors. Like I told Earl Wilson after he pitched his no-hitter, 'Don't forget this is only one ball game.' Sure, it's great to know you've achieved something outstanding, but there's a lot more to baseball than pitching one no-hit, no-run game."[17]

The man who made it possible for Wilson and Monbouquette to go all-out in every game, without worrying about completing each of their starts (still a point of pride among hurlers in the early 1960s), was another of Maglie's pupils, relief specialist and wide-body mound monster Dick Radatz. A man of awesome size—six-feet-six-inches tall, with his weight fluctuating between 235 and 280 pounds—Radatz first encountered Maglie in 1962, his rookie year with the Red Sox, when he enjoyed great success. He appeared in 62 games, had a superb 2.23 ERA (1.96 until a poor final outing), and won the *Sporting News* Fireman of the Year award as the best relief pitcher in the American League. Although saves were not yet an official statistic in 1962, by modern rules he would have had 24 saves that year, more than any other American League reliever.[18]

Radatz credited Maglie with making a change in his delivery that led to his success in the majors. As Sal watched the jumbo-size reliever work during spring training, he noticed that Radatz was not taking full advantage of his impressive bulk to get the maximum speed on his fastball. "He taught me how to use the lower part of my body," Radatz related. "He told me, 'you know, Dick, you're a big, tall guy, and you're strong, but you're not using your legs to drive off the mound, to get more velocity on your fastball.' He said that's an easy thing to learn, and he taught me how to do it. That probably put four or five miles an hour more on my fastball. If a pitcher stands straight when he delivers the ball, that means he doesn't use the lower part of his body. Nobody had ever brought it to my attention, till Sal saw me, and that sure was a big help. He showed me how to bend my back leg," Radatz continued. "Learning took me about a month—we did it in spring training, so I didn't have to fool with it during the season. It's an easy adjustment to make. In baseball terminology they call it 'drop and drive.' By the time the 1962 season began, I was all ready to go with a new motion." Maglie's help made a crucial difference in Radatz's subsequent success, and the pitcher never forgot what he owed Sal. "I think he was a fine pitching coach, I really do," Radatz stated. "He was very good with the pitchers, had a good rapport with all of them. He was a ballplayer's type of coach. He wasn't a management type—a real stringent, hard-core guy. You could always go to him with anything. If it was something personal you wanted to talk about, you could do that, too. What he taught me really helped me for the rest of my career. Without that, I don't think I'd have been the pitcher I was."[19]

Radatz also may have Maglie to thank, at least indirectly, for his memorable nickname, The Monster. After Radatz struck out Mickey Mantle on three 95–mile-an-hour fastballs, the Yankee slugger called him "the monster," preceding the word with a string of obscenities. A sportswriter overheard the tirade and began using the nickname, minus the vulgarities. When Radatz objected, a Boston paper ran a contest, asking fans to give the pitcher a new nickname. The winning entry was "Smokey Dick." Radatz, aware of the crude variations opposing players could invent on any nickname with the word "dick" in it, decided to stay with The Monster. Whether Maglie helped change Radatz's mind is unknown, but the experiences of the two men were similar. Just as Maglie initially felt insulted by the nickname "The Barber" but later came to see its value as a part of his intimidating image, so Radatz learned to love the frightening implications of being called The Monster.

The notable success of three of the hurlers under his supervision might seem like a good reason for the Red Sox to retain Maglie for 1963, but Sal learned that coaching is an even more precarious career than pitching as he fell victim to a managerial change that made his achievements irrelevant. The Boston team had performed so poorly under Higgins that owner Tom Yawkey came under strong pressure to change managers. Because Higgins was a personal friend, Yawkey was reluctant to cut him loose. Instead, he fired general manager Bucky Harris and installed Higgins in his place. He then called up former Sox star Johnny Pesky, who had made a second career managing in the Pacific Coast League, and installed him as the Red Sox manager. Pesky wanted to name his own coaching staff, and in mid-October of 1962, in his first act as the new manager, Pesky announced he was dropping three of the team's four coaches. He retained Billy Herman but fired Len Okrie, Rudy York, and Sal Maglie. With no warning, Sal found himself both out of major league baseball and out of a job.

ON THE HOME FRONT

The timing for Sal's firing could hardly have been worse. During the summer of 1963 the Maglies finally succeeded in adopting a long-desired second child, although they had been obliged to go out of the country to do it. They chose a child from Italy. In 1963, the year Sal and Kay adopted their second son, Italy was second only to Korea as a source of adoptable infants. Despite a postwar economic boom, poverty remained so severe in southern Italy that many orphanages there were full of abandoned children whose families were too poor to care for them.[20] Although the Maglies' second son came from the Abbruzzi province, which is not geographically in the south, in the 1960s it was still a remote, impoverished region included with the southern provinces in discussions of Italy's "southern problem." Sal kept the promise he had made to name his second son after his father. The little boy who joined the Maglie family in the summer of 1963 was baptized Joseph Louis Maglie and nicknamed Joey. Unlike their first son, who came to them as an infant, Joey was two years old when he arrived. He had a rough time at first, as he was old enough to be aware of his unfamiliar surroundings but not old enough to understand where he was, or why. The Maglies tried speaking to him in Italian, but the Pugliese dialect Sal and his mother spoke was of little use with a child who had heard only the Abbruzzese dialect. Furthermore, Sal's mother was in poor health and could not be of much help to her son. She died of a heart attack on May 27, 1964, at age 74.

Although the adult Joe Maglie has no recollection of his earliest years, the mistreatment and neglect of children in overcrowded Italian orphanages was widespread, so it is possible that he too had suffered unpleasant experiences before his arrival in America. The Maglies tried hard to make it up to him, and Mary Pileggi remembered Kay Maglie's loving, patient devotion to her initially frightened and difficult younger son. A local newspaper reported a story similar to the one that had appeared after the Maglies adopted their first son: that Sal lost no time in taking the toddler into the backyard and showing him the rudiments of baseball.

Sal and Kay had no sooner managed to settle down their second child, when a blow far worse than Sal's job loss fell on them. After five healthy years, Kay's cancer recurred in 1963, and this time it was inoperable. Doctors confirmed that the disease had spread to her bones. Informed of the verdict, the couple closed ranks against everyone outside their immediate family and even against younger family members, so no reports of Kay's illness appeared in the newspapers. "There was nothing they could do," Mary Pileggi recalled. "Bones don't grow back. She knew. She knew *everything*."[21]

During the next three and a half years Kay's health declined, until her death in February of 1967. At first she was not seriously disabled and kept up a cheerful front, particularly with her children. For three of those years (1963–1965) Sal remained at home in Niagara Falls, supporting himself and his family from what he earned through speaking engagements, the income he received from the local businesses in which he maintained an interest, and his latest attempt at a postbaseball career as a sales representative with a Buffalo investment firm dealing in mutual funds. Since Sal had put in the required 10–plus years in major league baseball, he may also have elected to receive the small pension granted to veterans. Unable to stay away from baseball, in 1965 Sal served as a part-time pitching coach for the Buffalo Bisons. Sal seemingly "forgot" that the Red Sox had fired him after the 1962 season. In February of 1963, local sportswriter Mike Quinlan insisted that Maglie had quit baseball on his own—not a word about the termination of his coaching position with Boston. Quinlan also noted that the one thing that would have kept Maglie in baseball was the offer of a manager's position in the majors, but no such offer was forthcoming. There was talk of Sal being hired as a coach for the Mets in 1963, but the deal fell through. In his 1968 memoir, Maglie claimed he took a three-year "break" (1963–1965) from baseball in order to stay home with his ailing wife, but at least during the first of those years, he had no choice.[22]

MEANWHILE, BACK IN BOSTON . . .

Team turbulence and futility continued into the mid-1960s. In 1963 the Red Sox finished seventh under Johnny Pesky's leadership, although Maglie pupils Bill Monbouquette and Dick Radatz continued to perform well.

Monbo had his only season as a 20–game winner, and Radatz finished with a 15–6 record and a superb 1.98 ERA. In 1964 the droopy Red Sox sank into eighth place despite the addition of brilliant teenage slugger Tony Conigliaro, and with two games left in the season Yawkey fired Pesky. At the same time he reluctantly dismissed Pinky Higgins and replaced him as general manager with the highly competent Dick O'Connell. Pesky's efforts to change the undisciplined clubhouse atmosphere and the players' slovenly work habits had been ineffective. The Sox went through the motions on the field, and afterward most of them headed for the bars. Pesky's replacement as manager was coach Billy Herman, whose only managerial experience in the majors consisted of piloting the 1947 Pirates to a seventh-place finish. Herman tried to rehire Maglie as one of his coaches for 1965, a move that came as welcome news in Boston, where Sal had been popular. A Red Sox player commented, "Sal has been out of baseball too long. We need guys like him in this game."[23] One of Pesky's problems as manager was the disrespect players had for his coaches. Boston sportswriter Larry Claflin pointed out that Maglie was one coach all the players could admire. "He earned the respect of all baseball for his courage and determination when he was a player, and he lost none of that respect in his previous tenure as a Red Sox coach," Claflin declared.[24]

Although Maglie was eager to return to his old position in Boston, another form of employment interfered. During 1964 Sal had made efforts to have himself appointed to the New York State Athletic Commission as deputy commissioner for Western New York. The post, which paid $10,900 a year, was a political appointment, and Sal received the support of the Niagara County Republican organization. According to Sal's nephew Pat Grenga, Maglie had no interest in politics and affiliated himself with the Republicans simply because they were in power in Niagara Falls. Sal won the position and was sworn in as a deputy commissioner in January of 1965. His responsibilities were to oversee professional boxing and wrestling in 17 northern counties of New York State. Asked about professional wrestling matches, Sal gave an answer that must have had the sport's promoters rolling in the aisles: "I imagine most of them are honest," said the naive new commissioner.[25] Sal soon found out that he could not hold both the Athletic Commission post and the coaching job with the Red Sox. Choosing between a post that allowed him to stay close to home and a position in his beloved baseball that would again take him away for much of the year was difficult for Sal, but he had two young children now, as well as a seriously ill wife. Furthermore, he had made a commitment to the Athletic Commission and did not wish to resign from a post he had worked hard to obtain. Regretfully, he turned down his chance to return to the Red Sox.

At least he had more time to spend with his children. No doubt at his father's urging, Sal Jr. played Little League baseball, although as an outfielder, not a pitcher. In an interview early in 1966 Kay Maglie made a significant observation about Little Sal—that he "tries to be perfect for his father,"[26] a futile, frustrating, and ultimately self-defeating enterprise for any child. Although, according to Kay, Sal stayed in the background at games when their son was playing, the mere presence of his major league father must have had a mortifying effect on the chubby, modestly talented boy, who could never be good enough—much less perfect—in the game where his father had excelled. Any failure or mistake would be magnified by the realization that his father had seen it. Sal Sr. had a mishap of his own at one of his son's Little League games in 1965. As he sat in the stands, Sal reached out a hand to grab a hard-hit foul ball, but his skills had grown rusty and he missed. The ball struck him on the left side of his nose, breaking bone and cartilage and sending blood gushing everywhere. Sal became woozy and nauseated, and he had to be helped out of the stands and hurried to a doctor. His nose healed with a dent in the left side (Figure 24). "He's supposed to catch those things," Kay quipped.[27]

Billy Herman was even less successful with the Red Sox than Pesky had been, as the team fell further back in the standings in 1965. Herman, 56 years old and a traditional type, had a generational problem with younger team members. The "Swinging Sixties" were now in full swing, and a new kind of free-spirited ballplayer who flaunted his off-field carousing and womanizing was becoming common. Pitcher Dennis Bennett, who joined the Sox in 1965, recalled players on other teams referring to the Bosox as "the country club" due to the team's high salaries, lax discipline, and reputation for postgame good times. "You'd party every night. You'd do just about what you wanted to do. There was no set curfew. There was no bed check." Bennett remembered players on the team bus bragging loudly about their all-night parties and sexual exploits within Herman's hearing. "He didn't have any control over the ball club whatsoever," Bennett declared.[28] The pitchers Maglie had worked hard to improve all deteriorated in 1965. Bill Monbouquette's record sank to a miserable 10–18; Earl Wilson ended the season at 13–14, and Dick Radatz fell to 9–11. To be fair to the pitchers, none had a bloated ERA—their teammates failed to score many runs for them. With a horrible 62–100 record, the Red Sox finished in ninth place.

In 1966 Maglie returned to Boston, taking up his old position as the Red Sox pitching coach. Billy Herman announced Maglie's rehiring in January of 1966. Sal resigned his post with the Athletic Commission and signed a two-year contract with the Red Sox. The lure of major league baseball proved too strong to resist. "Baseball is my first love," Sal told a reporter. "It has always been in my

24—Sal and his sons in 1966, when Maglie was the Red Sox pitching coach. Sal Jr., 11 years old, is on the left; Joey, 5, on the right. The dent in the left side of Sal's nose is where he was struck by a foul ball during one of his older son's Little League games. Photo: collection of John and Mary Pileggi.

blood and has been my whole life and always will be, I guess. As long as I feel I can be of some service to baseball and can contribute something, I want to remain in it." Sal confessed, "I missed baseball even more than I thought I would. I can hardly wait for spring training to begin."[29] Money was a consideration as well, since his salary with the Red Sox was reported at $20,000, almost twice what his post with the Athletic Commission had paid him.

There was another aspect to Sal's decision to return to baseball. He was having grave difficulties dealing with his wife's declining health. By the beginning of 1966 Kay was still mobile and looked well, but she was growing weaker. She spent much of her time on the living room couch, foggy from pain killers, as her mother took over running the household, and caring for Sal Jr. and Joey. Niece Kathy Pileggi Peller remembered being puzzled by her once-energetic aunt's lethargy. The explanation for Kay's condition was that she had the flu. "Uncle Sal didn't talk about aunt Kay's illness," Kathy recalled. "I really didn't know. Every time I went over there toward the end, she'd be on the couch, and she had the flu, the flu, the flu. I'd ask my mother how come aunt Kay always has the flu? And my mother would say, 'I don't know. She's just—weak.' I remember going over there, and she'd be on the couch, and uncle Sal would say, 'Whatsa matter—you layin' down again? Get off your fat ass!' That would get me right in my heart. I felt like telling him, 'Don't talk to my aunt like that!'"[30]

Sal was dealing with his wife's condition in the only way he knew how, by pretending to make light of it, kidding her with something like the reverse psychology he had used so successfully on Bill Monbouquette. But Monbo was a tough, healthy young pitcher, and Kay was a fragile, terminally ill woman. Although to the teenage Kathy Pileggi, Sal's behavior was insensitive and incomprehensible, at that time she did not know the burden Sal was carrying, the secret of Kay's true condition. In his 1968 memoir, composed less than a year after Kay's death, Sal explained: "She was very sick, but when I finally realized there was absolutely nothing I could do, I went back to the Sox in the spring of 1966."[31] Sal's despair, his sense of utter helplessness in the face of Kay's impending death, was one of the factors that sent him fleeing back to baseball.

In response to a local reporter's questions, Kay's composure never faltered. "Sal's going back to baseball is just wonderful," she declared, beaming. "Seeing him happy makes me happy."[32] If she felt any sense of abandonment, she kept it well concealed. The article also noted the lavish party Kay had hosted in mid-January of 1966 for Sal's niece Maria Grenga in honor of Maria's engagement to Joseph Rizzo. At the time of her engagement, Maria wrote Kay a letter, expressing the hope that she would have a marriage as wonderful as that of her aunt and uncle. The photograph accompanying the article about Kay in the *Niagara Falls Gazette* showed her holding up a sweater she had knitted for her own use during the summer fishing trips in Canada she always enjoyed with her two brothers. But there would be no more fishing trips for Kay Maglie. She is smiling in the picture, but the smile does not extend to her wide, frightened eyes.

The Red Sox did not do any worse in 1966, but they did not improve much, either, despite whatever Sal contributed. Dick Radatz was traded during the season, but promising young righty Jim Lonborg had joined the team the previous year. Despite the mediocre 10–10 record Lonberg compiled in 1966, Sal thought he had potential. On September 8, 1966, with the team in last place, owner Tom Yawkey fired Billy Herman and appointed former Sox star and current coach Pete Runnels as interim manager. Under his direction the team played .500 ball for the last 16 games of the season, a surge that enabled the Sox to finish ahead of the Yankees for the first time since 1948. Unfortunately, the Yankees finished dead last that year—in tenth place—and Boston again finished ninth, in front of the Yankees by a mere half-game. On September 28, the day after the regular season ended, the Red Sox announced the hiring of a new manager for 1967: Dick Williams. A fierce, hard-edged man with the temperament and demeanor of a Marine drill sergeant, Williams had been a utility player with the Dodgers in the early 1950s, where he was notorious for his bench-jockeying. At age 38, he would be the youngest manager in the league. Under his leadership, baseball's best-known country club was about to become a boot camp.

1967—Tragedy at Home, Triumph in Boston

20

In 1967 Sal was part of the "Impossible Dream" that culminated in the Boston Red Sox winning the American league pennant for the first time in more than 20 years. Jim Lonborg, a pitcher he had helped to develop, won 22 games, registered the pennant-clinching victory, then pitched a pair of brilliant World Series triumphs before going down with the ship, as the Sox lost the Series to the Cardinals in seven grueling games. But for Sal, conflicts and personal tragedy overshadowed the triumphs. Maglie did not get along with new Sox manager Dick Williams, which made the season difficult and frustrating for him. But the tragedy occurred at home. On February 22, a few days before Sal was due to report for spring training, Kay Maglie died.

THE FINAL ILLNESS AND DEATH OF KAY MAGLIE

Throughout the year, Kay's health had declined. She was still in fairly good condition when Sal left in February to join the Red Sox for the 1966 season, but by the time he returned home in late September, Kay's illness was reaching the terminal stage. Maria Grenga Rizzo, whose engagement party Kay had hosted a year earlier, remembered phoning her aunt shortly after she bought her wedding gown, which was a few weeks before Kay's death. "I was all excited," Maria recalled, "and wanted to give aunt Kay every detail. She never let you think she was sick. She acted totally interested in everything I was talking about. But now I realize—there she was—dying."[1]

Besides Kay's mother Mae Pileggi and Sal, the person most intimately involved with Kay at the end of her life was her sister-in-law Mary Pileggi. Kay
still confided in Mary, and from Kay, Mary learned that Sal had broken a
cardinal rule in baseball's code of personal behavior: he had become involved with a woman who lived in or near the same town where he and Kay
resided. Vern Stephens had put it crudely when he defined adultery for baseball players as "getting laid in the same town where your wife is," but his
quip contains a large element of reality. In return for their wives' turning a
blind eye to their on-the-road behavior, players are supposed to refrain from
affairs close to home. According to Mary Pileggi's recollections, Kay noticed
a change in Sal's behavior during the months he spent at home at the end
of the 1966 season. He had always passed most evenings in town, drinking
and playing cards with his male buddies, but this time Kay sensed something furtive and guilty about her husband's behavior. While she was still
able to drive, Kay followed Sal one night in her own car and saw him park
in front of a house and go in, as a woman answered the door. But she concluded it was not worth poisoning their last months by confronting her
husband. "Kay was heart-broken," Mary recalled. "She was crying when she
told me. Then she said, 'I'll be gone soon, and Sal can do what he pleases.'"
Shaking her head, Mary exclaimed, "He showed Kay *so* much love! You
wouldn't think he was *capable* of acting like that!"[2] Although it was hardly
the noblest moment of Sal's life, he was a healthy, virile man in his late 40s,
whose gentle nature would never have allowed him to force himself on his
ailing wife. An affair he hoped would remain secret must have seemed to
him the best course of action. According to Mary Pileggi's report, he at least
had the grace to feel guilty.

In her last weeks of life Kay begged Mary, who was a beautician, "Please,
don't let me go to my grave with my grey hair showing!"[3] Mary came to the
Maglie home in mid-February with her hair-dyeing supplies, but by the time
she finished her work, she realized Kay had fallen into a semi-comatose
state. Sal insisted on taking Kay to the hospital himself. After her mother
and Mary had wrapped her in a blanket, Sal took his dying wife in his arms,
carrying her down the stairs and out to his car. As they took Kay into the
emergency room of Mount St. Mary's Hospital, she revived enough to whisper a thank-you to Mary for tending to her hair.

Knowing Kay's end was near, Sal spent much of his time at his wife's bedside. Kay's mother and brothers visited daily as well. On the afternoon of
February 22, the day that Kay died, her mother was alone in the Maglies'
house when she heard a voice crying, "MA!!!" Later Mae Pileggi was certain
that happened at the very moment of Kay's death. The funeral, at Sacred
Heart church in Niagara Falls, was large and included television coverage.

Kathy Pileggi Peller recalled her own shock and grief at her aunt's death and found her uncle Sal's composure difficult to understand. "At Kay's funeral, Sal seemed almost cheerful," she recalled. "It was strange. Me being young, I was wondering, why isn't he crying his eyes out?"[4]

Sal had long ago learned not to display his emotions in public, and Kay's funeral, with its hundreds of mourners and the prying eyes of television cameras, was almost as public as the place he had once occupied at the center of a baseball diamond. Only one time in the days after Kay's death did Sal break down. Shortly after the funeral Mary Pileggi was in the hospital, and Sal stopped by to visit her. He sat with his head bowed, saying nothing, and after a while Mary realized he was silently weeping. A woman always ready to assist others, even from her own sick-bed, Mary asked how she could help him. Between sobs, Sal poured out his problems. He was at a loss for what to do about his boys. He had no idea of how to run a household and care for children. Their mutual mother-in-law, Mae Pileggi, was so sunk in grief over her daughter's death that she herself needed taking care of and could no longer provide the support she had given the Maglies for years. Furthermore, Sal had a contract with the Red Sox and had been expected at their spring training camp in Florida on February 25. And he could not bear to continue living in the house on Park View Drive, so full of memories of Kay. Mary responded, "You say you don't have anybody to take care of your kids? Well, you do now."[5] Mary offered to take them all in—Sal, his two sons, and Mae Pileggi. Within days, they had moved their personal belongings into John and Mary Pileggi's home, and a few days later Sal left for the Boston spring training camp.

Although Sal arrived a week or so late, according to family members who joined him there, he did not miss 1967 spring training entirely. Manager Dick Williams, however, insists that Sal *did* miss all of spring training and that bullpen coach Al Lakeman had to take over Sal's spring training duties, which started Sal off on the wrong foot with his new manager.[6] But it is unlikely that Maglie family members would be mistaken about the only year they visited Sal during spring training, especially as it was in the weeks just after Kay's death. Sal invited his two sons, his mother-in-law, his niece Kathy Pileggi, and his nephew Dennis Villani to stay with him in Winter Haven. Kathy recalled how Sal taught her the correct way to eat lobster. At first, she thought the ferocious-looking thing on her plate was horrible, and she protested, "I don't wanna eat this!" Sal, amused but patient and gentle as always, showed his niece the technique for cracking the shell. "He showed me how, and I've loved it ever since," Kathy declared.[7] "I remember going to the ballpark and watching them play," Dennis Villani recalled, "and there was this one pitcher who came over to the motel where we were staying. I said to this guy, 'Hey, you looked good out there today!' And my uncle Sal says to me, 'Aw, what do YOU know?' He was just kidding. He had a good sense of humor."[8] With his family around him, Sal tried to be cheerful. Unfortunately, those first weeks proved to be his happiest ones.

SAL'S SEASON WITH THE 1967 RED SOX

The appointment of Dick Williams as the Red Sox manager signaled fundamental changes. Williams laid down rules and enforced them, and he could not have given less of a damn whether the players liked him or his rules. "I'm not in a popularity contest," he growled to reporters. "I want to win, and I want a ball club full of other guys who want to win." Williams also wanted his own coaches, and in three out of four coaching positions Williams could bring in his own hires. He chose Eddie Popowski as his third base coach, former Sox second baseman Bobby Doerr as his hitting instructor and first base coach, and Al Lakeman, a former backup catcher, as his bullpen coach. Although Williams wanted to hire former reserve catcher Darrell Johnson as his pitching coach, that job already belonged to Sal Maglie, because Maglie had signed a two-year contract in 1966, before Williams took over as manager.

Although Williams continues to insist that there was never any ill feeling between himself and Maglie, according to Sal's account, Williams treated him badly throughout the season, and their relationship worsened, despite the team's success. Sal felt he was being ignored, and his advice brushed aside. He noticed that all the other coaches were with Williams after games and believed he was being excluded from these informal conferences. Already depressed and suffering from his recent bereavement, Maglie found his treatment even more distressing than he might have in happier days. Most players were too young to be interested in socializing with their 50–year-old coach. The 25–year-old Jim Lonborg, a friendly fellow who liked Sal, recalled spending an evening now and then talking with Maglie in hotel bars during road trips, but for the most part, Lonborg admitted, "I was single at the time, and when the ball games were over I was gone and out with my friends, so I didn't really hang around with him." Lonborg and the other players knew Maglie had recently been widowed, but it made little impression on them. "We were aware of it," Lonborg remembered, "but we were so intent on playing the game that we didn't really become personally involved with coaches' lives. Plus, Sal kept his sadness to himself."[9]

And so Sal went his lonely way. He had no close friends on the team. Although pitcher Dan Osinski, then in his mid-30s, was his occasional companion,[10] Maglie would often find himself drinking alone in hotel bars in the evenings. But Sal was rarely alone for long. Besides the bar flies and baseball groupies who sought his attention, there were sportswriters eager to hear his views. But during the regular season and up through the World Series, Sal refused to talk about his difficulties with Dick Williams. Instead, he brooded alone over the injustices he felt he was enduring. He was so often upset that his normally hearty appetite vanished, and he lost a large amount of weight off his already spare frame. He sounded so depressed and discouraged when he spoke with friends and family members that they grew concerned about his health. Pictures of him from that period show him looking drawn, gaunt, and grim (Figure 25).

As spring training began, Dick Williams wasted no time in whipping his charges into shape. The manager set up a weight chart, insisting that the team's assortment of gorgers and ale-boats meet their weight or be benched. He considered pitchers under-worked in spring training. Instead of shagging fly balls between workouts, Williams claimed, they usually stood around talking about "who's screwing who, who's mad, and whatever. Fly balls were

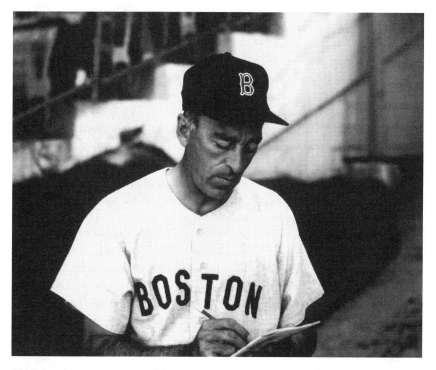

25—Sal making notes on a pad during his 1967 season with the Red Sox. Recently widowed, Maglie was also bitterly unhappy about his treatment by manager Dick Williams. Photo: Harold Kriessler/National Baseball Hall of Fame Library, Cooperstown.

the last thing on their minds."[11] Williams ordered the slothful pitchers to play volleyball. Since his retirement at the end of the 1960 season, Ted Williams had come to the Boston training camp as an unofficial batting instructor but spent most of his time regaling enthralled younger players with tales from his own career. The other Williams put a stop to that, sending Maglie to break up the confabs, putting Sal on the spot against the team's greatest hero. When Maglie's requests had no effect, Dick Williams *ordered* Ted Williams to cease his story hours. The elder Williams responded by packing his bags and stomping off in a huff, booming about fucking volleyball and what-is-the-game-coming-to. By the end of spring training the oddsmakers, who seem not to have noticed the changes Dick Williams had made, gave the Red Sox a 100–to-1 chance of winning the pennant.

Although the Red Sox won their Opening Day game on April 12, Boston soon sank to seventh place. In an effort to ignite the team, Dick Williams berated players, benched them, even criticized them to the press. Williams could be scathing—he once said that "trying to talk to [first baseman] George Scott is like talking to cement"—but he was impartial in his disdain.[12] White, black, and Latino players all came in for their share of criticism. It is of interest to note that the 1967 Red Sox were an integrated team that relied on players of all races. The departure of the bigoted Pinky Higgins, and his replacement in the front office by general manager Dick O'Connell, belatedly allowed the Sox to start acquiring first-rate black players. Although many players resented Williams' methods, they responded to them with better play, and on April 29 the Red Sox found themselves at the unfamiliar pinnacle of first place. They soon slid down from there, but by the end of June the team was in third place with a respectable 37–34 record. The pennant was up for grabs, and for once the Red Sox looked like contenders.

By July 1 Jim Lonborg had compiled a 10–3 record and was emerging as the ace of the staff. The six-foot-five-inch son of a California college professor, Lonborg was intelligent, well-educated, articulate, and cultured. He preferred symphonic music to country or rock and read history books rather than comic books. He had joined the Red Sox in 1965, when he acquired the nickname "Gentleman Jim," and posted a poor 9–17 record with a 4.47 ERA. Part of the problem was inexperience, some of it weak batting and fielding support, but a major part of Lonborg's inability to excel came from his failure to move hitters off the plate by throwing inside. That was before he met Sal Maglie. Under Maglie's tutelage in 1966 Lonborg improved, breaking even with a 10–10 record and a better ERA of 3.86. Maglie noticed that Lonborg lacked the control to throw his curve for strikes when he was behind in the count. Recalling how valuable the Cuban Winter League had been in his own development, Sal suggested to Lonborg that he play winter ball in Venezuela when the 1966 season ended, as a way of working on his pitching without the pressure of a big league season. Lonborg followed Sal's suggestion, and the result was a dramatic improvement in his performance.

Maglie also taught Lonborg what the pitcher called "an 'up' kind of fastball." The type of fastball he had thrown previously, Lonborg explained, "was a sinking fastball, one that moved around so much in the strike zone that I couldn't guarantee myself I could throw that fastball in the strike zone, and that it would stay there. Sal taught me what they now call a four-seam fastball. In those days they called it a cross-seam fastball. It was a pitch that went straighter. The dynamics of the pitch are this: when four seams are cutting through the air, it creates more resistance, and doesn't allow the ball to move as much. So when I got behind in the count, 3–0, I now had a pitch that I could throw very hard and it would stay in the strike zone, and I'd have more of a chance of getting the hitter out. That was really critical. It was one more pitch than I'd had before."[13]

Not surprisingly, Maglie also taught the big righthander the fine art of barbering batters' chins. Gentleman or not, Jim Lonborg was a tough-minded young man who shared Maglie's conviction that the pitcher owned the plate and that it was his job to enforce that possession. Lonborg explained: "Along with learning how to pitch in the big leagues came the matter of how hitters stood at the plate and how they reacted to certain pitches. I had no problems pitching from the middle of the plate to the third base side, because that's the way my ball naturally moved. Sal had taught me the cross-seam fastball, so now I could pitch from the middle of the plate to the first-base side and keep it on the outside part of the plate. But I needed to do something that would not allow hitters to stand in and wait for certain pitches. That's where he taught me the importance of pitching inside—the brushback pitch. This is how he explained it: he said you needed to get control of the outside corner of the plate, with right-handed hitters. And in order to do that, you had to be able to throw very hard *inside,* and create intimidation, because the more you threw inside, and created intimidation, the farther away the outside part of the plate looked to the batter."[14]

An apt pupil, Lonborg grasped that pitching inside was not only a mere mechanical technique but also a mental one. "The whole premise of the pitch," Lonborg continued, "is the psychological advantage. It actually expands the strike zone by making the outside part of the plate a little bit farther away, just because the hitter thinks the pitcher might be throwing inside. So, by teaching me the cross-seam fastball and keeping my two-seam fastball, which moved really hard on the inside part of the plate, that now made the plate, which is maybe 14 inches wide, look to the batter like it's 16 inches wide. And those two inches on the outside part of the plate are the difference between a home run and a lazy fly ball. I think because of Sal's history—being 'The Barber'—he knew the real importance of pitching inside was that now he could pitch *outside* easier, because hitters would be intimidated. It was something he'd learned through experience, and he was able to pass his experiences on to me."[15]

By 1967 Lonborg had absorbed Sal's lessons. In a game against the Yankees on June 21 at the Stadium, old-time fans could be forgiven if they thought they were back in the first half of the '50s. On the previous day Boston's Joey Foy had hit a grand slam, part of a Red Sox offense that had beaten the Bombers, 7–1. On the following day Yankee pitcher Thad Tillotson recalled Foy's slammer and threw at the Sox third baseman. The ball ricocheted off Foy's batting helmet. Lonborg, the Boston pitcher that day, waited until Tillotson came to bat, then hit him with a pitch. The two men exchanged sharp words, both benches emptied, punches flew, and it required a dozen policemen to break up the melee. When Lonborg came to bat, Tillotson hit him, and the benches emptied again. The game continued with both teams' pitchers throwing brushbacks, and Lonborg striking another batter, before it ended in an 8–1 Red Sox romp. After the game Lonborg told the press, "I was out to protect my teammates, and win the game. I don't give a damn about Tillotson." Asked if he was deliberately throwing at Tillotson, Lonborg retorted, "What do you think? I can't let him hit one of our guys."[16] In 1967 Lonborg struck a career-high 19 batters, almost twice the highest number (10) that Maglie ever hit. Lonborg was taking The Barber's lessons to heart and then carrying them further. He began marking the inside of his glove to note every hit batsman, although Maglie had never engaged in that kind of scorekeeping. Sportswriter Larry Claflin noted Lonborg's increased aggressiveness, that he was throwing closer to hitters more often than he used to, and that in his first nine games he had hit six batters. In his autobiography, Dick Williams praised Lonborg for his toughness in pitching inside but made no mention of Maglie's role in turning Lonborg into that kind of pitcher.

Dick Williams had a more difficult job keeping his team in line off the field than on it. His harsh methods produced wins, but his winning team in turn became a group of glamorous and desirable young men bent on having a good time. For a while Williams tried the old-fashioned method of bed checks, but he later gave that up as useless. On one occasion coach Eddie Popowski reported to Williams that Tony Conigliaro and Mike Ryan had two airline stewardesses in their room. Williams phoned the players and ordered them to report to his suite immediately. Once there, the two young men found not only Williams but also Popowski and Maglie awaiting them. It is easy to imagine Maglie's discomfort at being dragged into such a situation. A reserved, private man who resented intrusions into his own personal life, and no moralistic zealot, Sal would have seen little point in policing players' sexual behavior.

For Tony Conigliaro, the good times were almost over. On August 18, in a game against the Angels at Fenway Park, pitcher Jack Hamilton beaned the Boston star and nearly killed him. Ted Williams had warned not long before that Conigliaro crowded the plate excessively, but the carefree slugger laughed when the warning reached him. He was 22 years old, drop-dead gorgeous, rich, charming, talented, famous, and—he was sure—invulnerable. As Tony leaned far out over the plate Hamilton's 90–mile-an-hour fastball sailed in toward his skull. At the last instant, too late, he jerked his head back so hard that his batting helmet flipped off, and the ball struck him full-force on his left cheekbone and eye with a sickening thump. He crumpled to the ground, bleeding from his left ear, nose, and mouth, his left eye blackening and swelling, his cheekbone fractured, bone shards driven into his left eye, his jaw dislocated. He missed the rest of the 1967 season as well as the following one.

For all its horror, the beaning inspired the Red Sox rather than devastating them. They went on to win the game in which they lost Tony, swept the series from the Angels, and started a seven-game winning streak that carried them up to second place, just one game out. The race see-sawed through the month of August. As the season entered its final week, Boston was tied for first with the Minnesota Twins. But after two losses to the Indians on September 26 and 27, the Red Sox dropped back to third, their pennant hopes fading. Then Boston had a lucky break in the schedule: two days off on September 28 and 29 before facing the Twins on September 30 and October 1 at Fenway in their final games of the season.

In mid-September Phil Elderkin, sports columnist for the *Christian Science Monitor,* had reminded readers that "all season long people have been saying the one thing the Boston Red Sox don't have enough of to win the pennant is pitching." Maglie disagreed, telling the columnist that Jim Lonborg, Gary Bell, and Lee Stange "could start for any team in this league. And with [John] Wyatt, [José] Santiago, and [Sparky] Lyle in the bullpen, we've got three guys who can relieve under pressure. . . . How much more do you need coming down the stretch?" Sal asked. He added proudly that all his pitchers could work on three days' rest and that manager Dick Williams agreed. But at the end of the interview the author revealed one of the problems Sal faced. Although Sal was nominally in charge of the Boston pitching staff, "decisions as to who will start and who will relieve are made exclusively by Williams."[17] Such decisions are always the prerogative of the manager but usually are made in consultation with his pitching coach. In the case of Maglie, though, no consultations took place. "He never said a thing to me," Maglie revealed later. "It was as though I didn't exist. He never asked my advice, he never said a word. A couple of times I suggested things to him, but all I got were sarcastic answers."[18]

On September 30 Boston won the first of their games with Minnesota, 6–4, putting them in a tie with the Twins for first place. José Santiago, the winning pitcher in the game against the Twins, credited Maglie with correcting a flaw in his delivery that helped him win the crucial game. The pitcher said Maglie had noticed that "I was dropping my arm and not bending my back enough," adding that the pitching coach had told him in the third inning what he was doing wrong, "and I came back strong." When asked, Sal noted that he had also worked on Santiago's curve ball during the season and showed him how to mix it with his best pitch, a fastball. "One pitch has to help the other," he observed.[19]

For the final game of the regular season, on October 1, Dick Williams went with his ace, Jim Lonborg. Although Lonborg's record stood at 21–9, he had never beaten the Twins. In the first three innings the nervous Red Sox allowed two unearned runs, and the score was 2–0, Twins, going into the bottom of the sixth. With Lonborg scheduled to lead off, Williams faced a classic dilemma: should he allow a pitcher who was throwing a fine game to come to the plate or replace him with a pinch hitter who might have a better chance of getting a hit and scoring a desperately needed run? When Williams let Lonborg bat, the pitcher surprised everyone by laying down a bunt and beating it out. Two singles followed to load the bases. Carl Yastrzemski then smacked one up the middle to tie the score.

At this point the Twins started acting like a squad of spooked bushers. Pitcher Dean Chance became so agitated his whole body began to tremble. The next Boston batter, Ken "Hawk" Harrelson, hit a bouncer to Twins shortstop Zoilo Versalles. Instead of trying for the obvious out at second, Versalles threw home, but too late: no out, and another run for the Sox. Twins manager Cal Ermer then replaced Chance with Al Worthington. Now closing out his career, Worthington had been a Giants rookie back when Maglie was in his prime. Maybe the sight of Sal the Barber glaring at him from the Boston dugout unnerved him, or maybe it was the sound of 36,000 screaming Red Sox fans, but whatever the reason, the Twins reliever unloosed two wild pitches, allowing another run to score. A fifth run came in when Reggie Smith hit a hard grounder to Harmon Killebrew, and the first baseman fielded it with his knee. When the inning ended, the score was 5–2, Boston. The Twins scored a run in the eighth, and Lonborg took a 5–3 lead into the top of the ninth. He allowed a scratch single to the leadoff hitter but persuaded the next man to hit into a double play. When pinch hitter

Rich Rollins popped up Lonborg's first pitch to shortstop Rico Petrocelli for the third out, the fans at Fenway went crazy. Thousands poured onto the field, mobbing the Red Sox players, raising Lonborg to their shoulders, and practically stripping him. He lost his cap, uniform blouse, and shoelaces, all of them torn into pieces that fans reverently bore away with them like the relics of a miracle-working saint. The grounds crew finally cleared the field by turning on the sprinklers. The Red Sox had won the pennant for the first time since 1946 and for only the second time since 1918. Their opponents would be the same team they had faced in '46: the St. Louis Cardinals.

By using Lonborg to win the season's final, essential game, Williams had assured that his ace would not be available for the opening game of the World Series. Surrounded by celebrating team members, Dick Williams worried about how his team would fare in Game One against Bob Gibson. The Cardinals' future Hall of Fame fireballer was indisputably more intimidating than Sal Maglie had ever been. He was heavier and stronger, his fastball faster, his delivery more aggressive, and the anger that fueled his high-inside pitches born not of mere competitiveness but from a lifetime of bitter encounters with racism. On July 15, Gibson had suffered a broken bone in his right shin when struck by a line drive. It is an index of his astounding toughness that he pitched to three more batters, putting his full weight on his injured right leg, before collapsing. By World Series time Gibson was fully recovered, well rested, and ready to go.

THE END OF THE IMPOSSIBLE DREAM—THE 1967 WORLD SERIES

The Series opened on October 4 in Boston, with Fenway packed and fans almost literally hanging from the rafters—some were clinging to the supporting struts of two huge billboards beyond the outfield walls. Inside, Bob Gibson lived up to Dick Williams' nightmares, striking out 10 in a complete game, 2–1 victory. As for Sox slugger Carl Yastrzemski, whose batting average in Boston's final 12 games had been a stratospheric .523, Gibson held him hitless. "A good pitcher beat us," was all Sal Maglie had to say afterward.[20]

In Game Two on October 5, a well-rested Jim Lonborg pitched one of the most brilliant games in Series history, a one-hit shutout that was a perfect game until the seventh inning and a no-hitter until the eighth. He began it in true Maglie style, with a chin-grazing fastball to Lou Brock, who had scored both of the Cardinals' runs the day before, and he dropped three more St. Louis batters in the course of the game. The ball that sent Brock to the ground brought howls from the Cardinals' bench. Lonborg glanced over there and pulled another move from Maglie's bag of psychological tricks: he *laughed*. Yaz came back from his collaring by Gibson, accounting for four of

Boston's five runs with homers in the fourth and seventh innings. Boston's 5–0 victory evened the Series at a game apiece. After the game most reporters clustered around Lonborg and Yastrzemski, but a few sought out the team's quiet pitching coach, who sat unobtrusively in a corner. Sal Maglie spoke softly but with real pleasure, telling reporters that the game just completed had been the best Lonborg had pitched all year. "It was a great personal satisfaction to me to see Lonborg pitch like that," Sal declared. Maglie also expounded on the lessons Lonborg had learned, talking about how he had helped Lonborg gain control of his curve ball, his "strike pitch." "A strike pitch," Sal explained, "is a pitch you have enough confidence in that you can get it over anytime when you really need it. In spring training we worked on his fastball, and that in turn helped him master his curve, which is his 'strike pitch.'"[21] Sal's comments fit with the remarks, noted above, made by Lonborg years later. He had learned Sal's lessons well.

The Series moved to St. Louis for the third, fourth, and fifth games. In Game Three on October 7, the Cards' Nelson Briles outlasted a succession of Boston pitchers as St. Louis took the game, 5–2. In Game Four the Sox faced Bob Gibson again. As in Game One, his opponent was José Santiago, who had pitched a fine game in his first Series outing, giving up only two runs. But this time the overpowering Cardinal righthander tossed a five-hit shutout, while Santiago suffered an elbow injury and failed to make it past the first inning. The Cardinals won, 6–0, and now led the Series, three games to one. The Redbirds hoped to clinch the Series on their home turf, but Jim Lonborg had other plans for them in Game Five. On October 9 he tossed another gem, a three-hitter that defeated the Cardinals, 3–1. Lonborg set a new Series record for fewest hits allowed in two consecutive World Series games: four. As the Series went to Game Six the contests moved back to Boston, and at Fenway on October 11 the Sox clobbered the Cardinals, 8–4, as they smacked around eight St. Louis hurlers. The Series would go to seven games.

For the deciding contest on October 12 the Cards had the well-rested Bob Gibson ready, but Boston had to go with an exhausted Jim Lonborg, pitching on only two days' rest. Maglie tried to be optimistic as he spoke with a reporter: "With two such great pitchers as Jim Lonborg and Bob Gibson going today, I look for a real close game, and a break to win the World Series. . . . Lonborg will do okay if he has his stuff. He's determined and will be pitching on nerve as much as anything else," Sal admitted.[22]

Despite the positive spin from the Boston pitching coach, Game Seven proceeded along lines that experts had predicted and Red Sox fans dreaded. A foreboding silence descended on the sell-out crowd at Fenway as Dal Maxvill, the weakest hitter in the St. Louis lineup, smacked a triple in the third inning and scored on a single by Curt Flood. A single by Roger Maris followed, then a wild pitch by the frazzled Lonborg allowed Flood to score, and the Cards led, 2–0. St. Louis picked up two more runs in the fifth, although Lonborg was trying so hard that sometimes his cap flew off as he threw. Bob Gibson poled a home run into the center field bleachers. After that, Lou Brock singled to left, stole both second and third on Lonborg, and came home on Roger Maris' sacrifice fly, making the score 4–0, Cardinals. Boston cadged a run off Gibson in the bottom of the fifth, although it took a Cardinals throwing error for them to accomplish it.

In the sixth inning it all fell apart for Boston. With two men on, Dick Williams made a trip to the mound but left Lonborg in. The next batter, Julian Javier, clobbered the staggering pitcher for a three-run homer, making the score 7–1 and putting the game out of Boston's reach. When the inning ended, as all innings do sooner or later, Lonborg walked slowly off the mound, head bowed, shoulders sagging, tears streaming down his cheeks. Every fan in Fenway rose to give the battered hero a thunderous ovation. Too distraught to respond, Lonborg continued on his way through the dugout and back toward the locker room. Sal Maglie left the bench and caught up with him, trying to console the heartbroken hurler, telling him, "Jim, you got nothing to be ashamed of. You brought us here, and you took us this far. You did a hell of a job"[23]—all the usual conventions of comfort that were, as usual, no comfort at all. The final score, three innings later, was 7–2, but as Lonborg left the mound, everybody knew it was over.

The question of why Dick Williams left Lonborg in so long, when he clearly was too exhausted to be effective, remains controversial. In Lonborg's recollection, Williams came to the mound with the intention of taking the pitcher out, but he talked the manager into allowing him to continue. "Dick was thinking of taking me out in the sixth, but I wanted to pitch," Lonborg related. "I felt I could get those batters out."[24] When asked, Williams replied curtly, "I was the manager—I was going with my ace," and did not elaborate on the thinking that led him to leave Lonborg in the game.[25] Sal Maglie had a different story to tell. He remained convinced that Williams should have taken Lonborg out well before he did and should not have allowed him to take the terrible pasting he suffered in the sixth inning, regardless of what Lonborg himself might have wanted. "Williams should have yanked him sooner," Sal told Larry Claflin shortly after the Series ended. "It was degrading to let him take that beating after Lonborg did such a great job all season. I told [Williams] he should take him out, but he simply ignored me."[26]

A few months later, Maglie sat down with sportswriter Robert Boyle and related the incident in detail. Sal considered Williams' decision to leave Lonborg in the game when he was being blasted was a deliberate humiliation of a fine young pitcher, and if there was one thing that enraged Sal, it was any attempt to humiliate him or someone he cared about. This time, it was a young pitcher Sal liked, in whose career he had invested a great deal of time and effort. Sal claimed that already in the second inning it was clear that Lonborg had nothing. "I was hoping Williams would take him out of there. I think he owed it to Jim to do that. It was the decent thing to do. Besides, we had 10 other pitchers in the bullpen, and if one of them could hold the Cardinals we might win."[27] Years later another Red Sox pitcher, Gary Bell, confirmed Sal's judgment: "I do think [Williams] went a little too far with [Lonborg.] I really do. . . . He had five or six guys in the bullpen who were ready to pitch."[28] When Sal saw Lonborg's tears, he became even angrier at Williams. He knew, better than Lonborg might have suspected, how overwhelming the sorrow had to be to reduce a man to weeping. As he tried to comfort Lonborg, Sal was thinking "how lousy it was for a manager to do that to his ace pitcher. You just don't let a guy who pitched like Lonborg had get pounded like that."[29]

As the story came out, so did revelations of how miserable Maglie had been during the 1967 season. Sal had kept quiet about his conflicts with Dick Williams, but when the season ended there was no longer any reason for him to conceal the problems because, within 24 hours of the end of the Series, Williams fired Maglie. The firing itself did not upset Sal as much as the way it was done. He had been expecting it and had even offered to re-sign halfway through the season. On the day the Series ended, Maglie dropped in at Williams' office to say good-bye. The two men shook hands and, according to Maglie's recollection, Williams said, "I'll be in touch with you, buddy."[30] Instead, Maglie received a phone call at his Boston hotel the next evening from Sox general manager Dick O'Connell, who broke the news. "Dick [Williams] wants another pitching coach next year," O'Connell told Maglie, adding that he was personally sorry but that Williams had another man in mind.[31] At a press conference the next day, after Williams had signed a three-year contract with the Red Sox, he officially revealed the firing of Maglie. "I want a pitching coach who will spend more time teaching our young pitchers. The decision to replace Maglie was mine, and mine alone," Williams stated.[32] He then confirmed that his other three coaches, Eddie Popowski, Bobby Doerr, and Al Lakeman, would be retained. Only Maglie's services were no longer needed.

Although Dick Williams never provided any reasons for firing Maglie, beyond those just noted, Bobby Doerr suggested that Maglie was too independent for Williams' taste. "Sal knew what he wanted to do, and maybe that didn't go along with what Dick Williams wanted to do. Williams was a real organized type—he wanted to know exactly when guys were going to pitch; he wanted a chart of all that, and I don't think Sal was gung-ho about that. If there was a problem, that's what it would have been. Williams wanted *everything* on a chart, wanted to know exactly when particular pitchers were going to be ready. I don't think Sal liked that." Sal was old-fashioned —he relied on his intuition and instincts, honed by years of experience, and he refused to become involved with the tedious business of chart-making. "Sal just wasn't quite as organized as Williams," Doerr observed. "He never gave Williams the charts that Williams wanted. Sal knew the stuff, but he had it mostly in his head. He kept a little pad where he wrote things, but I don't think he had what Williams wanted. He wanted to know which pitchers would be ready one day, and then the second, third, and fourth day."[33]

Sal was furious about every aspect of the way his dismissal had been handled. Williams failed to do the job himself, handing it off to the general manager. He added a gratuitous swipe at Sal's competence by saying he wanted someone who would spend more time teaching young pitchers, when the molding of youthful hurlers into successful moundsmen had been Sal's proudest achievement as the Boston pitching coach. And to find out that Williams had replaced him not with another former pitcher, but with former backup catcher Darrell Johnson, was the final indignity. Maglie returned to Niagara Falls in a fuming rage.

He had been back in The Falls for only a week or so when he suffered still another misfortune: on the night of October 22 he was involved in a car accident that resulted in a minor whiplash injury. Ten days after the accident Sal checked himself into Memorial Medical Center in Niagara Falls, complaining of problems with his neck. While there Sal delivered himself of the longest and angriest tirade of his life, a blast against Dick Williams that began as a telephone interview with sympathetic Boston sportswriter George Sullivan and soon appeared in both the local paper and in baseball's bible, the *Sporting News*. The latter assured that everyone in the baseball world would hear Sal's side of the story.

"Dick Williams gave me the biggest disappointment I ever got in baseball," Maglie declared, referring both to his firing and the way it was carried out. "I don't like the way it was done. . . . Williams inked a three-year contract and then had me fired. . . . He didn't have the courage to tell me himself. . . . He should have done it like a man. . . . Williams never even had the courage or decency to tell me himself that I was fired. . . . I am well rid of Dick Williams and those around him . . . I got a bad deal from Dick Williams. I've kept quiet long enough. . . . I don't like being stepped on." Sal repeated the comments he had already made to the press about the error he believed Williams had made by leaving Lonborg in too long in the final game of the Series. Sal had been particularly insulted by Williams' implication that he had not done a good job of developing younger pitchers, and he cited not only Lonborg but also Bill Monbouquette and Earl Wilson as examples of pitchers he had helped to form. He could have included Dick Radatz and José Santiago as well. He concluded his remarks with a criticism of Williams' choice of a former catcher as his new pitching coach. "I think a pitching coach should be a former pitcher," he declared. "He should have that feeling—know what it's like to be out on the mound."[34]

Dick Williams refused to be drawn into a printed shouting match with his fired pitching coach. Asked for his response to Maglie's remarks, Williams said, "I have great respect for Sal as a pitcher and as a gentleman. But I made the decision to change coaches and Sal had to go."[35] He also admitted that he made a mistake in not calling Maglie personally to tell him of his dismissal. He claimed, however, that he told general manager Dick O'Connell that he would make the call to Maglie but that O'Connell wanted to phone Sal himself. Williams has stuck to his story with remarkable consistency. Asked about the issues 37 years later, he gave the same answers he had provided in 1967. Maglie, although he had gotten the matter off his chest, continued to dwell on its consequences for him. Asked about his future in baseball shortly after his firing, Sal responded, "Right now, I feel like quitting baseball for good, coming home and finding another job, but that is just bitter disappointment talking." Asked if there was any truth to the rumor that he might become the pitching coach with the New York Mets under new manager Gil Hodges, Sal said he had not been approached by the Mets. When asked about his immediate plans, he could only answer, "I don't know."[36]

1968–1969—Maglie's Stint with the Seattle Pilots

21

1968—A YEAR OF STRUGGLE AND RECOVERY

After the 1967 season Sal was in no hurry to go home, mostly because he no longer really had a home. The house on Park View Drive, which had been gathering dust and cobwebs since Kay's death, had been sold in July of 1967 for substantially less than Sal had paid to have it built, and its contents had been dispersed in a yard sale.[1] Sal and his two sons, as well as Mae Pileggi, were still living with John and Mary Pileggi, but Sal was not comfortable with the situation. So, instead of leaving for Niagara Falls as soon as the Series ended and Williams fired him, he lingered in Boston a few more days, hoping another coaching offer might come his way, but none did. This time, when he returned to Niagara Falls, there was no welcoming parade.

The reason Sal was less than eager to return to The Falls concerned the lack of privacy afforded him in the living arrangement with the Pileggi family. Sal was accustomed to coming and going as he pleased, and he kept late hours. Kay had disliked those habits but realized she could not change them. While Kay was alive, Mae Pileggi had put up with them as well, but with Kay gone, Mae was doubly indignant to find her son-in-law still going out nearly every evening and not returning until well past midnight. Sometimes he came in drunk, sometimes weary and lethargic from—Mae was sure—having to haul himself out of a woman's bed. This, she felt, was no way for a recent widower to behave. No matter how late or how quietly Sal crept into the house, Mae was there waiting for him, and a fight invariably erupted between them. Mary Pileggi recalled being awakened by their loud arguments. "My daughter's still warm in her grave," the inconsolable Mae Pileggi would shout, "and you're out chasin'!" According to Mae's thinking, Mary continued, "Sal was supposed to be sitting at home mourning. But what was he doing instead? Meeting the guys in the bars, chasing around with women. Every night, they'd wake up everyone. She'd yell at him, 'Where've you been?' And he'd yell, '*You leave me alone! Did Kay ever lack for anything from me? NO!!! You know I married Kay for love. I loved her so much, and I still do! Don't you think this is hurting me?'*"[2] By this point Sal would be close to tears, and even more furious at his mother-in-law for reducing him to that state than for her noisy monitoring of his private life, although he bitterly resented that as well. He had buried his grief over Kay's death deep inside him, but there was Mae, night after night, insisting he drag it out and dwell on it. The situation grew intolerable.

Within a few months Sal and his sons moved into the home of Sal's sister Carmen. The younger of Sal's two older sisters, Carm (as the family called her) had married late; her husband was a kindly Italo-Canadian named Dominick Mancuso, and the couple had no children. They owned a bungalow on LaSalle Avenue in Niagara Falls, and they remodeled the attic so Sal and his boys would have a place to live. Mae Pileggi stayed on with her son John and daughter-in-law Mary, and although Mae and Sal eventually patched things up, they were never close again. Carm, in contrast to Mae, did not interfere with her brother's life, and she relished the role of surrogate mother. "She was trying to be super-mom," Maria Grenga Rizzo recalled. "I'd go over there and she'd say, 'Look! I made cookies for the boys!'" Sal still did not spend much time around the house, day or night, nor did he spend a lot of time with his children. "He was always such a busy man!" Maria recalled.[3] Kay's death had left both boys bewildered and frightened, but Sal Jr., whose attachment to his adoptive mother had been intense, was particularly affected. Joey had joined the family just as Kay became ill again, and as a result, he had not known the full force of Kay's love to the extent that his older brother had, so he coped better with her death. Joey became a resilient and successful survivor, while Sal Jr. began a downward spiral into emotional chaos and self-destructiveness.

As the autumn of 1967 turned into the winter of 1968, Sal's spirits may have been lifted a little by the results of the Hall of Fame balloting. In a year when Joe Medwick was admitted with 240 votes and Roy Campanella received 205, missing election by only eight votes, Sal was twenty-ninth on the list, with 11 votes. That total came nowhere close to putting him within hailing distance of the Hall, but it was an honor even to be included among the names on the ballots. A March 1968 article in the *Sporting News* offered further consolation, noting that 1967 might have set a record for firings of coaches. Sal was hardly alone—there had been 35 coaching changes in the majors since the season's end.

The year 1968 proved tumultuous both for the country and for baseball. Across America protests against the Vietnam war increased, and president Lyndon Johnson announced that he would not seek another term; the assassination in April of the Rev. Martin Luther King Jr., and just two months later of Robert F. Kennedy, shook the country; and riots at the Democratic National Convention in Chicago made citizens wonder if the nation's basic political structures were collapsing. Even major league baseball, which usually stayed pretty much the same, began to change at an accelerated pace. In October of 1967 American League owners approved the transfer of the Kansas City Athletics to Oakland and their replacement in Kansas City by an expansion team, to be known as the Royals. They also awarded a franchise to Seattle. In late May of 1968, National League owners approved the entry of two more expansion teams for the 1969 season, the Padres in San Diego and the Expos in Montreal.

The 1968 season is called "The Year of the Pitcher," because of the way pitchers dominated it: there were 339 shutouts, including 82 games that ended in scores of 1–0; Los Angeles Dodgers ace Don Drysdale threw a record-shattering six consecutive shutouts and had a streak of 58 2/3 scoreless innings; the Cardinals' Bob Gibson tossed five consecutive shutouts, and his ERA was an almost invisible 1.12, while six other pitchers also had ERAs under 2.00; the Tigers' Denny McLain won 31 games; and all but one American League batter hit under .300. In response to complaints that fans wanted to see more long-ball hitting, major league baseball instituted rule changes after the 1968 season, aimed at curbing the power of pitchers. The mound was lowered from 15 inches to 10 inches, and the strike zone decreased: it had previously been defined as from the shoulders to the knees, but now it shrank to between the armpit and the top of the knees.

By 1968 the city of Seattle had a major league franchise, with its new team, named the Pilots because owner Dewey Soriano had once been a tugboat pilot, scheduled to begin play in 1969. In June of 1968 Maglie signed on as a pitching coach with the Pilots' minor league affiliate, the Newark (NY) Co-Pilots. The signing seems to have been a formality, since Maglie's contract called for a "salary" of one dollar per month. Sal's main duties consisted of scouting for the fledgling Pilots, the basis of his actual salary from the Seattle organization. Although Niagara Falls was not far from Newark, Sal lived at a motel in Newark during the 1968 baseball season. He wanted his privacy.

When Sal joined the Newark team as a coach, the manager was another utility player from the 1950s, but—unlike Dick Williams—one closer to his own age and background and much more congenial: the relaxed and good-humored Sibby Sisti. The two men had known each other while playing for different teams in the majors but became friends when they found themselves together in Newark. They kept each other company, keeping at bay the boredom of minor league life. Sisti remembered Maglie with affection. "He was a quiet type of guy—very serious at times, never loud or boisterous. I remember once when he got mad at me, though, because we both liked to do crossword puzzles. One night he bought the paper, but I'm working on the puzzle, and he got mad because I was filling up all the blank spaces. So from then on, we had to buy two papers, just so we could each do the puzzle. This was at night, after a game, back at the motel. There was nothing else to do. Have a bite to eat, and go back and read the paper. Sometimes in those small towns, it was tough even to find a paper in the evening." Quite a comedown from the big league life, but Sal did not complain. "Sal never griped about anything or anybody," Sisti continued. "He went out and did his work. Everybody had respect for him. His biggest asset was his pitching ability. He'd work with these young kids who were just coming out of high school or college, and he gave them a lot of valuable help. I thought he did a real good job."[4]

Sal did not talk about his personal life. "He never discussed his family," Sisti related. "I knew he had problems with his older boy, but he didn't talk about him. More or less we just talked baseball." Sisti's wife came to Newark on weekends when the team was at home, and so did Sal's girlfriend. Sisti assumed that the woman who spent weekends with Sal was his wife, and Sal did not correct him, but when reminded that Maglie did not remarry until 1971, Sisti chuckled, "I guess it was his girlfriend, then. I mean the one he married." Maglie's friend Benny Critelli recalled that even after Sal retired from baseball, "a lot of women would come up to Sal, right here in Niagara Falls, and ask for his autograph and his phone number. Just like that—give me your autograph and your phone number!"[5] Teenage boy, young buck, or balding, middle-aged man, Maglie never lacked for attention from women.

By the summer of 1968 Sal was more or less openly involved with Doris Ellman, the woman who became his second wife. When and how they met is uncertain, although Doris Maglie thought it was probably at one of the two Niagara Falls restaurants where Sal often passed his evenings: Macri's Palace or the Como.[6] Both establishments have a bar and lounge area, and that was where Sal spent his evenings. If he was hoping to find a woman who would *not* remind him of his first wife, he could hardly have done better than Doris. Kay was Sal's age; petite, curvaceous, and dark in coloring; she was Italian and Catholic; once married she never worked outside the home; other than her husband's career, she had few interests beyond home-making and child-raising; and she had been a lifelong baseball fan who knew the game thoroughly. Doris, in contrast, was 10 years younger than Sal; she was tall and trim; her background was German Lutheran; she was an independent woman, a divorcee raising a daughter, as well as handling a de-manding career as a legal secretary for a Buffalo law firm; and she could not have cared less about baseball.

When she first began spending time with him, Doris had no idea who Sal was or how famous he was, and with his typical modesty, he did not tell her. She found out when she mentioned him to her mother, who recognized the name and was delighted to learn that her daughter was dating Sal Maglie. Doris' ignorance may seem incredible in a woman who grew up in Tonawanda, a town next-door to Niagara Falls, but she seems to have been oblivious to baseball in a way that some women can be utterly oblivious to a sport in which they have no interest. In choosing Doris from among the many women vying for his attention, Sal chose wisely. He did not want a woman interested in him for his past glory and continuing fame; there were plenty of those wherever he went. Sal was happy to find a woman who was not a baseball fan, since that meant her interest in him was genuine. Even after she became aware of Sal's fame, Doris did not quite believe it was real. She recalled the first time she accompanied Sal to New York City. He warned her that he was going to receive a lot of attention at their hotel and on the street and that he would have to stop often to sign autographs. She thought he had "an awfully swelled head," but it turned out to be true.[7]

Sal loved that kind of attention and still had not entirely given up pitch-ing. Canadian sportswriter Bob Elliott spotted Maglie in Brantford, Ontario, in the late 1960s, in a charity game to raise money for the Shriners. He was a member of the Buffalo Simon Pures—one of his teams as a high school boy. Opposing him for Brantford was the even more ancient Negro League legend Satchel Paige. Elliott remembered, "In the first inning, Brantford's Al Dorstal laid down a bunt on the aging Maglie and beat it out easily. That didn't set well with Maglie." When Dorstal came to bat again in the third, "The Barber knocked him down, not once, but twice, on pitches right under the hair on his chinny-chin chin."[8] Sometimes, old dogs do not need to learn new tricks—the original ones still work.

Toward the end of the summer of 1968, when it became known that Sal was returning to major league baseball as a coach for the expansion Seattle Pilots, the town of Niagara Falls held another Sal Maglie Day. This one con-sisted of a recognition of Maglie's achievements between games of a double-header featuring the Buffalo Bisons and the Syracuse Chiefs at Hyde Park Stadium in Niagara Falls. There was a brief ceremony, with the presentation of gifts and a plaque. The event, held on August 29, also commemorated the

30th anniversary of Sal's first professional game, his (disastrous) debut with the Bisons in 1938. The large committee that planned the occasion included some of Sal's old friends, among them Dr. Salvatore Latona and Dominick Iannuzzi, but unlike past events in Sal's honor, this time the names were not predominantly Italian. Sal's fame and appeal had long ago transcended ethnic boundaries. A day or so before the event, Sal told a Buffalo reporter how happy he was to be returning to major league baseball. "I'm doing the thing I want to do the most," Sal declared. "I'm working in baseball."[9]

THE 1969 SEATTLE PILOTS

At the conclusion of the 1968 World Series Sal was officially hired as a coach for the Pilots, although he was already in Seattle's employ. Joe Schultz, formerly a coach with the Cardinals, had been chosen as the Pilots' manager. He announced that Maglie would be his pitching coach and former Yankee infielder Frank Crosetti his third base coach. Schultz did not know Maglie or Crosetti; their selection had been dictated by the team's general manager, Marvin Milkes, on the basis of the hoped-for gate appeal of their familiar and popular baseball names.

The Pilots front office was enthusiastic about Maglie. General manager Milkes said that one of Sal's prime duties would be to work with young pitching hopefuls selected by the Pilots in the free-agent draft, a relatively recent system where existing teams were required to make available a group of players from which the new teams could build their rosters. "The selection of Maglie culminates our search for the 'right man' to whom we can entrust the futures of these young athletes," Milkes declared. Sal was equally happy to see his selection as pitching coach made official. "I couldn't be happier returning to baseball," he declared, "especially with the opportunity to work with a young club again."[10]

Maglie displayed optimism about the Pilots' pitching, at least around reporters. "People are talking us third and picking us sixth," Sal stated in baseball shorthand, "[but] don't sell our pitching short. It's too early to tell—and all the teams seem to be in the same boat with a slow development of pitchers. Ours are getting the ball over the plate a little better every day. They're working out their problems. They'll be OK," Maglie concluded, sounding a little defensive.[11] Sal was working with individual pitchers, trying to help each one. "He sees those little things you do wrong without knowing," said Diego Segui, one of the team's relief pitchers. Marty Pattin, a Seattle starter, gave Maglie credit for spotting and correcting a fault in his delivery. In his first spring training start, Pattin had been ineffective, giving up six runs and four walks in four innings. "He changed my delivery," the pitcher said. "Before, I had a lot of wasted effort. . . . Sal got me to take less of a wind-up and to stop rearing back."[12] In his next start, Pattin pitched five shutout innings, giving up only two hits and one walk. So far, Sal seemed to be doing what he had been hired to do: correcting pitchers' problems, helping them improve—the same technique that had worked well with the Red Sox.

But the 1967 Red Sox had been a championship-caliber squad needing only to be jump-started, while the 1969 Seattle Pilots were for the most part as sorry a collection of has-beens, wannabe's, and never-was's as ever slunk onto a major league diamond. During the expansion draft, the Pilots had acquired a roster, but many of the players were injury-plagued rejects whom established teams had made available merely because they wanted to be rid of them. In contrast, the pitchers the Pilots acquired were a fairly promising crew. From Boston, Seattle picked up Gary Bell, who had averaged 10 wins a year during an 11–year career, had been an All-Star three times, and had contributed 12 wins to the Red Sox 1967 pennant. From the Angels they got Marty Pattin, a durable righthander. Another acquisition was Diego Segui, who had enjoyed a solid season with the Athletics in 1968, compiling a 2.39 ERA in 52 relief appearances. Mike Marshall, a righthander picked up from Detroit, had been brought up from the minors late in 1967 and posted a brilliant 1.98 ERA, but he was determined to complete a college degree and therefore arrived late for spring training in 1968, a sin for which Tigers manager Mayo Smith banished him to the minors and never recalled him. Steve Barber, acquired from the Yankees, had won 20 games for the Orioles before developing arm problems.

One of the Pilots' first-round draft picks was Jim Bouton, a free-thinking righthander acquired from the Yankees. After a so-so first season in 1962, he won 21 games in 1963 and 18 the next year, when he posted two World Series victories. But in 1965 Bouton developed a sore arm that ruined his fastball, and he tried to compensate by developing a knuckleball. He compiled a poor 9–24 record for the years 1965–68, before being shipped to Seattle. For Bouton, after his heady years with the Yankees, this was the baseball equivalent of being sent to Siberia. Restless, rebellious, articulate, and creative, Bouton channeled some of his energies into a diary of his 1969 season, much of it spent with the Pilots. Bouton's diary became *Ball Four,* the best-selling sports book ever written. The tell-all volume about sex, drug use, voyeurism, profanity, and general idiocy among major leaguers made a wealthy man of Jim Bouton and a fool of Sal Maglie.

Bouton was elated at first to learn that Maglie was the Pilots' pitching coach. Sal had been his hero when he was a kid, and now he hoped for a chance to learn something from his boyhood idol. Maglie, who had participated in the draft that chose the Pilots players, no doubt considered Bouton one of the stronger members of the team's pitching staff, but the two men were a mismatch, and relations between them quickly grew strained. Maglie concluded that Bouton was a washed-up whiner whose prized pitch, the knuckleball, was a trick unworthy of attention from a serious craftsman like himself, and he wanted Bouton to master other pitches. The quick-witted Bouton thought Maglie was a ludicrous-looking incompetent who was worse than useless as a pitching coach and dumber than a bag of hammers. What they had in common, neither man noticed. Bouton, hoping to coax a few more major league games out of his ruined right arm, and Maglie, still trying to repackage his pitching expertise as consistent coaching success, were both hanging on in desperation, trying to last one more year, one way or another, in the game they both loved.

In a year that saw a man walk on the moon and the once-hopeless New York Mets win the World Series, as well as the first divisional play and the experimental use of the designated hitter in spring training games, the brief existence of those one-year wonders, the Seattle Pilots, could have become a footnote to baseball history, were it not for Bouton's book, which brought the team unexpected immortality. For many team members, including Maglie, it was a form of immortality they could have done without. To be fair to Bouton, he did not single out Maglie. He was cruel to all the coaches, seeing them as annoying and irrelevant old coots hanging on in order to increase their pensions. Nonetheless, there is something uniquely nasty in Bouton's skewering of Maglie, a bitterness born of disillusion when his childhood hero failed to live up to his expectations. It is legitimate for a player to complain about a coach's competence but needlessly unkind to make fun of the man's appearance, something outside his control. Bouton noted Maglie's "big evil-looking black eyes." Once a vital part of Sal's intimidating image, Bouton thought they made Maglie look "like Snoopy doing his vulture bit." His teammates, Bouton reported, could not decide whether Sal looked more like an Indian chief or a Mafia enforcer. Bouton also thought Maglie's long, severe face made him look like "the friendly neighborhood undertaker. You can just see him standing in the mortuary doorway saying, 'Oh yes, we have something very nice for you in mahogany.'" Bouton relayed other unflattering nicknames for Maglie, including The Screaming Skull, after a character in a movie of the same name, and—sarcastically—My Pal Sal and Mother Maglie.[13]

All this may seem funny, except to the object of the humor. Sal had always hated being humiliated—it was one of the few experiences that could goad him to real fury. *Ball Four* was published in 1970, when Sal was no longer in major league baseball, but he soon found out about it, since the book created a national sensation. One can imagine Sal burning with embarrassment as he read Bouton's insulting portrayal of him. As with all things that upset him deeply, Sal avoided talking about the book. Friends and family members recalled that he disliked it but that he did not spend time discussing it. Nonetheless, when an interviewer asked him about it in 1974, Sal did not conceal his bitterness and anger. "Bouton, huh?" Maglie growled. "You want to know about Jim Bouton? I don't think you could print what I can say about him. [The book] was bullshit. I'll tell you about Bouton. He was like a spoiled little brat, always had to have things his own way. I had nine or ten other pitchers to worry about and he was forever comin' around botherin' me about his knuckleball. . . . If he'd still been useful as a pitcher he wouldn't be writin' books, would he? . . . Bouton was washed up—if it hadn't been for the expansion he'd of been in the minors. And even then he wouldn't've made it." Asked if he had read the book, Maglie retorted, "Yeah, I read it. Anybody who read that book and couldn't see Bouton for what he really is has got to be blind."[14]

Pictures of Maglie taken in 1969 convey an air of undisguised weariness and disillusion (Figure 26). He was back in the majors, but he had paid a high price for his return. There is some truth in Bouton's portrait of Maglie as a man too old and conservative for the game in the late 1960s. Sal furthermore found himself marooned for much of the year some 3,000 miles from home, out of touch with his children, and far from the woman who made his life more tolerable. His gray hair, deeply lined, haggard face, and tired eyes made him seem a decade or more older than his age of 52. It is unlikely that Bouton, as he scribbled notes about Sal's appearance and recorded his remarks, had any awareness of Maglie's personal troubles. As far as Bouton was concerned, Maglie was merely an exasperating old man

26—Sal in Seattle Pilots uniform, 1969. Maglie's final year in major league baseball, as pitching coach for the Pilots, was a frustrating one, as his air of undisguised weariness indicates. Photo: George Brace.

who specialized in pointless second guesses and blockheaded non sequiturs.

The Pilots played their home games at Sick's Stadium, its unfortunate name derived from local beer baron Emil Sick, who had purchased the team in 1937 when it was a minor league franchise. By 1969 Sick's had become a dreary place where the lack of water pressure was a constant problem. On days when more than 10,000 fans were in the stands, the pressure plummeted almost to zero, making it impossible to flush the toilets. On those days the players had to return to their hotels in order to shower after the game.[15] Maglie must have wondered if he had landed in a chillier and rainier version of Mexico.

The team began its regular season on the road and won three of its first four games, but a loss to the White Sox on April 20 put the Pilots below .500 forever. Home attendance was terrible. On April 29, only 1,954 fans watched Marty Pattin throw a complete, two-hit, 11–strikeout game, beating the Angels, 1–0. Although by early May the Pilots were in last place, by the end of June they had risen to third. Marty Pattin had a 7–5 record, and in the bullpen Diego Segui was 6–3 with a respectable 3.38 ERA. Relief pitcher Bob Locker gave Maglie credit for his improved performance, commenting that Sal had made him throw more across his body, enabling him to hide the ball better, get more of his body into his pitches, and stay in better control of them. On the negative side, Steve Barber (1–1) and Mike Marshall (3–9) were disappointments, as both were suffering from shoulder problems. Marshall, like Bouton, had no patience with Maglie's advice. An intelligent and well-educated man who later earned a doctorate in exercise physiology, Marshall believed that Maglie, "like every other college and professional baseball pitching coach before him and since," had no idea what he was talking about when he offered pointers on pitching.[16]

By mid-July the Pilots occupied fifth place, and as the team began a road trip on August 24, their record was 48–76, putting them in sixth. At that point Jim Bouton was traded to the Houston Astros, removing at least one thorn from Sal Maglie's side. Although the team climbed back into fifth, on September 14 they fell to last place, remaining in the divisional cellar for the rest of the season. The Pilots finished with a 64–98 record, 33 games behind the Western Division champion Minnesota Twins. At season's end the Pilots met a fate no other modern major league team had ever suffered: they went bankrupt and folded after a single season. The following year the franchise moved to Milwaukee, where it emerged as the still thriving Brewers. Manager Joe Schultz and all the coaches were let go when the team moved. There was a fleeting rumor that Sal might be offered a coaching position with the Cleveland Indians, but nothing came of it. The year 1969 was Maglie's final, frustrating season in major league baseball. His career in the Show—which as player and pitching coach had extended across a quarter of a century—was over.

The Rest of His Days

Sal's Life After Baseball

22

What to do after baseball? That question has haunted most of the men who made major league ball-playing the center of their lives. A few, such as Jim Lonborg, who became a successful dentist, make smooth transitions into satisfying and prosperous postplaying careers, but many ex-ballplayers flounder around looking for something—anything—that will provide a decent income and a satisfaction comparable to the pleasure they derived from the summer game. Sal Maglie was not among the fortunate few who found a comfortable niche when his playing and coaching years ended. He retired just before Curt Flood challenged the reserve clause in December of 1969, the beginning of a process that led to a tipping of the balance from the side of the owners to the side of the players. The huge financial advantages players eventually gained came too late to benefit Sal, who had to continue working because, like the vast majority of players of his era, he had not saved enough to cover his post-playing years. He tried a variety of jobs, but none brought him much satisfaction or financial success. More and more, he found his greatest pleasure in reminiscing about the past.

GENERAL MANAGER OF THE NIAGARA FALLS PIRATES

Maglie's dismal season with the Seattle Pilots in 1969 did not kill his love for baseball, but it seems to have dawned on Sal during that year that his children were growing up without him. "I'm tired of traveling," he told a local reporter. "I'd like to stay home, settle down, and watch my two boys grow up. I just want to stay around here now, and work in some sports or athletic capacity."[1] Fortunately for that wish, Niagara Falls was about to field a new minor league team, an affiliate of the Pittsburgh Pirates called the Niagara Falls Pirates, managed by former New York Yankee Irv Noren. In March of 1970 the team hired Maglie as its general manager. Although in the meantime Sal had taken a position as a sales representative with wholesale liquor distributor Mullen and Gunn, the lure of the old ball game was irresistible. He reported turning down coaching positions with major league teams, reiterating: "I'd rather do what I'm doing now, instead of running all over the country. I've got two boys and I want to stay home."[2] Sal Jr. was 15 and Joey nearly 9, but Sal had never expressed such sentiments when the boys were younger. His son Joe confirmed that his father had been absent most of the time in his early childhood. "This may sound weird," he remarked, "but I don't really remember him until about 1970."[3]

Sal offered a variety of ideas for drumming up interest in the Pirates. According to the *Sporting News,* Sal "likes the idea of a lady fan looking under her seat at refurbished Hyde Park Stadium and finding she won 10 pounds of salami." Sal had plenty of other plans: "We don't want baseball alone," he declared. "We want people to enjoy coming out to the park and meeting their friends there." To this end Maglie planned to enliven the evenings with bat nights, helmet nights, benefit nights, parades, fireworks, sky divers, and clowns. "It's a little different when you're starting an organization like we are here," Sal explained. "In the majors and in Triple A, you already have an organization. We're starting from scratch."[4] Here, Sal was more than a figurehead, and he put great effort into making the team's debut year a success. He also tried to interest his sons in the team. Despite Sal's sporadic efforts, which had begun when each of the boys was a toddler, neither cared much for baseball. Joey preferred football and hockey. Although Sal Jr. served as bat boy for the Pirates and helped out around the clubhouse, he had no enthusiasm for the game and could hardly have found a better way of hurting his father than by rejecting the sport that had been so long at the center of his father's life. Maglie did not continue as general manager after 1970. The pressures of holding down two jobs had become too great. But he left the team in good condition and it survived until 1979, longer than any other minor league team Niagara Falls ever had.

STARTING OVER—REMARRIAGE AND A BLENDED FAMILY

On April 16, 1971, in a quiet civil ceremony, Sal married Doris Ellman. She confirmed that the lack of a Catholic wedding bothered Sal not at all. In her recollection he had never been religious. His remarriage caused some ill feeling at first, and his sister Carm was especially upset. She worshiped her brother and felt that nobody was good enough for him. But Sal's family was not bigoted, and they did not reject him because of his choice of a Protestant wife and a civil marriage. A few of his old Italian friends also had reservations, but most accepted his decision. Sal's friend Joe Calato observed, "I think he enjoyed Doris because she gave him a way of life he wouldn't have had without her. I doubt he wanted to be alone."[5] In general, both friends and family were glad to see Sal happy and well taken care of by an energetic, competent woman. One old buddy, Charles Powley, recalling Sal's free-spending habits from his days as a baseball star, was glad Sal married a career woman with a good income, and remarked with a laugh, "He got a wife who could *afford* him!"[6]

About six months after their marriage the couple purchased a handsome, four-bedroom home on Grand Island, a large, sparsely populated island that splits the Niagara River just south of the city of Niagara Falls. The town of Grand Island is small and is a considerably more upscale and attractive community than Niagara Falls. There, the couple began the complicated business of creating their blended family. Sal had his two boys, age 16 and 10, and Doris had a daughter named Holly, who was about the same age as Sal Jr.[7] According to Doris Maglie's recollections, Sal told her she would have no trouble with Little Sal but that Joey would be "a handful." His predictions proved how little he knew his own children. Joey, who had lost two mothers—his birth mother and Kay Maglie—before the age of six, accepted Doris, but Little Sal never did.

The older boy had already begun drifting out of his family's control while he was still living in Niagara Falls, but after his father's remarriage and the move to Grand Island his behavior grew worse. He could not come to terms with Kay Maglie's death. "I don't think he ever recovered," observed Cecilia Grenga Anderson, Sal's great-niece and Little Sal's second cousin. "He tried, but then he just decided to stop trying."[8] He became slovenly and defiant, refusing to bathe or cut his hair, and his long, "hippie" locks made Sal furious. But Little Sal's behavior was not merely a passing phase of adolescent authority-testing. The boy was developing serious mental problems made worse by alcohol and illegal drugs. His presence in the Maglie home on Grand Island became so disruptive that he soon was sent back to Niagara Falls, where he drifted around, staying with friends and relatives.

IN THE WORKING WORLD

With the last of his baseball positions behind him, Maglie concentrated on his work for Mullen and Gunn. He drove around his territory, promoting the company's products and persuading the owners of bars and restaurants to purchase them. As with all Sal's jobs outside baseball, this one depended on his baseball reputation. Sal's friend Mickey Rizzo recalled: "He was a good salesman, but his problem was, every time he went to a place, he'd see all his friends and start talking, and they'd ask him about baseball, and he'd tell them about it. He never said no to anything like that."[9] Thomas Pratt, a retired sales manager for Mullen and Gunn, recalled Sal in the 1970s as a good employee but a man best known as a teller of entertaining stories about his days as a pitcher. "He liked to reminisce about baseball," Pratt recalled. "Every place he went, people would always say, 'Oh my goodness, Sal Maglie!'"[10]

Among the stories Thomas Pratt heard Sal tell is one that sheds new light on a notorious incident from Sal's career with the Giants: the time, on April 23, 1955, when he threw a pitch behind Jackie Robinson's head. Sal recalled how angry it made him when Robinson crowded the plate. "The guy was standin' there, and he was takin' up the whole plate," Sal recalled. While Robinson waited at bat, Sal called his catcher, Wes Westrum, to the mound, and told him, "Here's what I'm gonna do." When Westrum heard what Sal had in mind, he exclaimed, "Oh my God! You'll get thrown out of the league!" What Sal had in mind, Pratt related, was to throw the ball *deliberately* behind Robinson's head. Sal did indeed throw the ball there, but never admitted he had done so on purpose until this occasion, long after he was out of baseball. The tale could be a bit of drama added to spice up an old story, but Sal was not given to exaggerating, so it makes one wonder if other times when his pitches sailed behind batters' heads were intentional as well.

In 1972, when he was 55, Sal experienced the first in a series of health problems that plagued him in his later years. On August 29 he suffered an apparent heart attack. Since both his parents had died of sudden, massive coronaries, Sal had reason to be concerned. Doctors diagnosed his condition not as a heart attack but as pericarditis, an inflammation of the covering of the heart. He remained hospitalized for three weeks, recovered completely, and never suffered further heart problems. But the health crisis had shaken him up and given him a glimpse of a future where medical bills might cause him to lose his home. In 1976 he transferred ownership of the house in Grand Island to his wife.[11]

Sal always enjoyed participating in Old Timers games—any excuse to put on a baseball uniform again—and he never missed the gatherings of baseball's oldsters held at Yankee Stadium and Shea Stadium (Figure 27). In 1974 Maglie appeared in a commemoration of a game he had never been allowed to forget: Don Larsen's perfecto in the 1956 World Series, where he was the losing pitcher. The television program "The Way It Was," hosted by Curt Gowdy, brought together some principals from that historic game. In addition to Larsen himself, Duke Snider, Mickey Mantle, Sal Maglie, and Casey Stengel participated. As highlights of the game appeared on the screen, the faces of the former players were superimposed. The others smiled, but Maglie's face remained melancholy. That game would never be a pleasant memory for him. When asked about it at a different moment that same year, Maglie was less gracious than he had been at the time it took place. "I didn't root for [Larsen]," Sal growled. "I wanted to knock his brains out."[12]

In 1976 Sal left Mullen and Gunn for a job that seemed perfect for him: membership coordinator for the Niagara Falls Convention and Visitors Bureau. Local journalist Don Glynn recalled: "They'd have Sal go around the city—people just loved to see him, talk with him about baseball—and in the process he would sell memberships in the convention bureau."[13] But there was a hitch: the position's $12,000 salary came from a CETA (Comprehensive Employment and Training Act) grant from the federal government, and the grant required that the person who held the job be a resident of Niagara County. Since Sal had moved to Grand Island, in Erie County, he could not meet the residency requirement. In applying for the position, he gave his previous address at his sister Carm's in Niagara Falls as his residence, a misrepresentation sufficient to attract attention. As with any position funded

27—Sal poses between his former Giants teammates Monte Irvin (left) and Willie Mays (right) at an Old Timers game in the 1970s. Photo: collection of Eddie Gadawski.

by a government grant, there were politicians crowding around the pork barrel, and several had their own candidates for the post. "Sal was caught in the political cross-fire," insisted Niagara Falls broadcaster and businessman Tom Darro.[14] The *Niagara Falls Gazette* published a chilly editorial: "The federal funds that support jobs of the kind Mr. Maglie was given are intended to help reduce unemployment in the counties they are given to, not to help the unemployed in neighboring counties. . . . There are too many unemployed people in Niagara County to be giving away jobs to people who don't live here." The editorial alluded to the chronic problem of unemployment in Niagara Falls, which had begun in the 1960s as the city's chemical industries began closing down or moving away, gradually turning the town into a rust-belt ruin. The United States Department of Labor advised the convention bureau that they could not hire Maglie.

Newsday, a paper published in New York City and on Long Island, ran an article about Sal that appeared in papers across the country as well as in the *Niagara Falls Gazette.* In it, Sal claimed he had applied for the job in good faith. "I'm registered in Niagara Falls, I own property in Niagara Falls—three partners and I own the land where a General Tire store is, but it doesn't produce any profit; everything has to go toward the mortgage. I sure pay more taxes to Niagara Falls than I do here (Grand Island.)" "Everything went down," Sal reported sadly. "People ask me if I want to go back to baseball, that maybe I could find a place. I doubt it. And anyway, it's too hard—that traveling. I couldn't take it." Told that he sounded bitter, Sal snapped, "Of course I'm bitter. Wouldn't you be? It's ridiculous. They make me feel like a criminal." In order to hire Sal, the bureau redefined the job, creating a new "staff" position, since, according to CETA rules, if the job was defined as a staff position, the residency requirement did not apply.

Despite the bitter taste left by the controversy, Sal accepted the job and worked hard at it. Reporter Don Glynn recalled accompanying a group of bureau personnel, including Maglie, to Washington, D.C. They set up shop in a ballroom of the Mayflower Hotel, where a big reception was planned, and Sal busied himself with making sure everything was in order. That done, he invited the surprised Glynn to join him for drinks in the hotel bar. "It's amazing how well you can get to know someone over a couple of drinks," the journalist recalled. Sal talked about his fear of flying and how he had worked out ways to avoid it while he was a player. He even talked about his son. "He started telling me about talking with Mickey Mantle— how they'd both had problems with their sons, with drugs and so on, and how they tried to work it out," Glynn related.[15]

The thrilled reporter could hardly believe he was sitting with Sal Maglie, listening to the former star reminisce, and he was hoping their conversation would continue, but Sal returned to the ballroom to check on last-minute details. Glynn followed him. "Then, all of a sudden I heard two guys practically *screaming*," Glynn remembered. "They were speaking Spanish. They were Cuban waiters, carrying big trays with glasses and table settings. Suddenly I understood what it was—they recognized Maglie! They'd seen him when he played in Cuba. I vividly recall that one guy got so excited he dropped about half the stuff off his tray, just out of sheer excitement. Sal was really touched by it. He said to me, 'I'm surprised that those guys remember me—it's been a long time!' He autographed a baseball for them, and that really made their day. Later I was in the lobby and I overheard them—they were *still* talking about it, and telling other employees about their experience."[16] The episode is a perfect example of Sal's name recognition. Maglie put his fame to good use, continuing to work for the convention bureau until his retirement at age 62 in 1979.

THE PRINCE OF PINE AVENUE

Pine Avenue is the Broadway of the Niagara Falls Italian community. A wide, straight street that cuts across central Niagara Falls from east to west, it is still lined with restaurants, bakeries, and other businesses bearing Italian names. Local businessman Anthony Rendina recalled how, during the summer and autumn, Pine Avenue hosted an open market, "with everybody from the neighborhood promenading down the street. It was for shopping but even more for socializing. As soon as people saw Sal there, they'd rush to shake his hand."[17] Some of the people were personal friends, and many were acquaintances, but most were residents thrilled to encounter their local hero, shake his hand, say a few words, and perhaps get his autograph, something he was always willing to provide. According to Cecilia Grenga Anderson, Sal never became impatient or dismissive of fans. "He loved baseball, and he loved his fans," his great-niece observed. "He was always thrilled when people would ask him for his autograph, or introduce him to their kids. That was what he loved the most. It didn't matter how many people walked up to him on the street, or interrupted his dinner at the Como. He always smiled, talked with people. I never remember him being annoyed."[18]

Sal slipped into retirement with ease. As Doris continued to commute to Buffalo to work, Sal slept late and then on spring and summer mornings puttered in his backyard vegetable garden, a major domestic interest since his move to Grand Island. In 1979 Joey graduated from high school and decided to pursue a career in the Air Force, a decision approved of by his father. But Little Sal had dropped out of high school and continued to sink deeper into a haze of depression, drugs, and alcohol. His father paid the rent on an apartment for him in Niagara Falls and checked on him every day, often bringing him groceries. Sal never talked to his friends or family members about the anguish his older son was causing him, but the boy's behavior was public knowledge.

Since Sal had never learned to do even the most rudimentary cooking, he drove into Niagara Falls for lunch during the week in the cold months, meeting old friends at the Como or Macri's Palace for a midday meal and a few hours of reminiscing. Jimmy Macri related an episode concerning Sal that occurred during his restaurant's annual venison festival. Local hunters provided free venison that the restaurant cooked and sold to diners, with the profits going to charity. One year, a hunter included some bear steaks. Bears are not scavengers, Jimmy explained; their diet is wholesome and their meat excellent. When offered a bear steak, Sal refused vehemently, declaring in his best baseball vernacular, "I ain't eatin' no fuckin' *bear!*" Jimmy promised to serve Sal venison but served him bear instead. Sal devoured his steak, declaring it the best venison he had ever tasted, at which point Jimmy told him what he had actually eaten. Sal growled, "You son of a bitch!" and then announced to his dining companions that he was going into the men's room to stick a couple of fingers down his throat. But he returned a few minutes later with the sheepish admission that he had been unable to make himself throw up. No matter what his mind thought, his stomach had no objection to digesting bear meat.[19]

And so, with one group of friends or another, at one restaurant or another, Sal passed his afternoons. Sometimes he and Joe Calato drove to the nearby town of Lewiston to buy a special brand of caramel corn that Sal liked. His friend remembered how on those trips Sal often seemed "sort of sad—melancholy. We'd be driving, and he'd start talking about life, and how things turned out, and he seemed just—sad."[20] That was a side of Sal few people saw. By the time Doris returned home from work, Sal would be home as well, sitting in the living room with Doris' two dogs curled up on either side of him. It was a comfortable domestic life, and were it not for Sal's constant worry about his older son, it would have been a happy one.

A highlight of 1980 was the small part Sal had in a Hollywood movie. The film, *It's My Turn,* starred Jill Clayburgh as a professor and Michael Douglas as a washed-up baseball player, following the usual rocky road to love. The film contains a sequence set at an Old Timers game at Yankee Stadium. The camera pans across the weathered faces and out-of-shape bodies of 20 or so old ballplayers as they stand on the field during the playing of the national anthem. Most chat and smile, but Sal stands silent, his face full of sadness, his shadowy eyes far away, as if recalling his experiences as a player on that same field. It is the film's only moving moment. A few frames later, first a white-haired Roger Maris and then a porky, grinning Mickey Mantle come to bat. The pitcher they face is a wider-waisted but still wiry-armed Sal Maglie, who takes a full windup and has no trouble getting the ball to the plate.

Sal had always enjoyed golf, and after his retirement he spent a lot of time on the links. He was not an especially good golfer, or at least he was not as good as his friends expected him to be, given his past athletic prowess. "He and I spent a lot of years golfing together," Joe Calato recalled. "We figured he should have been a *great* golfer because he was such a great pitcher, but he wasn't." Sal belonged to the Niagara Frontier Golf Club, but Calato, a successful local businessman, belonged to the tonier Niagara Falls Country Club. "Every time I'd bring Sal with me [to the country club], oh God, the people would get all excited that he was there!"[21] Sal also played in celebrity tournaments organized by other players, which sometimes brought him back to his old stamping grounds in and around New York City. Ernie Aloi, who became friendly with Sal through Maglie's connection with Aloi's neighbor, former Giants backup catcher Sal Yvars, often hosted Sal at his home in White Plains, New York. "We played golf together in the '70s and early '80s," Aloi recalled. "He'd come over to my house, we'd have dinner, we'd sit and talk about baseball. That man knew the game! One time I played golf with him and Willie Mays. Sal came down especially to play in the Willie Mays tournament—that's how much he thought of Willie."[22]

Sal enjoyed golf so much he used to say that if he had to die, he wanted to die on the golf course—and he almost did. On July 18, 1982, a hot, sunny Sunday, Sal spent the day golfing with a group of friends and did not return home until well into the evening. When he finally appeared, he told Doris he must have had a heat stroke and had spent several hours sitting in the clubhouse drinking ice water, thinking that might help. He said he had the worst headache of his life and was going straight to bed. For the next two days Sal did what his great-niece Cecilia called "his stoic old Italian thing." He dragged himself around with his headache unabated, swallowing over-the-counter painkillers that barely took the edge off, but refusing to see a doctor.

Finally, on July 21, even Sal's formidable tolerance for pain gave way before the unrelenting agony inside his head. He went to his doctor, who promptly checked him into the hospital. A brain scan pinpointed the problem. Sal had an aneurysm, a thinning and bulging of the wall of a blood vessel that was leaking blood into his brain. The accumulating blood was causing his worsening headache. Luckily, the vessel was located in an operable part of the brain, just above the right temple. He underwent brain surgery on July 24 to drain the blood and "clip" the aneurysm before it burst. Sal was extremely lucky. A week had passed between the onset of his symptoms and his surgery, and at any moment during that period the aneurysm could have burst, causing a massive hemorrhage and certain death. Maglie remained unconscious for three days. Doris called Sal's son Joe, who was stationed with the Air Force in Guam, and asked him to fly home. When Sal regained consciousness, he saw his younger son at his bedside, and as he later quipped, "that's when I realized I must've been in bad shape."[23] Although he remained in Intensive Care for six days and in the hospital for three weeks, he made a remarkable recovery. "He's pretty weak," his wife told reporters after he had returned home, "but he'll be his old self before long."[24] She added that he was already up, walking around, and complaining about the weeds in his backyard garden.

News of Sal's condition appeared in newspapers all over the country, and the former pitcher was inundated with thousands of get-well cards, telegrams, and letters, as well as flowers and gifts from every part of the country but especially from fans in New York. In the *Post,* a paper that had covered Sal's games for all three New York teams, Jerry Izenberg's column recalled Sal's fierce fighting spirit, and ended with a question: "Who among us who lived those marvelous years cannot truly say that we are praying for one of the family?"[25] In later decades Sal the Barber no longer inspired fear but had become such a beloved figure that he seemed like a member of every fan's family.

For the next two and a half years Sal Maglie savored his life with the gratitude of a man who has received a reprieve when he was already against the wall with his hands tied behind him, the blindfold on, and the firing squad taking aim. He had experienced more than a mere brush with death. It had been, in every sense, a head-on collision. He bore the traces of it in the form of a curved, indented scar high on his right forehead, where the surgeons had sawed through his skull in order to save his life. Now, organizations vied to honor Maglie, realizing they had come close to being obliged to honor him posthumously. Within a month of his release from the hospital, plans were underway in Niagara Falls to organize another Sal Maglie Day, and the city council voted to rename Hyde Park Stadium, calling it Sal Maglie Stadium.

On November 11, 1982, Niagara Falls held its final Sal Maglie Day. Given the honoree's weakened condition, there was no parade, just a dinner in Sal's honor at the American Legion post in Niagara Falls. The master of ceremonies was former Yankees broadcaster Mel Allen. Two of Maglie's teammates from the New York Giants, Sal Yvars and Bobby Thomson, attended. Along with Sal's wife Doris and other family members, almost a thousand fans filled the hall. "This is the Sal Maglie family," Bobby Thomson observed in admiration, looking out at the throng. There were telegrams from President Ronald Reagan, former Yankee teammates Mickey Mantle and Whitey

Ford, singer Frank Sinatra, and Yankees owner George Steinbrenner. The evening included numerous speeches, but Sal's was the shortest and sweetest. In tears, he whispered to the gathering: "This is one of the greatest days of my life. Thank you."[26]

Maglie traveled to New York City in early May of 1983, where he received an award from the B'nai B'rith Sports Lodge at its annual dinner. Perhaps among the attendees were men who, more than 30 years earlier, had smuggled portable radios into their synagogues during High Holy Days services and hidden them under their prayer shawls in order not to miss the Dodgers-Giants playoff games in 1951. When Sal made his brief remarks to the group, he spoke of how happy he was "to be here" and explained that he meant more than merely here in New York on a dais at an awards ceremony. He meant "here" on this earth as opposed to six feet under it. He spoke briefly about his brush with death, mentioning the enormous amount of mail he had received from fans while he was in the hospital. "That'll heal you real fast," he told his audience.[27]

On June 21, 1983, Niagara Falls officially rededicated Hyde Park Stadium, naming it Sal Maglie Stadium. During the ceremonies, a bronze plaque with Sal's portrait, and an inscription noting that he had played for all three New York teams, was presented to him. It was to be placed on one of the stadium walls. Sal was delighted by the honor but surprised to see himself portrayed in a Yankee cap and uniform. He was too polite to say anything about it in public, but in private he mentioned that he would have preferred to be shown as a Giant or a Dodger. Recovered from his surgery and looking dapper and handsome as ever, Maglie thanked the crowd and the city officials who had made the rededication a reality. "I'm very thrilled," Sal said. "This is a great honor, the biggest ever bestowed on me."[28]

Less than a week later, on June 26, Maglie participated in a special Old Timers game, this one in Elmira, New York, where he had played in 1941 for the minor league Elmira Pioneers. A group of 52 former players came back for a reunion climaxed by a five-inning Old Timers' game. The man behind the reunion was Al Mallette, then sports editor of the *Elmira Star-Gazette*. Mallette recalled that Maglie was the most prominent former major leaguer to show up for the event and the most modest. "He came down from Niagara Falls to Elmira by bus!" Mallette exclaimed. "The organizers told him that if he wanted to fly down, they'd pay for it, but Sal refused. Sal was a great guy, not one of those arrogant types. Anybody who'd ride on a bus 145 miles, less than a year after having brain surgery—some guys would have demanded a limo! We offered to send someone to Niagara Falls to drive him to and from the event, but Sal said no; the bus was fine. Sal loved Elmira, loved the guys on the team. He could name them all, 45 years later."[29]

Also in 1983 Sal attended Old Timers Day at Shea Stadium, home of the New York Mets. Among the sportswriters in the clubhouse afterward was Donald Honig. Despite his fame as one of America's preeminent baseball writers, Honig felt as awed as a boy in the presence of his childhood heroes. He happened upon Sal Maglie, sitting alone on a stool in front of his locker. Although he had been an ardent Dodgers fan as a boy and recalled Maglie as the source of much long-ago heartache, Honig could hardly pass up the chance to talk with Sal. "He was cordial and soft-spoken," Honig recalled, "but he didn't seem well. He looked very tired, and seemed weak. I stood there and stared at him for maybe 30 seconds, trying to decide if we should bury the hatchet. What hatchet?" Honig exclaimed, laughing. "He didn't even know who I was."[30]

Maglie told Honig that he had not planned on coming to New York for the event, "but I guess I was feeling sentimental." When asked if he missed baseball, Maglie answered: "I don't miss pitching, but I do miss baseball."[31] A decade earlier a different interviewer had posed the same question, and Sal had given the opposite answer, replying: "Nope, not a bit. I miss pitchin', though. I sure did love to pitch."[32] Honig concluded that what Sal missed about baseball was not the actual games, but the camaraderie: "the ageless and rhythmic things that bonded these men. . . . The shape and sound and fabric of a game that had drawn them all together. . . . The uniting nationality of baseball—talent your certificate of membership."[33] With the passage of 10 years, had Maglie changed his mind? The likely answer is that Sal missed *both* his physical participation in the game and the companionship. The pleasure he had derived from the mastery of his craft, from pitching superbly in the fierce competition of major league pennant races—nothing else in his life had ever approached that, not love or sex, not parenthood, not family or friendship. At one time or another, he had put them all second to baseball. Now all that was in the past, and Sal's sad, weathered face, with its faint trace of a melancholy smile, revealed to Honig more powerfully than words the depth of the old pitcher's loss, the emptiness in the place that baseball once had filled.

Sal's remarkable recovery was not only a victory for himself; it also inspired others. On November 24, 1983, Sal traveled to New York for a baseball card signing at the Hotel Statler. It was not a big event. Only Maglie and former Brooklyn Dodger Cal Abrams participated—two old ballplayers, neither of them superstars, sitting in a near-empty room at an old New York hotel, still hoping to make a little money off their former fame, patiently waiting for the fans who never came. Maglie and Abrams chatted, trying to pass the time, pausing to sign an autograph now and then. But Sal's dull day was about to change.

Out on Long Island, in the suburb of Lindenhurst, a city parks employee named Augie Tumminia sat in a wheelchair, in constant pain and deepening despair after unsuccessful back surgery. Doctors had told him he would never walk again. He was 50 years old and had a wife and four children at home. Augie's brother Joe had seen a notice in the newspaper about the appearance of Maglie and Abrams. Knowing Augie was a life-long Giants fan who adored Maglie, Joe thought it might cheer up his depressed brother if he had a chance to meet the former star, so he offered to drive Augie into New York. Elated, Augie assembled his scrapbooks, with newspaper clippings about Giants games in the 1950s, and brought them with him to show to Sal.

Meeting Sal Maglie turned out to be a pivotal event in Augie Tumminia's life. To say the least, he was thrilled to meet his idol in person. "When I saw him," Augie recalled, "I got very emotionally *obsessed!* Here's this man I've loved since I was a kid. I'd never seen him except on the field and on TV. I didn't realize he was such a big man. What a pleasure when I met him! I was so in ecstasy, so in heaven, in paradise! But I was fighting my own personal battle. I couldn't walk, I was in a lot of pain, but I just couldn't believe it. I was huggin' him, and I said, 'Sal, I just can't believe I'm here!' I was in tears."[34] There were few other people around, so Sal invited his ardent admirer behind the table where he was sitting and settled down with Augie and his scrapbooks, poring over them for hours, reliving his games as Augie's clippings brought them to mind. Augie was in seventh heaven. "I loved Sal and I still love him. I *love* that man! I'm so glad I got to meet him, even if it was only that once. If I was ever a ballplayer, I'd love to be Maglie."

Augie's brother had brought a camera, and naturally Augie wanted his picture taken with Sal. But not sitting in his wheelchair. Because Augie could not stand up on his own, Sal helped him to his feet and held him up so his brother could take the picture. The contrast between one photo of the forlorn Augie in his wheelchair (Figure 28) and the other of an ecstatic Augie held up by the strong right arm of Sal Maglie (Figure 29) speaks volumes for the effect that being in Sal's presence had on his devoted fan. "He was *very* instrumental in my recovery," Augie declared. "When I saw him—I know he just got through with that brain operation, and he had a big indentation in his forehead from the surgery—I said, 'Sal, I know you've had your own problems.' And he said, 'Yeah, well, you gotta make it. You can't lay down and *die.*' And so I told him, 'I'm gonna go home and I'm gonna make it!' If he could recover from a hemorrhage in his head. . . . He told me, 'You gotta get well. You're 50 years old. Your life isn't over. You're gonna make it. You pray to God, go to physical therapy, and do what you gotta do. You're gonna get better!' And I *did* get better!" In his mid-70s today, Augie Tumminia is an exuberant and energetic man who long ago packed away his wheelchair.

28—A depressed, wheelchair-bound Augie Tumminia, holding his scrapbooks of 1950s New York Giants games. November 26, 1983, Statler Hotel, New York City. Photo: Joe Tumminia, collection of Augie Tumminia.

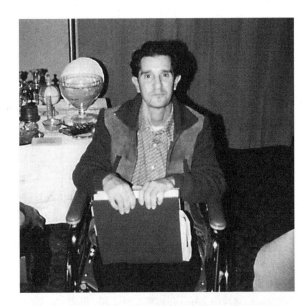

29—The transformation of Augie Tumminia. Supported by Sal, Augie glows with pleasure. Inspired by Maglie's encouragement, he learned to walk again. Maglie's forehead shows the dented scar from his brain surgery in 1982. Photo: Joe Tumminia, collection of Augie Tumminia.

Late in 1983, a new kind of baseball offer materialized for Maglie. A profitable spin-off from major league baseball in the 1980s was the development of fantasy camps, where, for a hefty fee, middle-aged men could pretend to be major leaguers, wearing big league uniforms, sharing clubhouse facilities, receiving instruction, playing games, and talking baseball with the heroes of their youth. A San Francisco businessman put together one such camp, held in Tempe, Arizona, in January of 1984. Among the ten former New York and San Francisco Giants on the staff was Sal Maglie. Monte Irvin, also on the camp staff, recalled Maglie's presence. "We asked him if he wanted to pitch a half an inning, but he said no. We said, oh, come on, so he got out there, and at least he could throw the ball from the mound to the plate."[35] For Sal, the camp was a chance to pick up some extra money, but just as important, a chance to go out on a diamond again, an experience that never grew stale for him.

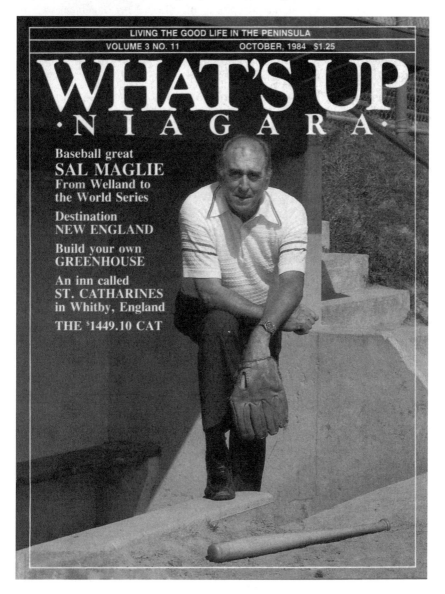

LIVING THE GOOD LIFE IN THE PENINSULA
VOLUME 3 NO. 11   OCTOBER, 1984 $1.25

WHAT'S UP
·N I A G A R A·

Baseball great
SAL MAGLIE
From Welland to
the World Series

Destination
NEW ENGLAND

Build your own
GREENHOUSE

An inn called
ST. CATHARINES
in Whitby, England

THE '1449.10 CAT

30—Sal Maglie looking fit and happy at age 67. That was in 1984, his last healthy year. Photo: Archie Hood.

Sal's health held steady through 1984 (Figure 30). He traveled to Brooklyn to attend inductions into the Brooklyn Dodgers Hall of Fame. That institution is the brainchild of Marty Adler, a lifelong Dodgers fan and retired principal of the Jackie Robinson Intermediate School in Brooklyn, located across the street from a housing project built on the site where Ebbets Field once stood. On June 7, 1984, a group of former Brooklyn Dodgers, as well as some of their traditional adversaries, the New York Giants, attended the first induction ceremony, held in Grand Army Plaza. Last to be presented, because he had played for both teams, was Sal Maglie. Inductees that year were Gil Hodges, Carl Erskine, and Carl Furillo. (Dodgers already enshrined in Cooperstown by 1984 were automatically members.) Maglie and Furillo had lost touch over the years, and according to Marty Adler, they greeted each other "like long-lost brothers. It was nice to see that, very nice. If they'd had weapons in the early fifties, they'd have killed each other."[36] Adler had forgotten that the two men *did* have weapons back then—bats and balls—and had used them against each other on numerous occasions.

Sal had bounced back from his near-fatal illness in a remarkable manner, but his healthy days were numbered. He continued to travel during 1983 and 1984, attending baseball-related events, and at home he still played golf, although less intensively—no more broiling his brain for hours under the summer sun—and worked in his garden. He still attended family functions, rarely missing the birthday parties for his steadily increasing brood of great-nieces and -nephews. He even learned of a way to combine golf and baseball. A different kind of fantasy camp had appeared, one where amateurs could spend a week golfing, rather than playing baseball, with former diamond greats. The organization, called "Golf with the Legends," signed up such baseball notables as Warren Spahn, Robin Roberts, Ralph Branca, and Enos Slaughter in addition to Maglie and planned its camp for Orlando, Florida, in October of 1985. But by that time, Sal was no longer in any condition to participate.

Twilight and Darkness

Maglie's Final Years

23

LOST BOY—THE DECLINE AND DEATH OF "LITTLE SAL"

Maglie's good health and good fortune lasted a few more months. But then, on March 9, 1985, he suffered the worst tragedy that can befall a parent: the death of one of his children. Little Sal's condition had worsened over the years. Mary Pileggi, who took care of Sal's sons during the months after Kay's death, believes Little Sal's problems began when Sal and his boys moved into the home of Sal's sister Carm. "Other kids got hold of him then," Mary declared, "and they got him on drugs. They were jealous of Sal Jr., because his father was Sal Maglie." John Pileggi added: "One year Little Sal went to Florida with some of his friends, and when he came back, his brain was gone from drugs. It broke his father's heart."[1]

Family members often pay the price of fame never exacted from the famous person himself. Whether the celebrity is a politician, rock star, actor, or athlete, his children are often pushed unwillingly into the same spotlight enjoyed by the celebrity. There was no way for Maglie's older son to escape, because he carried the spotlight around with him in the form of his father's name. Under its glare the boy withered. Sal and Doris had him committed to psychiatric centers and drug rehabilitation programs, but when he came out he always resumed his old life. He could not hold even a simple job. He worked at the Shredded Wheat factory in Niagara Falls, a job Sal secured for him, but soon was fired because he rarely showed up on time and often did not appear at all. Sal's nephew Paul Grenga, who owned a gas station, gave Little Sal a job pumping gas, but could not keep him on, as he was unable to make correct change. He became a local "street person." Everyone in town knew who he was—Sal Maglie's son, the local celebrity's boy gone bad. His cousin Kathy Pileggi Peller remembered, "You'd see him on the street, and he looked like a street urchin. I'd be scared to give him a ride if he asked me. I'd be scared because he was *not* the same kid any longer. Uncle Sal took care of him, though. Uncle Sal kept it all to himself, didn't talk to anyone about his son."[2] Little Sal's slipping-down life created a dark thread of sadness, anger, and anguish that ran through his father's life as surely as if they had been connected by blood. Sal's love for his son, and his deep sense of responsibility for him, never faltered. But like Jackie Robinson, whose namesake son also became addicted to drugs and died at a young age in an accident, Sal had more effect on other people's children than on his own.

On the evening of March 9, Sal and Doris were having dinner at the Como Restaurant, where they received a phone call telling them Little Sal was in the hospital after an accident. According to newspaper reports, the young man (he was 29) died in a fall from a window of his third-floor apartment in an old house. Police found a broken window but no signs of foul play. Apparently someone had thrown a snowball that shattered his window, and he was outside on the roof tinkering with it when he slipped and fell to his death. Although detectives concluded the death was accidental, rumors flew.[3] Little Sal's history of illegal drug use led some to suspect he had met with foul play. Others were sure alcohol must have been involved. There was even speculation he had committed suicide. After a private funeral, Sal Jr. was buried in St. Joseph's cemetery, where there is no marker for him, since he occupies the spot next to Kay, intended for his father, and nobody changed the inscription on the stone.

Sal Sr.'s health no doubt would have deteriorated, even without the shock of his older son's death. Ever since his brain surgery Sal had suffered bouts of dizziness and moments of disorientation, but the death of his son accelerated the breakdown of Maglie's physical and mental health. "He lost the will to live," observed his great-niece Cecilia. Kathy Pileggi Peller remembered attending the wake before Sal Jr.'s funeral, and she was surprised when her uncle did not recognize her and her brother. "I said, 'Uncle Sal. . .' and he was just staring at us. It was shocking. I guess something was already starting then. He was *not* himself. He'd just *stare*, with a blank look."[4] That blank, unnerving stare soon became all too familiar to Sal's family and friends.

Despite the blow of his son's death, Sal carried on for several more months. He garnered a few more honors, one of them a Sal Maglie Day organized by a local state representative and proclaimed in the New York State capital, Albany, on June 4, 1985. Sal spent the day being lauded and applauded by legislators, meeting governor Mario Cuomo, and listening to a proclamation in his honor that was read into the state senate record. He was introduced in the assembly, to a standing ovation. Governor Cuomo—another successful son of Italian immigrants—stated: "Sal Maglie has retained personal grace, quiet style, unremitting concern for his fellow man. . . . [He is] a native son who has contributed much to baseball and to the family of New York."[5] A newspaper article described Sal as "tall and straight at age 68" and still enjoying frequent travel to charity and sports events, but it also noted that Maglie wept as he listened to the applause in the senate chamber. Later, the long lines of legislators wanting to be photographed with Maglie held up state business. There was an honorary dinner that evening, and crowds eager for his autograph. It must have been a tiring day for the bereaved Maglie, the honors perhaps hollow in the face of his personal tragedy. A month later Sal attended the 1985 induction ceremony of the Brooklyn Dodgers Hall of Fame, where he was made a member, both as a teammate and a "worthy adversary." That evening, in a Brooklyn restaurant, Maglie made a last public appearance and managed a humorous quip. He thanked everyone "from the heart. And I found out from X-rays yesterday, I have a heart."[6] In late August Sal made a short trip up to Welland, Ontario. It was a private visit with friends from his wartime ball-playing days, but it made the local paper. That proved to be Sal's last unaccompanied outing. In September of 1985 he suffered a stroke, and from then on his health declined rapidly.

THE DYING OF THE LIGHT

Sal's memory lapses and spells of disorientation became more frequent and extended. He could no longer drive or handle money. If left unattended, he would wander off and not know where he was. Doris Maglie, who was still working, realized she could not leave her husband alone and hired caregivers to look after him. Many who knew Sal assumed he had Alzheimer's disease, because his symptoms resembled those of Alzheimer's: disorientation, confusion, memory loss, aimless wandering and rummaging, incontinence, inappropriate behavior, mood swings, changes in basic temperament. But Alzheimer's develops gradually, and Sal's condition came on quickly. The stroke he suffered in September of 1985 had a more profound effect on his mental than his physical functioning. Combined with the long-term effects of his brain surgery, these "insults" to the brain—and for once the medical term is both vivid and understandable—can result in the mental condition known as dementia. Speaking to a concerned Canadian reporter about her husband's condition, Doris Maglie noted sadly, "That poor brain has suffered so much damage that Sal can't remember things."[7]

For two years Doris struggled to care for her husband at home. She was loathe to place him in a nursing facility, because he still had periods of lucidity, and she could not bear the thought of him being aware that he was confined. "He would have been like a caged tiger!" she exclaimed.[8] One day in November of 1986, Sal escaped from the house. According to Louise Grenga's recollection, Sal walked into the downstairs bathroom while his companion was preparing lunch. When he did not come out, the caregiver investigated, only to find that Sal had taken the window off, squeezed out through the opening, and disappeared. The incident resembles the tale from Sal's childhood, related in Chapter 1, where as a boy Sal would wriggle out the bathroom window and run off to play baseball. "They couldn't find him," Louise continued. "It was winter, and snow was starting to come down. He didn't have a coat on, just a sweater. They called the police to search for him—they even used a helicopter. When they found him he was about a mile from the house, in a wooded area not far from the expressway. He'd lain down and fallen asleep. A little bit longer, and he'd have been covered with snow and died."[9] When found, he was cold, wet, dirty, and dazed, but otherwise unharmed. It was clear that Sal could not remain at home much longer. In April of 1987, on Palm Sunday, Sal suffered another stroke, and this time, after being hospitalized, he did not return home. He was briefly in a nursing facility on Grand Island and then was transferred to the skilled care facility at the Niagara Falls Memorial Medical Center, where he spent the final five and a half years of his life.

At first, Sal's presence lent an almost festive air to the nursing unit. The city's most famous citizen received a succession of visitors, and with a little prompting, he recognized most of them. The *Sporting News* reported he was "doing well." People brought him candy and flowers and little gifts. Old buddies dropped in, chatting about the past. Sal's wife and his sister Carm visited every day, and other relatives stopped by from time to time. He also had at least one famous visitor—Phil Rizzuto came to see Sal when he was in the area. Rizzuto and Maglie had become friendly after they retired, and several of Sal's friends remembered Rizzuto's visits.

While Sal was still relatively coherent, the Grenga family included him in family picnics. Sal's nephews would pick him up at the nursing home and drive "Unk," as they called Sal, to the picnic site. Sometimes he played a gentle game of catch with the younger children, and at other times, to the delight of the older ones, he would wind up and pitch to them a couple of times. With a bit of patience, Pat Grenga recalled, it was possible to hold a conversation with Sal, but most of the time he sat quietly, enjoying the presence of his family. He no longer remembered who was who, but he understood that he was surrounded by people who loved him. Only one thing could upset him, and that was when talk drifted to recollections of Kay. Although she had been dead for more than 20 years, and Sal had been happily remarried for more than 15 of those years, Kay's death was a wound that had never healed, and hers was the one name he never forgot. When he heard Kay's name mentioned, Sal would start to cry.

There was no reversing Sal's condition, and as the years passed, further small strokes did more damage to his physical functioning and mental faculties. In his last years the often agitated and uncomprehending Maglie turned into a six-foot-two-inch, 200-pound two-year-old. Until close to the end he remained extremely strong and was often difficult for the staff to handle. He threw things, and even at that late date, nobody wanted to be in the way of something thrown by Sal Maglie. He also flailed his arms at the nurses, nurse's aides, and orderlies, and when he hit someone, the force of the blow could send the person staggering. As a result of his unpredictably violent behavior, he often had to be kept in restraints, and visitors had the alarming experience of finding Sal strapped to his chair or bed. Sometimes he erupted into volcanic verbal rages, spewing streams of scorching obscenities.[10]

After a few years, Sal no longer recognized his old friends and often failed to recognize his wife. He mixed up his other relatives as well. He thought his sister Carm was his mother and that his niece Maria Grenga Rizzo was his sister Carm, or he sometimes confused Maria with her mother, Santa Grenga, Sal oldest sister, who had died in 1981. For many friends, their first visit to Sal was their last—they found his demeanor and behavior so distressing that few returned. Sibby Sisti was sure he could coax a response from his old friend, but Doris Maglie told him not to be surprised if Sal failed to recognize him. "But you know," Sisti reflected, "that sorta shocked me, because we were close friends. So I went up there, and he was sitting in a lounge chair in the hallway, and I says, 'Hi Sal,' and he just stared at me. I sat with him for a good half hour. It was tough sitting there that half hour, and I tried to talk to him about things we did together when we were playing, and also when he was a coach, tried to maybe bring back his memory a little bit, but he couldn't remember."[11] Sisti's experience was typical.

During his final year Sal could no longer get out of bed, no longer talked, and ate very little. Several times a week his sister Carm brought him rice mixed with homemade tomato sauce, patiently spooning it into her brother's mouth. Reporter Bill Wolcott also visited Maglie regularly. At first, Sal recognized him as the sportswriter from the local paper who had interviewed him often in the past, but as time went on, Wolcott's visits drew less and less response, and then no response at all. The reporter began to wonder if there was any point in continuing his trips to the nursing home.

"But then I saw the movie *Awakenings*," Wolcott related. "In the movie there are people who had strokes, and they give them drugs and they come back—they can talk to their families. One of the characters says, 'Visit your father—he knows you're there.' So I decided to go back and talk to Maglie, because I decided he knows I'm there, even if he doesn't respond." Seated at Sal's bedside, Wolcott reviewed Maglie's sports career. "I was determined I was really going to talk to him this time," Wolcott declared, "because *he knows I'm there*. I said to him, 'in 1970 you became the general manager of the Niagara Falls Pirates,' and then I added, 'now they have another Class-A team in Niagara Falls, the Niagara Falls Rapids.' When I said 'the Niagara Falls Rapids,' he lifts his arm and points toward the wall where there's a pennant pinned up, of the Niagara Falls Rapids, signed for him by all the team members. I had probably been talking for 25 minutes, and I didn't know if he was even hearing me, but I mention the Niagara Falls Rapids, and he points to the pennant those guys signed for him. That was the one thing in the room he could point to, like he was saying, 'Listen Bill, yes—I know what you're talking about.' It still gives me chills when I think about it."[12]

In his last months Sal sank into a semi-comatose state. His once powerful body began wasting away, and in that condition he was easy prey for the opportunistic infections that lie in wait for the severely weakened. When he contracted bronchial pneumonia in mid-December of 1992, no efforts were made to prolong his life. A Catholic chaplain administered Extreme Unction. Doris Maglie called her stepson Joe, stationed with the Air Force in Arkansas, and told him it was time for him to come home: his father was dying. All day on Sunday, December 27, they kept a vigil at Sal's bedside, along with his sister Carm, but they returned home in the evening, thinking Sal would live through the night. For a while, perhaps because the Manager approaching to take him out of his final game was no one he recognized, the old hurler refused to hand over the ball. Hour after hour he struggled on, but then, with the uncanny compassion the dying sometimes display toward those they leave behind, Sal seemed to wait until nobody was around before slipping away in the early morning hours of December 28.

The death of "Sal the Barber" made headlines not only in local papers but also in the big New York dailies that had covered his career decades earlier. The *Times* gave Sal a three-column obituary, and in the sports section Dave Anderson composed an additional appreciation. He was, Anderson recalled, a hard competitor who believed in throwing the "purpose pitch," but elsewhere he was a polite man "with a voice soft as a priest's in a confessional." *Newsday* also assigned two staff writers to cover Maglie's death. Joe Gergen recalled Maglie's influence on his own career—he had written his first sports story about Sal's no-hitter. In the same paper, Mark Hermann's article included a quotation from Sal's sister. "I know he had a sinister look on the mound, but he was a beautiful, generous person," declared Carmen Maglie Mancuso. "We went to see him on Sunday night and I said, 'He must have a strong heart.' His wife said, 'And a big one.'" In the *Daily News*, Bill Madden noted that Maglie had been ill for five years before he died, and added, "you have to think he regarded death in the same way he regarded Carl Furillo, Roy Campanella, Jackie Robinson, and Duke Snider—a formidable foe, to be sure, but one that would not be given in to." He ended his tribute by noting that Sal would never be elected to the Hall of Fame unless "there's a Hall of Fame just for pitchers whom you wanted to have the ball in a game you had to win."[13]

Three days after Sal's death, on New Year's Eve of 1992, a funeral Mass took place at Our Lady of Mount Carmel church in Niagara Falls. Sal had not been a regular churchgoer after his second marriage, but he had occasionally attended Sunday morning Mass at Mount Carmel in the company of a group of old friends. Msgr. Edward Scanlan, the wise and realistic priest who officiated at Sal's funeral, understood that what had drawn Sal to religious services in his later years was the prospect of going out to breakfast afterward with his friends. He never attended church alone.[14] The Maglie family wanted to keep the funeral as private as possible, and they excluded the media. Because he had not known Sal very long or well, Msgr. Scanlan kept his eulogy brief. "Remember the good things that Sal Maglie did. Keep those treasured memories alive," he urged the assembled mourners.[15] The funeral cortege was modest, and no crowds lined the sidewalks on the cold, misty day, as the procession of cars wound through the gloomy winter streets of Niagara Falls. The cortege made one detour, in order to pass the stadium that had been renamed in Sal's honor. Then the line of cars made a left turn onto Pine Avenue, toward St. Joseph's cemetery.

Sal Maglie's life lined up along Pine Avenue. Memorial Medical Center, in whose nursing unit Sal spent his final years, and where he died, is on the corner of Pine and Portage Avenues, across the street from the public high school he attended. Further down, on the corner of Pine and Fourteenth Street, where Sal lived as a child, stands St. Joseph's church, whose parish priest baptized the newborn Salvatore Maglie, and where Sal and Kay were married. Still further along are Macri's Palace and the Como, where he loved to eat, drink martinis, talk baseball, and play cards with his old pals. At the far end of Pine Avenue stands St. Joseph's Cemetery, where Sal's parents, his first wife, his sisters, and his older son are buried. Sal is there too. His body rests in a vault, in a building to the right of the cemetery entrance. Behind a simple rectangle of polished gray granite that bears only his name and the years of his birth and death, lies whatever was mortal of Salvatore Anthony Maglie. If there is any justice in this world or the next, his soul is in the sky with (baseball) diamonds.

PITCHING STATISTICS
FOR SAL MAGLIE

ABBREVIATIONS

YR	Year	BB	Bases on Balls
TM	Team	SO	Strikeouts
LG	League	H	Hits
G	Games	R	Runs
IP	Innings Pitched	ER	Earned Runs
W	Won	CG	Complete Games
L	Lost	SHO	Shutouts
PCT	Percentage	WP	Wild Pitches
ERA	Earned Run Average	HB	Hit Batsmen

Blank spaces in the tables indicate instances where no statistics are available. Further statistics on Maglie, including his performances as a fielder and batter, are available on the web sites noted on page 411.

MINOR LEAGUES

YR	TM	LG	G	IP	W	L	PCT	ERA	BB	SO	H	CG	SHO
1938	Buffalo Bisons	International (AA)*	5	12	0	1	.000	3.75	8	4	12	0	0
1939	Buffalo Bisons	International (AA)	39	101	3	7	.300	4.99	42	62	102	0	0
1940	Buffalo Bisons	International (AA)	23	54	0	7	.000	7.17	24	22	80	1	0
1940	Jamestown Falcons	Pony (D)	7	53	3	4	.429	2.73	15	41	54		
1941	Elmira Pioneers	Eastern (A)**	43	270	20	15	.571	2.57	107	148	231	23	
1942	Jersey City Giants	International (AA)	50	165	9	6	.600	2.78	74	92	142	4	0
1943–44 WAR WORK													
1945	Jersey City Giants	International (AA)	14	88	3	7	.300	4.09	33	41	91	7	0
	TOTALS		181	743	38	47	.447	4.01	303	410	712	35	0

* There was no Triple-A classification until after World War II, when the number of minor leagues expanded and they were reclassified.

** The Eastern League, later reclassified as C-level, was an A-level team in the pre–World War II era.

Sources: Johnson and Wolff, *The Encyclopedia of Minor League Baseball.* For 1938, 1939, 1940 (Buffalo), 1942, and 1945—Wright, *The International League Year-by-Year Statistics.* For 1940 (Jamestown) and 1941—"Sal Maglie, Pitcher Register," National Baseball Hall of Fame Library.

CUBAN WINTER LEAGUE, MEXICAN LEAGUE, PROVINCIAL LEAGUE (CANADA)

YR	TM	LG	G	IP	W	L	PCT	ERA	BB	SO	H	CG	SHO
1945-46	Cienfuegos Elephants	Cuban Winter	20		9	6	.600					9	
1946	Puebla Parrots	Mexican	47	285.1	20	12	.625	3.19	92	118		21	4
1946-47	Cienfuegos Elephants	Cuban Winter	N O S T A T S F O R T H I S Y E A R										
1947	Puebla Parrots	Mexican	39	285	20	13	.606	3.92	108	105		22	2
1947-48	Cuba	Cuban Winter	26		14	9	.609					20	
1948	Max Lanier's All-Stars		N O S T A T S F O R T H I S T E A M										
1949	Drummond- ville Cubs	Provincial (Can.)	37	266	23	9	.719		69	205	225	24	

Sources: For 1945–46, 1947–48—Figueredo, *Béisbol Cubano.* For 1946, 1947—Treto Cisneros, *The Mexican League.* For 1949—Young, "Sal Maglie: His Remarkable (But Forgotten) Year of 1949."

MAJOR LEAGUES

YR	TM	LG	W	L	PCT	G	IP	ERA	BB	SO	H	R	ER	HR	CG	SHO	WP	HB
1945	NYG	NL	5	4	.556	13	84.1	2.35	22	32	72	22	22	2	7	3	0	2
1950	NYG	NL	18	4	.818	47	206	2.71	86	96	169	71	62	14	12	5	4	10
1951	NYG	NL	23	6	.793	42	298	2.93	86	146	254	110	97	27	22	3	4	6
1952	NYG	NL	18	8	.692	35	216	2.92	75	112	199	80	70	16	12	5	2	6
1953	NYG	NL	8	9	.471	27	145.1	4.15	47	80	158	79	67	19	9	3	1	1
1954	NYG	NL	14	6	.700	34	218.1	3.26	70	117	222	83	79	21	9	1	4	3
1955	NYG	NL	9	5	.643	28	129.2	3.75	48	71	142	67	54	18	6	0	0	3
1955	CLE	AL	0	2	.000	10	25.2	3.86	7	11	26	14	11	0	0	0	0	1
1956	CLE	AL	0	0	.000	2	5.0	3.60	2	2	6	2	2	1	0	0	1	0
1956	BRD	NL	13	5	.722	28	191	2.87	52	108	154	65	61	21	9	3	1	5
1957	BRD	NL	6	6	.500	19	101.1	2.93	26	50	94	42	33	12	4	1	0	1
1957	NYY	AL	2	0	1.000	6	26	1.73	7	9	22	6	5	1	1	1	0	4
1958	NYY	AL	1	1	.500	7	23.1	4.63	9	7	27	12	12	3	0	0	0	0
1958	SLC	NL	2	6	.250	10	53	4.75	25	21	46	31	28	14	2	0	0	2
TOTALS:			119	62	.657*	303	1,723	3.15	562	862	1,591	684	603	169	93	25	18	44

* Maglie's winning percentage is 22nd on the all-time list—just below Randy Johnson and just above Sandy Koufax.

Sources: *The Baseball Encyclopedia*, Pitcher Register; <www.baseball-reference.com/m/maglisa01.shtml>; <www.baseball-almanac.com/players/player.php?p=maglisa01>; Thorn, Palmer, Gershman, and Pietrusza, *Total Baseball*.

WORLD SERIES

YR	TM	LG	W	L	PCT	G	IP	ERA	BB	SO	H	R	ER	HR	CG	SHO	WP	HB
1951	NYG	NL	0	1	.000	1	5	7.20	2	3	8	4	4	1	0	0	0	0
1954	NYG	NL	0	0	.000	1	7	2.57	2	2	7	2	2	0	0	0	0	1
1956	BRD	NL	1	1	.500	2	17	2.65	6	15	14	5	5	1	2	0	0	0
TOTALS:			1	2	.333	4	29	3.41	10	20	29	11	11	2	2	0	0	1

Sources: *The Baseball Encyclopedia*, Pitcher Register; <www.baseball-reference.com/m/maglisa01.shtml>; <www.baseball-almanac.com/players/player. php?p=maglisa01>.

ACKNOWLEDGMENTS

"Sal the Barber! He'll give them Dodgers another close shave today!" With those words my maternal grandfather who, for mysterious reasons, *hated* the Dodgers, would gleefully announce to me that my beloved Bums were as good as defeated. I was around eight years old then and already obsessed with baseball. I grew up on Long Island, about a 40-minute train ride from New York City and Brooklyn, and I grew up with baseball. One of my first life lessons, picked up from my avid Dodger-fan parents, was learning to loathe the New York Giants. From 1950 on, that included cultivating an intense hatred of the Dodgers' most devastating opponent, Giants pitcher Sal Maglie. And yet, such emotions move in mysterious ways, and perhaps because I was already quite a contrary little girl, Maglie was the very player who fascinated me the most, the man I silently and guiltily rooted for, even when he was beating my Dodgers. And so, before anyone else, I should thank my baseball-obsessed family for imparting a knowledge and love of the game to me and for marking Sal Maglie as a player of particular interest.

As a child I saw Maglie pitch at the Polo Grounds in New York City and at Ebbets Field in Brooklyn, and I watched him in action many more times on our family's grainy black-and-white television. But I cannot rely on those memories for anything more than the powerful and enthralling sense of menace that Maglie conveyed. For information about the games in which Maglie participated, this biography relies primarily on newspaper reports along with magazine articles, books, taped radio broadcasts, and the occasional, rare fragment of film footage. Although many of Maglie's teammates had passed on either shortly before or well before I began this book, and others died while the book was in progress, I was fortunate to be able to interview some of the survivors and to supplement written sources with their personal recollections. Their names are noted in the Bibliography. Team officials—in particular the amazing, 90-year-old Buzzie Bavasi—as well as several outstanding sportswriters from Maglie's era, including Robert Boyle, Robert Creamer, Frank Graham Jr., Donald Honig, Roger Kahn, and Jack Lang, were also kind enough to contribute their recollections, as was the observant Tom Villante, who produced radio and television broadcasts for the Brooklyn Dodgers in the 1950s and who sometimes happened to be in just the right place at the right time.

Among family and friends, many of those from Sal's generation are gone, but John and Carl Pileggi, and Mary Pileggi, Sal's brothers-in-law and sister-in-law from his first marriage, are still living in Niagara Falls and retain remarkably clear memories of Sal, not only during his time of stardom but also going back to his early years, long before he was famous. John and Mary Pileggi deserve special thanks. They spent many hours with me, in person and on the telephone, sorting through their memories of Sal and Kay Maglie, some happy, some sad, and some startlingly intimate. They also shared family photographs, several of which appear in this book. Sal's nephews Pat, Frank, and Joe Grenga, and Dennis Villani, Pat's wife, Louise, Sal's nieces Maria Grenga Rizzo and Kathy Pileggi Peller, and his great-niece Cecilia Grenga Anderson also extended themselves to help me, sharing memories, photographs, and newspaper clippings. Sal's widow and his son, Doris Ellman Maglie and Joe Maglie, agreed to be interviewed, and I am grateful for their help. A few of Sal's old friends still remain in his hometown, men whose memories extend back to Sal's childhood. Benny Critelli, Eddie Gadawski, and the late Chet Grochala sat and talked with me or spoke with me by telephone, recalling Sal as a young boy. Jimmy Briganti, Arthur Caggiano, Joe Calato, Jimmy Macri, Anthony Rendina, and Mickey Rizzo, Sal's younger contemporaries, also recalled their friend in his days of baseball stardom and in his later years.

A few other individuals deserve a special word of thanks. The volunteers at the Family History Center, Church of the Latter Day Saints, in Naperville, Illinois, offered help and access to census and immigration records. The staff of the Microforms Reading Room of the New York Public Library provided efficient although anonymous service during the week I spent poring over microfilms of 1950s New York newspapers. Ron Barshinger and his staff at Information Delivery Services, Founders Library, Northern Illinois University, batted at least .950—their success rate in tracking down old and new baseball books and half-century-old articles. Michele Dodde, of Lecce, Italy, a retired Italian army general and head of the Italian Baseball Association, helped with research on Sal Maglie's parents that would have been impossible for me to conduct independently. Ron Grossman, Chicago journalist and accomplished interviewer, gave me pointers on how to conduct interviews. John La Tourette, economist and president emeritus of Northern Illinois University, explained the rule-of-thumb formula for calculating the present purchasing power of Maglie's income at various points in his career. Lifelong friend and computer wizard Eric Marks provided valuable tips on internet research, particularly in the area of genealogy. Although some lines of internet research led to definite dead-ends—for example, my efforts to find out more about the history of the protective cup led me to a blog for jockstrap fetishists—for the most part the Internet provided an endless source of baseball statistics and other relevant information, available at the click of a mouse. The online archive of the *Sporting News* was of particular value. Baseball historian and archivist William Marshall of the University of Kentucky Library patiently answered my baseball questions, and searched his memory for details of his long-ago personal interview with Sal Maglie. Gabriel Schechter, baseball historian and research librarian *extraordinaire* at the National Baseball Hall of Fame Library in Cooperstown, where I practically lived for a week during 2003, was not only a great help while I was at that library but also later located material that eluded even the Barshinger team. Canadian baseball historian Bill Young was exemplary in his generosity, sharing his original research on Sal Maglie's obscure years of ball-playing in Canada. For help in sorting out and understanding Maglie's medical problems, I am grateful for the help of physical therapist Ken Olson and medical researcher Solomon Mowshowitz, as well as MDeities Roger Haab and Dirk Wassner.

For help in other ways too numerous and varied to list, I also thank the following individuals: Steve Acee, Paul Arthur, Larry Baldassaro, Daniel Bazzani, Ira Berkow, Robert Bireley, Bill Burdick, Carl Camann, Paula Carlson, Joe and Virginia Celenza, Al Chille, Marsali Classon, Craig Cleve, Cathy Comar, Deborah Cuttler, Vince D'Anna, Bill Dougherty, Bill Feder, Jorge Figueredo, Larry Freundlich, Sheri Gadawski, Steve Gietschier, Don Glynn, Peter Golenbock, Dick Gordon, Sean Graney, H. Roger Grant, Jim Grochala, Manny Hernandez, Jin-whi Hong, Archie Hood, Christopher Jennison, Yale Joel, Jim Joyce, Sean Kirst, Kathy Krolo, Cynthia Lucas, Rich Marazzi, Brenda Marinacci, Judie Mayer, James Meier, Carlos Montfort, Chris Nissen, Robin Nobone, Bill Nowlin, Tina Olsen, Jeannine Ouimet, Samuel Rousso, Stephen Schinnagel, Mark Shaw, Sue Shaw, Susan Slocum, Vince Staten, Jim Stewart, Jack Theobald, George Vecsey, Rich Westcott, Tim Wiles, Carolin Wilson, Bill Wolcott, and Adrian Zabala, Jr.

Mary Lincoln, director of the Northern Illinois University Press, has been an exemplary editor, skillfully combining critical acumen with tact—not an easy balance to achieve. The creative energies and talent of Julia Fauci, designer of the cover, and other aspects of the graphics in the book, deserve recognition as well, as does the conscientious work of Susan Bean, Managing Editor. William Marshall and Gabriel Schechter also merit a second and extra-special word of thanks for serving as preliminary readers of this lengthy manuscript. They made many helpful suggestions and saved me from numerous factual errors. Any remaining errors of fact, and all interpretations, remain my own responsibility.

ABBREVIATIONS

BCE	*Buffalo Courier-Express*
BDH	*Boston Daily Herald*
BE	*Brooklyn Eagle*
BG	*Boston Globe*
CSM	*Christian Science Monitor*
CST	*Chicago Sun-Times*
CT	*Chicago Tribune*
NBHOFL	National Baseball Hall of Fame Library
NFG	*Niagara Falls Gazette*
NFR	*Niagara Falls Reporter*
NYDM	*New York Daily Mirror*
NYDN	*New York Daily News*
NYHT	*New York Herald Tribune*
NYJA	*New York Journal-American*
NYP	*New York Post*
NYT	*New York Times*
NYWT	*New York World Telegram and Sun*
PDN	*Philadelphia Daily News*
PSS	*Pacific Stars and Stripes*
REG	*Reno Evening Gazette*
SN	*Sporting News*
WSJ	*Wall Street Journal*

1—THE MAGLIES OF ITALY AND AMERICA

1. The name "Maglie" is rare in every other part of Italy, but common in Puglia. "Maglie" is from the same root as the English word "mail," as in chain-mail, or armor, and it may indicate that the city once was known for producing armor.

2. Pat Grenga interview, February 24, 2004.

3. Harold Shelton, "Zero Man Sal," *Baseball Digest* 10 (1951): 7. For documents relating to Giuseppe Maglie's date and place of birth, the author is grateful to Michele Dodde of Lecce, who located the information in Italian military records.

4. Sal Maglie and Robert Boyle, "Baseball Is a Tough Business," *Sports Illustrated* (April 15, 1968): 86.

5. Pat Grenga interview, June 24, 2004.

6. For documents relating to Maria Immacolata Bleve and her family, the author is again indebted to Michele Dodde.

7. Pat Grenga interview, June 24, 2004.

8. Giuseppe's name does not appear in the federal census records of 1910, but he and his family appear in the New York State census records of 1915, where it is stated that he had been in the United States for five years.

9. Pierre Berton, *Niagara: A History of the Falls* (Toronto: McClelland and Stewart, 1994), 123; Patrick V. McGreevy, *Imagining Niagara: The Meaning and Making of Niagara Falls* (Amherst: University of Massachusetts Press, 1994), 121–23.

10. T. W. Kriner, *In the Mad Water: Two Centuries of Adventure and Lunacy at Niagara Falls* (Buffalo: J and J Publishing, 1999), 13.

11. H. William Feder, *The Evolution of an Ethnic Neighborhood that Became United in Diversity:*

The East Side, Niagara Falls, New York, 1880–1930 (Amherst, NY: BMP Inc., 2000), 450–53.

12. Ship's manifest, SS *Venezia,* online at the Ellis Island web site.

13. Maria Grenga Rizzo interview, May 28, 2003; Pat Grenga interview, June 24, 2004.

14. Parish register, St. Joseph's church, Niagara Falls, NY.

15. Italian military records consulted by Michele Dodde indicate that Giuseppe was drafted, and when he did not appear for induction (because he had emigrated to America), he was listed as a deserter.

16. Birth certificate, Salvatore Maglie, Niagara County Clerk's office; baptismal record, parish register, St. Joseph's church, Niagara Falls, NY.

17. New York State Census, 1915, microfilm, Family History Center, Church of the Latter-Day Saints, Naperville, IL.

18. United States Federal Census, 1920. Online, Family History Center, Church of the Latter-Day Saints, Naperville, IL.

19. Niagara Falls City Directories, 1921–1928.

20. United States Federal Census, 1930. Online, Family History Center, Church of the Latter-Day Saints, Naperville, IL. The reference to the junk yard appears in *NFG,* October 24, 1956.

21. Jimmy Macri interview, May 29, 2003. Feder, *Ethnic Neighborhood,* p. 384, also notes the numerous brothels.

22. Benny Critelli interview, June 28, 2004.

23. Maglie and Boyle, "Tough Business," 86.

24. *NYDM,* September 13, 1956.

25. Pat Grenga interview, June 24, 2004.

26. Louise Grenga interview, June 24, 2004.

27. Pat Grenga interview, June 24, 2004; Maglie and Boyle, "Tough Business," 86.

28. Chet Grochala interview, August 25, 2004.

29. *NYT,* May 25, 1952.

30. Eddie Gadawski interview, November 4, 2004.

31. *NFG,* October 25, 1956.

32. During the 1936–1937 season Teressa Archie, the girlfriend and later wife of team captain Dante Bazzani, kept a scrapbook of newspaper articles about the team. The author is grateful to Dante Bazzani's son, Daniel Bazzani, for making the scrapbook available. All references to team statistics and Sal's basketball record are from this source.

33. Sal Maglie and Dick Schaap, "I Always Threw Beanballs," *Cavalier* (September 1959): 33.

34. Milton J. Shapiro, *Sal Maglie Story* (New York: Julian Messner, 1957) 33–36; John Pileggi interview, October 12, 2003.

35. Comment attributed to Sal Maglie by his friend Mickey Rizzo. Dominic (Mickey) Rizzo interview, June 22, 2004.

36. *NFG,* October 25, 1956.

37. Eddie Gadawski interview, November 4, 2003.

38. *NFG,* January 30, 1966.

39. John Pileggi interview, June 2, 2003.

40. Sal Maglie, "I'm the Luckiest Guy in Baseball," *Sport* (September 1951): 15.

41. Cynthia Wilber, *For the Love of the Game: Baseball Memories from the Men Who Were There* (New York: William Morrow, 1992), 59.

42. John Pileggi interview, June 2, 2003.

2—THE NIAGARA NUGGET GOES NOWHERE

1. "The Niagara Nugget" was one of the nicknames given to Sal during his major league career.

2. Maglie and Boyle, "Tough Business," 86.

3. Joe Overfield, "Giant Among Men," *Bisongram* (April–May 1993): 26.

4. Maglie and Boyle, "Tough Business," 86; Shapiro, *Sal Maglie Story,* 38. It is not

clear when this game took place; it may have been at a later date, when Maglie had more experience. James D Szalontain suggests the game was in 1945, in *Close Shave: The Life and Times of Baseball's Sal Maglie* (Jefferson, NC: McFarland, 2002), 40.

5. Maglie and Boyle, "Tough Business," 86.

6. *NYDM*, September 13, 1956.

7. Ed Fitzgerald, "The Barber of the Giants," *Sport* (September 1952): 74.

8. Maglie and Boyle, "Tough Business," 86.

9. Dan Carnevale interview, October 29, 2004.

10. Buffalo Bisons program, 1940, 4. Collection of the author.

11. Herman Kaufman, "Sal Maglie: A Study in Frustration," *The National Pastime: A Review of Baseball History* (Vol. 2, no. 1, 1983):35.

12. Sal Maglie, "I'm the Luckiest Guy in Baseball." *Sport* (September, 1951): 14.

13. Maglie and Boyle, "Tough Business," 87; *NYHT*, March 28, 1959.

14. Certificate of Marriage Registration for Salvatore A. Maglie and Kathleen Piliggie [*sic*], copy from Lewiston Town Clerk, June 17, 2004.

15. James N. Giglio, *Musial: From Stash to Stan the Man* (Columbia: University of Missouri Press, 2001), 36–37. Musial began his career as a pitcher.

16. Maria Grenga Rizzo interview, August 5, 2003.

17. Al Mallette interview, January 20, 2004.

18. Overfield, "Giant Among Men," 26.

19. William Marshall, *Baseball's Pivotal Era: 1945–1951* (Lexington: University of Kentucky Press, 1991), 6.

20. Fitzgerald, "Barber of the Giants," 74.

21. *SN*, June 20, 1951:15

22. Details on the Welland Atlas Steels come from a Canadian newspaper, the *St. Catherines Standard*. The author is grateful to Canadian baseball historian Bill Young for this material.

23. Carolin Wilson, "Sal Maglie, Niagara's Greatest Pitcher," *What's Up Niagara* (October, 1984): 5.

24. Bill Gilbert, *They Also Served. Baseball and the Home Front, 1941–1945* (New York: Crown Publishers, 1992), 125, 165–66, 181–82.

3—A TASTE OF THE BIGS

1. Thomas Kiernan, *Miracle at Coogan's Bluff* (New York: Thomas Y. Crowell, 1975), 184.

2. *NYDM, NYDN, NYHT*, August 15, 1945.

3. *SN*, August 23, 1945: 15.

4. Rich Westcott, *Diamond Greats. Profiles and Interviews with 65 of Baseball's History Makers* (Westport: Meckler, 1988), 290.

5. Maglie and Boyle, "Tough Business," 88.

6. Gilbert, *They Also Served*, 249.

7. Fred Stein, *Mel Ott. The Little Giant of Baseball* (Jefferson, NC: McFarland, 1999), 154.

8. *NYHT*, August 14, 1945.

4—THE CUBAN WINTER LEAGUE AND THE MEXICAN BASEBALL WAR

1. Tom Meany, *The Incredible Giants* (New York: A.S. Barnes and Co.,1955), 98.

2. *SN*, May 14, 1952: 3.

3. Meany, *Incredible Giants*, 98.

4. Maglie's basic statistics appear in Jorge S. Figueredo, *Cuban Baseball. A Statistical History, 1878–1961* (Jefferson, NC: McFarland, 2003).

5. *SN*, May 14, 1952: 3.

6. Meany, *Incredible Giants*, 104.

7. Gilbert, *They Also Served*, 259–61.

8. *SN*, February 4, 1946: 4.

9. An article in *SN*, April 18, 1946, reported Maglie had asserted that his 1946 salary was around $5,000; Overfield, "Giant Among Men," 27, and Kaufmann, "Study in Frustration," 35, report Sal's 1946 salary as $6,000; Kyle Crichton, "Hot Tamale Circuit," *Collier's* (June 29, 1946): 119, gives Maglie's salary as $7,000; Fitzgerald, "Barber of the Giants," 37 and 44, reports his salary for that year as $7,500; Marshall, *Pivotal Era*, 53, gives the figure as $8,000. Sal himself at one time recalled the amount as $7,500, as noted in Meany, *Incredible Giants*, 104, and at another as $8,000, the latter reported by Stanley Frank, "How the Giants Found a Pitcher in the Doghouse," *Saturday Evening Post* (May 5, 1951): 152.

10. Frank, "Doghouse," 152.

11. Sal Maglie and Robert Boyle, "Great Giant-Dodger Days," *Sports Illustrated* (April 22, 1968), 41.

12. Kaufman, "Study in Frustration," 35.

13. Gerald F. Vaughn, "Jorge Pasquel and the Evolution of Mexican Baseball," *The National Pastime: A Review of Baseball History* (12, 1992), 9–11; John Phillips, *The Mexican Jumping Beans: The Story of the Baseball War of 1946* (Perry, GA: Capital Publishing, 1997), 3–5.

14. Harold Rosenthal, *The Ten Best Years of Baseball: An Informal History of the 'Fifties* (Chicago: Contemporary Books, 1979), 54.

15. Frank, "Doghouse," 152.

16. Fitzgerald, "Barber of the Giants," 37.

17. Frank Graham, Jr., "The Great Mexican War of 1946," *Sports Illustrated* (September 19, 1966), 119.

18. Craig Alan Cleve, *Hardball on the Home Front: Major League Replacement Players of World War II* (Jefferson, NC: McFarland, 2004), 80.

19. Roger Kahn recalled that the comment by Stephens was reported to him by sportswriter Harold Rosenthal of the *Herald Tribune*. Roger Kahn, e-mail to the author, October 6, 2003.

20. *NYT*, March 20, 1946.

21. *SN*, March 7, 1946: 2.

22. *NYT*, March 3, 1946.

23. Frank, "Doghouse," 152; Fitzgerald, "Barber of the Giants," 37–38; Meany, *Incredible Giants*, 104–105; Graham, "Great Mexican War," 119–20; Kiernan, *Coogan's Bluff*, 184–86; Phillips, *Mexican Jumping Beans*, 34; Stein, *Mel Ott*, 156; Sal Maglie interview, May 25, 1981, with William Marshall.

24. Kiernan, *Coogan's Bluff*, 185.

25. Frank, "Doghouse," 152.

26. George Hausmann interview, July 28, 2001, with Craig Alan Cleve, who kindly provided the author with a transcript.

27. *SN*, April 18, 1946: 2.

28. Ibid.

5—DOWN MEXICO WAY

1. Sal Maglie interview, May 25, 1981, with William Marshall.

2. Monte Irvin interview, September 29, 2003.

3. *BE*, April 1, 1946; *CT*, April 11, 1946; Frank, "Doghouse," 152.

4. Carl Pileggi interview, June 2, 2003.

5. John Pileggi interview, June 2, 2003.

6. Sal Maglie interview, May 25, 1981, with William Marshall.

7. Max Lanier interview, February 15, 2003.

8. In Winegardner's novel *The Veracruz Blues* (New York: Viking Penguin, 1996), 111, a fictionalized account of life in the Mexican League, the story is told by Danny Gardella. Asked if this really happened or if it was a novelistic invention based on knowledge that many American ballplayers had digestive problems in Mexico, Winegardner responded that Gardella "may well have told" him the Stephens anecdote, but he could not be persuaded to search for the tape of his interview with Gardella. Mark Winegardner, phone conversation with the author, July 21, 2004.

9. Mrs. Sal [Kay] Maglie, "My Best Years With Sal," *Parade* (November 25, 1956): 21.

10. Carl Pileggi interview, June 2, 2003.

11. Crichton, "Hot Tamale Circuit," 28.

12. Max Lanier interview, February 15, 2003.

13. Graham, "Great Mexican War," 126.

14. Adrian and Mary Zabala interview, March 2, 1989, with William Marshall.

15. Phillips, *Mexican Jumping Beans,* 30.

16. Max Lanier interview, June 26, 1987, with William Marshall.

17. Tom Gorman and Jerome Holtzman, *Three and Two!* (New York: Charles Scribner's Sons, 1979), 30.

18. Frank, "Doghouse," 153.

19. Fitzgerald, "Barber of the Giants," 72.

20. Frank, "Doghouse," 153.

21. Maglie and Boyle, "Giant-Dodger Days," 41.

22. Frank, "Doghouse," 153.

23. *SN,* April 19, 1947: 7.

24. Mickey Owen interview, May 27, 1989, with William Marshall.

25. Phillips, *Mexican Jumping Beans,* 40.

26. *SN,* June 27, 1994: 18.

27. Alvin Dark interview, August 26, 2004.

28. Monte Irvin with James A. Riley, *Nice Guys Finish First* (New York: Carroll and Graff Publishers, 1996), 60.

29. Graham, "Great Mexican War," 124. A version that does not include the gun episode appears in Angel Torres, *La Leyenda del Béisbol Cubano* (self-published, 1996), 135.

30. John and Mary Pileggi interview, June 2, 2003.

31. Mickey Owen interview, May 27, 1989, with William Marshall.

32. Art Pennington interview, August 21, 2003.

33. Sal Maglie interview, May 25, 1981, with William Marshall.

34. Mexican League statistics come from Pedro Treto Cisneros, *The Mexican League. Comprehensive Statistics, 1937–2001* (Jefferson, NC: McFarland, 2002).

35. Maglie and Boyle, "Giant-Dodger Days," 41.

36. *NYT,* May 25, 1946.

37. Max Lanier interview, February 15, 2003.

38. Art Pennington interview, August 21, 2003.

39. Maglie and Boyle, "Tough Business," 86.

40. Kay Maglie, "Best Years," 21.

41. Shapiro, *Sal Maglie Story,* 62.

42. Fitzgerald, "Barber of the Giants," 76.

43. *SN,* August 6, 1947: 22.

6—KNOCKING AROUND

1. Roberto Gonzalez Echevarria, *The Pride of Havana: A History of Cuban Baseball* (New York: Oxford University Press, 1999), 44.

2. Donald Honig, *Baseball When the Grass was Real: Baseball from the Twenties to the Forties Told by the Men Who Played It* (Lincoln: University of Nebraska Press, 1975), 219.

3. *SN,* April 14, 1948: 32, and June 2, 1948: 34.

4. Meany, *Incredible Giants,* 107.

5. Fitzgerald, "Barber of the Giants," 72.

6. Kay Maglie, "Best Years," 22.

7. Ibid.

8. Sal Maglie interview, May 25, 1981, with William Marshall; Fitzgerald, "Barber of the Giants," 72.

9. Richard J. Durrell, "The Night the Stars Nearly Fell in Minnesota," *Sports Illustrated,* October 17, 1988. Reproduced online at www.highbeam.com/library/doc3.

10. Fitzgerald, "Barber of the Giants," 72.

11. Maglie, "Luckiest Guy," 17; Fitzgerald, "Barber of the Giants," 72; Frank, "Doghouse," 153.

12. Fitzgerald, "Barber of the Giants," 72; Benny Critelli interview, June 18, 2004.

13. John and Mary Pileggi interview, June 2, 2003.

14. Mary Pileggi interview, October 30, 2003.

15. Maglie and Boyle, "Giant-Dodger Days," 41.

16. Merritt Clifton, *Disorganized Baseball: The Provincial League from LaRoque to Les Expos* (Richford, VT: Samisdat, 1982), 3–6; David Pietrusza, *Baseball's Canadian-American League: A History of Its Inception, Franchises, Participants, Locales, Statistics, Demise, and Legacy, 1936–1951* (Jefferson, NC: McFarland, 1990), 45.

17. *La Parole*, March 24, 1949. Translated by Bill Young. Unless otherwise noted, all material on Maglie's season with Drummondville comes from Bill Young, "Now Pitching for Drummondville: Sal Maglie," *Dominionball: Baseball Above the 49th*, ed. Jane Finnan Dorward (Toronto, Society for American Baseball Research, 2005), 80–84.

18. Szalontai, *Close Shave*, 72. The author fails to identify those "records."

19. Lee Lowenfish and Tony Lupien, *The Imperfect Diamond: The Story of Baseball's Reserve Clause and the Men Who Fought To Change It* (New York: Stein and Day, 1980), 161–62.

20. *SN*, June 15, 1949: 2.

21. Clifton, *Disorganized Baseball*, 8.

22. Kaufman, "Study in Frustration," 36.

23. Ibid.

24. Fitzgerald, "Barber of the Giants," 72.

25. *SN*, September 7, 1949: 15.

26. Frank, "Doghouse," 153.

27. Kay Maglie, "Best Years," 22.

7—WHILE YOU WERE GONE...

1. Harold and Dorothy Seymour, *Baseball: The Golden Age* (New York, Oxford University Press, 1971), 169.

2. Sal Maglie interview, May 25, 1981, with William Marshall.

3. As far back as the 1860s there had been rules barring the participation of "persons of color" in professional baseball games, and the history of such discrimination is more complicated than Anson's remark might suggest. Harold and Dorothy Seymour, *Baseball: The Early Years* (New York: Oxford University Press, 1960), 42.

4. The phrase comes from the title of a memoir by Brooklyn Dodgers broadcaster Red Barber: *1947: When All Hell Broke Loose in Baseball* (New York: Doubleday, 1982).

5. Donald Honig, *Baseball America: The Heroes of the Game and the Times of Their Glory* (New York: Macmillan, 1985), 252. Years before Rickey's move, black newspapers and the American Communist Party's *Daily Worker* had been calling for the integration of the majors. See Chris Lamb, *Blackout: The Untold Story of Jackie Robinson's First Spring Training* (Lincoln: University of Nebraska Press, 2004).

6. Scott Simon, *Jackie Robinson and the Integration of Baseball* (Hoboken, NJ: John Wiley and Sons, 2002), 6.

7. The version presented here is an effort to capture the verbal color of Durocher's speech by combining and adapting sentences and phrases quoted by the following sources: Leo Durocher and Ed Linn, *Nice Guys Finish Last* (New York, Simon and Schuster, 1975), 166–67; David Falkner, *Great Time Coming: The Life of Jackie Robinson from Baseball to Birmingham* (New York: Simon and Schuster, 1995), 152; Simon, *Jackie Robinson*, 106; Andrew Goldblatt, *The Giants and the Dodgers: Four Cities, Two Teams, One Rivalry* (Jefferson, NC: McFarland, 2003), 91; Gerald Eskenazi, *The Lip: A Biography of Leo Durocher* (New York: William Morrow, 1993), 205; Honig, *Baseball America*, 263.

8. Eskenazi, *The Lip*, 205.

9. Ibid., 210.

10. Stein, *Mel Ott*, 80.

11. Eskenazi, *The Lip*, 240.
12. Noel Hynd, *The Giants of the Polo Grounds* (New York: Doubleday, 1988), 305.
13. Eskenazi, *The Lip*, 234.
14. Marshall, *Pivotal Era*, 247.

8—THE BIRTH OF "THE BARBER"

1. Durocher and Linn, *Nice Guys Finish Last*, 306.
2. Bill Roeder, "Double Trouble," *True Magazine Baseball Yearbook* (1951): 74.
3. Frank, "Doghouse," 153.
4. Maglie and Boyle, "Giant-Dodger Days," 42.
5. *SN*, March 22, 1950: 17.
6. Ibid.
7. *SN*, March 23, 1950: 8.
8. Ibid.
9. Ibid.
10. Ibid. Maglie joined the Bisons in 1938, not 1942.
11. *NYDN*, April 19, 1950.
12. *BE*, April 19, 1950.
13. Russ Hodges and Al Hirshberg, *My Giants* (Garden City, NY: Doubleday and Co., 1963), 84; *NYHT*, June 5, 1950.
14. *BE*, June 20, 1950.
15. *NYHT*, June 20, 1950.
16. Fitzgerald, "Barber of the Giants," 74.
17. Roeder, "Double Trouble," 73.
18. Frank, "Doghouse," 154. In the 1951 article the expletive beginning the sentence is "Nuts," an unlikely choice of words by Maglie.
19. Hodges and Hirshberg, *My Giants*, 84.
20. Frank, "Doghouse," 154.
21. Robin Roberts and C. Paul Rogers III, *The Whiz Kids and the 1950 Pennant* (Philadelphia: Temple University Press, 1996), 248.
22. That record has been broken three times since Hubbell's mark of 1933: by the Cardinals' Bob Gibson in 1968 (47 innings), the Los Angeles Dodgers' Don Drysdale, also in 1968 (58 2/3 innings), and most recently in 1988 by the Dodgers' Orel Hershiser (59 innings).
23. Frank, "Doghouse," 151. The last phrase of Stanky's second sentence is rendered as "let's win this obscene game."
24. *BE*, September 14, 1950.
25. *NYDN*, September 14, 1950.
26. *NYT*, September 14, 1950.
27. *NYHT*, September 15, 1950.
28. Undated column from an unidentified newspaper, Sal Maglie file, NBHOFL.
29. The subject is discussed by Larry Baldassaro, "Dashing Dagos and Walloping Wops: Media Portrayals of Italian American Major Leaguers Before World War Two," forthcoming in *Nine: A Journal of Baseball History and Social Policy Perspectives*. Prof. Baldassaro kindly provided the author with a copy of his article.
30. Sheldon, "Zero Man Sal," 9.
31. Maglie and Boyle, "Giant-Dodger Days," 42.
32. Maglie, "Luckiest Guy," 17.
33. Carl Prince, *Brooklyn's Dodgers: The Bums, the Borough, and the Best of Baseball 1947–1957* (New York: Oxford University Press, 1996), 50.
34. Maglie and Boyle, "Giant-Dodger Days," 42.
35. Hodges and Hirshberg, *My Giants*, 84.
36. Fitzgerald, "Barber of the Giants," 76.
37. Roger Kahn, *Memories of Summer: When Baseball Was an Art and Writing About It*

Was a Game (New York: Hyperion, 1997), 189.

38. John Helyar, *Lords of the Realm: The Real History of Baseball* (New York: Villard Books, 1994), 417.

39. Wilson, "Sal Maglie," 6–7.

40. *BDH,* May 31, 1952.

41. Ray Robinson, *The Home Run Heard 'Round the World: The Dramatic Story of the 1951 Giants-Dodgers Pennant Race* (New York: HarperCollins, 1991), 22.

42. *NFR,* undated clipping.

9—AT THE AXIS OF EVENT, PART 1

1. Shapiro, *Sal Maglie Story,* 89.

2. David Halberstam, *The Fifties* (New York, Fawcett Columbine, 1993), 115.

3. Frank Graham, Jr., *A Farewell to Heroes* (Carbondale: Southern Illinois University Press, 2003), 231.

4. Roger Kahn, *The Boys of Summer* (New York: HarperCollins, 1998), 110. Dressen's theory defies common sense, since a pitcher who engages in sex while lying on his back would put a lot less strain on his elbows and knees than one who conducts his sex life in missionary position.

5. Durocher and Linn, *Nice Guys Finish Last,* 234; Irvin and Riley, *Nice Guys Finish First,* 141.

6. Roger Kahn, *October Men. Reggie Jackson, George Steinbrenner, Billy Martin, and the Yankees' Miraculous Finish in 1978* (New York: Harcourt, 2003), 14; Marshall, *Pivotal Era,* 414; Bobby Thomson, Lee Heiman, and Bill Gutman, *The Giants Win the Pennant! The Giants Win the Pennant!* (New York: Kensington Publishing, 2001), 94, 95.

7. Kiernan, *Coogan's Bluff,* 66.

8. Newspapers consulted were the *Times, Daily News, Herald Tribune,* and *Eagle.* The *Times* noted the incident briefly the next day.

9. Kiernan, *Coogan's Bluff,* 67, asserts that Robinson reached base; Robinson, *Home Run Heard 'Round the World,* 112, claims that Jackie "barged into Maglie with crushing force."

10. Doris Kearns Goodwin, *Wait Till Next Year* (New York: Simon and Schuster, 1997), 135; the author was 9 years old when she attended the game. Overfield, "Giant Among Men," 6; Szalontai, *Close Shave,* 130; Falkner, *Great Time Coming,* 238.

11. *NYT,* May 3, 1951.

12. Kiernan, *Coogan's Bluff,* 68–69.

13. Maglie, "Luckiest Guy," 75.

14. Irvin and Riley, *Nice Guys Finish First,* 142.

15. John Lardner, "Ned and the Barber," *Newsweek* (June 18, 1951): 39.

16. Frank Graham, *The New York Giants. An Informal History of a Great Baseball Club* (Carbondale: Southern Illinois University Press, 2002), 301; Irvin and Riley, *Nice Guys Finish First,* 148.

17. Robinson, *Home Run Heard 'Round the World,* 137.

18. John Lardner, "Razor Blades Amok," *Newsweek* (July 16, 1951): 77.

19. Szalontai, *Close Shave,* 153; Durocher and Linn, *Nice Guys Finish Last,* 255. It is unclear why Durocher thought such vulgarity confined to Italians, since he employed it himself. The man who carried such macho posturing to its ultimate degree several decades later was a notable non-Italian, President Lyndon B. Johnson. In an off-the-record conversation with journalists during the Vietnam conflict, a reporter asked Johnson why the United States *really* was in Vietnam. Johnson responded by unzipping his fly, hauling out what the writer described as his "substantial organ," and shaking it at the flabbergasted journalists. "*This* is why!" the Commander-in-Chief declared. Robert Dallek, *Flawed Giant: Lyndon Johnson and His Time 1961–1973* (New York: Oxford University Press, 1998), 491.

20. Thomson, Heiman, and Gutman, *Giants Win the Pennant,* 148.

21. *SN,* August 15, 1951: 21.

22. Harvey Rosenfeld, *The Great Chase: The Dodgers-Giants Pennant Race of 1951*

(Lincoln: iUniverse.com, 2001), 58.

23. Ibid., 107.
24. Ibid., 122.
25. Rosenfeld, *Great Chase,* 140.
26. *NYHT,* September 9, 1951.
27. Thomson, Heiman, and Gutman, *Giants Win the Pennant,* 192.
28. Sibby Sisti interview, August 20, 2004.
29. Rosenfeld, *Great Chase,* 192.
30. Ibid., 202.
31. Ibid., 210.
32. Ibid., 224.
33. Kiernan, *Coogan's Bluff,* 192.

10—AT THE AXIS OF EVENT, PART 2

1. A set of five videos about the Dodgers, produced by Pee Wee Reese's son, Mark Reese, is entitled *The Brooklyn Dodgers: The Original America's Team.*
2. Thomson, Heiman, and Gutman, *Giants Win the Pennant,* 194.
3. Ibid., 196.
4. Jules Tygiel, *Past Time: Baseball as History* (New York: Oxford University Press, 2000), 153.
5. Ibid., 152.
6. Alan Lelchuck, *Brooklyn Boy* (New York: McGraw Hill, 1990), 85, 87.
7. Gary R. Parker, *Win or Go Home: Sudden Death Baseball* (Jefferson, NC: McFarland, 2002), 88.
8. Ibid., 246.
9. *NYT,* October 3, 1951.
10. *NYDN,* October 3, 1951.
11. Robinson, *Home Run Heard 'Round the World,* 215.
12. Since McClendon's account of the game is available on CD, the author was able to purchase a copy and have it transcribed. The latter was a formidable task accomplished by Marsali Classon. Except where otherwise noted, the account of the game given here is from McClendon.
13. Alvin Dark interview, August 26, 2004.
14. Maglie and Boyle, "Tough Business," 88.
15. Parker, *Win or Go Home,* 93; Goldblatt, *Giants and Dodgers,* 112.
16. John Kuenster, *Heartbreakers. Baseball's Most Agonizing Defeats* (Chicago: Ivan Dee, 2001), 15.
17. Durocher and Linn, *Nice Guys Finish Last,* 247.
18. Thomson, Heiman, and Gutman, *Giants Win the Pennant,* 248.
19. Ibid., 250.
20. Although there were several claimants to the ball, none was ever authenticated. Don DeLillo's novel *Underworld* (New York: Scribner, 1997) opens with a chapter that follows the ball on a vivid, imaginary journey.
21. Robinson, *Home Run Heard 'Round the World,* 227.
22. *NYT,* October 4, 1951.
23. Maglie and Boyle, "Giant-Dodger Days," 47; Roger Angell, *Game Time* (Orlando: Harcourt, 2003), 143.
24. Dodgers photographer Barney Stein received permission to enter the closed Brooklyn clubhouse, where he shot several prize-winning photos of the weeping Branca.
25. *The All-Sport News,* January 2, 1952.
26. *NYDN,* October 3, 1991.
27. Fay Vincent, *The Last Commissioner: A Baseball Valentine* (New York: Simon and Schuster, 2002), 25–26.
28. Rosenfeld, *Great Chase,* 279.

29. Versions of the joke are reported by Kahn, *Boys of Summer,* 91, and Prince, *Brooklyn's Dodgers,* 74.

30. Kahn, *The Era,* 291.

31. *NYDN,* October 9, 1951.

32. Maglie and Boyle, "Giant-Dodger Days," 47.

33. Kahn, *The Era,* 292.

34. Sal Yvars interview, July 7, 2004.

35. *PDN,* February 6, 2001.

36. *NYT,* July 8, 2001. Yvars reiterated his position in conversation with the author. Sal Yvars interview, July 7, 2004.

37. Goldblatt, *Giants and Dodgers,* 118.

38. Ibid., 119.

39. Steve Kelly, "After 50 Years, 'Shot Heard 'Round the World' Still a Defining Moment in Baseball," *Baseball Digest* (October 1, 2001): 59.

40. Irving Rudd, *The Sporting Life* (New York: St. Martin's Press, 1990), 107; Carl Erskine, *Tales from the Dodger Dugout* (Champaign: Sports Publishing, 2001), 36–37.

41. *Newsday,* October 3, 2001. A brief, balanced discussion of the controversy appears in Glenn Stout, *The Dodgers: 120 Years of Dodgers Baseball* (New York: Houghton Mifflin, 2004), 174–75.

11—1952: A SEASON OF SUN AND SHADOWS

1. *NFG,* October 30, 1951.

2. John Pileggi interview, June 23, 2004.

3. Marty Appel, *Now Pitching for the Yankees: Spinning the News for Mickey, Billy, and George* (New York: Total Sports Illustrated, 2001), 169.

4. Maria Grenga Rizzo interview, August 5, 2003.

5. Kathy Pileggi Peller interview, June 1, 2003.

6. Dennis Villani interview, May 30, 2003.

7. Jansen stated that he and Sal never discussed family matters. Larry Jansen interview, October 28, 2003.

8. Larraine Day, *Day With the Giants* (Garden City, NY: Doubleday, 1952), 81.

9. Mickey McDermott with Howard Eisenberg, *A Funny Thing Happened on the Way to Cooperstown* (Chicago: Triumph Books, 2003), 124.

10. Jim Brosnan, *The Long Season* (New York: Harper, 1960), 101.

11. Roger Kahn, e-mail to the author, August 10, 2002.

12. Fitzgerald, "Barber of the Giants," 76.

13. *NFG,* February 15, 1952; Shapiro, *Sal Maglie Story,* 113; *NYHT,* February 12, 1952.

14. *NYHT,* February 12, 1952.

15. *NFG,* February 15, 1952.

16. Roger Kahn and Rob Miraldi, ed., *Beyond the Boys of Summer: The Very Best of Roger Kahn* (New York: McGraw Hill, 2005), 127.

17. *NYHT,* March 15, 1952.

18. *NYT,* April 21, 1952.

19. *BE,* April 21, 1952.

20. *NYP,* May 6, 1952

21. *SN,* May 14, 1952: 3.

22. *SN,* May 14, 1952: 3.

23. *NYDN,* May 15, 1952.

24. *NFG,* May 28, 1952.

25. Ibid.

26. Shapiro, *Sal Maglie Story,* 120.

27. Article from an unidentified newspaper, dated June 3, 1952. Sal Maglie file, NBHOFL.

28. *NYT,* June 16, 1952.

29. *NYWT,* June 18, 1952.

30. *NFG,* June 27, 1952.

31. *NYT,* July 17, 1952

32. Phil Allen, "Maglie's Lost Weeks," *Baseball Digest* (September 1952): 14.

33. The author is indebted to Dr. Ken Olson for explanation of Maglie's back problems and the treatments of them.

34. Mike Getz, *The Brooklyn Dodgers and Their Rivals, 1950–1952* (Brooklyn: Montauk Press, 1999), 153.

35. *NYDN,* September 7, 1952.

36. *NFG,* September 13, 1952.

37. *NYP,* August 4, 1952. Quotations in the following two paragraphs are from Gross's article.

38. Ted Irwin, "Hypnosis in Sports," *Sport* (October 1963): 83; Mary Bell, "Hypnosis in Sports: How to Slip into a Trance and out of a Slump," *Sport* (March 1974): 95.

39. Durocher and Linn, *Nice Guys Finish Last,* 255.

40. Whitey Lockman interview, August 24, 2004.

41. Monte Irvin interview, September 29, 2003.

42. Larry Jansen interview, October 28, 2003.

43. Roger Kahn, *The Era: 1947–1955—When the Yankees, the Giants, and the Dodgers Ruled the World* (Lincoln: University of Nebraska Press, 2002), 294.

44. Sal Yvars interview, July 7, 2004.

45. Alvin Dark interview, August 26, 2004.

46. Roger Kahn, *Memories of Summer,* 189.

47. Durocher and Linn, *Nice Guys Finish Last,* 256.

12—1953: SAL'S SEASON IN HELL

1. *SN,* October 1, 1952: 17; December 17, 1952: 6.

2. *NFG,* January 12, 1953.

3. *NFG,* January 13, 1953. Pulling a pitcher's teeth is not an unheard-of remedy for arm problems. In 1955, when Karl Spooner's arm went bad, the Dodgers paid to have all his teeth extracted, thinking that some mysterious poison might be leaking from his jaws into his shoulder. Jane Leavy, *Sandy Koufax: A Lefty's Legacy* (New York: HarperCollins, 2002), 150.

4. *NFG,* March 10, 1953.

5. *NYHT,* April 18, 1953.

6. *NYDN,* April 26, 1953. Presumably the word Young was looking for is *"paisani,"* an Italian term meaning fellow countrymen.

7. *NYHT,* April 26, 1953; *NYDN,* April 26, 1953.

8. Ibid.

9. *NYT,* April 26, 1953.

10. *NFG,* May 26, 1953.

11. *NYT,* June 25, 1953.

12. *BE,* July 11, 1953.

13. *PSS,* August 2, 1953.

14. *NFG,* August 6, 1953.

15. *NFG,* August 14, 1953.

16. Ibid.

17. *NYT,* August 23, 1953.

18. The incident is recounted by Monte Irvin in *Nice Guys Finish First,* 144. The gentlemanly Irvin does not include a great deal of profanity in his memoir, but since he included the phrase "dago prick," one can be certain the exchange between two of the game's most foul-mouthed men featured considerably more colorful language than what Irvin recorded.

19. Eskenazi, *The Lip,* 267.

20. Duke Snider and Bill Gilbert, *The Duke of Flatbush* (New York: Zebra Books, 1989), 70.

21. *NFG,* November 16, 1953.

13—1954: THE GIANTS TAKE IT ALL

1. *NYHT,* February 4, 1954.
2. *NYHT,* February 27, 1954.
3. *SN,* March 10, 1954: 4.
4. Neither Joseph nor Mary Maglie's name appears in Social Security Administration records.
5. Pat Grenga interview, June 24, 2004.
6. *SN,* March 10, 1954: 4.
7. Ibid.
8. *NYHT,* March 2, 1954.
9. Kahn, *Memories of Summer,* 154; *SN,* March 10, 1954: 26.
10. Charles Einstein, *Willie Mays: My Life In and Out of Baseball* (New York: E. P. Dutton, 1966), 151–53.
11. Kahn, *The Era,* 319.
12. *SN,* January 27, 1954: 19.
13. Kahn, *Memories of Summer,* 152–53.
14. *BE,* April 14, 1954.
15. *NYHT,* April 19, 1954.
16. Maglie and Boyle, "Giant-Dodger Days," 42.
17. Ibid.
18. *NFG,* July 9, 1954.
19. Roberts and Rogers, *Whiz Kids,* 103. According to the account of the game in the *Times,* Ashburn fouled off 13 of Maglie's 17 pitches to him.
20. *NYT,* September 4, 1954.
21. *NYT,* September 15, 1954.
22. Maglie and Boyle, "Giant-Dodger Days," 47.
23. Ibid. In his memoir, Maglie has Durocher saying "What the hell did you do that for?" but the chances are Leo used a stronger expletive.
24. Durocher and Linn, *Nice Guys Finish Last,* 255.
25. The author is grateful to Christopher Jennison for pointing out Maglie's right hand.
26. Alvin Dark interview, August 26, 2004.
27. Whitey Lockman interview, August 24, 2004.
28. *NYHT,* September 21, 1954; *NYP,* September 21, 1954.
29. *NYDN,* September 28, 1954.
30. Except where otherwise noted, the account of the game comes from the *Times,* the *Daily News,* and a recorded radio broadcast by announcers Al Helfer and Jimmy Dudley.
31. Arnold Hano, *A Day in the Bleachers* (New York: Da Capo Press, 1982), 47.
32. Kahn, *Memories of Summer,* 192.
33. Hano, *Day in the Bleachers,* 82.
34. Even a book as authoritative as John Thorn and Pete Palmer's *Total Baseball* (New York: Warner Books, 1991), 534, repeats the story.
35. Gene Fehler, *Tales from Baseball's Golden Age* (Champaign: Sports Publishing, 2000), 152. A similar version appears in John C. Skipper, *Inside Pitch: A Closer Look at Classic Baseball Moments* (Jefferson, NC: McFarland, 1996), 16.
36. *NYHT,* September 30, 1954.
37. Eskenazi, *The Lip,* 280.

14—1955: TROUBLES, TRAVELS, AND A TRANSFORMED FAMILY

1. *NFG,* Dec. 2, 1954.
2. *SN,* February 23, 1955: 7; March 2, 1955: 8.
3. *SN,* March 16, 1955: 3.
4. *NYP,* April 15, 1955.
5. Kahn, *Boys of Summer,* 395.

6. Ibid.

7. For a much later reference by Maglie to deliberately throwing behind Jackie Robinson's head, see Chapter 22.

8. Maglie and Schaap, "I Always Threw Beanballs," 34.

9. *NYHT,* July 3, 1955.

10. Carl Rowan and Jackie Robinson, *Wait Till Next Year: The Life Story of Jackie Robinson* (New York: Random House, 1960), 214.

11. Don Zimmer and Bill Madden, *Zim: A Baseball Life* (New York: McGraw-Hill, 2002), 28. The words are Zimmer's recollection of what Robinson said. Robinson's actual taunts probably included even more profanity.

12. Kahn, *Boys of Summer,* 396. Newspaper accounts indicate that Williams continued to play.

13. Ibid.

14. Kiernan, *Coogan's Bluff,* 189.

15. Roger Kahn, *The Head Game: Baseball Seen from the Pitcher's Mound* (New York: Harcourt, 2000), 213.

16. Rowan and Robinson, *Wait Till Next Year,* 216.

17. Kahn and Miraldi, *Beyond the Boys of Summer,* 259.

18. Irvin and Riley, *Nice Guys Finish First,* 145.

19. Rowan and Robinson, *Wait Till Next Year,* 216.

20. *NYP,* April 24, 1955.

21. Robert Creamer, "An Angel of Darkness Named Sal the Barber," *Sports Illustrated* (June 6, 1955): 44.

22. *SN,* June 29, 1955: 7.

23. *NYHT,* June 14, 1955.

24. *SN,* August 10, 1955: 7.

25. *SN,* August 10, 1955: 7; Maglie and Boyle, "Giant-Dodger Days," 47.

26. *NYP,* August 1, 1955; *NFG,* August 1, 1955.

27. Quoted in a column from an unidentified newspaper, August 1955, reproduced in *Baseball Nostalgia News,* 1985 edition, 10.

28. *SN,* August 10, 1955: 10.

29. Frank Graham, Jr., "They Were All Wrong About Maglie," *Sport* (February 1957): 82.

30. Richard Goldstein, *Superstars and Screwballs: 100 Years of Brooklyn Baseball* (New York: Dutton, 1991), 332.

31. Buzzie Bavasi and John Strege, *Off the Record* (Chicago: Contemporary Books, 1987), 66–67.

32. Michael Shapiro, *The Last Good Season: Brooklyn, the Dodgers, and Their Final Pennant Race Together* (New York: Doubleday, 2003), 2.

33. Mary Pileggi interview, October 30, 2003.

34. Larry Jansen interview, October 28, 2003.

35. Mary Pileggi interview, October 30, 2003.

36. Judith S. Modell, *Kinship With Strangers: Adoption and Interpretations of Kinship in American Culture* (Berkeley: University of California Press, 1994), 55.

37. *Child Welfare League of America: Standards for Adoption Service* (New York: Child Welfare League of America, 1958), 35–38.

38. Virginia Yans-McLaughlin, *Family and Community: Italian Immigrants in Buffalo, 1880–1930* (Ithaca: Cornell University Press, 1977), 91.

39. Mary Pileggi interview, June 2, 2003.

40. Sue Shaw (Catholic Charities of Buffalo) interview, September 21, 2004.

41. Shapiro, *Last Good Season,* 139.

15—1956: THE ARTFUL DODGER

1. Graham, "They Were All Wrong About Sal Maglie," 83.

2. *SN,* May 16, 1956: 12.

3. Mel Allen and Frank Graham Jr., *It Takes Heart* (New York: Harper, 1959), 149.

4. Ibid.

5. Shapiro, *Last Good Season*, 137–38; Buzzie Bavasi, e-mail to the author, January 25, 2005. In his autobiography, *Off the Record*, 204, Bavasi said that he paid $1,000 for Maglie, the same figure that appears in Szalontai, *Close Shave*, 307. Don Drysdale claimed the Dodgers paid only *one dollar* for Maglie: Don Drysdale and Bob Verdi, *Once a Bum Always a Dodger: My Life in Baseball from Brooklyn to Los Angeles* (New York: St. Martin's Press, 1990), 44.

6. *NYP,* May 17, 1956.

7. *NFG,* May 18, 1956.

8. Ibid.

9. Buzzie Bavasi, e-mail to the author, January 25, 2005.

10. Pat Grenga interview, June 24, 2004.

11. Eddie Gadawski interview, November 4, 2003.

12. Frank Graham, Jr., "Only Our Agent Watched as Maglie and Furillo Met," *Sport* (September 1956): 10; in an e-mail to the author, dated February 25, 2004, Graham suggested that the other reporter may have been fellow sportswriter Ed Linn, but he was unsure.

13. *NYDN,* January 29, 1989; Jack Lang interview, September 3, 2004.

14. Kahn, *The Era,* 330.

15. Tom Villante interview, July 6, 2004. A shorter version of the story appears in Shapiro, *Last Good Season,* 138.

16. Tom Villante interview, July 6, 2004.

17. George Vecsey, "The Barber and the Rifle," in Larry Freundlich, ed., *Reaching for the Stars: A Celebration of Italian Americans in Major League Baseball* (New York: Ballantine Books, 2003), 124.

18. Buzzie Bavasi, e-mail to the author, January 25, 2005.

19. Vecsey, "The Barber and the Rifle," 106–109; Donald Honig interview, February 3, 2004.

20. Tom Villante interview, July 6, 2004.

21. Vecsey, "The Barber and the Rifle," 121.

22. Roger Craig interview, March 5, 2005.

23. Ibid.

24. Maglie and Boyle, "Giant-Dodger Days," 48.

25. Graham, "They Were All Wrong About Maglie," 84. The columnist is not named.

26. Drysdale and Verdi, *Once a Bum,* 45–46.

27. Kahn, *Head Game,* 230.

28. Drysdale and Verdi, *Once a Bum,* 58.

29. Steve Gelman, *The Greatest Dodgers of Them All* (New York: G. P. Putnam's Sons, 1968), 47–48; Drysdale and Verdi, *Once a Bum,* 59–60.

30. Maglie and Boyle, "Giant-Dodger Days," 47.

31. Bob Chieger, *Voices of Baseball: Quotations on the Summer Game* (New York: Atheneum, 1983), 190.

32. In *Sandy Koufax: A Lefty's Legacy,* author Jane Leavy does not mention Maglie's influence on her subject.

33. *NFG,* June 5, 1956.

34. "Highlight," *Sports Illustrated* (June 18, 1956): 13.

35. Maglie and Boyle, "Giant-Dodger Days," 48.

36. "The Great Pastime," *Time* (July 30, 1956): 46.

37. *NFG,* August 6, 1956.

38. Details of Sal's reaction were provided by Jim Stewart of Niagara Falls, who attended the game. Jim Stewart, letter to the author, May 20, 2005.

39. Robert Creamer, "Three Clubs, and Only a Few Days to Go," *Sports Illustrated* (September 17, 1956): 14.

40. Larry Jansen interview, October 28, 2003.

41. *SN,* September 26, 1956: 5.

42. Graham, "They Were All Wrong About Maglie," 85.

43. Shapiro, *Last Good Season*, 247.

44. *NYT*, September 12, 1956; Shapiro, *Last Good Season*, 247.

45. Marshall Smith, "The Meanest Face in the Pennant Race," *Life* (October 1, 1956): 122.

46. J. Ronald Oakley, *Baseball's Last Golden Age, 1946–1960: The National Pastime in a Time of Glory and Change* (Jefferson, NC: McFarland, 1994), 240.

47. Maglie and Boyle, "Giant-Dodger Days," 47.

48. *NYHT*, September 22, 1956.

49. Robert Creamer, "Cocky Nationals and Mighty Yanks," *Sports Illustrated* (October 1, 1956): 12.

16—1956: MONEY PITCHER

1. *NYDN*, September 26, 1956.

2. Graham, "They Were All Wrong About Sal Maglie," 86.

3. Milton Shapiro, *Sal Maglie Story*, 184; Michael Shapiro, *Last Good Season*, 268.

4. Rich Coberly, *The No-Hit Hall of Fame: No-Hitters of the 20th Century* (Newport Beach: Triple Play Publications, 1985), 97.

5. *NYP*, September 26, 1956.

6. Nancy Seely, "No-Hitter? Kay Maglie Had to Wake Sal Jr.," *NYP*, September 26, 1956.

7. Confidential interview.

8. Pat Grenga interview, June 24, 2004.

9. Shapiro, *Last Good Season*, 271.

10. Ibid.

11. Ibid., 278. The newspaper is not identified.

12. Ibid., 282.

13. *NYT*, October 4, 1956.

14. *NYP*, October 4, 1956.

15. Graham, "They Were All Wrong About Sal Maglie," 86.

16. *NYHT*, October 4, 1956.

17. *NFG*, October 4, 1956; *NYT*, October 4, 1956.

18. *NYP*, October 4, 1956.

19. *NYT*, October 4, 1956.

20. Kahn, *The Era*, 331.

21. Don Larsen and Mark Shaw, *The Perfect Yankee: The Incredible Story of the Greatest Miracle in Baseball History* (Champaign: Sagamore Publishing, 1996), 30.

22. Ibid., 32.

23. Bob Neal, 1956 World Series, Game 5, Disk 1, The Miley Collection: radio broadcast transferred to CD.

24. *NYP*, October 9, 1956.

25. Larsen and Shaw, *Perfect Yankee*, 47.

26. Ibid., 107.

27. *NYP*, October 9, 1956.

28. Bert Randolph Sugar, *Baseball's 50 Greatest Games* (New York: Exeter Books, 1986) 49.

29. Larsen and Shaw, *Perfect Yankee*, 169.

30. *NYP*, October 9, 1956.

31. Years later, Sal acknowledged that reality, saying: "In effect, [1956] was my last season as a player." Maglie and Boyle, "Giant-Dodger Days," 48.

32. Rudd and Fischler, *Sporting Life*, 180; Paul Adomites, *October's Game* (Alexandria, VA: Redefinition, 1990), 53.

33. *NYHT*, October 9, 1956.

34. Robert Creamer, "And Then...," *Sports Illustrated* (October 15, 1956): 28–29.

35. Larsen and Shaw, *Perfect Yankee*, 190.

36. James Buckley, Jr., *Perfect: The Inside Story of Baseball's Sixteen Perfect Games* (Chicago: Triumph Books, 2002), 80–81.

37. Dr. Solomon Mowshowitz, e-mail to the author, December 16, 2002.

38. *NYP,* October 9, 1956.

39. Buzzie Bavasi and Tom Villante, e-mails to the author, May 20, 2005.

40. *NYP,* October 9, 1956.

41. *NYHT,* October 9, 1956.

42. Glenn Dickey, *The Great No-Hitters* (Radnor, PA: Chilton Books, 1976), 19.

43. "Baseball: The Way it Went," *Newsweek* (October 8, 1956): 61.

17—1957: "THE CALENDAR NEVER KILLED ANYBODY"

1. *SN,* November 14, 1956: 1.

2. Ibid.

3. *NFG,* November 2, 1956.

4. *NFG,* December 12, 1956.

5. Ibid.

6. *SN,* February 6, 1957: 16.

7. Dennis Villani interview, May 30, 2003.

8. John R. Tunis, *Schoolboy Johnson* (New York: William Morrow, 1958, reprinted 1991), 26.

9. Ibid., 11, 13.

10. Ron Briley, "'Do Not Go Gently [*sic*] into That Good Night': Race, the Baseball Establishment, and the Retirements of Bob Feller and Jackie Robinson," in Joseph Dorinson and Joram Warmund, eds., *Jackie Robinson. Race, Sports, and the American Dream* (Armonk, NY: M.E. Sharpe, 1998), 198.

11. *SN,* February 6, 1957: 9.

12. *SN,* March 6, 1957: 22.

13. In *The Last Good Season,* Michael Shapiro offers a thoughtful reassessment of the issue that does not exonerate O'Malley but distributes the blame for the Dodgers' departure from Brooklyn more evenly between O'Malley and Robert Moses.

14. *SN,* May 1, 1957: 9.

15. *NYJA,* April 23, 1957.

16. *NYWT,* July 6, 1957.

17. John P. Rossi, *A Whole New Game: Off the Field Changes in Baseball, 1946–1960* (Jefferson, NC: McFarland, 1999), 152.

18. *NYHT,* September 2, 1957.

19. *SN,* September 11, 1957: 7.

20. "Double Indemnity," *Newsweek* (September 16, 1957): 104.

21. Fred Stein, *Under Coogan's Bluff: A Fan's Recollections of the New York Giants under Terry and Ott* (n.p., 1981), 145.

22. Peter Golenbock, *Bums: An Oral History of the Brooklyn Dodgers* (Chicago: Contemporary Books, 1984), 448.

18—1958: SUNSET AT THE SHOW

1. Milton Richman, "Does a Ballplayer Know When He's Through?" *Sport* (July 1957): 12.

2. *SN,* October 16, 1957: 21.

3. *NYHT,* March 20, 1958.

4. "Kinescope" film fragment, contained in a video from Rare Sportsfilms of Naperville, IL. The film fragment is also the source of quotations from Mel Allen and Phil Rizzuto's commentary on the game.

5. *SN,* June 25, 1958: 5.

6. Joe Calato interview, June 22, 2004; Jimmy Briganti interview, May 27, 2003; Benny Critelli interview, June 18, 2004; Jimmy Macri interview, May 29, 2003.

7. Mickey Rizzo interview, June 22, 2004; Eddie Gadawski interview, November 4, 2003.

8. Leavy, *Sandy Koufax*, 69.

9. Jean Hastings Ardell, *Breaking into Baseball: Women and the National Pastime* (Carbondale, Southern Illinois University Press, 2005), 51–78.

10. Glenn Dickey, *The Jock Empire: Its Rise and Deserved Fall* (Radnor, PA: Chilton Books, 1974), 5; George Gmelch, "Groupies and Baseball," *Journal of Sport and Social Issues* (February 1998): 33.

11. Ross Morrow, "Ballplayers versus Bobbysoxers?" *Sport* (September 1950): 97.

12. Roger Kahn, *A Season in the Sun* (New York: Harper and Row, 1976), 110; and *Games We Used To Play* (New York: Ticknor and Fields, 1992), 214–18. Although Kahn concealed the player's identity in the latter book, in the former he had already revealed it was Wynn.

13. Larry Jansen and Sal Yvars both declared that during his years with the Giants, Sal never engaged in extramarital affairs. Larry Jansen interview, October 28, 2003; Sal Yvars interview, July 7, 2004.

14. Gussie Moran, "The Ten Most Exciting Men in Baseball, *Sport* (October 1955): 68–69.

15. Hank Aaron and Lonnie Wheeler, *I Had a Hammer* (New York: HarperCollins, 1991), 90.

16. The conversation, date unspecified, was mentioned to the author by Steve Acee, who spoke with Skowron during an event at the Baseball Hall of Fame in Cooperstown. The allegation perhaps should be filed under "hearsay history," although there is no reason to believe it is untrue. The author's attempts to contact Bill Skowron were unsuccessful.

17. The story was related to the author by Kay Maglie's sister-in-law and confidant Mary Pileggi, who heard it directly from Kay. Mary Pileggi interviews, June 23, 2004, and September 12, 2004.

18. Prince, *Brooklyn's Dodgers*, 80–81. No doubt other factors were involved; Casey's reluctance to play with Jackie Robinson was likely a more pressing reason for his being traded.

19. Danielle Gagnon-Torres and Ken Lizotte, *High Inside: Memoirs of a Baseball Wife* (New York: G.P. Putnam's Sons, 1983), 97.

20. John Pileggi interview, June 2, 2003.

21. Maglie and Boyle, "Giant-Dodger Days," 49; John Pileggi interview, June 2, 2003.

22. Bob Gibson and Lonnie Wheeler, *Stranger to the Game: The Autobiography of Bob Gibson* (New York: Penguin Books, 1994), 52–53.

23. *SN*, February 4, 1959: 21.

24. *NYHT*, March 18, 1959.

25. Jim Brosnan, *The Long Season* (New York: Harper, 1960, reprinted 2002), 17.

26. Ibid., 18.

27. Ibid., 45.

28. Ibid., 46.

29. Ibid.

30. *SN*, April 1, 1959: 34.

31. *NFG*, undated clipping.

32. "Opening Day: High Hopes—Heartaches," *Newsweek* (April 13, 1959): 71.

33. *NFG*, April 11, 1959.

34. *REG*, April 14, 1959.

35. Kahn, *October Men*, 159.

36. *NFG*, undated clipping.

19—1960–1962, 1966: COACHING THE KIDS

1. Sal Maglie and Dick Schaap, "I Always Threw Beanballs," *Cavalier* (September 1959): 31–32.

2. Excerpted in *SN*, November 4, 1959: 11.

3. *SN*, December 16, 1959: 8.

4. *SN*, November 11, 1959: 19; Maglie and Boyle, "Giant-Dodger Days," 49.

5. Mickey Rizzo interview, June 22, 2004.

6. Confidential interview.
7. *NFG,* May 8, 1960.
8. *SN,* Janaury 4, 1960: 18.
9. *SN,* May 24, 1961: 28.
10. Bill Monbouquette interview, September 24, 2004.
11. Ibid.
12. Frank Graham Jr., "The Education of Bill Monbouquette," *Sport* (August 1962): 71.
13. William M. Simons, "Pitcher at Twilight: Bill Monbouquette and the American Dream," *Cooperstown Symposium on Baseball and American Culture* (Jefferson, NC: McFarland, 2002): 45.
14. Bill Monbouquette interview, September 24, 2004.
15. *SN,* July 7, 1962: 9.
16. Clipping from an unidentified newspaper, NBHOFL.
17. *SN,* August 25, 1962: 2.
18. Gabriel Schechter, "Dick Radatz: Baseball's Supernova," www.baseballhalloffame.org/library/columns/gs_050309.htm.
19. Dick Radatz interview, October 8, 2004.
20. Mary Kathleen Benet, *The Politics of Adoption* (New York: Macmillan, 1976), 86.
21. Mary Pileggi interview, September 12, 2004.
22. Maglie and Boyle, "Giant-Dodger Days," 49.
23. *SN,* October 24, 1964: 19.
24. Ibid.
25. *NYT,* January 12, 1965.
26. *NFG,* January 30, 1966.
27. Ibid. Kathy Pileggi Peller remembered Sal being hit in the nose with "blood all over the place." Kathy Pileggi Peller interview, June 1, 2003.
28. Peter Golenbock, *Fenway: An Unexpurgated History of the Boston Red Sox* (New York: G.P. Putnam's Sons, 1992), 288–89.
29. *NFG,* January 24, 1966; *SN,* February 26, 1966: 22.
30. Kathy Pileggi Peller interview, June 1, 2003.
31. Maglie and Boyle, "Giant-Dodger Days," 49.
32. *NFG,* undated clipping, 1966.

20—1967: TRAGEDY AT HOME, TRIUMPH IN BOSTON

1. Maria Grenga Rizzo interview, August 5, 2003.
2. Mary Pileggi interviews, October 3, 2003, June 24, 2004.
3. Ibid.
4. Kathy Pileggi Peller interview, June 1, 2003.
5. Mary Pileggi interview, June 23, 2004.
6. Dick Williams interview, August 16, 2004. Williams's words were: "Maglie wasn't even *in* spring training! His wife was seriously ill. He was at home with his wife, where he *should* be."
7. Kathy Pileggi Peller interview, June 1, 2003.
8. Dennis Villani interview, May 30, 2003.
9. Jim Lonborg interview, July 1, 2004.
10. Dan Osinski declined to be interviewed.
11. Dick Williams and Bill Plaschke, *No More Mr. Nice Guy: A Life of Hardball* (New York: Harcourt Brace Jovanovich, 1990), 85.
12. Glenn Stout and Richard A. Johnson, *Red Sox Century: One Hundred Years of Red Sox Baseball* (Boston: Houghton Mifflin, 2000), 320.
13. Jim Lonborg interview, July 1, 2004.
14. Ibid.
15. Ibid.
16. *BG,* May 5, 1967.
17. *CSM,* September 14, 1967.

18. Maglie and Boyle, "Tough Business," 80.

19. *NFG*, October 1, 1967.

20. *NFG*, October 5, 1967.

21. *NFG*, October 6, 1967.

22. *NFG*, October 12, 1967.

23. Maglie and Boyle, "Tough Business," 79.

24. Bill Reynolds, *Lost Summer: The '67 Red Sox and the Impossible Dream* (New York: Warner Books, 1992), 270.

25. Dick Williams interview, August 16, 2004.

26. *SN*, November 18, 1967: 36.

27. Maglie and Boyle, "Tough Business," 79.

28. Golenbock, *Fenway,* 316.

29. Maglie and Boyle, "Tough Business," 79.

30. *SN*, November 18, 1967: 36.

31. *NFG*, October 15, 1967.

32. *SN*, October 28, 1967: 16.

33. Bobby Doerr interview, February 11, 2004.

34. *SN*, November 18, 1967: 36; *NFG*, November 2, 1967.

35. *SN*, November 18, 1967: 36.

36. *NFG*, November 2, 1967.

21—1968–1969: MAGLIE'S STINT WITH THE SEATTLE PILOTS

1. Sal's friend Benny Critelli recalled that it had cost Sal around $60,000 to have the house built. Benny Critelli interview, June 18, 2004. The house was sold for $42,000. E-mail to the author from Niagara County Clerk's Office, July 10, 2003. Kathy Pileggi Peller recalled the yard sale. Kathy Pileggi Peller interview, June 1, 2003.

2. Mary Pileggi interviews, June 2, 2003, and October 30, 2003.

3. Maria Grenga Rizzo interview, August 5, 2003.

4. Sibby Sisti interview, August 20, 2004.

5. Benny Critelli interview, June 18, 2004.

6. Doris Maglie interview, May 31, 2003.

7. Doris Maglie interview, April 25, 2003.

8. Bob Elliott, *The Northern Game: Baseball the Canadian Way* (Wilmington: Sports Media, 2005), 193.

9. *BCE*, August 21, 1968.

10. *NFG*, October 14, 1968.

11. Undated clipping from unidentified newspaper.

12. *SN*, April 12, 1969: 41.

13. Jim Bouton, *Ball Four: The Final Pitch* (North Egremont, MA, Bulldog Publishing, 2000), 16, 85, 116, 152.

14. Kiernan, *Coogan's Bluff,* 182–83.

15. Carson van Lindt, *The Seattle Pilots Story* (New York: Marabou Publishing, 1993), 20–23, 154.

16. Mike Marshall, e-mail to the author, July 16, 2004.

22—THE REST OF HIS DAYS

1. *NFG,* January 16, 1970.

2. *NFG,* June 7, 1970.

3. Joe Maglie, e-mail to the author, January 29, 2003.

4. *SN*, June 27, 1970: 47.

5. Joe Calato interview, June 25, 2004.

6. Charles Powley interview, August 4, 2004.

7. Holly Jager declined to be interviewed.

8. Cecilia Grenga Anderson interview, June 19, 2005.

9. Mickey Rizzo interview, June 22, 2004.
10. Thomas Pratt interview, December 18, 2003.
11. Quit Claim Deed, signed by Salvatore A. Maglie on July 27, 1976. Copy from Niagara County Clerk's office.
12. Clipping from an unidentified newspaper, dated July 21, 1974.
13. Don Glynn interview, June 2, 2003.
14. Tom Darro interview, July 22, 2003.
15. Don Glynn interview, June 2, 2003.
16. Ibid.
17. Anthony Rendina interview, May 29, 2003.
18. Cecilia Grenga Anderson interview, June 17, 2005.
19. Jimmy Macri interview, May 29, 2003.
20. Joe Calato interview, June 25, 2004.
21. Ibid.
22. Ernie Aloi interview, August 15, 2004.
23. *NYT,* May 3, 1983.
24. *NFG,* August 15, 1982.
25. *NYP,* July 29, 1982.
26. *NFG,* November 12, 1982.
27. *NYT,* May 3, 1982.
28. *NFG,* June 22, 1983.
29. Al Mallette interview, January 20, 2004.
30. Donald Honig interview, February 3, 2004.
31. Donald Honig, "A Special Breed," in Freundlich, *Reaching for the Stars,* 41.
32. Kiernan, *Coogan's Bluff,* 192.
33. Honig, "Special Breed," 41.
34. Augie Tumminia interview, September 12, 2003.
35. Monte Irvin interview, September 29, 2003.
36. Marty Adler interview, August 25, 2003.

23—TWILIGHT AND DARKNESS

1. Mary and John Pileggi interview, June 2, 2003.
2. Kathy Pileggi Peller interview, June 1, 2003.
3. The Maglie family declined to release the coroner's report on Sal, Jr.'s death.
4. Cecilia Grenga Anderson interview, June 17, 2005; Kathy Pileggi Peller interview, June 1, 2003.
5. *NFG,* August 16, 1992.
6. *Newsday,* December 29, 1992.
7. Clipping dated 1987, from an unidentified Canadian newspaper.
8. Doris Maglie interview, April 25, 2003.
9. Louise Grenga interview, June 24, 2004.
10. Confidential interview.
11. Sibby Sisti interview, August 20, 2004.
12. Bill Wolcott interview, May 28, 2003. Wolcott first told the story on a television show and then published it in one of his columns for the *Niagara Falls Gazette.* A version also appears in Sean Peter Kirst, *The Ashes of Lou Gehrig and Other Baseball Essays* (Jefferson, NC: McFarland, 2003), 54–57.
13. *NYT,* December 29, 1992; *Newsday,* December 29, 1992; *NYDN,* December 29, 1992.
14. Msgr. Edward Scanlan interview, June 22, 2004.
15. *NFG,* January 1, 1993.

UNPUBLISHED MATERIALS

Birth and marriage records, Town Hall, Faggiano, Italy.

Military draft record, Giuseppe Luigi Maglie, State Historical Archive, Lecce, Italy, and Documentation Center of the Military District, Lecce, Italy.

Birth certificate, Salvatore Maglie, Niagara County Clerk's office, Lockport, NY.

Marriage registration, Salvatore Maglie and Kathleen Pileggi, Town Clerk's office, Lewiston, NY.

Parish records, St. Joseph's Roman Catholic church, Niagara Falls, NY.

Sal Maglie—Pitcher Register, National Baseball Hall of Fame Library, Cooperstown, NY.

Art Pennington scrapbook, National Baseball Hall of Fame Library, Cooperstown, NY.

Baldassaro, Larry. "Dashing Dagos and Walloping Wops: Media Portrayal of Italian American Major Leaguers Before World War II." Unpublished paper presented at Society for American Baseball Research conference, Cincinnati, 2004.

Young, Bill. "Sal Maglie: His Remarkable (But Forgotten) Year of 1949." Unpublished paper presented at Society for American Baseball Research conference, Cincinnati, 2004.

GOVERNMENT DOCUMENTS

New York State Census records, 1915, 1925. Mf# 0523311, 0523312, Family History Center, Salt Lake City, Utah.
Niagara Falls City Directories, 1910–1960. Polk City Directories, Livonia, Mich.
United States Federal Census records, 1910, 1920, 1930. <www.ancestry.com>
SS *Venezia*, September 16, 1913, manifest, United States Immigration Service. <www.ellisisland.org>

FILMS, FILM CLIPS, AND VIDEOS

1958 Film clip, fragment of game between New York Yankees and Detroit Tigers; Maglie pitching for Yankees; Rare Sportsfilms Video.
1974 "The Way It Was." Sal Maglie, Mickey Mantle, Clem Labine, Don Larsen, Duke Snider, and Casey Stengel; announcer, Curt Gowdy; discussion of Larsen's perfect game in 1956 World Series.
1980 "It's My Turn," Columbia Pictures, 1980; movie starring Jill Clayburgh and Michael Douglas; cameo appearance by Sal Maglie.
1984 Video of Brooklyn Dodgers Hall of Fame inductions ceremony, June 7, 1984; Sal Maglie among guests; videotape from Marty Adler.

SOUND RECORDINGS OF GAME BROADCASTS

1951 National League Playoff, Game Three, Brooklyn Dodgers vs. New York Giants; Sal Maglie and Don Newcombe, starting pitchers; Gordon McClendon, announcer; The Miley Collection.
1951 National League Playoff, Game Three; three "calls" of Bobby Thomson's home run; "Great Sports Moments"; The Miley Collection.

1954   World Series, Game One, New York Giants vs. Cleveland Indians; Sal Maglie and Bob Lemon, starting pitchers; announcers Al Helfer and Jimmy Dudley; The Miley Collection.

1956   World Series, Game Five, Brooklyn Dodgers vs. New York Yankees; Sal Maglie and Don Larsen, pitchers (Don Larsen's perfect game); The Miley Collection.

INTERVIEWS

A. B. Chandler Oral History Project, University of Kentucky Library, Lexington; interviews conducted by William Marshall: Danny Gardella, Monte Irvin, Max Lanier, Sal Maglie, Mickey Owen, Adrian and Mary Zabala.

Interview conducted by Craig Allen Cleve: George Hausmann.

Interviews conducted by the author (recorded unless otherwise indicated): Marty Adler, Ernie Aloi, Cecilia Grenga Anderson, Buzzie Bavasi (e-mail), Robert Boyle, Ralph Branca (e-mail), Jimmy Briganti (not recorded), Ann Bright, Jim Brosnan (not recorded), Arthur Caggiano, Joe Calato, Dan Carnevale, Al Corwin, Roger Craig, Robert Creamer, Benny Critelli, Carol D'Anna, Vince D'Anna, Alvin Dark, Tom Darro, Bobby Doerr, Carl Erskine (letter), Charlie Feeney, Fern Furillo, Eddie Gadawski, Don Glynn, Frank Graham, Jr., Frank Grenga (not recorded), Joe Grenga (not recorded), Louise Grenga, Pat Grenga, Chet Grochala, Donald Honig, Monte Irvin, Stan Isaacs (e-mail), Larry Jansen, Roger Kahn (e-mail), Clem Labine, Jack Lang, Max Lanier, Joe Latona, Whitey Lockman, Jim Lonborg, Jimmy Macri (not recorded), Doris Maglie (not recorded), Joe Maglie (e-mail), Al Mallette, Bill Monbouquette, Irv Noren, Kathy Pileggi Peller, Art Pennington, Carl Pileggi, John Pileggi, Mary Pileggi, Johnny Podres, Charles Powley, Thomas Pratt, Dick Radatz, Anthony Rendina, Maria Grenga Rizzo (not recorded), Mickey Rizzo, Edward Scanlan, Sibby Sisti, Augie Tumminia, Dennis Villani, Tom Villante, Dick Williams, Mark Winegardner (not recorded), Bill Wolcott, Sal Yvars, Mary Zabala, and two confidential interviews.

NEWSPAPERS

Boston Daily Herald, Boston Globe, Brooklyn Eagle, Buffalo Courier-Express, Chicago Sun-Times, Chicago Tribune, Christian Science Monitor, Newsday, New York Daily Mirror, New York Daily News, New York Herald Tribune, New York Journal-American, New York Post, New York Times, Niagara Falls Gazette, Niagara Falls Reporter, Pacific Stars and Stripes, Reno Evening Gazette, Sporting News, Wall Street Journal, Welland (Ontario) Tribune.

BOOKS

Aaron, Hank, with Lonnie Wheeler. *I Had a Hammer: The Hank Aaron Story.* New York: HarperCollins, 1991.

Alexander, Charles C. *Our Game: An American Baseball History.* New York: Henry Holt, 1991.

Allen, Lee. *The Giants and the Dodgers: The Fabulous Story of Baseball's Fiercest Feud.* New York: G. P. Putnam's Sons, 1964.

Allen, Mel, and Frank Graham, Jr. *It Takes Heart.* New York: Harper, 1959.

Alston, Walter, with Si Burick. *Alston and the Dodgers.* Garden City: Doubleday, 1966.

Appel, Marty. *Now Pitching for the Yankees: Spinning the News for Mickey, Billy, and George.* New York: Total Sports Illustrated, 2001.

Ardell, Jean Hastings. *Breaking into Baseball. Women and the National Pastime.* Carbondale: Southern Illinois University Press, 2005.

Barber, Red. *1947: When All Hell Broke Loose in Baseball.* New York: Doubleday, 1982.

The Baseball Encyclopedia: The Complete and Definitive Record of Major League Baseball. New York: Macmillan, 1996, tenth edition, rev.

Bavasi, Buzzie, with John Strege. *Off the Record.* Chicago: Contemporary Books, 1987.

Benet, Mary Kathleen. *The Politics of Adoption.* New York: MacMillan, 1976.

Berton, Pierre. *Niagara: A History of the Falls.* Toronto: McClelland and Stewart, 1994.

Bjarkman, Peter C. *Baseball with a Latin Beat.* Jefferson, NC: McFarland, 1994.

Blake, Mike. *Baseball Chronicles: An Oral History of Baseball through the Decades.* Cincinnati: Betterway Books, 1994.

———. *The Minor Leagues: A Celebration of the Little Show.* New York: Wynwood Press, 1991.

Bouton, Bobbie, and Nancy Marshall. *Home Games: Two Baseball Wives Speak Out.* New York: St. Martin's Press, 1983.

Bouton, Jim. *Ball Four: The Final Pitch.* North Egremont, MA: Bulldog Publishing, 2000.

Brosnan, Jim. *The Long Season.* New York: Harper, 1960. Reprinted 2000.

Bryant, Howard. *Shut Out: A Story of Race and Baseball in Boston.* New York: Routledge, 2002.

Buckley, James, Jr. *Perfect: The Inside Story of Baseball's Sixteen Perfect Games.* Chicago: Triumph Books, 2002.

Cataneo, David. *Tony C.: The Triumph and Tragedy of Tony Conigliaro.* Nashville: Rutledge Hill Press, 1997.

Child Welfare League of America Standards for Adoption Service. New York: Child Welfare League of America, 1958.

Cleve, Craig Allen. *Hardball on the Home Front: Major League Replacement Players of World War II.* Jefferson, NC: McFarland, 2004.

Clifton, Merritt. *Disorganized Baseball: The Provincial League from LaRoque to Les Expos.* Richford, VT: Samisdat, 1982.

Coberly, Rich. *The No-Hit Hall of Fame: No-Hitters of the 20th Century.* Newport Beach: Triple Play Publications, 1985.

Cohen, Marvin A. *The Dodgers-Giants Rivalry 1900–1957: A Year by Year Retrospective.* New York: MC Productions, 1999.

Cohen, Richard, and David Neft. *The World Series: Complete Play-By-Play of Every Game, 1903–1985.* New York: Macmillan, 1986.

Coleman, Vince, and Dan Valente. *The Impossible Dream Remembered: The 1967 Red Sox.* Lexington: The Stephen Greene Press, 1987.

Cramer, Richard Ben. *Joe DiMaggio: The Hero's Life.* New York: Simon and Schuster, 2000.

Creamer, Robert. *Baseball in '41: A Celebration of the Best Baseball Season Ever in the Year America Went to War.* New York: Viking Press, 1991.

Crehan, Herbert F., and James W. Ryan. *Lightning in a Bottle: The Sox of '67.* Boston: Brandon Publishing, 1992.

Day, Laraine, with Kyle Crichton. *Day with the Giants.* Garden City, NY: Doubleday, 1952.

DeLillo, Don. *Underworld.* New York: Scribner, 1997.

Dickey, Glenn. *The Jock Empire: Its Rise and Deserved Fall.* Radnor, PA: Chilton Books, 1974.

———. *The Great No-Hitters.* Radnor, PA: Chilton Books, 1976.

Dickson, Paul, *The New Dickson Baseball Dictionary.* New York: Harcourt Brace, 1999.

Dorinson, Joseph, and Joram Warmund. *Jackie Robinson: Race, Sports, and the American Dream.* Armonk, NY: M. E. Sharpe, 1998.

Drysdale, Don, and Bob Verdi. *Once a Bum Always a Dodger: My Life in Baseball from Brooklyn to Los Angeles.* New York: St. Martin's Press, 1990.

Dumych, Daniel M. *Niagara Falls.* 2 vols. Charleston, SC: Arcadia Publishing, 2003.

Durant, John. *Baseball's Miracle Teams.* New York: Hastings House, 1975.

Durocher, Leo, with Ed Linn. *Nice Guys Finish Last.* New York: Simon and Schuster, 1975.

Einstein, Charles. *Willie Mays: My Life In and Out of Baseball.* New York: E. P. Dutton, 1966.

Eizen, George, and David K. Wiggins, eds. *Ethnicity and Sport in North America: History and Culture*. Westport: Greenwood Press, 1994.

Elliott, Bob. *The Northern Game: Baseball the Canadian Way*. Wilmington: Sports Media, 2005.

Enders, Eric. *100 Years of the World Series*. New York: Barnes and Noble Books, 2003.

Erskine, Carl. *Tales from the Dodger Dugout*. Champaign: Sports Publishing, 2001.

Eskenazi, Gerald. *The Lip: A Biography of Leo Durocher*. New York: William Morrow, 1993.

Falkner, David. *Great Time Coming: The Life of Jackie Robinson from Baseball to Birmingham*. New York: Simon and Schuster, 1995.

Feder, H. William. *The Evolution of an Ethnic Neighborhood that Became United in Diversity: The East Side, Niagara Falls, New York, 1880–1930*. Amherst, NY, BMP, Inc., 2000.

Fehler, Gene. *Tales from Baseball's Golden Age*. Champaign, IL: Sports Publishing, 2000.

Figueredo, Jorge S. *Cuban Baseball: A Statistical History, 1878–1961*. Jefferson, NC: McFarland, 2003.

———. *Béisbol Cubano: A un Paso de las Grandes Ligas, 1878–1961*. Jefferson, NC: McFarland, 2005.

Flood, Curt, with Richard Carter. *The Way It Is*. New York: Trident Press, 1971.

Freundlich, Larry, ed. *Reaching for the Stars: A Celebration of Italian Americans in Major League Baseball*. New York: Ballantine Books, 2003.

Frommer, Harvey. *Baseball's Greatest Managers*. New York: Franklin Watts, 1985.

———. *Baseball's Greatest Rivalry: The New York Yankees and the Boston Red Sox*. New York: Atheneum, 1982.

———. *New York City Baseball, 1947–1957: The Last Golden Age*. New York: Harcourt Brace Jovanovich, 1992.

———. *Rickey and Robinson: The Men Who Broke Baseball's Color Barrier*. New York: Macmillan, 1982.

Gagnon Torrez, Danielle, with Ken Lizotte. *High Inside: Memoirs of a Baseball Wife*. New York: G. P. Putnam's Sons, 1983.

Gelman, Steve. *The Greatest Dodgers of Them All*. New York: G. P. Putnam's Sons, 1968.

Getz, Mike. *The Brooklyn Dodgers and Their Rivals, 1950–1952*. Brooklyn: Montauk Press, 1999.

Gibson, Bob, with Lonnie Wheeler. *Stranger to the Game*. New York: Penguin Books, 1994.

Giglio, James N. *Musial: From Stash to Stan the Man*. Columbia: University of Missouri Press, 2001.

Gilbert, Bill. *They Also Served: Baseball and the Home Front, 1941–1945*. New York: Crown Publishers, 1992.

Gmelch, George. *Inside Pitch: Life in Professional Baseball*. Washington, DC: Smithsonian Institution Press, 2001.

Goldblatt, Andrew. *The Giants and the Dodgers: Four Cities, Two Teams, One Rivalry*. Jefferson, NC: McFarland, 2003.

Goldstein, Richard. *Spartan Seasons: How Baseball Survived the Second World War*. New York: Macmillan, 1980.

———. *Superstars and Screwballs: 100 Years of Brooklyn Baseball*. New York: Dutton, 1991.

Golenbock, Peter. *Bums: An Oral History of the Brooklyn Dodgers*. Chicago: Contemporary Books, 1984.

———. *Dynasty: The New York Yankees 1949–1964*. Englewood Cliffs: Prentice-Hall, 1975.

———. *Fenway: An Unexpurgated History of the Boston Red Sox*. New York: G.P. Putnam's Sons, 1992.

Gonzalez Echevarria, Roberto. *The Pride of Havana: A History of Cuban Baseball*. New York: Oxford University Press, 1999.

Goodwin, Doris Kearns. *Wait till Next Year*. New York: Simon and Schuster, 1997.

Gorman, Tom, with Jerome Holtzman. *Three and Two!* New York: Charles Scribner's Sons, 1979.

Graham, Frank. *The New York Giants: An Informal History of a Great Baseball Club*.

Carbondale: Southern Illinois University Press, 2002; reprint of 1952 edition.

Graham, Frank, Jr. *Great No-Hit Games of the Major Leagues*. New York: Random House, 1968.

Gutman, Dan. *It Ain't Cheatin' If You Don't Get Caught: Scuffing, Corking, Spitting, Gunking, Razzing, and Other Fundamentals of Our National Pastime*. New York: Penguin Books, 1990.

Halberstam, David. *The Fifties*. New York: Fawcett Columbine, 1993.

———. *Summer of '49*. New York: William Morrow, 1989.

Hano, Arnold. *A Day in the Bleachers*. New York: Da Capo Press, 1982.

———. *Sandy Koufax: Strikeout King*. New York: G. P. Putnam's Sons, 1967.

Hano, Arnold, Dave Weiner, and Bill Gutman. *When the Cheering Stops: Ex-Major Leaguers Talk About Their Game and Their Lives*. New York: Macmillan, 1990.

Helyar, John. *Lords of the Realm: The Real History of Baseball*. New York: Villard Books, 1994.

Higbe, Kirby, with Martin Quigley. *The High Hard One*. New York: Viking Press, 1967.

Hirshberg, Dan. *Phil Rizzuto: A Yankee Tradition*. Champaign: Sagamore Publishing, 1993.

Hodges, Russ, and Al Hirshberg. *My Giants*. Garden City, NY: Doubleday, 1963.

Honig, Donald. *Baseball America: The Heroes of the Game and the Times of their Glory*. New York: MacMillan, 1985.

———. *Baseball in the '50s. A Decade of Transition*. New York: Crown Publishers, 1987.

———. *Baseball When the Grass Was Real: Baseball from the Twenties to the Forties Told by the Men Who Played It*. Lincoln: University of Nebraska Press, 1975.

House, Tom. *The Jock's Itch: The Fast-Track Private World of the Professional Ballplayer*. Chicago: Contemporary Books, 1989.

Humber, William. *Diamonds of the North: A Concise History of Baseball in Canada*. Toronto: Oxford University Press, 1995.

Hynd, Noel. *The Giants of the Polo Grounds*. New York: Doubleday, 1988.

Irvin, Monte, with James A. Riley. *Nice Guys Finish First*. New York: Carroll and Graff Publishers, 1996.

Irwin, William. *The New Niagara: Tourism, Technology, and the Landscape of Niagara Falls, 1776–1917*. University Park: University of Pennsylvania Press, 1996.

Izenberg, Jerry. *The Rivals*. New York: Holt, Rinehart and Winston, 1968.

Jennison, Christopher. *Wait 'Til Next Year: The Yankees, Dodgers, and Giants 1947–1957*. New York: W. W. Norton, 1974.

Johnson, Lloyd, and Miles Wolff. *The Encyclopedia of Minor League Baseball*. Durham: Baseball America, 1993.

Kahn, Roger. *The Boys of Summer*. New York: HarperCollins, reissued 1998.

———. *The Era 1947–1957: When the Yankees, the Giants, and the Dodgers Ruled the World*. Lincoln: University of Nebraska Press, 2002.

———. *Games We Used To Play*. New York: Ticknor and Fields, 1992.

———. *The Head Game: Baseball Seen from the Pitcher's Mound*. New York: Harcourt, 2000.

———. *Memories of Summer: When Baseball was an Art and Writing about It was a Game*. New York: Hyperion, 1997.

———. *October Men: Reggie Jackson, George Steinbrenner, Billy Martin, and the Yankees' Miraculous Finish in 1978*. New York: Harcourt, 2003.

———. *A Season in the Sun*. New York: Harper and Row, 1976.

Kahn, Roger, and Rob Miraldi, eds. *Beyond the Boys of Summer: The Very Best of Roger Kahn*. New York: McGraw Hill, 2005.

Kaplan, Jim. *Baseball's Great Dynasties: The Giants*. New York: W. H. Smith, 1991.

Kiernan, Thomas. *Miracle at Coogan's Bluff*. New York: Thomas Y. Crowell, 1975.

Kirst, Sean. *The Ashes of Lou Gehrig and Other Baseball Essays*. Jefferson, NC: McFarland, 2003.

Koppett, Leonard. *The Man in the Dugout: Baseball's Top Managers and How They Got That Way*. New York: Crown Publishers, 1993.

Kriner, T. W. *In the Mad Water: Two Centuries of Adventure and Lunacy at Niagara Falls*.

Buffalo: J & J Publishing, 1999.

Kuenster, John. *Heartbreakers: Baseball's Most Agonizing Defeats.* Chicago: Ivan Dee, 2001.

LaGumina, Salvatore. *Wop! A Documentary History of Anti-Italian Discrimination.* Buffalo, NY: Guernica Press, 1999.

Lally, Richard. *Bombers: An Oral History of the New York Yankees.* New York: Crown Publishers, 2002.

Lamb, Chris. *Blackout: The Untold Story of Jackie Robinson's First Spring Training.* Lincoln: University of Nebraska Press, 2004.

Lautier, Jack. *Fenway Voices from Smoky Joe to Rocket Roger.* Camden, ME: Yankee Books, 1990.

Leavy, Jane. *Sandy Koufax: A Lefty's Legacy.* New York: HarperCollins, 2002.

Lelchuk, Alan. *Brooklyn Boy.* New York: McGraw Hill, 1990.

Light, Jonathan Fraser. *The Cultural Encyclopedia of Baseball.* Jefferson, NC: McFarland, 1997.

Linn, Ed. *Hitter: The Life and Turmoils of Ted Williams.* New York: Harcourt and Brace, 1993.

Lowenfish, Lee, and Tony Lupien. *The Imperfect Diamond: The Story of Baseball's Reserve System and the Men Who Fought To Change It.* New York: Stein and Day, 1980.

Mangione, Jerre, and Ben Morreale. *La Storia: Five Centuries of the Italian American Experience.* New York: HarperCollins, 1992.

Mantle, Mickey, with Phil Pepe. *My Favorite Summer: 1956.* New York: Doubleday, 1991.

Marshall, William. *Baseball's Pivotal Era: 1945–1951.* Lexington: University Press of Kentucky, 1999.

McDermott, Mickey, with Howard Eisenberg. *A Funny Thing Happened on the Way to Cooperstown.* Chicago: Triumph Books, 2003.

McGreevy, Patrick V. *Imagining Niagara: The Meaning and Making of Niagara Falls.* Amherst: University of Massachusetts Press, 1994.

McKelvey, G. Richard. *Fisk's Homer, Willie's Catch and the Shot Heard Round the World: Classic Moments from Postseason Baseball, 1940–1996.* Jefferson, NC: McFarland, 1998.

McSweeney, Bill. *The Impossible Dream: The Story of the Miracle Boston Red Sox.* New York: Coward-McCann, 1968.

Meany, Tom. *The Incredible Giants.* New York: A.S. Barnes, 1955.

Melosh, Barbara. *Strangers and Kin: The American Way of Adoption.* Cambridge, MA: Harvard University Press, 2002.

Mills, Dorothy Jane. *A Woman's Work: Writing Baseball History with Harold Seymour.* Jefferson, NC: McFarland, 2004.

Modell, Judith S. *Kinship with Strangers: Adoption and Interpretations of Kinship in American Culture.* Berkeley: University of California Press, 1994.

Moffi, Larry. *This Side of Cooperstown: An Oral History of Major League Baseball in the 1950s.* Iowa City: University of Iowa Press, 1996.

Neft, David S., Richard M. Cohen, and Michael L. Neft. *The Sports Encyclopedia: Baseball.* 24th edition. New York: St. Martin's Griffin, 2004.

Niagara Falls Historic Photo Album. 2 vols. New York: Pediment Publishing, 2000.

Oakley, J. Ronald. *Baseball's Last Golden Age, 1946–1960: The National Pastime in a Time of Glory and Change.* Jefferson, NC: McFarland, 1994.

Obojski, Robert. *All-Star Baseball Since 1933* (Briarcliff Manor, NY: Stein and Day, 1980.

———. *Bush League: A History of Minor League Baseball.* New York: Macmillan, 1975.

Overfield, Joseph. *The 100 Seasons of Buffalo Baseball.* Buffalo, Partners' Press, 1985.

Parker, Gary R. *Win or Go Home: Sudden Death Baseball.* Jefferson, NC: McFarland, 2002.

Parrott, Harold. *The Lords of Baseball.* Atlanta: Longstreet Press, 2001.

Patterson, A. E., ed. *Dodgers Year Book 1957.* Brooklyn, n.p., 1957.

Peary, Danny, ed. *We Played the Game: 65 Players Remember Baseball's Greatest Era 1947–1964.* New York: Hyperion, 1994.

Phillips, John. *The Mexican Jumping Beans: The Story of the Baseball War of 1946.* Perry, GA: Capital Publishing, 1997.

Pietrusza, David. *Baseball's Canadian-American League: A History of Its Inception, Franchises,*

Participants, Locales, Statistics, Demise and Legacy, 1936–1951. Jefferson, NC: McFarland, 1990.

Prince, Carl E. *Brooklyn's Dodgers: The Bums, the Borough and the Best of Baseball 1947–1957.* New York: Oxford University Press, 1996.

Rader, Benjamin G. *In Its Own Image: How Television Has Transformed Sports.* New York: Macmillan, 1984.

Regalado, Samuel O. *Viva Baseball! Latin Major Leaguers and Their Special Hunger.* Urbana: University of Illinois Press, 1998.

Reynolds, Bill. *Lost Summer: The '67 Red Sox and the Impossible Dream.* New York: Warner Books, 1992.

Ritter, Lawrence. *Lost Ballparks: A Celebration of Baseball's Legendary Fields.* New York: Penguin Studio, 1992.

Roberts, Robin, with C. Paul Rogers III. *The Whiz Kids and the 1950 Pennant.* Philadelphia: Temple University Press, 1996.

Robinson, Ray. *The Home Run Heard 'Round the World: The Dramatic Story of the 1951 Giants-Dodgers Pennant Race.* New York: HarperCollins, 1991.

Rosenthal, Harold. *The Ten Best Years of Baseball: An Informal History of the 'Fifties.* Chicago: Contemporary Books, 1979.

Rossi, John P. *A Whole New Game: Off the Field Changes in Baseball, 1946–1960.* Jefferson, NC: McFarland, 1999.

Rowan, Carl, with Jackie Robinson. *Wait Till Next Year: The Life Story of Jackie Robinson.* New York: Random House, 1960.

Rucker, Mark, and Peter C. Bjarkman. *Smoke: The Romance and Lore of Cuban Baseball.* Kingston: Total Sports Illustrated, 1999.

Rudd, Irving, and Stan Fischler. *The Sporting Life.* New York: St. Martin's Press, 1990.

Shapiro, Michael. *The Last Good Season: Brooklyn, the Dodgers, and Their Final Pennant Race Together.* New York: Doubleday, 2003.

Shapiro, Milton J. *The Sal Maglie Story.* New York: Julian Messner, 1957.

Shaw, Mark, with Don Larsen. *The Perfect Yankee: The Incredible Story of the Greatest Miracle in Baseball History.* Champaign: Sagamore Publishing, 2001.

Simon, Scott. *Jackie Robinson and the Integration of Baseball.* Hoboken: John Wiley and Sons, 2002.

Skipper, John C. *Inside Pitch: A Closer Look at Classic Baseball Moments.* Jefferson, NC: McFarland, 1996.

Smith, Curt. *Storied Stadiums: Baseball's History Through Its Ballparks.* New York: Carroll and Graf, 2001.

Smith, Red. *Red Smith on Baseball: The Game's Greatest Writer on the Games's Greatest Years.* Chicago: Ivan Dee, 2000.

Snider, Duke, with Bill Gilbert. *The Duke of Flatbush.* New York: Zebra Books, 1989.

Snowden, Frank M. *Violence and Great Estates in the South of Italy: Apulia, 1900–1922.* Cambridge, England: Cambridge University Press, 1986.

Staten, Vince. *Why is the Foul Pole Fair? (Or, Answers to the Baseball Questions Your Dad Hoped You'd Never Ask).* New York: Simon and Schuster, 2003.

Stein, Fred. *Mel Ott: The Little Giant of Baseball.* Jefferson, NC: McFarland, 1999.

———. *Under Coogan's Bluff: A Fan's Recollections of the New York Giants under Terry and Ott.* n.p. 1981.

Stein, Fred, and Nick Peters. *A Century of Giants Baseball in New York and San Francisco.* Berkeley: North Atlantic Books, 1987.

Stout, Glenn. *The Dodgers: 120 Years of Dodgers Baseball.* New York: Houghton Mifflin, 2004.

Stout, Glenn, and Richard A. Johnson. *Red Sox Century: One Hundred Years of Red Sox Baseball.* Boston: Houghton Mifflin, 2000.

Stuart, Jeffrey. *Twilight Teams.* Gaithersburg, MD: Sark Publishing, 2000.

Sugar, Bert Randolph. *Baseball's 50 Greatest Games.* New York: Exeter Books, 1986.

Sullivan, Neil J. *The Dodgers Move West.* New York: Oxford University Press, 1987.

————. *Minors: The Struggle and Triumph of Baseball's Poor Relation from 1876 to the Present.* New York: St. Martin's Press, 1990.

Szalontai, James D. *Close Shave: The Life and Times of Baseball's Sal Maglie.* Jefferson, NC: McFarland, 2002.

Thomson, Bobby, with Lee Heiman and Bill Gutman. *The Giants Win the Pennant! The Giants Win the Pennant!* New York: Kensington Publishing, 2001.

Thorn, John. *Baseball's 10 Greatest Games.* New York: Four Winds Press, 1981.

Thorn, John, and John B. Holway. *The Pitcher.* New York: Prentice Hall, 1987.

Thorn, John, Peter Palmer, Michael Gershman, and David Pietrusza. *Total Baseball: The Official Encyclopedia of Major League Baseball.* Fifth edition. New York: Penguin Books, 1997.

Thornley, Stew. *Land of the Giants: New York's Polo Grounds.* Philadelphia: Temple University Press, 2000.

Torres, Angel. *La Leyenda del Béisbol Cubano, 1878–1996.* Privately printed, 1996.

Treto Cisneros, Pedro. *The Mexican League: Comprehensive Statistics, 1937–2001.* Jefferson, NC: McFarland, 2002.

Tunis, John R. *Schoolboy Johnson.* New York: William Morrow, 1958; reprinted 1991.

Turner, Frederick. *When the Boys Came Back: Baseball and 1946.* New York: Henry Holt, 1996.

Tygiel, Jules. *Baseball's Great Experiment: Jackie Robinson and His Legacy.* Second edition. New York: Oxford University Press, 1997.

Vincent, Dave, Lyle Spatz, and David W. Smith. *The Midsummer Classic: The Complete History of Baseball's All-Star Game.* Lincoln: University of Nebraska Press, 2001.

Vincent, Fay. *The Last Commissioner: A Baseball Valentine.* New York: Simon and Schuster, 2002.

Westcott, Rich. *Diamond Greats: Profiles and Interviews with 65 of Baseball's History Makers.* Westport: Meckler, 1988.

Westcott, Rich, and Allen Lewis. *No-Hitters: The 225 Games.* Jefferson, NC: McFarland, 2000.

Wilber, Cynthia. *For the Love of the Game: Baseball Memories from the Men Who Were There.* New York: William Morrow, 1992.

Williams, Dick, with Bill Plaschke. *No More Mr. Nice Guy: A Life of Hardball.* New York: Harcourt Brace Jovanovich, 1990.

Winegardner, Mark. *Veracruz Blues.* New York: Viking Press, 1996.

Wright, Marshall D. *The International League: Year-by-Year Statistics, 1884–1953.* Jefferson, NC: McFarland, 1998.

Wright, Russell O. *A Tale of Two Leagues: How Baseball Changed as the Rules, Ball, Franchises, Stadiums, and Players Changed, 1900–1998.* Jefferson, NC: McFarland, 1999.

Yans-McLaughlin, Virginia. *Family and Community: Italian Immigrants in Buffalo, 1880–1930.* Ithaca: Cornell University Press, 1977.

Zimmer, Don, with Bill Madden. *The Zen of Zim: Baseballs, Beanballs, and Bosses.* New York: St. Martin's Press, 2005.

————. *Zim: A Baseball Life.* Kingston, NY: Total Sports Publishing, 2001.

Zoss, Joel, and John Bowman. *Diamonds in the Rough: The Untold Story of Baseball.* New York: Macmillan, 1989.

ARTICLES AND ESSAYS

Allen, Phil. "Maglie's Lost Weeks." *Baseball Digest* (September, 1952): 13–16.

Angell, Roger, "The Flowering and Subsequent Deflowering of New England." *The New Yorker* (October 28, 1967): 176–205.

"Antique Series." *Time* (October 15, 1956): 69–70.

"The Barber." *Newsweek* (May 19, 1952): 97–98.

"Baseball: A Time for Elders." *Newsweek* (October 15, 1956): 75.

"Baseball: The Way It Went." *Newsweek* (October 8, 1956): 61.

"Baseball's Greatest Final Week." *Life* (October 8, 1951): 35–39.

Bell, Mary. "Hypnosis in Sports: How to Slip into a Trance and out of a Slump." *Sport* (March 1974): 92–96.

Breslin, Jimmy. "Meet Sal Maglie, New York's Miracle Man." *Inside Baseball* (October 1952): 11–13, 70–72.

Briley, Ron. "'Do Not Go Gently [sic] into That Good Night.' Race, the Baseball Establishment, and the Retirements of Bob Feller and Jackie Robinson." In Joseph Dorinson and Joram Warmund, eds. *Jackie Robinson: Race, Sports, and the American Dream* (Armonk: M. E. Sharpe, 1999): 193–213.

Cohane, Tim. "Maglie . . . They Call Him Unfrivolous Sal." *Look* (July 29, 1952): 54–58.

Creamer, Robert. "An Angel of Darkness Named Sal the Barber." *Sports Illustrated* (June 6, 1955): 43–44.

———. "And Then . . . ." *Sports Illustrated* (October 15, 1956): 28–29.

———. "The Curtain Rises." *Sports Illustrated* (October 15, 1956): 18–29.

———. "Three Clubs, and Only a Few Days to Go." *Sports Illustrated* (September 17, 1956): 13–14.

Creamer, Robert, and Roy Terrell. "Cocky Nationals and Mighty Yanks." *Sports Illustrated* (October 1, 1956): 10–12.

———. "The Great Drama, Last Act." *Sports Illustrated* (October 8, 1956): 14–16.

Crichton, Kyle. "Hot Tamale Circuit." *Collier's* (June 29, 1946): 27–29.

"Double Indemnity." *Newsweek* (September 16, 1957): 104.

Durrell, Richard. "The Night the Stars Nearly Fell in Minnesota." *Sports Illustrated* (October 17, 1988), reproduced online at <www.highbeam.com/library.doc3>.

"Events and Discoveries—Robinson, the Avenger." *Sports Illustrated* (May 2, 1955): 11.

Fitzgerald, Ed. "The Barber of the Giants." *Sport* (September, 1952): 34–37, 72–76.

Frank, Stanley. "How the Giants Found a Pitcher in the Doghouse." *Saturday Evening Post* (May 5, 1951): 29, 151–54.

Gmelch, George. "Groupies and Baseball." *Journal of Sport and Social Issues* (February 1998): 32–45.

Graham, Frank, Jr. "The Education of Bill Monbouquette." *Sport* (August 1962): 42–43, 69–71.

———. "The Great Mexican War of 1946." *Sports Illustrated* (September 19, 1966): 117–34.

———. "Only Our Agent Watched as Maglie and Furillo Met." *Sport* (September 1956): 10–12.

———. "They Were All Wrong About Maglie." *Sport* (February 1957): 12–13, 81–86.

"The Great Pastime." *Time* (July 30, 1956): 46.

Gross, Milton. "The Pitcher Who'd Brush Back His Grandma!" *See For Men* (May 1957): 38–40, 46–48.

Helfer, Al. "Make Mine Maglie!" *Complete Baseball* (September 1952): 30–33.

"Highlight." *Sports Illustrated* (June 18, 1956): 13.

"Highlight." *Sports Illustrated* (April 29, 1957): 10.

Irwin, Ted. "Hypnosis in Sports." *Sport* (October 1963): 33, 83–85.

Jares, Joe. "Look! It's The Monster!" *Sports Illustrated* (April 9, 1965): 101–5.

Kates, Maxwell. "Of Horsehides and Hexagrams. Baseball as a Vehicle for American Jewish Culture." *The National Pastime. A Review of Baseball History* (Vol. 24, 2004): 118–26.

Kaufman, Herman. "Sal Maglie: A Study in Frustration." *The National Pastime. A Review of Baseball History* (Vol. 3, 1983): 34–38.

Kelly, Steve. "After 50 Years, 'Shot Heard 'Round the World' Still a Defining Moment in Baseball." *Baseball Digest* (October 1, 2001): 58–60.

King, Joe. "Pitcher from Nowhere." *Complete Baseball* (Winter 1950–1951): 10–12, 70.

Lardner, John. "Ned and the Barber." *Newsweek* (June 18, 1951): 39.

———. "Razor Blades Amok." *Newsweek* (July 16, 1951): 77.

Maglie, Kay [Mrs. Sal]. "My Best Years with Sal." *Parade* (November 25, 1956): 20–23.

Maglie, Sal. "I Can't Pitch Forever." *Saturday Feature Magazine, New York World Telegram and Sun* (July 1957): day and pages not provided in copy.

———. "I'm the Luckiest Guy in Baseball." *Sport* (September 1951): 14–17.

———. "My Book on National League Hitters." *Sport* (September 1954): 12–17.

Maglie, Sal, and Robert Boyle. "Baseball Is a Tough Business." *Sports Illustrated* (April 15, 1968): 78–88.

———. "Great Giant-Dodger Days." *Sports Illustrated* (April 22, 1968): 40–42, 47–49.

Maglie, Sal, and Dick Schaap. "I Always Threw Beanballs." *Cavalier* (September 1959): 31–34, 81–82.

Maglie, Sal, and Roy Terrell. "Sal Maglie on the Art of Pitching." *Sports Illustrated* (March 17, 1958): 35–38, 43–45.

———. "One League Is Just Like the Other." *Sport* (July 1959): 32–33, 75–77.

"Mean Man in a Clutch." *Life* (October 4, 1954): 34.

Moran, Gussie. "The Ten Most Exciting Men in Baseball." *Sport* (October 1955): 68–69.

Morrow, Ross. "Ballplayers versus Bobbysoxers?" *Sport* (September 1950): 14–16, 97–100.

"One More World Series?" *Newsweek* (September 24, 1956): 71–72.

"Opening Day: High Hopes—Heartaches." *Newsweek* (April 13, 1959): 71.

"Out of the Bullpen." *Time* (September 25, 1950): 59–60.

Overfield, Joseph. "Giant Among Men." *BisonGram* (April–May, 1993).

Richman, Milton. "Does a Ballplayer Know When He's Through?" *Sport* (July 1957): 12–13, 74–76.

Roeder, Bill. "Double Trouble." *True Magazine Baseball Yearbook* (1951): 50–51, 72–74.

Rosenthal, Harold. "The 'War' with Mexico." *Baseball Digest* (December–January, 1963–1964): 53–56.

Schechter, Gabriel. "Dick Radatz. Baseball's Supernova." <www.baseballhalloffame .org/library/_columns/gs_050309.htm>.

Sheldon, Harold. "Zero Man Sal." *Baseball Digest* 10 (1951): 5–10.

Simons, William M. "Pitcher at Twilight: Bill Monbouquette and the American Dream." *Cooperstown Symposium on Baseball and American Culture* (Jefferson, NC: McFarland, 2002): 40–60.

Smith, Marshall. "The Meanest Face in the Pennant Race." *Life* (October 1, 1956): 119–21.

Stedler, Dick. "Ace Pitcher Overcomes Years of Heartbreak." *Open Road* (May 1952): 2, 30–33.

"Stretch Run." *Time* (October 8, 1956): 66.

Testa, Judith. "Maglie Mole in Dodgerville." *Elysian Fields Quarterly* (Vol. 22, No. 1, 2005): 62–66.

Vaughn, Gerald F. "George Hausmann Recalls the Mexican League of 1946–47." *Baseball Research Journal* (1990): 59–63.

———. "Jorge Pasquel and the Evolution of Mexican Baseball." *The National Pastime: A Review of Baseball History* (Vol. 12, 1992): 9–13.

"The Way It Went." *Newsweek* (October 8, 1956): 61.

Wendel, Tim. "An Ill-Fated Night." *USA Today Baseball Weekly* (August 13–19, 1997): 8–11.

Will, George. "Liddle Big Man." *National Review* (June 7, 2000), reproduced in <www.national review.com/will/will060700.html>.

Wilson, Carolin. "Sal Maglie, Niagara's Greatest Pitcher." *What's Up Niagara* (October 1984): 5–11.

INDEX

SALARY AND INCOME: 1946 Giants salary, 51, 418n9; 1950 Giants salary, 93, 105; 1951 Giants salary, 129; 1952 Giants salary, 183–84; 1953 Giants salary, 206–7; 1954 Giants salary, 221; 1955 Giants salary, 242; 1956 Cleveland Indians salary, 261; 1957 Brooklyn Dodgers salary, 311–12; 1957 World Series half share, 325 1958 World Series half share, 338; 1959 St. Louis salary, 339; Buffalo Bisons contract, 20; Canada, Provincial League, 92; during Depression, Union Carbide, 17; highest salary, 1952, xiv; loss with All Stars, 86; Mexican League, 49, 55, 59–60, 62; product endorsements, 184, *185*, 186, 309–10, 316; Red Sox coaching salary, 356; Sal Maglie Day, 1950, gifts, 122; Sal Maglie Day, 1951, gifts, 147; Sal Maglie Day, 1952, gifts, 198; Sal Maglie Day, 1956, gift, 308; semi-pro ball, 17, 20; unwise financial decisions, xviii; wealth, comparative to boyhood friends, xiv, 182

Maglie, Salvatore Anthony, Jr. "Little Sal" (son), 287, *356*, 357; adoption of, 256–60; appearance, 259, *267*, 349; baseball and, 386; death of, 402, 435n3; mother's death and, 375, 376, 387; problems of, 376, 378, 387, 390, 391–92, 401–2; relationship with Sal, 355, 386

Maglie, Santa Maria (sister). *See* Grenga, Santa Maria Maglie (sister)

Major League Baseball (MLB): in 1917, description of sport, xvii; 1941 season, 30; 1946 season, 95–97; 1947 season, 97–100; 1949 season, 100–102, 102–4; 1950s as finest decade, xviii; 1951 New York sweep, 155; 1951 playoff, third game as most dramatic ever played, 158–74; 1956 season, bad behavior by players, 275–76; 1956 World Series, perfect game, 296–306; 1960s, discipline problems, 355; 1967, firing of coaches, record, 377; 1968, Year of the Pitcher, 377; in 1992, changes in sport, xvii; American League breaks color line, 100; Babe Ruth homerun record broken, 1961, 347; banning of Mexican League jumpers, 57–58, 61, 78, 81, 83, 84; banning of Mexican League jumpers, lifted, 1949, 90, 102, 103; "Baseball Annies," 18, 332–33; batting helmets, 47, 111, 188, 243; beanballs, 111, 125, 243; bias against Italian players, 122, 127, 128; Black Sox scandal, 34; Branch Rickey signs Jackie Robinson, 43; career ending, players and, 325, 333; Commissioner Chandler, 34, 57, 98; Commissioner Frick, 134, 174, 307; Commissioner Landis, 30–31, 33, 34, 98; Cuban players in, 81; Curt Flood's challenge to reserve clause, 385; Cy Young Award, 307; Dodgers and Giants move their franchises, 315; Dodgers last Brooklyn pennant, 1956, xii; domination of the game by New York teams, 102; employment issues, postwar, 50; ethnic abuse accepted in, 42; expansion of leagues, 346–47, 377; expulsion for glove throwing, 150; Gardella's lawsuit against ban and reserve clause, 90–91, 102; GenDouglas MacArthur and, 130; headhunters, 47; integration of, 57, 95, 96, 97–98, 324; Japan's enthusiasm for, 218; "knockdown" defined, 210; Lanier and Martin lawsuit against ban, 91; lifting of ban, 1949, 91; Maglie and gaining of players' pension plan, 96; Mexican Baseball war, 52–60; National Federation league, Cuba, 76; new balk rules, 1950, 107; no-hitters, 286; perfect game, Don Larsen, 296–306; perfect games, 304; pitchers feared by batters, xii; pitchers leading in hitting batters, 245–46; pitchers weeping after losses, 302, 306; pitching record, consecutive scoreless innings, 119; pitching record, shutouts, 119; players or managers on all three NYC teams, 320; players pension, 314; players' rights, 95, 96; players' salaries, 1946, 95–96; racial quota system (informal), 135; racism in, 81, 96, 98, 154, 421n3; reserve clause, 50, 54, 58, 91, 385; rivalry between Dodgers and Giants, 39; rule changes, pitching, 377; salaries, post-war, 50, 54, 56; sign-stealing, 177–79; status in mid 1950s, 219–20; television and, 95, 219–20; television coverage, playoffs 1951, 155; "The Cub Factor," 179; transforming events, 1946 through 1949, 95–104; unionization of baseball, 96, 219–20; waiver system, 252, 253, 319;